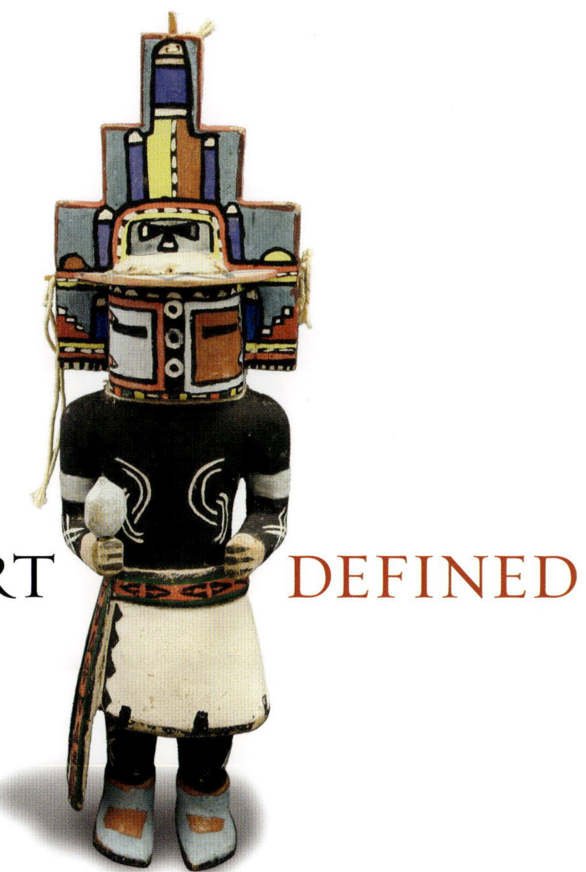

SOUTHWEST ART DEFINED

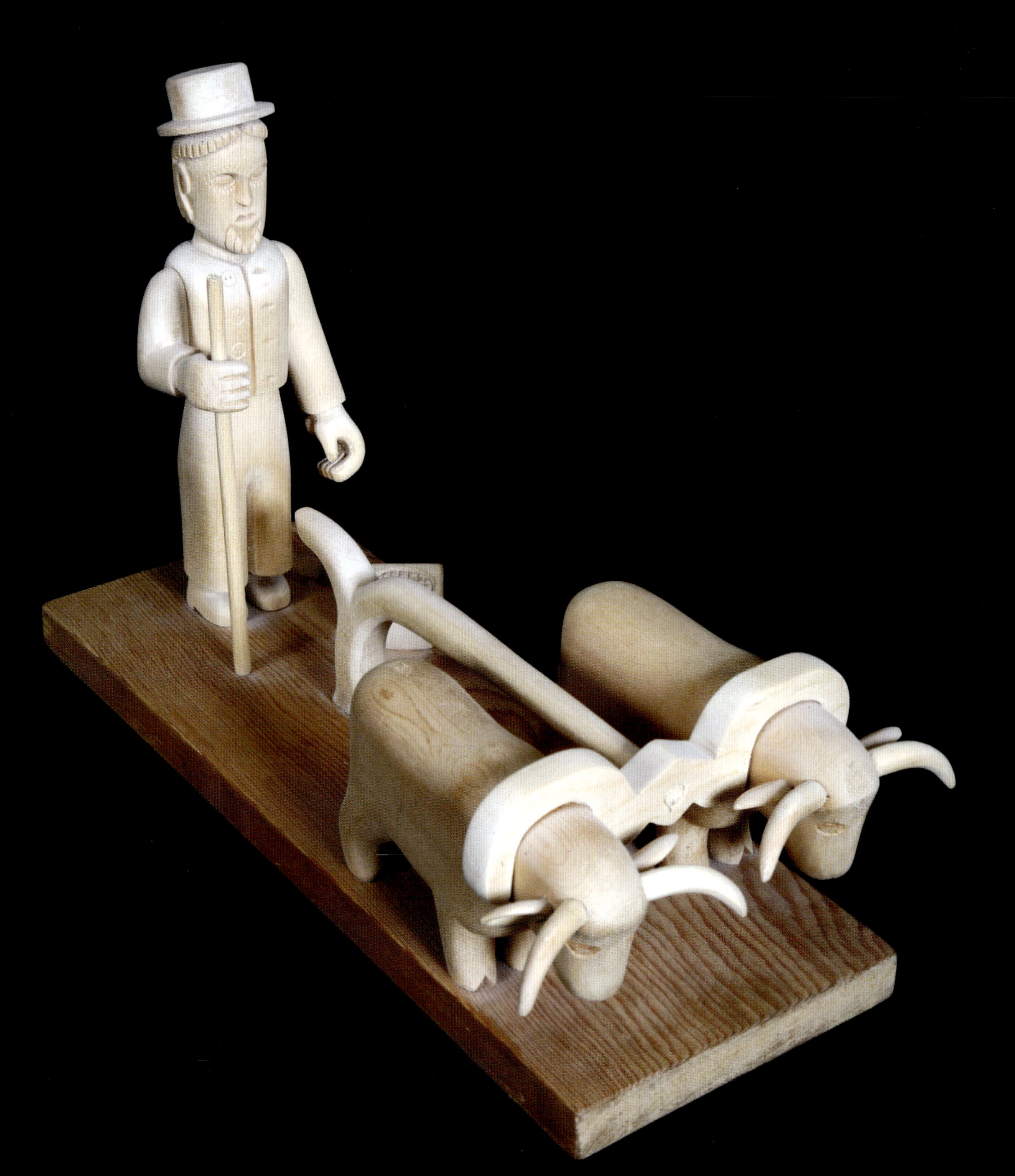

SOUTHWEST ART

DEFINED

{ AN ILLUSTRATED GUIDE }

Margaret Moore Booker

RIO NUEVO PUBLISHERS

Tucson, Arizona

PHOTOGRAPH ON PAGE i: Hopi Hemis Katsina doll, ca. 1930.
PAGE ii: José Mondragon (New Mexico), San Isidro bulto, ca. 1959–1990.
PAGE iii: Navajo rug, courtesy Peabody Museum, Claffin Collection.

Rio Nuevo Publishers®
P.O. Box 5250
Tucson, AZ 85703-0250
(520) 623-9558, www.rionuevo.com

Text © 2013 by Margaret Moore Booker.
See page 197 for photography credits.
Map by Tom Jonas.
Basket weaving illustrations on p. 186 by Jake Page.
Navajo loom illustration on p. 187 by Jessica LeMar.
Book design: David Jenney.

Printed in China.

10 9 8 7 6 5 4 3 2 1

Library of Congress Cataloging-in-Publication Data

Booker, Margaret Moore.
Southwest art defined : an illustrated guide / Margaret Moore Booker.
pages cm
Includes bibliographical references and index.
ISBN 978-1-933855-75-2 (hardcover : alk. paper) -- ISBN 1-933855-75-4
(hardcover : alk. paper)
1. Indian art--Southwest, New. 2. Hispanic American art--Southwest, New.
3. Folk art--Southwest, New. I. Title.
E78.S7B66 2013
709.79--dc23
2012026385

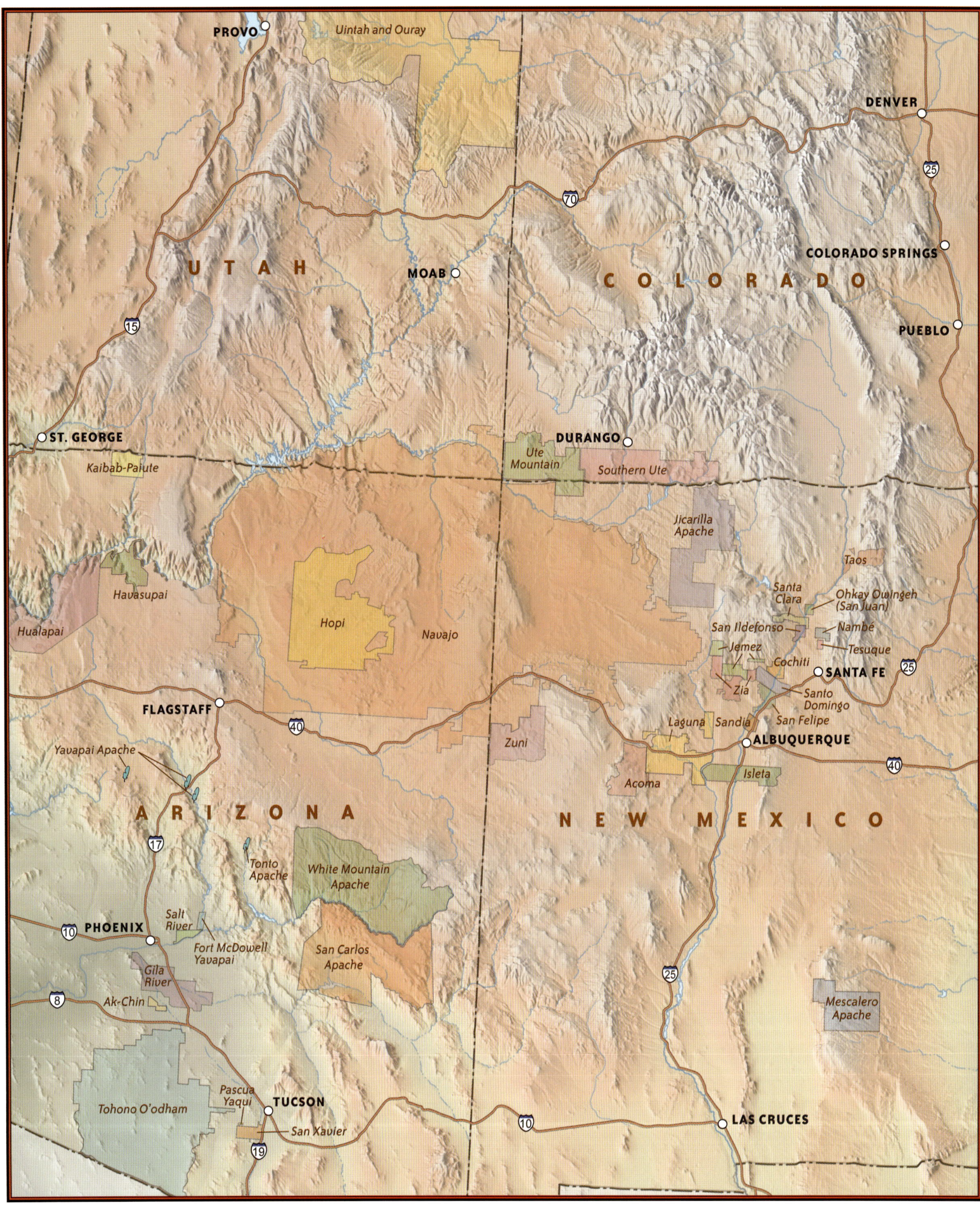

PROVO
Uintah and Ouray
DENVER
25
MOAB
COLORADO SPRINGS
U T A H
C O L O R A D O
15
PUEBLO
ST. GEORGE
DURANGO
Kaibab-Paiute
Ute Mountain
Southern Ute
Jicarilla Apache
Taos
Santa Clara
Ohkay Owingeh (San Juan)
Havasupai
Nambé
San Ildefonso
Hualapai
Hopi
Navajo
Jemez
Tesuque
Cochiti
Zia
SANTA FE
25
Santo Domingo
San Felipe
Laguna
Sandia
FLAGSTAFF
40
Zuni
Acoma
ALBUQUERQUE
Isleta
40
Yavapai Apache
A R I Z O N A
N E W   M E X I C O
17
Tonto Apache
White Mountain Apache
Salt River
25
PHOENIX
Fort McDowell Yavapai
San Carlos Apache
10
Mescalero Apache
Gila River
8
Ak-Chin
Pascua Yaqui
Tohono O'odham
TUCSON
LAS CRUCES
San Xavier
10
19

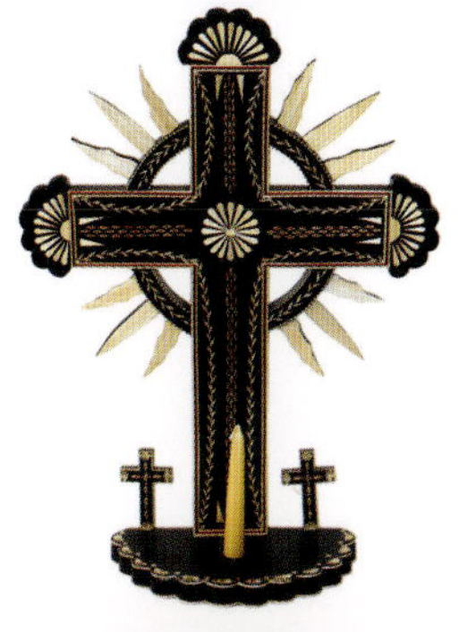

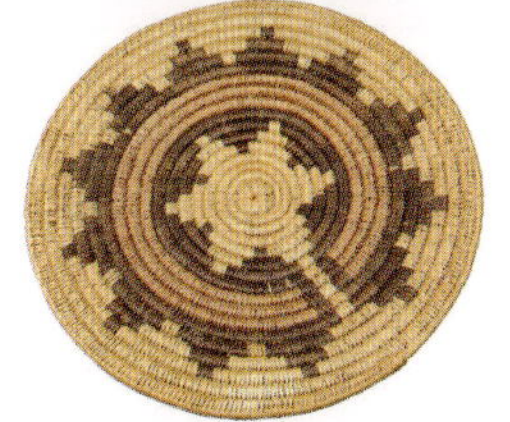

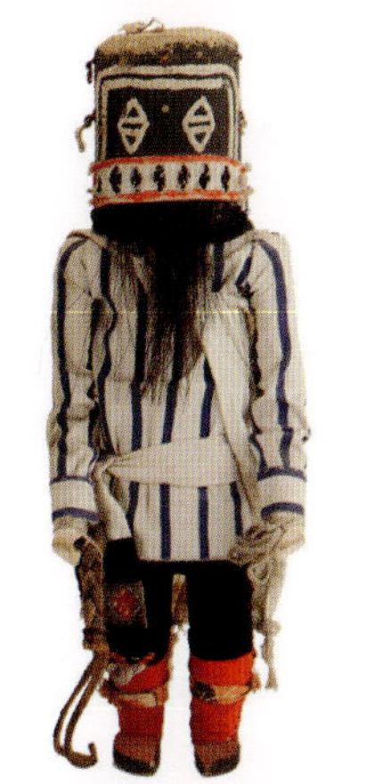

CONTENTS

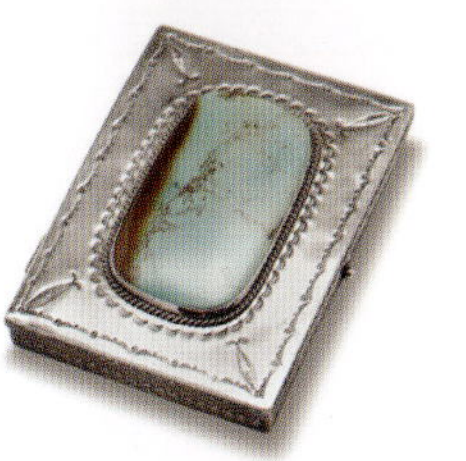

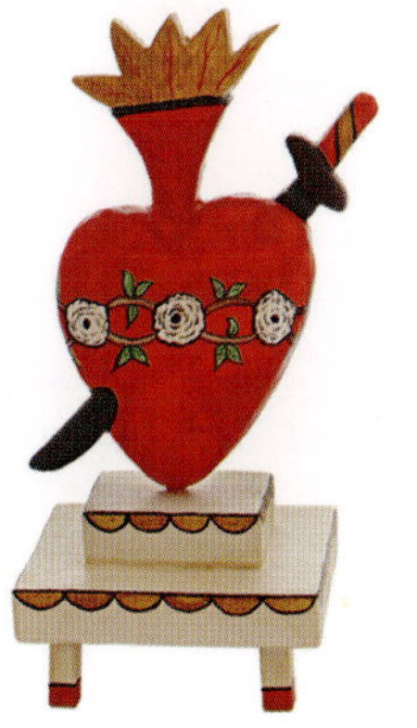

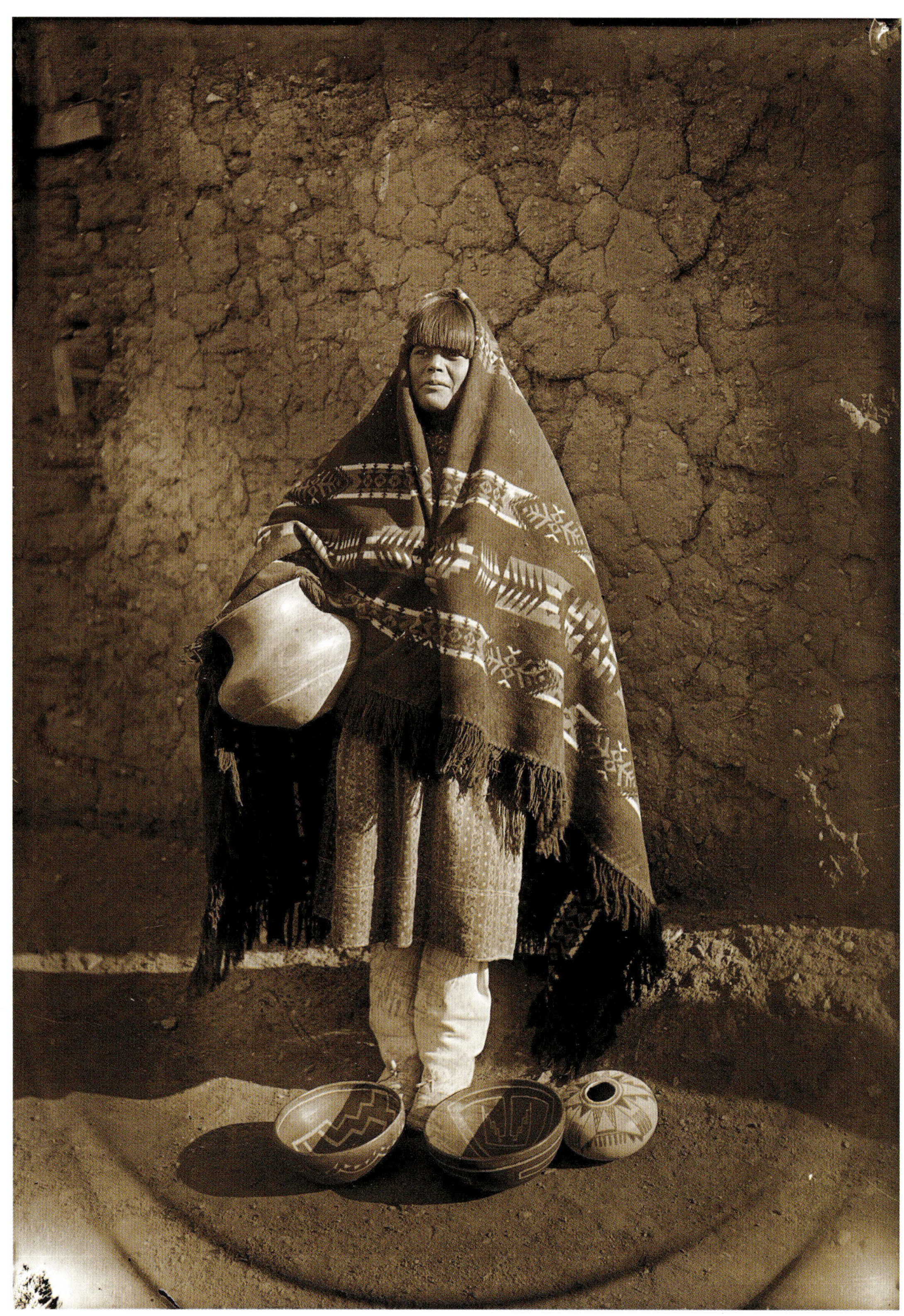

Susana Aguilar, San Ildefonso Pueblo, ca. 1925.

PREFACE

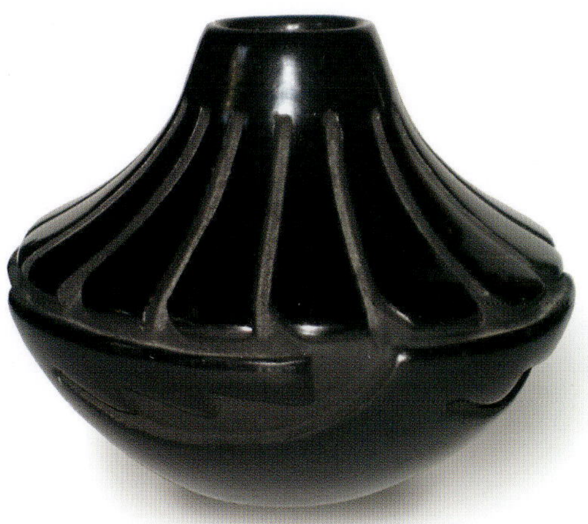

ALMOST TWENTY YEARS AGO, during my first visit to New Mexico, I took a much-anticipated trip to the ancient adobe pueblos situated just north of Santa Fe. On a winding, dusty road leading to San Ildefonso Pueblo, I stumbled across the picturesque Babbitt's Cottonwood Trading Post, nestled among giant cottonwood trees. Inside the post, displayed on a glass shelf amongst a collection of fine Pueblo pottery, was a miniature black-on-black pot that immediately caught my eye. It was intricately carved with traditional feather and kiva-step patterns and was polished to a high sheen. I gingerly held the pot in my hands, admiring its beauty and the technical skill it took to make it, and marveling at the history and culture embodied in this superbly crafted little form. I wondered if I could afford it, and once I learned the price (which seemed exorbitant at the time) I hesitated over purchasing it only for a few short moments. I had to have it. This pot, with its black-as-the-night-sky surface and culturally significant design, "spoke to me." Little did I realize that this piece of pottery by Denise Chavarria of Santa Clara Pueblo would spark a passion in me, and later in my husband, for collecting Native American (and eventually Hispano) arts and crafts of the Southwest.

In 2004, while living on Nantucket Island, thirty miles off the coast of Massachusetts, my husband and I came to the conclusion, after several life-altering events, that "life is too short" and made plans to move to a place we had long desired to be: Santa Fe, New Mexico. Once we settled in and began to develop a kinship with this sunbaked landscape of red-hued earth and an abundance of prickly-pear cacti, chamisa bushes, and piñon trees, we sought familiarity with the multifaceted culture and history of the area. It seemed only natural with my art history background and my husband's expertise in jewelry and silver that our first step in the process was the studying and collecting of art and artifacts of the region—objects that tell the story of the human face of the Southwest.

In an era when most of our goods are mass-produced in foreign countries, it has been refreshing to meet people who create utilitarian and/or decorative items by hand in home studios. For many of these artisans, who have a deep respect for tradition and history, making art is a family affair and one that has been carried on from generation to generation. In a time

ABOVE RIGHT: Denise Chavarria (Santa Clara), miniature black-on-black pot.

when it is commonplace for Americans to change addresses frequently, it was (and still is) remarkable to witness cultures that have remained regionally intact for centuries.

My husband and I found that certain pottery, baskets, textiles, retablos, wood carvings, and other art forms could be recognized as being from a particular village or community—places where young people were taught traditional techniques under the watchful eyes of their elders. We also learned, however, that there is really no such thing as a "pure" local style. Intermarriage, educational opportunities, exposure to contemporary techniques and materials, interactions with outsiders, and other forces have led to the combining of traditions and the development of new styles and innovative art forms. There is nothing static about the art and architecture of the Southwest!

Over the years, as I developed my career in freelance writing and editing, and my love of all things Southwest increased, I searched in vain for a definitive sourcebook on terms relating to the distinctive art, architecture, decorative arts, and jewelry that has been produced over the centuries and in recent times in the American Southwest. I found that definitions of the region's art and built environment—truly personal expressions reflecting rich traditions and cultures— were scattered in numerous individual books published on a wide variety of topics. Trying to locate the answers to my seemingly simple questions about the art my husband and I were collecting (or admiring in museum, gallery, and personal collections), or about the architecture we passed by everyday, was an extremely frustrating and often fruitless endeavor.

And so, beginning in 2010, from our home in the high-desert landscape of Santa Fe—where our hearts and our feet are now deeply embedded—I embarked on a journey that culminated in *Southwest Art Defined*, in which I have brought together for the very first time, in one single volume, close to five hundred expanded definitions of terms for the art, architecture, decorative arts, and jewelry of the American Southwest, as well as terms for the techniques and materials used to create them, and the styles and prominent designs displayed in them. This enormous task could not have been completed without the generous assistance of scholars in the various fields, to whom I am eternally grateful.

By defining everything from the natural dyes used for textiles and basketry to the tools used by Hispano artisans in making furniture to the designs used in Pueblo pottery to the mud recipe used in building adobe homes, this book serves to preserve, celebrate, and honor the Southwest and its multicultural history. Many of these art forms have changed very little over time and some, such as silver and turquoise jewelry and tinwork, have become synonymous with the Southwest.

 Whether you are an avid art collector; a museum, gallery, or auction professional; an art appraiser, art history or history enthusiast; a resident of the region, frequent visitor, or someone who plans to journey to the Southwest, this volume will prove to be invaluable as a research tool and as a source of continual pleasure. Through reading this book, I hope you will come to appreciate, as I have, the remarkably diverse and endlessly fascinating artistry, history, and traditions of this unique region. And my husband and I sincerely hope that along the way you discover a work of art or craft that "speaks to you."

—Margaret Moore Booker, June 2012

NOTE TO THE READER

The American Southwest is defined in various ways depending upon the source consulted; for the purposes of this book it is narrowly defined as covering the geographic area of southern Utah, southern Colorado, Arizona, and New Mexico. Although many of the terms included relate to art, decorative arts, architecture, and jewelry that are made throughout America and indeed worldwide, the definitions presented here relate specifically to the terms' usage in the aforementioned regions.

Furthermore, the focus of this book is on the traditional indigenous arts and architecture of the Southwest, with mention of contemporary trends. The "fine arts" such as easel painting, printmaking, and bronze or marble sculpture are not included. Readers should also take note that although the definitions are thorough explanations, due to space constraints, they are relatively brief and some local traditions unfortunately had to be left out. The many scholars consulted for this project have provided guidance when it comes to the entries included. To further assist the reader, an extensive list of sources for additional reading/research is featured at the end of the book. These publications, as well as insight gleaned from specialists in the various fields, museum exhibition texts, and the author's own experience as a collector, were the basis for the definitions provided herein.

Throughout the book the terms "Anglo American" and "Hispano" appear. The former refers to people with European and American backgrounds living in (or visiting) the Southwest and the latter refers to Americans of Spanish or Mexican descent living in the Southwest.

Some terms have various spellings depending on the source consulted. Presented here are the generally accepted spellings, with the variations in parentheses after the term. For instance "Heishi (Heishe)" for the shell beads used to make jewelry. Also, if more than one term is used for the same object, the generally accepted word is placed first, followed by the alternatives in parentheses. For instance, "Filigree (Metal Lace)" or "Wedding Jar/Vase (Double-necked Jars)." And finally, the scientific name of plants appears in parentheses after the popular name.

While the definitions for most techniques, such as the coil method of pottery making or the weaving of Hopi plaques, are straightforward, the explanations for many patterns and designs are less clear cut. Many of the designs have symbolic meaning (or multiple meanings) for the artists and their communities. For instance, an incised wavy line on a piece of pottery may mean one thing to a Santa Clara Pueblo artisan and something else entirely to a potter from Nambé. Also, meanings may have changed with time. As far as techniques and materials, artists in the region are constantly experimenting, so it is difficult to provide "definitive" explanations for these categories. In all of the aforementioned instances, the explanations are based on the general consensus of scholars, museum curators, and artisans and are meant as a guide. For contemporary art, the best description you will ever receive for a certain design, pattern, or technique is from the artist who made the work, as well as possibly from a knowledgeable dealer, trader, museum curator, or salesperson.

Concerning religious and ceremonial imagery, they rarely appear on art produced for the consumer/collector, and when they do appear, the artisan who made the piece will not likely divulge its sacred meaning. Thus, in many instances we will never know what certain designs truly symbolize. Tribal leaders today are concerned about making their religious traditions public; most oppose recording or further disseminating sacred material. As Mark Bahti—renowned dealer, cultural historian, and writer—states, this protective attitude is not surprising considering that most Pueblo religions were suppressed, even banned, from Spanish Colonial times up until 1934, when religious freedom was finally extended to the original inhabitants of the American Southwest.

On a final note, for easy cross-referencing, any terms included within other term definitions are highlighted in bold.

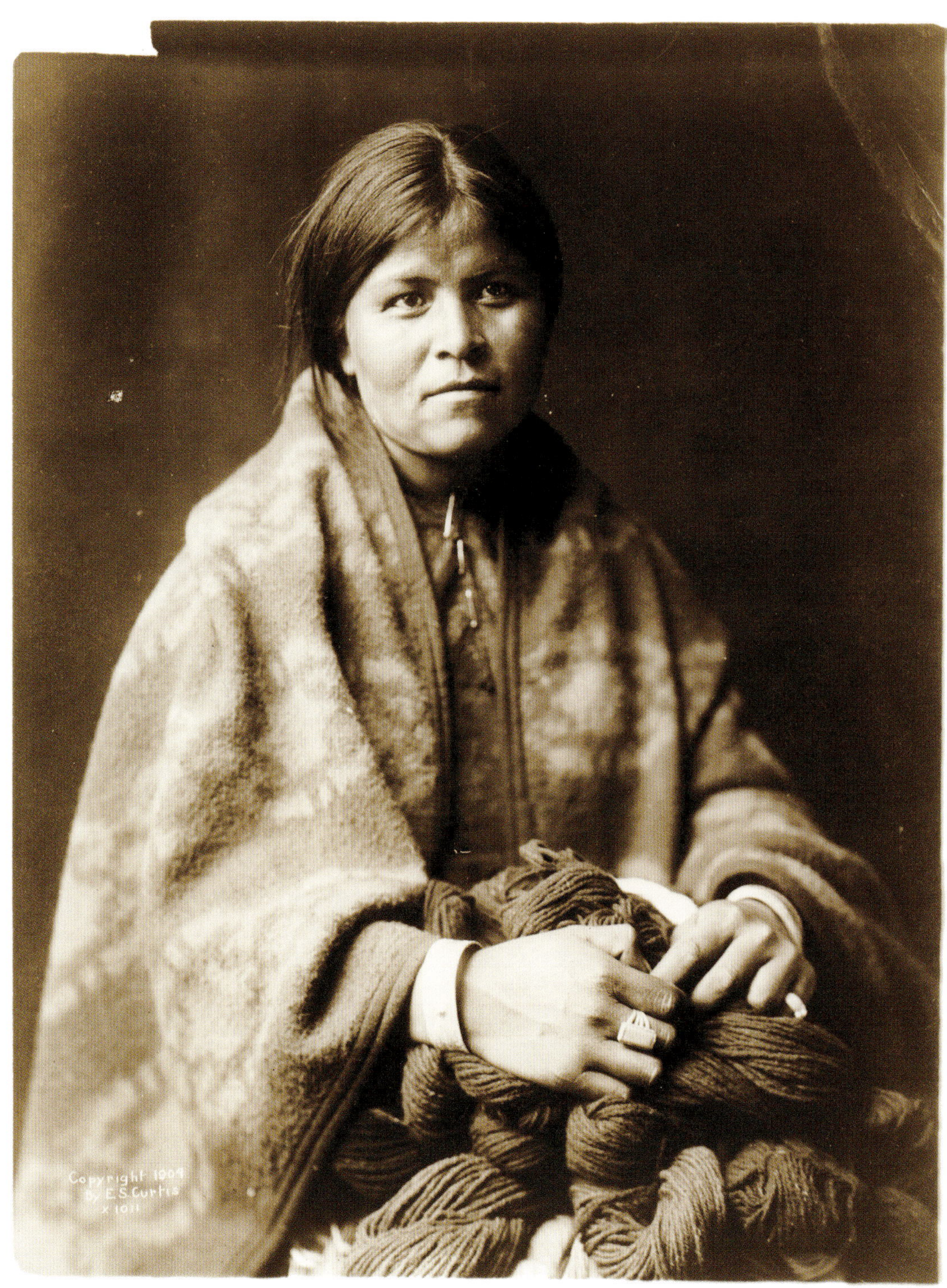

Navajo woman holding yarn, ca. 1904.

INTRODUCTION

If you have an art passed down, you have a responsibility. I remember my mom telling me when I was little, even if you don't become a weaver as a vocation, you still need to learn it. It's part of who you are and part of what we do. It's something you're going to have to carry on to your kids.

— SIERRA NIZHONII TELLER ORNELAS
Navajo [Marshall, Home: 97]

THE ART OF WEAVING, like so many other crafts, has indeed been "carried on" in the Southwest for thousands of years, in part because of a deep respect and honor for preserving the tradition and history of one's ancestors. As this book illustrates, much of the art, decorative art, architecture, and jewelry of the Southwest can be traced back to the region's prehistoric and historic peoples: the Native Americans, the Hispanos, the Anglo Americans, and those of other cultural and multi-cultural backgrounds. The continuation of traditional styles in architecture and crafts, some more than one thousand years old, reflects the strength, vitality, and enduring legacy of these people.

The people of the Southwest have a shared land and a shared history. Archaeological evidence indicates that human habitation of the American Southwest dates back at least 12,000 years and possibly longer. The first Southwesterners were descendants of immigrants from Asia, and as time passed, other people came from Asia, Europe, and Africa, to make this land their home. This mix of people with different traditions resulted in the rich and vibrant cultural diversity characteristic of the modern Southwest.

Since the beginning, the people of the Southwest have had a close relationship with the land—a diverse terrain that ranges from white desert sands and sage-covered mesas to high mountains graced by towering piñons and aspens. This land has provided plant species, rocks and minerals, animals, and even soil that have sustained human life for thousands of years by offering food as well as raw materials for making medicines, tools, clothing, building supplies, and various utilitarian and ceremonial objects. Through time, this connection between the people and the land has only deepened, producing a spiritual bond that continues today in many communities.

By using native materials of the region, as well as trade items and later manufactured supplies, the many cultures who have resided here (and continue to do so) have expressed themselves through their arts and crafts: in the weaving of baskets and textiles, the hand-crafting of personal adornments such as jewelry and ceremonial clothing, the carving or painting of historic events and symbolism in rocks, in the building of shelters and furniture, in the hand-coiling and painting of clay vessels, and in many other artistic and utilitarian formats. For these cultures of the Southwest, "art" has always been (and continues to be) an integral and inseparable part of daily life.

THE PEOPLE

The first of the varied cultures to have lived in this region are the Native Americans, whose communities have remained intact in the Southwest more than anywhere else in the country. Still connected to the lands that have been their homes for centuries, today's Native Americans reside on several million acres of land in present-day New Mexico, Arizona, southern Utah, and southern Colorado. Some live in ancient villages, such as the old adobe pueblos of the Rio Grande Valley; others live on reservation lands that were designated by the U.S. government; and many can be found residing in towns and cities of the region that are outside the boundaries of their homelands.

In search of gold and riches for the Spanish Crown and souls for the Catholic Church, the Spanish were among the first Europeans to arrive in the Southwest. In 1538–39, Fray Marcos de Niza (a Frenchman also known as Frerè Marc de Nice) was sent north from Mexico City by Viceroy Mendoza to search for wealthy cities rumored to be north of the frontier of La Nueva España (New Spain). He returned in the summer of 1539 and wrote a report indicating that "good and prosperous" lands existed in a province called Cibola (present-day Zuni Pueblo). His report led to the expedition of Francisco Vasquez de Coronado who made the first entrada into northern New Spain (now New Mexico) in the winter of 1540. Although gold and riches were never found, the Spanish continued to explore and settle in the region. Coronado was followed later by Juan de Oñate, who in 1598 established the first Spanish colony in New Spain near Ohkay Owingeh Pueblo (renamed San Juan Pueblo by the Spanish) called San Juan de los Caballeros. In 1610 the seat of government was permanently established in Santa Fe (called Villa Real de la Santa Fé de San Francisco de Asís), which then became the Spanish capital. The Spanish dominated New Mexico until 1821 (when Mexico achieved independence from Spain) a time period referred to as the Spanish Colonial period.

Early explorers and settlers in the Southwest were not all from Spain, for there were people from various other cultures among them: Europeans from different countries, Indians from Michoacán in Mexico, Afro-Hispanos, and so on.

Coronado's explorers also ventured into the lands of present-day Arizona, in 1540, in search of great riches or Indian communities willing to convert to Christianity. They were followed later by Antonio Espejo in 1582, Juan de Oñate in 1605, and in 1629 four Franciscan missionaries led by Father Francisco de Porras established missions on the Hopi mesas. The Spanish missionary, explorer, and scholar Father Eusebio Francisco Kino, on a campaign of peaceful conquest, made the first of nine expeditions into Arizona in 1691, encountering Tohono O'odham and Pimas living in clusters of houses in and near present-day Tucson. Eventually he established more than twenty missions, including San Xavier del Bac in 1700, and Tumacácori and Guevavi in 1701. Immigrant families soon followed the Spanish missions and presidios and settled along the Santa Cruz and San Pedro rivers in what is now southern Arizona.

OPPOSITE: Man wrapped in trade blanket, Zia Pueblo, ca. 1925–1945.

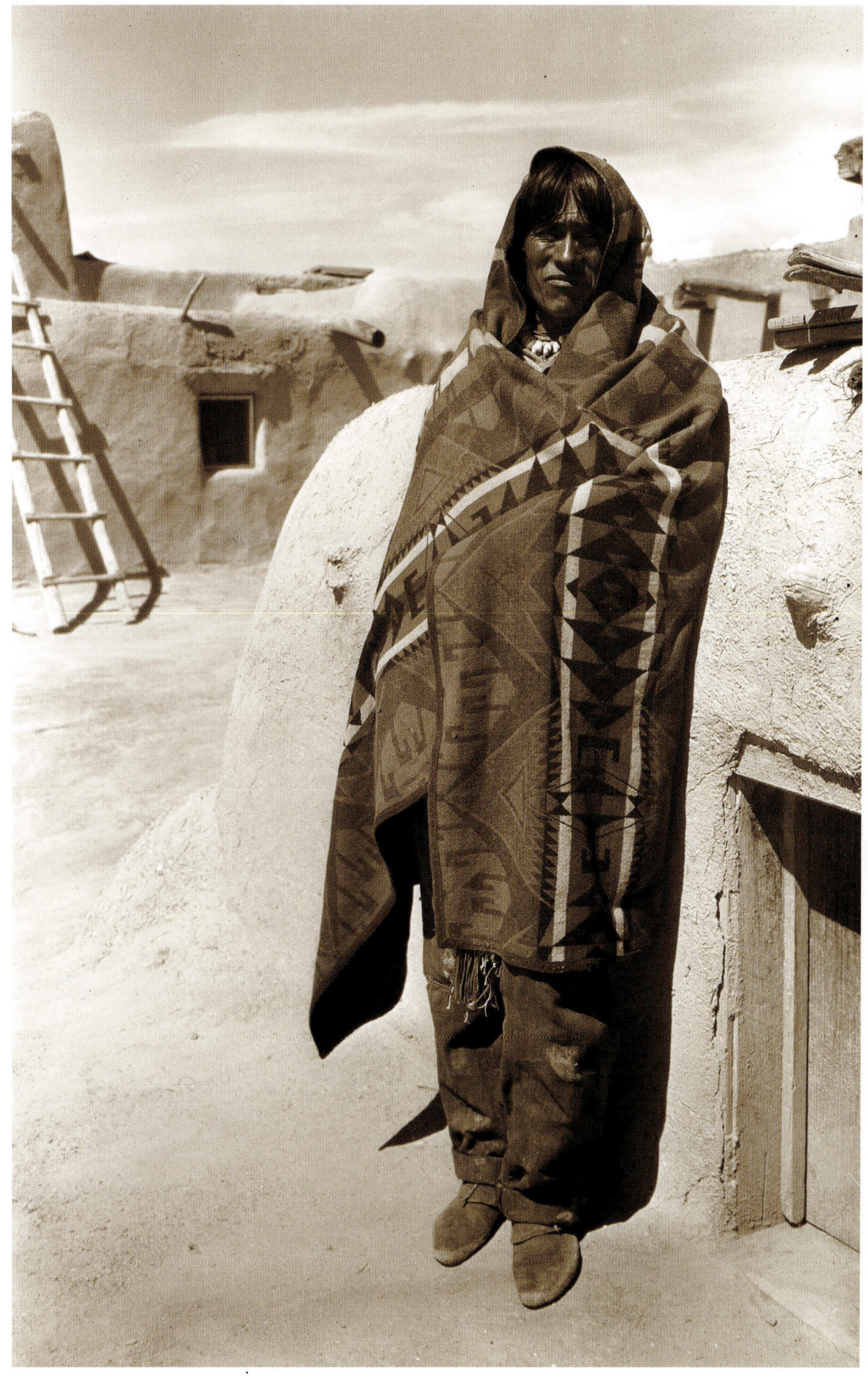

Under Juan de Oñate, who had been appointed governor of the province of New Mexico, the Spanish journeyed into Colorado in the late 1500s. Oñate's expedition brought him to the San Luis Valley and eventually as far north as the site of present-day Denver. It was not until 1706 that Juan de Ulibarri made the first recorded claim to Colorado soil in the name of the Spanish Crown. Seventy years later, two priests, Padre Silvestre Vélez de Escalante and Fray Antanasio Domínguez, on their journey to find a new route linking Santa Fe (Spanish for "Holy Faith") with the Spanish missions in California, explored much of western Colorado, as well as Utah, Arizona, and New Mexico.

Colorado, which encompasses much of the Rocky Mountains and northwestern portion of the Colorado Plateau, was named for the Colorado River, or Río Colorado—so-called by early Spanish explorers for the *colorado* (red) silt the river carried from the mountains.

When the Spanish arrived in the area we know today as the Southwest, they found Native Americans residing in small adobe villages (which the Spanish called *pueblos*, the Spanish word for villages) scattered throughout the Rio Grande valley. Of primary importance to the Spaniards was the conversion of the indigenous people to Christianity. The Spanish also instructed the Native peoples in the European skills needed to further the colonizing goals of the Spanish Crown. A period of great artistic activity followed: large mission churches were built and filled with didactic murals and Native artists were trained in European painting techniques.

The Spanish brought many innovations to the Native peoples: horses, churro sheep, new foodstuffs (such as fruit trees), blacksmithing and carpentry skills, ceramic styles, and more. Over time, the Spanish settlers also introduced the arts, decorative arts, and building methods of their homeland to New Spain. For instance, they taught Native builders how to use wooden forms to make adobe bricks for erecting houses; formerly the Pueblo people had used the time-consuming process of hand puddling to create earthen walls.

Hispano families settled in the Rio Grande Valley from the river's headwaters in the San Luis Valley of southern Colorado, throughout the river's length in New Mexico, and south to El Paso del Rio on the Texas border. Spanish (and later Mexican) governments established ninety-six land grants for Spanish settlers, between 1701 and 1829, which were concentrated along the Rio Grande and its tributaries. These grants encouraged the formation of large sheep ranches in some areas. Many land grants surrounded or heavily encroached upon Pueblo territory; the land and the resources within (such as firewood and pasture) could only be used by the Spanish grantees.

Among the earliest crafts made by Hispanos in New Mexico were pottery and weaving; the latter developed around organized workshops *(obrajes)*, as well as in less formal household operations.

When the Spanish settlers, soldiers, and priests rode into the lives and lands of the people of sixteenth-century New Mexico, they changed the indigenous residents' lives forever. They named

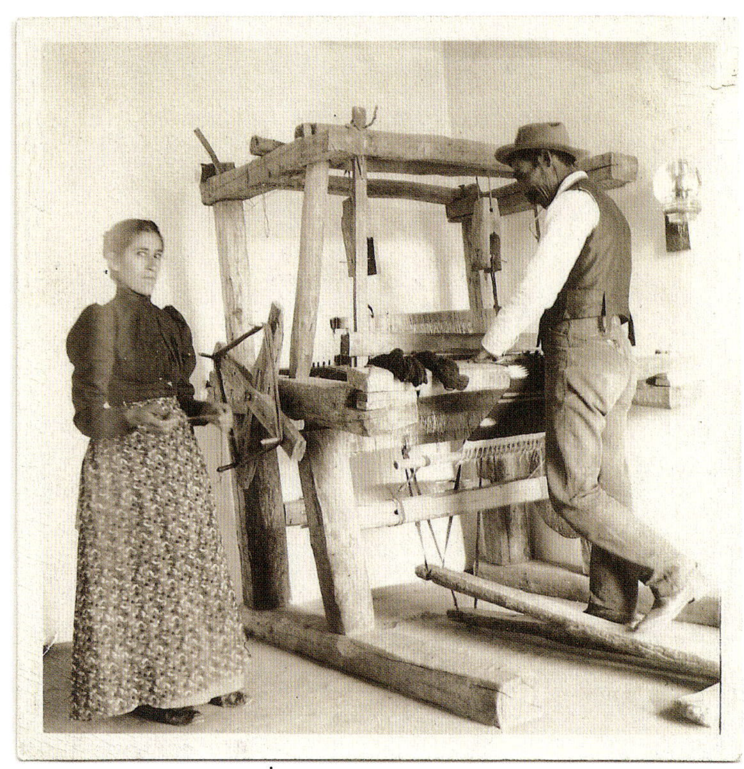

Hispano weavers, Mr. and Mrs. Esquipula Martínez, Plaza del Cerro, Chimayó, New Mexico, ca. 1910.

the rivers and mountains they passed while exploring the region, and they renamed many of the centuries-old multi-story pueblos in honor of Catholic saints, including Santa Clara, Santa Ana, San Felipe, San Ildefonso, San Juan, and Santo Domingo, to name a few. When the Spanish first arrived, there were about one hundred Pueblo villages, some of which had been established as early as AD 1300, and the Native population was between 80,000 and 100,000 people.

Drought and famine strained relations between the Spanish and the Pueblo people in the 1670s, and by 1680, following decades of cultural and political domination—which included servitude, loss of land, threatened ancestral traditions, starvation, and loss of life from European-introduced diseases—Pueblo villagers (who by then only numbered about 11,000 souls living in 31 villages) sought to expel the Spanish from the Southwest in what has become known as The Pueblo Revolt. Under the leadership of Popé, from San Juan Pueblo, Catholic priests were killed, mission churches burned, and the Spanish were driven out, first to Santa Fe and then to El Paso, Texas. Twelve years later, following numerous attempts at reconquest, Don Diego de Vargas was successful in returning Spanish settlers to New Mexico.

In the eighteenth century, the northern Pueblos and the Spanish increasingly became allies against raids from well armed, neighboring Native Americans. Among them were Utes, Comanches, Navajos, and Apaches. Continued religious suppression by the Spanish led to a dual religious life for Pueblo people, who openly worshipped the Catholic religion and secretly observed their own religious practices. In Arizona there was also unrest among the Native peoples; in 1751 the Pima Revolt pitted Pimas and Tohono O'odham against the Spanish, who quelled the rebellion with a pitched battle at Arivaca in January of 1752.

After achieving its independence from Spain, in 1821, through the Treaty of Córdoba, Mexico colonized the Native homelands and people of New Mexico and Arizona. Major trade routes opened up that brought together Mexican and American traders, resulting in a blended Southwestern economic and cultural frontier. Mexico held power over the region until 1846, when the United States took over control, during the U.S.–Mexican War. The Spanish–Mexican Era in the Southwest officially ended with the Treaty of Guadalupe Hildago in 1848, when Mexico surrendered its northern territory, including New Mexico, most of Arizona, and Colorado, to the United States.

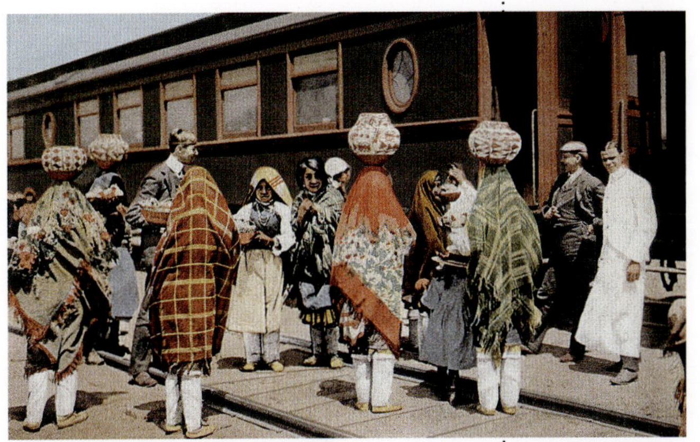

Laguna vendors meet the train, 1883.

Anglo influence in the Southwest region was realized as early as 1821, when Missouri trader William Becknell opened the Santa Fe Trail, connecting the area with much of the rest of the United States. Long freight wagons made their way across the frontier to Santa Fe, bringing an influx of manufactured goods, as well as building supplies for erecting structures in Eastern and Midwestern styles of architecture. New routes of trade also brought much-needed goods to the remote villages of southern Arizona.

In 1880 the Transcontinental Railroad reached the heart of the Southwest, bringing tourists and entrepreneurs in ever-increasing numbers on the new railway cars. The effects of the railroad on the Hispano and Native American inhabitants of the Southwest were many and profound; in particular, the utilitarian arts of the region had to compete with the arrival of less expensive and readily available commercial goods. For instance, due to the new availability of metal pots and pans, the quality and quantity of pottery being made and used at pueblos declined. Likewise, weavers of

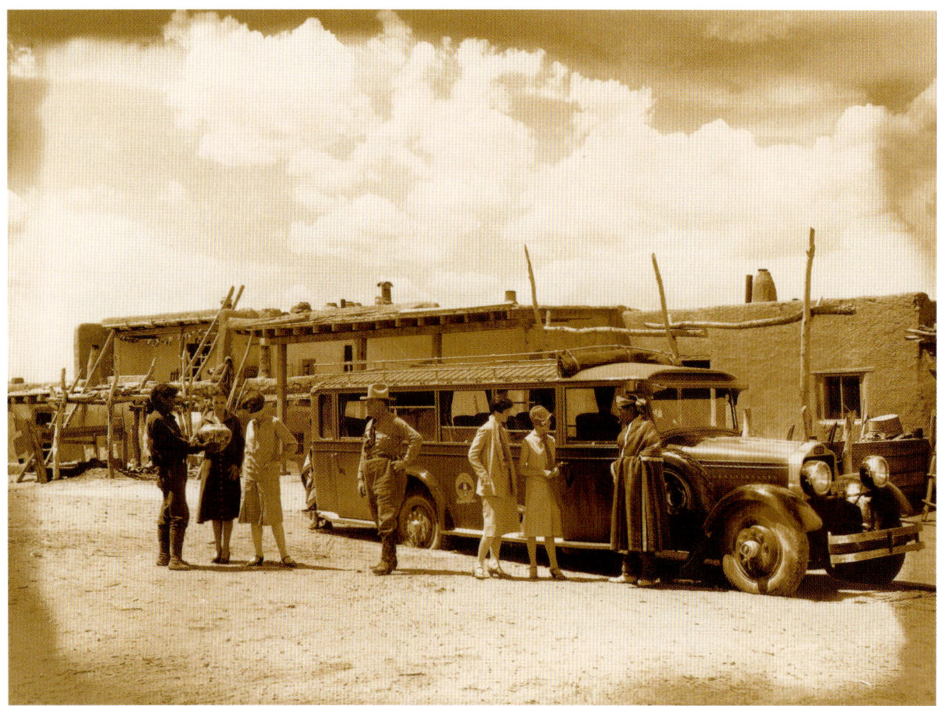

Fred Harvey Indian Detour car, San Juan (Ohkay Owingeh) Pueblo, 1925.

the region had to vie with ready-made textiles and Hispano tinsmiths were faced with competition in the form of commercially made objects such as lighting fixtures.

In 1912 New Mexico and Arizona were officially admitted to the Union as the forty-seventh and forty-eighth states, respectively. By this time, the increasing flood of tourists and traders to the Southwest had broadened the market for the region's indigenous arts and crafts. These supportive outsiders encouraged the improvement of ceramics, textiles, tinwork, basketry, and other local art forms, and provided a ready market for them. Creative and talented Native and Hispano artisans responded by making the transition from producing pieces made for domestic use or trade to those made for sale. Gradually, the economic and artistic control of these crafts shifted away from traders, dealers, and others to the artists themselves, who began selling their own work at fairs, markets, and from home studios/shops, directly to collectors and tourists.

In the following decades, world events and modern economic developments would have a profound impact on the peoples of the Southwest. During World War II, large numbers of Hispano men were drafted into the army and many regional cultural and family traditions went into decline. Following the war, a large number of people who once lived in Hispano villages, pueblos, or other small communities moved to urban cities in the Southwest or elsewhere, places where they entered the wage economy. Eventually, some transitioned back to their homelands to live a more "traditional" life and to revive or continue the arts and crafts of their ancestors, devoting their lives to creating and selling their work. In tight-knit families and communities, these elders taught and encouraged the next generations to create indigenous crafts; each generation added its own innovations relating to the materials, techniques, and subject matter used. For many, their work was (and still is) a spiritual endeavor as well as a cultural one.

In recent years, as commercial products have gradually replaced native materials in some crafts of the region, valuable information is in danger of being lost—such as the best type of desert plant to use for particular dyes or sewing strands for baskets; the special clay potters should utilize for colored slips to paint designs on pottery; and the ingredients for making piñon-sap varnish for retablos. Hence, the importance of writing and publishing a book such as *Southwest Art Defined:* to help preserve knowledge relating to the materials, techniques, and recipes used by Southwestern artists and artisans over the centuries.

NEW MEXICO

Throughout this book, the term "Pueblo people" is used to refer to all the Native Americans who today live in villages in northern New Mexico and along the Rio Grande. They are the descendants of the Ancestral Puebloans (formerly called the Anasazi), who occupied the northern Southwest, including the Colorado Plateau and Rio Grande Valley, beginning as early as AD 600. Archaeologists defined this cultural group based on particular forms of pottery, architecture, and lifestyle.

There are twenty surviving Pueblo villages scattered throughout parts of New Mexico, each with a population ranging from about one hundred to several thousand. Although many cultural and architectural features unify these villages, or pueblos, eight different language groups have been spoken in the New Mexico villages.

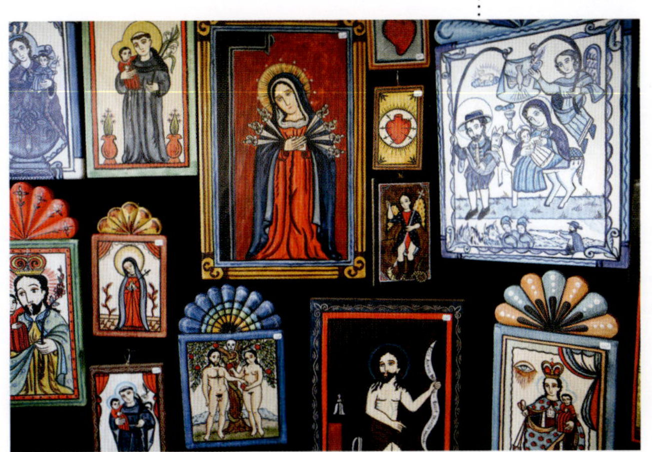

Retablos by Charlie Carrillo, New Mexico.

Many Pueblo groups in New Mexico are still known by their Spanish names. However, in recent years, some have rejected this sign of Spanish colonial domination and have resumed their tribal names. For example, San Juan has reverted to the name Okhay Owingeh.

Today there are three Tiwa-speaking villages in New Mexico. Isleta Pueblo, whose name is a Spanish word for "little island" (for reportedly when the Spaniards first saw the pueblo in 1540 it appeared like a little island in the Rio Grande) and is known to its people as Tuei, was originally established in the 1300s. Today it is situated on a 244,000-acre reservation in the Rio Grande Valley, thirteen miles south of Albuquerque. Taos Pueblo, whose name derived from the Tiwa word *tua*, meaning "houses," is located just north of the town that bears its name, on a 95,000-acre reservation, with its main village divided in half by the Taos River. The third Tiwa-speaking village is Picuris Pueblo (the name is a Spanish corruption of the Keres word *pikuria*, meaning "those who paint"), situated about twenty-four miles southeast of Taos in the Sangre de Cristo Mountains. Once the largest Tiwa pueblo, Picuris is today one of the smallest, with about 1,800 residents.

Two of the region's pueblos are Towa-speaking: Jemez, who call themselves hee Mish and call their village Walatowa ("the people of the canyon"), is situated on a 89,000-acre reservation at the foot of the Jemez Mountains west of Santa Fe; and Pecos Pueblo, which is no longer inhabited, and today is a National Historic Landmark and part of the National Park Service.

With a population of about 7,000, the largest of the Keresan-speaking villages is Laguna Pueblo, located forty-five miles west of Albuquerque, New Mexico, on a 460,000-acre reservation, including homelands occupied by Laguna people since at least AD 1300. Laguna is Spanish for "lake," and is named for the lake on the reservation. The Keres name for the pueblo is Kawaik, which also means "lake." The southernmost Keresan-speaking pueblo is the ancient village of Acoma ("people of the white rock"), built atop a 367-foot-high mesa in west-central New

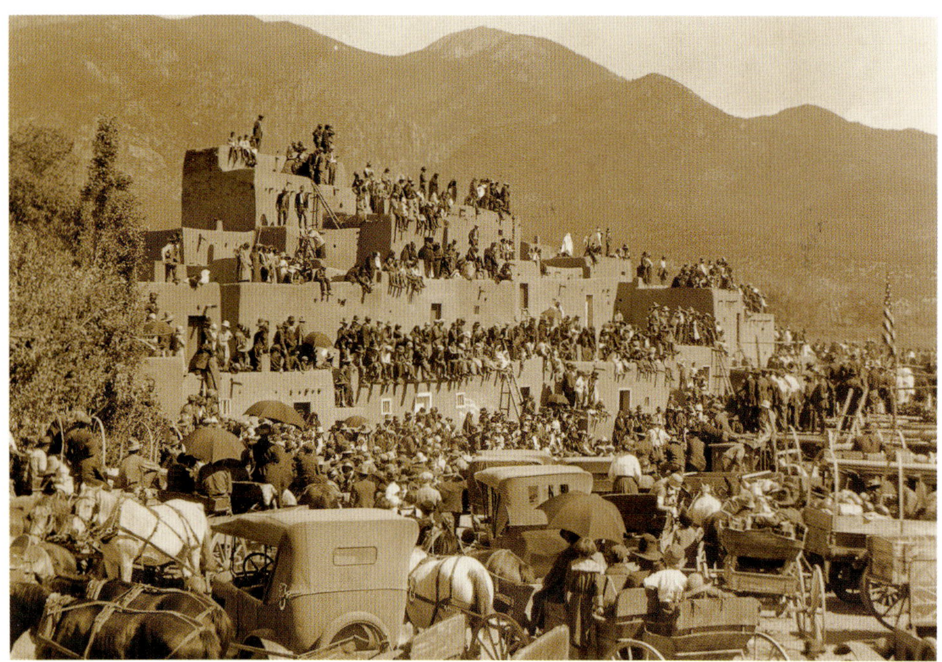

San Geronimo Feast Day, Taos Pueblo, 1920.

Mexico, occupied since at least AD 1150. The mesa is part of the tribe's present 431,664-acre reservation. The northernmost Keres pueblo is Cochiti (a mispronunciation of its native name Ko-tyit, meaning "stone kiva"), a village settled in AD 1250. Today Cochiti encompasses about 53,779 acres of land about forty miles south of Santa Fe on the Rio Grande River, which flows through its reservation.

Other Keresan-speaking villages are Zia Pueblo (whose Keresan name is Tsiya), situated on an isolated basalt-capped mesa on the north bank of the Jemez River, and Santa Ana Pueblo (whose Keresan name is Tamaya), whose people have occupied their current site in central New Mexico, about twenty-seven miles west of Albuquerque, since at least the late 1500s. The original Santa Ana village lies against a craggy mesa wall on the north bank of the Jemez River and is primarily used for ceremonies. Perhaps the most culturally conservative of all the Keresan-speaking pueblos is San Felipe Pueblo, situated about twenty-eight miles north of Albuquerque; the tribe's traditional name is Katishtya.

Five pueblos in New Mexico are Tewa-speaking: Santa Clara (whose Tewa name is Kha'po, "where the roses grow near the water"), with a village dating to the 1300s, and nearly 46,000 acres of reservation land along the Rio Grande (just south of Española); San Ildefonso (or Po-hogeh Oweengeh, meaning "where the water cuts through"), which has occupied its village since the fourteenth century, located on 26,000-acre reservation, just south of Santa Clara Pueblo; Nambé (the Spanish interpretation of the Tewa name Nambay-ongwee, roughly meaning "people of the roundish earth"), was established around the 1300s, now located on a 19,000-acre reservation north of Santa Fe, at the base of the majestic Sangre de Cristo Mountains, with a population of about 1,800 people; Tesuque (a Spanish derivation of the native name Tetsugeh, meaning "cottonwood tree place"), with a 17,000-acre reservation, just outside Santa Fe; and Ohkay Owingeh ("place of the strong people"), named San Juan de los Caballeros by the Spanish, once the largest of all the Tewa pueblos (today consisting of about 6,700 people), established around AD 1300, and now located on a 12,000-acre reservation, twenty-five miles north of Santa Fe, on the Rio Grande River just north of the confluence with the Chama River.

The Zuni people, who call themselves the A:Shiwi, speak a language unrelated to that of any other tribe in the Southwest. Their present village, built in 1662 on the site of earlier villages, is located about forty miles southwest of Gallup, and its reservation land now encompasses 400,000 acres.

The Athabascan-speaking Mescalero Apaches and Jicarilla Apaches reside in New Mexico. The Apache name most likely comes from a Zuni word, *apachu*, meaning "enemies." The Jicarilla Nation (headquartered in Dulce) is located in the north on a diverse landscape of mountains, rugged mesas, sagebrush flats, and seven lakes. The population is about 2,700. Jicarilla, a name of Spanish origin, has been translated by the Jicarillas as meaning "little basket;" this culture is indeed known for its fine basketry skills. The Mescalero Apaches (including the sub-tribes Chiricahua and Lipan) are located in south-central New Mexico. Their home consists of a 720-square-mile reservation and mountainous terrain, including the 12,000-foot-high Sierra Blanca peak that is sacred to the Mescalero people. The name Mescalero is Spanish for "mescal eaters."

ARIZONA

Among the prehistoric cultures that once flourished in Arizona are the Ancestral Puebloans (in the Four Corners region), the Hohokam (who settled in central and southern Arizona along the Gila, Salt, and Santa Cruz rivers), the Mogollon (who founded villages in the mountainous region of eastern Arizona and the Mimbres Valley of southwestern New Mexico), and the Sinagua (who inhabited central Arizona between the Little Colorado River and the Salt River).

At present there are at least twenty-one Native cultures that call the state home. The Hopis, who speak a Uto-Aztecan language, have a 1,600,000-acre reservation on three mesa tops in northeastern Arizona that is encircled by the much larger Navajo Reservation. The population today is about 7,000 people. Believed to be descendants of the ancient cliff-dwelling people of northern Arizona and the Four Corners Region, the Hopis have lived for centuries in compact villages on the southern edge of a plateau called Black Mesa. The Hopi village of Oraibi, on Third Mesa, was founded around AD 1200 and is considered the oldest continuously inhabited community in North America. The village of Hano was settled by Tewa people from the Rio Grande Valley after the Pueblo Revolt of 1680.

The two Piman-speaking groups in Arizona are the Pima (Akimel O'odham, or "The River People") and the Tohono O'odham ("The Desert People," formerly known as Papago). Descendants of the prehistoric Hohokam people, both groups live in the southern part of the state in small, scattered family groups that unite for ceremonies and other special occasions. The Pimas have long inhabited the areas adjacent to the Gila and Salt Rivers and the Tohono O'odham are residents of the Sonoran Desert of southwestern Arizona and northwestern Mexico.

Two bands of Paiutes reside in Arizona. The Kaibab Paiutes have a reservation on the Arizona/Utah border and the San Juan Southern Paiutes live on traditional lands of high-desert terrain within the Monument Valley–Navajo Mountain area of the Navajo Reservation. A small

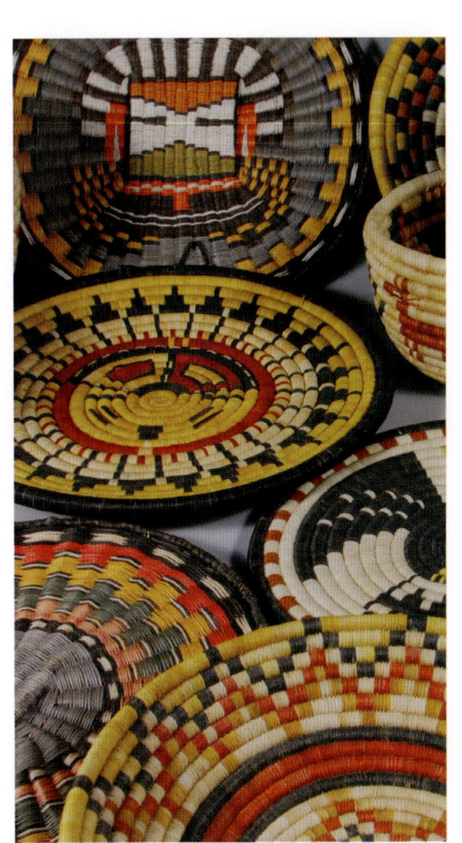

Group of Hopi baskets.

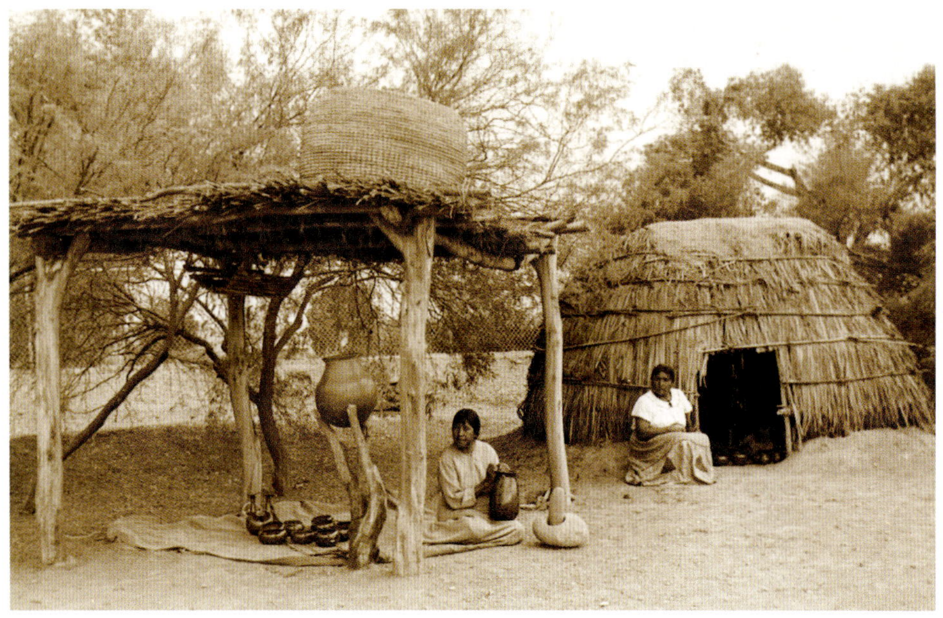

Maricopa potters Mary Juan and Ida Redbird selling pottery at Pueblo Grande Museum, 1940.

tribe of several hundred people, the San Juan Southern Paiutes received tribal recognition from the United States government in 1989 and are working toward having their lands designated for their own reservation. They belong to the Southern Numic branch of the Uto-Aztecan family. In an effort to maintain its cultural identity and distinctive traditions, the Southern Paiutes continue to make and use utilitarian and ceremonial baskets.

The Maricopas (or Piipaash), a Yuman-speaking tribe, migrated from the lower Colorado River region to the confluence of the Gila and Salt rivers, where by the mid-nineteenth century, most of them lived in the vicinity of their present tribal location among the modern Pimas. Today several hundred Maricopas have informally clustered in specific areas of two predominantly Pima communities: on the south side of the Salt River near the town of Lehi and at the Gila River Indian Community, on the west side around the town of Laveen.

At the turn of the twentieth century, Cahitan-speaking Yaqui refugees fled north from Mexico during the Mexican Revolution, escaping persecution by the Mexican government and Pancho Villa and his rebel armies. The Yaquis established small colonies near Scottsdale, Tempe, and Tucson, where they found work and where they eventually became known as the Pascua Yaqui tribe. In 1964 the U.S. government granted the Yaquis two hundred acres of land near Tucson for the community of New Pascua, and in 1978 the tribe received federal recognition. The Yaquis in Arizona retain ties to the Yaqui homelands along the Yaqui River in Sonora, Mexico.

The Yuman-speaking Hualapai and the Havasupai were once part of the same group, living in adjoining communities. Basketry has played an important role in both tribes' history and traditions. Since 1883 the Hualapai (or "People of the Tall Pine") have resided on a reservation of almost one million acres along the Grand Canyon/Colorado River in present-day northwestern Arizona. The largest community with five hundred or so residents is in Peach Springs. The Havasupai (or "People of the Blue Green Waters") have resided in the Grand Canyon and the rest of north-central Arizona for over 1,000 years. Their reservation, established by the United States government in 1880 and enlarged in 1975, today consists of 188,077 acres of canyon land and plateaus abutting the western edge of the Grand Canyon's south rim.

The Navajos, who call themselves Diné, meaning "The People," are Athabaskan speakers who migrated late to the Southwest from Canada sometime between AD 1200 and 1500. They made their home in the vast plateau lands between the Rio Grande pueblos in New Mexico and the Grand Canyon. The Treaty of 1868 established the Navajo Reservation, which was later enlarged by executive orders and acts of Congress. Today's Navajo Nation inhabits a 17.2-million-acre reservation, encompassing much of the Four Corners area of Arizona, New Mexico, Colorado, and Utah. With close to 300,000 enrolled members, it is the largest Native American tribe in the United States. Window Rock, Arizona, is the capital.

The homelands of the Apaches (Indé, "The People") range across a vast and rugged territory in the Southwest. The Athabascan-speaking Western Apaches, linguistic relatives of the Navajos, live in Arizona. In the mid-nineteenth century, when Americans first occupied Western Apache territory, the six thousand or so people were divided into five distinct groups: White Mountain Apache, Cibecue Apache, San Carlos Apache, Southern Tonto Apache, and Northern Tonto Apache. Because of their semi-nomadic lifestyle, Western Apaches, who moved on foot with their belongings packed on their backs in burden baskets, developed few of the arts that more sedentary cultures of the region did. Even their dome-shaped brush-covered dwellings were easily reconstructed and set up in a new place when necessary. At present, through the teaching of language, the establishment of tribal cultural centers, and other avenues, the Apache people, who live in communities across the region, are currently working hard to preserve their cultural and historical heritage.

COLORADO AND UTAH

By AD 700 Ancestral Puebloan people were cultivating crops for food in the Four Corners Region (where present-day Utah, Colorado, Arizona, and New Mexico meet) and by AD 1000 they were inhabiting the multi-story masonry and adobe homes, or "cliff dwellings" (such as Mesa Verde in Colorado) for which they are known today. People in this region eventually moved on from these communities in search of more water, fertile land, firewood, and game animals. By AD 1300 most had abandoned the northern parts of the Colorado Plateau. Pueblo people of the Southwest have numerous stories of the migration journeys their clans made towards their present-day homes in Arizona (Hopi) and New Mexico (Zuni, Acoma, the Rio Grande Valley).

Historically, the Southern Paiutes and Utes lived on the high plateaus and on the flanks of the southern Rockies at the northern edge of the Southwest, along the borders of today's Utah and Colorado. Utah, which joined the Union in 1896 as the forty-fifth state, derived its name from the Ute tribe whose name means "land of the sun" in the Ute language. Today the Ute people (with a population of about 3,500) live on three reservations consisting of about 1,300,000 acres of land in Colorado and Utah: the Southern Utes (headquartered in Ignacio, Colorado); the Ute Mountain Utes (headquartered in Towaoc, Colorado, with a small group living at White Mesa, Utah); and the Northern Utes on the Unitah and Ouray Reservation (headquartered in Fort Duchesne, Utah).

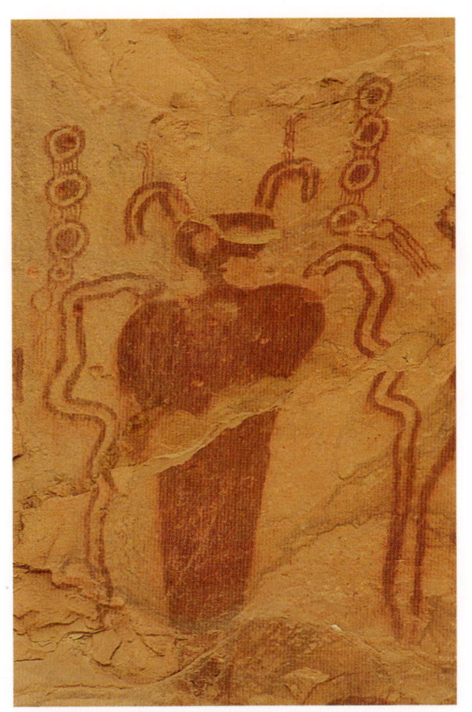

Pictograph at Sego Canyon, Utah.

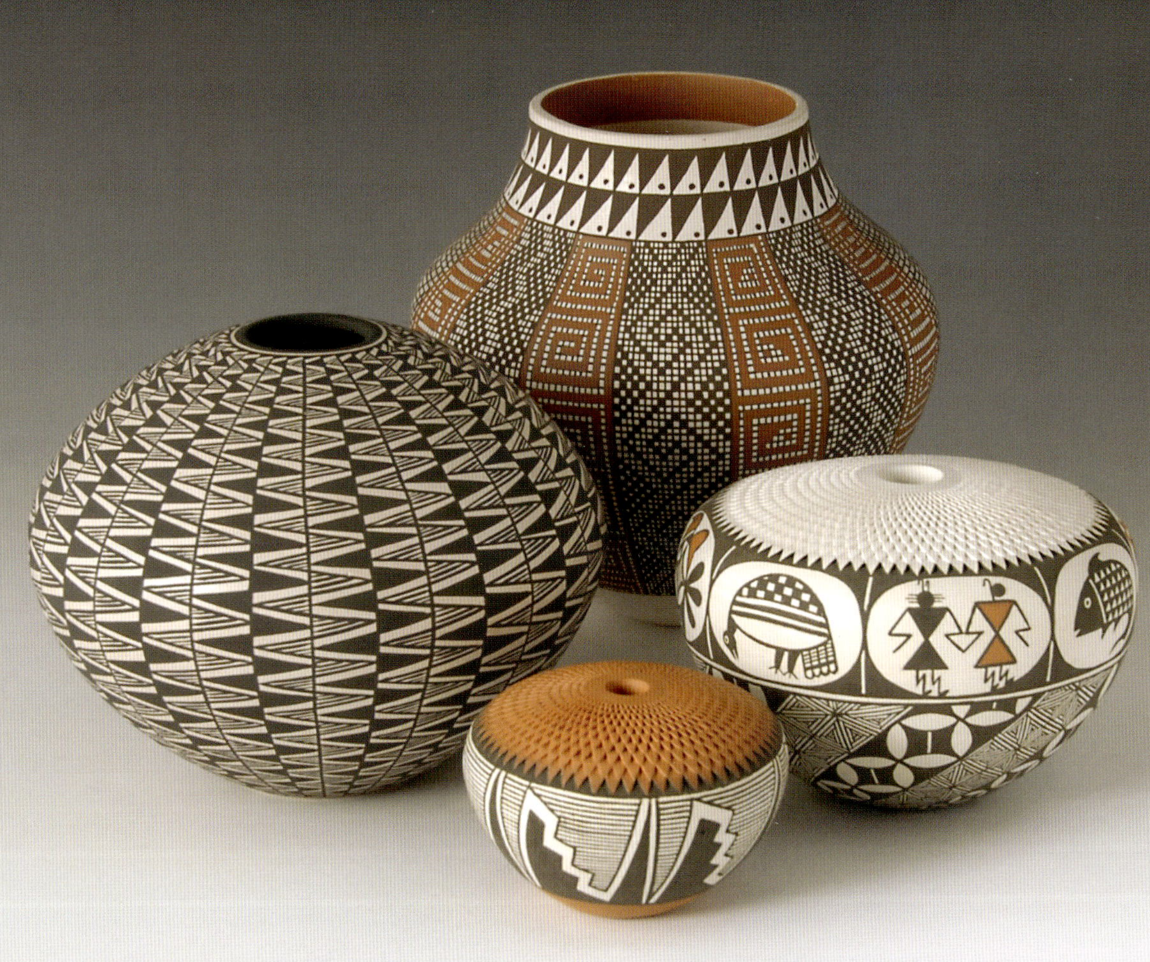

Acoma pottery (clockwise from left): Paula Estevan, Frederica Antonio, Adrienne Roy-Keene, Adrienne Roy-Keene.

ACOMA PUEBLO POTTERY / Acoma Pueblo is known for its revival of prehistoric pottery styles, especially vessels distinguished by intensely white, thin walls and black (or black and red-brown) fine line geometric decoration. In the nineteenth century Acoma potters also made **polychrome** pottery with a **slip** of white **kaolin** (fine, soft, white **clay**) as the ground and painted designs with red, orange, black, and sometimes yellow slips. Historically, Acoma potters made clay vessels for ceremonial purposes, jars to carry water from the springs in the valley floor to the mesa top (where the pueblo is situated), and other utilitarian forms.

Acoma clay, dark gray and very dense, must be ground to a powder before being mixed with ground **potsherds** for **temper**. The sherds are recycled from a potter's own pieces or gathered from ancient ruins at the base of the mesa. By using the ancient sherds, each pot contains several generations of ceramics within its clay and has a connection to the "ancient ones."

In preparation for shaping, the local clay is cleaned, soaked, dried, crumbled, sifted, ground, and soaked again. (Because of this time-consuming process, some Acoma potters use commercial clays today.) Using the traditional coil and scrape method, the potters form the vessels; the type of clay they use is so pliable that it can be stretched very thin. Pots are then covered with a white slip using a rag or brush, the surface is stone-polished, and then the potters use natural paints (such as powdered black mineral base with boiled-down **beeweed**) to brush on complex polychrome designs. Originally, Acoma potters used the outdoor **firing** method, but once electric kilns became available, most have preferred to kiln-fire their vessels (in part because kilns provide more controlled heat). Today only a handful of Acoma potters use the risky outdoor method.

In addition to fine-line geometric designs, Acoma potters are known today for white-matte clay vessels decorated with flowers, animals, and abstract creatures inspired by the **Mimbres** culture. Anthropologist Kenneth Chapman is credited with being the first to encourage modern Acoma potters to revive the Mimbres style, in 1958.

Stylized parrots often appear on Acoma pottery. The parrot was venerated by the Acoma culture as a gifted creature that could converse with the gods, and it also symbolized the sun and the coming of the rains. In prehistoric times, traders brought parrots and **macaws** to the region from tropical Mexico. They appear on historic (and contemporary) pottery made at other pueblos in the region as well, including Zia, Zuni, Laguna, and the Hopi villages.

Some modern potters at Acoma have been inspired to reintroduce another historic style of pottery—**corrugated**—on their white-slipped wares, based on the utilitarian wares and small potsherds of their ancestors.

In recent decades many potters at Acoma have been purchasing (or making) **greenware**—unfired clay forms that are produced in molds and then painted, etched, and/or glazed by the artisans, and then fired. Many Acoma potters prefer greenware because it is easier and faster than collecting, processing, and hand-shaping their own clay. They use a variety of shapes, including jars (**ollas**), bowls, plates, figures, and animals, and typically use hematite mixed with beeweed juice to paint their elaborate black designs with **yucca**-leaf brushes on the white background of kaolin slip.

It is interesting to note that Acoma pottery, generally made with extremely thin walls, rings if the rim is tapped gently. Dazzling fine-line designs—tight narrow lines that cover the pots in interlocking frets and hachures based on historic potsherds found at Acoma or in museum collections, made famous by Acoma matriarchs Marie Z. Chino and Lucy M. Lewis—are still an Acoma trademark. See also **black-on-white pottery** and **pottery—Pueblo**.

ADOBE / a name that derives from the ancient Egyptian hieroglyph *dbt*, meaning "brick," later translated by Arabs as *al-tub* ("the brick"), and finally in Spain it became *adobe* (or "brick made from earth"), the name and definition generally used today. In the Southwest the term is used to refer to the soil that makes the bricks, the bricks themselves, and the houses made from these bricks. One of the oldest and most common building materials known to mankind, and still a construction material in the Southwest, adobe is made from clay, sand, water, and binders—such as straw, manure, or grass—mixed together by hand, placed in wooden molds, and then removed from the molds and dried in the sun. Adobe walls, generally two- to three-feet thick, are laid with mud mortar of the same composition as the bricks and commonly finished with a **mud plaster** (especially in New Mexico) or a lime plaster. Many traditional adobe structures had no foundation; later, adobe walls were built on a foundation of stone and mortar, poured concrete, or concrete block. Adobe bricks, which slowly absorb the heat of the sun during the day and slowly release the heat into the interior at night, make this material perfect for homes built in moderate and hot climates. Thus, unlike wood-frame construction, adobe has thermal mass.

Adobe was a traditional building material in both the Spanish and Pueblo cultures of the Southwest. When Francisco Vásquez de Coronado

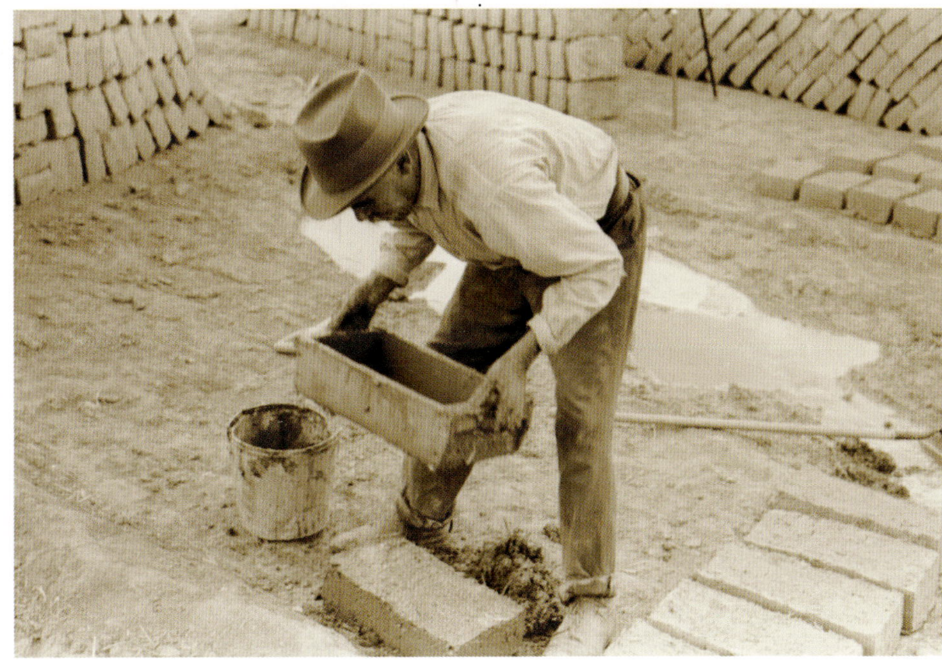

Making adobe bricks, Chamisal, New Mexico, 1940.

entered New Mexico's Rio Grande Valley in 1540, he found indigenous peoples experienced in mud construction and living in **pueblos** several stories high. The Spanish taught them a different way to make adobe bricks (for the Puebloans "**puddled**" their mud into monolithic walls): to use wooden molds to form the bricks and the sun to dry them. In some instances, adobe bricks were combined with sod **terrones**—dried dirt bricks cut from grassy river bottoms or marshlands.

Euro-Americans adopted adobe construction when they took control of the region in the mid-nineteenth century. Over the next decades, the popularity of adobe construction rose and fell, especially after World War II. Since the 1970s, when an interest in building environmentally friendly and energy-efficient homes emerged in the United States, there has been a renewed interest in adobe, which is so well suited to the climate of the Southwest.

Today most homeowners purchase premade adobe bricks from commercial suppliers; however, some owners/builders, especially in Santa Fe and small villages of rural New Mexico, prefer to make adobe bricks the traditional way on the actual building site, using the soil on the property and wood forms to shape the bricks. In order to do this, the soil must be tested first; the most desirable soil composition for adobe bricks is equal parts of sand and clay. In addition to its energy efficiency, adobe is admired by today's homeowners, builders, and architects because of its romantic associations and sculptural qualities. However, few "true" adobe buildings are being erected today, due in part to regulations in certain jurisdictions that require the material be treated with certain additives and the high price of labor and transportation costs related to building adobe homes. See also **adobe—stabilized** and **puddled adobe**.

ADOBE / Burnt / mud bricks (the same size, shape, and material as adobe bricks) placed in a kiln and fired, achieving greater cohesive stability and reduced moisture infiltration and a degree of ceramic vitrification, a favored building material in southern Arizona (and occasionally in New Mexico) from the 1930s through the 1960s, as an economical alternative to fired clay bricks, cement block, or wood-frame construction. Burnt **adobe** was used as early as the eighteenth century in the Mission San Xavier del Bac outside Tucson, but did not become prevalent in southern Arizona until the twentieth century. In New Mexi-can Spanish they are known as *adobe quemado* and in Mexico and Arizona they are called *tabique* or *ladrillo* (meaning "brick"). Burnt or fired adobes are primarily made in small villages of northern Mexico, where they are fired in kilns fueled by **mesquite** (as well as other local woods and/or brush), cooled, and then shipped north. This has resulted in the deforestation of mesquite bosques in the region. The use of burnt adobe, therefore, is considered by many to be less environmentally friendly than sun-dried adobe and is not recommended for new dwellings. Today the use of burnt adobe is primarily limited to decorative accents such as the **coping** in garden or **parapet** walls and to repairs and remodels of the thousands of homes built with it.

ADOBE / Stabilized (Treated Adobe) / a type of **adobe** brick developed by large-scale adobe producers, to which a stabilizer (also known as "amendments") such as asphalt emulsion, Portland cement, lime, or other chemical is added to make adobe bricks more water-resistant. Both fully and semi-stabilized adobe bricks are readily available from commercial manufacturers. Because this type of adobe is resistant to erosion, the walls do not need a mud or lime plaster finish. The majority of adobe bricks produced in the Southwest today have been stabilized; these bricks are not considered "true" adobe. In the building industry, adobe bricks with no amendments are called "natural adobes."

ADOBERO / from the Spanish, a mason or other person engaged in the production and/or laying of **adobe** bricks for adobe structures.

ADZE (azuela) / a carpenter's hand tool with a thin, arching blade set at right angles to the handle, used for hand hewing, trimming, or decorating wood surfaces. For example, the adze has traditionally been used in the Southwest to shape or decorate the surface of furniture, boards for **retablos**, **vigas**, and **corbels**.

AGAVE / a desert plant with succulent, spine-tipped leaves and a single towering flower stalk. Agave fibers have historically been used by Native Americans of the Southwest for making bow-strings, paintbrushes, cradles, nets, sandals, skirts, mats, rope, baskets, and snares. To make pliable strands for weaving/producing these items, the agave leaves were soaked and pounded to release the fibers that were then dried and separated by

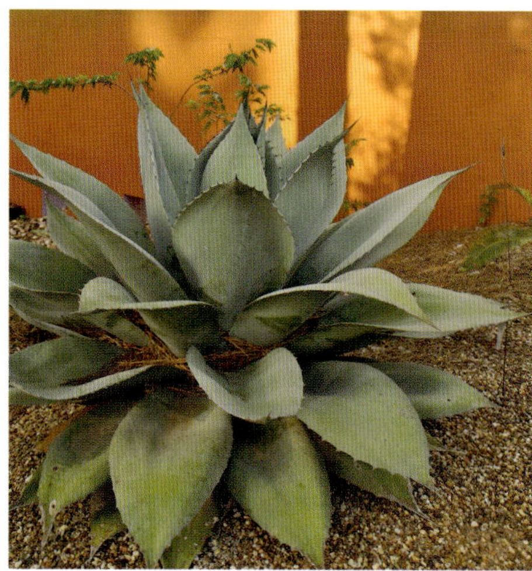

Agave plant.

combing. Some artisans of the Southwest continue to use agave fibers to create paintbrushes and weave baskets. See also **gího** and **Hohokam pottery**.

ALACENA / a Spanish word for "cupboard," the term refers to recessed wood shelving or cupboard built into the **adobe** wall of a house (particularly in a kitchen or dining room), sometimes covered with single or double rough-hewn wooden doors or shutters that hang on **pintle hinges**. Used in the homes of Spanish Colonial New Mexico for storing foods, alacenas later became popular in the early twentieth century when architects featured them in **Spanish Pueblo Revival–style** houses. They have remained a favored element in New Mexican architecture.

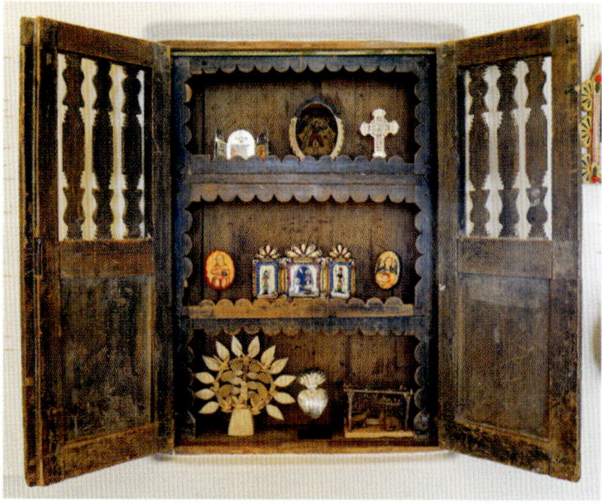

Nineteenth-century alacena, Museum of Spanish Colonial Art, Santa Fe, New Mexico.

ALTAR SCREEN / a large, wooden architectural framework typically featuring columns and arched niches in which are placed individual painted panels or carved images of saints and holy personages. In New Spain and in Spanish Colonial-era documents, a large, main altar screen was known as *"retablo major"* and a smaller side or nave altar screen was called *"retablo collateral."*

Set behind the altar in churches, chapels, and missions, altar screens are part of a long tradition of religious art making in New Mexico. Initially, screens were carried up to New Mexico along the Camino Real from urban artistic centers in Mexico. By the seventeenth century a number of mission churches had imported gilded altar screens made in Mexico City. A fine example of an early altarpiece brought to New Mexico, painted by one of New Spain's preeminent painters of the late eighteenth century, José de Alcíbar, is still on view at the Santuario de Guadalupe in Santa Fe, New Mexico.

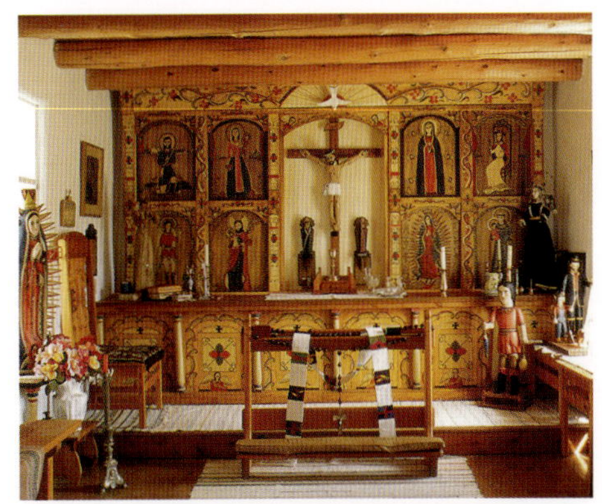

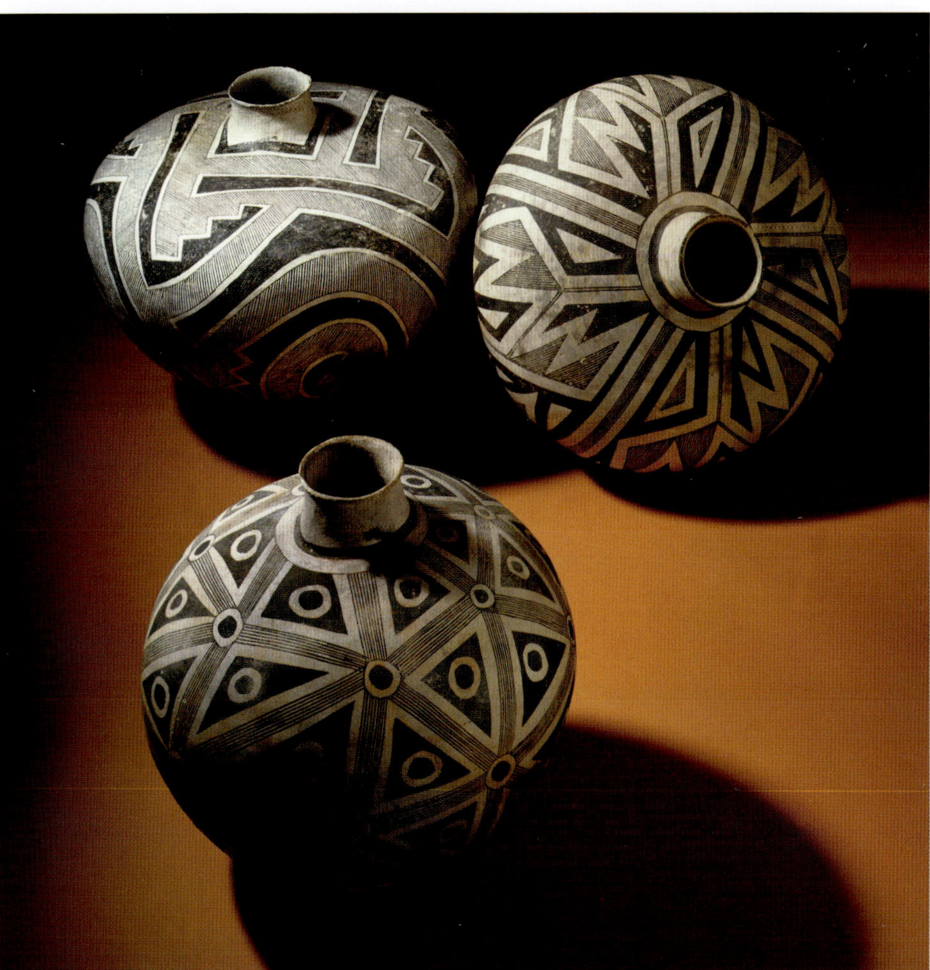

ABOVE: Anasazi (Ancestral Puebloan) black-on-white storage jars, ca. 12th–13th centuries.
LEFT: Altar screen in private chapel of Eulogia and Zoraida Ortega, Velarde, New Mexico.

In the early eighteenth century and especially from the 1780s onwards, Hispano **santeros,** and possibly some Pueblo artists trained by them, made altar screens for Spanish villages and Indian Pueblo mission churches in New Mexico. These santeros maintained certain design elements of the Mexican altar screens, while at the same time they created a local version of the baroque style. Among the modifications they made, for instance, were to create altar screens that were smaller in size (because of limited resources) and simpler designs (likely due to the varying skill levels of emerging New Mexican artists).

The Saint Joseph altar screen by the Laguna Santero (active ca. 1787–1808) at Laguna Pueblo and the carved- and painted-stone altar screen featuring an image of Our Lady of Valvanera, made in 1761 by Bernardo Miera y Pacheco (1713–1785) for La Castrense, the mili-

tary chapel that once stood on the **plaza** in Santa Fe (and later installed in the Church of Cristo Rey when it was built in 1940), are among the finest early screens by New Mexicans extant. A number of contemporary santeros/santeras carry on the tradition today, creating new altar screens for sale in the mainstream marketplace, or restoring antique ones for northern New Mexico churches. In addition, many have painted miniature versions of altar screens for sale. See also **reredos**.

ANASAZI ART/CULTURE (Ancestral Puebloan Art/Culture) / a term used historically by archaeologists to refer to the art and culture of the ancestors of modern Pueblo Indian peoples, who occupied the northern Southwest, including the Rio Grande Valley and the Colorado Plateau, beginning as early as AD 600. Particular forms of architecture, pottery, and other objects found at archaeological sites in the Southwest have been used to define the Anasazi people and their culture. Among the renowned early archaeologists who used this term were Richard Wetherill (1858–1910) and Alfred V. Kidder (1885–1963).

In recent decades there has been much controversy over the use of the term "Anasazi" and its definition. The word has been defined at least thirty different ways. One describes it as a Navajo word meaning "enemy ancestors." Another definition that most archaeologists sanction suggests "Anasazi" is an Anglicization of a Navajo term for "those who came before us"—a translation that many leaders of the Navajo Nation confirm. However, since the early 1990s, because of the influence of archaeologists and Puebloan and Hopi tribes who find the use of a Navajo word for their ancestors to be offensive, the National Park Service, archaeologists, historians, scholars, and others now use the preferred term, "Ancestral Puebloans."

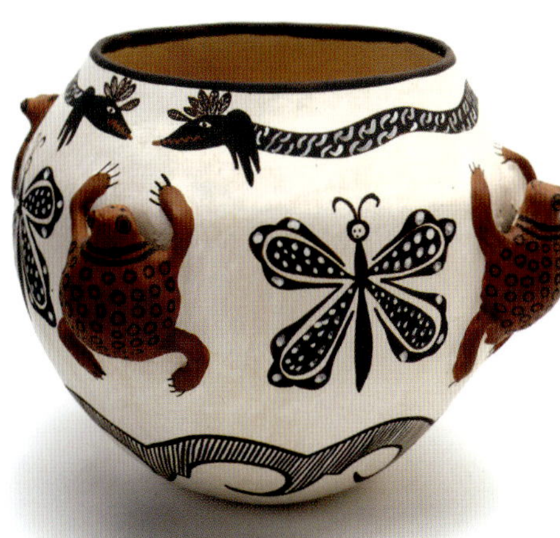

Jennie Laate (Acoma), frog pot, 1983.

APPLIQUÉ (Applied Decoration) / a decorative technique in which cutout or molded decoration—of fabric, straw, clay, metal, silver, or other material—is applied to another surface. For instance, the cutting-out of straw and applying it to a wood surface with glue; the soldering of silver leaves, feathers, or other cutout silver forms to an article of silver jewelry; or the molding of clay into a form and attaching it to the surface of vessels (or figures) with clay. The latter is a decorative method long common in Pueblo ceramics and also used since the 1970s by Navajo potters. Faye Tso (1934–2004), a Navajo herbalist and healer, was one of the first to break with Navajo tradition and appliqué figures of animals, **Corn Maidens**, **Yé'iis**, dancers, and other unconventional forms to her clay pots. Her appliqué-style pottery is carried on by contemporary Navajo potters such as Elizabeth Manygoats (b. 1972). Historically, and at present, appliqué is one of the basic techniques used by Native American, especially Navajo, silversmiths and jewelers. Precious and semi-precious stones, as well as silver or gold forms are appliquéd onto bracelets, buckles, earrings, pendants, and many other items of adornment. In furniture, the term appliqué refers to molding, turning, or other types of cut decoration fastened to the surface of a piece of furniture with glue, pegs, or nails; it is commonly used in Spanish Colonial and Spanish Colonial Revival-style pieces. See also **straw appliqué**.

ABOVE: Sunshine Reeves (Navajo), Number 8 turquoise and sterling silver stamped bracelet with appliqué designs.

ARAÑA / a Spanish word for "spider," which nicely describes the form and flow of most Spanish, Mexican, and New Mexican chandeliers that consist of many arms that hold rows of candles (or later, lightbulbs). In New Mexico the term was used beginning in the nineteenth century for chandeliers constructed of tin that featured one or more circular bands supporting extended arms terminating in six to twelve candleholders. Often the tin is decorated with painted designs. Beginning in the 1920s, tinsmiths made electrified tin arañas for residential and commercial buildings. Contemporary tinsmiths continue to make elaborate arañas today.

ARIZONA ROOM / **Sleeping Porch** / a screened porch attached to the rear of a house, historically used in Arizona (especially before the advent of air conditioning) as a place in which to sleep or lounge and take advantage of the cool evening breezes during the hot desert summer. This "outdoor" living room was adapted during the American Territorial period from the previous tradition of sleeping outdoors in **courtyards**, or on the roof.

ARMARIO (Wardrobe) / in seventeenth- and eighteenth-century colonial New Mexico and Arizona, and elsewhere in the Spanish Americas, a freestanding closed cabinet typically used for storing clothing. Beginning in the nineteenth century it was called *ropero*. See also **trastero**.

ARTS AND CRAFTS STYLE ARCHITECTURE/ MOVEMENT / a movement founded in the United States in the mid 1890s, to revive the production of finely handcrafted furniture, decorative objects, and architecture, as a revolt against the ornamental excesses of the Victorian period and the increasingly mass-produced goods of the era. Inspired by the Arts and Crafts Movement in England, based on the writings of philosopher and critic John Ruskin and the work of designer William Morris, the American Arts and Crafts Movement was disseminated in the U.S. by craftsmen Elbert Hubbard and Gustav Stickley, among others. Early twentieth-century **Spanish Pueblo Revival–style** buildings in the Southwest, with their austere simplicity, straightforward construction, and use of natural materials, colors, and textures, reflect Arts and Crafts characteristics. Additionally, the **bungalow**—a type of house that proliferated throughout the Southwest in

the early to mid-1900s—perhaps best embodied the Arts and Crafts philosophy in its simplicity, harmony with nature, and craftsmanship.

AVANYU (Awanyu) / the Tewa word for the plumed or horned water serpent—considered the guardian of waterways—and one of the most important figures in Pueblo cultures of the Southwest. According to legend, this mythological figure is said to have carried water down the streams and arroyos to the Native peoples of the region. In particular, the serpentine shape of the Rio Grande in New Mexico is believed to be linked to the legend of avanyu.

As a symbol and a prayer for flowing water, a crucial element for life in the desert, avanyu is represented in a variety of Native American art forms, including ceramics, paintings, and ceremonial clothing.

The serpent's name, attributes, and meaning vary among Pueblo cultures. For instance, at Zuni Pueblo he is known by the name Kolowisi. At Pecos he was a terrible war-like figure who gouged out huge channels in the ground (later known as arroyos) as he was defeated.

Avanyu has long been portrayed on the painted or **carved pottery** of Tewa-speaking Pueblos—particularly at San Ildefonso and Santa Clara—usually on vessels that carry water. The serpent is typically shown with a wave-like body and a lightning-shaped "tongue," and he is often accompanied by cloud and water motifs. At Santa Clara Pueblo, where it is believed that avanyu once saved the village from a flood, potters there have painted, carved, or etched the water serpent (with its tongue and tail intersecting) encircling vessels. A plumed version of the avanyu also appears in the jewelry of Hopi silversmiths.

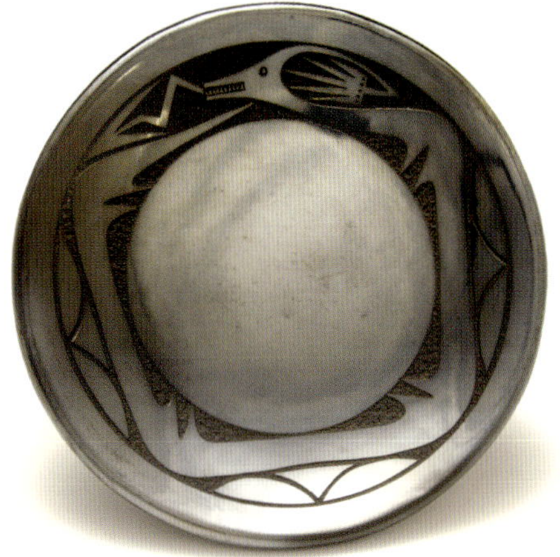

Tony Da (San Ildefonso), gunmetal plate with sgraffito avanyu design, ca. 1968.

AWL / a sharp-pointed tool used to make holes in hide, wood, and natural fibers such as **yucca** or wicker. Originally made of thorns or sharpened pieces of animal bone, awls were (and continue to be) used by Native American hide workers to puncture holes in hide for sewing and by basket weavers for separating foundation fibers in order to insert the weaving fibers (or sewing elements). These useful tools were often carried in tanned-hide cases sewn together with **sinew**; the cases were sometimes decorated with glass beads and tin cones known as **tinklers**. Particularly fine beaded awl cases were made by various Apache tribes in the Southwest. In the twentieth century, wood and bone awls were replaced by needles or other sharp metal implements ground to a point and set in wooden handles. Today most Native basket makers and hide workers use commercially made awls, available at leather or fabric stores. Some, however, continue to fashion their own awls by pounding a nail into wood (often **mesquite**); the wood is shaped into a handle and the head of the nail is ground off to a point.

AZUELA / See **adze**.

AZULEJOS / See **tiles—Mexican/Spanish**.

BANCO / a Spanish word for "bench," referring to both freestanding wooden benches with or without arms or back, and **adobe** benches comprised of mud bricks covered in **mud plaster**, built along the base of adobe walls, sometimes beside fireplaces. In eighteenth- and nineteenth-century New Mexico, built-in adobe bancos were covered with rugs and carpets for sitting and sleeping. Built-in furniture of this type was a tradition inherited from Moorish Spain. The term is also generally applied to built-in plastered benches placed adjacent to corner fireplaces, along walls, or under windows in **Spanish Pueblo Revival–style** homes of the Southwest.

BANGLE / a rigid bracelet constructed of wood, shell, metal, or other materials shaped into a ring or band and worn around the wrist or ankle. This jewelry type can be traced to prehistoric times in the Southwest. The ancient Hohokam people of Arizona crafted bangles from *Glycymeris* (clam) shells from the Gulf of California; band/ring forms were cut from the shell, then abraded and polished. Made in various sizes, the Hohokam bangles were worn by everyone from children to adults. Bangles were among the early jewelry forms made by Navajo silversmiths; their bangles were constructed from heavy wire that they decorated with file work or **stamp work**.

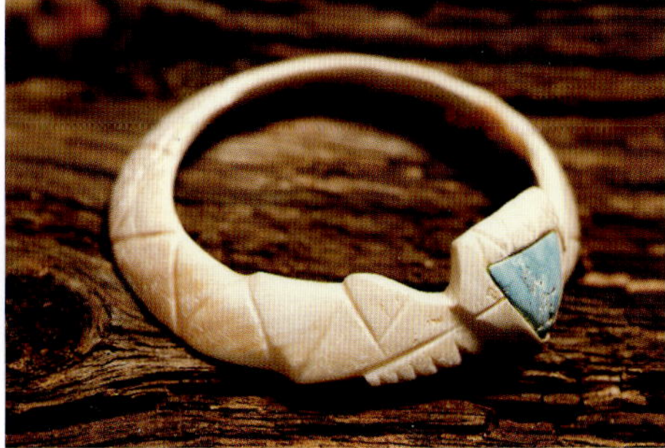

Hohokam carved shell bangle with turquoise.

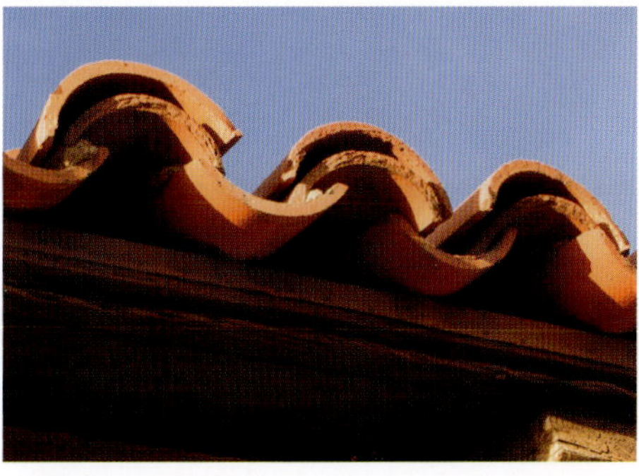

BARREL TILES / half-round, primarily red, clay roof tiles, originally formed by molding clay over sections of logs or across the tile maker's thigh, particularly popular in the Southwest from about 1915 through the 1930s. Barrel tiles were inspired by the barrel-tiled roofs of eighteenth-century Spanish Colonial **missions** in California, and used mostly on California **Mission Revival–style** houses. Production of these roof tiles was mechanized by the 1920s. After decades of exposure to the elements, these tiles gain a dark patina that was much prized by architects of the era. In addition to being used on roofs, they were incorporated into California Mission Revival homes as gable vents and patio screens.

BASKETRY / Ceremonial / handwoven ceremonial baskets have been made by the Native people of the Southwest for centuries. These baskets are used in ceremonies ranging from the Hopi Basket Dance to Navajo rites in which the baskets hold cornmeal for prayers/blessings. They are also used to hold prayer sticks/prayer offerings. The Tohono O'odham use them as resonators for rasps and as drums (inverted and beaten with a short stick). See also **Hopi plaques**, **wicker**; **sifter baskets**; **spirit line**; **wedding baskets**; **and wickerwork baskets**.

BASKETRY MATERIALS / the first step in traditional Native American basket weaving is the gathering of raw materials, which is done respectfully and only at appropriate times of the year, reflecting the basket weaver's intimate relationship with the natural world. The variety of native plant materials used for basketry include:

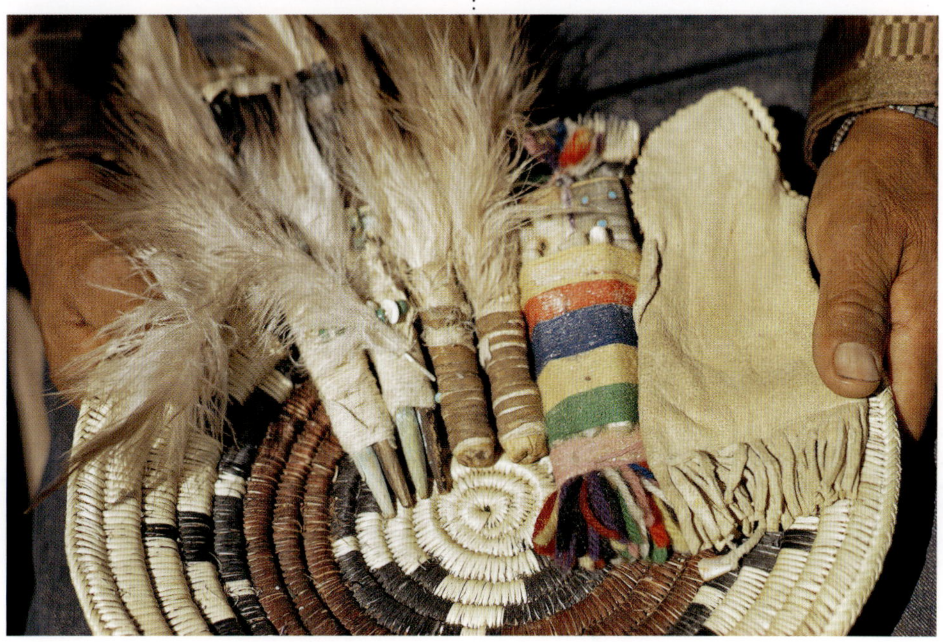

A basket holds a Navajo medicine man's tools.

beargrass, for the foundation of **coiled** Tohono O'odham baskets; cattail stems, for the foundation of coiled Pima baskets; desert **willow**, in rare instances in Tohono O'odham coiled baskets; dune broom (*Parryella filifolia*, called *siwi* by the Hopi), for the foundation of Hopi (Third Mesa) **wicker** baskets; **chamisa** (or rabbitbrush), for the sewing element in Hopi (Third Mesa) baskets; **devil's claw** as the sewing element and design of Tohono O'odham baskets (also used as coiling material in early Western Apache baskets); galleta grass, for the foundation of Hopi (Second Mesa) coiled baskets; three-leaf **sumac**, for the foundation and coiling material of Navajo, Jicarilla, Apache, and **San Juan Paiute baskets**; willow, for the coiling material for Pima, Western Apache, and occasionally Navajo and Jicarilla Apache baskets; red willow, for Pueblo bowl-shaped baskets; and white or green **yucca**, for coiling material/the sewing element for Hopi (Second Mesa), Pima, and Tohono O'odham baskets.

BASKETRY TECHNIQUES / Native American / See **close stitch**, **coiling—basketry**, **dyes**, **Hopi plaques**, **plaiting**, **split stitch**, **twining**, and **wickerwork baskets**.

BAYETA / a Spanish word, referring to a coarsely woven, usually wool, textile. In the Southwest it specifically refers to the commercially manufactured red-woolen trade cloth from European, Mexican, and American mills imported into the Southwest, first appearing in the late 1700s in New Mexico. The cloth originated in France and was introduced to England, where it was known by the word "baize." The wool used to weave bayeta was predominantly dyed red with either **lac** or **cochineal**; however, some yellow, green, and brown bayeta cloth was also available. In the nineteenth century, prior to the wide availability of red commercial **yarns** or synthetic red dyes, it was **raveled** and then re-spun by Navajo artisans (and to a limited extent by Pueblo and Hispano weavers) to make crimson-red yarn for their own textiles. Bayeta also refers to American-made flannel and woolen cloths made after the War of 1812. See also **chief's blanket**, **cochineal**, **lac**, and **raveled yarn**.

BEADS / made since prehistoric times, beads have long been used by Native Americans to ornament clothing, accessories, and jewelry. The earliest beads were made out of a variety of natural materials—shells, stone, bird or animal

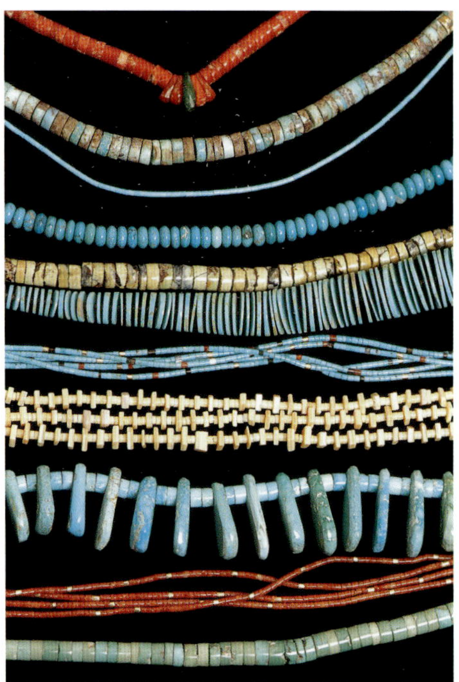

Beaded necklaces by Ray Lovato, Percy Reano, and other artists (Santo Domingo).

bones, claws, horns, wood, seeds, berries, nuts, and baked mud (or **clay**)—all of which had to be patiently hand-drilled or ground into shape. Flat disk beads—made from bits of **shell**, **turquoise**, **jet**, or other semi-precious stones that were drilled in the center and then strung and rolled back and forth on abrasive stone to smooth and shape them into round, flat shapes—were made by the thousands by the Hohokam, Ancestral Puebloans, and other ancient cultures.

In 1540 the Spanish introduced European-made glass beads to the Southwest, and in 1598 the Oñate expedition carried close to 80,000 glass beads into New Mexico as trade items and gifts. Glass beads were also introduced to the region by fur traders and missionaries who used them for trade with Native people. Most of these early glass beads were produced in Murano, Italy, and in Czechoslovakia.

Seed beads, so named for their tiny size and resemblance to plant seeds, became the favored bead among Plains and eastern groups, as well as Southwestern cultures such as the Apaches and Utes. By the late nineteenth century, trading posts began to stock a large selection of beads; the beads, along with finished beaded pieces, became important trade items. When tourists began flocking to the Southwest at the end of the nineteenth century, beadworkers adapted their work for the new market.

After World War II, the revival of Native American powwows and other ceremonies increased the demand for beads and beadwork. Contemporary artisans created beaded items for the regalia and outfits worn in powwows, for high-end collectors, and smaller, less expensive items for tourist shops.

Beadwork traditions are still popular among the Southwestern tribes today; among the beads they use are "greasy yellows" (an old type of glass bead named for its buttery yellow color); hex beads (glass beads with faceted surfaces); white hearts (an old type of glass bead with a white core and red outer layer); silver beads, plain or with **stamp work**; and seed beads—the most commonly used, consisting of tiny, flattened, globular shaped glass beads ranging in size from about 1/16 to 1/8 inch in diameter, made in Europe and Japan and imported by retailers and traders in the Southwest. See also **beaded bags**, **beaded folk art**, **beadwork—Ute**, **doming**, **heishi**, **pony beads**, **beads—silver**, and **shells**.

BEADS / Silver / have been made by soldering together two dome-shaped silver pieces that are polished to hide the joint and create a smooth finish, since the 1870s, by Navajo silversmiths and other Native artisans at the pueblos of Zuni, Laguna, Acoma, and Isleta. These bead makers learned the art of silver making from their Hispano neighbors. Some of the earliest beads were made from Mexican *pesos* or American coins; the coins were melted into ingot form and then hammered out into the desired shape. Eventually, Navajo-made silver buttons were embellished with **stamp work** or other decorative techniques.

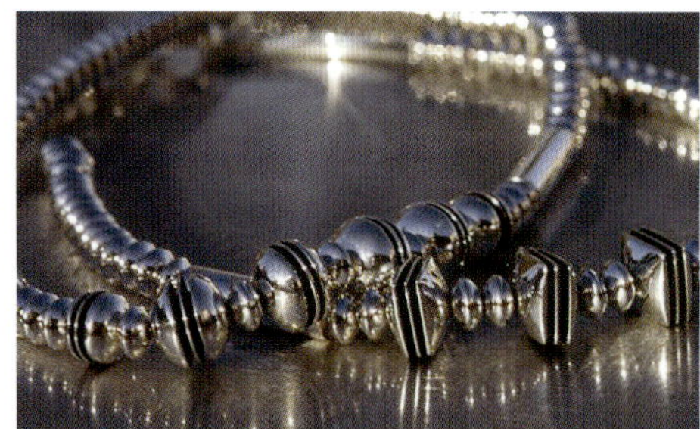

Jack and Mary Tom (Navajo), necklaces with silver beads.

Silver beads were an important feature of the **squash blossom** necklaces made by Navajo smiths beginning in the 1870s–80s, still popular at present. By the turn of the twentieth century large, showy silver beads had become fashion and status symbols for Native Americans in the Southwest, and remain so today. The Navajo-made beads in today's antique stores, museums, or private collections made directly from old coins with still-visible images and wording were made after World War II. When made into necklaces, Navajo silver beads are strung on plastic-coated metal wire, called "tiger tail" in the trade, or on braided-steel wire known as "fox tail." See also **beads**, **doming**.

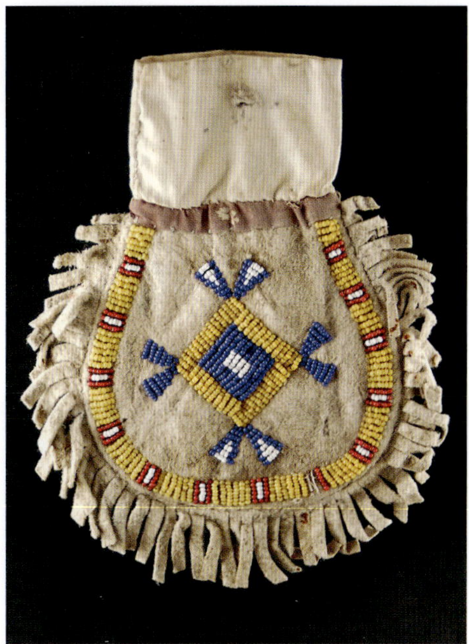
Ute beaded "possibles bag," ca. 1880.

BEADED BAGS, POUCHES, PURSES / decorated with both **loom** and stitched beading and long used and made by Native peoples of the Southwest, they were (and continue to be) distinct to the Ute people of Colorado. Historically, the Utes traded beaded bags along with hides, robes, and horses for Navajo blankets, silver, and crops. Through trading, the Ute's designs and methods of beading spread to other tribes in the region. Artisans of the tribe, situated in present-day southern Colorado, still make, use, and sell beaded bags, pouches, and purses. Although Pueblo beadwork remains largely unstudied, it is known that Tesuque Pueblo also became renowned for its beaded bags. By the late nineteenth century Santa Fe **curio** dealer Jake Gold had supplied this pueblo with beads he ordered from S. A. Frost of New York and commissioned them to make beaded purses and other beaded items for his store. Curio dealer J. S. Candelario (1864–1938) is also known to have commissioned Pueblo Indians to make beaded purses for him to sell at his shop in Santa Fe. By the early twentieth century artisans

at both Tesuque and Santa Clara Pueblo made beaded purses and watch fobs by the hundreds for sale. Mescalero Apaches are also known for beaded purses.

BEADED BASKETS / the Southern Paiute and Pima peoples of the Southwest were famous for this type of basket. The Pimas decorated both miniature and full-sized finely handwoven baskets with glass trade **beads**, primarily in the 1920s to '40s, for the tourist market. They typically wove their baskets with **willow**, **devil's claw**, and **beargrass** and the large beads were mainly sewn around the rim usually with willow as the "thread." Turquoise blue was the favored color of the larger beads used; smaller seed beads were more suitable for decorating the miniature baskets.

BEADED FOLK ART / armatures made of metal, found objects, sheep's vertebrae, and other items that are surrounded with cotton stuffing or other material, formed into various miniature shapes—figures, animals, and **hogans** or other buildings—and wrapped with strings of tiny seed and/or glass **beads** (today often attached with super-glue) that give the impression of traditional beadwork. Highly skilled artisans can create these figures using one continuous thread. This type of folk art is primarily made by artisans at Zuni Pueblo, New Mexico, and on the Navajo reservation. Among them is Navajo Sheila Antonio, a resident of the Four Corners region, whose figures display a wonderful sense of humor. See also **dolls**—**Zuni**.

BEADED JEWELRY / created in the Southwest by Native peoples since ancient times, from disk-shaped (and later round) beads, typically small in size, made from a variety of materials—especially **shell**, **turquoise**, **jet**, and **coral**—and used for personal adornment and ceremonial purposes. To make the beads the raw material is cut, drilled with a pump drill (more often today with an electric drill), strung on cotton, and shaped by rolling against sandstone slabs (or shaped with electric saws, drills, and sanders). For the final necklace, bracelet, or earring, the shaped beads are strung on cotton, silk, or braided-nylon thread. Beaded jewelry continues to be an important form of artistic expression for some Native Americans today. These artisans have taken the art form of using seed beads to new levels of creativity. For example, Kiowa-Comanche beadworker Teri Greeves of Santa Fe, New Mexico, is known for her

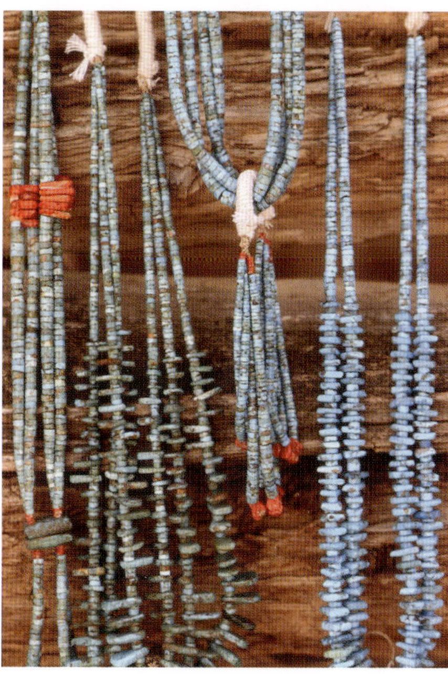
Ray Lovato Sr. (Santo Domingo), beaded necklaces.

pictorial beadwork on tanned-hide cuff bracelets. Another is Marcus Amerman, a Choctaw artisan and also a resident of Santa Fe who has become known for his intricate, realistic, pictorial images created with beads.

BEADWORK / Ute / although the date Ute artisans first began to use **beads** is unknown, according to one historic account the Spanish did trade beads to the tribe in the late eighteenth century. The Utes are among the few Native American cultures of the Southwest that have a rich bead-working tradition, dating back to at least the mid-nineteenth century. Tiny, European-

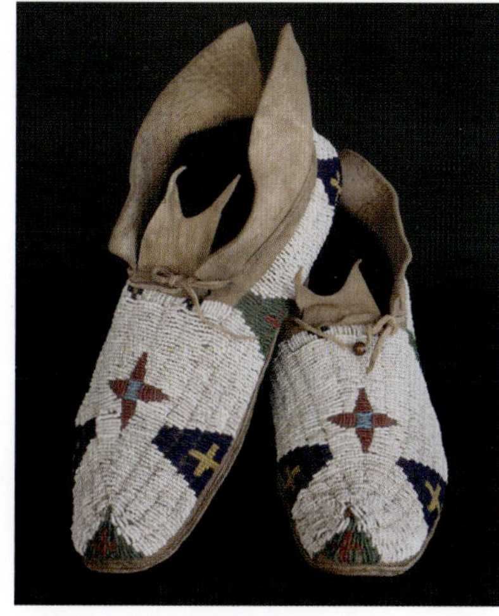
Ute moccasins with classic "morning star" design, ca. 1875, native tanned elk hide with Italian glass trade beads.

manufactured glass seed beads, initially acquired through trade with the Plains Indians, were used by Ute women by 1860 (and possibly earlier) to embellish finely tanned leather trade goods, utilitarian items, and garments—for example, carrying pouches, knife cases, moccasins, and tobacco pouches.

The women wove their beadwork on a loom or sewed the beads directly onto the garments or objects. One of the signature background colors in Ute beadwork is pale blue and typically the forms depicted were straight-edged: blocks, crosses, and triangles. By the turn-of-the-twentieth century floral patterns appeared in Ute beadwork. The craft continues today, as Ute women create bright floral and geometric beadwork patterns using a loom or sewing the beads directly on traditional regalia that are worn for ceremonies, celebrations, and community events such as the Bear Dance.

BEADWORK / **Western Apache** / sewn beadwork, resembling that of Southern Plains tribes, characterized by linear patterning. The Western Apaches, who arrived in the Southwest sometime between 1400 and 1600, made clothing and accessories from animal hides, which they initially decorated with vegetal-based pigments and later, once they were introduced to the region by traders, with glass **beads**; in some instances they used a combination of both. By the 1850s, Apache women used the "lazy stitch"—also called lane stich, for the manner in which short rows of beads are stitched into lanes—sewing technique to create beadwork designs on buckskin shirts, ponchos, shirts, moccasins, and on items such as pouches, awl cases and sheaths, hats, and hair ornaments. They also used netting—an ancient technique that creates large areas of beading strung in a net-like pattern—for beadwork on collars and small bags/pouches. For making necklaces and to cover handles of objects such as riding quirts,

Apache women implemented the "peyote" stitch, so-named for its use to decorate objects used in peyote ceremonies by Native Americans (although the stitch itself was used as early as ancient Egypt and Africa), in which beads are woven together by hand in an offset row method, so that when completed, no thread shows between the bead or row.

Clothing was typically bordered with narrow bands of diagonal stripes in alternating colors; pouches and moccasins often had bands encircling a central pattern; and geometric forms were common. Beginning in 1880, when soldiers from nearby reservation forts started collecting Western Apache beadwork, and the railroad reached the region bringing increasing numbers of tourists, the styles and techniques were altered to suit the tastes of the outside market. The Apaches made specific items for the tourist trade, including watch fobs, necklaces, hat bands, and napkin rings. By 1920, when loom-bead weaving was popularized, Western Apache women used the loom for beading necklaces, belts, and hatbands. Beadwork, primarily necklaces and small items such as key chains, continue to be produced today for Apache use and the tourist market. In addition to providing economic assistance, beadworking helps perpetuate the distinct Apache culture.

It is important to note that other Apachean groups (such as the Chiricahua, Jicarilla, Mescalero, and Kiowa) have made beadwork, but their work has gone largely unstudied.

BEADWORK TECHNIQUES / traditionally, Native American beadworkers stitched their designs onto a surface with animal **sinew** and later cotton thread. For stitching, the artisan punched holes with a bone **awl** in soft, brain-tanned buckskin

or rawhide, and eventually in woven wool fabric such as baize or cotton calico, and then applied the **beads**. Later, **loom** beading was used, a method in which a bow was strung with **warp** thread to serve as a loom. Eventually, looms were handmade from a variety of materials, and today they are often store-bought.

Contemporary beadworkers, when using the stitching method, use specially made needles, nylon or cotton thread, and a variety of backing materials, including leather, vinyl, chamois, canvas, and velvet. The most common stitches employed are: the appliqué or overlay stitch (two threads are used, one carrying the beads, and a second to tack down the beads at intervals); the lane or lazy stitch (six or so beads are strung on the thread at one time, laid in, and stitched down, making the work go faster); and the peyote or gourd stitch (used to create a diagonal pattern).

BEAR / among Southwestern Native cultures, animals have been given a spiritual nature and are believed to have powers that humans do not, and the bear, whether the much-feared grizzly or the more common black bear, has always been given special regard. Most of these cultures (including Hopi, Zia Pueblo, and Taos Pueblo) associate the bear with healing powers and for others (such as the Navajos) it represents supreme strength and power. Each of the tribes has their own legends and rituals regarding this animal. The bear has long been a popular motif in Native art, from jewelry to pottery to textiles. Representations may range from only a paw (see **bear paw design**) to various body shapes.

ABOVE: Western Apache beaded T-necklace, ca. 1900.
BELOW: Russell Sanchez (San Ildefonso), clay bear.

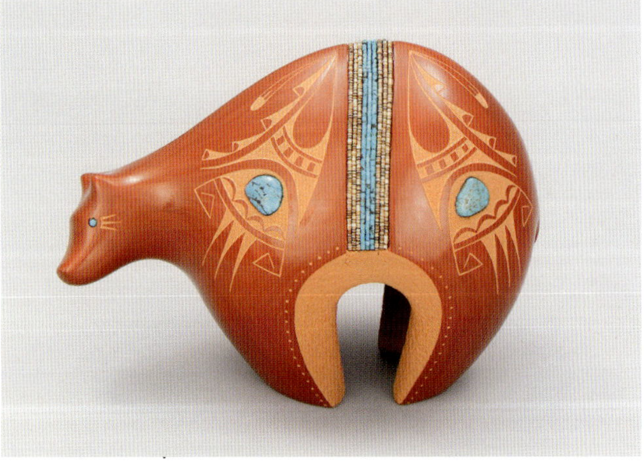

The bear is one of the most important animals carved into **fetishes** by Pueblo artisans, particularly at Zuni Pueblo where the bear is regarded as the guardian of the West and as the second-most powerful animal (after the puma or mountain lion). In Navajo cosmology, the bear is considered so powerful that the Navajo people avoid them, including the paths the bears use and tree trunks they rubbed up against. Several Southwestern cultures honor the bear in Bear Dances, including the Jicarilla Apaches and the Utes of Colorado. Bear Societies (or clans) exist at Hopi and several pueblos, including Zuni, Taos, and Santo Domingo (Kewa). One of the Hopi **Katsinaam** who participates in dances is called White Bear (or Qötsahònkatisna) and is considered to have curative powers.

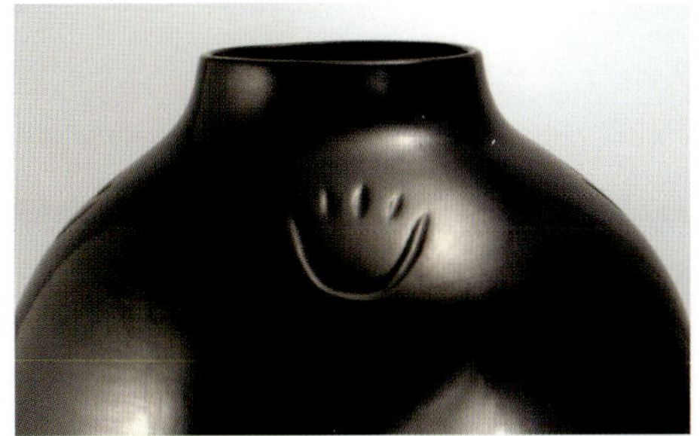
Margaret Tafoya (Santa Clara), black storage jar with bear paw design.

BEAR PAW DESIGN / a stylized image used on the pottery of Santa Clara Pueblo since at least AD 1200. It is a deeply significant symbol from an old legend: during a time of drought at the pueblo, a bear led the people to a freshwater spring and saved them. Because of the bear's association with water, the bear paw design—created by impressing into wet clay a U-shape line for the paw and three indentations above to indicate the claws—traditionally appeared most often on vessels that could store or carry water. Among the first modern potters to revive the design was Sara Fina Tafoya (ca. 1863–1949) of Santa Clara. It continues to be immensely popular among contemporary Pueblo potters and collectors.

BEARGRASS (Nolina microcarpa) / a plant that grows in thick clumps with long, narrow, razor-sharp leaves that are shredded and used by Tohono O'odham artisans in Arizona for use in the bundle foundation of their **coiled** baskets. The plant is called *moho* in the Tohono O'odham language.

BEEWEED (Cleome serrulata, stink weed, spider flower, guaco) / iron-rich wild spinach used by Pueblo potters as black-mineral paint for decorating clay vessels. To make the paint, a few drops of juice from beeweed concentrate are placed in a depression in a stone, then a nodule of hematite is rubbed into the depression and mixed with the beeweed. The paint is applied to the hard **clay** surface with a **yucca**-leaf brush and then the pot is fired. Some contemporary potters mix the beeweed with other substances, for instance Virgil Ortiz of Cochiti Pueblo uses sugar, while others, such as Sandra Victorino at Acoma mix the beeweed with enough iron oxide to create a more reddish-brown paint instead of black.

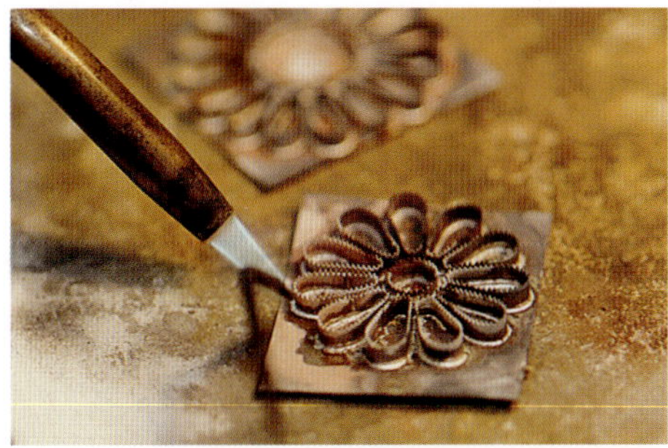
Jennie Vicenti (Zuni) creates a bezel.

BEZEL / in jewelry, a thin strip of silver or gold rimming a stone and holding it into the backing; often the upper edge is serrated or scalloped, so the bezel can be bent inward more tightly around the stone. The bezel is anchored to the ring, bracelet, pendant, or other type of jewelry by soldering.

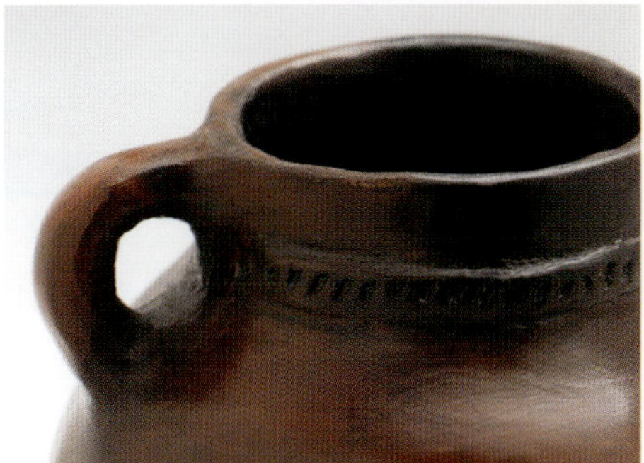
Rose Williams (Navajo), two-handled jar with biyo', 2006, clay with varnish.

BIYO' (Biyoo') / a Navajo word referring to the traditional beaded "necklace" of textured clay **appliquéd** to the area just below the rim of a clay pot, a feature seen primarily in **Navajo pottery**. A tiny break in the biyo' called *atiin*, meaning "the road," is similar to the **spirit line** in hand-woven textiles and the break in designs on baskets that offers a path of escape for the energy and spirit that the artist put into creating the piece.

BLACK POTTERY / a type of pottery resulting from an exacting process in which iron-rich red **clay** pots are fired in the absence of oxygen; the chemical and physical reactions that occur in the clay turn the pot black. This is usually achieved by covering the clay vessel in such a way that the oxygen in the atmosphere immediately surrounding it cannot be replaced as the temperature rises during the **firing**. This is called "reduction" firing. In traditional outdoor firings, some Native American potters smother the hot fire with pulverized manure to achieve the reduction. Others place a metal bucket over the pot on the ground and seal the edges with manure or dirt.

In Pueblo cultures the process dates back at least to the twelfth century; some scholars in the twentieth century speculated that it was nearly forgotten until about 1730, when it experienced a revival. The scholars identified these clay vessels with the Tewa name for Santa Clara Pueblo, "Kapo," and called the pottery Kapo Black. The Tewa-speaking villages of Santa Clara and San Ildefonso remain the primary sources for this style of pottery today. Other techniques for producing black pots include simply painting the entire pot with black paint and firing it in an oxidation firing. A variation of this is the use of a graphite solution on the pot surface. See the **Mata Ortiz** section of **black-on-black pottery**.

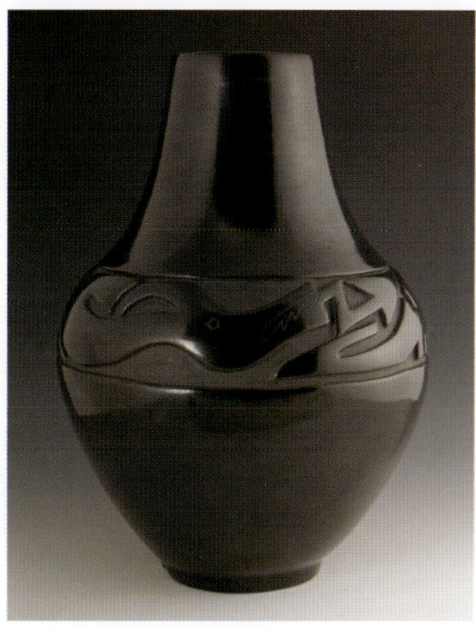
Margaret Tafoya (Santa Clara), tall jar with avanyu.

BLACK-ON-BLACK POTTERY / clay vessels with a black matte design on a highly polished black surface. This subtle and elegant style of pottery was developed around 1919 by Maria Martinez (ca. 1880–1980) and her husband Julian Martinez (1897–1943) of San Ildefonso Pueblo. Techniques vary, but basically an unfired vessel is stone-**polished** to a high sheen and then designs are painted on the polished surface with an iron-rich clay **slip** that becomes matte when fired. Many of the motifs used on the black-on-black wares made by Maria and Julian Martinez and other Pueblo potters were inspired by ancient Southwestern sources, such as animals and stylized feathers used by **Mimbres** potters. Some

potters in **Mata Ortiz**, a village in Chihuahua, Mexico, make a black-on-black ware known as "graphite" or *grafito* work. After polishing they cover the pot with a solution of graphite. When this dries, the painted designs are applied. The result after firing is a metallic-like sheen on the pot surface under the matte designs. Macario Ortíz of Barrio Porvenir discovered this technique in the late 1980s.

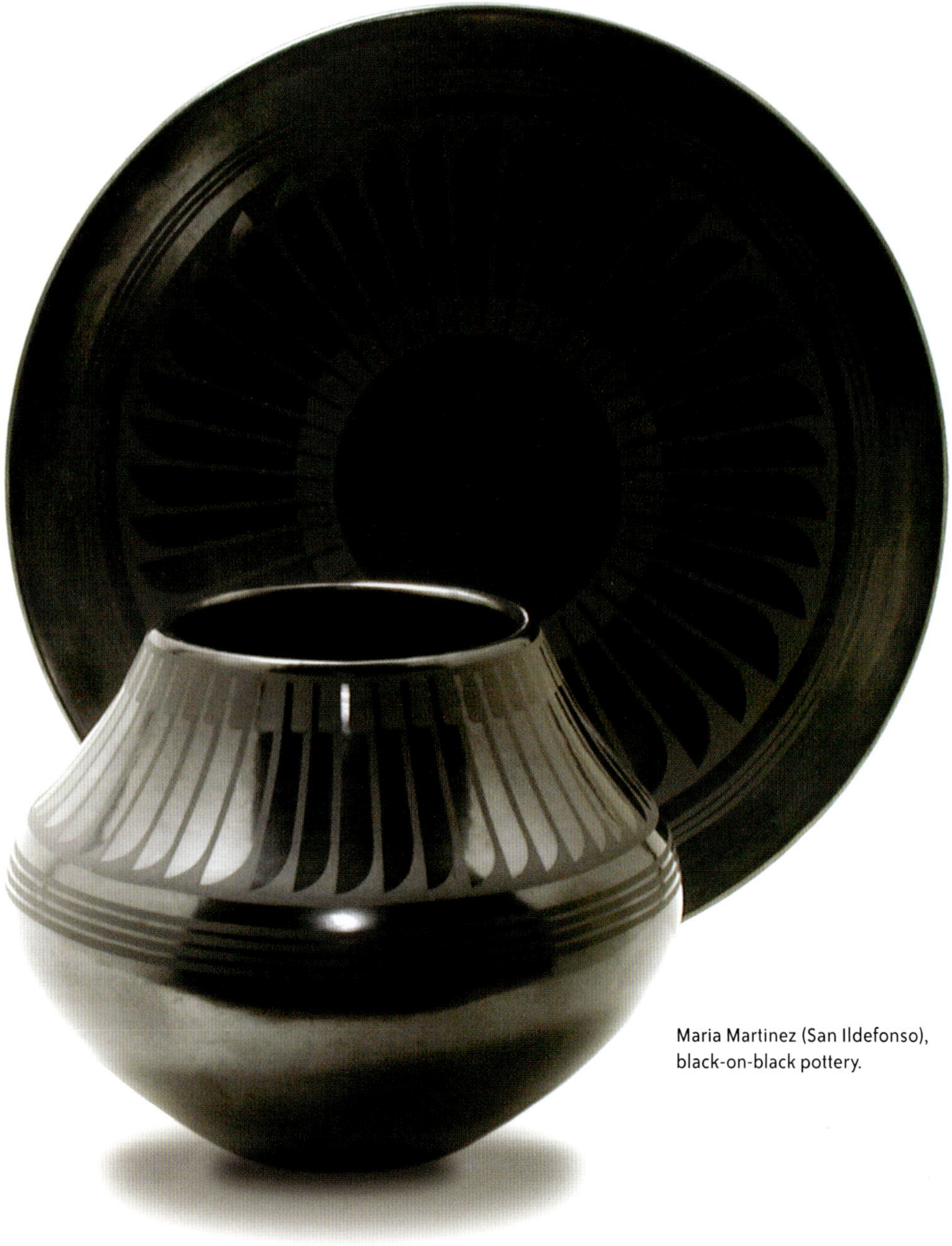

BLACK-ON-WHITE POTTERY / white-slip ceramic vessels decorated with geometric black designs executed in **mineral pigments** derived from hematite (or other iron oxides) or with carbon **pigments** derived from plants (such as

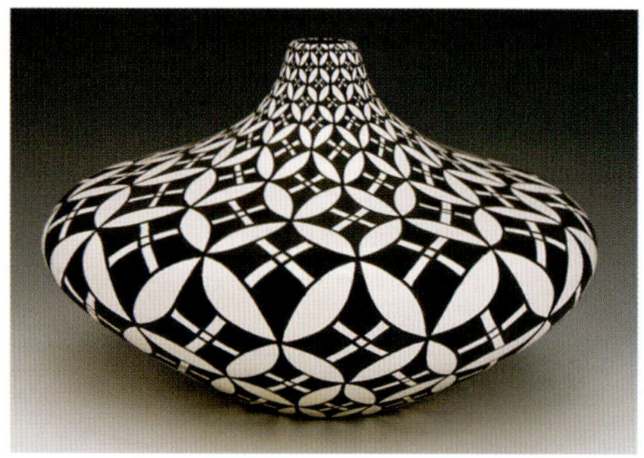

Dorothy Torivio (Acoma), large black-on-white jar.

beeweed). These pots were made by prehistoric peoples of the Southwest, including those at Chaco Canyon (northwestern New Mexico), **Mesa Verde** (southwestern Colorado), and the **Mimbres**. Although the design motifs and layouts changed through time, black-on-white pottery typically featured **hatched** and/or solid motifs that repeat and encircle the interiors or exteriors of the forms. Among the patterns commonly used: stepped or fringed triangles; interlocking scrolls, frets, or diamonds; and dotted lines, zigzags, and checkerboards. The black-on-white vessels found at Ancestral Puebloan ruins include globular jars, cylinder jars, mugs, bowls, pitchers, **canteens**, and cooking ware. A similar black-on-white style of pottery is made today at **Acoma Pueblo**.

BLANKET / from the French word *blanquete*, a soft, handwoven fabric (usually of wool or cotton), historically used for draping around the body, as well as for bed coverings, carrying sacks, and saddle covers. Either plain or decorated with stripes arranged in bands (and later with more elaborate patterns), blankets were made by both Native American and Hispano weavers. Hispanos generally called them **mantas** or **sarapes** (for wearing) and **frazadas** (for bedding). See also **Rio Grande textiles** and **trade blanket**.

BLANKET STRIP / a strip of hide ranging in width from three to six inches, heavily decorated with **beadwork** or quillwork, generally sewn over the center seam or along the edges of a hide or cloth robe, or blanket. By the 1870s the Utes of Colorado favored robes—usually commercially made blue wool blankets—decorated with Plains-style beaded blanket strips made by Ute artisans.

BOARD CHEST / See **caja** and **chest-on-legs**.

Maria Martinez (San Ildefonso), black-on-black pottery.

BOLO TIE (Bola Tie) / an iconic symbol of life in the West and Southwest, the bolo tie is a type of neckwear consisting of a jewelry element, generally **silver** but occasionally gold, and often enhanced with **turquoise** or other stones or **shells**, attached to a length of braided leather or other type of cord ending with metal tips that keep the cord from unraveling. The jewelry element is backed with a fitting that may be a slide or clasp that slides up and down to adjust for fit.

The origin of the bolo tie has been overlooked by most scholars, museum curators, and others. Some have attributed its history to Arizona silversmith Victor Cedarstaff (1904–1985), but Native American examples predate Cedarstaff's first bolo. It is generally agreed that the bolo tie was in common use by the late 1940s in the Southwest, and was likely developed from "scarf slides"—simple or elaborate metal rings or bands that may or may not have a decorative front attachment, used to slide up on a scarf to fasten the scarf around the neck.

The earliest bolo ornaments were isosceles trapezoid shapes that later served as the backings for decorative plates. Over time the bolo designs became increasingly elaborate: with small ornaments dangling from the tips; enhanced tips that elaborate on the theme of the main bolo ornament; and intricate **inlay** designs on the ornament of turquoise, **coral**, and other gemstones.

Traders in New Mexico and Arizona helped spread the interest in Native American bolo ties, which they sold, manufactured, and distributed. By the 1950s, when Native American silver and turquoise jewelry had gained popularity as the perfect accompaniment for western clothing, the bolo tie became an increasingly important Native American art form. Bolo tie ornaments have been created using a variety of techniques including **tufa casting**, silver **overlay**, **stamp work**, and several types of complex stone inlay. Some bolos, especially those made by Hopi, Zuni, and Navajo artisans, reflect the maker's cultural heritage, while other examples are purely artistic creations. Among the important modern Native artisans to make bolos was the master Hopi jeweler Charles Loloma (1921–1991), whose use of unusual techniques and non-traditional materials and designs influenced a generation of bolo tie makers. Initially worn by men and occasionally women in the West and Southwest, the bolo tie's popularity has spread to all parts of the country and continues to be made in a variety of materials and techniques by skilled jewelers and artisans.

BOVEDA / a Spanish word for "vault," the term refers to a brick shallow-domed ceiling, a visually appealing architectural element that has become popular in recent decades in the Southwest and Mexico. An ancient technique practiced by a small number of craftsmen today, boveda ceilings are hand built by laying bricks in such a way that the bricks support themselves. Similar to a barrel or cloister vault, bovedas have a square or polygonal base from which curved segments rise to a central point. In Mexico, the craft is often passed down from one generation to the next.

BOW GUARD / See **ketoh**.

BUCKSKIN / See **burden basket**, **conchas**, **hide clothing**.

BULTO / a Spanish word meaning "statue," used in the Southwest to refer to a three-dimensional sculpture of a saint or holy personage. Historically, bultos were carved from indigenous wood—**cottonwood**, cottonwood root, aspen, or cedar—covered with **gesso** (a white plaster-like substance made from gypsum), painted with water-based paint made from local and imported vegetal and mineral **pigments**, and sealed with a native varnish, such as the sap from a **piñon** tree. Sometimes the statue is clothed, and other materials such as tin are applied to the surface.

Prototypes or models for the bultos included images of saints in woodcut prints and engravings in bound books, as well as religious sculptures, brought into the New World by early settlers and priests. The earliest known **santero** working in New Mexico in the late eighteenth century was Bernardo Miera y Pacheco (1713–1785), who created bultos in the late Mexican baroque style—a style that also incorporated many rococo elements and was distinguished by robust and stocky figures with heavy draperies, naturalistic poses, and a subdued palette.

Created by artisans in the region up to the present, the production of bultos waned somewhat after the arrival of the railroad in the 1880s, when plaster saints began to replace handmade santos. In the early decades of the twentieth century there was a marked transition from painted to unpainted bultos, made by such renowned carvers

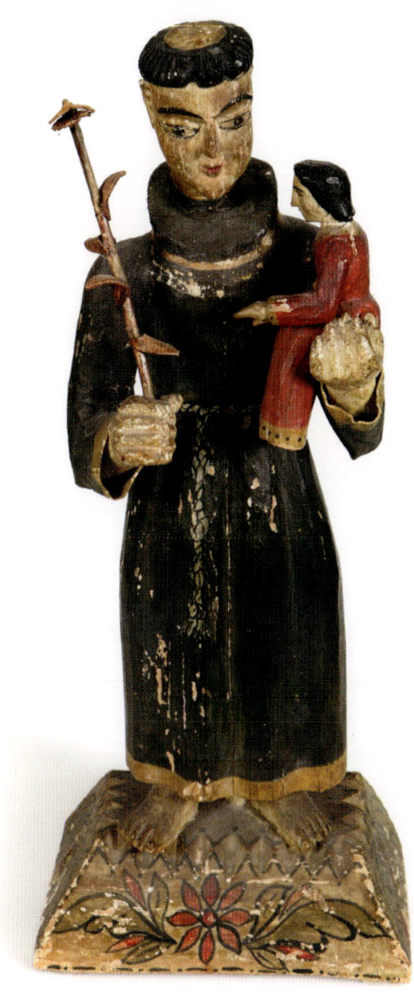

LEFT: Navajo thunderbird bolo-tie ornament, ca. 1940s, sterling silver with stamp work, turquoise stones set in bezels, on braided leather cord. **BELOW:** Juan Sanchez (New Mexico), Saint Anthony bulto, ca. 1935–1942.

as Patrocino Barela, Jose Dolores López, and Celso Gallegos. The Spanish Market and Indian Market in Santa Fe, New Mexico, encouraged the production of these unpainted religious figures. However, some, like Juan Sanchez, continued to create **polychrome** bultos in the traditional Spanish Colonial style during the WPA (Works Progress Administration) period.

In the 1970s, artists such as Luis Tapia began pioneering new expressions in bulto subjects and styles. For example, Tapia, as well as Horacio Valdez, started painting their bultos, reviving the eighteenth- and nineteenth-century tradition which by the '70s had largely been replaced with unpainted bultos. Tapia intentionally used bright colors to paint his bultos, instead of subdued tones that would have made the bultos look like antiques.

Today many artists continue to expand the art form and create non-traditional figures. These contemporary santeros/santeras use traditional materials and/or modern materials, such as oil or acrylic paints and manufactured varnishes and imported woods.

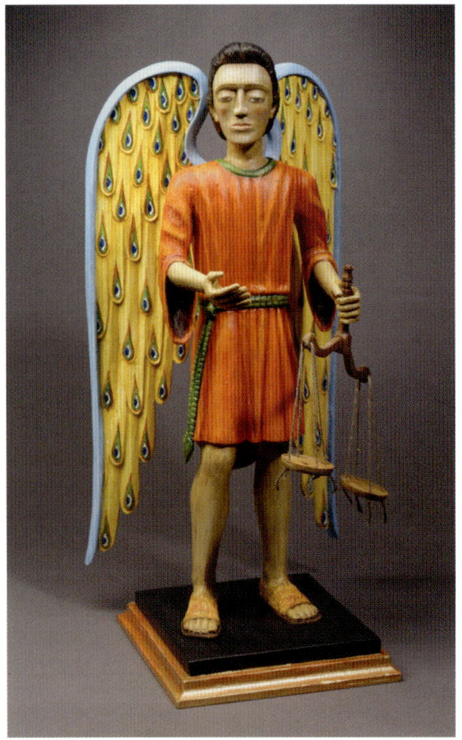

Luis Tapia (New Mexico), Angel of Color (San Miguelito) bulto, 2002, carved and painted wood.

BULTO DE VESTIR / a statue with a carved head and torso that is dressed in clothing; the lower half of the figure is sometimes referred to as "candlestick"—an armature made of wooden sticks.

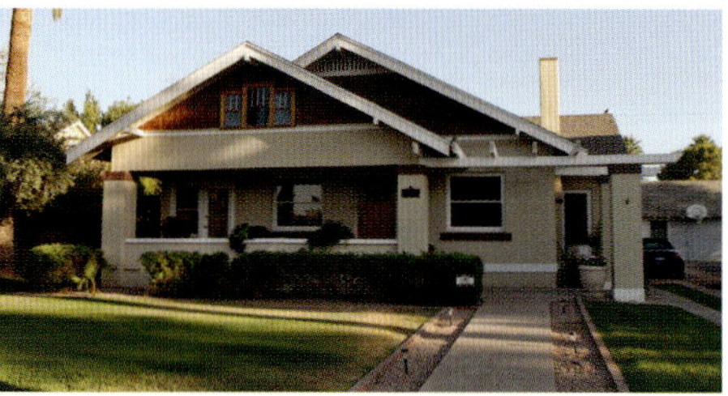

BUNGALOW / a simple house type, popular in the Southwest (and elsewhere in the country) from about 1900 to the 1940s, with origins in India and much admired by the English **Arts and Crafts Movement**, that was transported to the United States by proponents of the type. Relatively small in size, bungalows are generally of wood-frame or brick construction (and in rare instances of adobe brick) and range from a single-story with a single gable facing the street to two-story houses with perpendicular and multiple gables. They also typically have the following distinguishing features: low-pitched gable roofs with wide overhangs, exposed rafter ends, deep-set front porches often with stone or wood piers (sometimes tapered), and a rubble-stone foundation. Usually, bungalows were erected in the center of a lot, leaving space on all sides for landscaping. Interiors were often designed in the Arts and Crafts style with built-in wood cabinets, shelving, window seats, and plate rails; glazed-tile floors and fireplace surrounds; and metal light fixtures with mica shades. In fact, one type of bungalow is specifically known as "Craftsman" and represents the three main points of the Arts and Crafts movement's philosophy: simplicity, harmony with nature, and craftsmanship. Some bungalows were designed by architects, but most of these modest houses were copied from pattern books, plans published in magazines, or constructed from mail-order kits.

Part of a "bungalow fever," which originated in California and swept across America, these houses reflect the Anglo-American influence on the architecture of the Southwest. Before the advent of mechanical cooling systems, the bungalow—with its banks of windows, generous-sized porches with cooling breezes and deep shade, and large attic vents (that allowed built-up heat to escape)—made this house form particularly appealing to residents of the sun-baked Southwest. They were also admired by health seekers who flocked to the region seeking the dry, healing climate, as well as residences with good ventilation and porches for sleeping outdoors.

Bungalows declined in popularity in the post–World War II housing boom, when ranch homes became the favored house form. However, they are much in demand today, throughout the Southwest, by house restorers and homebuyers devoted to this type of dwelling.

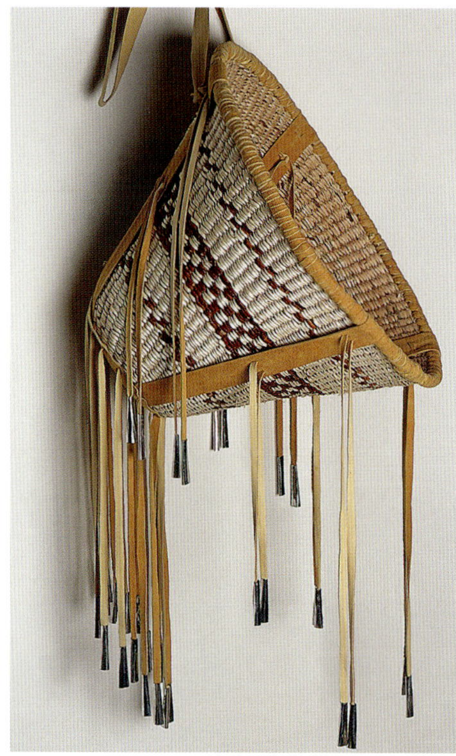

Signed "Enfield" (Western Apache), burden basket.

BURDEN BASKET / U- or cone-shaped, finely **twined** basket originally made by Southwestern Indian cultures for carrying berries, seeds and other wild foods, and for transporting crops and firewood. They were usually made with U-shaped frames consisting of two heavy rods of **cottonwood** or **willow**, and often were decorated with buckskin fringes.

After contact with Anglo traders, **tinklers** (small tin cones) became a traditional part of these baskets; they were a feature, for instance, of late-nineteenth-century Mescalero Apache burden baskets. Before the advent of metal, some basket makers used deer dew claws and later sheep hooves to make tinklers. According to scholar Mark Bahti, the noise the tinklers made was intended to warn bears of the person's approach when gathering berries or passing through mountainous areas. The Western Apaches have long excelled at making twined U-shaped burden baskets for storage, transport, and ceremonial purposes.

Burden baskets play an important role in the Apache Sunrise Ceremony, which celebrates a girl's change from childhood to womanhood. During the sunrise, the girl being celebrated and her witnesses are blessed and wished prosperity and long life. Today the form is made for sale as well; they are twined with willow, cottonwood, or mulberry splints, featuring horizontal patterns of animal or geometric designs, with long commercial-hide fringes tipped with tinklers. See also **gího**.

BURNISHING / See **polishing**.

BURNTWATER RUGS / a Navajo rug style, developed in the 1960s by Don Jacobs at the Burntwater Trading Post near Sanders, Arizona, characterized by intricate bordered patterns with central terraced diamonds, pastel colors derived from native vegetal **dyes**, and fine weaving. Navajo artisan Philomena Yazzie is credited with creating the first Burntwater-style rug in 1968; six years later, an article in *Arizona Highways* magazine made the style famous. The early Burntwater textiles had a small number of colors; however, by the mid-1980s, Bruce Burnham, owner of the Burnham Trading Post in Sanders, was encouraging weavers in the area to include as many as forty colors in one rug. Another trader who encouraged the development of the Burntwater style is Steve Getzwiller, who featured the rugs of Navajo women working in this style in his landmark 1984 book, *The Fine Art of Navajo Weaving*. The Burntwater style is still being woven today; some contemporary Navajo weavers of the style continue to use the vegetal-dyed **yarns**, while others use commercially dyed yarns.

BUTTERFLY / a design motif that signifies beauty and rebirth and transformation, and sometimes a symbol of springtime, the butterfly has long been important to inhabitants of the arid Southwest, for it is one of the primary insect pollinators in the region. For centuries, it has also been a significant ritual symbol for many Native peoples of the area because of the remark-able transformation it undergoes from caterpillar to cocoon to butterfly, and also for its association with fer-tility and rain. The Hopis honor it with the Butterfly Maiden dance; the Apaches once used butterfly motifs on their courting flutes; and Tohono O'odham women painted their upper bodies with but-

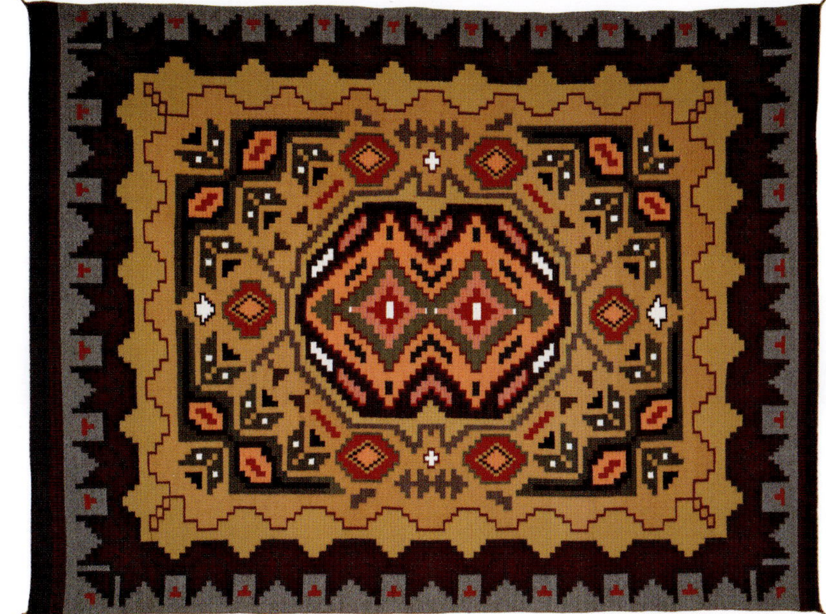

ABOVE: Maggie Price (Navajo), Burntwater textile, vegetal dyes, 72" x 54".
BELOW: Rosella Shack (Zuni), butterfly fetish, 2012, jet with turquoise and coral inlay.

terfly designs for the Nawait ceremony (held to bring life-giving summer rains). According to a To-hono O'odham legend, I'itoi (one of several beings who helped create the world) made butterflies to make the hearts of children happy. The butterfly appears in prehistoric **pictographs**, early pottery, and ancient **kiva** murals. Today it is appliquéd on **quilts**, carved or painted on pottery, woven into baskets, formed into **silver** jewelry, carved as **fe-tishes**, painted onto **tablitas**, and incorporated into other art forms. The Butterfly Dance still occurs in many Hopi and Pueblo villages. For the Hopis, these dances are a petition for rain, good health, and long life for all living things; they are also meant to honor the butterfly for its beauty and contribution in pollinating plant life.

BUTTONS / the Navajos, who wore clothing with silver buttons as early as 1824 (a style likely adopted from Mexicans, who in turn acquired it from the Spanish), were, according to the reports of early ob-servers, making **silver** and **copper** buttons by the 1860s. Silver buttons were initially made using American coins and Mexican *pesos* that were usually melted into a mold forming an ingot that was ham-mered into the desired button shape. Some buttons were made directly from coins; on early examples, the coin imagery is still visible. Later, Navajos used the **doming** method in which disks

of metal are forced into hollowed-out depressions (usually of wood) by means of a die with a rounded head. The slightly convex buttons had two holes in the center through which a leather thong or twist of woolen yarn was passed to fasten it to clothing or leather items. After Navajo smiths learned to solder, they attached a loop of copper or brass to the underside of the buttons. Usually made in multiples (the number depending on the article to be ornamented), buttons were used to fasten cloth-ing (such as a woman's dress, at the shoulders) and as decoration on leather pouches, belts, saddles, bridles, bowguards, and other items. Used spar-ingly at first, buttons were eventually incorporated as decoration more lavishly, especially on men's heavy leather pouches with leather straps (worn over the shoulder), in which were kept tobacco, fire-making materials, and other necessities.

Early on, buttons were decorated with very simple patterns that were chased (or scratched) into the silver by a pointed tool, or with file marks radiating from the center, or were deeply grooved with a **cold chisel**. Later, smiths improved the button-making technique by fashioning their own dies and by enhancing the button surfaces with filing, **stamping**, **embossing** (**repoussé**), and casting. Eventually, the Navajo smiths set silver buttons with **turquoise**. Some of the simple decorative effects found on Navajo silver buttons influenced the design of silver **souvenir spoons**. For example, the fluting (or deeply ridged surfac-es) so popular in late-nineteenth-century Navajo buttons was incorporated by Navajo smiths in the

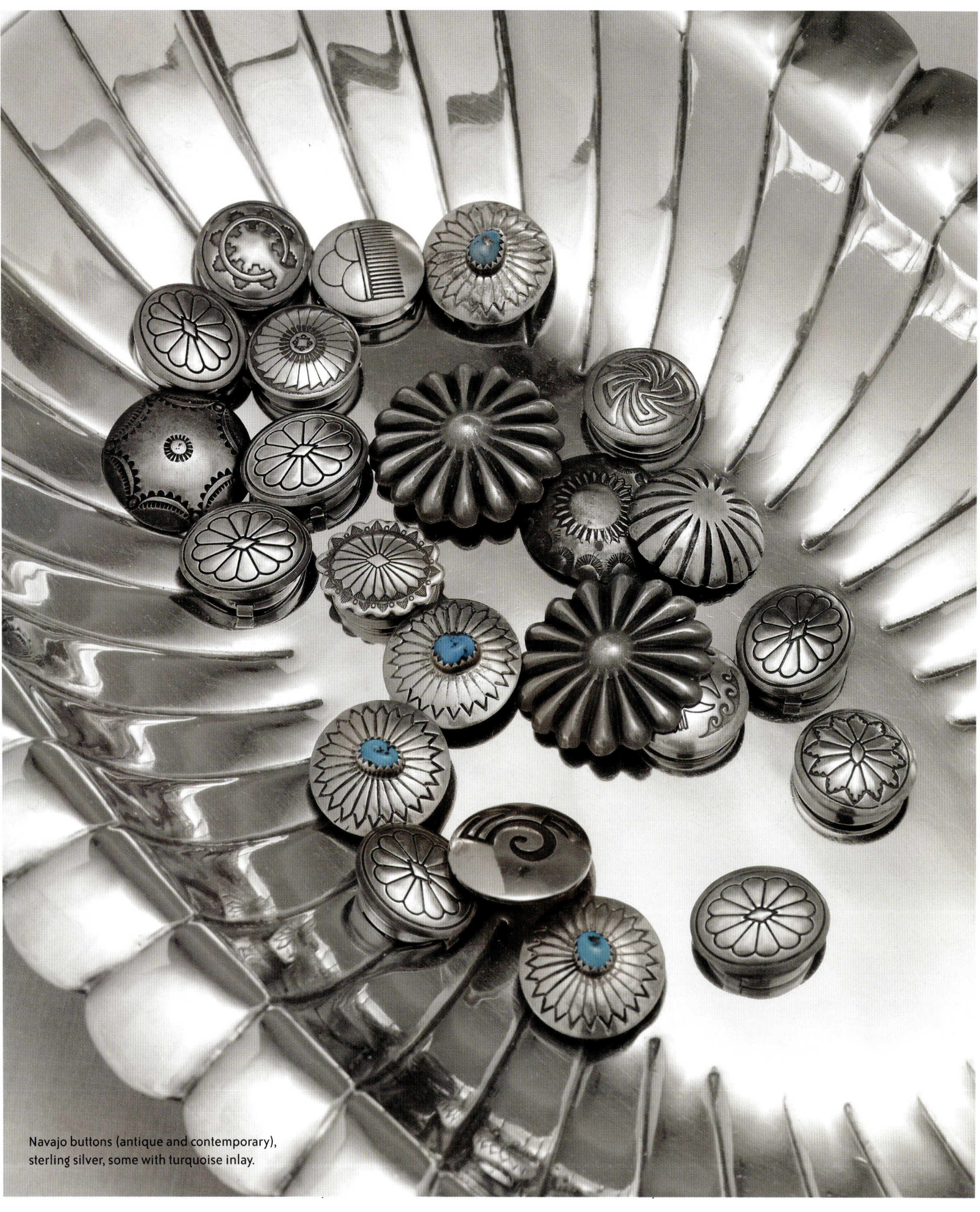

Navajo buttons (antique and contemporary),
sterling silver, some with turquoise inlay.

bowls of sugar spoons by about 1890.

Buttons, as well as button covers—that snap over existing buttons on clothing, an innovation Navajo smiths established in the 1970s—continue to be hand-fashioned by Native silversmiths today. Among the types being made are silver buttons with stampwork and/or stones such as turquoise or coral and Hopi silver **overlay**, often with pictorial designs.

BUTTRESS / an architectural term referring to an element, usually vertical, built against a wall to support it. The buttress acts as a counter force to the horizontal force exerted on a wall from the roof, to effectively distribute the load to the ground. In the Southwest it specifically refers to **adobe** buttresses built on the exterior corners of adobe buildings to stabilize them. However, buttresses for churches and other building types may be built of stone, brick, or other materials. Buttresses were common in the first **mission churches** built in New Mexico beginning in the early 1600s.

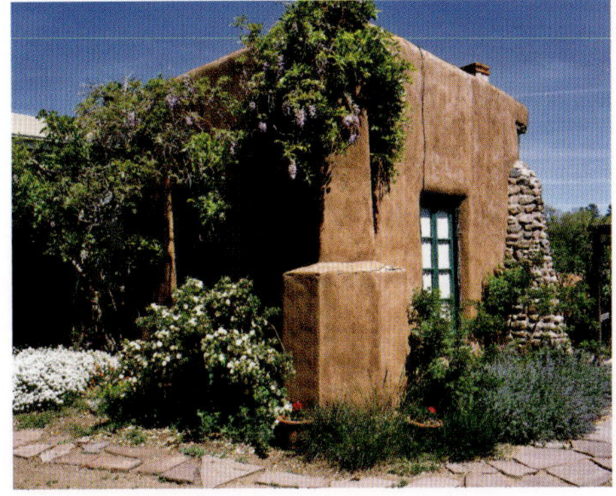
Buttresses on El Zaguán, ca. 1854/renovations 1928, Santa Fe, New Mexico.

Some of the early mission churches remain standing, such as San Esteban del Rey Church at Acoma Pueblo (begun in 1630). Its buttressed design influenced many early-twentieth-century architects working in the **Spanish Colonial Revival style** in New Mexico, including renowned architect John Gaw Meem (1894–1983). Another important buttressed church in the region is **San Francisco de Asís** (early 1800s), in Ranchos de Taos, New Mexico, which has long been known for its enormous sculptural buttresses made famous in the paintings of Georgia O'Keeffe and photographs of Ansel Adams and Paul Strand. In recent decades, buttresses have become an adobe aesthetic added to the exterior of homes in the region purely for visual effect.

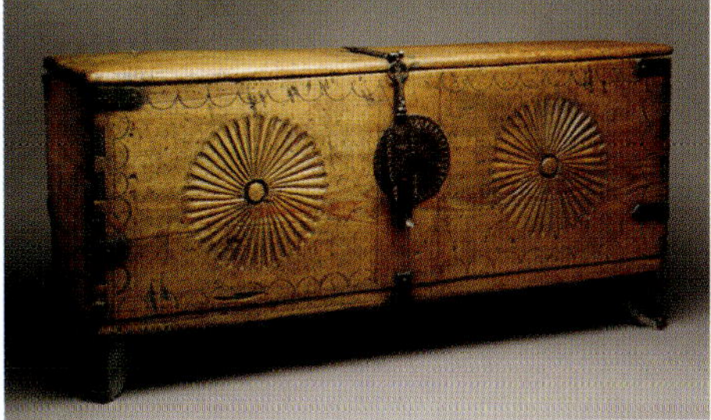
New Mexican caja with rosettes.

CAJA (Caxa) / the Spanish word for "box" or "chest." Decorative wood-board chests—typically made from native ponderosa pine—have **mortise-and-tenon** or **dovetail** joinery and are reinforced with hide glue or nails or wood pegs, with iron hardware, and occasionally with small drawers inside. Generally, they were adorned with **chip-carved** geometric designs or low-relief figural carvings, and often painted with decorations using water-based paint. These chests, also referred to as "board chests," were used to store valuables, clothing, and food. During the Spanish Colonial era, they were the most common furniture item in a Hispano New Mexican home and are often found listed in wills and estate inventories of that period.

Among the traditional Spanish motifs appropriated by New Mexican furniture makers in cajas, as well as in other woodwork, are: rampant lions, pomegranates, **rosettes**, scallop shell patterns, and bird-like forms. These designs are still used in the cajas and other wood furniture constructed by contemporary Hispano artisans of New Mexico.

CAJITA / the Spanish word for "little box," often referring to a container for notions. Some nineteenth-century examples made by Hispano artisans of New Mexico consist of an elaborate **tinwork** frame, glass walls, and scraps of commercial wallpaper or hand-painted paper for decoration.

CALICHE / a Spanish word originally from the Latin *calx* meaning "lime," it refers to the naturally occurring hardened deposits of calcium carbonate found in many soils of semi-arid regions, especially the American Southwest. It was used by prehistoric Hohokam and Salado cultures, as well as by present-day Native Americans as a waterproof finish coat on exterior walls and interior floors. A surviving early example of a caliche building is Casa Grande, Spanish for "Great House" (a national monument since 1918), a four-

story, eleven-room structure dating to about 1350 BC that was built in the Sonoran Desert of Arizona by Hohokam people.

Caliche—actually a mixture of clay, sand, and calcium carbonate, and almost as hard as concrete when dry—is generally light-colored, but can range from white to light pink to reddish-brown. It is usually found on or near the surface, but also can be found in deeper deposits. Layers of caliche can vary in depth from a few inches to one or more feet. Building structures on soil with caliche can be challenging; a tool called a "caliche bar"— a heavy steel tool usually about five feet long with one end cut like a chisel and the other with a point—is often used today to break through deposits of caliche. See also **mud plastering** and **puddled adobe**.

CALIFORNIA MISSION REVIVAL STYLE / See **Mission Revival style**.

CANAL / **Canales** / a Spanish word referring to a drain spout (or scupper) originally constructed from hollowed-out log sections, pottery, metal, or stone, extending out from the **parapet** wall of a flat roof on an **adobe** structure, and designed to prevent water from pooling on the roof and falling onto the vulnerable adobe walls. Historically, to further help deter the erosive effects of water on the walls, "splash" stones were placed on the ground below where the canal drops the roof water. Because adobe bricks are highly susceptible to moisture and erosion, these prominent, oversized

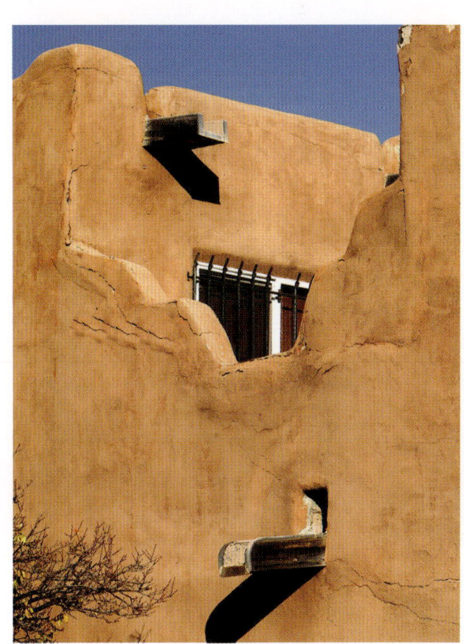

drain spouts are common architectural features in Southwestern adobe buildings. They also appear on flat-roofed homes with walls of material imitating adobe (plaster, concrete block, and so on), to give the look of an authentic adobe and to keep rainwater from pooling on the roof. Sometimes wooden canales have decorative features, such as carved zigzags along the bottom edge. In recent decades, functional canales have been made in a variety of sizes and styles from metal, or wood lined with sheet metal or roofing tar, or from concrete.

CANTEEN / a container used for the transportation of water, made by Native peoples of the Southwest since ancient times from fired clay or hollowed-out **gourds**, with straps of woven native-plant material or leather. Pueblo potters in New Mexico have created canteens with an opening at the top and two eyelets through which a leather strap is drawn. Some canteens were (and continue to be) made for ceremonial purposes: rain priests need them to carry water from the sacred springs. Today, this largely functional form has evolved into a purely aesthetic form and made primarily for sale. See also **tobacco canteens/ flasks** and **wedding jar/vase**.

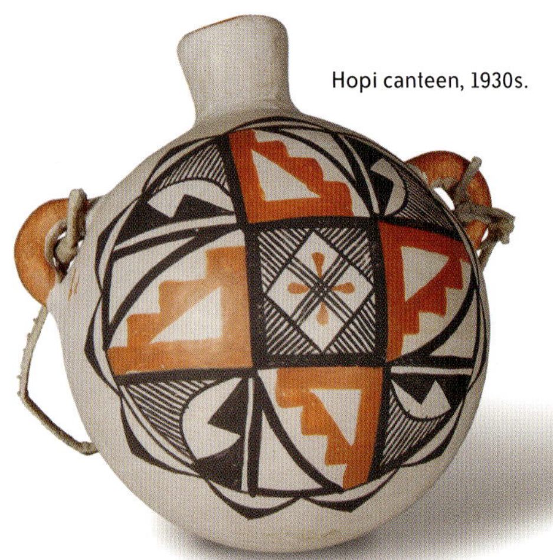

Hopi canteen, 1930s.

CANTERA (Piedra de cantera) / a Spanish word that alternately refers to quarry or the sedimentary quartz-based stone found there. The stone is formed from volcanic ash that settled over time in ancient silt beds, and then was compressed over the ages. It is found primarily in several regions of southern Mexico, as well as in New Mexico (for example, in Jacona). A strong, porous, and lightweight stone that comes in a variety of textures and colors (depending on the impurities present in the stone) including pink and white,

cantera is easily mined and carved. Artisans use it to carve structural and decorative architectural elements, as well as fountains, benches, and garden sculptures, in some regions of Mexico and in the American Southwest.

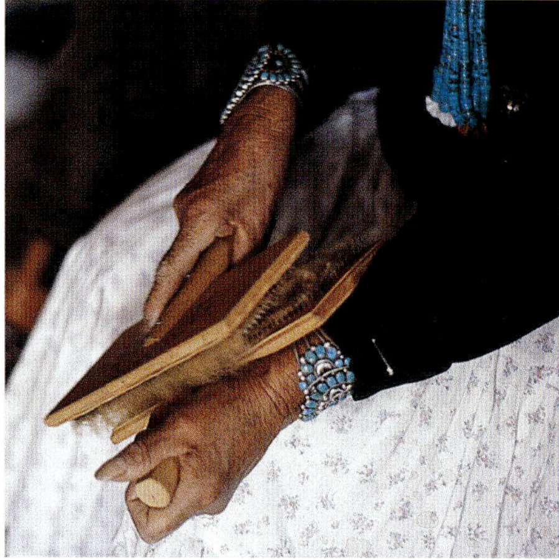

CARDING WOOL / Before sheep wool can be used for weaving it must be carded, which is done by drawing wool through parallel rows of metal teeth (a carder) to align the fibers into a soft mat (or an ordered roll or sliver) in preparation for spinning. The weaver twists the fluffy carded mats of wool with the aid of a spinning wheel or **spindle** into one continuous thread (or **yarn**). Several colors of wool can be carded together to produce certain colors; for example, brown, black, and white wool can be carded together to make tan or gray. The carding of wool is also part of the process of cleaning wool, as a lot of detritus falls out during carding. Weavers who still handspin their wool place a heavy cloth or canvas across their laps while carding to catch the debris. See also **yarn—handspun**.

CARPINTERO / a Spanish word for "woodworker" that can refer to either a carpenter or furniture maker. Historically, in Spanish Colonial New Mexico and Arizona, carpinteros also framed wooden houses, carved the decoration on ceiling beams of **adobe** homes, crafted doors and window frames, and framed the **altar screens** (or **retablos**) behind church altars. The first carpintero in the Southwest came with the explorer Juan de Oñate, who settled in northern New Mexico in 1598. The carpin-

tero, along with six other men in the expedition, brought with them rudimentary carpentry tools such as axes, saws, and an assortment of chisels, augers, and **adzes**. By the early seventeenth century, some Pueblo Indians were being trained in carpentry shops at local missions, such as Pecos and Cochiti; they became known for producing particularly fine furniture. Many furniture makers in the Southwest today still use traditional tools and early methods of wood construction. See also **dovetail joint**, **mortise-and-tenon joint**, and **Spanish Colonial furniture**.

CARVED POTTERY / a popular technique used by Pueblo potters since the 1930s, in which the designs are drawn on the dry or "leather hard" clay surface, then gouged out with a sharp tool, ranging from an X-ACTO® knife to a sharpened screwdriver. Then the carved areas are painted with a mineral clay **slip**, which is left unpolished so it has a **matte** finish after firing, while the uncarved areas of the surface are **polished** so they will appear shiny after firing. The technique is used on both redware and blackware. Some potters are known for creating sharp-edged carving, while others are known for their soft, rounded edges.

Among the popular designs carved into the pottery are **avanyu** (the water serpent) and geometric shapes with important symbolism, such as the cloud or rain pattern. Santa Clara Pueblo potter Sara Fina Tafoya (ca. 1863–1949) is credited with originating this innovation in 1922. The technique is carried on today by her talented descendants, as well as other potters. Rose Gonzales (1900–1989) introduced carved pottery to San Ildefonso Pueblo about 1930.

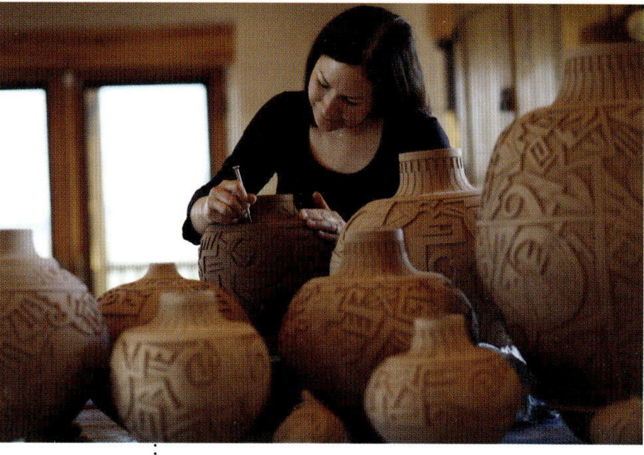

Tammy Garcia (Santa Clara) carves pottery, and a finished black carved pot by Garcia is shown at right.

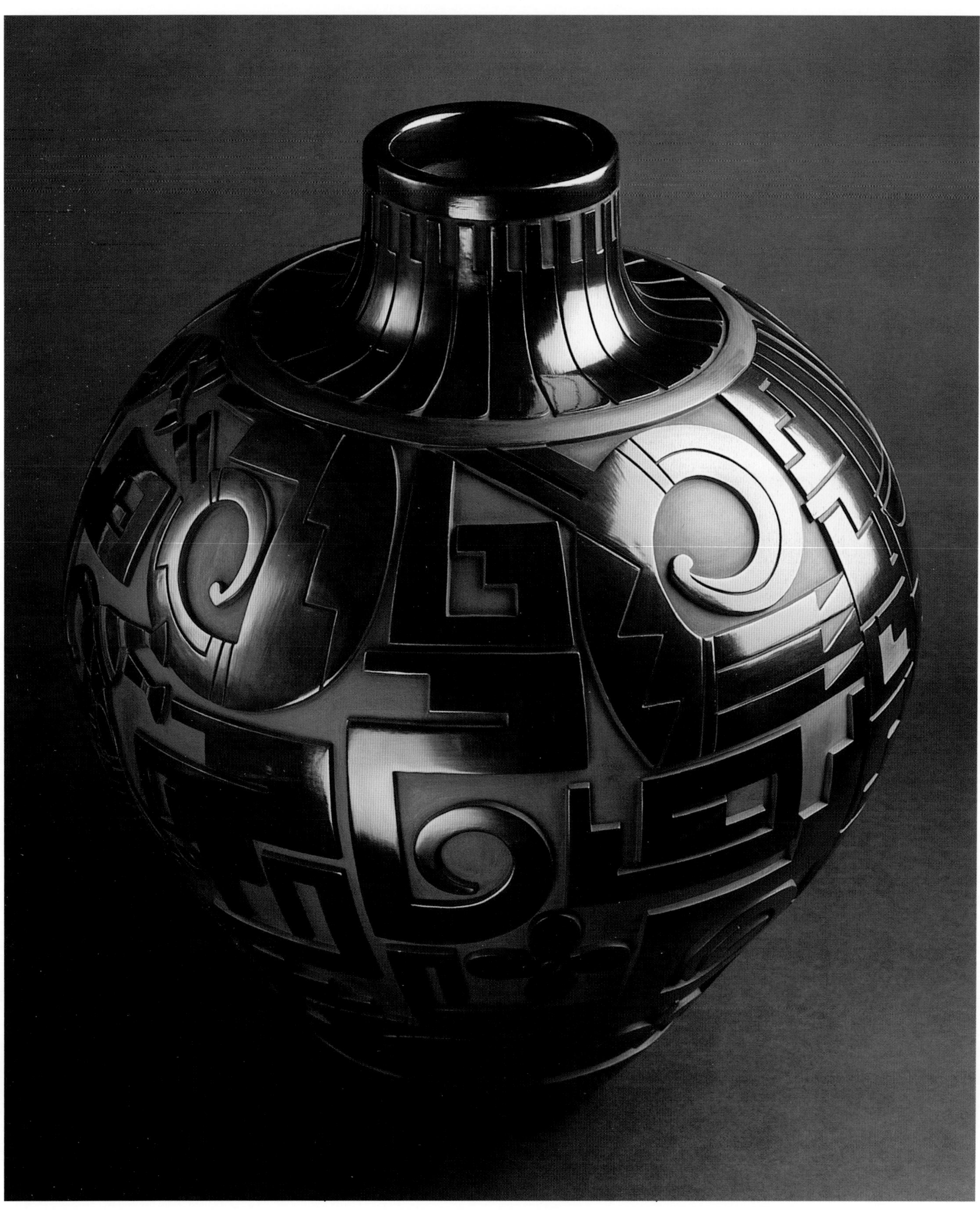

CASA / Casita / casa is the Spanish word for "house," and the term casita generally refers to a small, Southwest-style cottage which may be freestanding or attached to a main house.

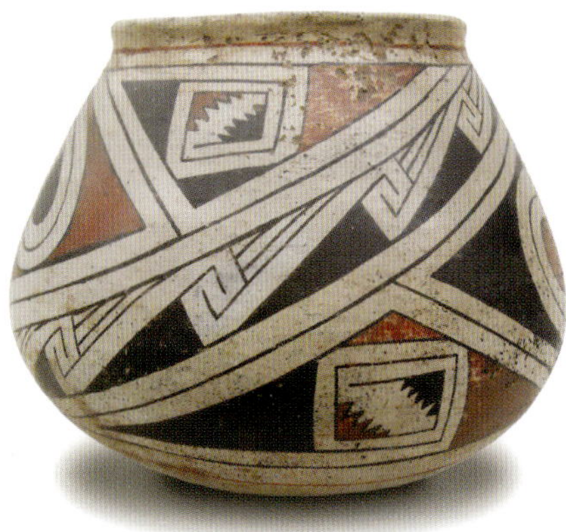
Casas Grandes pot.

CASAS GRANDES POTTERY / polychrome pottery from the prehistoric culture of Casas Grandes, centered in a large city in northern Chihuahua, Mexico, known as Paquimé, built of **rammed-earth adobe** that resembles the multistory **pueblos** of the Southwest. Investigations of the ruins began in 1884 with the Swiss ethnologist Adolph Bandelier. Subsequent archaeologists and scholars discovered that during the Viejo period (ca. AD 700–1200), Casas Grandes potters made mostly plain brown wares such as jars and bowls and decorated pottery by creating textures in the clay and painting with red pigment. During the Medio period (AD 1200–1450), potters collected high-quality local clays to hand form a wide variety of vessels and **effigies**. They decorated the pots with bold geometric designs and representational imagery (**macaw** heads, serpents, birds, humans, and animals) painted in red and black on the light clay backgrounds. The Medio potters also made some polished black wares. Casas Grandes pottery inspired the contemporary modern ceramic art movement that originated in the village of **Mata Ortiz**, located sixteen miles from Paquimé.

CAST IRON / iron shapes formed by pouring molten iron with alloys into molds. During the Victorian era, after the railroad reached the Southwest, a multitude of new building materials were brought to the region, including cast-iron facades and decorative ornaments. In some instances, the mass-produced cast iron replaced the more costly and time-consuming decorative wrought

ironwork, which continued to be made in the region, especially in New Mexico.

CERAMICS / See **pottery**.

CHAIRS / See **silla** and **sillón frailero**.

CHAMISA (_Chrysothamnus nauseosus_, rabbitbrush) / a silver-blue deciduous shrub with pungent yellow flowers in the fall, which thrives in the Southwest, and whose flowering tops produce various shades of yellow dye used for Hispano textiles and Native American basketry and textiles. Peeled and dyed chamisa stems are also used as the **weft** (weaving over and under the **warp**) in **Hopi wicker plaques,** and some San Juan Paiute weavers use chamisa as foundation filler in their baskets.

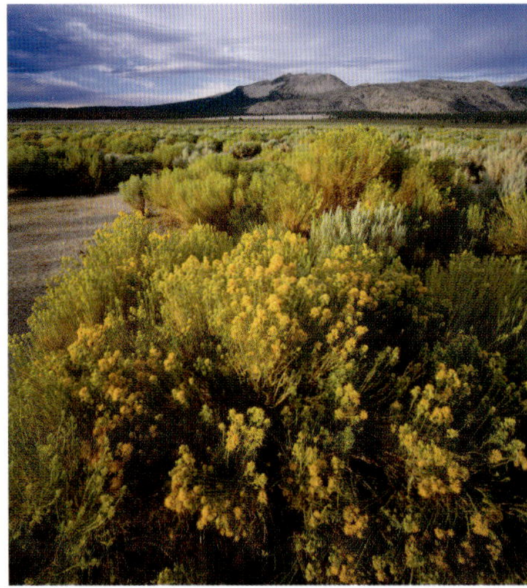

CHANGING WOMAN (White Shell Woman) / the spirit being who, according to Apache belief, brought the arts of basketry, sewing, and ceremony to the Apache people. She is also called White Shell Woman because she came ashore in a shell. In puberty dances or ceremonies such as the Apache Sunrise Ceremony, Keesda Ceremony of the Jicarilla Apache, or the Navajo Kinaalda ceremony, the young girls being initiated into womanhood wear a specially made hide dress as well as a bone necklace and a shell to represent White Shell Woman.

CHANNEL INLAY / a technique of setting a decorative pattern into **silver** jewelry, developed in Native American culture by silversmiths at Zuni Pueblo, New Mexico, by the

mid-1920s. Precut stones (usually **turquoise** and/or **shell**) are glued and set individually into small spaces separated by thin strips of silver that have been soldered perpendicular to the base. Then the stones/shells are ground down (using a hand grinder) until they are flush with the surface. The silver dividers remain visible and are part of the overall design. Originally silver was hand-hammered into the desired thickness for the dividers; by the 1920s sheet silver was readily available, although some jewelers used 8-gauge silver and thinned it by hammering or running it through a rolling mill.

Among the earliest Zuni jewelers to use the technique was Juan de Dios (1882–1940s). Beginning in the 1930s, post trader C. G. Wallace encouraged Zuni artisans to make channel jewelry. His influence can be seen in the massiveness of the pieces, in the materials used (high quality turquoise and **coral**), and in the designs (strongly geometric). During the Depression era, Zuni jewelers experimented with ways to make the jewelry lighter and less expensive for their customers; one method involved constructing hollow cuff bracelets with the channel work set in a linear fashion along the top.

In the 1950s, Zuni jeweler Annie (Quam) Gasper (b. 1926) created innovative channel inlay designs using Blue Gem and Last Chance turquoise, including the hummingbird and the spiderweb patterns, still used by the Quam and Quandelacy families today. Over the decades Zunis have used channel inlay to create **conchas**, pins, cuff bracelets, **squash blossom** necklaces, earrings, **najas**, buckles, and other forms. Popular motifs include geometric or flower-shaped cluster patterns, birds, butterflies, and designs drawn from prehistoric pottery motifs. See also **inlay** and **mosaic inlay/overlay**.

CHEST-ON-LEGS / a Spanish Colonial–style wooden chest, usually constructed of pine with iron hardware, on wooden legs (or stiles). Chests with short stiles, and writing desks that rested on tall stands, were common in northern Spain, but the extension of stiles to form tall legs is unique to New Mexico. This style of chest is believed by some scholars to have been invented by the Valdez family of Velarde, New Mexico, in the late eighteenth century. A wavy-line, chip-carved design is a common motif

Zuni channel-inlay bracelet.

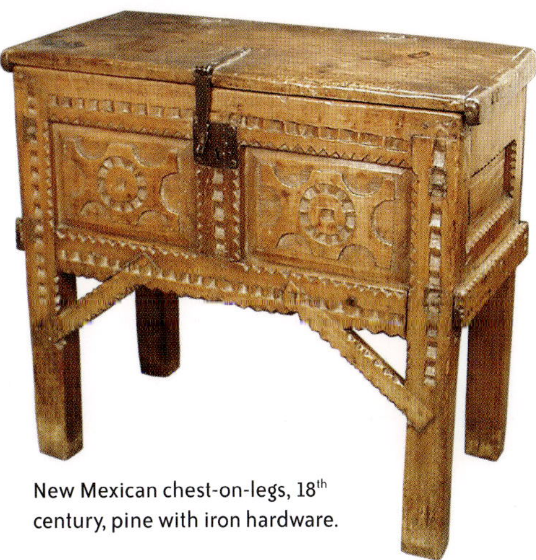

New Mexican chest-on-legs, 18th century, pine with iron hardware.

on these chests—a design innovation sometimes credited to the Valdez family. Contemporary New Mexican **carpinteros** have reinvented their own version of the chest-on-legs. See also **caja**.

CHIEF'S BLANKET / the commercial term for a Navajo shoulder blanket usually worn by men, woven wider than long in a **weft**-faced weave with a distinctive striped design, made beginning around 1750. The proportions come from ancient Pueblo women's **mantas** or shawls. The name derives from the knowledge that this style of blanket was once highly favored by the "chiefs" or powerful members of many Plains Indian tribes; there are no "chiefs" in the Navajo social and political structure. By 1800 these blankets had become coveted and valuable barter items; the Navajos traded them with other Native Americans, Spaniards, and Euro-Americans. They were worn by men, and sometimes women, of different tribes as symbols of prestige and pride. Plains tribes traded buffalo robes and horses for them. Beginning in the late 1880s, post traders on the reservation acted as middlemen for the Navajo weavers and supplied chief-style blankets (and later chief-style rugs) to **curio** dealers and other retailers.

Today old chief-style blankets are the most recognizable and valuable of all Navajo textiles, which have been categorized by scholars into three (and sometimes four) broad overlapping design phases. First phase: the simplest and rarest of the blankets, made around 1800 to 1850, woven from handspun natural **churro wool** and incorporating a horizontal, zoned layout with alternating **indigo** blue, brown, and white stripes or bands, with wider stripes/bands at the ends and in the center. Second phase: made from around the 1850s, this style has the addition of

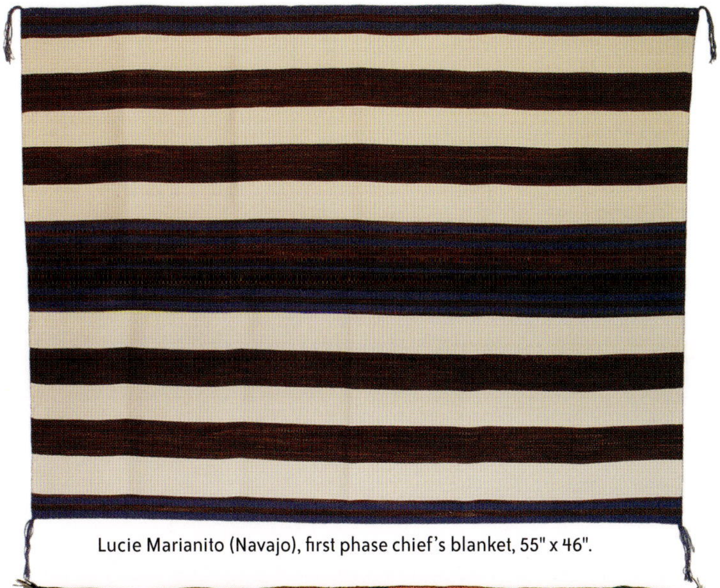

Lucie Marianito (Navajo), first phase chief's blanket, 55" x 46".

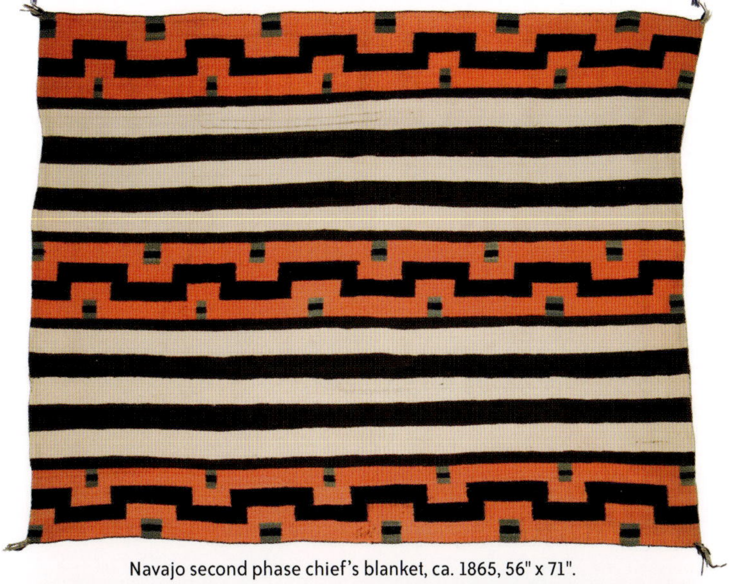

Navajo second phase chief's blanket, ca. 1865, 56" x 71".

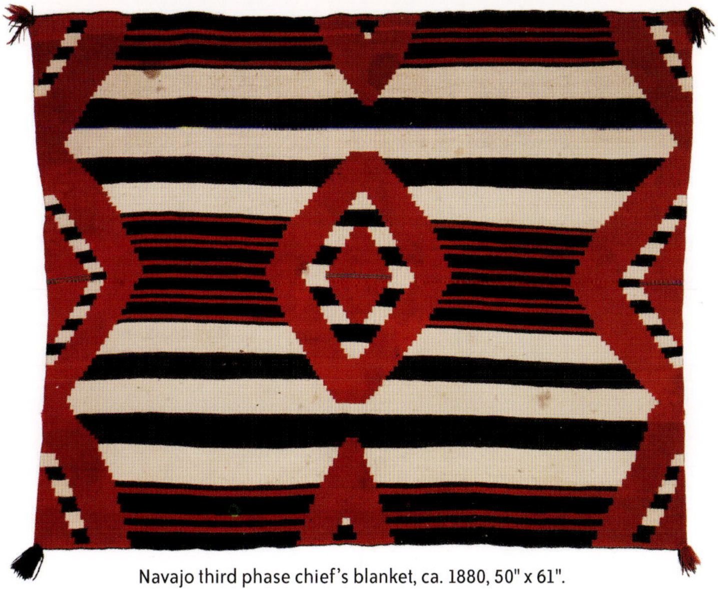

Navajo third phase chief's blanket, ca. 1880, 50" x 61".

small bars or rectangles of red at the ends and down the middle of the indigo blue and brown stripes of the blanket. Third phase: much more elaborate and artistic with a terraced diamond placed in the center with quarter diamonds (right-angle triangles) at each corner and half-diamonds (isosceles triangles) within the center of the bands at each end, generally made between 1860 and 1880. Some scholars include a fourth phase, in which the diamond motifs are larger and have become the main focus, with the background less important, made circa 1870 through the early twentieth century. Navajo weavers are still making traditional chief's-style blankets today.

CHIMAYÓ TEXTILES / textiles distinguished by a central motif such as a diamond or chevron and bordered on either end by horizontal bands or stripes, usually with visible warp fringe (hand-knotted) on both ends, produced in northern New Mexico, primarily by descendants of the original Spanish settlers. The style is named after the small village of Chimayó, where artisans have been weaving these textiles on horizontal **treadle looms** since at least the 1700s. Originally they were utilitarian forms, such as blankets and rugs, and were woven using handspun, natural or hand-dyed wool **yarn**.

Beginning in the 1880s, after the railroad reached the region, weavers in the village created textiles for the **curio** trade using four-ply commercially-manufactured wool yarn (initially supplied by curio dealers) and simplified **Rio Grande** and Native American designs. One of the popular **pictorial** motifs used was the fanciful **thunderbird**. Among the dealers who promoted and sold Chimayó textiles were Jake Gold and J. S. Candelario in Santa Fe, New Mexico, and the **Fred Harvey Company**, which distributed them throughout the United States. To meet the high demand for these textiles, some dealers provided artisans with new looms and materials, such as commercially processed wool and cotton dyed in a wide variety of colors with synthetic dyes.

By the early twentieth century Chimayó had become one of the largest weaving centers of the Southwest; families such as the Trujillos, Ortegas, Jaramillos, and others opened up their own weaving shops and sold directly to tourists. The term "Chimayó" became used in the curio trade to describe all Hispano-made New Mexican textiles. Popular sellers in the tourist market were rugs, table covers, table runners, chair throws,

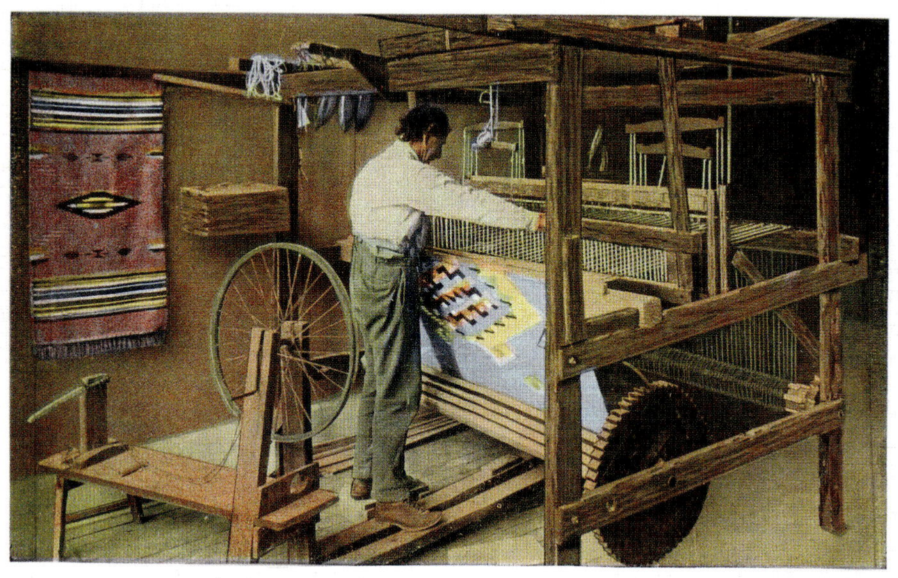

Antique postcard of a Chimayó weaver at his treadle loom.

purses, pillows, jackets, and curtains. Traditional Chimayó colors and patterns finely woven in a wide range of forms from placemats to table runners to vests remain popular among tourists and residents alike. In addition, finely woven rugs and wall hangings featuring highly original designs, or sometimes reinterpretations of older patterns, are being produced in Chimayó today; these expressive works are highly prized by collectors and museum curators across the country. Among the renowned Chimayó weavers who are combining traditional techniques and looms with modern aesthetics and personal vision are Irvin and Lisa Trujillo and Karen Martinez.

CHINLE STYLE / a Navajo rug style made since the early twentieth century, named for a region of the Navajo reservation situated in Apache County, Arizona, at the mouth of Canyon de Chelly, consisting of a banded pattern and vegetal-dyed yarns, largely indistinguishable from the **Wide Ruins** pattern.

CHIP-CARVING / a technique of hand-incising designs into the surface of smooth, planed wood by using a sharp skew-bladed knife or a rigid chisel, and a mallet. The incisions are grouped to form various designs, including geometric patterns with the triangle often used as the base. Typically, woods that have a straight, even grain without pronounced color, knots, or wavy grain are used for chip-carving; soft woods such as pine, cedar, or

redwood, and medium-hard woods such as walnut or mahogany are preferred. Chip-carving was often used by carpenters in colonial New Mexico, due in part to the limited availability of tools and the soft nature of New Mexico pine and cedar woods; in the twentieth and twenty-first centuries, contemporary woodcarvers, especially those of **Córdova**, New Mexico, still use the technique.

CHURRIGUERESQUE STYLE / an elaborate Baroque-style architectural design featuring ornate, high-relief ornament of stone, **terra cotta**, or molded-clay brick, most often found in Spain and Latin America in the late seventeenth and eighteenth century, named after the profusely decorated buildings of the seventeenth-century Spanish architect and sculptor José Benito Churriguera (1650–1723). One of the finest examples in the Southwest of this rich and exuberant Spanish Baroque mode is the late-eighteenth-century San Xavier del Bac Mission Church, built

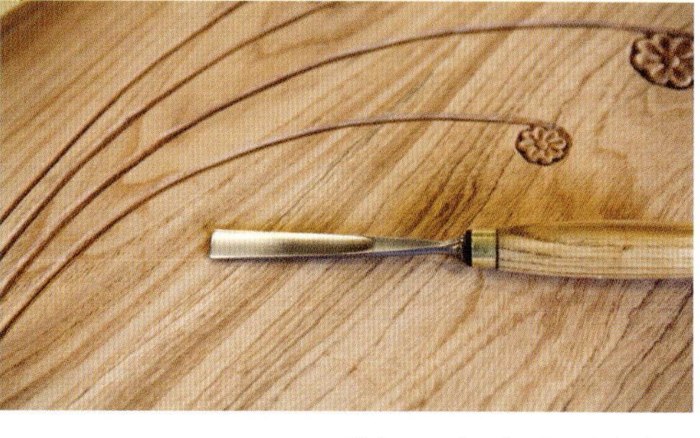

Chip-carving tool and design.

nine miles outside Tucson, Arizona, which has a central, highly ornate Churrigueresque-style portal, flanked by relatively austere, white **stucco**-over-brick twin towers. A central element of the Churrigueresque style is the distinctive **estípite** pilasters, as seen on the façade of San Xavier del Bac and in the interior of the church on the five **retablos.** The Churrigueresque style gained further notice in the West and Southwest after East Coast architect Bertram Grosvenor Goodhue (1869–1924) designed buildings with Churrigueresque decoration for the 1915 Panama-California Exposition in San Diego, California. Today this architectural style is usually referred to as "estípite baroque."

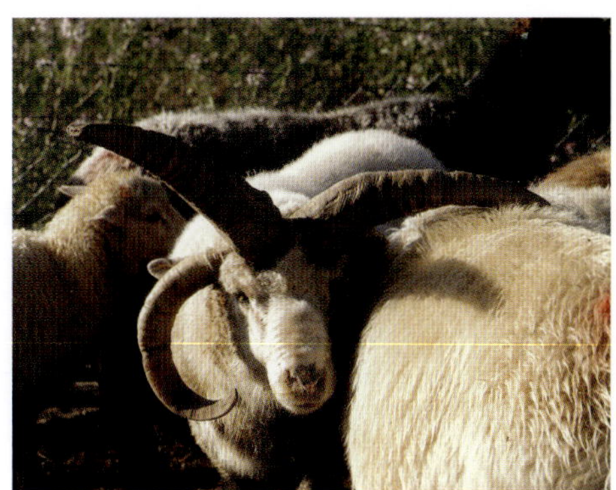

CHURRO WOOL (Navajo-Churro Wool) / the double-coated fleece (outer coat is long and coarse, while inner coat is soft and fine) of churro sheep has been transformed into **yarn** and used to weave textiles in New Mexico and throughout the Southwest since this breed (which originated in Rome) was introduced to the region by the Spanish in the sixteenth century. Churro fleece was also handspun into single-ply **yarn** and used by Spanish colonial women in New Mexico for their **colcha** embroidery and by the men to weave **sabanilla**—yardage used to make sheets, bedcovers, the ground cloth for colcha work, and other items. An ancient, hardy Iberian breed from the areas of Castile and León, churro sheep (known as *churra* in Spain) are good for meat and milk as well as for wool. Churros adapted well to the harsh dry conditions of the region and played an important role in sustaining the economy and daily life of early Spanish settlers in New Mexico.

Churro wool occurs in a variety of natural colors from black-brown to a creamy white and has long, lustrous, straight fibers with low lanolin or grease content making it excellent wool for spinning, dyeing (it easily absorbs vegetal dyes), and weav-ing. The silky yet durable yarn made from churro wool was initially prized by Spanish weavers of the Southwest and eventually became a favorite of Navajo weavers, who acquired churro sheep through raiding and trade. (Today churro sheep are also known as "Navajo-Churro" sheep, since the breed was widely adopted by the Navajos in the early years of Spanish settlement.) Over time, due to a variety of reasons from extensive cross breeding to the decimation of the Navajos' churros by the U.S. government (in 1864), this once-prevalent breed became scarce in the Southwest.

Beginning in the 1970s, several individuals began acquiring churros with the purpose of preserving the breed and revitalizing Navajo and Hispano flocks. Among those who helped revitalize the breed were the Navajos, who successfully maintained original flocks in remote areas of the Navajo Nation; Dr. Lyle McNeal, who formed the Navajo Sheep Project (1977); trader and collector Steve Getzwiller, who recognized the superior quality of historic textiles woven with churro wool and supplied churro lambs to prominent Navajo weaving families, and also submitted Navajo churro textiles in competitions; and the non-profit organization Ganados del Valle, in Los Ojos, New Mexico, which began a successful movement in the early 1980s to encourage Hispano sheep growers and weavers to produce churro sheep and wool (the weaving cooperative Tierra Wools was part of this effort). In addition, El Rancho de las Golondrinas living history museum, just outside Santa Fe, has raised churro sheep and used their wool in a weaving program for many years.

Today, finely woven textiles made from churro sheep wool is a thriving art form, among both Hispano and Native American weavers. In addition, a handful of Hispano women still wash, card, spin, and dye churro wool to create yarn for their colcha embroidery work. See also **Rio Grande textiles**.

CLAY / a natural silicate earth material composed of various minerals and found in deposits at various locations throughout the Southwest (as well as throughout the world) ranging from recent sediments in lakes and streambeds to geological deposits that are millions of years old. Clay is the result of decomposing rock in which the particle size is very small and structured in such a way that the mass, when wet, can be formed into shapes. The material contains varying amounts of iron and other colorants.

Pottery was the primary purpose for clay among Native Americans, however some have also used it to decorate wooden figures and for ceremonial purposes. For instance, white clay is used by some Navajo woodcarvers to create the "whites" in their wood pieces; the same clay is used by Navajos to paint their bodies white for certain ceremonies.

Clay is considered by most Pueblo potters of the Rio Grande to be a living substance, and when "Mother Clay" is gathered, some potters offer prayers and cornmeal. The laborious process of preparing clay for making vessels and other forms begins with the potter—whether Pueblo, Hopi, Navajo, or Hispano—gathering the clay. Skilled potters know where to find the best clay (and often will not divulge the location to others). During these trips, the potter may also collect plants and minerals to make paint, as well as **potsherds**, sand, or volcanic tuff for **temper**.

After the clay is gathered, it is dried in the sun for several months (and in some instances for an entire year). Then it is soaked in buckets of water up to four days and sieved through a screen to remove impurities and foreign matter like pebbles and twigs. (Impurities in the clay, such as a blade of grass or a large grain of sand could cause the pot to crack in the firing process.) The **temper** is then added to the clay and the mixture is set aside and kept damp—a process called "curing"—until ready for use. Modern potters wrap the clay in plastic to prevent further drying. Throughout the process, the mixing is generally done by "feel" rather than by measuring ingredients. The origin of a piece of Pueblo pottery can be determined by the type of clay and temper used; in fact, archaeologists have used this technique to discover the source of ancient pottery found at prehistoric sites.

Because the process of gathering and preparing natural clay is so laborious, some contemporary potters use commercial clay. However, potters in the region who strive to preserve their Native culture and tradition in their work refuse to do so. See also **coiling**, **firing**, **mica/micaceous pottery**, **Navajo pottery**, **pottery—Hispano**, **pottery—Pueblo**, **puki**, and **slip**.

CLIFF DWELLINGS / Ancestral Puebloan sites where residences were built right into the sheer cliffs of mesas, escarpments, or mountains. Using nature to their advantage, the **masonry** dwellings were skillfully constructed by carving into the soft stone (**tufa** or limestone) and extending outward with **adobe** walls and/or sandstone-block walls using a mortar of dirt and water. The ceilings and roofs were supported by wood beams.

In multistory cliff dwellings, tapering pole ladders provided access to the different levels. In some instances, these early architects built underneath existing sandstone-cliff overhangs; in other instances they scaled the high cliffs to carve out recessed areas. In both cases, these difficult-to-reach cliff dwellings were almost impossible for enemy tribes to penetrate.

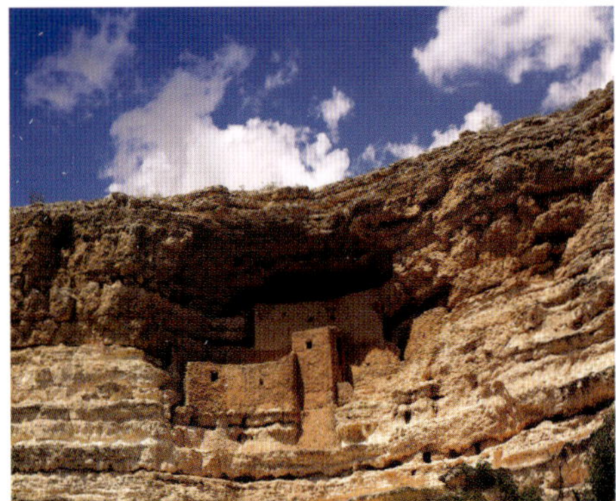

Montezuma Castle, Sinagua cliff dwelling, Arizona.

Important cliff-dwelling sites are preserved by the National Park Service, including the Gila (western New Mexico) occupied by the Mogollon people between circa AD 1275 and 1300; Bandelier (north central New Mexico) occupied from about AD 1150 to 1325 by Ancestral Puebloan groups; Tonto (southeastern Arizona) occupied during the thirteenth, fourteenth, and early fifteenth centuries by the Salado people; Montezuma Castle (Verde Valley, Arizona) occupied from the early 1300s into the 1400s by the Sinagua people; and Mesa Verde (southern Colorado) where the dwellings were built in the cliff face between AD 1100 and 1200 (and abandoned by about AD 1300). Present-day multistory adobe Pueblo architecture of the Southwest evolved from these early building types.

CLOSE STITCH (Close Work, Covered Stitch) / a centuries-old technique used in the **coiled** basket forms of all Native basket makers, in which the sturdy inner coil is completely covered by hundreds and sometimes thousands of tight stitches, which are woven directly next to one another. In close-stitch coiled **trays**, weavers have incorporated a variety of desert plant fibers, such as **devil's claw** and **yucca**, to create bold designs and patterns, including the traditional **squash blossom**, fret (also called "Greek key," a continuous pattern of angular bands repeated within a border), and "**man-in-the-maze**" motifs.

CLUSTER WORK / a style of jewelry featuring well-matched small stones, often **turquoise** or **coral**, or small **shell** pieces, set into individual delicate silver **bezels** in elaborate oval, circular, or flower-like patterns arranged around a central (and often larger) stone. Developed by jewelers at Zuni Pueblo, New Mexico, in the early twentieth century, cluster-work jewelry can include up to 150 or more small stones in one piece.

Some believe the cluster style may have an iconographic connection with the sunflower medallion seen on Zuni pottery. The technique has been used to create **conchas**, **squash blossom** necklaces, bracelets, earrings, rings, and pins. By the 1930s, cluster work had become a favorite style with Zuni jewelers and the tourist market. Since then, Zuni jewelers have gained widespread recognition for this fine and meticulous work.

Eventually, Navajo smiths also created cluster-style jewelry, but never as elaborate or as fine as the Zuni examples. **Petit point** (made with exceptionally tiny round or teardrop-shape stones) and **needlepoint** (with stones shaped into points at both ends) are even more elaborate variations of the cluster technique developed by the Zunis. See also **row work**.

Zuni cluster-work concha belt, sterling silver and turquoise.

COCHINEAL (Cochinilla) / a natural red-purple dye derived from the dried and crushed (or scraped and boiled) body of the female insect *Dactylopius coccus* that lives on the *nopal* (prickly pear) cactus (*Opuntia*). About seventy thousand of these dried insects are required to produce one pound of dye material. The small insect is native to the Sonoran Desert of the Southwest. In colonial New Mexico, the dye was imported from Central America and from Mexico, where it was a major industry and main export second only to silver. Navajo and Pueblo weavers used yarn **raveled** from commercially made cloths such as **bayeta** that were dyed with cochineal; they did not use this dye on their own native handspun **yarns**.

COCHITI PUEBLO POTTERY / this pueblo has a long history of making utilitarian pottery, as well as three-dimensional, hollow figurines. The tradition of making the figures dates back to pre-contact times in the Southwest, when Puebloan cultures created a large variety of clay forms—**fetishes**, **figurines**, and **effigy** vessels. Around 1880, Cochiti potters began making large, hollow figurines in great abundance for the tourist trade; these figurines were embraced by consumers as "curiosities" that reflected an unfamiliar culture.

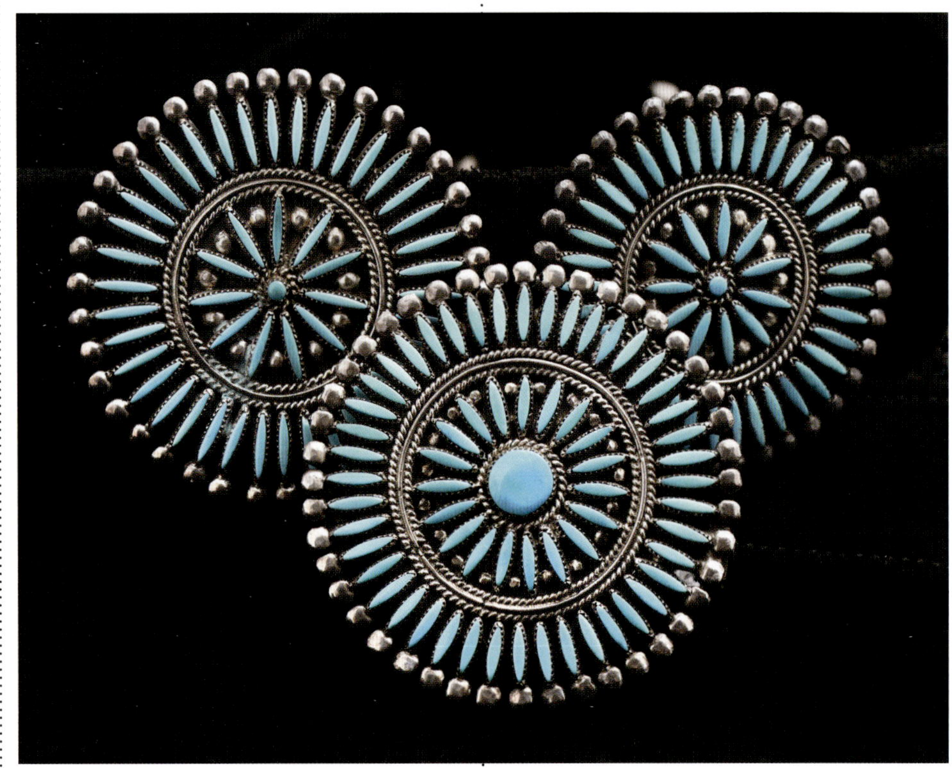

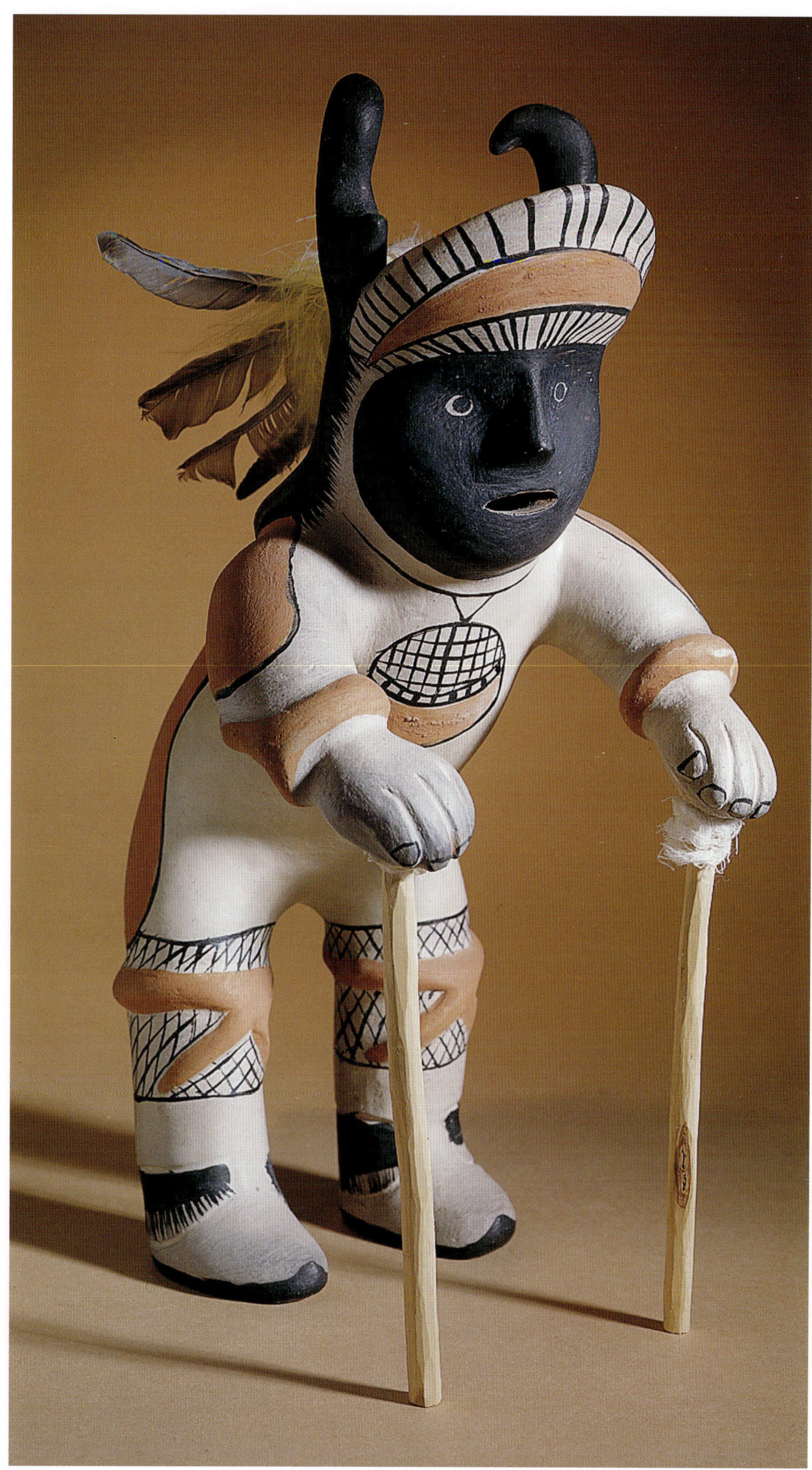

Louis Naranjo (Cochiti),
deer dancer figurine.

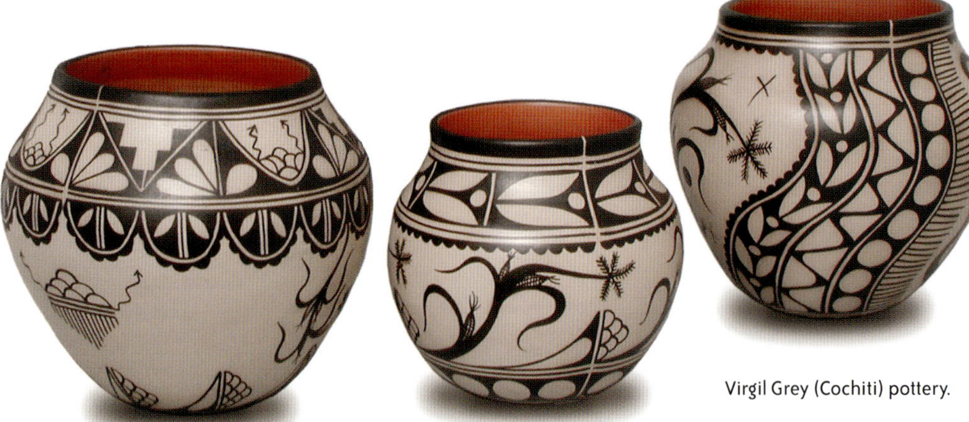

Virgil Grey (Cochiti) pottery.

In the late 1800s, potters at the pueblo were also making utilitarian pots and other ceramic forms for sale. As with many other pueblos in the region, Cochiti potters believe that they were taught to make pottery by Clay Woman.

Traditionally, Cochiti's figures have been made by **coiling** and pinching out the different clay parts, adhering the parts together with clay **slip**, and then refining the figures with pieces of **gourd** and other tools. Colored slips are used to embellish the figures with details and then the piece is fired. The figures can stand as tall as thirty inches and typically have white/off white slip with details painted in black and red. To prevent breakage during the firing process, hollow Cochiti figures have open mouths to allow the gases to escape.

By 1880/81, Cochiti potters had developed a distinctive style that included caricatures of animals, as well as of the people Cochiti people came in contact with—cowboys, priests, carnival and vaudeville figures, businessmen, and tourists—humorous figures that were promoted and marketed by curio dealers such as Aaron and Jake Gold in Santa Fe. Carnivals, circuses, and vaudeville companies were brought to New Mexico by wagon train, and later by the railroad in the 1880s. Some ethnologists of the period rejected these figures as debased or even pornographic, as some of the clay caricatures had genitals clearly depicted. Some scholars believe these "clown-like" figures, which are also called "munos" (similar to the Spanish term *mono* which colloquially can mean "cute" or "endearing"), were a way for women potters at Cochiti to use their traditional arts as a means to cope with (or "strike back" at) the invasion and oppression of outsiders.

At present, Cochiti potters continue to create a remarkable array of figures, including comic book characters, **nacimientos,** animals, and the unique **storytellers**, a tradition begun in 1964 by Cochiti potter Helen Cordero (1914–1994). Around 1990, Virgil Ortiz (b. 1969) revived the tall standing figures that had not been made in nearly a century at Cochiti. Ortiz, as well as Lisa Holt (along with her husband Harlan Reano of Santo Domingo Pueblo), and M. J. Ortiz are among the highly talented Cochiti potters who are continuing the figurative tradition with its humor and social commentary into the twenty-first century.

COILING / Basketry / a technique used for basket making in the Southwest since at least 2000 BC, in which the basket maker creates a spiral foundation out of natural materials and then adds successive circles that spiral outward from the center to the rim; the circles are sewn together with pliable splints of natural fibers such as **sumac**, **cottonwood**, **willow**, or **yucca**. These splints are left natural, bleached, or dyed with commercial or plant **dyes**. The different stitching methods include: **close stitch**, in which each stitch of natural fiber closely buttresses against

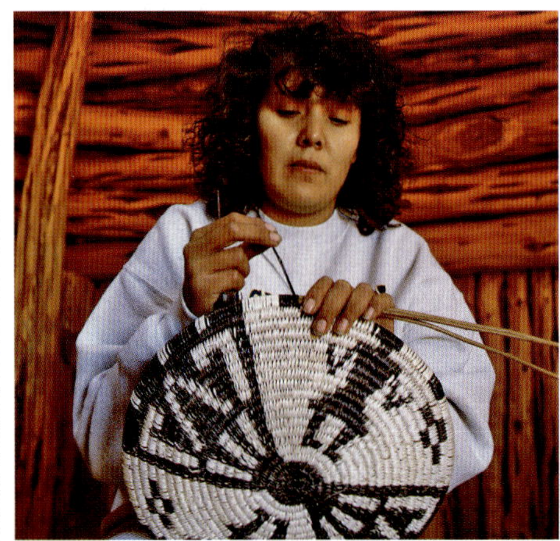

Lorraine Black (Navajo) finishes weaving a large coiled basket.

its neighbor, completely covering the foundation; and **split stitch**, in which the stitches are spaced wide apart, exposing the foundation coil for contrast (a faster weaving technique generally used for utilitarian baskets, notably the large storage baskets among the Pimas). The Hopis, Tohono O'odham, and Pimas use a "bundle" foundation—bundles of plant material wrapped with a single piece of plant material. Other Native peoples use a "rod" foundation, with one or more solid rods around which a single piece of plant material is wrapped. The coiling technique is primarily used for making shallow bowls, **ollas**, **plaques**, **trays**, and **water jars**. See diagram on page 186.

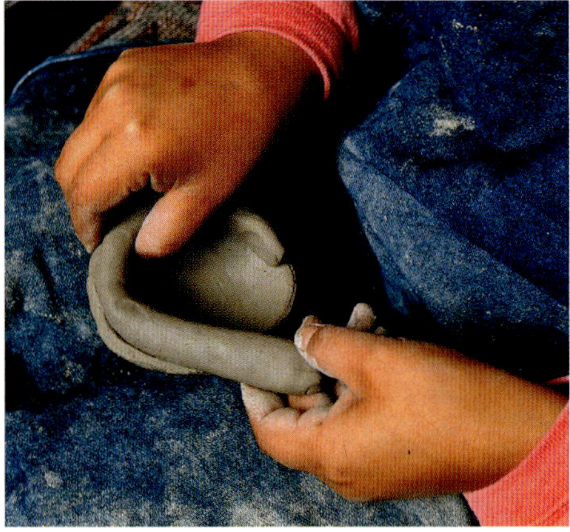

Dawn Navasie (Hopi) uses coils of clay to form a vessel.

COILING / Pottery / a centuries-old traditional method of creating clay vessels, in which the walls are shaped and built up by laying rope-like coils of clay one upon the other, with a round slab (or circular coiled shape) of clay as the base. The walls of the pot are thinned and heightened by pinching the coils and then smoothing them out with a scraping tool—traditionally a piece of **gourd**, a **potsherd**, or stone—which also helps eliminate air bubbles and prevent cracking during the drying or firing process. Contemporary potters have been known to use their fingers, a letter opener, a spatula, a rock, a knife, a tongue depressor, or a myriad of other objects to help smooth the walls of the pot.

The base of the vessel is typically placed in a "**puki**"—the Tewa name for a small dish-like form used to form the base of a new pot; during the coiling process the puki is turned to ensure symmetry. After smoothing the surface, potters may decorate the vessel by attaching pieces of clay in the form of animals, ears of corn, or other forms (see **appliqué**). When completely dry, the vessel is sanded to smooth the surface. In earlier times potters used natural materials like corncobs dipped in water or pieces of sandstone rock, but by the 1930s most potters were using various grades of sandpaper. The pot may then be simply **polished**, or decorated with painted or carved designs before polishing. (Some potters use a pencil to draw out the design on the surface first.) Coil-building large vessels might take weeks, while smaller pieces might take only a few days. Most Pueblo potters continue to use this method today. See also **firing**, **polishing**.

COLCHA / the Spanish word for "bed covering" or quilt, in New Mexico the term refers both to the embroidered textile and the stitch used to cover it. This distinctive style of embroidery has been made by Hispano women in the northern Rio Grande Valley of New Mexico since the mid-1700s. Colcha is a type of self-couching (or "filling") stitch, also called Bokhara or Romanian Couching, in which a long base stitch is held flat along the ground cloth by two or three smaller stitches taken with the same needle and thread. In the earliest examples of the embroidery in New Mexico, found on bedspreads, coverlets, and altar cloths, colcha was created with hand-spun wool that was un-dyed or vegetal-dyed and applied to **sabanilla** backing—a loosely woven, plain-weave, off-white wool fabric—using an easy and flexible stitch to create free-flowing patterns of floral and other naturalistic motifs, **pictorial** elements, and geometric shapes. The wool used for both the yarn and the backing (or ground cloth) typically came from **churro** sheep, introduced to New Spain about 1598. The early wool-on-wool, fully embroidered colchas are known today as *sabanilla labrada* (or fully worked cloth). Wool-on-wool colcha embroidery work is likely one of the few textiles both developed and made in New Mexico during the Spanish Colonial period.

The dominant design sources for these colorful floral and paisley designs of eighteenth- and nineteenth-century New Mexican colchas were East Indian chintz (known in New Mexico as "indianilla") and the linen and silk embroideries imported to Spanish Colonial New Mexico from Mexico, Spain, and Asia. When the Santa Fe Trail trade route opened in the early 1820s, thin-plied commercial-wool **yarns** and cotton-twill cloth became available in New Mexico and were used by some women for colcha. These wool-on-cotton colchas were lightly embroidered with new, free-standing designs such as small birds, insects, and elaborate floral motifs scattered across the textile.

Considered high-value items, wool-on-wool and wool-on-cotton colchas from this period became an important part of the trade with Mexico. Colcha embroidery declined in the late nineteenth century, after the railroads brought new products and trade goods including fabrics to New Mexico. However, in the 1930s the tradition was revived, due in part to Arte Antiguo—a social club founded by twelve Hispano women in the Española Valley, active until 1995—as well as the Native Market, a privately owned store in Santa Fe (1933–1940) that specialized in traditional Spanish Colonial art forms and techniques. Also, beginning in 1930, Frances Varos Graves (b. 1910), of Carson, New Mexico, helped revive the medium by making wool-on-wool colcha embroideries of flowers, birds, animals, "wild west" images, and Catholic saints. Graves, who was self-taught, introduced new figurative and narrative elements to colchas, a departure from traditional colcha designs. In addition, she created a style of colcha in which the entire backing cloth is covered with embroidery; today this is called Carson-style colcha for the town that made it popular.

Another group that contributed to the resurgence of the craft is Artes del Valle—a woman's craft cooperative founded in 1973 in La Garita, in the San Luis Valley of Colorado. The technique is still employed today, primarily by women of northern New Mexico and southern Colorado. Together they are following the old Spanish custom of embroidering items for churches, family *oratorios* (chapels), and household use, as well as on articles of dress such as scarves and shawls. Some of these women embroiderers continue to

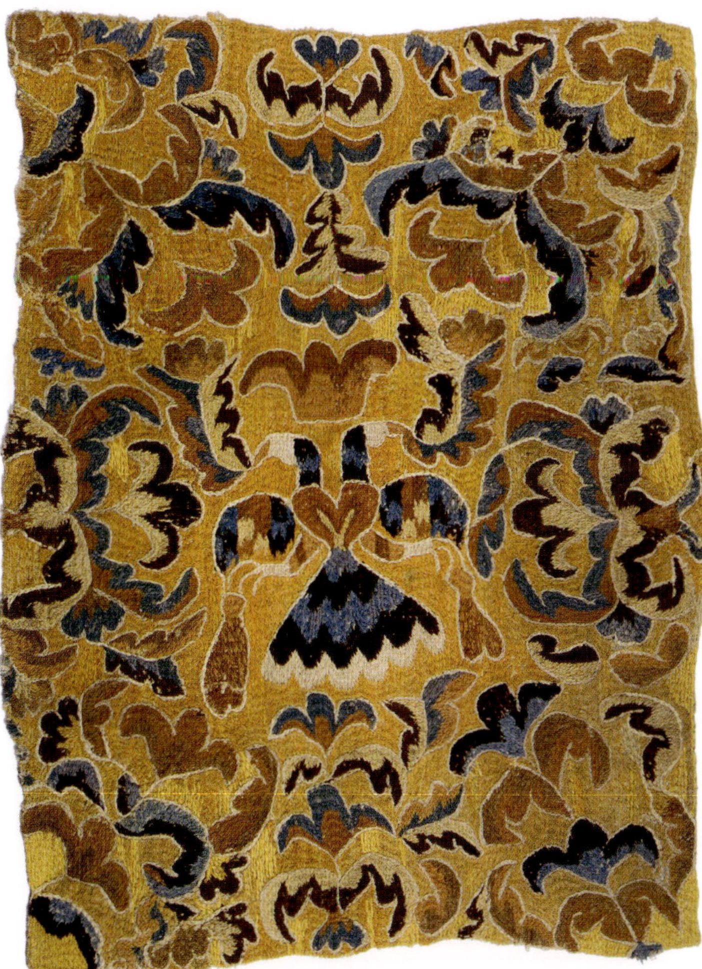

New Mexican colcha, late 18th–early 19th century, wool embroidery on wool background.

wash, card, spin, and dye churro wool to make yarn for their colchas. Fine examples of colcha are exhibited at the annual Spanish Market in Santa Fe, New Mexico. Among the prominent women who are carrying on the historic art form and sell there is María Fernández Graves, niece of Frances Varos Graves. See also **tinwork**.

COLD CHISEL / a hardened steel tool often made of scrap metal, with a ½-inch to ¾-inch straight cutting edge, used to shape/cut/decorate early metalwork including **silver** jewelry, before saws became readily available in the 1900s. Cold chisels were used for some of the earliest Navajo decorative work on silver. Still used by some Navajo jewelers today, cold chisels can make angles, flutes, and edges in silver that cannot be achieved by saws or **stamp work**. See also **buttons**.

COLUMNS / See **estípite column** and **Solomonic column**.

COMBED GLASS / a decorative technique created by painting glass in reverse with oil paint and then "combing it" to create wavy designs, primarily used to decorate **tinwork** items made by Hispano artisans in New Mexico, beginning in the late nineteenth century. It was also a common technique in tinwork made in Mexico. One of the earliest known New Mexican artists to use this technique is known as the "Mesilla Combed Paint Tinsmith." Little information has been discovered about the artist except that he/she was active from about 1890 to 1920; examples were collected in Mesilla, New Mexico, and southern Arizona; the tinwork (of **crosses**, frames, and other forms) is distinguished by reverse-painted combed glass, backed by either foil or colored paper. Among the contemporary tinsmiths using combed glass in the traditional manner is Nicolas Madrid of northern New Mexico, who has won numerous awards for his work at the Spanish Market in Santa Fe.

CONCHAS (Conchos) / from the Spanish word for "shell," slightly domed silver forms, usually oval or circular in shape (and today sometimes rectangular), with surface decoration and sometimes set with stones such as **turquoise** and **coral**, made by Navajo silversmiths who adopted this type of ornament in the mid-nineteenth century. Originally shaped by a technique called **doming**, conchas were decorated by the Navajos with engraved, **stamped**, or punched designs and used on leather belts, for jewelry, or attached them to the sides of leather **horse bridles**.

Beginning in the 1880s, turquoise stones were set in the middle of some Navajo conchas. Objects that display a silversmith's creativity and ability, conchas are most often attached in a series to a leather belt. Older conchas have a diamond-shaped slot in the center separated by a bar, through which the leather belt strap was passed. Later, when metal loops were attached to the reverse to accommodate the leather strap belt, silversmiths emulated the slots by creating patterns in the centers of conchas.

One of the standard features is the traditional scalloped edge, an adaption of early Mexican conchas that decorated horse bridles. The Navajo smiths were also influenced by the oval and round plaques of German silver worn by the Comanches, Utes, and Kiowas as hair decorations, as ornaments strung on leather belts, and as fasteners for the sides of buckskin leggings. Silver adornments such as conchas were also traditionally used by the Spanish and Mexicans to decorate their horse bridles/**headstalls**.

Today silversmiths create conchas by cutting a sheet of silver into a round or oval shape before doming, or they melt silver and then form an ingot by pouring the molten metal into a mold, and once the metal has cooled, it is hammered into the desired shape. Then the concha is decorated with stamp work or other techniques. In recent decades Navajo smiths have used the concha form on rings, pendants, earrings, brooches, **bolos**, and buckles.

Concha belts were originally worn primarily by Navajo men, and then eventually by women, low around the hips. Initially fastened by tying leather thongs, concha belts early on became secured with buckles. The latter were simple at first, but soon became more elaborate, and like the conchas, a major object of display of a silversmith's imagination and skill. **Stamp work**, **repoussé**, filing and **cold-chisel** work, **appliqué**, and inlaid stones are among the decorative techniques implemented on concha belt buckles. The buckle either echoes the design of the individual conchas or is treated as a separate ornament with an unrelated design. These belts have been a uniquely Southwestern adornment for more than a century.

COPING / a covering at the top of a **parapet** wall used to protect the wall from water damage, typically made of brick, tile, metal, or concrete. See also **dentils**, **Sonoran Transformed**, **Sonoran Transitional**, **Territorial style—New Mexico**, and **Territorial Revival style.**

COPPER / a reddish brown malleable metal, used since prehistoric times to fashion various utilitarian objects and jewelry. Copper items were used and possibly made by prehistoric peoples at sites such as Paquimé (Casas Grandes) in northern Chihuahua, Mexico, and in the area of present-day Jerome, Arizona, where copper and **turquoise** deposits were discovered by Spanish explorer Antonio de Espejo in 1583. Ornaments such as **crosses** and utilitarian objects made of copper and brass were brought to the Southwest, including to the trade fairs held in Pueblo centers like Taos and Pecos, New Mexico, by Spanish explorers and settlers and then by Mexicans. Hispano blacksmiths and artisans, who taught the Native people blacksmithing skills, fashioned various utilitarian objects out of copper, such as **tobacco flasks** (*tabaquera*) and cooking implements.

By the 1840s Native artisans of the Southwest were fashioning jewelry out of copper. For instance, early metalworking at Zuni was primarily confined to copper and brass items such as twisted wire bracelets and rings with simple decorations of file and chisel marks. They also made **buttons**, bracelets, pendants, **beads**, and **ketoh** mountings out of old copper pots and pans that had been melted and pounded into the desired shape.

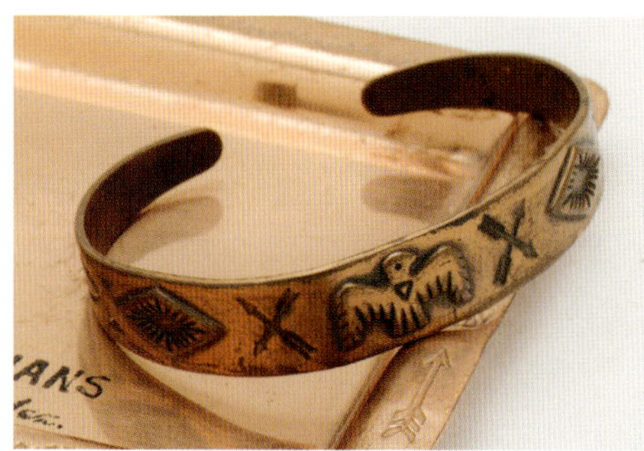

ABOVE: Souvenir tray (Mescalero Apache), ca. 1930s, and child's cuff bracelet (Bell Trading Post, Albuquerque, NM), ca. 1940s, both copper with stamp work.
ABOVE LEFT: Nicolas Madrid (New Mexico), Mesilla combed glass and tinwork cross.

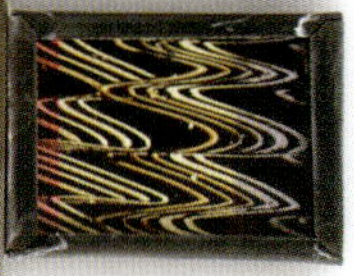

Later, brass and copper were obtained in the more convenient form of wire, which was supplied by traders. The early copper and brass jewelry was uneven in workmanship and simple in design; decoration generally consisted of file marks scratched on to the surface to create geometric patterns. Some Navajo smiths fashioned copper bracelets with simple diagonal marks or chevrons made by cutting into the metal with **cold chisels.** Mexican residents of the region took brass and copper to Zuni Pueblo and asked the smiths there to make jewelry for them, as many believed that these metals warded off rheumatism.

The Zunis made crosses for the Mexicans, who wore them around their necks. Although less desirable than silver, copper was more readily available in the mid-nineteenth century and easily worked by Native craftsmen. Among the

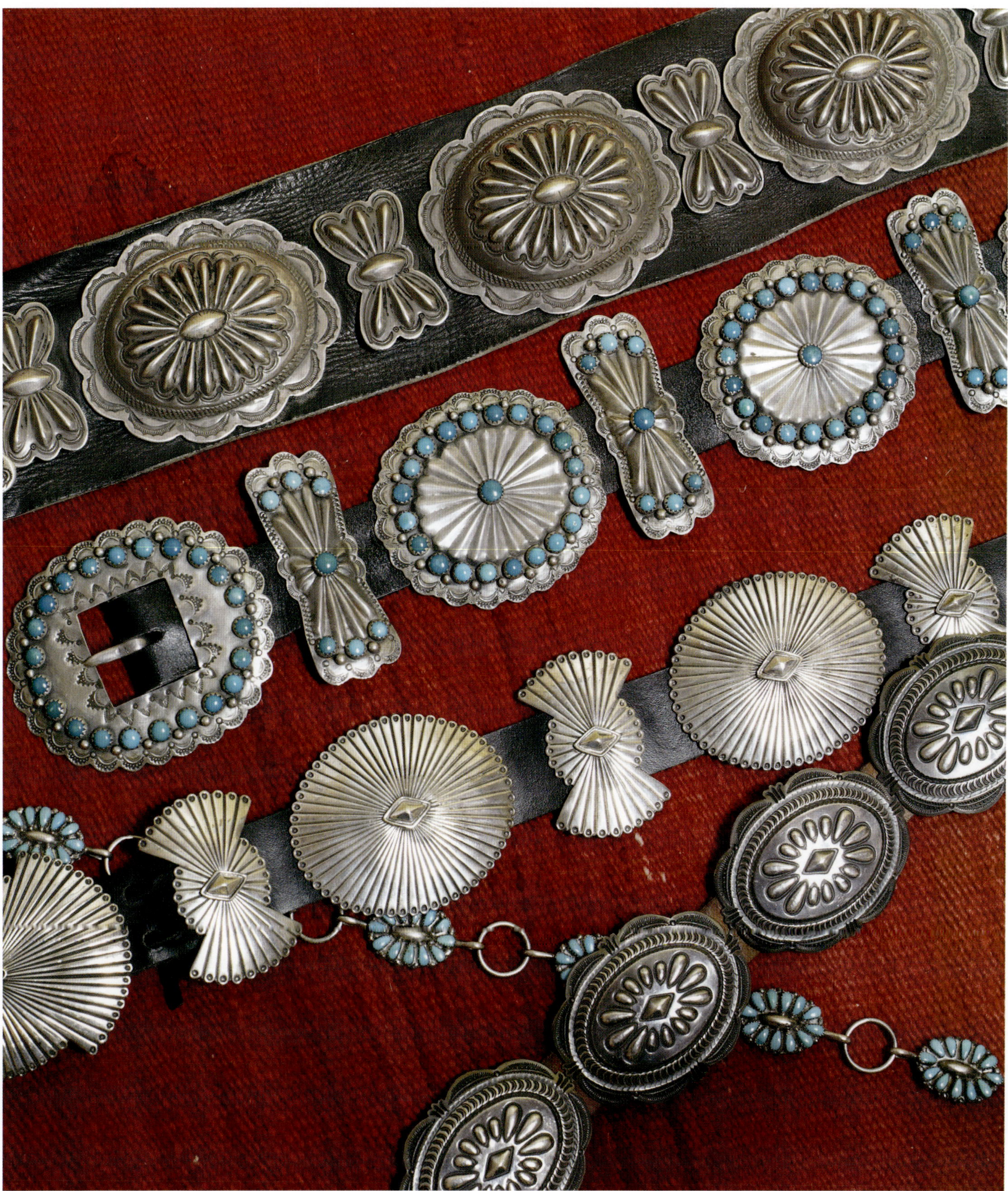

Navajo concha belts (contemporary and antique), made of sterling silver (some with inlaid turquoise) and leather.

sources for copper were the few small copper mines in southern New Mexico and the mines at Jerome, Clifton, and Bisbee, Arizona, in the largest copper-producing state in the United States. Native smiths, especially Navajo, pounded copper into bracelets or into rods that were formed into hoop earrings. In some instances, Navajo smiths made hoop earrings by flattening and then stamping commercial copper wire. When silver became available, it quickly replaced copper as the preeminent ornamental metal in the Navajo and Pueblo cultures; many of the earliest silver jewelry pieces, such as bracelets, followed the same shape and decorative patterns as the brass and copper ones.

However, during the Great Depression and World War II when there was a shortage of silver supplies, some Zuni, Navajo, and other smiths experimented with copper. Among the copper items made for sale at trading posts such as Julius Gans's Southwest Arts & Crafts in Santa Fe, in the 1930s, were hand-hammered ashtrays shaped into birds with stampwork decoration. Copper cut into forms such as **thunderbird**, deer, or **knifewing** figures was also used during this time by some smiths as templates to outline jewelry patterns on sheet silver; and some smiths use copper templates today. The use of copper for items sold at trading posts along **Route 66** and elsewhere, such as cuff bracelets, pendants, **conchas**, and ashtrays with **stamped** designs (thunderbird, rain clouds, etc.), continued into the 1950s and '60s.

In recent decades, copper, used by fledgling Native American silversmiths to practice on and sometimes as an accent metal in their silver pieces, has once again become a favored material for jewelry. This is due in part to the popular belief that copper helps ease symptoms of arthritis and

because the soaring price of silver makes copper items more affordable.

CORAL / a living sea organism consisting of calcium carbonate with small amounts of magnesium carbonate and traces of iron, semi-translucent to opaque with a rock-like hardness and ranging in color from white to pale pink to blood red. Introduced into the Southwest by the Spanish, coral was frequently used as **beads** for necklaces and for inlay in Native American jewelry. Also, some artisans polished thin branches of coral and used them unaltered in jewelry such as brooches and pendants.

When coral was first introduced to the region it was in bead form, drilled and strung. For example, pre-drilled pink coral beads were available on the Navajo reservation by the 1870s. Beginning in the 1920s trader C. G. Wallace (1898–1993) was offering through his trading post at Zuni deep-red Mediterranean coral, much of it harvested from reefs near the islands of Sardinia and Corsica. Most of Wallace's coral was made into beads. Another trader, J. S. Candelario, who owned a curio business in Santa Fe, New Mexico, also imported large quantities of coral from suppliers in Italy in the early twentieth century. Famed Zuni artisan Leekya Deyuse (1889–1966) was using coral sparingly in his **fetish** carvings beginning in the 1920s. Some highly skilled jewelers hand-drilled their own coral beads in the mid to late 1970s.

Coral remains a highly valued commodity by the Navajo, Hopi, and Pueblo tribes today. Due to over-harvesting in the Mediterranean, coral has become a rarity and prices have soared. Now it is primarily imported from the Sea of Japan

(though some Native artisans still purchase raw coral from Italy), in the form of pre-drilled beads or natural branches. Faced with a lack of quality coral, Zuni fetish carvers tend to use "apple coral" or "bamboo coral," a resin-stabilized, orange-red dyed coral from the South China Sea.

CORBEL / a supporting projection on the face of a wall, made from a variety of materials including stone, wood, brick, and cement, and in a variety of shapes from simple blocks to highly decorated elaborate forms. In the Southwest the term refers to a scroll-shaped carved or molded wood bracket, with one end embedded in the wall, extending outwards from one to three feet, and used to support roofing, ceilings of **vigas** or beams, or the wood-beam joints on exterior **portals**.

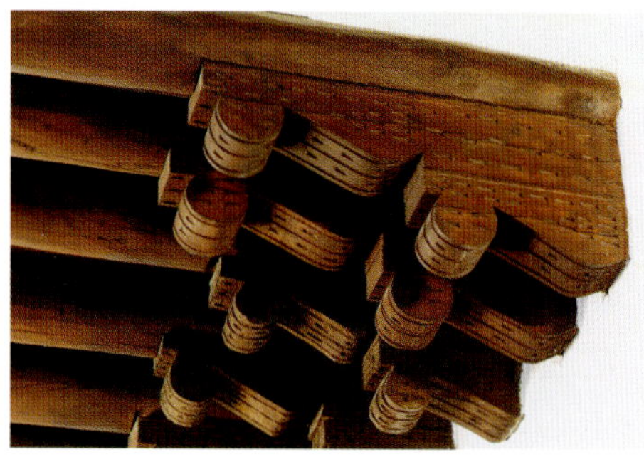

In some instances, corbels, usually painted or carved with decoration, are used purely for ornamental purposes. The most commonly used corbel shape in the region derives from the scrolled volute that originated in corbels associated with the Mujédar architecture of Moorish Spain, imported to the New World by the Spanish. They were intended to perform the essential function

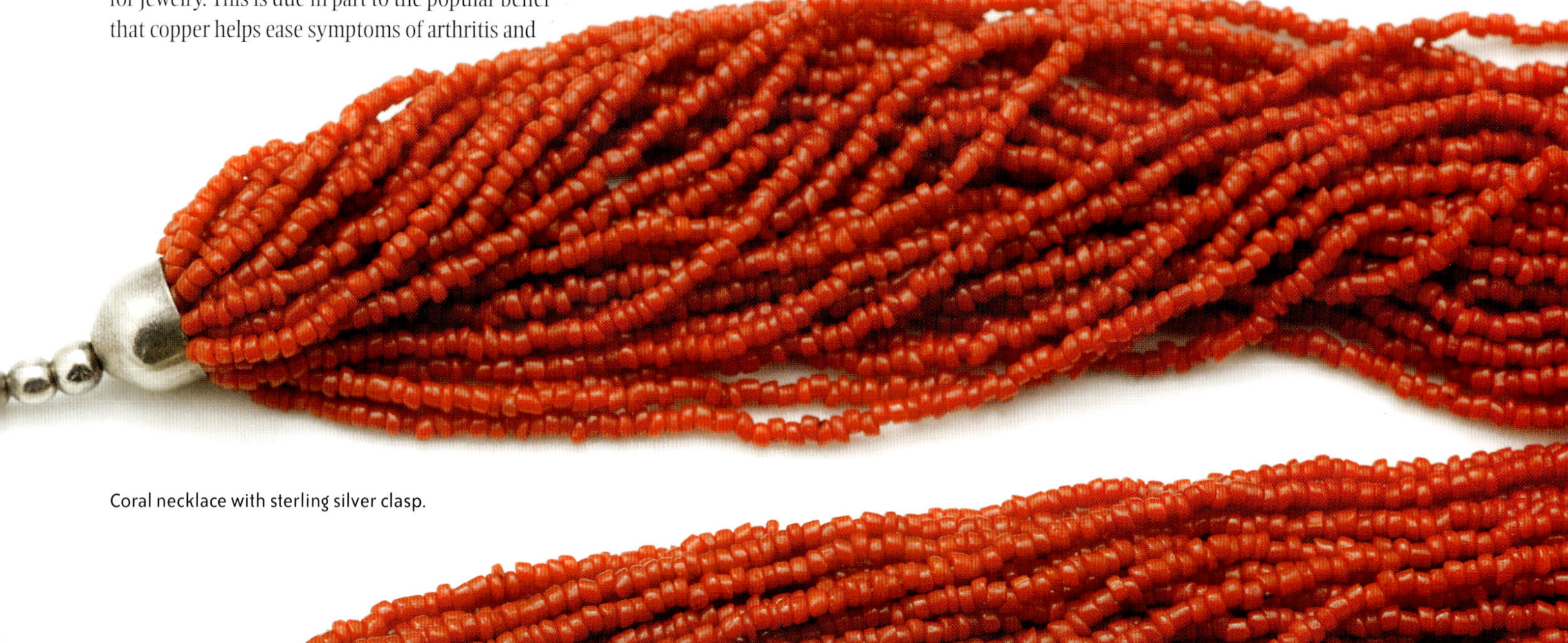

Coral necklace with sterling silver clasp.

of distributing the heavy load of the flat roof system of **adobe** and other types of buildings, and also provided a surface area for carved and painted decoration. Because handcrafted corbels require much expense and effort to produce, they have always been highly valued and often salvaged from ruined buildings and reused. Originally handcrafted with **adze** and chisel, wood corbels are largely mass-produced today and remain a key feature of architectural design throughout the Southwest. See also **zapata**.

CÓRDOVA WOODCARVING /

an original style of wood carving developed by José Dolores López (1868–1937) in the tiny isolated village of Córdova, situated in the picturesque mountains of northern New Mexico. Córdova style, as it is known today, consists of unpainted, smooth-grained wood figures with intricate **chip-carved** and **incised** details executed with a sharp knife. Soft white aspen is the primary wood used, but in some instances it is combined with pinkish-red cedar for contrast, or cedar is used as the main wood. If the figure requires separate pieces, wooden pegs and/or glue are used to join them together.

A furniture-maker by trade, López began carving small animal figures during many sleepless nights while worrying about his son serving in World War I. By the time his son returned safely home he had become an inventive woodcarver. His style was shaped by the wide tradition of Hispano wood sculpture. In the last decade of his life, López created wooden religious figures; in 1929, Santa Fe artist Frank Applegate encouraged López to adapt the chip-carved style of his furniture to the religious figures.

Through their work, José López and his son George López (1900–1993) established a New Mexico folk art carving tradition, which continues to thrive to this day among their descendants and other artisans living in the region. Among the items they have carved are **santos,** crucifixes, **Trees of Life**, **nacimientos**, death carts, and whimsical animals. In the early days of the technique men did the carving and the women completed only detail work and sanding; today the work is no longer strictly divided. Trademarks of the style are fine carving, high polish created by different grades of sandpaper, and exquisite details.

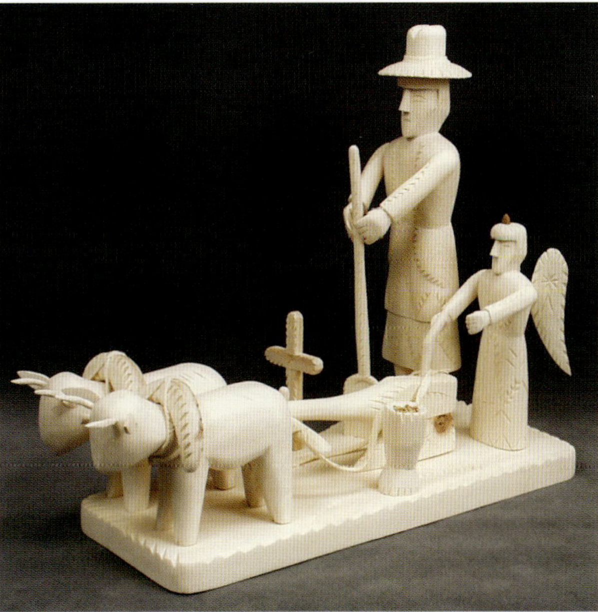

Sabanita Lopez Ortiz (Córdova, New Mexico), San Ysidro carving, 2000, aspen.

CORN / the most important crop and staple food for Native Americans in the Southwest since about 1000 BC, and a powerful and significant symbol for many Native people. For the Hopis, corn literally signifies life. For Pueblo people, corn is equally important in part because of the nurturing relationship of planting corn—unlike most other domesticated plants of the New World corn cannot re-seed itself and must be replanted each year. A perfect ear of corn is an important personal **fetish** that is given during the naming ceremony and kept

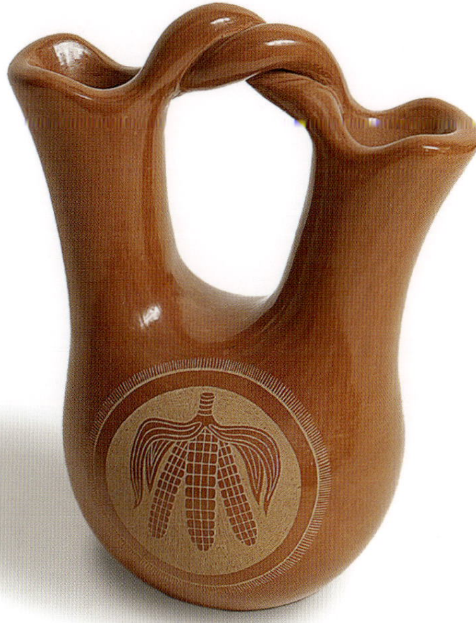

Celestina Naranjo (Santa Clara), redware wedding vase with sgraffito corn design.

for life by the Pueblo and Hopi people. When an image of a corncob appears beside a signature on a piece of pottery, silver jewelry, or other piece of art, it serves as a **hallmark** and indicates that the artist is a member of the Corn Clan. Corn motifs that appear on Native-made clothing, in religious dances, and on various art forms—such as jewelry, pottery, baskets, fetishes, and textiles—are usually intended to indicate a respect for, and prayer for, fertility and/or a good growing season.

CORN MOTHER / Corn Maidens / among the Pueblo and Navajo peoples, they are considered divine figures who are summoned to watch over the crops. Corn is called "the Mother" because of the peoples' dependence on corn and because of corn's emergence from the primary mother, Earth. Among the earliest forms symbolizing and honoring the power of Corn Mother are stone **fetishes** resembling an ear of corn. Some were carved with eyes and mouths that were inlaid with **turquoise** or **shell**, others would simply be dressed in shell and stone beads and wrapped with feathers. These

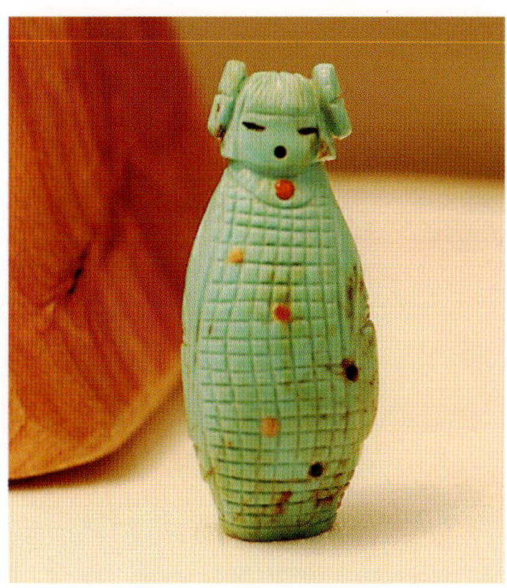

Sandra Quandelacy (Zuni), double Corn Maiden fetish.

Corn Mother fetishes would never have been sold or made for sale.

Corn Maidens are important to the Zunis, who believe that the maidens once saved their people from starvation. Beginning in the mid-1970s, Zuni fetish carvers began fashioning Corn Maidens out of a variety materials often inlaid with tiny pieces of turquoise, **coral**, or **jet;** artist Faye Quandelacy is credited with popularizing the form. Zuni Corn Maidens are usually depicted with a corn-like body and a human head. In addition to fetishes, representations of the Corn Mother and Corn Maidens can be found today in pottery, jewelry, and other art forms. As a representation of the earth, the seasons, and other aspects, Corn Mother appears in Navajo sandpaintings created for the Blessingway—the oldest of Navajo ceremonies held to secure a blessing and ensure a long and good life.

CORNMEAL / Corn Pollen / used in prayers, blessings, offerings, and ceremonies by Native Americans as an affirmation of the connection between Earth and all life. It is often carried by Pueblo people in a small leather pouch. Cornmeal or corn pollen is also used to metaphorically "feed" carved **fetishes** made by the Zunis. The Navajos use cornmeal and corn pollen in their religious observances as ceremonial food to fuel both the spiritual and physical bodies. Hopi women have traditionally dusted finely ground cornmeal on their faces during ceremonies, as a prayer for future bountiful corn harvests.

CORRUGATED POTTERY / an ancient technique for creating textured clay vessels, used by Ancestral Puebloans of the Southwest, in which the clay coils of the pot (when still moist) are pinched with fingers, or notched using a stick or other pointed tool to produce a rippled or "corrugated" effect.

Many examples of corrugated pottery vessels found near hearths in prehistoric Puebloan sites have soot on the interiors, suggesting they were likely used for cooking. The corrugated surface may have aided in heat transfer and reduced cracking in cooking pots that were exposed to frequent heating and cooling. Modern potters at Acoma Pueblo, New Mexico, including Lucy M. Lewis (ca. 1890–1992) and Stella Shutiva (1935–1997) were inspired by the corrugated utilitarian pots and **sherds** of their ancestors to reintroduce this decoration on their white-slipped wares.

Today Acoma potters use a variety of methods to create the corrugation on the moist clay, from a deer antler to a thumbnail to a pointed tool. Among the accomplished living artists carrying on the corrugated style at Acoma is Jackie Shutiva Histia, who learned the art at the age of nineteen from her mother Stella. Potters at other Pueblos also have used the corrugated method; for instance, the late Garnet Pavatea (1915–1981) of Hopi (First Mesa) used a band of corrugation around the shoulders of her red bowls, which she created by imprinting the tip of a metal can opener.

Stella Shutiva (Acoma), corrugated seed pot.

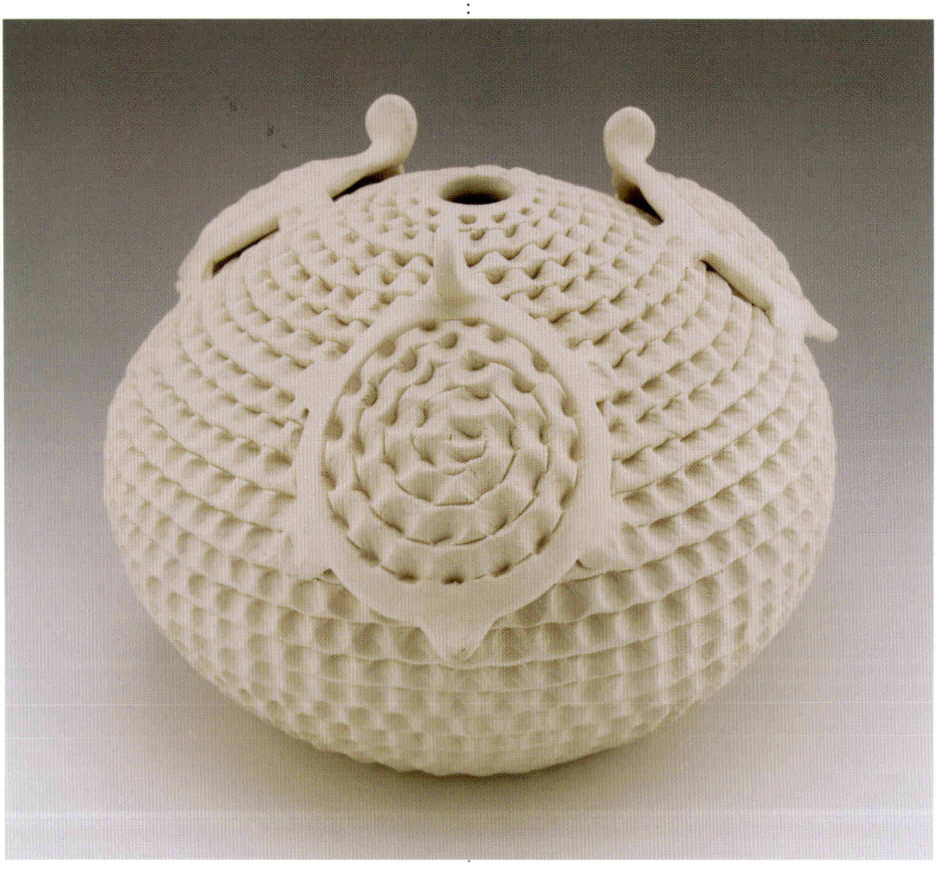

COTTONWOOD / a large deciduous tree with at least three species, the most common in the Southwest being *populous fremontii*, named for Major John C. Fremont (1813–1890), explorer and governor of territorial Arizona (1878–1883). The common name derives from the fruit the tree bears each spring: green pods that have hairy and cotton-like seeds. Found growing near streams, rivers, springs, or seeps throughout the Southwest, this tree (its branches and roots) has been used by residents of the region for a variety of crafts, clothing, utilitarian wares, and building needs for centuries.

Historically, Native Americans used the forked branches as the framework for houses and **ramadas**—the bottom of a branch was buried in the ground and the fork provided support for beams (branches from cottonwoods or other trees such as the **willow**) placed above. Traditionally, and in recent times, the Hopis have used the soft, lightweight root of the cottonwood to carve **katsina** dolls. **Navajo woodcarvers** have favored cottonwood for their folk-art figures, and the Yaquis of Arizona use cottonwood to carve their **Pascola masks**.

In addition, cottonwood trees have provided material for both **coiled** and some **twined** baskets (such as **burden baskets**) made by the **Havasupais** and **Hualapais**, the Apaches, and other groups. The handles of **rattles** made for various Native American ceremonial dances are often carved from cottonwood branches; and hollowed-out trunks have been used as ceremonial drum frames. Lastly, but no less importantly, the Hispano **santeros/santeras** of New Mexico have traditionally carved **bultos** from the branches or root of the native cottonwood tree (as well as from other native trees).

COURTYARD (Patio) / an area in a house or other structure that is open to the sky and enclosed by three or four walls (or a building), an architectural feature particularly suited to homes built in hot and arid climates such as the American Southwest. The courtyard is a design concept brought from Spain to central Mexico in the 1500s and then north to New Spain (specifically, southern Arizona and southern New Mexico) in the late seventeenth century. Building a house around an open courtyard originated with the ancient Mediterranean civilizations; early examples dating from 2,000 to 3,000 years old can be found in Egypt, Greece, and Rome. Considered to be the "heart" of a house, courtyards provide a central area for privacy, fresh air and ventilation, and light. A **portal** usually borders the courtyard, providing shelter from the elements (especially the intense summer heat). Historically, the courtyard, often the largest room in the house, was used for multiple purposes. For instance, in Arizona, during the nineteenth century and later, courtyards were used for gardening, cooking, eating, entertaining, and during the hot summers for sleeping. A privy and/or well were often situated in the courtyard. Historic courtyard homes of the American Southwest are built primarily with **adobe** walls, a stone foundation, and traditional flat earthen roofs. Typically, in these homes, the courtyard is accessed from the street through a **zaguán**. See also **placita.**

COYOTE / from the Nahuatl (Aztec) word *coyotl,* an animal that plays a prominent role in Native American mythology and, as a result, has long been portrayed in various Native American arts and crafts, especially in the Southwest. Many tribes credit the clever Coyote with bringing fire to them; others, including some Apache groups, believe Coyote taught people how to prepare and cook foods, tan hides, make moccasins, and weave baskets; and to several cultures the Coyote is known as a trickster. One of the most common myths has to do with the placement of the stars in the heavens: the curious and meddlesome Coyote is believed to have disrupted the process, leading to the scattering of stars in a willy-nilly manner across the night sky. Among the artisans who have portrayed the Coyote are Zuni Pueblo carvers, who have made **fetishes** of the animal standing on all four legs with its bushy tail stretched out, as well as in the howling position (with its head thrown back). Some Navajo basket makers, such as Sally Black, are known for portrayals of the Navajo Creation Story during which Coyote haphazardly places the stars in the

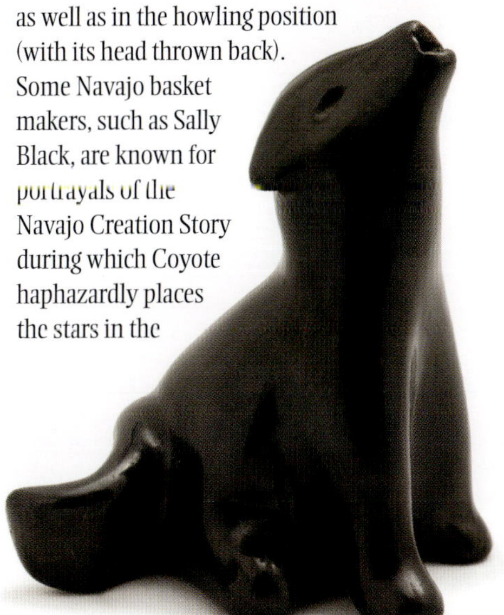

night sky. In traditional **sandpaintings**, Navajo medicine men have depicted the part of the Creation Story when First Coyote brings back fire to First Man and First Woman. The Coyote also appears on occasion in Hopi silverwork, **Tohono O'odham baskets**, **Santa Clara Pueblo** black clay figurines, and Navajo **pictorial** textiles and wooden folk carvings. Like the **Kokopelli** figure, the coyote has become an iconic image of the Southwest and its Native cultures. As a result, beginning in the late twentieth century, the coyote has been mass produced on everything from magnets to dish towels to t-shirts, thereby diluting the figure's significance.

COYOTE FENCES / a style of fence traditionally made in New Mexico of **latillas** (slender peeled or unpeeled logs or branches) that are firmly placed in the ground and wired together; these fences were originally erected to protect livestock from coyotes. They can be seen built around numerous properties in Santa Fe and northern New Mexico today.

CRACKLING (Crazing) / fine cracks that appear in the **slip** of **clay** vessels during the firing process, which are caused by a difference in the ratio of expansion and contraction between the slip and the body of the vessel.

CRADLEBOARD (Cradles, Basket Cradles) / a device for transporting babies on a mother's back, made by the Utes, Apaches, San Juan Paiutes, and other Native Americans. They are typically constructed with a **willow** or **sumac** basketry frame—or wood-board backing of thin, hand-**adzed** boards—covered with brain-tanned hide and hide lacing in the front. Usually a hood made of **twined** willow or sumac, or hide, was attached to the front to shield the baby's head from the elements and provide decoration. Cradleboards may be either plain (Apache cradleboards, for instance, are sparsely ornamented) or heavily ornamented with beadwork (such as those made by the Utes) and hide fringe. The front flap that covered the lacing and the high backboard above the hood was a blank canvas for colorful beadwork designs. The Utes often hang elaborately beaded **umbilical cord bags** from their cradleboards. Additionally, miniature or toy-size cradleboards ornamented with lazy-stitch beadwork were produced by the Utes as early as the 1880s and likely intended for the **curio** trade. An important and constant aspect

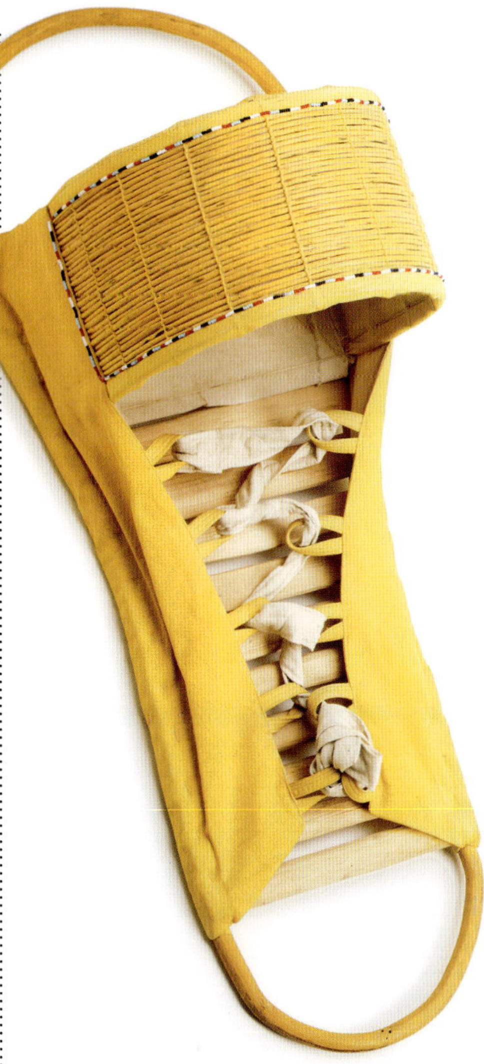

ABOVE: Alma Gusta Thompson (San Carlos Apache), cradleboard, ca. 1956. **LEFT:** "Cresencia" (Santa Clara), coyote, clay.

of Ute culture since the 1860s, cradleboards continue to be made and used today. Hopis have woven miniature **wicker** cradleboards for the flat style **katsina dolls**, generally given to women of child-bearing age during certain Hopi katsina ceremonies. Pueblo Indians have also traditionally made simple wooden cradles, many carved with a symbolic stepped "cloud" at the top; however, this subject has largely gone unstudied.

CROSSES / consisting primarily of two forms—the Latin/Christian in which the crossbar is shorter than the vertical piece, and the equilateral in which the vertical and horizontal arms are the same length—crosses appeared in Native American and Pueblo arts and crafts prior to Spanish contact. Based upon the traditions explained by current Southwest Indian cultures, it seems most likely that they represent stars. It is clear, however, that beginning in the seventeenth century, Spanish missionaries converted this symbol into the Christian cross in their efforts to convert the Native peoples of the New World.

For some Pueblo people, the double-barred cross was significant, for it represented a **dragonfly**—an ancient emblem associated with water found in **rock art** and on pottery designs; this cross type was also likely introduced by Spanish missionaries as a religious symbol. Necklaces featuring crosses and beads were brought by the Spanish from Mexico and Spain to New Mexico both for personal use and for trade with Native peoples to inspire their conversion to Christianity. These crosses influenced Pueblo artisans who copied their designs. For the Navajos, an equilateral cross with two squares at each point on both side arms is referred to as a **Spider Woman cross**. Some Pueblo- or Navajo-made cross pendants are embellished with hearts at the bottom, also likely an influence of Spanish- and Mexican-made crosses. In Catholocism, this heart is the Sacred Heart, and for some Pueblo people, it can represent the heart of a dragonfly.

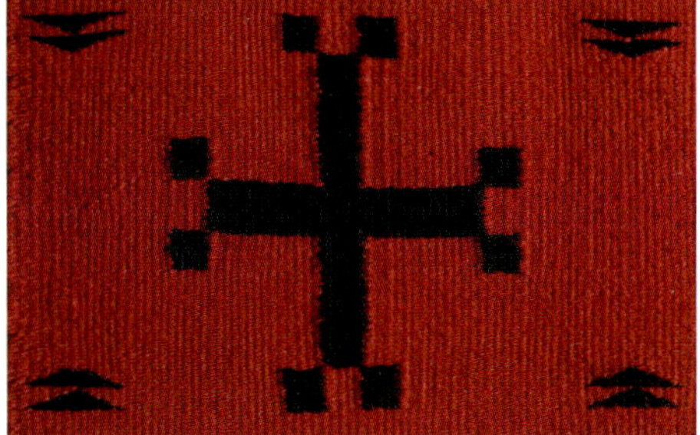

ABOVE: Louise Reed (Navajo), Spider Woman cross (detail of rug), 2003, handspun yarns, synthetic dyes. **TOP:** Bobby Garcia (New Mexico), tin cross with Sacred Heart center, vintage Chimayó tin. **RIGHT:** Irene Clark (Navajo), Crystal-style textile, 44" x 61".

Beginning in the nineteenth century, **tinwork** crosses were also made by Hispano tinsmiths in New Mexico; they were produced in a variety of sizes and were intended to hang on the wall, be freestanding, or used for carrying in processions. Typical decorative elements on these tin crosses are strips of wallpaper or cloth placed under glass, as well as oil-painted panels, mirrors, or reverse-painted glass. In the mid-twentieth century, pieces of **colcha** embroidery were used to ornament tin crosses. This technique has been attributed to New Mexican artisans Emilio and Senaida Romero (Emilio crafted the tinwork and Senaida made the colcha). Other popular embellishments are cut-out tin shapes such as crescents that are attached to the ends of the horizontal arms; the center of the cross, where the horizontal and vertical arms meet, may be covered with a tin **rosette** or other tin circular shape; and the space between the arms may have quarter-round tin brackets representing rays. Crosses, as religious symbols and as decorative motifs, continue to play an important role in the designs of Native American and Hispano artisans today.

CRYSTAL TRADING POST / Crystal-style Rugs / built at an elevation of eight thousand feet at the edge of the Chuska Mountains north of Window Rock, Arizona, in the east-central part of the Navajo reservation, this remote post was founded in 1894 and purchased by Irishman John B. Moore in 1896, who renamed the post after the crystal-clear spring nearby (called Tó Niltsilí in Navajo). The post eventually became associated with a Navajo rug style called "Crystal."

In the mid-1890s, Moore, an influential trader, encouraged Navajo weavers to create new styles of textiles in designs he favored and to improve the quality of wool they used. In 1904 he was one of the first traders to produce a mail-order catalogue advertising Navajo rugs, silverwork, and other items. Early examples of the Crystal rugs made by Moore's expert weavers are characterized by hand-spun wool and a bold central pattern and borders, often accompanied by hook motifs and other shapes influenced by Oriental rug designs. Moore owned the post until 1911, but the early Crystal style was carried on in the region for another twenty to thirty years. By the latter part of the 1930s, a new Crystal style had developed, consisting of banded patterns in vegetal colors and including the use of wavy lines.

The newer style was promoted by Don Jensen when he took over the Crystal Trading Post in 1944. Crystal rugs from that period were usually made with yarns of muted earth tones, and sometimes pastels, and included such design elements as bands of **squash blossoms**, diamonds, triangles, or stars between narrow bands of wavy lines. Currently, the Crystal Trading Post lies in ruins. However, Crystal-style rugs are still woven by Navajo artisans. Contemporary versions are banded and not bordered; woven with vegetal-**dyed** yarns in warm golds, browns, greens, and sometimes black; and are distinguished by bands composed of rows of alternating colors. See also **souvenir spoons**.

CURIO TRADE / the curio trade in the Southwest was established simultaneously with the completion of the transcontinental railroads, and

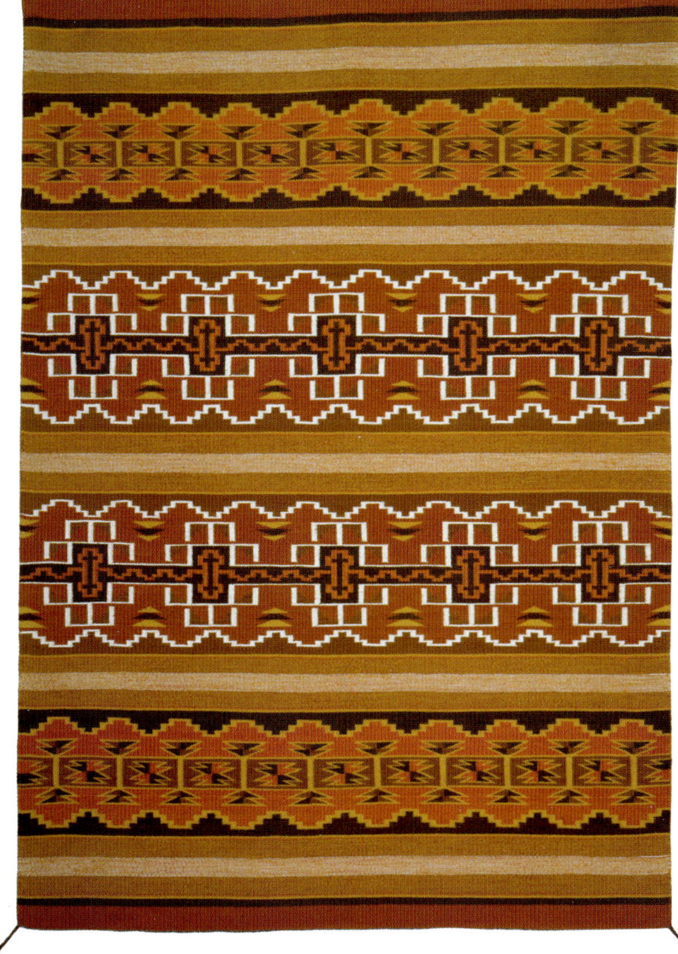

their branch routes, in the late nineteenth century. Tourists and other interested persons could purchase Hispano and Native American artifacts and "curiosities" made in the Southwest through mail-order catalogues and from curio dealers, who acquired pottery, baskets, textiles, silverwork, and other crafts directly from artisans through barter or purchase. By February of 1880, the year the Atchison, Topeka and Santa Fe Railway arrived in New Mexico, Aaron Gold had established the first known curio shop in Santa Fe. In the first years of the twentieth century, curio collecting was so popular that new curio stores emerged at an astonishing rate in major cities throughout the Southwest. These early curio dealers contributed to the commodification of traditional Native American artifacts and the invention of entirely non-traditional ones.

CUTTLEFISH BONE CASTING / one of the oldest methods of casting, in which a cuttlefish bone serves as the casting medium, used by some contemporary Native American artisans to create **silver** or gold jewelry. It is used in the same way as a carved **tufa** stone, the difference being that the natural curvature of the cuttlefish bone forms the pattern on the silver. Admired for the textured effects it creates, cuttlefish bone casting is utilized for a variety of jewelry forms, ranging from rings to cuff bracelets to earrings to pendants and pins. Among the contemporary Native smiths using this technique in the Southwest are Larry Golsh (Pala Mission), Robert Sorrell (Navajo), Samuel Great-walker LaFountain (Turtle Mountain Chippewa), and Althea Cajero (Santo Domingo/Acoma).

DAY OF THE DEAD (El Día de los Muertos) Figures / skeletons, skulls, and allegorical figures created from wood, ceramic, sugar, or papier-mâché, made by Mexican artisans in Oaxaca City and other places, for a celebration of ancient Mexican origin, occurring on October 31 and November 1 and 2, when dead souls return to earth to celebrate with friends and family. Day of the Dead may have originated with the ancient Aztecs, who believed that the dead returned to visit the living each year. Initially celebrated during the month of August, it was moved to autumn by the Spanish conquerors after arriving in Mexico in the 1500s, to correspond with All Saints' Day and All Souls' Day of the Roman Catholic calendar.

Day of the Dead is still observed in Mexico and in various cities across the American Southwest. During the three-day event families honor their

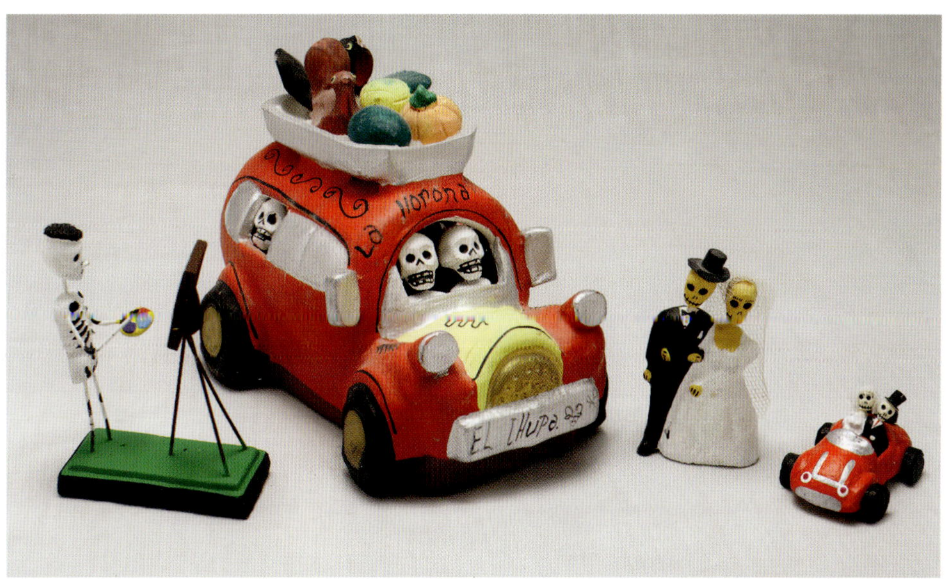

Mexican Day of the Dead figures, early 21st century, painted clay, some metal, netting.

deceased relatives by: preparing special meals; dancing and playing festive music; gathering in cemeteries and decorating the graves of the deceased with flowers; and creating and displaying colorful crafts and decorations, including handmade figurines. The most popular of these figures are grimly humorous *calaveras* (skeletons) that are portrayed enjoying the afterlife, engaged in the midst of everyday activities—smoking cigarettes, painting a picture, dancing, playing music, and getting married. Sometimes these miniatures are placed inside painted tin or wood **nichos**.

These skeletal figures recall the imagery of nineteenth- and early twentieth-century Mexican engravings, including those by José Guadalupe Posada (1852–1913), a Mexican illustrator and artist whose satirical and religious images have influenced a large number of artists and their Day of the Dead figures. In particular, Posada's images of the finely dressed La Catrina figure (often clad in Victorian garb holding a parasol) and her counterpart El Catrin (a gentleman dressed in top hat and tails) have inspired artists. Many Hispano residents of the Southwest display Day of the Dead figures on home altars built for the occasion, along with votive candles, marigolds (the "flower of the dead"), **santos**, and other offerings for the deceased. In recent decades, the popular skeleton revelers and other Day of the Dead figures have been used by Hispano artisans on a variety of items including ceramic tableware, painted furniture, and fine art.

DENDROCHRONOLOGY (Tree-Ring Dating) / from the Greek words *dendros* (tree) and *chronos* (time), a scientific dating technique developed by Andrew E. Douglass (1867–1962) of the University of Arizona, Tucson, in which the pattern of annual growth rings in a tree is matched to a master long-term growth-ring chart (created by Douglass) and used by historians and archaeologists to date wood and the structures built from wood. This research method has been particularly helpful in the Southwest, where more than 5,000 ancient and historic sites have been dated, including many pueblos constructed of mud, stone, and wooden posts and beams.

Most trees add a ring of growth each year, with the width depending on the climate. For instance, dry years produce narrow rings and wet years produce wider rings. To date a timber, such as a ceiling **viga** in a home, a cylindrical boring tool (called an "increment borer") is used to remove a sample of wood that cuts across all growth rings from the outer surface to the central core. The sample taken, typically only about as wide as a dime, is called a "core." Then the annual growth ring specimen is compared with Douglass's master chart and used to determine a "cutting date" and hence the approximate date a building was constructed.

When using this dating technique, it is important to remember that in prehistoric and historic times, timbers were typically reused in other buildings constructed later—especially in places where timber was scarce—and some timbers were cut and stockpiled several years before used in construction.

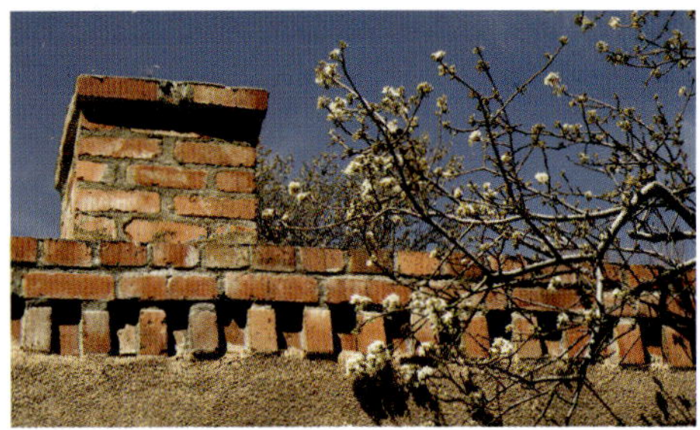

DENTILS / from the Latin *dentes*, small, square, tooth-like blocks placed in a series to form a molding often under Ionic and Corinthian cornices (the projecting section at the top of a wall or pediment). Dentils are a typical feature of the Greek Revival style—a style echoing classical Greek temples that dominated American architecture from about 1818 to 1850—recreated in the Southwest (especially New Mexico) by the mid-1800s with kiln-fired red bricks laid in rows as **coping** on homes built of **adobe** (and much later, of material imitating adobe). Brick dentils or coping was an important feature in New Mexican homes built in the **Territorial Style** (ca. 1846–1875) and **Territorial Revival Style** (ca. 1910s–1940s, and later), and in Arizona homes known as **Sonoran Transitional** (ca. 1880–1900).

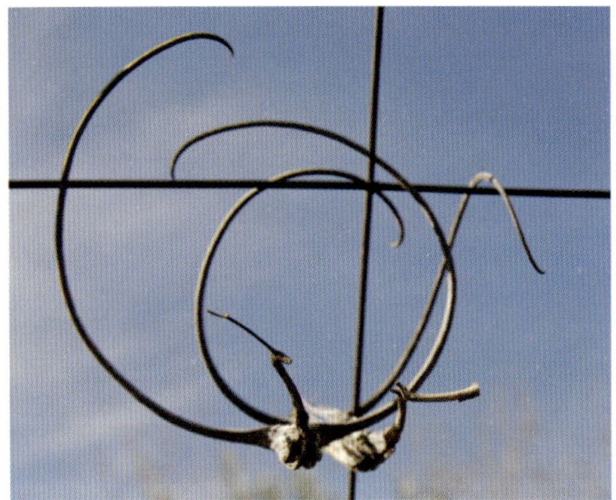

DEVIL'S CLAW (*Martynia a parviflora*, *Proboscidea parviflora*) / a crawling vine with claw-like pods, of both wild and cultivated varieties, which flourishes in the desert environments of the Southwest. Sewing elements are made from devil's claw and used to work the black designs in handwoven baskets made by Native American artisans of the Southwest including the Apache, Tohono O'odham, Pima, Hualapai, Havasupai, San Juan Paiute, and other peoples. Called *eehuk* by the Tohono O'odham, devil's claw pods are harvested in the fall, soaked, and then split into thin strands before using. Combined with white **willow** or **yucca** sewing elements (as well as splints of other colors) in baskets, the devil's claw is used to create striking, contrasting designs. See also **close stitch** and **man-in-the-maze**.

DIE (Stamp) / a steel or iron rod with a design on one end that is used for striking an image (or stamping) on sterling silver and other metals, as well as on leather. Making detailed designs on the end of a small piece of iron is painstaking work. Beginning in the 1870s, Navajo smiths used any bit of scrap iron that had a flat surface, such as leftover bolts, railroad nails, and worn-out chisels to make a die. The earliest ones were simple, such as the ends of files impressed into **silver** to create simple lines; later, after mastering die cutting, the Navajo created more elaborate designs—including crescents, animals, **rosettes**, and wavy and zigzag lines. Following the arrival of the railroad in the Southwest in 1880, the **Fred Harvey Company** and possibly other companies introduced new designs for Navajo silver that appeared on dies: arrows, **swastikas**, and other images. Some dies with ornate designs may have been imported from Germany. Today dies are still heavily used by Navajos and other silversmiths in the region to create designs, borders, and complex patterns on metal surfaces. See also **stamp work**.

The progressive steps in making a stamped concha.

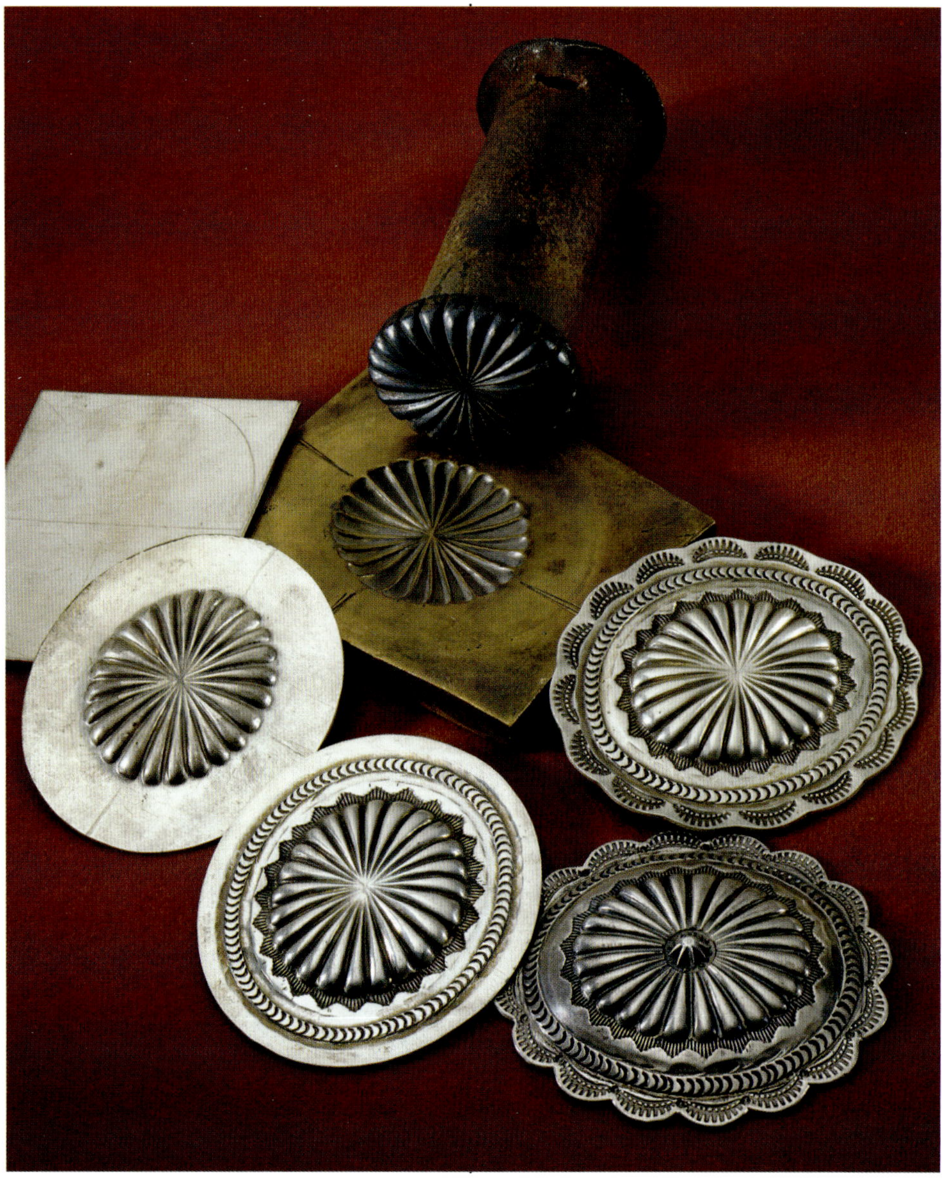

DOLLS / Native American / usually made from cloth, basketry, or wood and often embellished with **beadwork**, rawhide, or cloth details, featuring replicas of traditional Native clothing and hair styles, made by Native peoples of the Southwest as children's toys and for sale as tourist souvenirs since the nineteenth century. Traditionally, the Navajos did not make dolls as children's toys. Representations of the human form were used primarily in a few religious contexts, but this sensitivity relaxed somewhat in the twentieth century. In the early 1960s, for instance, Navajo Kay "Kaibah" Bennett (1922–1997) began making "Navajo" dolls by hand, and later made dolls portraying other Native people.

Apache artisans in New Mexico and the Western Apaches of Arizona made male and female dolls with elaborate buckskin clothing, beaded necklaces, and hair in traditional styles. In addition, some Apache artisans have made dolls in dresses worn during a girl's puberty rite; some are buckskin with beading, cone **tinklers**, real hair, and beaded necklaces and earrings. In more contemporary versions the dresses are cloth. Pima and Tohono O'odham basket makers began producing basketry dolls in the 1930s, using traditional techniques and materials, such as **yucca** and **devil's claw**. See also **beaded folk art**, **katsina dolls**, **mud toys**, and **storytellers**.

Kay Bennett (Navajo), doll, 1965.

DOLLS / Zuni / dolls made by painstakingly stringing tiny seed and/or glass beads on cotton string, made at Zuni Pueblo in western New Mexico since at least 1918, later developed into popular inexpensive curios for tourists in the 1930s, and still a thriving folk art today. New Mexico post trader C. G. Wallace is credited with first encouraging the Zunis, in 1918, to make beaded dolls for tourists because the Pueblo's remoteness made it difficult and expensive to ship pottery or other large crafts from Zuni. Among the earliest beaded pieces made by Zuni women were cow heads and Comanche figures. To make a cow head, a sheep's vertebra was used as a framework, around which strings of beads were wrapped to portray the cow's face, and pointed extensions of the vertebra were left exposed to represent the horns.

Today women, as well as some men, at Zuni Pueblo have transformed the craft from beaded trinkets into vibrant, detailed figures that are expressions of Pueblo life and beliefs. Among the subjects portrayed are deer and elk, ceremonial dancers, **katsinas**, and Zunis wearing traditional clothing and jewelry. Those highly skilled at the craft can create the figures using one continuous thread of seed and glass beads. In recent decades, Navajos and artisans from other Pueblos have experimented with beaded figures, creating subjects ranging from Native American dancers to **storytellers** to birds to nativity scenes. See also **beaded folk art**.

Jeanne Melikan (Zuni), beaded "olla maiden," 2012, seed beads, cotton string.

DOMING / a historic jewelry technique in which a Mexican *peso*, American coin, or disk of silver is placed into a hollowed-out depression (usually in a stump of wood), and hit with a hammer until the silver conforms to the shape of the depression. Navajo smiths have used this method to create silver **conchas**, **beads**, and **buttons** since at least the 1880s. Silver beads and buttons were formed by soldering together two dome-shaped pieces; most silversmiths polished the joint to create a smooth finish.

DOÑA SEBASTIANA / an allegorical figure of death portrayed as a skeletal woman holding a bow and arrow, spear, knife, axe, sickle, or other instrument in her bony hands, with a menacing smile, often riding in a two- or four-wheel cart called *la carreta* (the "death" cart), a subject often depicted by New Mexican **santeros/santeras**. This figure, intended as a reminder of death, is among the religious art found in the Pentitente Brotherhood's **moradas** in remote villages of New Mexico. The carreta with Doña Sebastiana is traditionally taken along in Holy Week processions by the Penitente, as a reminder of the ephemerality of life. Her name may be a reference to Saint Sebastian, who was martyred by being shot with arrows.

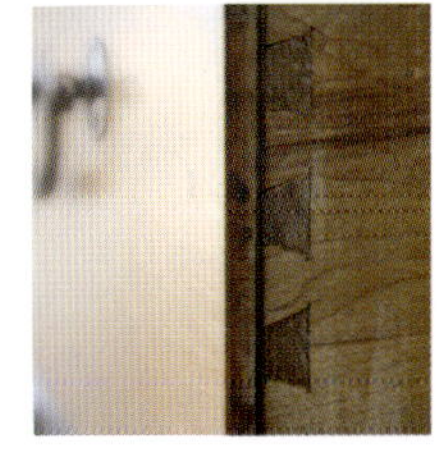

DOVETAIL JOINT / one of the strongest types of wood joints, constructed by cutting one piece with "tongues" or tenons (fan-shaped like the tail of a dove) that fit tightly into corresponding cutouts on the side or end of the second piece of wood. Typically, this method is used to construct wood chests, drawers, and cabinets of all kinds, including those made by craftsmen/women in the Southwest.

DRAGONFLY / an ancient symbol associated with water, represented in early rock art, pottery designs, and in **kiva** murals by Native peoples of the Southwest. It is one of many insects recognized in Native American lore for their importance in fertilizing plants. The dragonfly, which resembled the double-barred Christian **cross**, was later incorporated into metal jewelry by Pueblo and Navajo silversmiths. The dragonfly has different meanings among the Native groups; for instance, at Zuni, where some carvers make dragonfly **fetishes**, it is symbolic of the late summer rains.

DRESS ORNAMENTS / silver pins, brooches, buttons, and narrow tips to outline the points of a collar made primarily by Navajo silversmiths to

Rubel Jaramillo (Colorado), Doña Sebastiana and death cart bulto.

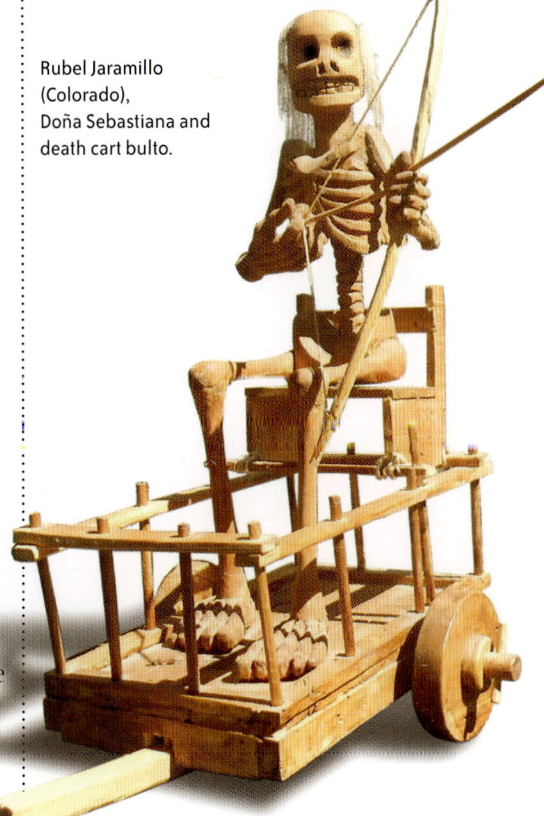

adorn women's clothing. There was a revival of these forms in the 1930s, when Navajo women had adopted the long full skirt of calico or velveteen and a velvet blouse with pointed collars; the **silver** ornaments were considered a sign of the wearer's wealth and prestige. These silver forms continue to be fashionable today.

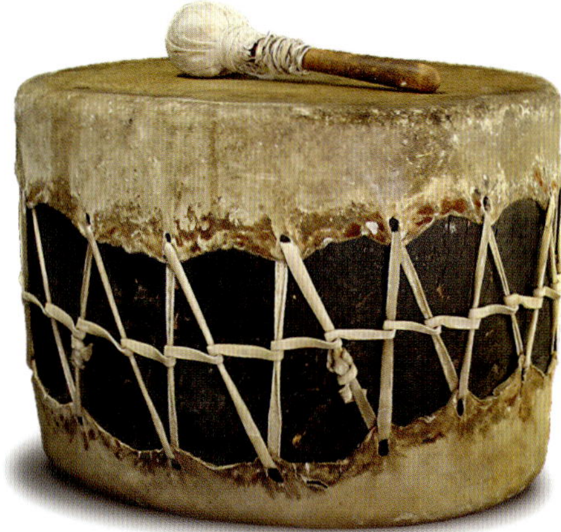

Hopi drum, ca. 1900.

DRUMS / the most well known of Native American musical instruments, used in both ceremonial and social contexts for hundreds of years, and made since the late nineteenth century for sale. Native Americans use drums in various ways to interact with a higher spirit known to many as the Great Spirit. Made in a circle, drums are said to represent Mother Earth.

The style and construction of drums depends on the tradition of each tribe as well as the artisan's individual style. Western Apaches and Navajos traditionally made drums for ceremonial use with a piece of buckskin tied over the mouth of a pottery jar with water inside to keep the buckskin damp and to create certain tones. Pueblo people, historically and continuously to the present, have made drums from hollowed out and sanded wood—typically **cottonwood**, aspen, or another native tree—in oval or cylindrical shapes with tanned animal hide stretched taut across the opening with **sinew** thongs. The type of wood, the depth and diameter of the wood shell, and the thickness and tightness of the hide all affect the tone.

Large Pueblo drums, two to three feet in diameter, are played communally by groups of men who stand or sit around them in a circle. Smaller wood and rawhide hand drums are held by individual drummers. In making Pueblo-style drums, artisans cut a log into the desired shape and size, strip off the bark, hollow it out, and then allow the wood to dry slowly to prevent cracking. The

dried wood is then leveled, rounded, and sanded. To fashion the drum top, a hide—from cow, deer, elk, or goat—is cleaned, scraped, and soaked in water to make it soft and pliable. The hide is then hand-scalloped, stretched over the wood shell, and secured with rawhide lacing. As the hide dries, it tightens further and conforms to the wood. Some antique and contemporary drums have painted decorations of animals, geometric patterns, and other motifs on the hide and/or wood sides.

An unusual type of hand drum was made at Tesuque Pueblo, New Mexico, in the early 1880s and into the early twentieth century, from a wooden cheese ring or cheese box (the container in which cheese was shipped) covered with either goatskin or sheepskin. Intended for trade and the tourist industry, these hand drums were often painted with designs, some of which derived from **Spanish Colonial arts**. Today both Taos and Cochiti pueblos are known for their fine drums—a craft handed down through the generations and still hand-fashioned in the traditional way. According to legend, Cochiti was once the place where all other tribes in the region obtained their drums; today the drum serves as the pueblo's official seal. Drums are still made for various Native ceremonies. For instance, because they make the sound of thunder that comes with rain, drums are the main instrument used to accompany song-prayers for rain in Pueblo rituals.

DYES / a source of color derived from plants, minerals, animals, insects, or chemicals used to dye the fibers of **yarn** for weaving textiles and of sewing splints for baskets. See also **dyes—aniline**, **dyes—vegetal**, and specific plants.

DYES / Aniline (Chemical Dyes) / a synthetic dye derived from aniline—a colorless, oily, slightly water-soluble type of coal tar—used to inexpensively produce bright colors in **yarns** for weaving textiles and in splints (sewing strands) for weaving baskets. First available through imported yarns and fabric and later in packet form, aniline dyes were available in the Southwest from European sources by about 1857. They were being used in Navajo-made blankets and Hispano textiles by about 1860 and the first American aniline-dye factory was founded in 1864. Among the available colors were bright purple, green, orange, and red. By the 1880s, when the railroad had arrived in the Southwest and was increasingly transporting manufactured goods to the region, the dyes were in wide use throughout the area.

Textile and basket weavers, accustomed to the many hours it takes to gather and prepare and boil vegetal dyestuffs, welcomed the commercially made chemical dyes. Some preferred the vivid hues, a change from the softer hues achieved with vegetal dyes. However, not all artisans were pleased with the results; for example, Native American basketweavers who used aniline dyes to color **sumac** or **willow** reeds for their baskets discovered that the color faded unless kept out of sunlight. The term "aniline" has also been used in reference to dyes made with a variety of chemicals, not just aniline; today it is used in the decorative arts field mainly to differentiate between synthetic and vegetal dyes.

DYES / Vegetal / natural dyes derived from plants and berries and used to color yarn, plant fibers, thread, and other materials used to weave rugs, blankets, fabric, and baskets, and to make **colcha** embroidery and other items. Until 1860, when **aniline** synthetic dyes became available, natural vegetal dyes were the only colorants in existence. For textiles, previous to 1860, colors of wool were primarily limited to the natural colors of sheep (white, black, brown, and blended shades).

Preparing vegetal dyes involves gathering of the plants and berries (usually in the early summer and dried for later use), splitting or grinding of the natural material, boiling, cooling, and drying. It is a time-consuming process. Then the wool yarns are placed in the dye and left for minutes to hours depending on the desired depth of color, rinsed in fresh water, and hung from shade trees or another place to dry.

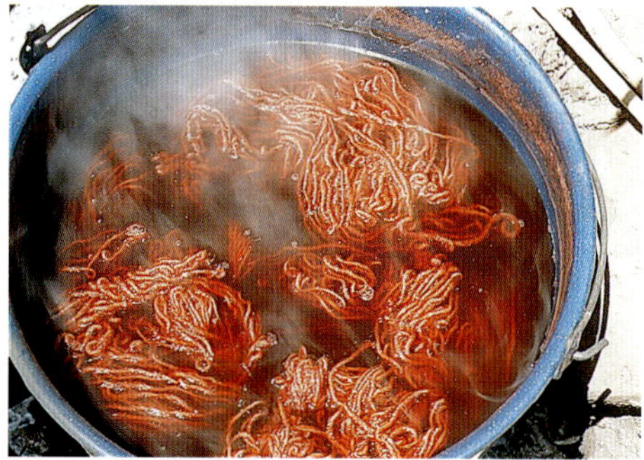

Although generally the colors are more muted than those in commercial aniline dyes, materials dyed with vegetal tints actually retain their color better. Some materials used for dyes were considered highly valuable; a 1739 will and estate inventory for Cristóbal Baca, a Spanish settler in New Mexico, includes a single piece of wood from

Mexico called "logwood" that was used for making a reddish-brown or purple-black textile dye.

Here are just a few examples of the natural dyes that can be made from native plants of the Southwest: yellows from snakeweed, canaigre, Cota, Indian paintbrush, barberry root, Oregon grape, and **chamisa**; gold from Indian tea; gray from **sumac** berries; black from sumac bark or sunflower seeds; lavender from dandelion roots and stems; oranges and rusts from Cota and alder bark; soft reds and corals from the madder root; pink from chokecherries and hollyhocks; and reds, mauves, roses, purples, magentas, and crimsons from hollyhock flowers, currants, **mountain mahogany** bark, and chokecherry.

In Navajo handwoven textiles the range of vegetal-dye colors was relatively limited to yellow, green, and reddish brown until the year 1940, when Navajo weaving teacher Nonabah Bryan wrote a pamphlet on how to create eighty-four different plant dyes. Vegetal-dyed yarns are commercially available and some Navajo weavers re-dye them to obtain special colors. The Navajo weavers who continue to dye their own yarns often keep their family recipes a secret.

EFFIGY VESSELS / a type of clay vessel formed into a human or animal shape and intended for ceremonial use, made by Native peoples of the Southwest since prehistoric times. Among the earliest peoples to make them were the **Mimbres** and Chacoans in New Mexico and the potters of **Casas Grandes** in Chihuahua, Mexico. Generally the body of the clay container is hollow with an opening on the top so that it could be filled with a liquid or with a dry material such as **cornmeal**. Effigy jars were produced in a wide range of bird, amphibian, and animal shapes—including ducks, frogs, fish, turtles, bears, bighorn sheep, and badgers. In some instances Ancestral Pueblo potters added small effigy-figure handles to clay **canteens** or pitchers.

Human-shaped effigy vessels, which were relatively rare in the prehistoric American Southwest (but common in the Casas Grandes culture), provide historians with valuable information about prehistoric personal dress and adornment: figures have facial decoration, which may indicate tattooing or body paint; pierced ears; sandals, sashes, leggings, and other textiles; and ornaments such as bracelets, anklets, armbands, and headbands. Beginning in the late nineteenth century, effigy jars were made for the tourist market in the

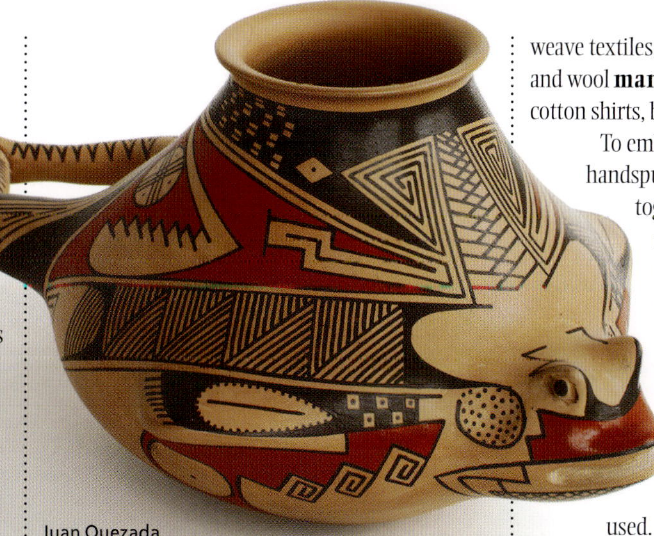

Juan Quezada (Mata Ortiz, Mexico), effigy pot, ca. 1987.

Southwest, a custom that continues to this day. Maricopa and Pueblo potters have all made effigy vessels. Additionally, the skillful potters of **Mata Ortiz**, in the state of Chihuahua, Mexico, have traditionally made (and continue to make) animal- and human-shaped effigy pots called *figuras*.

EMBOSSING / See **repoussé**.

EMBROIDERY / a method used to decorate cloth, in which **yarns** are inserted into cloth with a needle, a common technique in the Southwest by AD 1400 and still in use today. Archaeologists found cloth fragments decorated by running-stitch embroidery at Ancestral Pueblo sites (AD 1100–1300), and cloth fragments with more complex embroidered designs at Sinagua sites (AD 1100–1300) in central Arizona, and at Salado ruins in Tonto National Monument (AD 1250–1400), in southern Arizona.

Embroidery became an increasingly important decorative technique in historic times, particularly among artisans of the Rio Grande Pueblos. This was due in part to the eventual availability of new dyes, commercial **yarn**, and metal needles. Ancestral design elements combined with other motifs were employed by these needle workers. Among the early influences on Pueblo embroidery was the needlework designs of Spanish settlers in the region; for example, a small, stylized flower was adopted from the Spanish and used in the embroidered fabrics of Zuni, Acoma, and Jemez pueblos. During the period of about 1848 to 1880, Pueblo artisans of New Mexico created embroidered designs on the borders of plain-weave or **twill**-weave textiles, including Zuni and Acoma black and wool **mantas**, white cotton mantas, white cotton shirts, breechcloths, and kilts.

To embroider designs, they used a pair of handspun or **raveled yarns**, often twisted together between insertions of the needle, and a pair of flat wooden pins fastened to the cloth to hold a small area of cloth flat for stitching. At the pueblos today, a single four-ply commercial **yarn** is used with stitches that create large areas of solid color on the cloth; other stitches, such as outline, satin, and herringbone also may be used. A regular embroidery hoop is generally now used to stretch the cloth in the work area.

Many design motifs of prehistoric and historic woven textiles are incorporated into contemporary Pueblo needlework, including the use of "negative space"—when narrow lines of the background fabric are allowed to show between the embroidered elements of the pattern. Among the commonly embroidered designs on Hopi kilts and Pueblo clothing today are terraced triangles (said to represent clouds) and the triangle-and-hook pattern. Contemporary Hopi quilters incorporate embroidered designs of animals, stars, and many other images on their hand- or machine-stitched **quilts**, and some contemporary Pueblo women use cotton floss to cross-stitch (an "X" stitch) designs on gingham-fabric aprons that tie at the waist. The aprons are worn on special occasions only. See also **colcha.**

ENCRUSTED STRAW / a term introduced by New Mexico artisan Jimmy Trujillo, who studied old pieces of **straw appliqué** and determined that they were made by pressing pieces of straw into wet varnish, followed by the application of additional varnish to coat the straw and seal the piece. As a result, Trujillo and his students make pieces with a very thick coat of varnish. Jimmy, his wife Debbie, and daughter Cordelia have won many awards for their work at the annual Spanish Market in Santa Fe and at other events.

ENJARRE / See **mud plastering**.

ENTRADA / a Spanish word meaning "entrance," used to describe the formal entryway into a house of the Spanish Colonial period. The term also refers to the Spanish entry into the New World. See also **zaguán.**

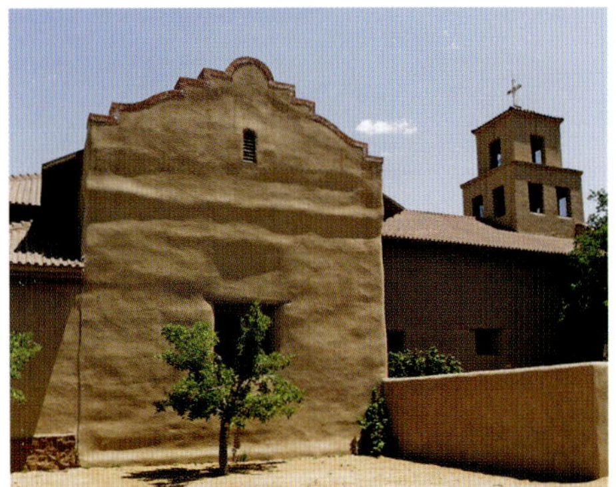

Espadaña feature on Santuario de Guadalupe, 1700s (espadaña added 1922), Santa Fe, New Mexico.

ESPADAÑA / a Spanish word for "belfry," used to describe the curvilinear **parapet** of a church façade, with hollow arches designed to hold bells. An architectural element borrowed from the historic mission churches of California, it was commonly used in late nineteenth-century and early twentieth-century **Mission Revival**–style buildings in the Southwest.

ESTÍPITE COLUMN / Pilaster (Pilastras Estípites) / a Baroque-style, richly decorated column or pilaster that has the shape of an inverted cone or obelisk and was used, either freestanding or attached/engaged, as a central element of the **Churrigueresque** style of architecture in eighteenth-century Spain and Spanish America. The history of the estípite can be traced to the pattern books of the German architect Wendel Dietterlin (1550/51–1599), who may have originated the form. Fine examples can be seen on the facade and the altarpieces of the late-eighteenth-century San Xavier del Bac mission church outside Tucson, Arizona. In addition, estípite columns with gilded decorative motifs were used to decorate **altar screens** in New Mexico in the late 1700s. For example, columns of this type appear in the 1761 altar screen originally placed in La Castrense military chapel in Santa Fe, New Mexico, and now housed in Cristo Rey Church, Santa Fe.

ESTOFADO WORK / a decorative technique in which a carved wooden figure is covered with **gesso**, a layer of red bole (clay pigment) as a ground, then completely or partially covered with thin gold leaf (except for the flesh areas), and the areas of clothing/fabric completely or partially painted in oils, and finally the painted areas are all scratched, etched, or stamped to reveal the gold underneath in patterns that reflect the rich brocade clothing of the Baroque and Rococo eras. The technique was used in Spain, Italy, and Latin America from the late sixteenth through the early nineteenth century for religious imagery. This style of religious figure was copied by New Mexican artists in the early nineteenth century.

EX-VOTO / a Latin term meaning "from a vow," ex-voto is an offering made by the faithful to their favorite saint, Jesus Christ, or the Virgin Mary, as a request for divine intervention or to publicly express gratitude for a miracle. An ex-voto may consist of flowers, photographs, religious medals, holy cards, handwritten notes, rosaries, or **milagros**, and are typically placed by the faithful on statues or altars in Catholic churches, *oratorios* (chapels), home shrines, and pilgrimage sites in Mexico, elsewhere in Latin America, and in the southwestern U.S. Additionally, the term ex-voto commonly refers to Mexican folk art oil paintings on tin (and sometimes on wood, paper, or canvas) that use words and images to depict narrative scenes of a miraculous cure, rescue, or a supplicant praying for a miracle.

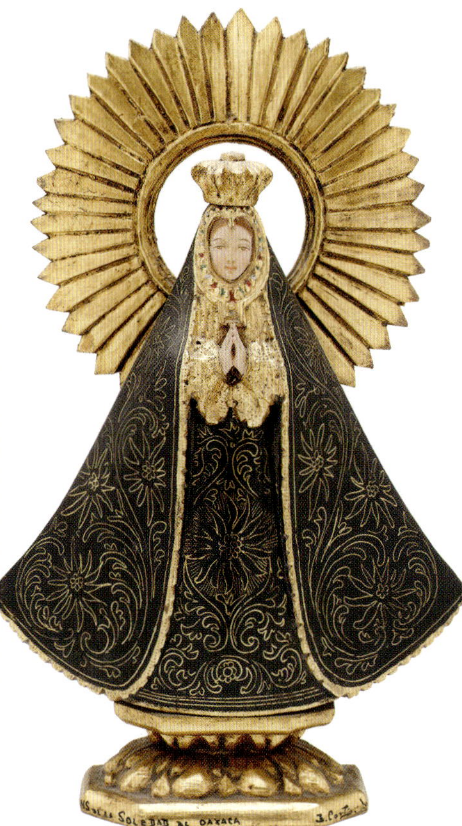

E. Cortes (Oaxaca, Mexico), Nuestra Señora de la Soledad (Our Lady of Solitude), ca. 1950s, carved wood with gilt, paint, and estofado work (on dress).

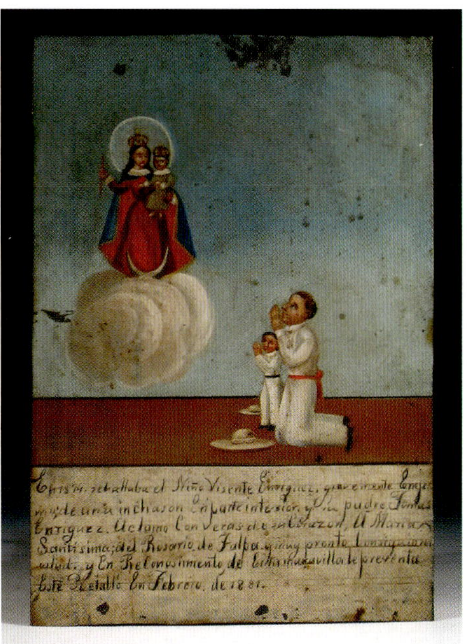

Mexican ex-voto, 1881, oil on metal.

Popular in Mexico in the nineteenth and early twentieth century, ex-voto paintings—deeply rooted in personal faith—have played a role in Hispano religious practices of the American Southwest since at least the nineteenth century. Ex-votos were traditionally small in size, painted by self-taught anonymous artists who lived in or nearby a popular pilgrimage site, and were divided into two parts: a pictorial representation of the occurrence being commemorated and devotional text (including the date and time of the event). This Catholic folk tradition, which has its roots in ancient Mediterranean cultural practices and beliefs, has continued into the twenty-first century. Many contemporary examples are made by highly skilled artists working in formal styles. See also **milagros**.

EYEDAZZLER / a term generally used for a style of Navajo blanket, **tapestry**, or rug woven beginning in the 1870s, featuring a profusion of bright and often contrasting aniline-dyed colors and complex patterns—such as serrated diamonds and triangles—that together create a design that is "dazzling" or "dizzying" to the eye. The earliest **yarns** used were aniline-dyed and machine-spun from **Germantown**, Pennsylvania; the **warp** was commercially manufactured cotton or wool. (Beginning about the mid-1880s, post traders encouraged Navajo weavers to use commercial cotton for the warp instead of handspun wool, in order to speed up weaving production. However, the use of cotton warp for Navajo textiles was never widespread.) The eyedazzler designs were not dictated by the taste of post traders or tourists; instead they were uniquely Navajo inventions, developed when a new range of commercial colors became available to them. Popular with weavers and collectors today, the style often features small, serrated diamond patterns influenced by Hispano textiles such as **Saltillo blankets/sarapes** and **Río Grande-style blankets**. In some respects, Hispano weavings of the Southwest (especially of northern New Mexico) that incorporate intricate designs such as the **Vallero star** and brightly colored handspun or commercial **yarns** could also be called "eyedazzlers." See also **Germantown yarns/rugs**.

FAROLITOS / See **luminarias**.

FEATHERS / highly prized by Pueblo Indians and other Native cultures of the Southwest for ceremonial and religious purposes, often attached to ceremonial clothing and objects—including mantles (turkey), on shields and shield covers (eagle), on **tablitas**, and **katsina dolls.** Birds are considered messengers to the cloud spirits and thus their feathers are important in prayers for rain. Historically, eagle feathers were worn in the Southwest by the Jicarilla Apaches on headdresses worn for battle and used in ceremonial fans with beaded handles; and turkey feathers were attached to arrows by the O'odham and Maricopa peoples of Arizona. Some artisans made wood boxes specifically for storing single, precious feathers. Feathers from brightly colored tropical or temperate-weather birds, such as parrots and **macaws**, have been found in prehistoric Southwestern archaeological sites. Since at least the 1300s, birds and feathers, because of their association with prayers for rain, fertility, and new growth, have been an important design component on Pueblo pottery, especially on **water jars.**

When federal laws prohibited the possession or resale of feathers of all migratory birds, including eagles, hawks, and owls, in 1973, with the Endangered Species Act, Native artisans had to replace the migratory feathers in their works with feathers of turkeys, pheasants, and other exotic species. In some instances, artisans have replaced real feathers with carved stone or wood versions. See also **Acoma Pueblo pottery**.

FETISHES / **Carvings** / the term commonly used to describe small animals carved by Native

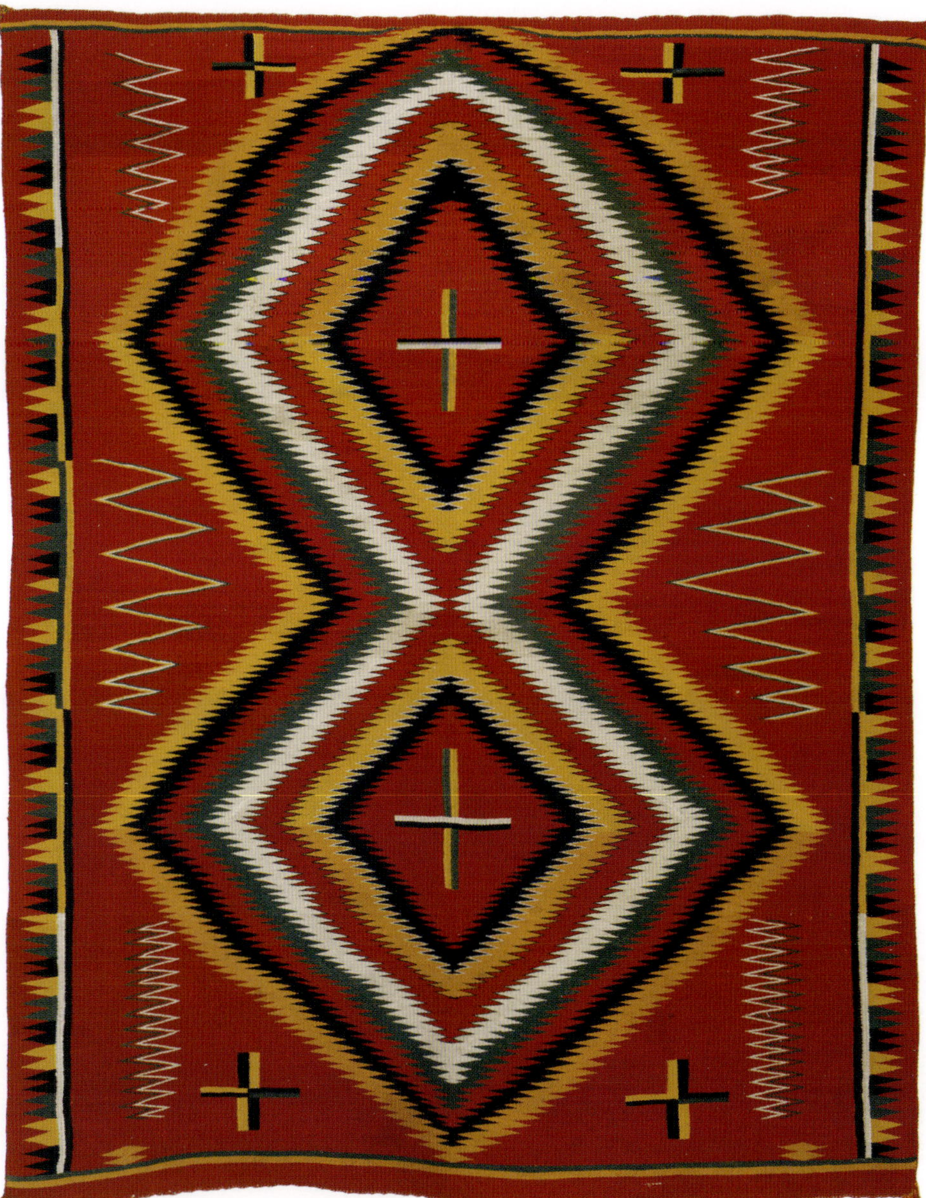

Navajo eyedazzler textile, ca. 1875, 72" x 58".

Americans from natural materials—typically precious and semi-precious stones such as **turquoise,** as well as **shells**, antlers, **coral**, and bone—that represent the spirit and natural traits of the animals they portray. Fetishes can be any size, but most are made for personal use and so they are relatively small in size. Traditionally, they were worn or carried by some Native cultures in pouches; today they are also collected and displayed (mostly by non-Native Americans) as fine art in the home. Authentic or "true" fetishes used for religious purposes require a blessing by a Native American priest; they are considered too sacred to be sold and are kept in protected places.

Therefore, the fetishes created today that are made as art objects for sale should more properly be called "carvings."

Many Native American cultures produce and use fetishes, but they are particularly important to the Zuni people of southwestern New Mexico. Many prehistoric animal carvings of local stone (some of which have painted designs) have been found at Zuni Pueblo. Using only simple hand tools, carvers at Zuni have historically made animal fetishes for their families and friends. They were made as blessings for hunters to catch game, for curing ceremonies, to protect individuals or the community as a whole, or to ensure fertility,

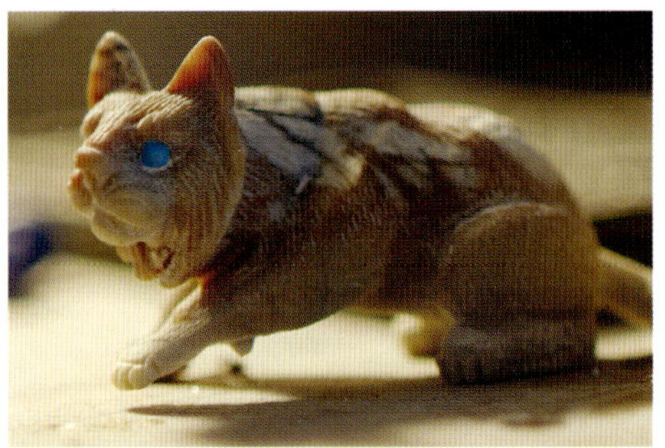

Dan Quam (Zuni), bobcat fetish, 2009.

rain, and bountiful crops. The Zunis call fetishes *wema:we* and believe it is the spirit within the fetish that is of value, not the object itself.

The prominent category of carved fetishes is animals. The Zunis believe that animals are more like their deities and have more spiritual power than humans. These powers reside in their fetishes. The first fetishes were stones that naturally looked like animals (and sometimes humans or deities)—they are often called concretion fetishes—left alone or carved slightly by an artisan to more fully resemble an animal. The Zunis and other Native peoples carried these, believing they would bring good fortune, power, or protection. Naturally shaped fetishes, which the Zunis believe represent the "ancient stone beasts" of their mythology, are thought to have more power than carved ones.

By the 1890s, encouraged by traders such as C. G. Wallace and others, Zuni carvers began making fetish-like figures for the tourist market. Some were based on animal shapes similar to the stone fetishes discovered at prehistoric and historic sites. For instance, Zuni fetish carver Leekya Deyuse (1889–1966) participated in the archaeological dig at Hawikuh (1917–1920s), where he gained first-hand knowledge of pre-contact Zuni carvings. Leekya created freestanding fetishes that were produced entirely with hand tools in the beginning (later in life he adopted electrical tools); some are considered by collectors today as among the finest stone sculptures ever made in the Southwest.

By the 1930s the fetishes became increasingly well-crafted and realistic depictions of animals and figures. Among the latter are **Corn Maidens**—a female figure shown with the body of an ear of corn—an important figure to the Zuni people, who believe that long ago Corn Maidens saved their pueblo from starvation. Making fetishes is labor intensive, involving hand tools (and sometimes electrical tools), intricate inlay,

and exacting polishing work. First the stone is sawed into a small slab, and then some carvers draw an outline on the stone. This is followed by grinding off the stone into a rough-finished stage; smoothing the surface with a rubber-bond polishing wheel; polishing it with a polishing compound on a buffing wheel; and finally, hand polishing and attachment of offerings. The inlaying of stones (such as turquoise for eyes and coral for noses and mouths) is typically done during the rough-finished stage. Some skillful carvers take advantage of a stone's natural markings—for instance, a stripe in the stone might represent a badger's stripe. Others add **sgraffito** (or incised) decoration to the surface.

Traditional-style fetishes are often wrapped with "bundles" consisting of **sinew** (or cotton thread/twine) with tiny beads, shells, gemstones, feathers, arrowheads, or actual tiny hide **medicine bundles** tucked into it. The bundles serve as an offering to the animal spirit that resides within the fetish, empowering the fetish to better aid the user, and to serve as a gift to the fetish, which the fetish will in turn give back. To gain access to the animal spirit and its powers, the Zunis ceremonially or metaphorically nourish or "feed" fetishes with blue **cornmeal**, crushed turquoise and shell, or other foods.

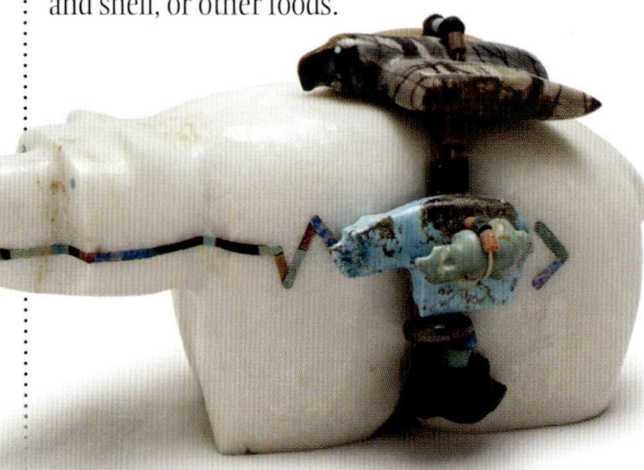

Daniel Weahkee (Zuni), bear fetish with smaller fetishes attached to back, 2005, alabaster (large bear) with inlaid heart line of lapis, onyx (or jet), turquoise, malachite, and jasper.

Since about 1980 there has been a rapidly growing appreciation for fetishes among collectors, some of whom are interested in them as objects of healing and others as examples of fine Native American art. To meet the demand, an ever-increasing number of Zunis make a living by carving. Originally they scoured their own countryside for stones or were provided a limited range from traders. Today an enormous variety of interesting stones are available to Zunis from

around the world (although many collectors prefer the use of locally obtained stones). Among the ones most often seen: Picasso marble (a type of limestone from southwestern Utah), serpentine, alabaster, pipestone, turquoise, and **jet**. Coral, horn, antler, and glass are also used. Some carvers are expanding the craft by carving non-traditional animals such as dolphins, donkeys, beavers, fish, lizards, and skunks, and using unusual materials like fossilized ivory from Alaska. Others are reverting to the older and plainer style of fetishes, and carving them out of sandstone or other local stones. Pueblo cultures associate certain attributes to the specific animals portrayed. For instance, the **bear** is said to have the greatest curative abilities. See also **coral, Corn Mother/ Corn Maidens**, **heart line**, **shells**.

FETISHES / For Stringing / tiny hand-carved animal or figure fetishes of precious or semi-precious stones, drilled with holes and intended for stringing on a necklace of single or multiple strands of **heishi** beads (on cotton cordage and sometimes on **sinew**), handmade by artisans at Zuni Pueblo, New Mexico, since at least the 1930s, for the tourist market. Typically, a larger-size fetish is carved and placed like a pendant in the center (or bottom) of the necklace string(s). The heishi—finely made **shell** or gemstone beads—used in the necklaces are usually made and supplied by Santo Domingo Pueblo jewelers. In some instances earrings have been made to match. Unlike individual fetishes (see previous entry), fetish necklaces are not used for religious purposes; from the standpoint of Zuni religion, fetishes by definition cannot be jewelry.

Possibly the earliest Zuni lapidarist to create fetish jewelry was Leekya Deyuse (1889–1966); he was encouraged to drill and string the small carvings into necklaces, bracelets, and other types of silverwork by the trader C. G. Wallace (1898–1993), who also provided Leekya with raw materials and tools. These "stringing fetishes" were among the first small-scale Zuni carvings made for sale outside the Pueblo. In most instances, traders like Wallace and others purchased the diminuitive animals, already pierced and individually priced, and then strung them according to their own taste or that of a particular customer. Additionally, Wallace and other traders arranged for Navajo or Zuni smiths to set the tiny fetish carvings into elaborate handmade silver bezels for pins, rings, and bracelets; and they had the smiths drill the carvings with holes in the more

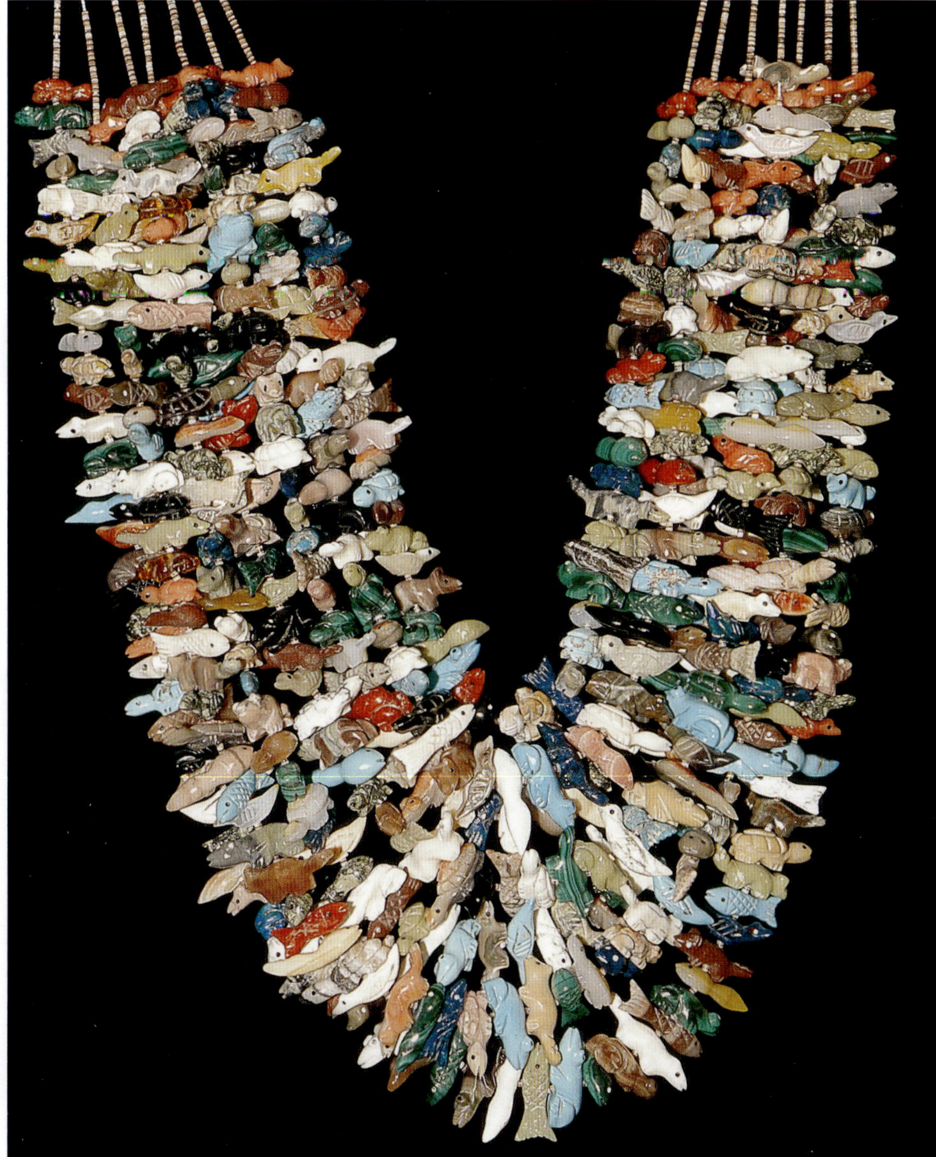

ABOVE: Dinah and Pete Gaspar (Zuni), elaborate fetish necklace. **ABOVE RIGHT:** Martha Arquero (Cochiti) bear, ca. 1960s, clay with natural slips; unknown maker (Cochiti Pueblo), rabbit, ca. 1950s, clay with natural slips.

Figurines representing the human form were rare at ancestral Pueblo sites; the earliest documented example is a Zuni canteen of a man astride a horse from 1851.

By 1880, human and animal clay figurines were once again being made at Cochiti, Laguna, San Ildefonso, Santa Clara, and Tesuque pueblos; the small seated figures created at Tesuque became known as **Rain Gods**. These Pueblo clay figures were not religious in nature. During the 1880s, Indian art traders and shopkeepers in the Southwest aggressively marketed figurative Pueblo pottery to the increasing number of tourists visiting the region. These consumers embraced the figurines as curiosities that reflected an unfamiliar culture. From this period onwards, clay figures became mainstays of the curio trade; they remain popular today. See also **effigy jars**, **Cochiti Pueblo pottery**, **Rain Gods**, **Santa Clara Pueblo pottery**, and **storyteller bowls** and **storyteller figures**.

FILIGREE (Metal Lace) / an intricate, openwork metal jewelry technique that originated more than four thousand years ago when metals were first soldered; it was brought to southern Spain by the Phoenicians during the Bronze Age, and then the Spanish brought filigree to the New World. It was (and continues to be) fashioned by using pliers or a similar tool to twist, curl, braid, or plait fine pliable metal wires—of high-karat gold, **silver**, or gold-plated **copper**—into complex floral or geometric designs—such as **rosettes**, spirals, scrolls, arabesques, and vines—that are soldered onto a framework of flat wire. Small grains of metal, called *guachaporo* beads, as well as small pieces of **coral**, **turquoise**, lapis, or other semi-precious stones are sometimes added to accent the work.

Filigree was made in New Mexico by the early nineteenth century and taught in workshop settings. Hispano artisans working in this technique were called **plateros**, even though most of them worked primarily with gold. The most frequently made items were pendants, earrings, necklaces, hairpins, chains, and brooches. Earrings shaped like half moons called *las media lunas* and earrings topped with fan or shell motifs were among the

traditional manner for **bolo ties**, scarf slides, and pendants. Single and multi-strand fetish necklaces became increasingly appreciated by and popular with Anglo-American collectors beginning in the 1960s, and remain so today.

Highly prized for their beauty, high polish, detail, and overall craftsmanship, stringing fetishes for necklaces continue to be made by the Zunis. The highly collectible fetish necklaces sometimes feature a single animal repeated throughout, such as bears or birds, while others incorporate a variety of animals. A wide array of materials are used for carving the animals and figures, purchased from trading posts and supply stores or collected

from local sources, including **turquoise**, **coral**, **jet**, shell, serpentine, fossilized ivory, pipestone, and marble.

FIGURATIVE CERAMICS / made by prehistoric people for at least two thousand years in North America, in a variety of forms, such as human **effigy** figures, animal figures, animal-shaped pitchers, duck-shaped **canteens**, and bird pots. They were made either by modeling or more often by the coil-and-scrape method, and most likely used in ceremonial rituals (including those held to pray for rainfall, bountiful crops, or human or animal fertility), as well as purely for amusement.

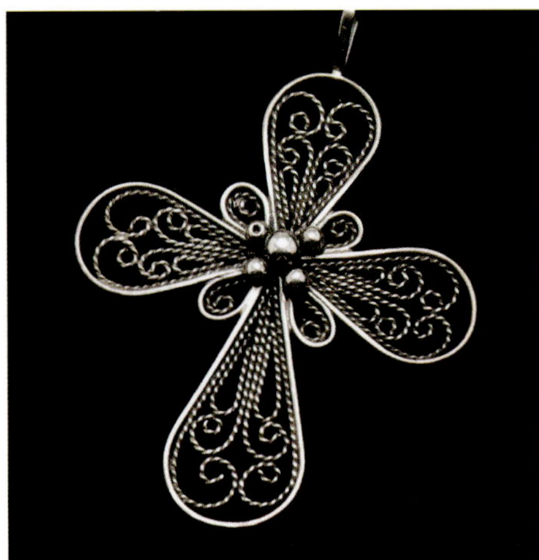

Racheal Roybal-Montoya (New Mexico), filigree cross, 2011, sterling silver.

common early gold filigree designs. Initially, ingots made from melted coinage and precious metal scrap were stretched to create the fine thin wire needed for filigree. After 1867 major gold strikes in central New Mexico provided new supplies of 20-karat gold, leading to increased production of filigree jewelry.

During the late Victorian period, this jewelry style became popular with both the indigenous population and early Anglo-American tourists, who increasingly visited New Mexico after the railroad reached the region in 1880. By this time gold had been discovered in the hills of Cerrillos and Golden (just south of Santa Fe), which encouraged the production and expansion of filigree-style earrings, rings, and necklaces in Santa Fe. Often these pieces were set with colored gems made of paste (glass), as well as with locally mined turquoise.

In the late 1800s and first decades of the 1900s, curio dealers and shop owners in the Southwest helped spread the popularity of filigree work by selling both Mexican and New Mexican examples. By the 1920s a small number of Pueblo jewelers had begun producing silver filigree work. Lacking the proper tools, they used a variety of techniques to replicate the looped wire decoration. Like the Hispano versions, some have precut turquoise stones **appliquéd** or inlaid on the jewelry.

The interest in filigree jewelry faded around World War I, though a few jewelers continued to make the traditional work into the 1960s. At present, a small number of plateros are active and producing this unique craft in the Southwest. Their exquisite work in silver and/or gold can be seen at the annual Spanish Market held in Santa Fe each July and December, as well as in shops and galleries throughout the region.

FIRE CLOUDS / irregular smudges or dark areas on the surface of a clay vessel usually caused when something touches the vessel during **firing**, such as another pot or a piece of burning fuel. Sometimes rejected as an unsightly blemish, fire clouds are often sought after by collectors as aesthetically pleasing and/or as proof that a pot has been fired outdoors in the traditional manner and not in a commercial kiln. Some Pueblo potters consider them a detriment, while others, such as Jody Folwell at Santa Clara Pueblo, Navajo potters Alice Cling and Sammy Manymules, and Hopi potter Mark Tahbo intentionally create or "allow" the fire clouds to be formed as a decorative effect. Likewise, the award-winning Hispano potter Jacobo de la Serna (b. 1965) creates minimalist, sculptural pieces in which fire clouds are a prominent feature. Today fire clouds on **micaceous** clay pots, both historical and contemporary examples by Native American and Hispano potters, are generally considered a highly prized feature. See also **firing**, **Navajo pottery**, **Picuris Pueblo pottery**, **Pottery—Hispano**, and **Taos Pueblo pottery**.

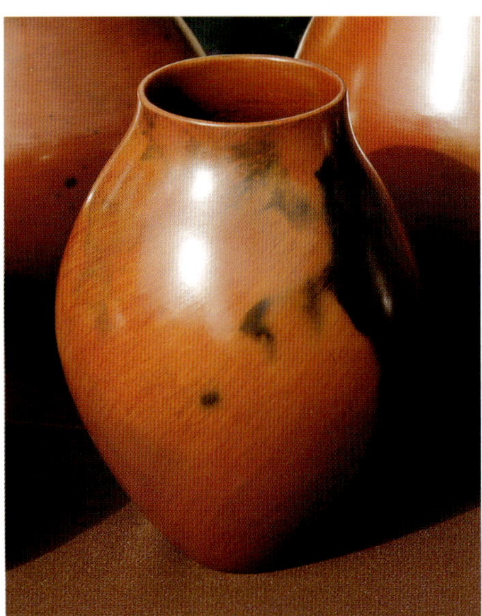

Samuel Manymules (Navajo), pottery with fire clouds.

FIRING / the final step in pottery making when the clay piece is baked and hardened by the application of heat in either a commercial kiln or in an outdoor fire—using wood (typically juniper, **mesquite**, pine, or sometimes cedar) and/or animal dung (cow, sheep, or horse) as the fuel. By using an electric or gas kiln, the potter can produce controlled heat with temperatures 500–1,000 degrees F higher than outdoor firing and can reduce the risks involved in firing. Many

Pueblo and Hispano potters of New Mexico, however, prefer to use the traditional outdoor method; likewise, many collectors prefer to purchase pottery of this type.

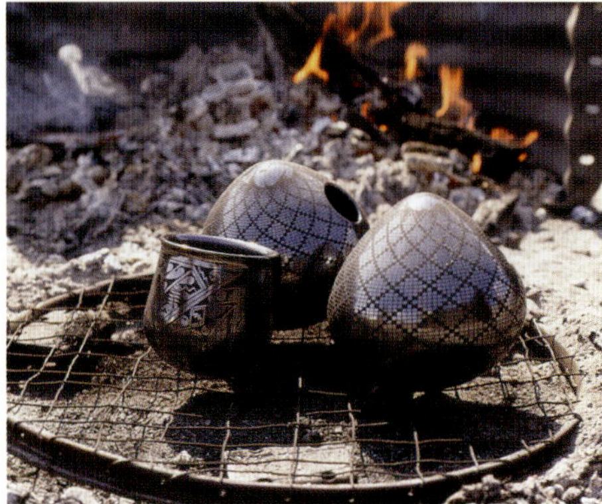

Graphite-style firing of pottery by Macario Ortíz (Mata Ortiz, Mexico), 1996.

Approaches to outdoor firing vary widely, depending on the traditions of the Pueblo, Hispano village, or family of the potter, as well as each potter's individual style and preference. For example, Ancestral Hopi potters fired their ceramics at a high temperature with coal, producing durable pieces that were traded widely among Pueblo people; some contemporary Hopi potters still use this method. Historically, Hispano potters also fired their wares at a high temperature, using local wood placed in an open, shallow depression in the ground.

Most potters prefer to fire on sunny, windless days. Some preheat their pots in an oven before taking it outdoors for firing. This ensures that the clay is completely dry and reduces the chances of cracking when heat is applied to a cold vessel. The pot or group of pots (depending on the potter's technique) is placed on a ceramic or metal grate, bricks, rocks, or other foundation, and surrounded by metal sheets, grates, **potsherds**, or a ceramic cover (again depending on the artist's style) to protect the piece from the direct flames and to confine the heat. The fuel (dry wood and/or dry dung) is then piled around and over the covered pots to form a beehive-shaped mound and then set on fire. Potters use various techniques to determine when a vessel is ready to be removed from the fire: some can judge by just looking at the pot (based on years of experience); others wait for the vessel to begin to "glow;" and some wait for the fuel to turn to ash. Once the process is complete, the potter dismantles the outdoor "kiln" and allows the fired pieces to cool.

Firing outdoors is risky: if the ground is too

damp or the weather suddenly changes (a frequent occurrence in the Southwest), the pots may absorb moisture and crack. A poorly laid fire may cause cracking should the heat rise too quickly, and a poorly constructed piece containing air bubbles might explode during the process, ruining other pieces in the firing. When a clay vessel is destroyed during firing, some Native American potters say that "Mother Earth is taking back the piece for herself." In rare instances, Pueblo potters have been known to use a **horno** oven to fire their pots. See also **black-on-black pottery**, **fire clouds**, **greenware**, and **Mata Ortiz**.

FLASKS / See **tobacco flasks/canteens**.

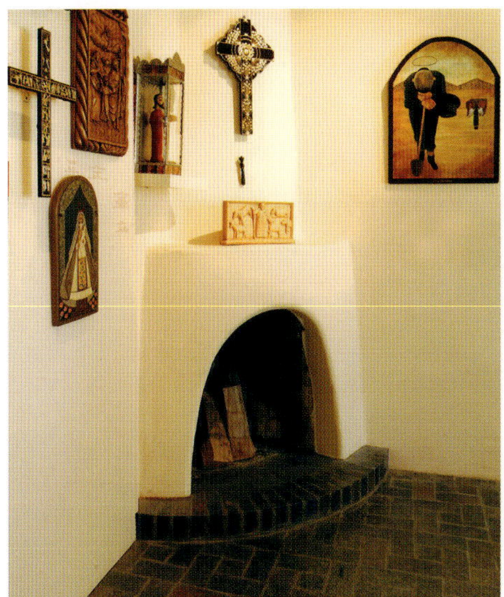

Fogón, 1930, in the Museum of Spanish Colonial Art (architect John Gaw Meem), Santa Fe, New Mexico.

FOGÓN / a Spanish word for "fireplace" or "firebox," and a term that in New Mexico and Arizona has come to refer to a corner fireplace with an arched opening, typically constructed of **adobe** bricks with a **mud-plaster** finish, used for heating and cooking. This fireplace design was introduced to the area by Spanish settlers in the sixteenth/seventeenth centuries; previously, the indigenous peoples of the region used fire pits placed in the center of each room. Fogones became the predominant fireplace form in the region; for instance, they were built in every room in Sonoran-style homes. Some fogones have attached **bancos**.

Traditionally, these fireplaces were (and continue to be) made by women in the Hispano and Pueblo villages of New Mexico; the name for a woman who undertakes the craft of fireplace building is *fogonera*. These corner fireplaces have also long been called "kiva fireplaces," a name devised by Anglo builders/owners in the early twentieth century, which erroneously suggests that this was the type of fireplace used in a **kiva**, the traditional underground ceremonial rooms of New Mexican **pueblos**. See also **mud plastering** and **Sonoran row house**.

FRAZADA (Frezada) / see **Rio Grande textiles**.

FRED HARVEY COMPANY / founded in 1876 in Topeka, Kansas, the company built and ran restaurants, hotels, and souvenir shops along the tracks of the Atchison, Topeka and Santa Fe Railway, from Kansas to California. In 1915 Harvey Cars provided tours of the Grand Canyon and by 1925 the company had established its Indian Detour Cars—three-day automobile excursions that took visitors all over the Southwest to visit archaeological sites, **pueblos**, and beautiful natural vistas. Native Americans sold their pottery and other crafts outdoors beside the Harvey businesses and along the railroad tracks.

Beginning in 1902, when the Indian Department of the company was established (and headquartered at the Alvarado Hotel, Albuquerque, New Mexico), the Harvey company shipped boxcar loads of Indian-made crafts from **Hubbell Trading Post** to their Albuquerque headquarters on the Santa Fe lines. They also sold jewelry and other items in the Harvey hotel shops and on the trains. By the early twentieth century the Fred Harvey Company had become one of the largest distributors of Indian arts in the United States. They purchased a range of items—baskets, silver jewelry, pottery, textiles, and other crafts—through reservation traders and directly from the artists.

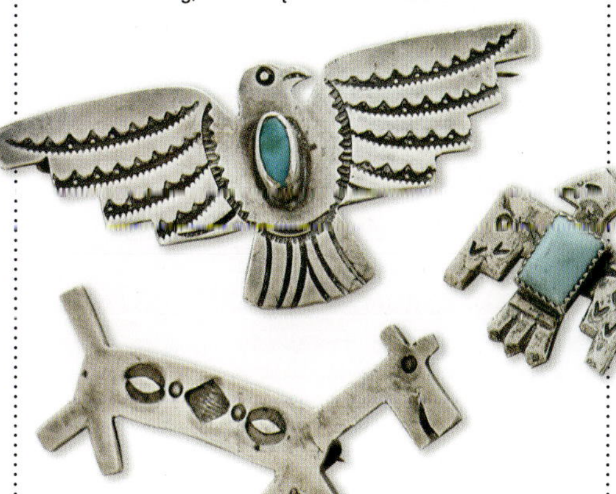

Fred Harvey–era jewelry: thunderbird and "Hopi Horse" pins, ca. 1920s/'30s, sterling silver with stamp work and/or hand tooling, and turquoise set in bezels.

The company also employed silversmiths and other artisans to demonstrate their craft at the Alvarado; they found that the Indians' presence helped sell the crafts and promote travel to the Southwest. Significantly, the company introduced new design ideas for the tourist trade. Indian jewelry, made between 1900 and 1930, and featuring thin sheet-silver bracelets, pins, and other forms stamped with arrows, **swastikas**, **thunderbirds**, chevrons, and other "Indian" designs thought to appeal to tourists were erroneously termed "Harvey House" jewelry, but were actually made by many different companies throughout the Southwest. Whatever its origin, this type of jewelry is highly collectible today. In addition, the Fred Harvey hotels played a significant role in the arts and crafts production of the Southwest by hiring local artisans to create the furniture, wrought-iron fixtures, and other handcrafted items for hotel and restaurant interiors; they also hired local artists to paint murals and other decorations on wall surfaces.

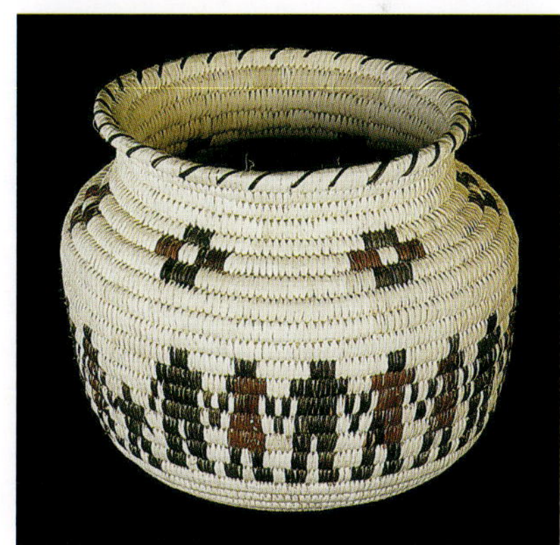

Tohono O'odham friendship basket.

FRIENDSHIP BASKET / a woven basket pattern that has become increasingly popular on Tohono O'odham and Pima baskets, in which a group of men and/or women, usually shown from the back and holding hands, encircle the perimeter of the basket. The friendship design on Southwestern baskets was influenced by an indigenous design of the California Yokuts, who had developed the pattern by the 1890s.

FRIENDSHIP BOWL / a type of clay bowl with **polychrome** decoration, made primarily by the Tohono O'odham people of Arizona, in which adult figures—generally alternating men and women—shown from the back, holding hands, and encircling the rim of the bowl, representing a social round dance, in which Indian and non-Indian alike are invited to participate.

This design, called Nawoj Hah'ah by the Tohono O'odham, has come to symbolize the strength that comes from "unity of purpose" in a community. Often accompanying the dancing figures (with smiling faces painted on the interior of the pot), are a desert mountain landscape, symbols/design motifs, detailed clothing, and sometimes **appliquéd** hats (on the male figures). Friendship bowls were first made by Rupert Angea in the late 1970s, and are currently made by the Angea family and Manuel family of Hickiwan Village. They use **clay** from a deposit near White Horse Pass to hand form the bowls; they make red paint from hematite and black paint from the sap of the **mesquite** tree to paint the design on the light-colored clay; and to fire the bowls, they use the traditional outdoor method with mesquite wood as fuel.

GAAN (Gaa'he) / an Apache word referring to the four benevolent mountain spirits who keep the Apache world in balance and ensure the well-being of the people, and the dancers who are manifestations of the Gaan in ceremonies. Apache artisans have depicted Gaan dancers in various art forms, including paintings and coiled **pictorial baskets.** The Gaan—who also represent the powers of the Apache universe, including the sun, moon, wind, lightning, thunder, and rain—appear during certain ceremonies, including the Sunrise Ceremony held to celebrate a girl's transition from childhood to womanhood. Also known as Mountain Spirit Dancers or Crown Dancers, the Gaan impersonators dance around a fire, accompanied by singing and drumming, bringing the spiritual world into physical manifestation. They wear painted-wood slat headdresses and belts decorated with bells, hold wooden swords (or dance wands) decorated with lightning patterns, and their bodies are painted with various symbols, including lightning. They also wear distinctive, colorful masks that entirely cover their faces. The Gaan are accompanied in the ceremonies by a fifth figure, L'ubaiye, the Gray One, who whirls a bull-roarer—a short piece of wood on a length of string that when whirled around produces a distinctive sound resembling thunder and stormy winds. The Western Apaches call these dancers Gaan, while the Eastern Apaches call them Gaa'he and do not use a bull-roarer.

GALLUP THROW / an inexpensive, relatively small, and loosely woven textile, originally made by Navajos during the first decades of the twentieth century, named after the town of Gallup, New

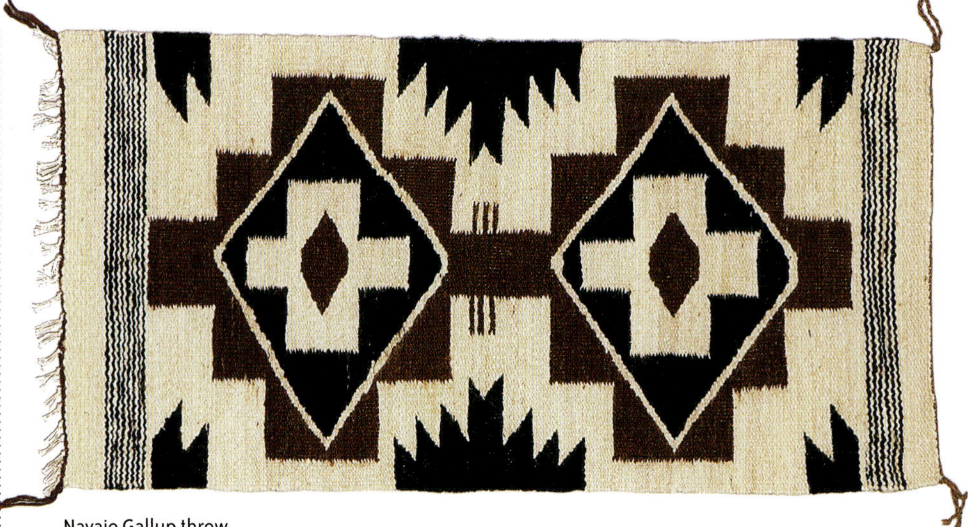

Navajo Gallup throw.

Mexico, a railroad stop and tourist town where they were sold as souvenirs. Featuring simple, abstracted pictorial images such as **corn** stalks or **Yé'ii** figures and/or bold geometric patterns such as diamonds, **crosses**, and stepped designs, these rugs were typically made on commercial cotton **warps** with commercially spun and dyed **yarns.** They are often left unfinished with an exposed cotton-warp fringe at one end. Generally measuring about one-and-one-half feet by three feet and too small for use on the floor, Gallup throws served as chair or sofa backs, tablecloths, and other informal purposes. A favorite and easy-to-transport souvenir among visitors to the Southwest, these rugs were, on occasion, made with homespun yarns.

GANADO STYLE / a type of Navajo rug identified by its deep red background, a dominant central motif usually consisting of one or two terraced diamonds, and at least one border, named after a community in the south-central part of the Navajo reservation. Traditionally, the red and black were aniline-**dyed**, and the other colors—gray, white, black, and sometimes brown—were from natural wool. Occasionally the background color in these rugs is white or gray. Ganado rugs are associated with the **Hubbell Trading Post** and owner Juan Lorenzo Hubbell, who by 1902 marketed Ganado-area handwoven textiles through the **Fred Harvey Company**. The "Ganado red" of the region's early textiles continues to be used by Navajo artisans today, although most are woven with commercially dyed **yarn.**

GANADO TRADING POST / first operated by Clinton N. Cotton and then by Juan Lorenzo Hubbell sometime after 1876, on the Navajo Reservation in Arizona, this post was instrumental in encouraging the work of Navajo weavers and silversmiths. For instance, Cotton, recognizing the potential market for jewelry, hired a Mexican silversmith to teach the art form to the Navajos. Both Cotton and Hubbell provided Native artisans of the region with materials, designs they believed would appeal to tourists, and a steady marketplace. Cotton published at least three mail-order catalogues, the first in 1896; the last was entitled *The use of Navajo Blankets as a home decoration.*

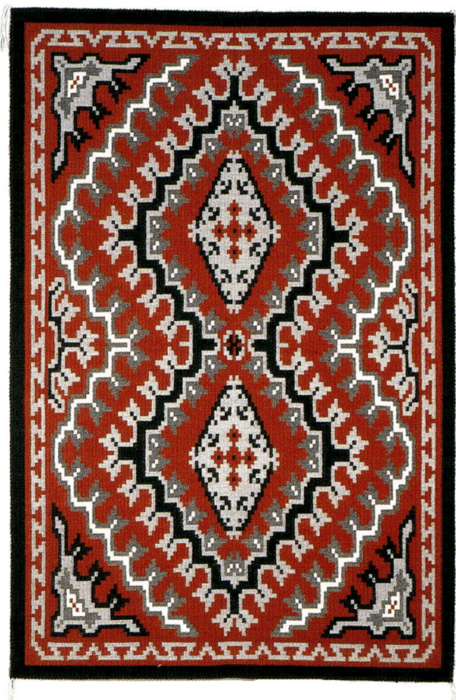

Beth Tapaha (Navajo), Ganado-style textile, 72 ½" x 49 ½".

During his nearly fifty-year career, he supplied thousands of Navajo rugs to curio dealers and other retailers.

Hubbell was also influential regarding rugs woven during the period. There are several rug patterns associated with the Ganado post—including the **chief-style**, **Moki style**, and the "pine tree"—all based on Hubbell's textile study at the turn of the twentieth century, when he commissioned one hundred paintings of copies of old blanket patterns that could be used as templates for weavers.

GEOGLYPHS (Intaglios, Earth Glyphs) / images created by scraping away surface material on the desert floor, executed by ancient peoples of the Southwest. Usually very large, the designs are best viewed from the air. A number of geoglyphs have been discovered in the Mojave Desert. One of the few examples in the Southwest can be viewed at the Bouse Fisherman site in west-central Arizona, which was discovered in 1984 by pilots flying over the Colorado River canyon. About thirty feet long, it features a male figure holding a spear (with the spear point filled in with chips of white quartz) and he appears to be running or dancing across water; a series of stylized waves beneath his feet represent water. The date, meaning, and identity of the artists of this type of paleo-art remain a mystery. See also **petroglyphs** and **pictographs**.

GERMAN SILVER (Nickel Silver, White Brass) / an alloy of **copper** (60 percent), zinc (20 percent), and nickel (20 percent) that was used by the mid-nineteenth century by Plains Indians to fashion **concha**-style belts, hair plates, bracelets, rings, and **horse bridles**. The Navajos, who acquired many of these objects through trade with the Plains Indians, were influenced by the designs and forms of the Plains German-silver jewelry when making their own silverwork. See also **conchas**.

GERMANTOWN YARNS / **Rugs** / a type of rug made beginning in the 1870s by the Navajos and named after the **yarns** used to weave them—three- or four-ply machine-spun wool yarn, **dyed** with aniline tints in a wide variety of hues, originally manufactured in woolen mills in or near Germantown, Pennsylvania, beginning in 1864. The Germantown aniline-dyed commercial **yarns** gradually replaced the earlier Saxony commercial yarns imported from Europe. Some Germantown rugs were very colorful, with multiple outlined, serrated shapes—rugs of this type are known today as **eyedazzlers**. The range of colors available included yellow, green, brown, red, orange-red, blue, white, tan, and lavender-purple.

The Germantown rug style was established by Navajo weavers around 1869, when thousands of pounds of Germantown yarns were distributed to them by the U.S. government; they frequently incorporated these yarns into their blankets, and later into rugs woven for sale. About the mid-1880s, due to the influence of post traders who wanted to speed up the weaving production, Navajo weavers began using cotton **warp** instead of handspun wool in their Germantown-style rugs. According to some scholars, the term "Germantown" has often been incorrectly associated with all antique textiles woven with commercially made yarns. The Navajos continued to weave in the Germantown style into the 1930s. Since the 1980s there has been a revival of this rug tradition. See also **yarns—commercial**.

GESSO (Yeso) / a plaster traditionally made from gypsum, baked to eliminate moisture, mixed with homemade rabbit-skin glue, and applied to the wood surface of New Mexican **retablos** and **bultos** as a ground for painting. Gesso fills in any

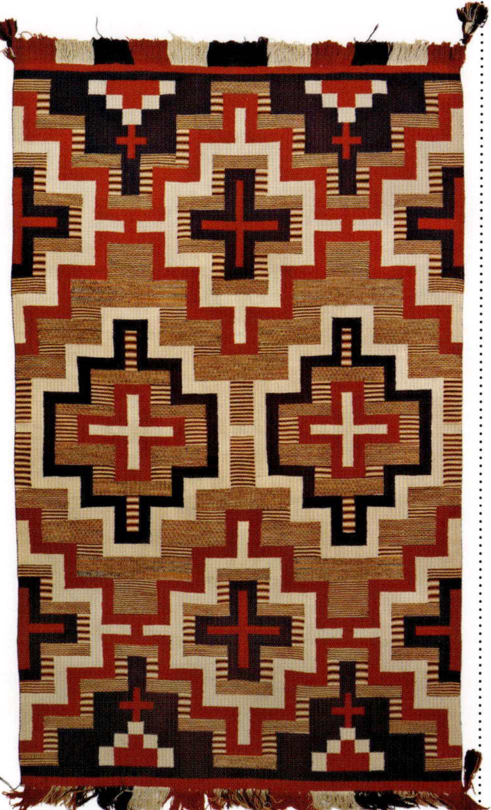

Navajo Germantown textile, 1880s, 78" x 48".

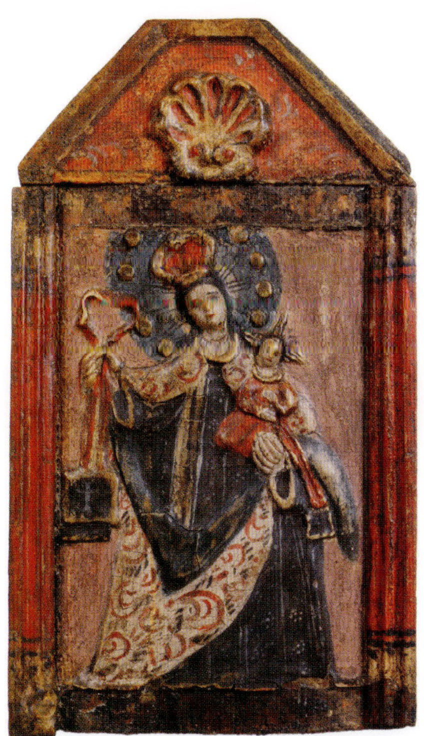

School of Laguna Santero, Our Lady of Mount Carmel, gesso relief panel, late 18th–early 19th century, wood, gesso, water-based paint.

cracks and holes in the wood, providing a smooth surface. Although commercially made gesso is available today, many **santeros/santeras** continue to make gesso the old-fashioned way.

GESSO RELIEF PANEL / a **retablo** rendered in bas-relief through the use of gesso made into a thick paste and applied, molded, and allowed to dry and then painted; sometimes cloth soaked in gesso is used and sometimes the gesso is carved. Common in Europe, the method was used in Spain into the sixteenth century, and is documented as being used by at least one **santero** in nineteenth-century New Mexico. Today the Spanish Market, held annually in Santa Fe, New Mexico, in July and December, offers an award for gesso reliefs. Among the contemporary santeros/santeras making them today are Charlie Carrillo, José Armijo, Nicolás Otero, Ramón José López, Cruzito (Cruz) Flores, and David Nabor Lucero.

GÍHOS / the name given to **burden baskets** made by the Tohono O'odham and Pima (Akimel O'odham) of Arizona, by hand-weaving or almost "crocheting" **agave** fibers (by looping the fibers with fingers, sharpened stick, thorn needle, or other tool) into a large conical shape with a lacelike pattern. Then the shape is bound with a cord to a circular stick to form the rim, and dampened and stretched to fit a framework of four **saguaro**-rib poles, to which the basket is tied with a horsehair or human-hair cord. Also attached are a **twilled** back mat and headband. Often the basket's pattern was highlighted with red paint derived from a native **clay** and blue paint created from the juice of prickly pear cactus fruit. Historically, these light, strong baskets were used by women to carry heavy loads on their backs.

GLAZEWARE / pottery decorated with glazes—mineral paints with fluxes, such as lead and **copper**, which become glossy when **fired**—was produced in many New Mexico pueblos from about 1250 to 1700. The glaze paints were not used to seal the clay to make it waterproof, rather they were used purely for aesthetic purposes. The glazes produced were primarily dark brown, light brown, black, and green. A significant feature of glazes, which helps identify its use on older pieces, is that glaze paints tend to run during the firing process, creating droplets, globules, puddling, or streaks on the surface. After about 1700, possibly due to European influence (after the reconquest of the region by the Spanish in 1692, officials cut off the supply of vital resources to Indians, which likely included materials for glaze paints) indigenous potters replaced the lead glazes with matte-**mineral** or **vegetal pigment paints**, used continuously at **pueblos** into the present day.

GOURDS / a trailing desert plant bearing large fruit with a hard rind or shell, used by Native peoples of the Southwest since prior to European contact as a source for food, medicine, soap, musical instruments, vessels for carrying foods or water, and for shaping pottery. Dried gourd shell pieces were (and continue to be) used by Native potters to scrape, shape, and smooth the walls of traditionally made pinched- or **coiled**-clay vessels. Whole shells were used as molds for **paddle-and-anvil**-style clay vessels. Additionally, hollowed-out gourd shells were (and continue to be) used by the Hopis for utensils (such as a ladle) and to make **rattles** for ceremonial dances and celebrations, musical instruments, and **canteens**. Gourd canteens, used by both Native Americans and Hispanos in the nineteenth century, were sometimes covered in rawhide. The practice of using gourds for utilitarian and ceremonial purposes is a tradition that can be traced to cultures across North America.

GREENWARE / any unfired **clay** form. In the Southwest greenware is sometimes mass-produced in molds and then painted, etched, and/or glazed, and then kiln-fired by artisans. Traditional Pueblo potters, who say it is not "true" pottery, frown upon using pre-made greenware.

However, many potters at **Acoma Pueblo** (situated on a 357-foot-high mesa) do purchase or make greenware because it is easier and faster than collecting, processing, and shaping their own **clay**. Acoma potters use a variety of pre-made shapes such as jars, **ollas**, and animals, and typically use acrylic paints or the more classic hematite mixed with **beeweed** juice to paint elaborate black designs on the white surface. The features to look for in a piece of pottery that indicate it was made in a mold are: a perfectly symmetrical shape; a chalky, dead white, very smooth surface; and visible seams from the mold, most noticeable on the inside or bottom of the piece. When asked, potters at Acoma will be truthful about whether a piece is handformed or a molded "ceramic" piece.

GRILLE (Reja) / wrought-iron or wood-spindled grating placed over windows, initially used in eighteenth- and early-nineteenth-century New Mexico in the small windows of **Spanish Colonial–style** homes, as well as in **Sonoran** homes of Arizona; primarily used for protection and eventually for ornamental purposes. Sometimes the Spanish word for grille, *reja*, is used in the region. In the 1920s and '30s they became popular decorative features in windows and balcony railings in **Spanish Colonial Revival–style** homes, ranging from modest dwellings to mansions, built in the Southwest (also in California and Florida). Window grilles can be traced back to the screened projecting bays of Islamic houses. These turned-wood grilles and latticework provided ventilation without admitting much sun.

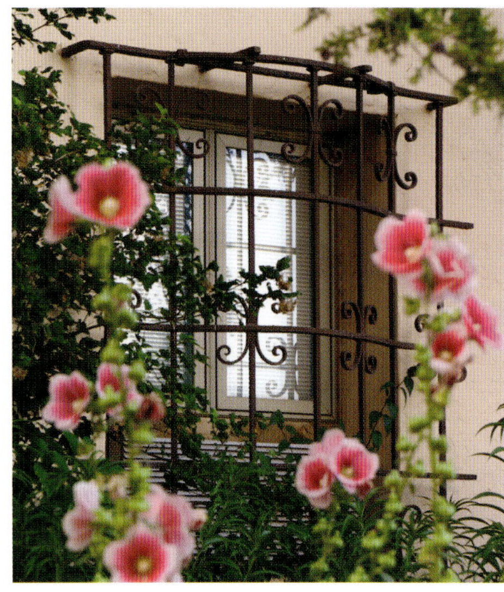

Wrought-iron grille.

HACIENDA / a Spanish word for "country estate," used in the Spanish Colonial era throughout the Americas to refer to a large landed estate or property owned by wealthy merchants or ranchers. Hacienda can also describe an architectural style, patterned after the Spanish-Mediterranean home, featuring a square plan of rooms surrounding and opening into one or more interior **courtyards** (with a **portal** running the length of the courtyards), typically constructed of **adobe** brick, or a combination of stone and adobe. The courtyards were connected through a breezeway called a **zaguán**. The Hacienda de los Martinez in Taos, New Mexico, is one of the few remaining examples of a typical hacienda of the late Spanish Colonial period in the region. This fortress-like massive adobe-walled complex (of twenty-one rooms surrounding two **placitas**) was built in 1804 by Severino Martin (later changed to Martinez) and became an important trade center for the northern edge of the Spanish Empire.

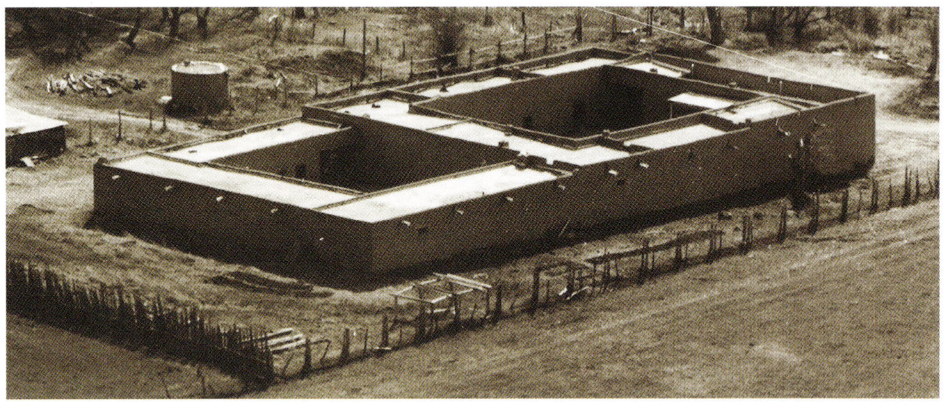

Aerial view of Hacienda de los Martínez, Taos, New Mexico.

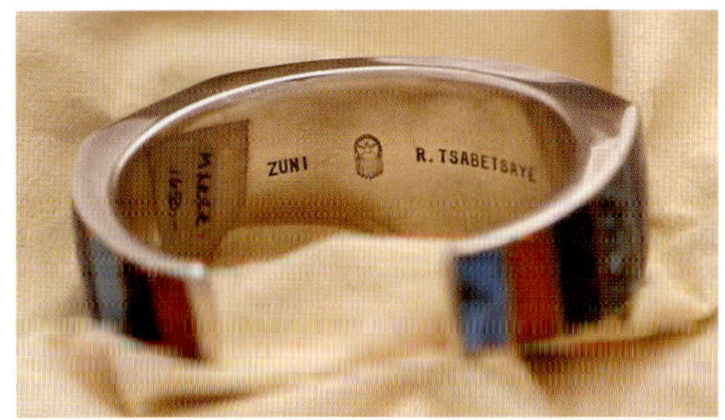

Hallmark of Roger Tsabetsaye Sr. (Zuni), on the inside of a bracelet.

HALLMARK / a cast, engraved, or stamped mark of a name, initials, or symbols on jewelry and silverwork, usually located on the reverse or underside of the item, that indicates the artisan or studio that made the piece. Hallmarks not only help authenticate pieces, they also help date them, because artists and studios would change their marks over time to protect their authorship. Most individual Native American jewelers did not hallmark their work until after World War II; by the 1970s it had become commonplace. The use of hallmarks was two-fold: to indicate who produced the piece and as a sign of authentic Indian craftsmanship. In fact, many traders and collectors see the hallmark as a stamp of quality in modern Native American jewelry and silver pieces.

HAND-ADZED / See **adze**.

HAND WROUGHT / a piece of jewelry, **silver**, or other metalwork that was shaped by hand using a hammer or other implement or tool.

HANDS / **Hand of Fatima** / hands, an ancient symbol in the Southwest (as well as elsewhere around the world), appear frequently in prehistoric and historic art and artifacts including **petroglyphs** and **pictographs**. A stylized hand is a common motif in jewelry, pottery, tiles, and other works of art made by Native American artisans today. Its specific meaning varies depending on the culture, traditions, and aesthetic preferences of the maker. One particular design used in the region is known as the "hands of Fatima," which originated with the Moors and was used by Spanish silversmiths on the crescent-shaped pendants of their silver **horse bridles**. The design made its way to the Southwest through the Spanish; Navajo silversmiths adopted and adapted this motif into small hand-shaped forms that appear as terminals on their **najas** and bracelets. In some instances, the terminations of najas are flattened and scratched with four perpendicular lines to suggest fingers of the hand.

The hand (or hand amulet) has many different connotations to cultures around the world. For instance, called *hamsa* in Arabic, the hand amulet—an open right hand often with an eye in the palm—was believed to offer protection and ward off evil. The hand amulet remained popular among Spanish Catholics long after the Moors were defeated and left Spain. With the advent of Islam, the amulet became known as the "hand of Fatima" to commemorate the Arab prophet Muhammad's daughter Fatima Zahra, who according to Islamic legend, dipped her hand in blood during a battle and printed it on a standard, proclaiming "Let this be your symbol." Christians came to call it the hand of Mary, for the mother of Jesus. Today the "hand of Fatima" is generally considered a good luck charm.

HAVASUPAI BASKETS / extremely fine **coiled** baskets of **willow**, **cottonwood**, and **devil's claw**, with particularly crisp, mostly geometric designs in black (and sometimes other colors) on a natural white background. Most are flat, oval, plaque forms; some coiled bowls, **trays**, and **ollas** have also been woven in recent decades. **Twined** baskets of catclaw, **sumac**, Apache plume, arrowweed, and serviceberry are also being made by the Havasupais in trays, **burden baskets**, bowls, and **water jugs**.

Historically, because of their isolated location in Havasu Canyon where their main village of Supai is located, baskets were a necessity in every home. The early Havasupais primarily made

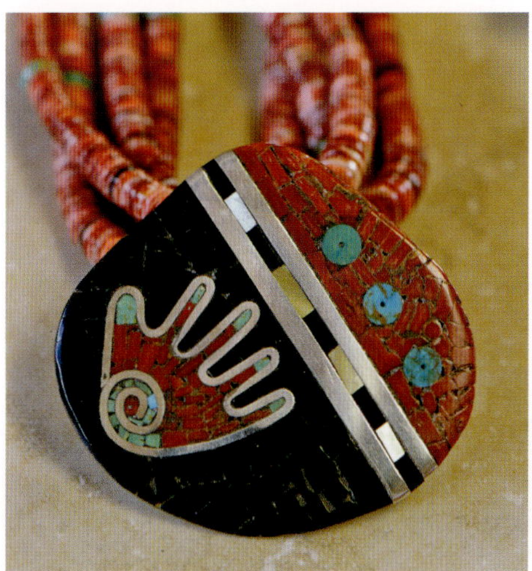

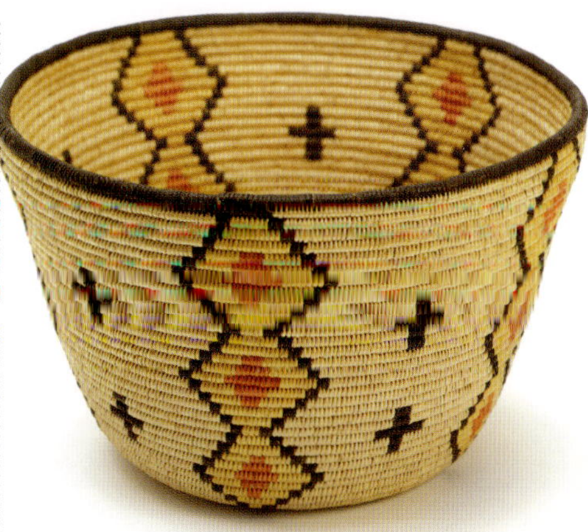

Havasupai basket, ca. 1920.

twined utilitarian wares. After about 1870 they made increasing numbers of coiled baskets, due to the introduction of the **awl**, the use of devil's claw for creating designs, the encouragement of teachers, and increased demand for their baskets by the Hopis and Anglo tourists. Following a surge in basket weaving from 1929 to 1940, when the Havasupais perfected the quality of their craft and made baskets for sale, there was a decline in weaving until the 1970s.

At that time, the unspoiled beauty of Havasu Canyon began to attract numerous hikers and tourists and once again coiled baskets were purchased in increasing numbers as souvenirs. At present, the Havasupai Tribal Museum's exhibition and sale of baskets is helping preserve a basket-making tradition that otherwise could be in peril.

HEART / **Indented (Bruised Heart, Lazy Heart)** / a term used to describe the heart-shaped terminal of some double-barred **crosses** hanging from silver-**bead** necklaces, made by Pueblo jewelers in New Mexico beginning around 1900.

HEART LINE (Spirit Line, Breath Line) / a historically important symbol to Zuni Pueblo, New Mexico, consisting of a line running between the heart and mouth in representations of animals. Found etched, carved, inlaid, or painted on Zuni pottery and **fetishes**, on one or both sides of the

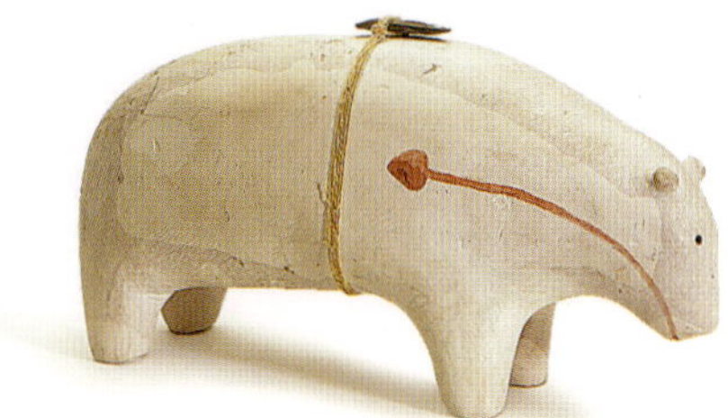

animal, it is said to represent the path of breath, which contains the animal's spiritual essence. Many Zuni fetish carvers include an inlaid heart line on hunting animals like mountain lions, for the hearts of hunting animals are believed to have magical power over the hearts of their prey (game animals). The heart line has been adopted by other Pueblo and Navajo artisans for carvings, jewelry, pottery, and paintings. There are other interpretations of what the heart line represents, including that it "points to the soul of the animal."

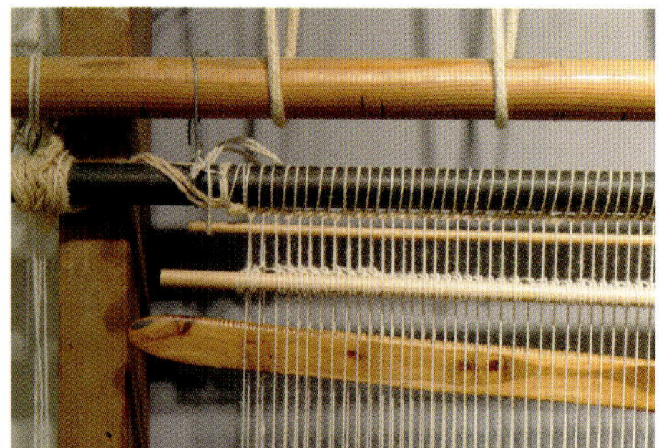
Detail of loom showing (top to bottom): tension beam, upper warp beam, shed stick, string heddle, and batten.

HEDDLE / a wooden rod used during the traditional weaving process on a **loom**, to pull certain **warp** threads up or forward in order to slide a shuttle—a small wood stick on which the wool or other fiber was wrapped—through. In Navajo and Pueblo weaving, the heddle stick holds a cord that is wrapped around the selected warps to pull them forward. See diagram on page 187.

HEISHI (Heishe) / the Keres word for "shell," a term referring to flat, disk-shaped **beads** of **shell** originally made by drilling holes in the shells with a cactus needle and sand, or a basic pump drill. Heishi also refers to necklaces consisting of hundreds or thousands of shell beads strung together. Both the heishi beads and necklaces have been made by Native Americans since ancient times; the tradition is carried on today at the New Mexico pueblos of Santo Domingo and San Felipe.

Today the term is also commonly used to describe tiny handmade beads of any material. Among the shells commonly used for authentic heishi are olivella, **spiny oyster**, abalone, and **coral;** often used in combination with turquoise. The traditional way to make a heishi bead begins with rubbing a small piece of shell or semi-precious stone against a course slab of sandstone to flatten it, then a hole is drilled in the bead using a hand-powered pump drill (with thicker pieces

requiring drilling from both sides). To make the beads round, they are strung on a wire and then rolled back and forth across sandstone, or pulled through a groove in a rough stone. Fine sandstone is used to smooth the beads and buckskin is used to polish them. The heishi are then strung on cotton or nylon; they are finished with a clasp of **silver**, or the traditional white-string cotton wrap, or a single strand of tied string. In some instances the artisan will add another smaller loop or two of strung heishi at the bottom of the necklace that hangs like a pendant, called a **jacla**.

Since the advent of power tools, some Pueblo jewelers have used electric drills and grinding machines to make heishi, while others have continued to make them completely by hand. Necklaces made with single or multiple strands of heishi have long been a trademark style of jewelers at Santo Domingo Pueblo. Some of their finest necklaces contain over 10,000 miniscule beads, most often made from dark olive, white clam, and melon shells, as well as **silver**, **turquoise**, and **coral.** In recent decades some Pueblo artisans have been experimenting with gold beads and various semi-precious gemstones in their heishi.

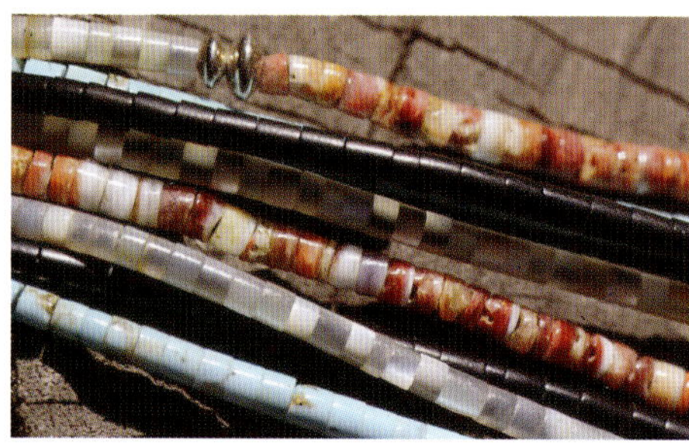
Joseph and Mary Calabaza (Santo Domingo), heishi necklaces.

In addition, some Pueblo potters inlay strings of shell and turquoise heishi beads, purchased from Santo Domingo jewelers, into their clay vessels—an innovation credited to Tony Da (1940–2008) of San Ildefonso Pueblo. He carved grooves into the clay surface before the piece was fired, and then after it was fired he would set the heishi string into the grooves with glue. Among the artisans currently carrying on this technique are the award-winning potters Caroline Carpio of Isleta Pueblo and Russell Sanchez (b. 1963) of San Ildefonso. See also **beadwork**, **fetishes**, **jaclas**, and **shells**.

HEMATITE / an earth iron ore widely used by Native Americans of the Southwest to make red paint. Pueblo and Hopi (First Mesa) potters com-

bine local hematite with **beeweed** juice to make a black paint used to paint designs on **clay** vessels. See also **Acoma Pueblo pottery**.

HERRINGBONE (False Braid) / an ancient, complex, and time-consuming method of finishing basket rims that is still used today on Navajo, San Juan Paiute, and Jicarilla **coiled** baskets.

HIDE CLOTHING (Buckskin Clothing) / the Utes of southern Colorado and northern New Mexico were renowned from an early date as experts in the preparation of hides for clothing. In the mid-1700s, Spanish explorers and settlers visited Ute villages or attended the annual Ute trade fair held at Abiquiu, New Mexico, to exchange **beads**, knives, metal tools, horses, and other items for the highly valued deer skins and leather clothing. Using deerskin, mountain sheep, antelope, or elk, the Utes made clothing in styles reminiscent of their Plains neighbors. Women's full-length dresses and men's shirts and leggings were often beautifully decorated with glass beads.

In the winter the Utes wore skin clothing, moccasins lined with bark or fur, and heavy tanned bison or bear hides as robes. In the summer, they wore lighter skin clothing (of deer or antelope) and lighter skin robes.

The Apache people also have a long tradition of making hide clothing. Hide dresses, decorated with elaborate fringe and minimally with beading and/or **tinklers** and German silver spots, were made and worn for ceremonies such as the Apache Sunrise Ceremony that marks a young girl's entry into womanhood. The dresses are handed down from generation to generation, and the Sunrise Ceremony continues to be an important part of the Apache culture.

Surviving examples of 1880s Apache-made buckskin men's shirts are decorated with long fringes, color-staining, and minimal **beadwork**, and show the influence of southern Plains fashion. Deerskin jackets patterned after the coats of American military were popular among the Western Apaches during the Indian Wars of the 1870s. Other buckskin items made by the Apaches are boots with color-staining and beadwork and moccasins with beadwork, tinklers, and fringe.

Animal hides were important to the early Spanish settlers in the region, as well; hides and buckskin clothing were popular trade items at colonial New Mexico fairs and carried along the Camino Real (Royal Road) to other trade fairs and markets in Mexico. Largely out of necessity, by the seventeenth century buckskin clothing was worn by some Hispano residents of the Southwest. See also **leatherwork**.

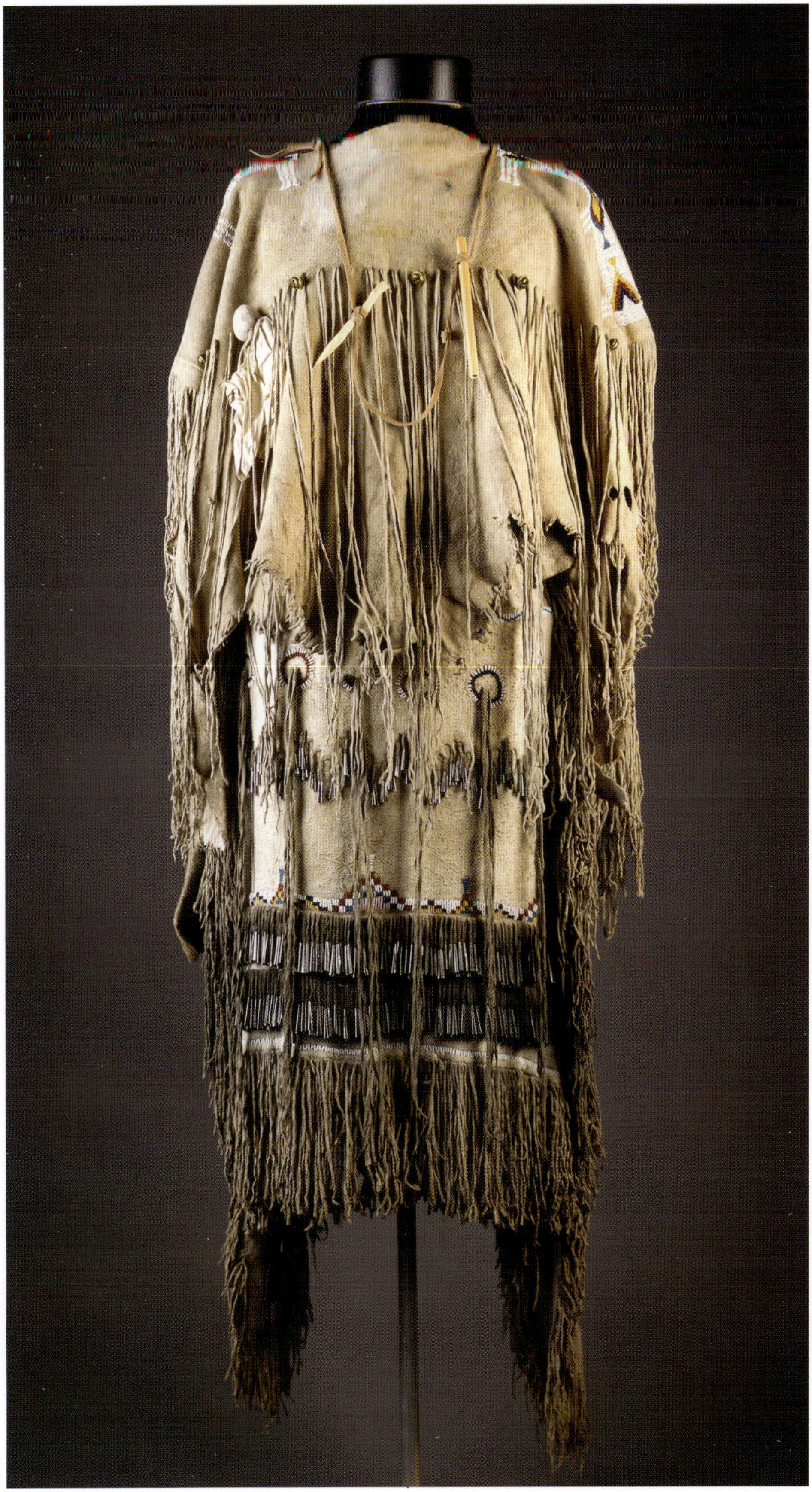

HIDE PAINTINGS / *See* **paintings on hide**.

HOGAN (Hoogan, Hoghán) / a traditional Navajo dwelling consisting of a single small, round or six or eight sided room of wood or mud walls with a central hearth, log roof with smoke hole in the center, and hard-packed earthen floor. Most hogans are built of log construction with chinking of mortar, but in areas with limited supplies of timber, the walls may be made from stone, mud, or a combination of these and other materials. The round hogans with a cone-shaped roof (with forked poles) are referred to as "male" hogans, and the more spacious six- or eight-sided hogans with domed roofs are called "female." Traditionally hogans were only inhabited during the winter months and abandoned in the summer, when Navajo families moved to temporary homes near sheepherding areas.

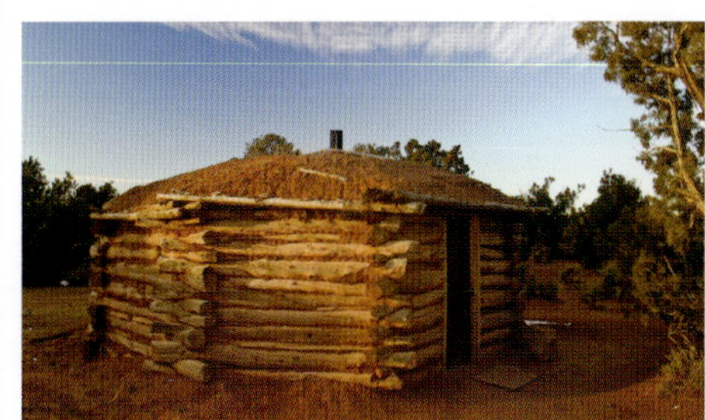

In the early 1900s, when metal saws and axes were plentiful and cutting larger timbers was easier, octagonal hogans constructed of horizontal notched logs topped with log roofs were favored. Eventually, wood-burning metal stoves replaced the open hearths. These single-room dwellings are sacred spaces to the Navajos and even the building of them is a ceremonial act performed in a proper order. When completed, a hogan is blessed by a ceremony that includes sprinkling **cornmeal** and powder from prayer sticks in the four cardinal directions.

Every part of the house has a special significance: the door faces east towards the sunrise to receive the benedictions of the Dawn People who come with the sun's first rays; it is customary for the Navajos to emerge from this door to greet the dawn with a pinch of corn pollen to bless the day. The south side is for storing the tools of daily

Mescalero Apache Coming of Age ceremony hide skirt and poncho, early 1900s.

life and for weaving in winter; the west side is for visiting, storytelling, and sleeping; and the north is for things used in taking care of the family, such as herbs and hunting equipment. Hogans continue to be built into the present day, generally from modern materials—wood frame walls, exterior siding, drywall, windows, and metal roofing—and remain a central part of Navajo ceremonial and cultural life. Even if Navajo families have contemporary dwellings of a different sort, they usually still have a hogan for ceremonial purposes. For instance, healing ceremonies that include the making and use of **sandpaintings** still take place in a Navajo family's hogan; some Navajo women weavers continue to set up their **looms** on the floor of a hogan.

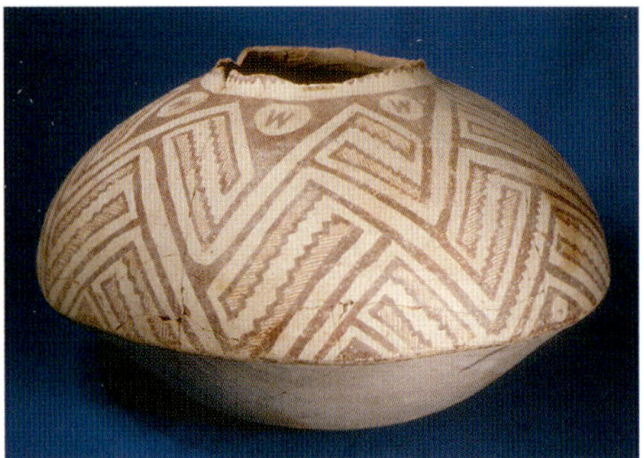

Hohokam large Sacaton red-on-buff jar, ca. AD 900–1100.

HOHOKAM POTTERY / pottery created by prehistoric Hohokam people—using the **paddle and anvil** construction method and pit-kiln firing. They created plainware, polished redware, redware with black-and-white decoration, and clay figurines of humans and animals. For daily use, they created cookware, serving dishes, containers for storage and carrying water, and firedogs for propping cooking pots near fires. For their ceremonies, they produced **effigies**, censers for burning incense, and funeral jars for cremated remains. Among the standard features of Hohokam pottery is red paint made with an iron oxide pigment applied with an **agave**-fiber brush. They also developed a unique painted pottery now well-known as Snaketown **red-on-buff**—clay pots painted with a light tan- or buff-colored **slip**, decorated with animal and human figures (often shown dancing) as well as geometric and hachure (shading consisting of multiple crossing lines)-filled designs.

Scholars speculate that the Hohokam potters were women and worked near home. Their wares differed from that of the Ancestral Puebloans and Mogollon people in manufacture and color. Hohokam pottery was usually red-on-buff rather than **black-on-white** or red-on-brown. Also,

their decorations were different: most having curvilinear elements and small repeated animal or bird motifs instead of geometric patterns. Bird designs were particularly popular images on Hohokam pottery. Some Hohokam pottery designs appear in **petroglyphs** of the period; see for example Sears Point in southwestern Arizona. See also **shell etching**.

HOPI PLAQUES / Coiled / a type of close-**coiled** basket form made by women at the Hopi villages on Second Mesa (Shungopovi, Shipaulovi, and Mishongnovi). The coiled plaques consist of a bundle foundation of galleta grass (*söhö* in Hopi) sewn with cleaned, split, and dyed fiber splints of narrow-leaf **yucca**. They are woven in a round plaque shape and feature traditional centuries-old designs such as **katsina** faces and figures, turtles, and star and floral patterns. Used the same way within the Hopi community as wicker plaques (see next entry), they are also made for sale. The

yucca leaves employed in these and other baskets made by Hopi weavers cannot be gathered until mid- to late July after the Niman Ceremony.

The sewing element for traditional coiled plaques consists of only five colors: white splints, made from center leaves of a yucca plant gathered in late summer and allowed to bleach in the sun; yellow splints, from yucca leaves exposed to the sun and rain; green splints, from the outside leaves of the yucca; red splints, from yucca leaves colored with commercial or natural plant **dye**; and black splints, from yucca leaves colored with commercial or plant dye.

HOPI PLAQUES / Wicker (Yungyapu) / a style of **wickerwork** basket that is round and flat, made by women in the Hopi villages of Third Mesa (Oraibi, Kykotsmovi, Hotevilla, Lower Moenkopi, and Upper Moenkopi). Wicker baskets range in size from a few inches to up to sixteen inches in diameter, are executed using a rigid

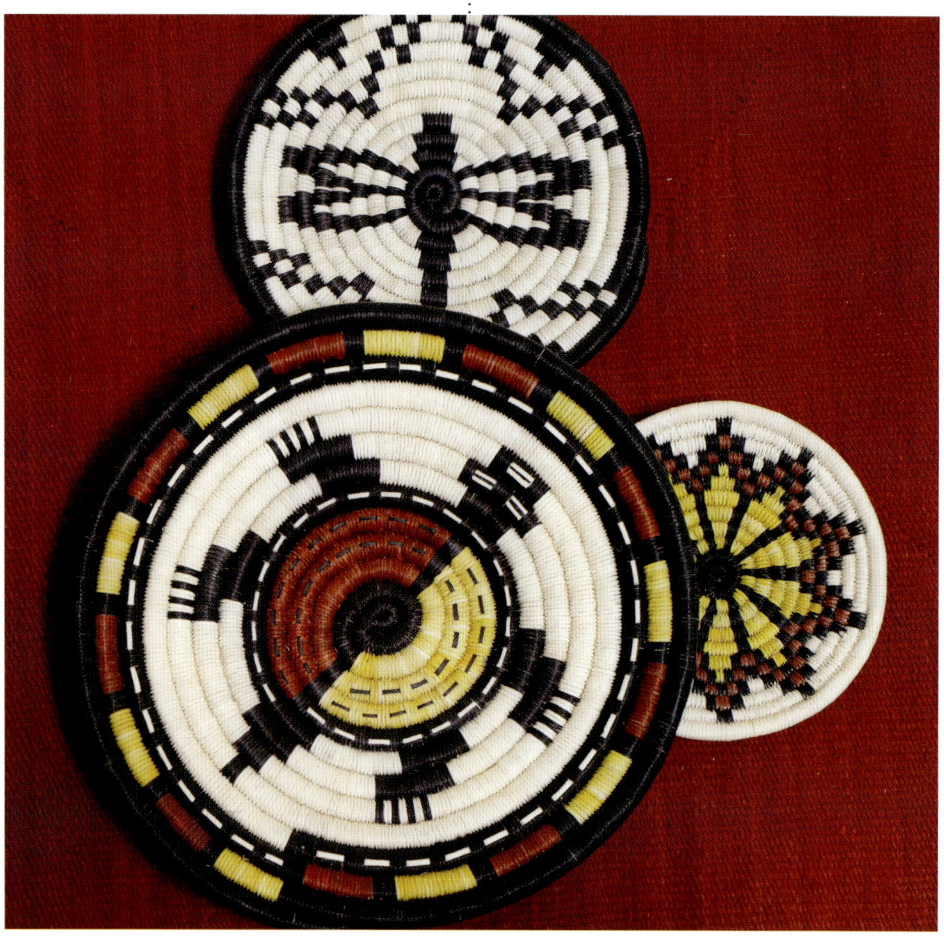

Top: Kathryn Kooyahoema (Hopi, Second Mesa), dragonfly coiled plaque, 2010, yucca, natural dyes; bottom left: Griselda Saufkie (Hopi, Second Mesa), turtle coiled plaque, 2005, yucca, natural and synthetic dyes; bottom right: unknown weaver (Hopi, Second Mesa), flower coiled plaque, ca. 2002, yucca, natural and synthetic dyes.

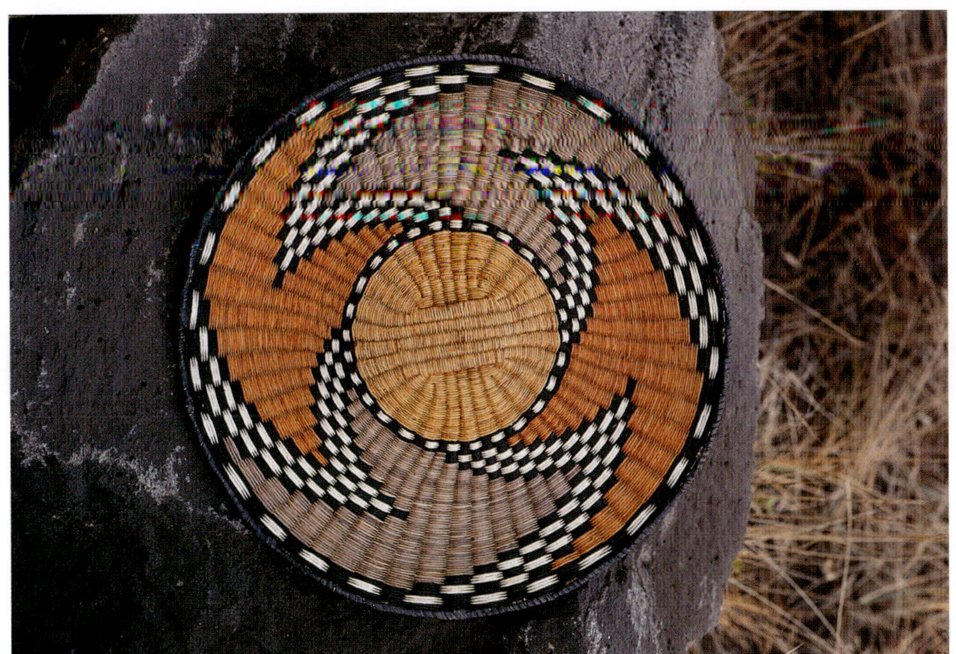

Hopi (Third Mesa) wicker plaque.

foundation of scrub **sumac** stems (*Rhus trilobata*, or *suuvi* in Hopi) and a rigid **weft** of rabbit brush stems (*Chrysothamnus*, or *siváapi* in Hopi), and are dyed bright colors. Synthetic or aniline **dyes** are often used to create the array of bright colors, though a few weavers continue the arduous task of making and using natural vegetal dyes. Both geometric forms and representational imagery of symbolic significance are woven into the plaques. Among the frequently used designs are clouds, rain, turtles, and **katsina** faces.

Wicker plaques, called *yungyapu* in Hopi, are an important aspect of Hopi culture: they are used as gifts, payment for work, prizes for footraces, and as ceremonial items in the **kiva** or in the Basket Dance of women's societies. During the Hopi Pow-amuya or Bean Dance, basket plaques are among the special gifts girls receive from the Katsinas, intended to encourage the girls to behave properly in the Hopi Way.

Additionally, wicker plaques are made for what the Hopi call "payback" in social occasions. For instance, when the groom's parents make the wedding robes for a bride, in return the bride's family will make the appropriate number of plaques as payback to the groom's family. The recipient of the plaque may keep it, give it away, or sell it. The "doll katsina"—a flat decorative piece woven in the shape of a **katsina doll** wearing a headpiece—is one of the more unusual and particularly difficult to make of the Hopi plaques. One of the few master Hopi weavers alive who can make

the latter is Abigail Kaursgowva of Hotevilla. Flat wicker katsina dolls are given to Hopi infants as presents, and, like other wicker plaques, they are made for sale.

HOPI AND HOPI-TEWA POTTERY / a tradition going back centuries, beginning with ancient Hopi potters making gray utility ware as early as AD 700 and then developing over the centuries **black-on-white** styles, black-on-red styles, and finally **polychromes** in both utilitarian and decorative forms. Around 1700, following the Pueblo Revolt,

Tewa immigrants arrived at Hopi and became known as Hopi-Tewa people (settling on First Mesa); they also made pottery and some of their descendants, such as Nampeyo (ca. 1860–1942), became renowned for their clay vessels.

In the late 1800s, Hopi and Hopi-Tewa pottery experienced a revival period, when traders, tourists, and others began to appreciate the artistry of their polychrome wares.

Today the Hopis are known for their distinctive orange pottery with black and red designs inspired by the pots of their ancestors (see **Sikyatki pottery**).

Initially, pottery was made in all the Hopi villages. Gradually the mesas specialized in crafts and the ancient villages of First Mesa—Walpi, Sichomovi, and Hano, as well as the modern village of Polacca at the base of the mesa—became the centers of Hopi pottery (although potters can be found living throughout the Hopi mesa villages today).

Perhaps the most famous Hopi-Tewa potter is Nampeyo, who fashioned elegant jars and bowls for sale to visitors, in which she interpreted designs (including anthropomorphic figures) and shapes of pottery found in the ancient Sikyatki ruins. Nampeyo also successfully influenced other Hopi-Tewa potters to begin reviving pre-contact styles.

Hopi potters begin the process by hand digging **clay** on the Hopi mesas and then processing it by hand. They use the ancient technique of **coiling** and scraping to form their vessels. The Hopis **fire** their pots in the open air on the mesa using sheep dung and cedar as the heat source. Their clay is gray before firing and can turn a range of colors

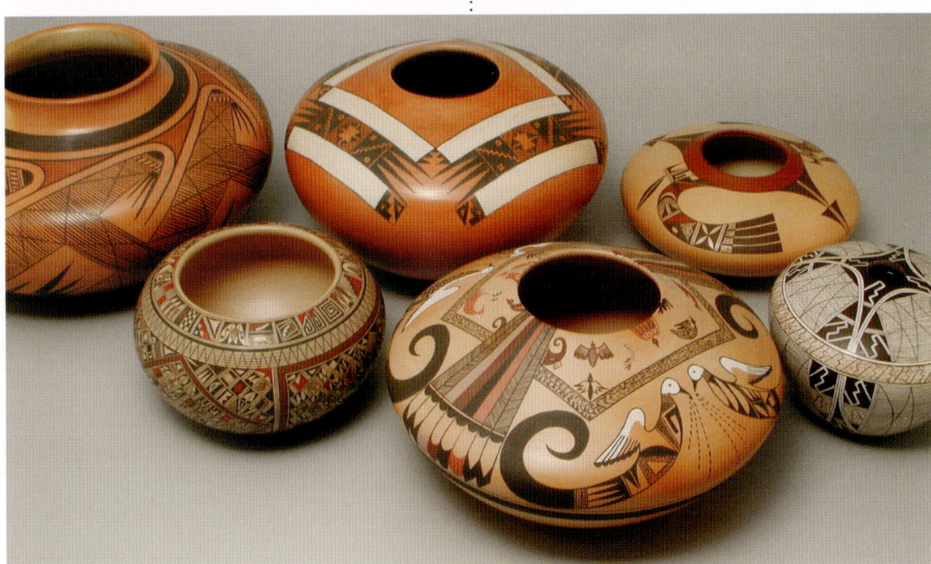

Hopi pottery: back row (left to right), Fannie Nampeyo, Dextra Quotskuyva, Steve Lucas; front row (left to right), Rondina Huma, Mark Tahbo, Rainy Naha.

from cream, buff, or yellow to apricot, peach, or light red depending on its iron content and the firing temperature. For example, higher temperatures with local coal (lignite) as fuel yield the lightest colors. To make rich red pottery, Hopi artisans use yellow clay or yellow **slip**; the more iron in the clay, the redder the pot fires. Some Hopi clays need **temper** and others do not. Paints for decorating the pots are made from natural materials; for instance, Hopi potters boil **beeweed** for black paint. They use the traditional **yucca**-leaf brushes to apply their intricate designs.

Among the characteristic Hopi pottery forms are the tall, straight-sided vases; Hopi potters may have been encouraged to make this form by Santa Fe writer and ceramic artist Frank Applegate, who visited the mesas in 1922. Among the forms made today are **tiles**, wide-shouldered flattened jars, bean pots, stew bowls, ladles, **seed jars**, standing figures, and bowls in which to mix batter for the paper-thin blue-cornmeal piki bread. Inventive designs ranging from traditional to abstract to contemporary are painted with **yucca**-leaf brushes (or commercially made brushes). A few potters specialize in white-slipped (**kaolin** clay) ware. See also **Keams Trading Post**.

HOPI QUILTS (Tavupu) / the best-known quilters of the Southwest are Hopi women (and some men). The Hopis first learned the craft in the 1880s from Mennonite missionaries and teachers. These quilts (or tavapu in the Hopi language) eventually replaced the cotton, wool, and fur coverings once made by the Hopis and used for warmth and bed coverings. Sewing, knitting, and weaving were traditionally male occupations among the Hopis, but quilting became primarily a female activity, providing Hopi women with important social occasions.

When first learning the craft, Hopi women attended quilting bees where they pieced together quilt tops using small blocks (3 ½ x 5 ½ inches) of material of various colors, patterns, and fabrics that had been sent to the Hopi villages and mission churches from around the country. With the availability of factory-made fabrics (usually brightly colored and patterned calico) at trading posts and the free quilt patches from the missionaries, quilting became a widely practiced craft on the Hopi mesas. Later, fabric from worn-out or second-hand clothing and flour or grain sacks was used. Because quilt patterns were scarce in the region, the Hopis passed hand-drawn patterns from generation to generation.

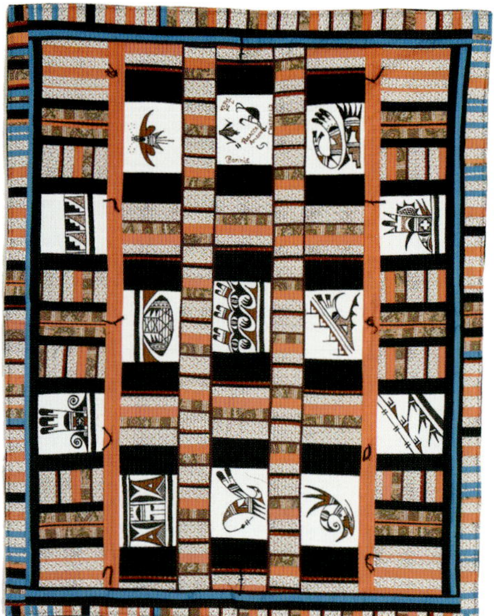
Bonnie Nampeyo Chapella (Hopi-Tewa, First Mesa), "painted pottery" quilt, 43" x 35".

In the 1960s and '70s, when there was a revival of quilting around America, Hopi women joined the movement. Quilts served a practical purpose as blankets, bed coverings, ground cloths, window or door coverings, and couch throws. In addition, they are an important aspect of Hopi culture. They are given to infants during baby-naming ceremonies *(tipos' asni)*, as a remembrance of home and family to sons and daughters when they leave the reservation, and for celebratory events such as weddings. Quilts also serve as chronicles of important events and are used as burial shrouds.

At present there are third- and fourth-generation women quilters in the Hopi villages who learned the craft by attending Arizona Quilt Guild workshops, or by working side-by-side with female members of their family and community. Still holding weekly quilting bees to make machine- or hand-pieced quilts from brightly colored, worn-out clothing and fabric scraps, these women combine traditional quilt patterns (log cabin, pinwheel, spools, Irish chain, nine patch) with painted, **appliquéd**, or embroidered images important to Hopi culture—**butterflies**, **katsinas**, **koshares**, basket shapes, bows and arrows, rain clouds, lightning bolts, dance rattles, and clan symbols such as **bear**, **coyote**, eagle, **corn**, or sun.

The Hopi women do not make "presentation" quilts, rather they make quilts as gifts or for themselves to be used as a wrap or bed covering and worn out. As a result, very few old Hopi quilts have survived.

Beginning in the latter part of the twentieth century, there has been increased interest in historical and contemporary Native American quilts, making quilts by Hopis and other Native artisans highly desirable and collectible. See also **quilts**.

HORNO / an outdoor beehive-shaped oven with arched opening and no chimney, traditionally made of sun-dried mud bricks, mud mortar, and finished with a layer of **mud plaster**, introduced to the Pueblo people of the Southwest by early Spanish settlers, and still in widespread use at **pueblos** today. Hornos can be traced back to the Muslims of North Africa, from whom the

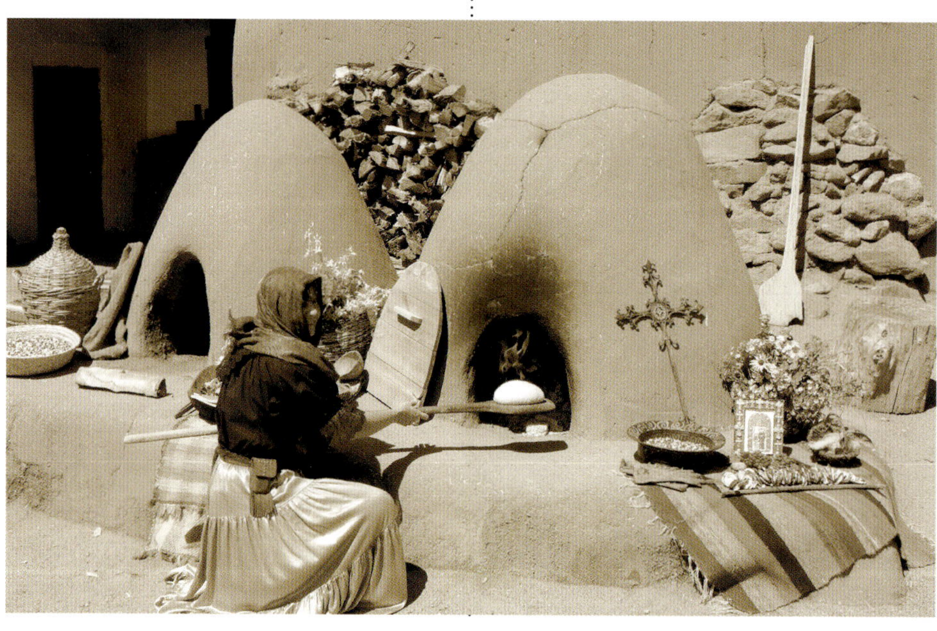

Spaniards adopted the custom. With walls 5 to 8 inches thick, these ovens are built on an elevated foundation of stone or **adobe** to keep it above the potentially wet ground. They also have a small opening near the top, on the side away from the prevailing wind, to allow the smoke to escape.

After a fire is started in the horno, the wood and/or coals and ash are swept out, and a wooden paddle with elongated handle is used to place the food inside. To enclose the heat, the smoke hole is stopped-up with a rag, or piece of wood, and the arched opening is closed with a large stone or piece of wood and mud for sealing the edges. The thermal mass of the adobe walls can store enough heat to cook the food for one-and-a-half to two hours. Originally used for baking, roasting *chicos* (dried **corn**) and green and red chile, and cooking meat by Hispano and Pueblo peoples of the Southwest, the horno is primarily used today by Pueblo people for baking bread.

In rare instances, Pueblo potters have used the horno for the outdoor **firing** of their clay vessels, for it creates even heat and retains heat longer than other outdoor firing methods.

In recent decades, the functional horno has become a popular ornamental accent in the patios and **courtyards** of Southwest homes. Beginning in the late nineteenth century and continuing to the present, miniature versions of hornos have been fashioned out of **clay** by Pueblo potters and sold to the tourist market.

HORSE BRIDLES (Headstalls) / Native American / horse gear that goes over the horse's head and behind the ears, and holds in place the iron or steel bit that goes into the horse's mouth. In the Southwest, bridles evolved from simple braided hair ropes or plaited-buckskin straps to more elaborate leather straps ornately decorated with **silver,** or in rare instances **copper**. Horses were introduced to the Southwest by Spanish explorers in 1598 and by the mid-1600s large numbers of horses populated the region. The earliest known examples of Navajo-made silver headstalls date to the early 1870s. They were similar in construction and decoration to the Plains Indian versions, who adopted from the Spanish and Mexicans the tradition of silver-mounted bridles/headstalls. By 1880 the Navajos had developed their own bridle designs. The neighboring Utes also fashioned silver and leather headstalls.

The earliest Navajo-made bridle ornaments were made from Mexican or American silver coins that were melted and poured into a mold forming

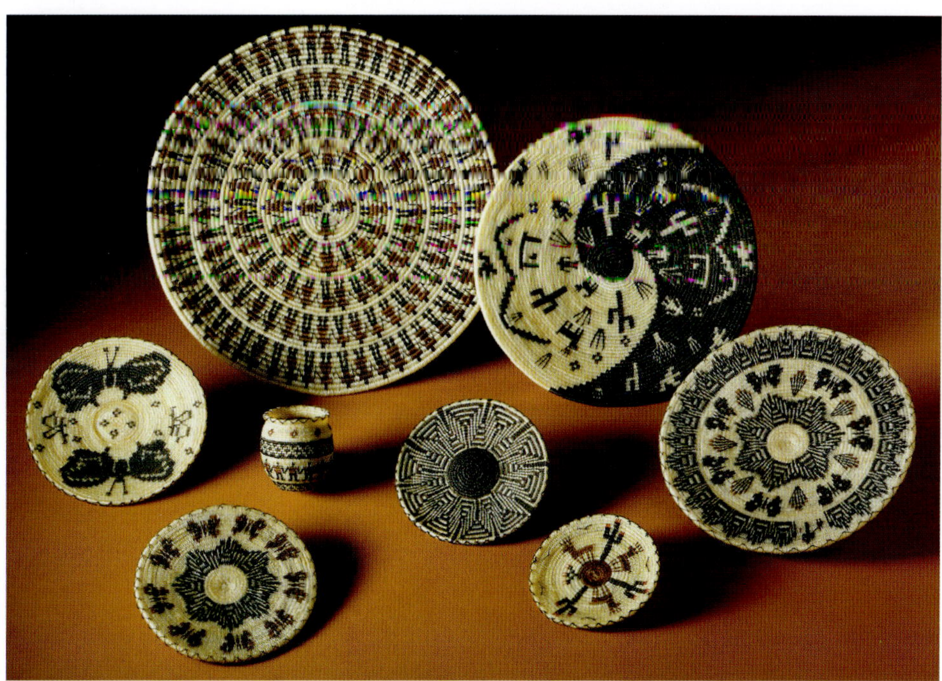

Tohono O'Odham miniature horsehair baskets. Top left: Leana Antone; top right: Elizabeth Juan; front row (left to right): Norma Antone, Linda Hendricks, Charlene Juan, Norma Antone, Rudy Thomas, Linda Hendricks.

an ingot, which was then hammered into shape. Once the silver was shaped, the parts were joined together by soldering and then lightly decorated with etched or **rocker-engraved** designs made with a sharpened iron tool (files, chisels, or **awls**). Later **sand** and **tufa casting** were employed to mold silver elements for the bridle decoration.

As time passed and the smiths' skills improved and better tools became available, the designs on the bridles became more elaborate. Bridle decoration evolved along with the jewelry styles being fashioned by silversmiths of the time. Navajo bridles were (and continue to be) constructed from buckskin, sometimes braided or plaited, and then much of the leather is sheathed in plates of silver—the more elaborate ones are incised with a row of **die** or **stamp** work and may have stamped or scalloped edging. Some plaited-rawhide bridles are decorated with silver buttons.

Almost every Navajo bridle has a silver **concha** on each side and a curved, tapering silver strap end. The conchas were decorated in a variety of ways, but typically have a scalloped-edge with stamped pattern. The plate that rested on the horse's forehead, called a frontlet, the central feature of the bridle, was usually rectangular in shape and sometimes curved to conform to the horse's brow; the frontlet is often embellished with stamp, **repoussé**, and **embossing** work. A wrought or cast silver crescent-shaped pendant, called a **naja**,

or another type of silver pendant usually hung from the frontlet, a fashion the Navajo originally adopted from Mexicans bridles, who in turn copied it from the Spaniards.

By the 1880s **turquoise** was used as a decorative ornament on Navajo bridles, and by the twentieth century it became more common. The stones were typically set in high-shouldered **bezels** in the center of the conchas, and sometimes on the frontlet and naja. By the turn of the century, Navajo-made silver-mounted headstalls were widespread and sold through trading posts such as Hubbell's.

HORSEHAIR BASKETS / very fine, **coiled** basket forms miniature in size, usually created with the **close stitch** method, made since the early twentieth century by the Tohono O'odham and Pima peoples of Arizona, from the hair of horses' tails and manes. The idea for using the material in baskets may have been inspired by horsehair bridles, **quirts**, and other equine accessories made by Tohono O'odham men. A technique that requires great skill, patience, and much time, horsehair baskets are generally woven in the form of tiny plaques, pottery shapes, and sometimes boxes. The designs vary from simple geometric shapes such as frets to more complex figures, **squash blossom** patterns, and **man-in-the-maze**. The tough, coarse horsehair provides an ideal combination of thinness and elastic strength, and is available in the natural colors of red, black, brown, and white. Both the foundation and sewing element are woven from horsehair. The material is relatively abundant and inexpensive, and much easier to obtain than **willow, yucca,** or **devil's claw** (the traditional materials used to weave Tohono O'odham and Pima baskets), especially for weavers living in or near cities today. High quality examples are frequent winners at various Indian art shows and markets held throughout the Southwest.

HORSEHAIR-FIRED POTTERY / a decorative ceramic technique discovered in the 1980s and used by some Pueblo and Navajo potters since then, in which individual strands of horsehair are carefully laid on the hot surface of a polished **clay** vessel as it emerges from the fire, after which the hair turns to carbon and singes or burns the surface, leaving black and/or gray streaks of residue in unique patterns. The technique is tricky, for there is a small window of opportunity when the surface of the clay pot is hot enough for applying the horsehair. How the technique was discovered is still being debated. Some believe it first happened when a woman potter at **Acoma Pueblo** was removing a hot piece of pottery from a kiln and her long hair accidentally fell against the pot leaving an interesting mark that led her to explore using the method for decoration. Others believe the innovation was borrowed from Euro-American potters working at Ghost Ranch near Abiquiu, New Mexico.

After much experimentation by potters, it was discovered that hair from a horse's mane should be used to create fine lines and hair from a horse's tail should be used to achieve thicker, bolder lines.

Over the years, both Native and non-Native potters have experimented with the technique. In addition to horsehair, they have used straw, feathers, pine needles, other types of animal hair, and human hair. Among the potters to use this method today are Jicarilla Apache/Hispano potter Felipe Ortega (b. 1951) and Hispano artisan Annette Morfin of Youngsville, New Mexico, both of whom incorporate horsehair decoration into their golden-hued or black **micaceous pottery**.

Navajo potters (who highly regard the horse) excel at making horsehair-decorated vessels; they create large numbers of different pottery forms (typically **greenware**) in buff, white, orange-red, sienna, and other hues embellished with black or gray horsehair striations.

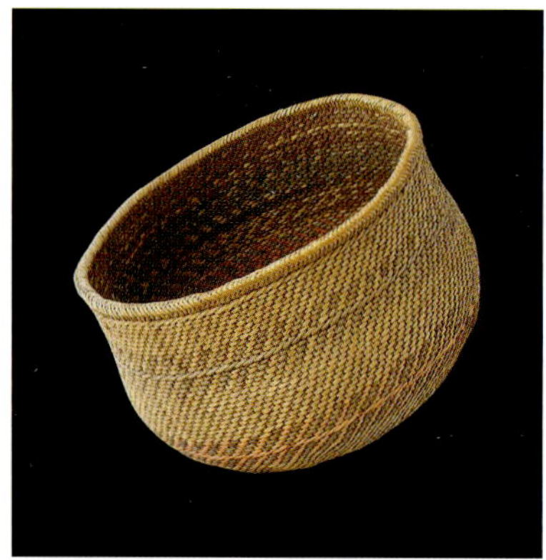

Hualapai storage basket, 1920s, sumac.

HUALAPAI BASKETRY / **twined** baskets of **sumac** twig **warps** and sumac splint **wefts** or **coiled** baskets of **willow** and **cottonwood**. By the early twentieth century, the Hualapais stopped weaving twined baskets in favor of the more saleable coiled baskets. This was due in part to Frances Calfee, a teacher who arrived in 1894 to open a school and encouraged Hualapai women to make coiled baskets for sale. The Hackberry railway station and shops at the Grand Canyon were outlets for their baskets.

By the 1930s the basket weavers increased their production of twined-sumac baskets—mostly small- or medium-size bowls—largely because they took less time to make and thus were more profitable. After experiencing a decline in the decades following WWII, in the late 1960s and early 1970s, Hualapai basket makers enjoyed a revival and once again created utilitarian twined baskets, including **trays**, conical **burden baskets**, and **water jugs**. The revival was encouraged by Mrs. Tim McGee, who taught a basket-making class in 1966 in Peach Springs, Arizona, and by the owners of a new store there. Twined Hualapai baskets are distinguished by their designs of simple rows of diagonal slashes or zigzags. These motifs are executed using sumac dyed with Rit dye for reds, oranges, and browns, and **devil's claw** for black. In recent years, the art of basket making among the Hualapai has come dangerously close to extinction.

HUBBELL TRADING POST / in Ganado, Arizona, nestled in a small valley along the banks of the Colorado Wash, this post was first owned by Clinton N. Cotton and then beginning in the late 1870s by Juan Lorenzo Hubbell, who ran it for over fifty years. Hubbell sold a variety of Native American artifacts; in 1902 he acquired a large inventory of Hopi (First Mesa) pottery from Thomas V. Keam, and for years supplied the curio trade with this pottery. Hubbell influenced the development of Navajo textiles by encouraging weavers to produce rugs with natural wool colors and a deep aniline red (see **Ganado Style**) and by hiring Anglo artists to paint examples of the earlier blankets and then hanging them in his post for the weavers to use as guides. The post remained in family hands until 1967, when it was purchased by the federal government as a national historic site. Today it is operated as a living history exhibit, where exquisite examples of Navajo jewelry, rugs, and baskets can be purchased within the well-preserved thick **adobe** walls of the post building. Hubbell Trading Post is also still the hub of Ganado, much like it was in 1876.

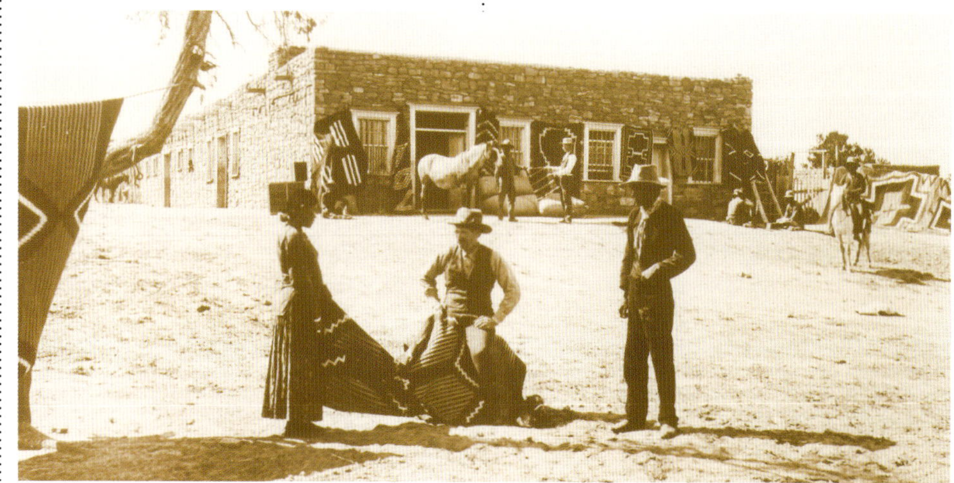

ABOVE: Juan Lorenzo Hubbell in front of Hubbell Trading Post. **RIGHT:** Painted rug designs commissioned by Hubbell.

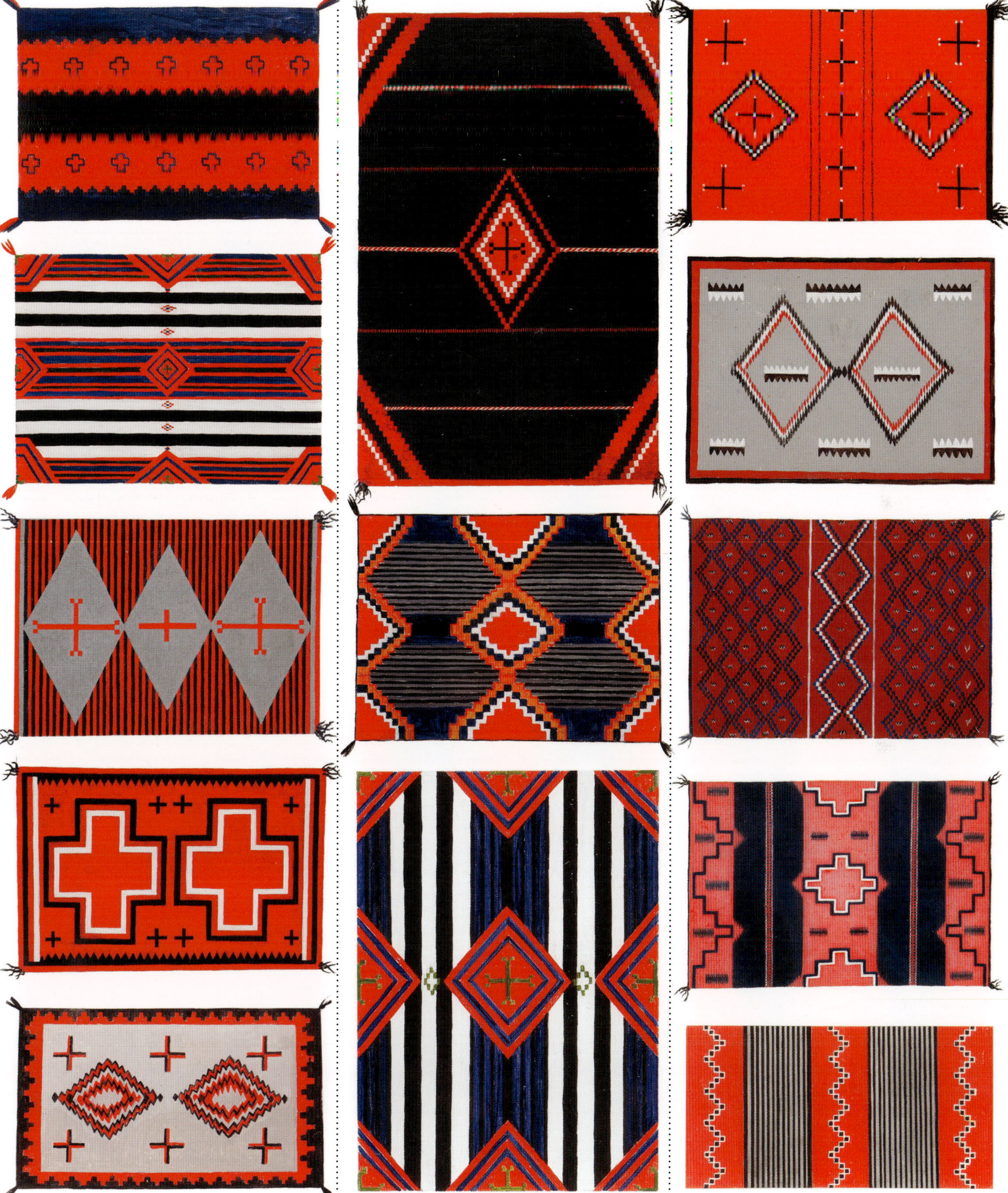

INCISING (Etching, Scratching) / a method of decoration in which the surface of a wood figure or piece of furniture, or piece of **silver** (or other metal) jewelry is scratched with a sharp tool to make closely spaced lines and designs. A similar process is used to decorate pottery, which is called **sgraffito**. In jewelry it was one of the earliest forms of decoration on Navajo silver bracelets, consisting of grooves made with files.

INDIAN ARTS AND CRAFTS BOARD (IACB) / established by the U.S. Department of the Interior in 1935 to promote and preserve Indian arts and crafts and foster their revival. IACB was founded in part due to complaints about machine-made and non-Indian made crafts being sold at national parks. Jewelry was the first art form to be promoted and protected. To identify authentic Native American jewelry from the imitation, the IACB established the stamping (with **dies**) of "U.S. Navajo" and "U.S. Zuni" on silver jewelry they deemed of superior craftsmanship, heavy in weight, and traditional in design. These marks were accompanied by numbers that designated the trading post or Indian school where the items were crafted. In some instances, items deserving of the stamp were just too small for the die.

INDIGO (Añil) / a natural blue **dye** ranging from almost blue-black to pale blue, obtained by processing the stems and leaves of the herb *Indigofera suffruticosa*, which is grown in Mexico and elsewhere. Indigo has been found in some AD 1100 prehistoric Mogollon sites. During the Spanish-Colonial period, it was imported into New Mexico in the form of lumps or cakes from Mexico and South America. It was (and continues to be) used by Hispano, Navajo, and Pueblo weavers to dye their own handspun **yarn.** For the Navajos, it was a popular trade item from the Spanish.

INLAY / method of jewelry construction in which designs are carved into **shell**, **silver**, gold, stone, or other materials and then set or "inlaid" with small pieces of stones, shells, and other fine materials. Jewelers at Zuni Pueblo, New Mexico, developed a technique of setting a decorative pattern of stones into silver referred to as **channel inlay**. Another type of inlay is more sculptural and comprises irregularly shaped stones

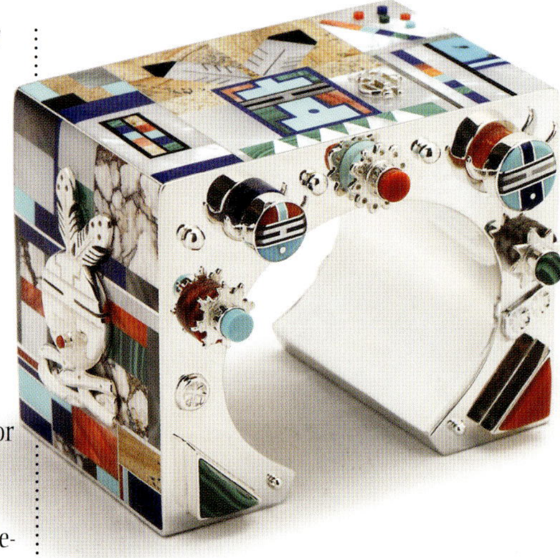

Benson Manygoats (Navajo), inlay cuff bracelet, 2009, sterling silver with intricate inlay (turquoise, coral, mother-of-pearl, lapis lazuli, malachite, and onyx).

that rise above the silver base. For example, Hopi jeweler Charles Loloma (1921–1991) created inlay bracelets in the 1960s and 1970s that feature vertical slabs of varying height of colorful non-traditional stones and materials—such as rosewood, lapis lazuli, malachite, fossilized ivory, ironwood, and **coral**. Today Native jewelers are creating remarkable inlay work. Among them is Benson Manygoats, a self-taught award-winning Navajo silversmith, who creates jewelry and boxes with contemporary, highly intricate designs inspired by traditional motifs such as rug patterns or **katsinam**. He cuts fragile gemstones into perfect geometric shapes for his inlay. See also **mosaic inlay**.

IRONWORK (Herraje) / an ancient craft consisting of techniques that have changed little over time, in which a special kind of malleable or wrought iron is heated in a furnace or forge, then hammered or chiseled on an anvil into shapes that are joined by hammer welding, riveting, or collaring. The early Spanish colonists who migrated to New Mexico in the late 1500s, in the Oñate expedition that included several trained blacksmiths, brought with them small hand-forged iron implements, tools, hardware, and other trinkets for their own use and to trade with the Pueblo people. Once established, the Hispano settlers used recycled old ironwork or iron in the form of bars and sheets imported from Spain to create tools, weapons,

Verma Nequatewa (Hopi), gold inlay bracelet.

horse gear, **crosses**, scissors, spatulas, *chispas* (strike-a-lights), and other vital utilitarian objects; they also hand-forged brass altar bells and copper **tobacco flasks**.

Throughout the colonial period, Santa Fe was the center of the blacksmithing trade in New Mexico. The blacksmiths who came to New Mexico in the early 1600s to aid in building the Franciscan **missions** taught Pueblo people how to work iron. By the mid-nineteenth century, blacksmith workshops had been established at pueblos and among the Navajos. Among the items made under the friars' supervision were hinges, candle snuffers, horse and mule bits, as well as crosses, church ornamentation, and church gates.

After the Santa Fe Trail opened in 1821, more bar iron was imported and ironworking flourished. At that time, animal tallow such as bear grease was used to protect the iron from water and corrosion. In the 1850s, a Mexican blacksmith at Washington Pass (now Narbona Pass, New Mexico) taught the first Navajo, Atsidi Sani, or "Old Smith," how to work iron. It is generally agreed among scholars that it was Atsidi Sani who later became the first Navajo silversmith.

During the Victorian era, decorative wrought iron was largely replaced by mass-produced cast iron. Toward the end of the nineteenth century, however, the **Arts and Crafts Movement** brought medieval crafts such as ironwork back into vogue. Then, in the 1910s through the 1930s, wrought-iron crafts experienced a renaissance, as a lavish amount of decorative iron—railings, window **grilles**, strap hinges, locksets for doors and gates, weathervanes, downspout straps, and lighting fixtures—was cre-

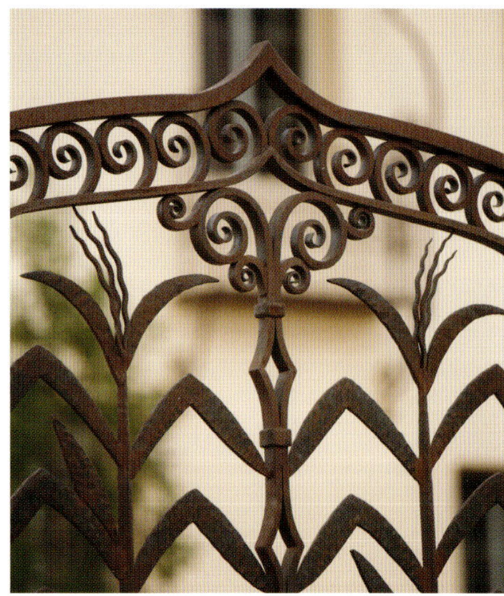

Wrought-iron gate with corn design, La Posada Hotel, Winslow, Arizona.

ated for **Spanish Colonial Revival–style** and **Spanish Pueblo Revival–style** homes. The ironwork was inspired by the increasingly widespread availability of photographs and drawings featuring traditional Spanish and Mediterranean architecture.

Wrought-iron fixtures were popular in early twentieth-century hotels as well; for example, architect Mary Elizabeth Jane Colter (1869–1958) hired Mexican and Indian craftsmen to make wrought-iron lamps shaped like **yucca** plants and smoking stands that resembled jackrabbits for La Posada Hotel, which she designed and built for the **Fred Harvey Company** at the railway station in Winslow, Arizona, in 1930.

Today blacksmiths in the region ply their trade by making a variety of hand-forged iron objects that are prized for their irregular, rustic, hand-worked appearance—including tools, branding irons, fireplace screens and tools, architectural hardware, ornamental work, and other household objects such as kitchen implements and cooking utensils.

JACÁL / Jacales (Wattle-and-Daub) / an early method of construction that evolved out of the **pit house**, built by Ancestral Puebloans of the Southwest by at least AD 1000. Dwellings of this type were built with sticks or logs that are usually five to eight inches in diameter, placed vertically side-by-side in a trench and capped by horizontal bond beams. The sticks/logs were filled in with earthen chinking, brush, stones, or **adobe** and often coated with adobe plaster on both sides. Roofs were either thatched or constructed of **vigas**, **latillas**, grasses, and firmly packed dirt, and sometimes with mud adobe. After the Spanish settled in New Mexico in the late 1500s, some Hispano residents of the region also adopted this building method. In addition, jacales were built by Pima, Spanish, and Mexican people in Arizona as temporary structures; they were the precursor to **Sonoran row houses** (built about 1850–1890). Like most of the region's earliest structures, few examples of jacales survive—these homes of mud and sticks eventually disintegrated into the earth from whence they came.

JACLAS (Zhocla, Jokla, Joclas) / from the Navajo word for "earring," a short loop consisting mostly of **turquoise** and/or **shell** disc **beads**, usually from three- to four-inches long, originally worn strung through pierced ears by Navajo men and women, now principally used for ornamental

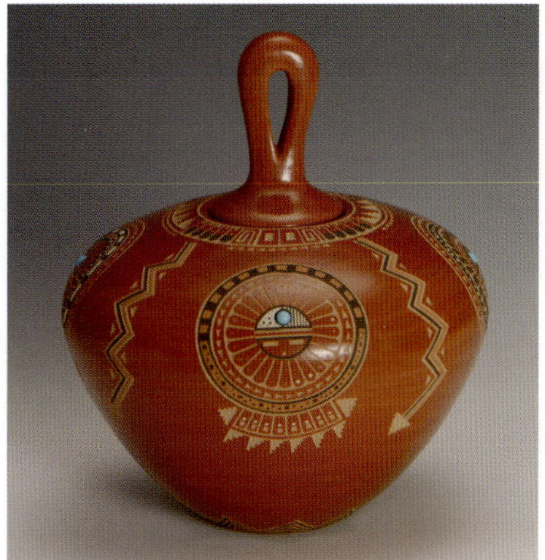

Ray Lovato (Santo Domingo), jacla with turquoise, red coral, and spiny oyster.

pendants on turquoise- and shell-bead necklaces. Most jaclas are tapered and have larger-sized or wedged-shaped red **spiny oyster** or white shell beads— called "corn" for their resemblance to corn kernels—strung at the bottom of the loop. Like beaded necklaces, the beads for jaclas are either drilled by hand or with a power tool and strung on cotton, silk thread, or braided nylon thread.

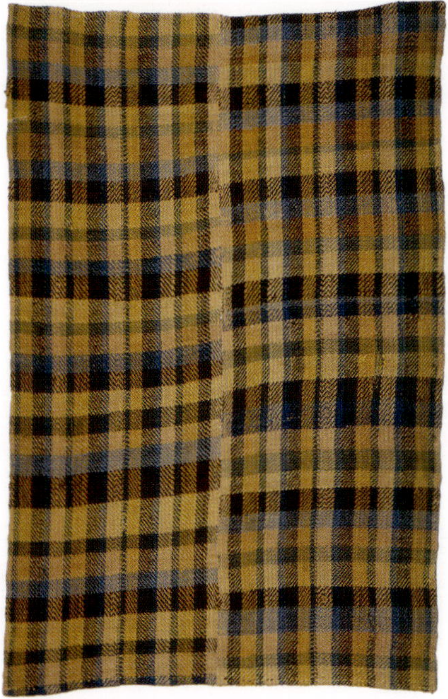

Glendora Fragua (Jemez), redware lidded jar.

JEMEZ PUEBLO POTTERY / once known for its painted fine-line, **black-on-white** designs (before 1700) and today known for a multitude of highly inventive pottery styles and forms. In the eighteenth and nineteenth centuries, Jemez relied on pottery made at nearby **pueblos,** for which they traded food and crops. Then, around 1900, recognizing the opportunity for a new source of income, potters began making vessels for the tourist trade, in which they combined elements of the classic styles of their ancestors with a variety of new ideas. These jars and other forms made in the early 1900s, with a thick, light-colored **slip** and designs painted in brightly colored poster paint, are known today as "revival" pieces.

Later, the craft was almost lost at Jemez, but by the late 1970s, the pueblo was experiencing an-

other dramatic pottery revival. Some made low-quality vessels from sun-dried clay decorated with poster paint, while others produced quality pottery using traditional materials and kiln firing. Currently, Jemez potters are continuously experimenting with design and form; they excel at making **melon pots**, **wedding vases**, vessels with intricate **sgraffito** designs, and **storytellers**.

JERGA / a coarse woolen cloth, usually **twill**-woven with a plaid or check pattern, made by Hispano weavers on a four-harness **treadle loom**, and used as a floor covering, under mattresses, for clothing, for blanket batting, and for wrapping cargo in the trade caravans that traveled the Santa Fe Trail. The material played an important role in the trade and economy of the Southwest. The earliest jerga consisted of a natural, undyed, white-and-brown wool yarn combination. When commercial dyes became available after the 1860s, synthetic shades of red, green, pink, and orange were mixed with the natural-colored and vegetal-dyed yarn. The tradition of using jerga as a wall-to-wall floor covering for the **sala** continued well into the 1930s in some of the more isolated villages of northern New Mexico. On their **upright looms**, Hopi weavers created similar check-pattern textiles that were used as a man's or boy's wearing blanket.

New Mexican jerga, ca. 1850, hand-spun wool with vegetal dyes.

JET (lignite, "cannel coal") / often mistakenly called a stone or mineral, jet is actually fossilized wood—a solid, durable type of lignite coal that is derived from wood subjected to chemical action in stagnant water and subsequently flattened by great pressures. In the American Southwest, it has been used since the prehistoric era, especially among Pueblo people, for certain types of jewelry and carvings. It has been mined for centuries in various places, including on Acoma Pueblo land and is therefore sometimes referred to as "Acoma jet." With its intense black color and capacity for high polish, jet has long been favored by Zuni Pueblo artisans for **inlay** jewelry and **fetish** carvings. However, it is difficult to work with, for it fractures easily. Some of the jet used by contemporary Zuni carvers comes from Pennsylvania and Africa. Jet is also used to make **heishi** beads by Santo Domingo jewelers. A variety known as "Silverado" jet, which produces a "gunmetal" sheen when polished, is mined in Colorado and used by some Zuni fetish carvers.

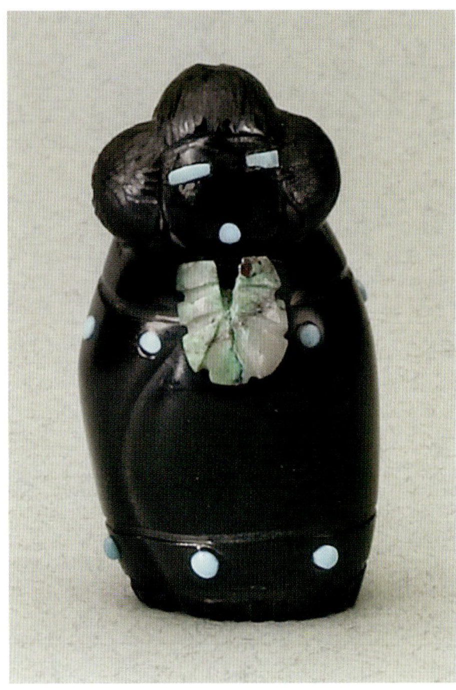

ABOVE: Gayla Eriacho (Zuni), Hopi maiden fetish, jet and turquoise inlay. **ABOVE RIGHT:** Jicarilla Apache basket.

JICARILLA APACHE (Indé) BASKETRY / an important part of the Jicarilla Apache's identity since at least 1500; the tribe's name means "little basket." Before the twentieth century, they made coiled utilitarian baskets of natural **willow** or three-lobed **sumac** splints, boiled with the bark on to create a soft amber finish or with the bark removed. In addition, tightly coiled water jars, coated on the interior with **piñon pitch** to make them waterproof, with braided horsehair handles and rawhide thongs for decoration, were also a common early basket form.

Established on a reservation in northern New Mexico since 1886, Jicarilla weavers have also traditionally made large, strong, thickly-**coiled** baskets characterized by bold colors and geometric designs. Nineteenth-century Jicarilla baskets, highly valued for their durability and decoration, were traded and sold to the Pueblo villages of New Mexico and to Hispano settlers in the region. In the early 1900s, Jicarilla basket makers made items specifically for the tourist trade, including hampers, wastebaskets, and fishing creels. The art of basketry almost disappeared completely among the Jicarillas, until it was revived by the establishment of a tribal museum and the Jicarilla Arts and Crafts Shop on the reservation. In the 1950s the Jicarillas revived the brightly-colored clothes hampers and waste baskets, popular with Anglo collectors and homeowners.

Today Jicarilla Apache artisans make a variety of coiled baskets using sumac or willow sewing elements and sumac foundations, in forms that range from shallow bowls (or **trays**) to water jars to wastebaskets to miniatures. For decorative patterns, the Jicarillas use natural vegetal **dyes** to create subtle colors on the sumac or aniline dyes for bolder colors. Mountain and **butterfly** designs are among the designs that appear on their baskets, both of which derive from the Jicarilla origin narrative.

Some Jicarilla Apache weavers, including Molly Pesata (a fourth generation basket maker), incorporate vertical lines of double-coiled overstitching in their traditional water jars. These ascending stitches are the "**spirit line**" that allow a basket maker's creativity to escape and not be trapped inside, and also may symbolize the "sun ladders"

that play an important role in the Jicarilla creation story. Baskets with spirit lines/ladders are usually not produced for the marketplace. Water baskets that are made for sale, however, are often rubbed with **kaolin** clay to give them an attractive white color.

JICARILLA APACHE (Indé) POTTERY / historically, the Jicarilla Apaches in northern New Mexico have been known for their pottery-making skills. Since at least the early 1700s, they have made utilitarian **micaceous** ware, using the traditional **coiling** and scraping technique and outdoor **firing** method. By the nineteenth century, Jicarilla Apache potters were particularly noted for their cooking vessels. Their pottery of this period shared many traits with the micaceous pots of Hispano potters living in nearby villages, as well as with the pottery produced at the neighboring pueblos of Taos and Picuris. Like the Navajos, Jicarilla potters have traditionally coated their vessels with **piñon pitch** immediately after being fired outdoors; the pitch seals the clay and makes it watertight. Unlike other Native potters of the region, however, Jicarilla Apache potters, who lived in relative isolation in northern New Mexico, were not strongly influenced by the tourist and curio trade brought to the region by the railroad beginning about 1880.

Pottery making went into serious decline at Jicarilla in the mid-twentieth century, but beginning in the late 1970s was revived by Lydia Pesata (b. 1942) and her family, and Felipe Ortega (b. 1951) of Jicarilla Apache and Hispano descent. Ortega taught many classes that inspired other Pueblo and Hispano potters in the region to work with micaceous clay. The Jicarilla Apaches are secretive about their sources for clay in the region. Still making the wares today, potters at Jicarilla tend to sign them "J.A.T." for Jicarilla Apache Tribe. Micaceous bean pots, teakettles, pitchers, cups, and other pieces are used by the Jicarilla Apaches regularly, as they have been for more than two hundred years. See also **pottery—Hispano**.

KACHINA / See **katsina**.

KAOLIN / natural white **clay** used by Native American artisans to enhance the white color of moccasins, wedding robes, and baskets, or for the surface of their pottery.

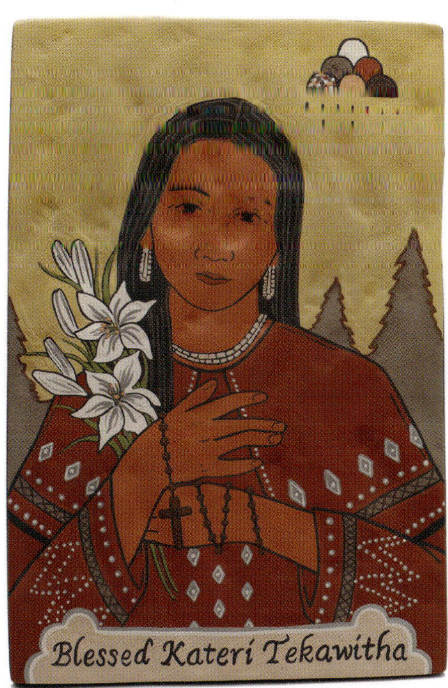

Jason Garcia (Santa Clara), Kateri Tekawitha, 2010, clay tile with natural slip paint.

KATERI TEKAKWITHA / a Mohawk woman (1656–1680) born to a Christian Algonquin mother and a Mohawk father in the Mohawk Valley in New York State, baptized a Catholic by a French Jesuit missionary in 1676, to whom many miracles are attributed, and the first Native American saint in the Catholic Church. Laid to rest in a tomb in her community of Kahnawake, Mohawk Territory in Quebec, Canada, Kateri was beatified on June 22, 1980, by Pope John Paul II. In December 2011 Pope Benedict XVI signed a decree approving a miracle attributed to Kateri. Her canonization took place at the Vatican in 2012. The miracle approved by the Pope involved Kateri's intercession on the behalf of a child in Washington state who developed necrotizing fasciitis, a flesh-eating disease. When gravely ill in the hospital, the boy's parish priest asked his family and other church members to ask Kateri for an intercession; soon after, the bacteria stopped spreading and the boy recovered.

It was reported that Kateri had a horribly scarred face since childhood from a bout of smallpox, but when she died her face cleared and she became beautiful. Known as the patron saint of ecology and the environment, she has been deemed "The Lily of the Mohawks," the "Fairest Flower among True Men," and "The New Star of the New World." She is typically portrayed as a young woman wearing buckskin clothing, holding a cross, and accompanied by blooming lilies. Shrines dedicated to her have been established near her birthplace, across Indian Country, and in the Basilica of the National Shrine of the Immaculate Conception, Washington, D.C. Her image also appears on many altars and in churches with a predominantly Native American congregation, such as the Saint Nicholas Indian Center in South Tucson, Arizona. In 2011 the Museum of Contemporary Native Arts, Santa Fe, New Mexico, presented an exhibition in her honor: "Soul Sister: Re-imagining Kateri Tekakwitha," featuring about twenty works of art portraying the Blessed (now Saint) Kateri.

KATSINA (pl. Katsinam) / the benevolent supernaturals or spirit beings who reside from early July to February on the San Francisco Peaks near Flagstaff, Arizona, where they "rehearse" dances. In Hopi belief, the term also refers to the physical form the katsinam assume when they come for the ceremonies that have been practiced for at least a thousand years in the **kivas** or **plazas** of many different pueblos in the Southwest, and to the Hopi wooden carvings that represent them (see **katsina dolls**). Although the katsina religion exists in all modern pueblos, it is most central to the Hopis. The katsinam, or ancestral spirits, serve as mediators between the gods and people.

The Hopis, who live on semi-arid mesas above the desert in northeastern Arizona, believe their survival as a people depends upon maintaining good relationships with the katsinam, inhabitants of the spiritual realm. They provide a place for the spirits to come and dance; during these occasions, the "father" of the katsinas (an older man in the village) feeds the spirits, sprinkling them with **cornmeal**, the spirit food. There are over two hundred different types of Hopi katsinam; the attire of each is highly elaborate and symbolic. Among them are Angwusnasomtaka (Crow Mother), Honànkatsina (Badger katsina), Hon (Bear katsina), Mongwukatsina (Great Horned Owl katsina), and Soyoko wuuti (Ogre Woman). Two of the major katsina ceremonies are Powamuya, or Bean Dance, in early February, and the Niman, or Home Dance, which takes place in mid-July each year and marks the end of the katsina season.

Katsina faces and figures have appeared in **rock art** dating back to the eleventh and twelfth centuries; as stone figures in the 1100s and as carved-wooden figures beginning about 1300; on Hopi pottery since about 1400; and on Hopi baskets since the late nineteenth century. Hopi artists today represent katsinam in paintings, as **gourd rattles and gourd banks**, on jewelry, pottery, baskets, and bronze sculptures, and on a variety of other items made for tourists, collectors, and the Hopis themselves. It should be noted that some Hopi (First Mesa) potters believe it is not ethical to use katsina designs on pottery, because during the firing process, the katsina is burned and one should not do such a thing.

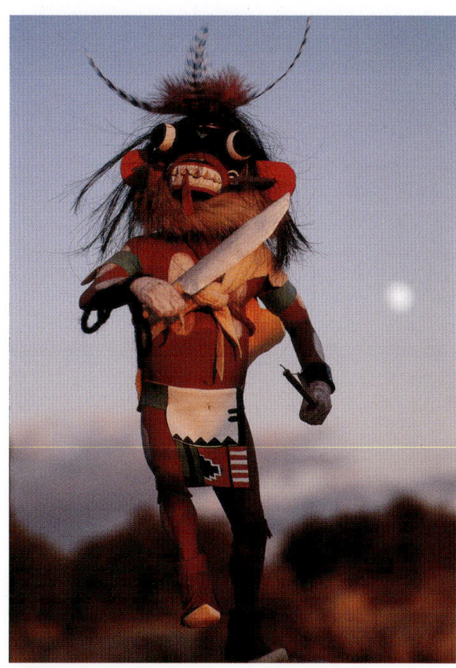

Hopi Ogre katsina doll.

KATSINA DOLLS (or Katsin Tihu, pl. Tithu) (Kachina) / personifications of **katsinam** (spirit beings of the Hopi world) called *paako* by Hopis—traditionally carved by hand by initiated Hopi men from the root of a **cottonwood** tree, sanded with a stone, primed with a thin coat of white **clay** (or **gesso**), and then painted with natural mineral and vegetal pigments. Some are also adorned with **feathers** on the top of the head. Formerly called "kachinas," the name changed to "katsina" about twenty years ago, as a more phonetically correct spelling of the word as it is spoken in Hopi. (There is no "ch" sound in the Hopi language.) A katsina doll is called *tihu* in Hopi. According to traditional Hopi culture, the *tithu* are carved by the katsinam themselves in their own likeness.

The dolls were (and continue to be) given to infants, and young boys and girls during the **plaza** dances as a teaching tool and as a religious

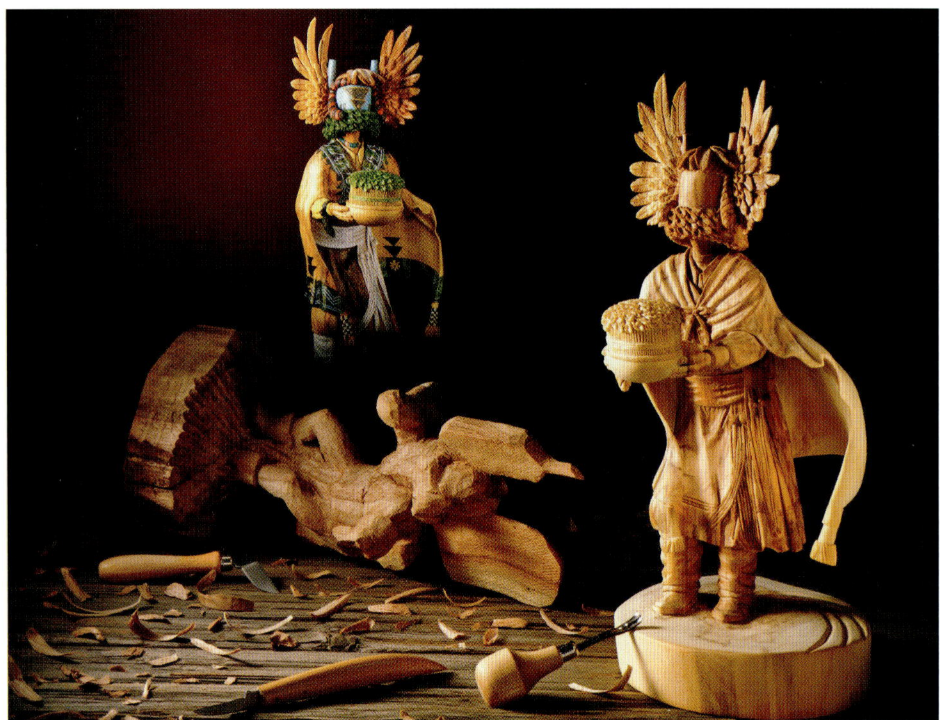

ABOVE: A "one-piece" katsina doll carved from cottonwood root in its early stages (left), a nearly completed carving (right), and a completed piece (in background), by Dennis Tewa (Hopi). **BOTTOM LEFT:** Hopi Motsin katsina, pre-1901. **BOTTOM RIGHT:** Larry Melendez (Hopi), traditional-style Hilili katsina.

item during a child's rite of passage. Katsina dolls are given, for instance, as special presents to girls during the Hopi Powamuya or Bean Dance, to encourage the girls to behave properly in the Hopi Way. They are also given to brides to denote their new special status. Originally, these figures were carved in the **kiva** during the weeks preceding the ceremony at which they were to be distributed. A child's first doll is usually a simple, flat doll (also called a cradle doll) representing Hahay'iwuti, the mother of katsinam, and as the child grows older he or she receives dolls that are more and more three-dimensional. The more realistic dolls have arms, legs, and other features.

As katsina dolls were intended to be played with, it was expected that they would eventually wear out and be discarded. The hanging of katsina dolls on the wall is a very old Hopi tradition; a string or leather strip was tied around the neck of the wooden doll for this purpose. Among the earliest Anglo collectors of katsina dolls were U.S. Army surgeons who came to Hopi in the 1850s. Many Hopi elders took a dim view of selling ceremonial dolls to outsiders; as a result, some carvers made dolls that combined symbols, costumes, and features of several katsinam.

By the early 1880s, when the Atchison, Topeka and Santa Fe Railway had reached northern Arizona, it had become acceptable and popular for Hopi men to make katsina carvings to sell to tourists. Eventually, carvers were encouraged to place the figures on bases and sign them on the bottom. Older dolls were largely simple, flat forms until the early 1900s, when shapes grew more complex and included rudimentary arms and legs, with the arms running down the sides and meeting in front (a type of katsina the Hopi sometimes refer to as "stomachache dolls"). From about World War II, the figures were carved in action, with a knee bent or a foot raised, and they began to be painted with commercial paints (such as tempera and poster paints) that allowed for brighter colors and more intricate details. This coincided with an increased interest in collecting katsina dolls and making them for sale.

Some modern Hopi carvers have experimented with new materials and tools, such as electric carving tools, acrylic paints, and yarn for the "ruff" that a katsina has around its neck. The 1970s saw the advent of the highly detailed, so-called "one-piece" carvings of katsinam; by the early 1990s older style carvings experienced a revival. More recently, carvers have created highly realistic, extremely detailed, and complex figures or multi-figure tableaus with elaborate bases. These wooden sculptures are often finished with color stains rather than paint.

Katsina dolls are also made by the Zunis, and occasionally by other Native Americans including the Navajos; the latter are considered folk art or by some scholars "fakes"—mere imitations of those made by their Hopi neighbors. Today, both the older styles and modern katsinas are carved in homes or studios by Hopi men, and some women, who have developed their own distinctive styles. Cottonwood has become scarcer, so the artisans have to travel farther afield to get it; in some instances, cottonwood root from hundreds of miles away is sold to Hopi carvers. For carving, artisans are using pocket knives, chisels, X-ACTO™ knives, and sandpaper; for painting they are using mineral or vegetal pigments gathered from the land, or poster paints and acrylics. Some katsina makers clothe their figures in fur, yarn, cloth, leather, and/or feathers. (Since the use and sale of feathers from migratory, song, and endangered or threatened birds was made illegal by federal wildlife laws in the early 1970s, carvers have used feathers from turkeys, starlings, or other common birds, or have carved the feathers out of cottonwood root.) Or, clothing is carved onto the doll and details such as the designs on the sashes are intricately painted. Those made for ceremonies are never signed, while those made for sale are usually signed. See also **Hopi plaques**, **mudheads**, and **Route 66**.

KEAMS CANYON TRADING POST / in 1875 Englishman Thomas Varker Keam purchased an established trading post in a canyon in northern Arizona (originally called Peach Orchard Spring and Keams Canyon by 1882), situated just east of the Hopi mesas and a few miles from the Navajo reservation. Keam became a highly influential figure in the historic development of both Hopi and Navajo arts and crafts, for which he provided a ready market. He was, for instance, one of the first traders to sell Hopi **katsina dolls**. In the mid-1870s he began purchasing large numbers for resale to museums as well as to private collectors. He also encouraged the production of **Hopi pottery**; in the 1880s he commissioned copies of several prehistoric pottery styles including **corrugated** and **Sikyatki**-style. Around the same time, he encouraged Hopi potters to hand-shape and hand-decorate slab pottery **tiles,** including those with old designs such as katsina faces. These were made strictly for sale to Anglo consumers.

Keam provided all his Native American artists and customers with much-needed goods for trade. He sold large collections of Native-made items to the Smithsonian Institution, the Field Museum, and the Peabody Museum. In 1889 the federal government bought Keam's original trading post to be used as a boarding school and Keam moved his operations to the mouth of the canyon, where he ran the new post until 1902. That year he sold the enterprise to noted trader Juan Lorenzo Hubbell. Since 1937 the McGee family has owned and operated Keams Canyon Trading Post.

KETOH (Bow Guard) / the Navajo word for bow or wrist guard, originally a plain strip of hide about four inches in width, held together by lacing, that was worn on the wrist and used to protect Native American archers from the snap of a bowstring. When metals—brass, **copper**, sheet tin, and finally **silver**—became available, Navajo silversmiths began attaching decorative metal plaques to the leather bands. In some instances a large shell ornament was attached to the band. By the 1870s ketohs with rectangular-shaped silver plaques were common; initially they were simply handwrought from tinned sheet iron, and later more ornate silver plaques were cast. Early on the silver was decorated with simple patterns impressed by a **cold chisel**, file, or primitive stamps. Later, they were embellished more elaborately with inlaid **turquoise** stones, intricate **stamp work**, and **repoussé** (the latter often

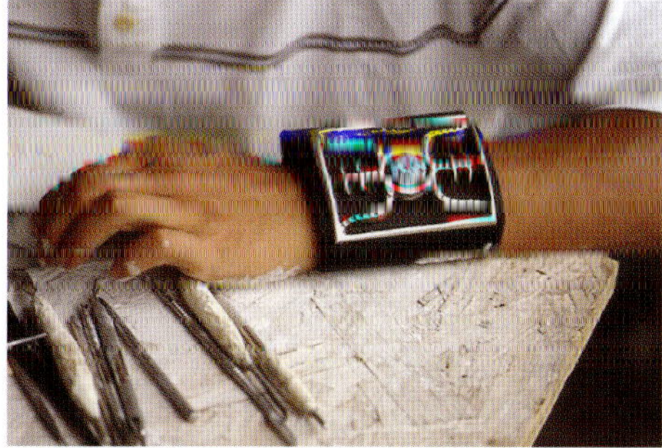

Mark Roanhorse Crawford (Navajo) wears a ketoh.

accented with a line chiseled around the design). Sometimes **buttons** might be fastened at one or both sides of the silver plaque. Long after their use as wrist guards ceased, ketohs continued to be made; they became an essential part of ceremonial dress for Navajo, Hopi, and Pueblo men. Today the ketoh is still an important piece of jewelry worn during ceremonial dances and other special occasions. They are also sold in the commercial and tourist markets.

KILT / a short, cotton, rectangular loom-woven cloth, with embroidered ends, still made by Pueblo and Hopi artisans today. They are worn on ceremonial occasions by men and boys and sometimes attached to a long pole and carried as a banner in ceremonies. Prehistoric examples of kilts were found in Hohokam and Sinagua burials in Arizona and appear on the figures in early Pueblo murals of New Mexico. Kilts are worn around the hips and extend down to the knees, with the embroidered ends meeting along the right thigh or sometimes in the back.

The design of Pueblo embroidered kilts has essentially remained the same since the late nineteenth century. It consists of a main or outer area with motifs (typically terraced triangle motifs said to represent clouds and stripes representing rain) worked in black, red, and green; a single black line separating the main area from the inner zone; an inner zone traditionally containing triangle-and-hook repeats or simple triangles; a bottom edge with small embroidered rectangles and pairs of broad green lines; and a narrow black braid is sewn on the border with slanting black stitches. The design is said to represent rain, while the white area of the kilt is said to represent a cloud.

The Hopis weave their kilts today from commercial cotton and embroider them with traditional designs. A Hopi boy's initiation kilt is called *kokom vitkuna*, worn by a young man when he begins to participate in ceremonies. Since the late 1800s, Pueblo dancers have worn kilts made from commercial cotton cloth embroidered with decorations.

KIVA / a circular, rectangular, or square chamber, often built partially underground, with **adobe** and stone walls and wood pilasters supporting a beam-and-mud roof. Kivas, accessed from the top by ladder, have been used at Hopi and Pueblo villages for religious ceremonies and some social occasions for more than 1,500 years. Kivas reflect structural ties to earlier **pit structures**, as well as the Pueblo peoples' spiritual connection to earth and the underworld. In the packed-dirt floor is a small floor pit called *sipapu*—a Hopi word for "place of emergence"—that represents the sym-

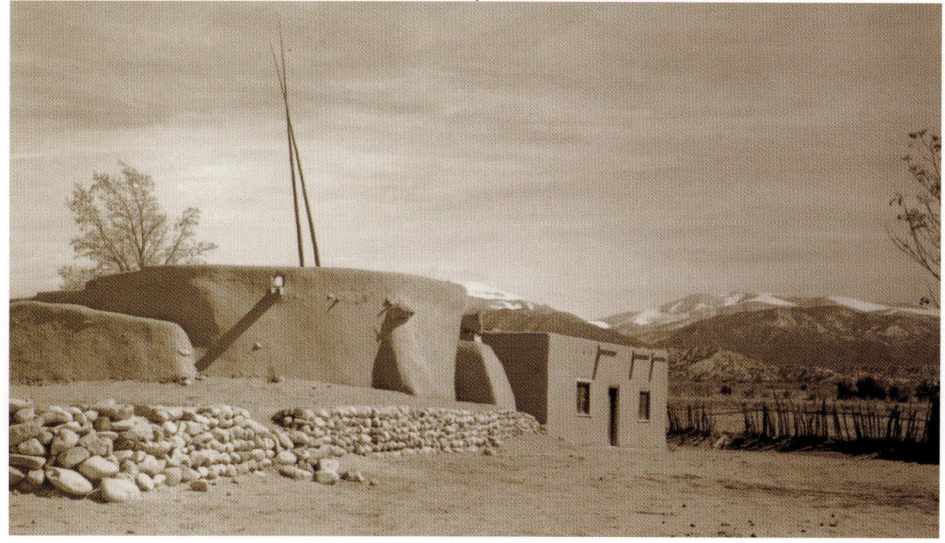

Kiva at Nambé Pueblo, New Mexico.

bolic place where the Ancestral Puebloan people emerged from the previous world into this one. Other features of early kivas are a fire pit, an encircling masonry bench on the interior perimeter, a ventilator for drawing fresh air into the chamber, and a stone or wood screen used as a deflector between the fire pit and ventilator. Historically, the number of kivas varied from village to village, and were used for **katsina** ceremonies, healing rites, prayers for rain, and other religious events, as well as for social purposes, such as weaving, preparing clothing and paraphernalia for ceremonies, and informal gatherings. Traditionally, the kiva (a Hopi word for "ceremonial room") is the place for the men to gather in; however, in the otherwise matrilineal and matrilocal Hopi society, women and children may be present during katsina ceremonies held in the kiva.

KIVA FIREPLACE / See **fogón**.

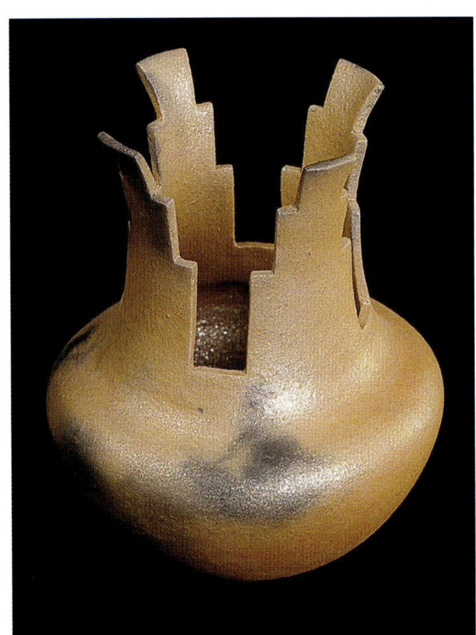

Angie Yazzie (Taos), kiva-steps pattern pot.

KIVA-STEPS PATTERN / a symbol of the **kiva** where religious ceremonies take place at the pueblos, kiva steps are often incorporated into Hopi silverwork, pottery, basketry, and textiles, and in ceramic cornmeal bowls made by Zunis. In addition, since the early 1900s, potters at Santa Clara Pueblo, Taos Pueblo, and elsewhere have created "kiva step" or ceremonial bowls with terraced edges, often with holes at the top of the terrace for the attachment of eagle feathers. Some Native Americans have also identified the so-called step pattern as "terraced clouds" or thunderheads.

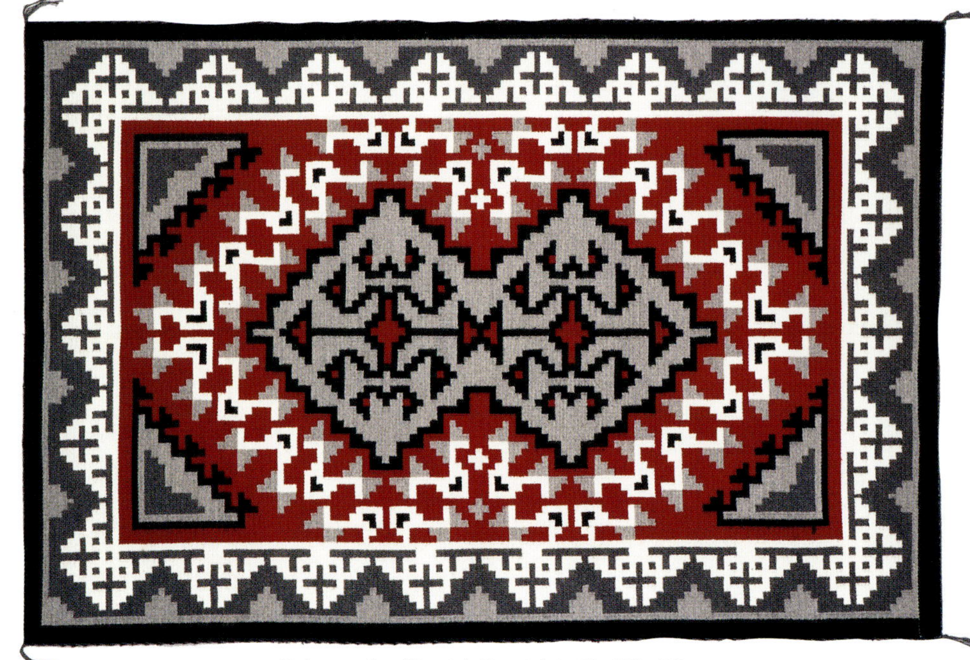

Katherine Nez (Navajo), Klagetoh textile, 70" x 47".

KLAGETOH RUG STYLE / named after a community in the south-central part of the Navajo reservation, twelve miles south of Ganado, near Defiance Plateau, Arizona, this style of rug usually has one border, features a dominant central motif of one or two diamonds, and primarily gray, dark red, black, and white **yarns**. Typically, natural and vegetal-**dyed** and aniline-dyed wool was used to weave these rugs. Originating sometime in the 1920s and still made today, Klagetoh-style rugs were sold at Klagetoh Trading Post, which no longer exists. Some scholars argue that Klagetoh is not a separate regional style, and consider **Ganado** and Klagetoh as one regional weaving area. In fact, there is no significant difference between Ganado and Klagetoh rug patterns.

Dave Chavarria (Santa Clara), knife sheath, 2005, tanned hide with beadwork, sinew, and tin tinklers.

KNIFE SHEATH / a covering made to protect the handle and blade of a knife from moisture and to keep the knife secure when carried, traditionally created by Native Americans in the Southwest. They are made from one piece of heavy tanned hide (usually deer) folded over and sewn together with **sinew**, often embellished on one or both sides with tiny glass beads sewn on with sinew, or sometimes painted with earth pigments. Also, they are decorated along the curved edge with rawhide fringe or tin cones (**tinklers**). The Southern Utes of Colorado and the Western Apaches of Arizona have made beautiful examples.

KNIFEWING (Knife Wing) / a Zuni Pueblo deity with outstretched arms or wings and legs set in a crouching position, wearing a terraced cap, that has appeared in **silver** and gem-set jewelry and boxes, sold by traders and popular with tourists since the late 1920s/early '30s. Today Knifewing figures are among the most prized and highly valued

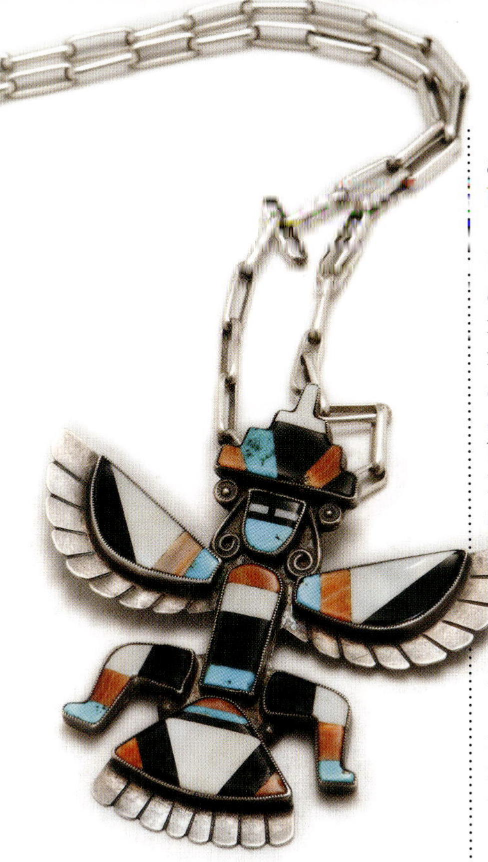

pieces of jewelry from that period, and continue to be made by Zuni jewelers and artisans of other Native cultures.

This mythical and religious form, believed to represent the War God or God of the Zenith, called Achiya:lataba by the Zunis, has a long history in Zuni culture. It was first documented by anthropologist Frank Cushing, who lived with the Zunis from 1879 to 1884, and who saw the form, along with **Rainbow God**, in the shield of the Zuni Bow Priesthood (or Bow Priest Society). Cushing described the figure as a god and hero of hundreds of folklore tales who is represented as possessing a human form with a tail and flint-knife feathers, a terraced cap (symbolizing his dwelling place among the clouds), and flint-knife weapon and bow of the skies (the rainbow).

Zuni artisan Horace Iule (ca. 1901–1978) is credited with fashioning the first Knifewing design in silver in 1928. His first attempt was made of wrought, cut, and filed silver; in 1930 he began casting the figure. The **Fred Harvey Company** adopted the symbol for various uses, including replicating it on their Indian Buildings (Albuquerque, New Mexico) and even on a set of their playing cards. In the 1940s post trader C. G. Wallace encouraged the casting of Knifewing figures by Zuni jewelers, and he pictured the figure on his own business card and stationery. The figure's popularity continued through the 1970s and '80s. Since then, the Knifewing has appeared on pins, necklaces, rings, pendants, buckles, and **bolo ties**.

KOKOPELLI (Humbacked Flute Player) / a name applied to a mystical male fertility figure portrayed with a humpback and playing the flute that appears in prehistoric rock art (both **petroglyphs** and **pictographs**), ancient ceramic wares (**Mesa Verde**, **Mimbres**, **Hohokam**, **Sikyatki**), and Ancestral Puebloan murals. The flute player—a simple stick or outline human figure usually shown in profile—probably first emerged about AD 500–700, in the Four Corners area of the Southwest, and by AD 1000 the figure had been etched or painted in rock throughout much of the region (Arizona, New Mexico, and Utah). As time went on, the figure became increasingly rare and by the Spanish **entrada**, in the 1500s, images of the flute player ceased to be made. The vast number of flute players created over a large area, and for almost one thousand years, indicates it was a significant figure in the prehistoric Southwest. However, the origin and meaning of the flute player in rock art is still debated among scholars and historians. He has been variously identified as a fertility symbol, roving minstrel, trader, rain priest, storyteller, hunter, trickster, and seducer of maidens.

It is likely the figure is a result of a merging of various myths, deities, and personalities that evolved over a thousand years or more. Among the possible associations is: Kokopölö, a Hopi **katsina** (or "spirit being") associated with the rain that brings good crops and with human fertility (he's usually portrayed with a "hump" believed to be full of seeds), and the Zuni legend about a flute-playing cicada known as Paiyatemu, whose "song" marked the beginning of the rainy season, a time of planting and a safe time to travel and be able to count on finding water. The flute-player of rock art is at times shown with animals, sun and cloud motifs, and abstracted figures. And he appears in a variety of poses: standing (sometimes with a cane or staff), sitting, lying on his back, running or dancing to his own music, hunting (and holding a bow and arrow), wearing a dramatic headdress or sporting horns like a ram, or even copulating. He is often depicted with a prominent phallus—a symbol of fertility. In recent times, for the sake of public decency, the figure has been "emasculated" in modern Native and non-Native works of art.

Kokopelli's humpback has been interpreted by some scholars as indicative of a physical abnormality that resulted from a disease, while others suggest it was not a humpback at all but instead was a basket that the figure carried on his back and related to the active trading network of the ancient Southwest. Whatever the origin and meaning of the figure, scholars agree that Kokopelli clearly served more than one culture and probably more than one purpose.

In addition to the hundreds of prehistoric flute-player images pecked into rocks across the Southwest, many contemporary Native artists of the region have portrayed the figure in their baskets, **overlay** silverwork (Hopi), paintings, textiles, and other art forms. Beginning in the late twentieth century, because the kokopelli is considered by many to be an iconic image of the Southwest and its Native cultures, a simplified, homogenized version of the figure has been, and continues to be, mass produced on everything from magnets to dish towels to t-shirts, thereby diluting the figure's significance.

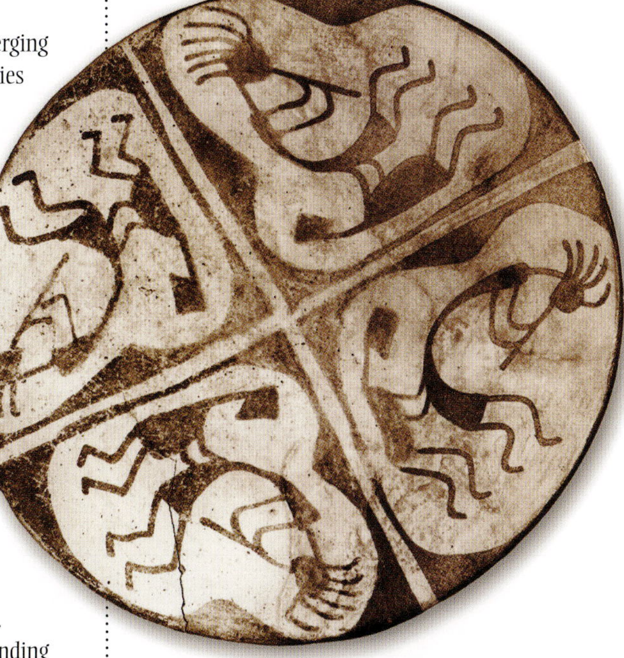

ABOVE: Hohokam red-on-buff plate featuring the flutist, kokopelli. **TOP LEFT:** Zuni Knifewing pendant, sterling silver with inlay (coral, turquoise, jet, and shell).

KOSHARES (Clowns) / ritual clowns known for their mischievous behavior, who appear in Pueblo and Hopi feast day ceremonies. Each linguistic group has its own name for them; for instance the Hopis call them Koyaala. These clowns sometimes appear at Hopi dances along with the **katsinam**. Traditionally, koshares wear black- and white-striped clothing, or paint their bodies with stripes of black (from soot or corn smut) and white (from **kaolin**). They also wear matching skull caps with conical horns and cornhusk tassles, and often their hair is braided. A similar type of figure has been found on ancient **Mimbres** pottery, thus suggesting the presence of similar ritual roles nearly one thousand years ago in southwestern New Mexico.

As sacred and profane figures, the Koshares' role is to entertain the audience at dances and ceremonies, as well as to instruct through comedy. Often they present an example of how *not* to behave. One of their favorite games is to play "toss and catch" with a watermelon. Sometimes their risqué and irreverent acts serve as social commentary. For example, they often mock the behavior of spectators, especially Anglos. Shown doing everything from riding bulls to eating

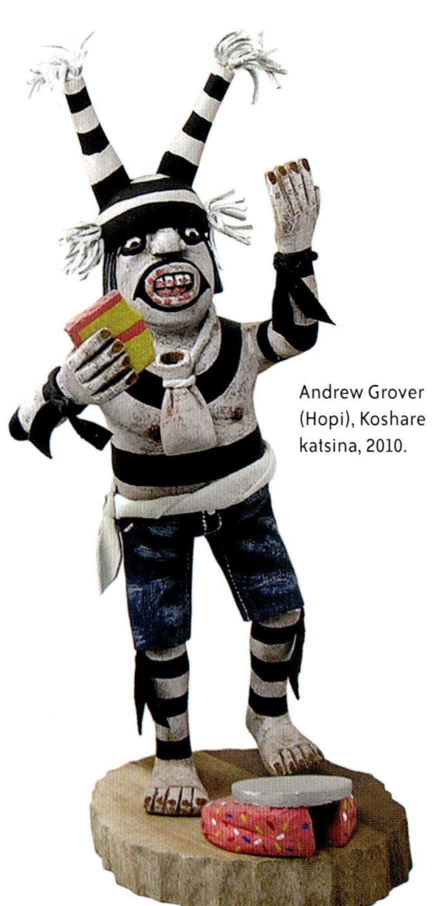

Andrew Grover (Hopi), Koshare katsina, 2010.

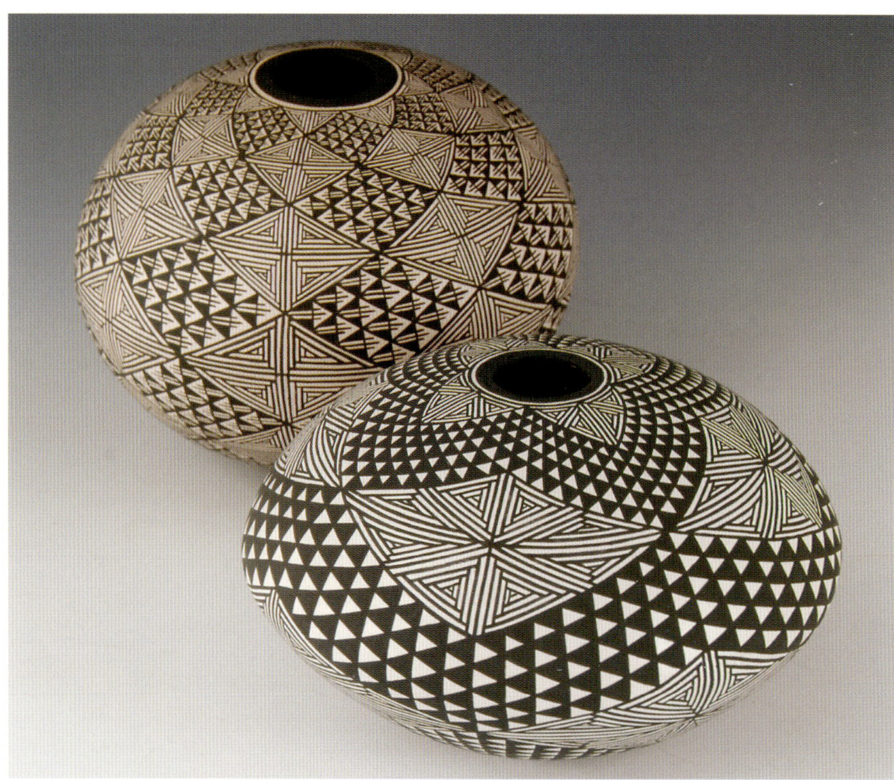

Roger Kasero (Laguna), pair of seed pots.

watermelon to shooting basketballs, the Koshares are one of the most frequently represented figures today in Pueblo and Hopi wood carvings, jewelry, ceramics, **quilts**, paintings, and other forms of art intended for sale. Among the well-known potters to make **clay** koshares is Kathleen Wall of Jemez Pueblo; she uses natural clays under glazes, kiln fires her work, and sometimes uses acrylic paints to decorate them.

LAC / the term commonly used for a crimson-red dye derived from a sticky resinous substance secreted by the female scale insect, *Tachardiella larrea* (related to the **cochineal** beetle). Navajo and Pueblo weavers **raveled yarns** dyed with lac (and cochineal/lac combinations) from imported cloths such as **bayeta** and rewove these fibers into their own blankets. The earliest lac-dyed yarns found in Navajo textiles date to about 1800; by 1870, after the invention of **synthetic dyes**, its use was obsolete.

Lac secretions were also collected from the surface of creosote-bush branches in the desert Southwest and used as an adhesive. When the secretions or encrustations of lac "scale" are heated, it softens to a plastic state and can be used as a bonding material. When it cools, it is hard and impenetrable. Early Native Americans used

lac to mend pottery, to waterproof baskets, and to inlay **turquoise** chips, **shells**, and other natural elements onto shells.

LAGUNA PUEBLO POTTERY / as at other pueblos in New Mexico, early potters at Laguna created **glazeware** clay vessels (for utilitarian and ceremonial purposes) and by 1700 began decorating their wares with paints that fired to a **matte** finish, producing **black-on-white** and **polychrome** (typically black and red or black and orange on white) pottery with designs ranging from simple to highly complex (including cross hatching, geometric shapes, plant forms, and figures).

Much later, about 1870 to 1880, modeled-clay animals were made at Laguna. Also around this time, potters increasingly made small, inexpensive wares for the tourist market. After 1880, when the Santa Fe Railroad reached Laguna and a station was built there, potters sold their wares directly to train passengers. In 1899 Josephine Foard moved to the pueblo to help the potters improve their wares; she encouraged them to glaze/waterproof the interiors of their vessels.

During the 1930s and '40s, potters sold small pieces with traditional motifs alongside

Route 66, which crossed Laguna lands.

The craft declined severely at the pueblo in the early to mid-twentieth century; its revival, in the early 1970s, is credited to Evelyn Cheromiah (b. 1928), who researched historic techniques/designs and taught the craft to others at the pueblo (including her daughter, LeeAnn).

Among the prominent potters working at Laguna today are Gladys Paquin (b. 1936) and her son Andrew Padilla (b. 1956), Thomas Natseway (b. 1953), and Max Early (b. 1963). Most carry on the historic methods of using local clay tempered with crushed rock or **potsherds**, as well as natural paints (red clay for red, wild spinach for black, and clay for white). Both kiln-firing and outdoor-firing techniques are used.

LAPIDARY WORK / the highly technical and labor-intensive art of cutting and setting of stones in **silver** or other metal; usually for jewelry forms. Native American artisans of the Southwest, especially at Zuni Pueblo, have long been known for their lapidary skills. Early on, the primary stone used by the Zunis in their jewelry was **turquoise**—a stone that was venerated by the Pueblo and assigned a vital place in their religion and mythology—that they cut, hand-polished, and set into silver bezels. Eventually, the Zuni smiths set pre-cut and pre-polished stones that were acquired from trading posts in the region, resulting in designs dictated by the size and shape of those stones.

Also, the Zunis originally used simple hand-held tools. Beginning in 1950, when electricity was brought to the village, motor-driven wheels and diamond-tooth saws could be used, vastly improving Zuni fine lapidary work. Today many artisans cut their own stones and thus have greater control over their designs. Now that they are no longer dependent on traders for tools and materials, Zuni silversmiths are free to explore different designs and a wide range of new materials such as diamonds, gold, malachite, lapis lazuli, rubies, and other precious and semi-precious stones. Navajo and Santo Domingo artisans are also well known

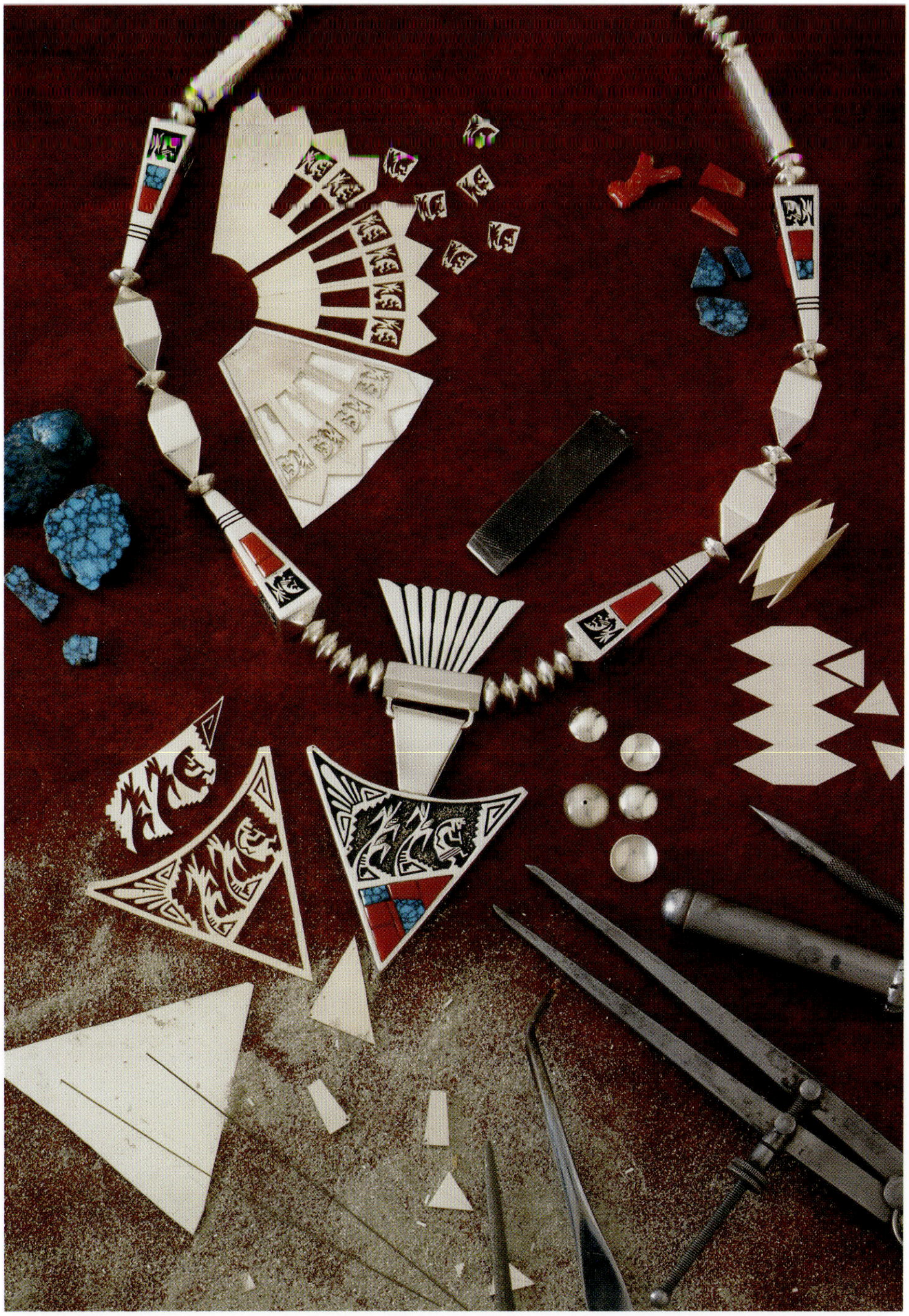

An example of lapidary work by Alvin and Lula Begay (Navajo). The finished necklace with reversible pendant combines the techniques of overlay, granulation, fabrication, and mosaic inlay. Components of a matching piece demonstrate the process of overlay. The handmade stamp used is shown directly above the pendant.

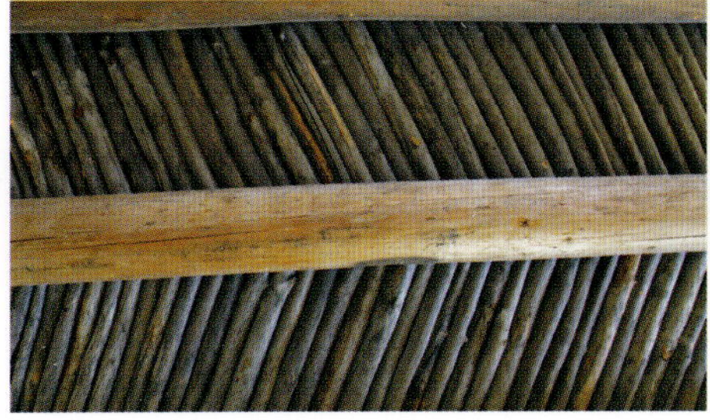

Detail of latillas on a ceiling.

for mastering lapidary work. See also **inlay**, **Navajo silverwork**, and **Zuni Pueblo jewelry**.

LATILLAS / slender peeled logs, branches, or wood saplings (1½ to 2 inches in diameter) that are placed across **vigas** (wood beams) to form the ceiling and support the flat earthen roofs of **adobe** structures. The latillas are laid perpendicularly across (on top) of the vigas, or diagonally to form a herringbone pattern. In New Mexico, the poles usually come from aspen trees; in Arizona, **saguaro ribs** or **ocotillo** branches are more common. Still used in the ceilings of Southwestern homes today, latillas have become primarily decorative rather than functional. See also **coyote fences** and **living fences**.

LAZY LINES / a visually subtle diagonal break or joint in solid color areas of the weave of most Navajo and some Zuni textiles, so-called because it is a labor-saving technique that allows a weaver to build up wedge-shaped sections of a textile and avoid having to weave the entire width of a fabric all at once. The break marks the line along which the independently woven sections meet.

LEATHERWORK (Buckskin) / in the Spanish Colonial period, and through the nineteenth century, Native Americans and Hispanos (who adopted the practice from Pueblo and Plains people) depended on animal hides—deer, elk, and buffalo—for fine leatherwork or buckskin clothing and other utilitarian items, including saddles and other horse gear; shields, coats, shirts, jackets, leggings, and moccasins; and chests, boxes, sacks, and bags. Some of the buckskin clothing and other items were embellished with hide fringes, glass beads, pieces of woolen cloth, and embroidery designs of cotton thread. In most instances, the early Hispano settlers in the region initially relied on the Native Americans to provide them with raw and tanned hides. For instance, they used and reused Indian painted rawhide—**parfleches**—for traveling cases for **santos,** grain sacks, document pouches, and other utilitarian purposes. Franciscan missionaries reused pieces of early painted Plains Indian rawhide to make bindings for church records and Hispano artisans used hide as a painting surface in lieu of canvas throughout the colonial period.

Eventually, the Hispanos learned from the Pueblo Indians the indigenous method of brain-tanning to make soft, supple buckskin for clothing and footwear. They made hide moccasins which they called *teguas,* after the Tewa Indians from whom they were adopted. Hispano leatherwork in turn influenced Native Americans: Apaches and other tribes adopted saddles and other leather horse gear and protective clothing worn by Spanish soldiers (such as the sleeveless buckskin coat called *cuera*); they decorated soldier's hide bandolier bags with silver **buttons** and **beadwork**; and were inspired to copy the braided-leather traveling chests (*petacas*) of the Hispanos by constructing similar items out of rawhide, wood, and woolen cloth. Pueblo people of the region made certain ceremonial items from hide; among the more important were (and continue to be) wooden **drums** stretched with hide.

"Lazy line" (detail of Navajo saddle blanket), early 20th century, handspun wool with natural and commercial dyes.

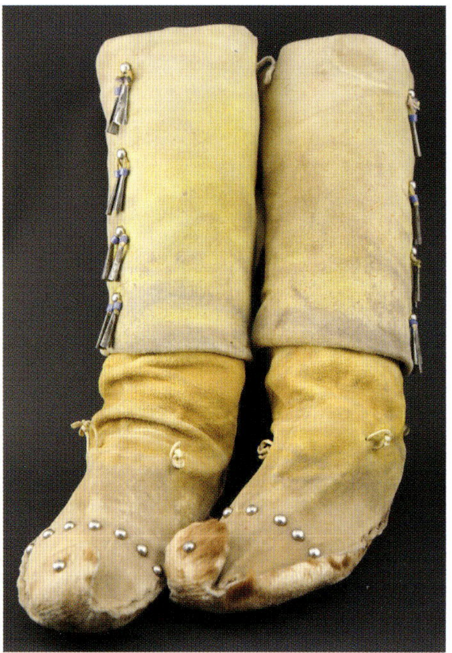

Apache leather "Cactus Kickers" moccasins, ca. 1940.

LEDGER DRAWINGS / a term referring to nineteenth-century drawings of graphite or colored pencils, ink, or watercolor rendered on the lined paper of account books, made by Plains Indians in the western United States. Today the term has become shorthand for all drawings done on paper by Native Americans, even those done on unlined paper in notebooks or artists' tablets, on ordinary lined writing paper, and on antique invoices or other historic documents. Among the subjects portrayed in the historic ledger drawings of Plains Indians and other Native peoples are warfare, significant events in the tribe's history, scenes from daily life, and nature studies. Today many contemporary Native American artists have been inspired by these historic ledger drawings to draw or paint on antique lined-paper again; some portray images that are social commentaries.

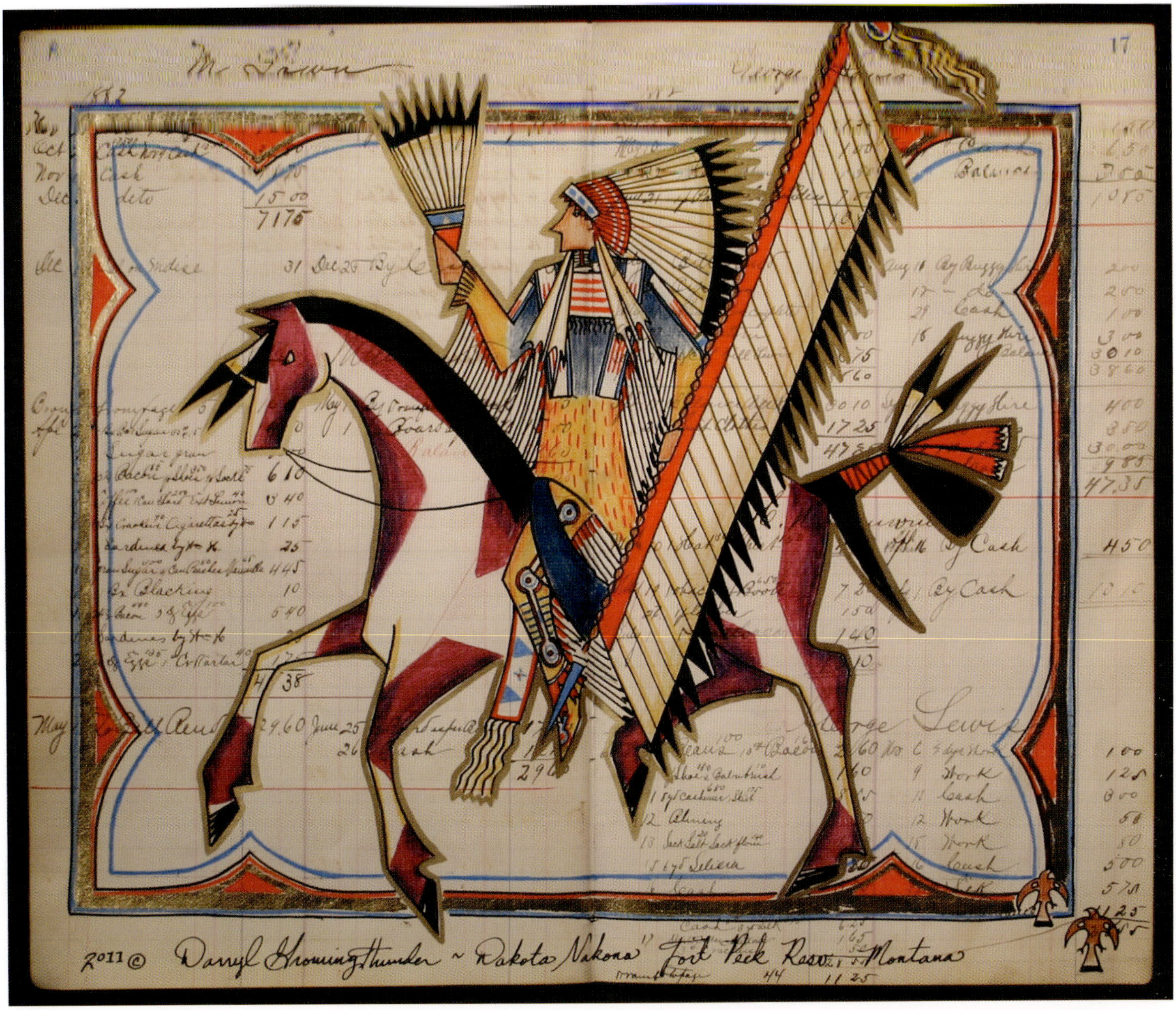

Darryl Growing Thunder (Assiniboine/Sioux), "Leading the Way," 2011, contemporary ledger drawing, colored pencil, India ink, and metal leaf on vintage lined paper.

LINTELS / horizontal beams that support the weight of the wall above a window or door. In the Southwest the term refers to the horizontal, rough-hewn wooden beams placed for support above windows, doors, or other wall openings, which are left exposed and sometimes hand-carved and/or painted with various designs. The lintel- (or post-) and-beam building system—two vertical posts supporting a horizontal beam—is one of the world's oldest construction techniques.

LIQUID SILVER / a jewelry technique in which necklaces or bracelets are created from very thin,

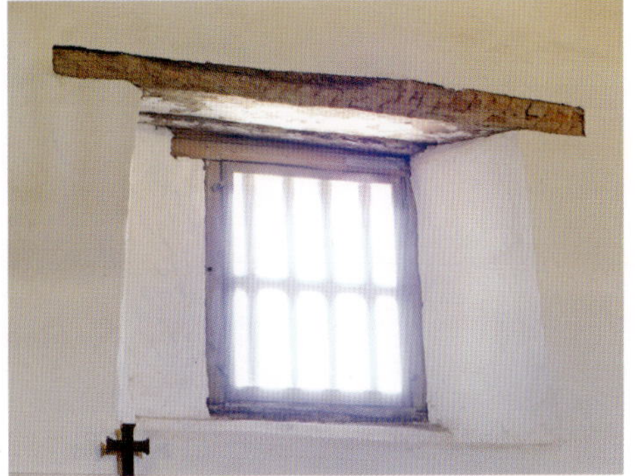

Hand-adzed wood lintel over window.

fine, small commercially extruded cylinders (or tubes) of sterling **silver** strung on catgut. Today the cylinders are more often strung on fine wire. They are named for the "fluid" appearance of the tiny beads. Invented and perfected by Ray and Mary Rosetta of Santo Domingo Pueblo around 1958–59, the technique involves cutting sheet silver into long, narrow bands and then scoring a channel down the middle so each strip can be folded over, leaving a hollow center. Then the folded lengths are hand pulled through smaller and smaller holes in a drawplate until the required size is achieved. These tiny tubes of silver are cut into miniature **beads**, then the ends of each bead are polished and smoothed ready for stringing. Small-diameter, silver, tubular beads were incorporated into **coral** and **turquoise** bead necklaces before the 1950s, but no one had ever handcrafted an entire necklace from these beads nor made such fine ones. The Rosetta children have carried on the tradition by making liquid-silver-bead necklaces, which typically include twelve beads per inch. Very few artists make hand-pulled silver today; the majority of liquid silver is manufactured.

LIVING FENCES / a style of enclosure made by Native peoples of Arizona, consisting of **ocotillo** branches placed in the ground, side by side, and watered so the branches take root. These fences were used as an effective barrier against rodents and burrowing animals such as rabbits that tried to invade Native gardens. The term "living" refers to the ocotillo branches that have re-rooted and begun to grow again.

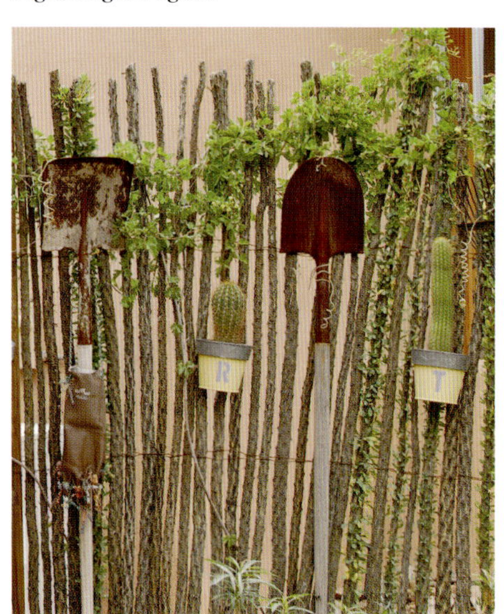

LOOM / Backstrap (Waist Loom, Belt Loom) / used for narrow fabrics such as belts or sashes, it consists of two sticks about 1½ to 2½ feet long between which **warps** are stretched; one end is fastened to a strap around the weaver's waist and the other end is fastened to a tree, wall, or other object. The weaver begins work at the waist bar and winds the finished cloth around it as necessary, to keep the unfilled warps within easy reach. This indigenous loom form was used by prehistoric weavers when making narrow cotton fabrics. Today it is still used by the Navajos, Hopis, and other Native peoples of the region to weave belts

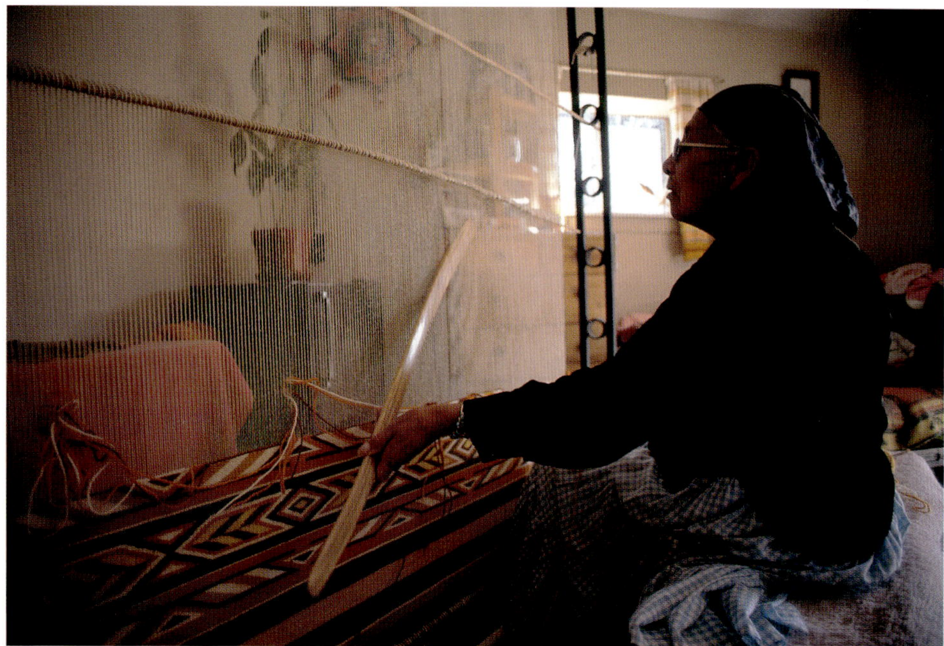

Glenibah Hardy (Navajo) weaves on an upright loom.

and sashes worn primarily on ceremonial occasions. See also **rain sash**.

LOOM / Horizontal (Treadle, Telar, or Floor Loom) / a massive horizontal loom of European origin, brought to the New World by Spanish colonists in the late sixteenth century; this loom is larger, less portable, and more mechanized than the upright indigenous loom of the Southwest (see next entry). This important tool made the weaving of almost infinite lengths of cloth possible. In New Mexico, horizontal treadle floor looms (known as a *telar*) were locally constructed of ponderosa pine or **cottonwood**. They were largely used by men in Hispano households, in the tradition of the regulated cloth guilds of old Spain. However, when milled lumber was brought over the Santa Fe Trail and sawmills were established in New Mexico in the 1850s to 1860s, looms could be made with smaller frames, making them more suitable for women. In rare instances, Native American weavers have adopted the horizontal loom; some **"slave"** or "servant" blankets were woven on this type of loom and some contemporary weavers (such as Ramona Sakiewtewa) have used them.

In the horizontal loom, foot-powered treadles, or pedals, are used to move an overhead system of semi-permanent heddles strung onto harnesses (or wood beams), separating individual **warp** threads from each other, and freeing the hands

to manipulate the **weft**. The warps were passed between the dents of a reed, used to space the warps and to beat the weft into place. The width of the fabric was constrained by the structure of the treadle loom and its reed; the length, however, was not constrained in any way. Weavers usually stand in front of this type of floor loom; as the textile is woven, it is wound progressively around a front beam near the weaver's knees. When the fabric is finished, it is cut from the loom, and the warp ends are knotted together to form a fringe at each end of the piece, or run back into the fabric. See also **Rio Grande textiles** and **Chimayó textiles** and the photograph on page 4.

LOOM / Upright (Vertical) / an indigenous loom form used since prehistoric times by Native peoples of the Southwest, originally made by setting two wood posts in the ground and two cross-pieces or braces lashed to the posts, used to weave various textiles including wearing and utility blankets, dresses, **mantas**, **sarapes**, breechcloths, shirts, and **belts**, and later rugs and **tapestries**. The length of the **warp** is limited to the distance between the upper and lower bars to which the cloth and yarn beams are secured.

Navajo weavers sit on the ground in front of the loom and roll the completed work onto the lower beam to maintain a consistent height. On some old Navajo blankets, a row of puckers on the surface indicates a place where the weaver had rolled down the blanket and sewed it to itself to maintain tension on the warps.

The warp sets are controlled by a string loop heddle and a shed rod that are manipulated by hand, and the **weft** is tapped into place with a wooden weaving comb or long wooden, sword-shaped batten. The Navajos use a weaving comb—considered a treasured heirloom that is passed down from generation to generation. Early Pueblo weavers typically used frameless looms that were often anchored into the floor, walls, or ceiling of a room.

The Navajos, who learned to weave from the Pueblos in the last half of the seventeenth century, generally used trees for steadying outdoor looms; later they built portable, free-standing frames of lumber and metal pipes. Selvages neatly finished with twined (or twisted) edging cords, often with knotted or braided tassels at each corner, are typically found in Navajo and Pueblo textiles made on this type of loom. In addition, **lazy lines,** a result of sectioned weaving, are often found in Navajo textiles made on upright looms. See diagram on page 187.

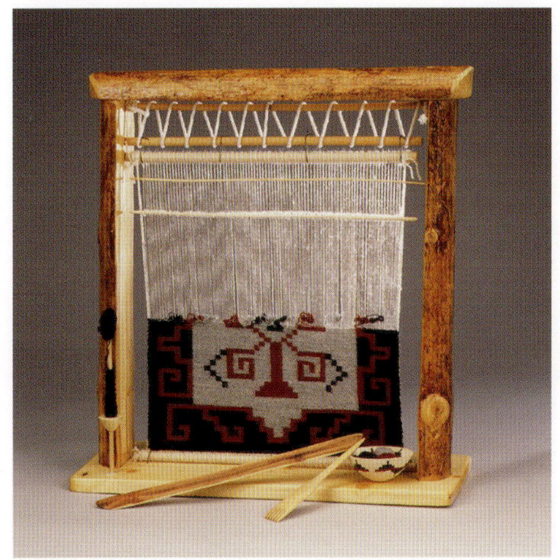

ABOVE: Katherine Cleveland (Navajo), loom sampler.
RIGHT: Luminarias (farolitos) along a street in Santa Fe, New Mexico.

LOOM SAMPLERS / miniature wood looms with small incomplete **tapestries** still attached, sold from 1890 to the present. First sold by reservation post traders, these popular tourist curios may be purchased at a variety of stores and galleries in the Southwest, and directly from the artisans. They serve as illustrations of the traditional weaving process and often include a doll seated before the loom engaged in weaving.

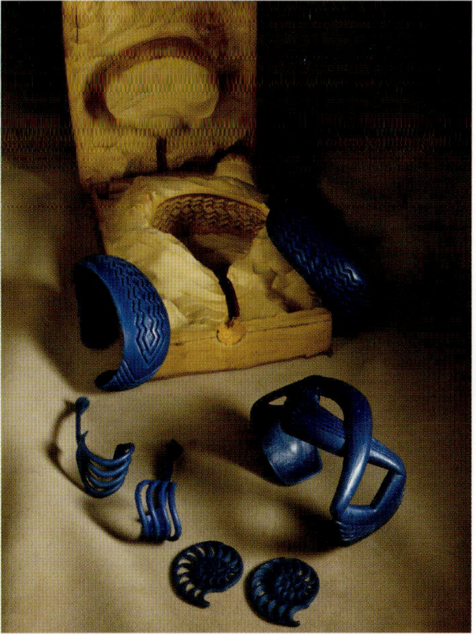

Mold and wax models used by Harvey Begay (Navajo) in the lost-wax process.

LOST-WAX CASTING (Cire Perdu) / a traditional jewelry technique in which a wax model is used to create a mold from which the wax is melted away and molten metal poured in to create the final piece. The method has been used for one-of-a-kind works, as well as multiple copies. Some contemporary Native American artisans have explored new uses of this ancient technique. For instance, some of Hopi jeweler Charles Loloma's (1921–1991) lost wax-cast rings are comprised of free-flowing shapes that are very different from traditional Native American jewelry.

LUMINARIAS / farolitos / terms used in parts of the Southwest for lanterns comprised of candles anchored in dirt- or sand-filled paper bags (usually beige in color, folded at the top, and sometimes featuring punched designs) that are set along pathways, roadsides, and on rooftops during the Christmas season. For some the lanterns are a time-honored tradition meant to welcome the Christ Child into the world or to guide His spirit to one's home, while for others they are merely festive, secular decorations. They are sometimes used for religious processions, such as the one held on the feast day of **Nuestra Señora de Guadalupe**, on December 12, in Santa Fe, New Mexico, at the church named in her honor. Usage of these terms varies according to region. For instance, in Albuquerque and southern New Mexico and in Arizona, the word luminarias from the Spanish *luminaria*, meaning "illumination" and/or "festival lights," is the preferred term. In Santa Fe and northern New Mexico, the lanterns are called farolitos, from the Spanish *farolito*, or "little lantern." In this region, the term luminaria refers to a pile of split logs stacked in a square and set ablaze; some local historians believe these small bonfires are a Spanish tradition that dates back to the early 1600s in Santa Fe and were meant to guide the way for the Wise Men from the East seeking their Newborn King, or to guide people to Midnight Mass. Today luminarias/farolitos are also made commercially and consist of plastic beige-colored, bag-shaped containers with electric lightbulbs inside. In addition, some Hispano artisans in the region make **tinwork** luminarias/farolitos with punched designs.

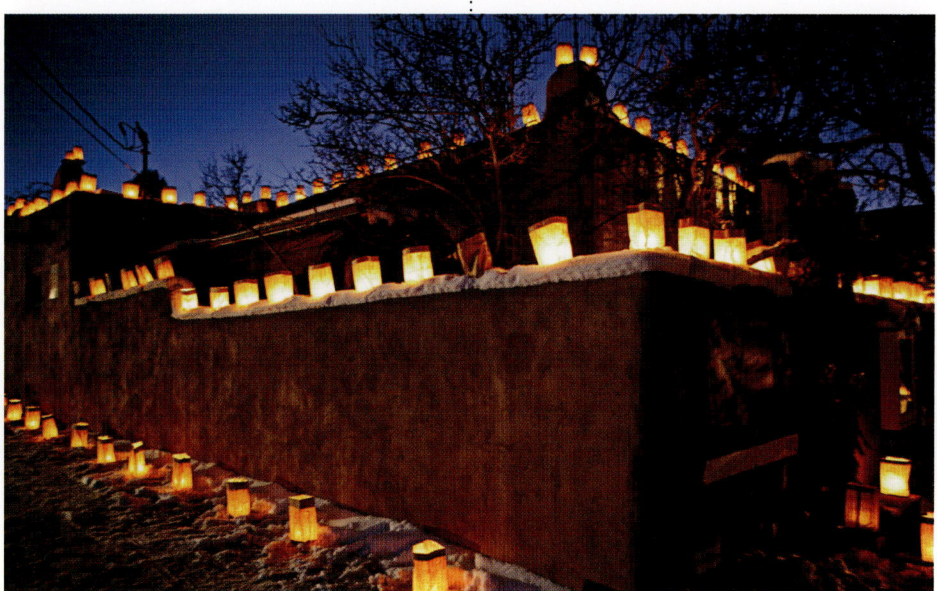

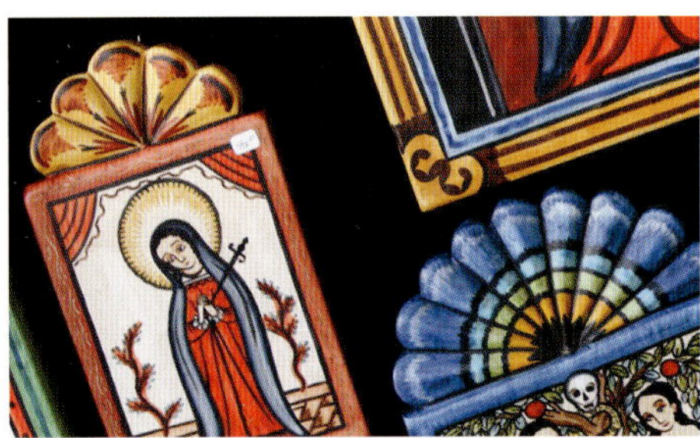

Lunette detail on retablos by Charlie Carrillo.

LUNETTE (Media Luna) / a French word for "little moon," a half-moon or semi-circular shape often placed at the top of **retablos**, **altar screens**, **tinwork** (mirrors, frames, sconces), **trasteros**, **chests**, and other decorative objects made by Hispano artisans of the Southwest. A frequently used motif in Spanish Colonial–era art and crafts, the lunette continues to be popular today. In wood furniture or works of art the lunette (or *media luna* in Spanish) may be left flat and plain or further articulated with deeply carved grooves, scalloped edges, and/or elaborate painted designs. In some instances, the lunette is carved or painted to represent half a **rosette** or shell. In architecture, it may also be called a tympanum and refers to a semi-circular space or opening in a wall or ceiling, framed by an arch or vault.

MACAW / brightly colored **feathers** of macaws (a bird native to the rainforests of Mexico and Central and South America) have been found in prehistoric Puebloan, Hohokam, Chacoan, and Mogollon archaeological sites. For example, scarlet macaws were present in sites of the Hohokam and other cultures by AD 500, and macaw burials have been found at Tuzigoot Pueblo, built by the Sinagua people in circa AD 1000, in central Arizona (now the Tuzigoot National Monument). Archaeological evidence suggests that macaws were brought to the Southwest from Mexico beginning in prehistoric times. Much later, in the sixteenth century, Spanish explorers recorded an active trade in feathers among Puebloan people. Macaws were an important early design element in southwestern art; for instance, they were depicted on **Mimbres pottery**, in prehistoric rock art, and in paintings on the walls of Pueblo **kivas**. Today macaw and parrot feathers continue to be incorporated into the ceremonial objects and regalia used by Pueblo people. However, because the macaw is an endangered species in the wild, acquisition of their feathers is strictly controlled by laws designed to protect the species.

MACHINE-SPUN YARN / See **yarn—commercial**.

MAIDEN'S SHAWL / See **manta**.

MAN-IN-THE-MAZE (Home of the Elder Brother, Maze of Life) / a historic design consisting of a black geometric maze (or labyrinth) and a single simplified figure standing at the entrance to the maze, with deep significance to the Tohono O'odham, who have traditionally used the pattern on their pottery and finely woven baskets. The latter are generally made from a coil whose foundation is a bundle of **beargrass** and with sewing elements of **willow**, or bleached-white **yucca**, and black splints from **devil's claw** seedpods. Occasionally, the maze is made from sewing elements of green, unbleached yucca.

Sometimes also referred to as the "Maze of Life," this pattern is found in ancient Hohokam **petroglyphs** of the Sonoran Desert. For the Tohono O'odham, it has many layers of meaning, some of which are related to the Creation stories. According to tradition, the design is believed to represent the path that I'itoi (also known as Elder Brother and one of several beings who helped create the world) took to his home near the base of Baboquivari (or *Wa:w Giwulk*), a steep volcanic mountain in southern Arizona that is a sacred place to the O'odham. In recent times the maze has come to symbolize one's journey through life, which contains many challenging twists and turns, but ultimately reaches the "center" where one's life is complete. Contemporary Tohono O'odham artisans depict the man-in-the-maze in jewelry, **beadwork**, **horsehair baskets** and other types of handwoven baskets, and in other art forms.

MANTA / the Spanish word for "blanket," used in textile literature to describe a wider-than-long woven piece of fabric that was worn as a shawl or wraparound dress—fastened at the right shoulder with a **manta pin**—by the early Navajo, Hopi, and Pueblo people. Often associated with women's dresses and shawls, mantas were also once worn as clothing by both sexes. Woven on a vertical **loom** in **twill** or plain weave, mantas often had decorative borders along the top and bottom edges. The term is also used in Spanish Colonial documents to describe a cloth used as a tax

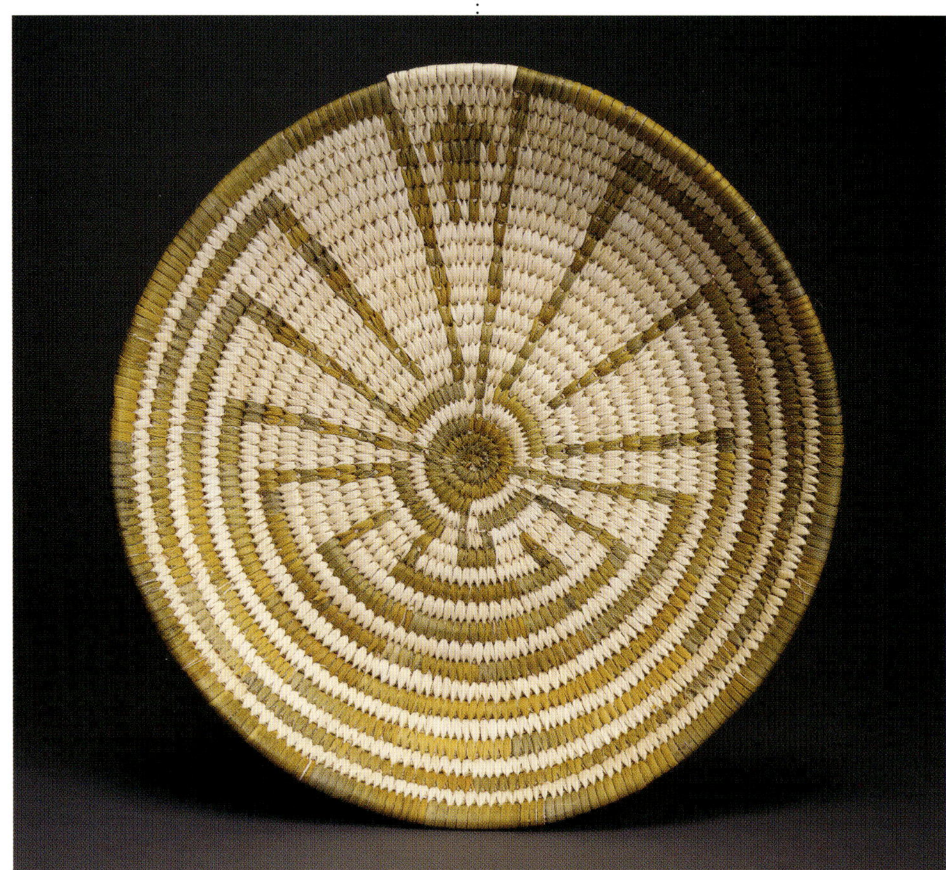

Anita Antone (Tohono O'odham), man-in-the-maze basket, 1997.

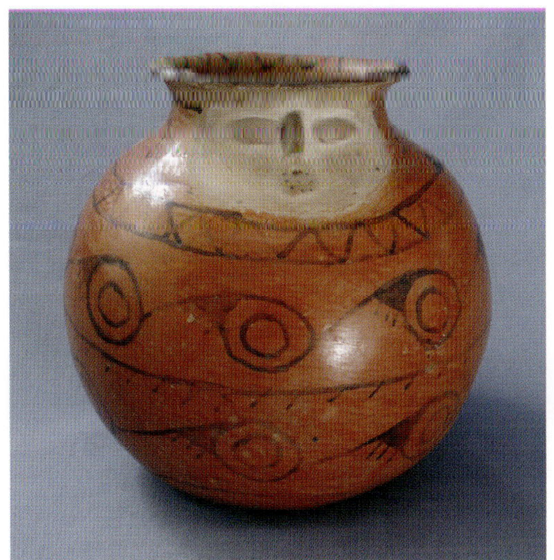

Maricopa polychrome jar with human-face effigy, ca. 1885–1912.

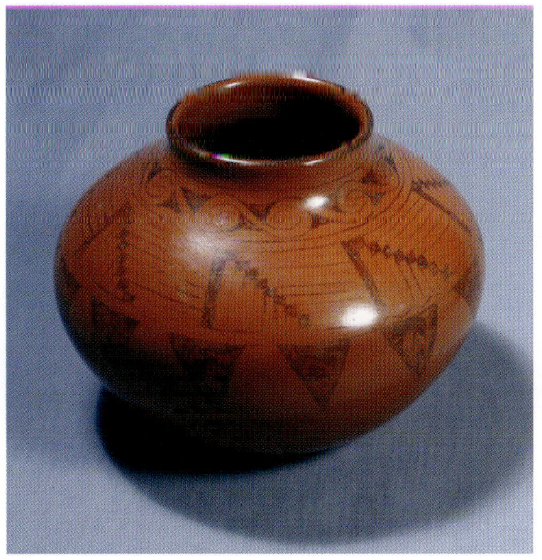

Maricopa black-on-red jar by Mary Juan, ca. late 1930s.

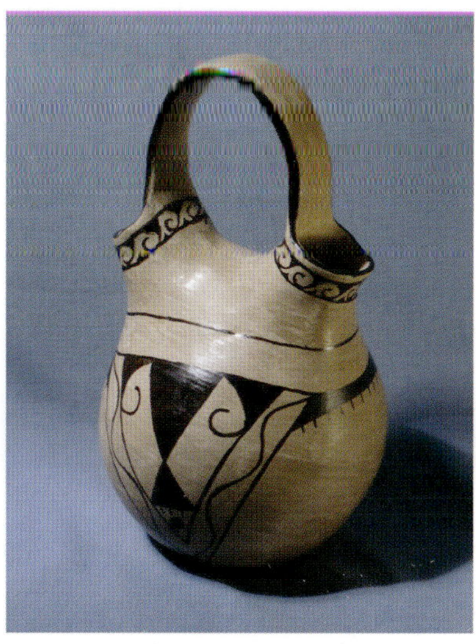

Maricopa black-on-cream wedding vase by Dorothea Sunn-Avery, 2007.

payment or tribute—such as the *repartimiento* that was paid to the Spaniards by Native Americans. In addition, manta can refer to treadle-loom-woven commercial cloth or unbleached sheeting that was made in large quantities for the commercial trade. In Arizona the term is also used to refer to a ceiling cloth that was attached to the **vigas** (wood beams) in the ceiling of early **Sonoran** homes, to hide the exposed roof system and to prevent insects or mud from falling from the earthen roof onto furniture or occupants in the room.

The earliest Native American-made mantas were cotton; after sheep were introduced to indigenous weavers by the Spanish settlers in the late sixteenth century, wool replaced the cotton. The designs ranged from terraced diamonds, triangles, zigzags, and crosses to later serrated-edged motifs. Pueblo weavers made a type of manta called a "maiden's shawl," made of cotton with patterned wool borders. The earliest Navajo mantas are natural brown with blue borders. The Navajos, who drew some motifs from their own basketry patterns, made many of these shawls; they often sold or traded the mantas to the Pueblos.

The Hopi term for a wool or cotton blue-bordered, blue and red-bordered, or black-and-red-bordered white manta is *atö'ö*; they also call them "maiden's shawls." The Zuni term for a black or brown wool manta-dress is *bi:sale'*.

MANTA PIN (Shawl Pin) / a long functional pin, usually of brass or **copper** soldered to a decorative panel of **silver** (sometimes **German silver**), sometimes set with **turquoise**, used in the nineteenth-century to fasten together a Pueblo or Navajo woman's **manta** (a woven shawl or wraparound dress) at the right shoulder. The decorative panel (or head) may be square, oblong, or oval, with plain or notched edges and decorated with simple **stamped** or scratched designs. After dress styles altered, this early form disappeared, replaced by silver and turquoise plaques with basic pin clasps.

MARICOPA (Piipaash) POTTERY / distinctive cream- and red-colored pottery made for a century and a half. Late-nineteenth-century Maricopa wares—with colors of black-on-red, brown-on-tan, black-on-tan, **red-on-buff**, and **polychrome**, and of forms such as jars, pitchers, **canteens**, bowls, **effigy** jars, and figurines—are similar to the pottery made by the Tohono O'odham and Pimas during that time.

In the first decades of the twentieth century, the Maricopas were making pottery for the increasing number of tourists visiting the region. On these highly polished polychrome or black-on-red wares they often replicated ancient **Hohokam** pottery designs, and experimented with scalloped rims and different forms such as cups and saucers, sugar bowls with carved lizards and frogs, unusually shaped effigy bowls, and other items suited to the tourist trade.

Perhaps the most renowned and influential Maricopa potters of the period were Lena Mesquerre, Mary Juan (1920–1972), and Ida Redbird (1892–1971). Among their favorite design motifs was the arrowhead. Redbird played a major role in the revival of Maricopa pottery in the late 1930s: she was the first president of the Maricopa Pottery Makers Association, an organization founded to market the members' wares. Taught by her mother, Redbird formed polychrome and black-on-red bowls, jars, **wedding vases**, effigy bowls, ash trays and other forms using the ancient **paddle and anvil** method, decorating them with simple geometric patterns, and giving them a high polish. With the exception of Redbird and a few others, Maricopa potters rarely signed their pieces until the 1970s, when a second revival of Maricopa pottery occurred. During that period frogs, lizards, and insects were frequently used design motifs. Only a handful of potters carry on the tradition today, creating mostly small-scale tourist pieces. These simple polychrome or black-on-red vessels are made from **clay** collected at various locations in the community and are decorated with geometric designs of natural dyes.

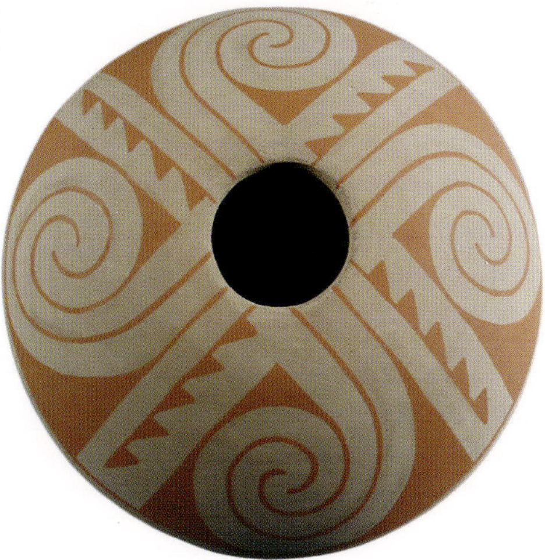

Maricopa red-on-plain jar by Ron Carlos, 2010.

MARQUETRY / a decorative technique in which elaborate patterns are created by applying pieces of wood, **shell**, ivory, and sometimes metal into a wood veneer, either through **inlay** or **mosaic overlay**. For inlay, the pattern is placed in an indentation made in the wood; for mosaic overlay, pre-cut materials are glued directly on the surface, then ground down to a smooth finish, and polished. The technique was firmly established in Spain during the Moorish occupation (711–1492); in the sixteenth century the Spanish introduced marquetry to Mexico. Examples of marquetry-decorated furniture were likely imported to New Mexico from Mexico. Spanish Colonial artisans (possibly as early as the seventeenth century) in New Mexico embellished their furniture and wood objects (such as crosses) in a similar manner, but because of a lack of ivory or rare woods they utilized indigenous materials such as straw and cornhusks to create marquetry-like patterns. Common early motifs used by New Mexican artisans were geometric shapes (especially stars and chevrons) and floral motifs, reminiscent of the intricate marquetry patterns seen on early Spanish and Mexican furniture. See also **straw appliqué**.

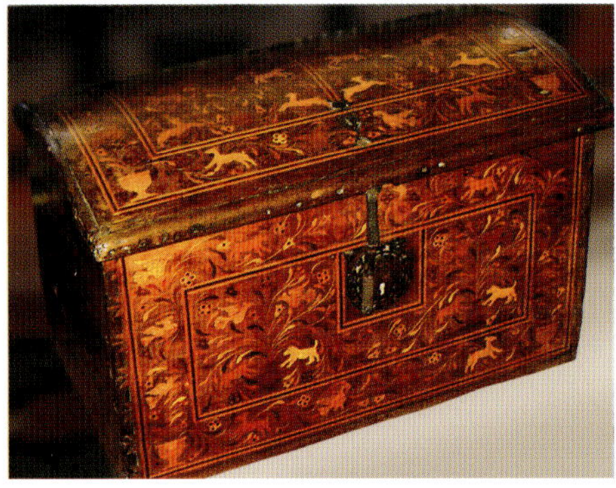

Spanish Colonial chest with marquetry, 18th century.

MASONRY (Stone Masonry) / a building method used throughout the world, in the Southwest beginning with prehistoric peoples including those of Chaco Canyon in northwestern New Mexico, consisting of large rocks gathered from the local landscape, laid up in courses or piled into wooded forms (that are later removed), covered and set in abundant amounts of mud mortar, and sometimes finished on both sides with a thick **mud plaster**. There are several variations of the technique. In some instances, the mortar joints are chinked with small stones to create a smooth surface. In other cases, the masonry walls have a "rubble" stone core that is covered with a veneer of a layer of finished or dressed stone. The latter has been called core-and-veneer masonry by archaeologists.

MATA ORTIZ (Casas Grandes) POTTERY / a thin-walled, finely painted, hand-formed ceramic ware typically decorated with geometric patterns, made in the small village of Mata Ortiz in northern Chihuahua, Mexico, less than 100 miles from the U.S.–Mexico border. Acclaimed by the international art market, this work is sometimes known as "**Casas Grandes**" pottery, after the prehistoric culture that flourished 16 miles north of Mata Ortiz, between about AD 1000 and 1450. In the 1970s, Juan Quezada found Casas Grandes **potsherds** in the countryside near his home. Inspired by the elaborately painted red or black geometric and figurative decorations, he taught himself to form, fire, and decorate the pots. Other interested family members learned his techniques, and soon Quezada and his siblings and their children and neighbors became the core of a new pottery movement.

Mata Ortiz pottery is hand-shaped using local **clays** and the coil-pinch technique, decorated with hand-ground **mineral paints** using human-hair paint brushes, painstakingly **polished**, and **fired** in an outdoor kiln with cow manure, bark, or wood as the fuel. Oxidation firing yields pots of colors (white, red, tan, etc.), while the reduced-oxidation technique (in which an elevated level of carbon circulates around the pot and turns the surface black) is used to create **black pottery**. Polychrome and **black-on-black** pots are produced in a wide variety, ranging from one-inch-high miniatures to three-foot-high vessels. Colors range from metallic black to bright white, and include all the earth tones from cream to yellow to brown and chile-pepper red.

Prominent styles include black-on-black wares (made with either the oxygen-reduction firing method or graphite), red clay with black designs, white vessels with black and red designs, and more elaborate color combinations. Typical forms are **ollas** (or jars), animal- and human-shaped **effigy** pots, plates, vases, and bowls. Beginning in 1976, Spencer Mac-Callum, an American trained in anthropology and art history, worked with Juan Quezada and other potters to market their work to museum

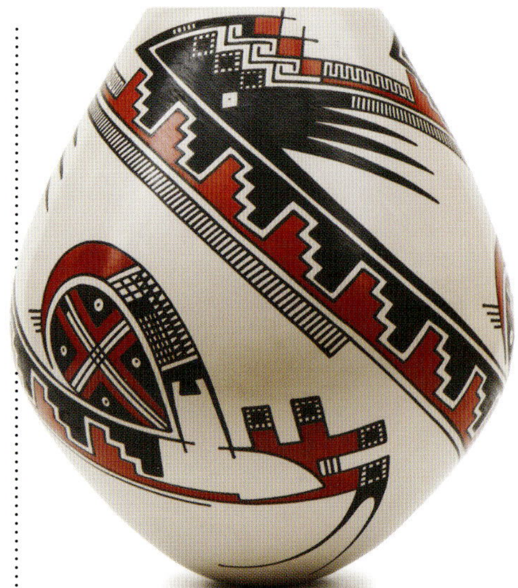

curators, academicians, gallery owners, and others, convincing them that the Mata Ortiz pottery movement was a noteworthy phenomenon. The movement gained momentum and interest in the U.S. during the 1980s, and an increasing number of U.S. traders and dealers visited the village and brought the pottery north to an expanding market that included the Southwest.

The pottery experienced a flowering of styles and skills in the 1990s, with new generations of young potters taking up the clay and creating pots with traditional, abstracted, or completely new designs ranging from geometric patterns to stylized animals. They also experimented (and continue to do so) with new clays, paints, forms, and patterns. For example, some artisans are using subtle green and blue paints made from local minerals; Juan Quezada developed the "Quezada style" of pottery, a time-consuming process of painting exact mirror images on opposite sides of the vessel; and Reynalda Quezada is known for pieces with sculpted lizards or snakes encircling the rims.

In 1999 Juan Quezada was awarded El Premio Nacional de Ciencias y Artes, the highest Mexican honor given to living artists. Today more than five hundred villagers in Mata Ortiz have followed his success and have become potters, providing a much-needed economy and important artistic heritage to this remote village. Contemporary Mata Ortiz ceramics reflect the evolving diversity and creativity of the individual potters.

LEFT: Effigy by Juan Quezada, 1986. **ABOVE AND RIGHT:** Ollas by Juan Quezada, ca. 2000.

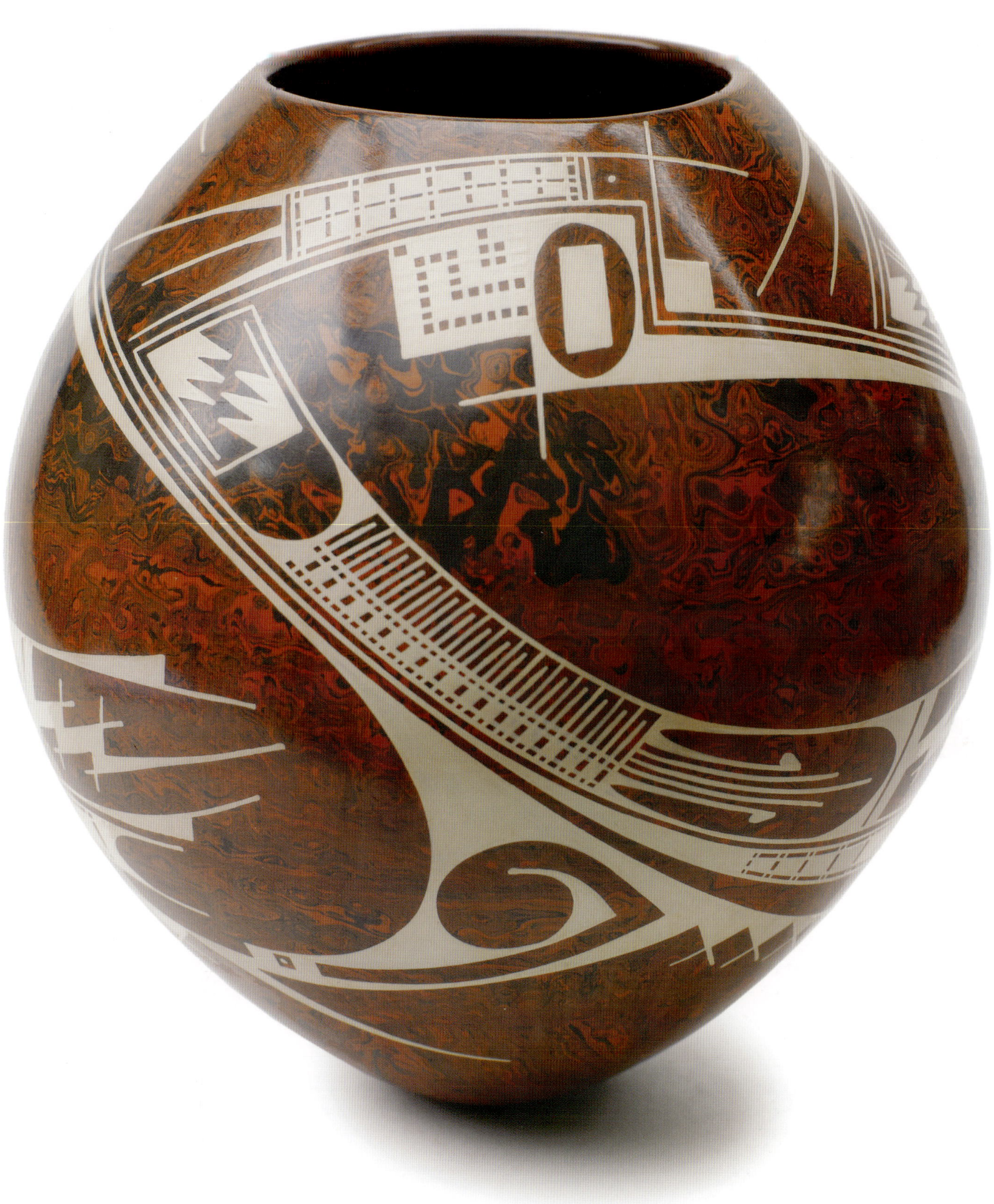

MATACHINES DANCE (Danza de los Matachines) / derived from the Italian word *mattaccini* and originally used beginning in the sixteenth century as a generic European term for a wide variety of strange dances, los Matachines is one of the oldest ritual, religious, dance dramas of New Mexico that is performed on certain saint's days and at Christmas and New Year's by both Hispano and Pueblo communities in the Upper Río Grande Valley. It is also performed by the Pascua Yaquis outside Tucson, Arizona, and in Guadalupe, at the southern edge of Phoenix, and across Mexico. Some scholars see it as a symbolic ritual of the cultural syncretism of the region: an expression of the Indo-Hispano culture.

The origins of the Matachines remain shrouded in mystery. Some scholars believe it originated in medieval Spain in the twelfth century and was introduced to the American Southwest by early Spanish missionaries who used it to Christianize Indian converts, while others believe the dance is of Native American origin. Performed on key winter and summer feast days, the ritual varies widely in detail, style, and meaning depending on where it is performed, with each community applying its own unique interpretation. Generally enacted in several musical and choreographic sets by a king, a young girl, and a bull, with clowns and two lines of eight to ten dancers, it is said to portray "the triumph of good over evil," the Virgin's conversion of a pagan king, or the Aztec Indian resistance against foreign invaders.

In Hispano communities, it has a strong sacred character (and often devoted to the Virgin of Guadalupe), and is accompanied by violin and guitar music. In Pueblo communities, it is danced to native drums and rattles, and in the Yaqui villages, the matachines and their musicians (violin and harp players) are sacred ritual performers. Usually, the *danzantes* (dancers) wear scarves masking the lower part of their faces and silky fringe attached to their headdresses hides their eyes. Their heads are crowned with tall highly decorated *cupiles* (headdresses) from which hang brightly-colored ribbons or paper streamers; and they hold a *palma* (a three-pronged dance wand) in one hand and a highly decorated *guaje* (**gourd rattle**) in the other hand.

MATACHINES DANCE WAND (Palma) / a simply constructed, three-pronged, painted-wood dance wand (sometimes also highly decorated with colored feathers and other items), held in the right hand and waved in time to the music

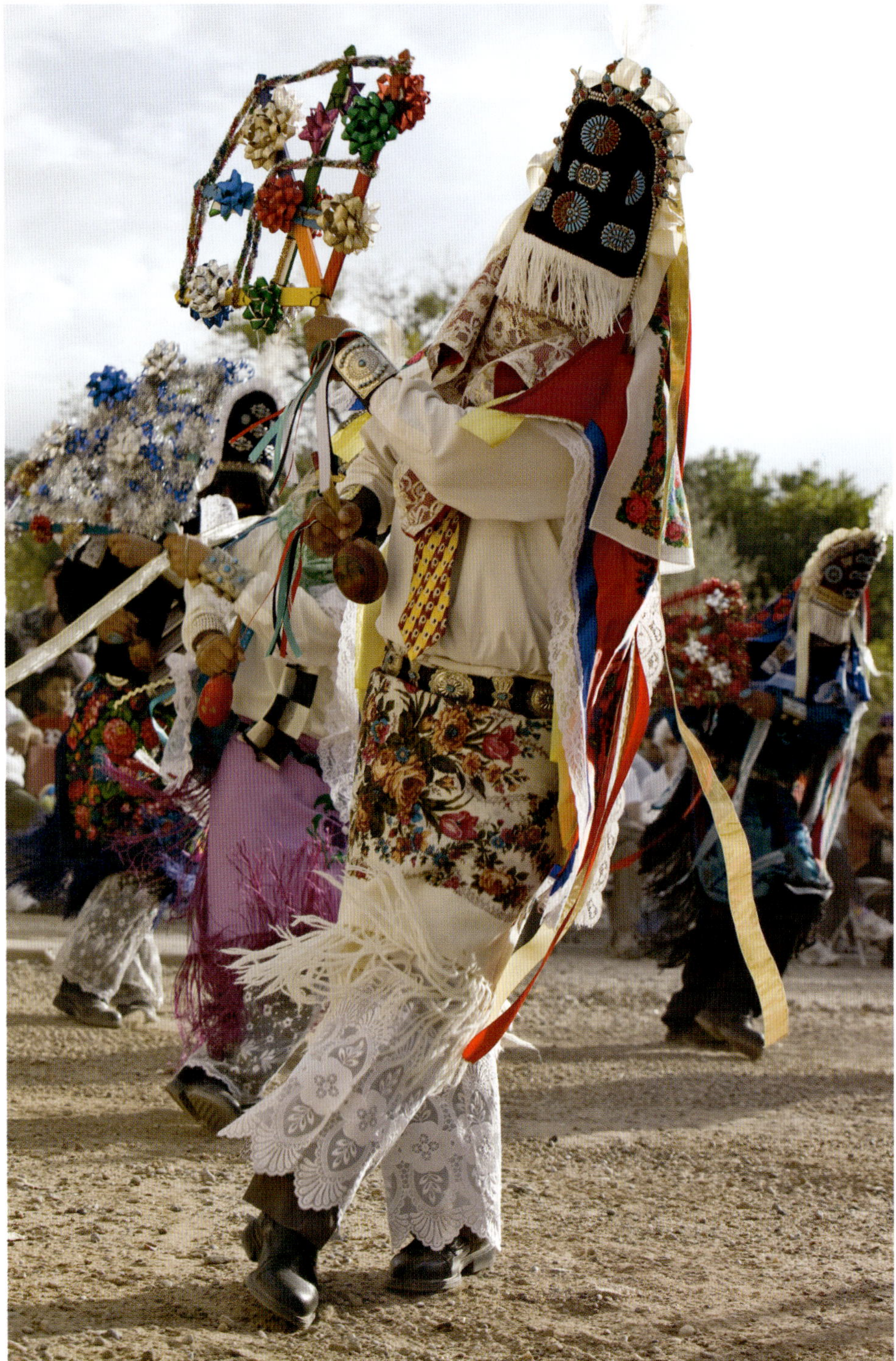

ABOVE: Matachines dancers perform at the National Hispanic Culural Center in Albuquerque, New Mexico.
OPPOSITE: A Matachín dancer holds a dance wand.

during the **Matachines dance** performed in the Southwest by both Native Americans and Hispanos since the colonial period. Also called *palmas*, the Spanish word for "palm leaf," the wands represent the Trinitarian belief that God is one and three at the same time. Palmas are still used today in performances of the Matachines in Hispano villages, in some pueblos of New Mexico, as well as in the Yaqui villages in Arizona. See also **Matachines Dance**.

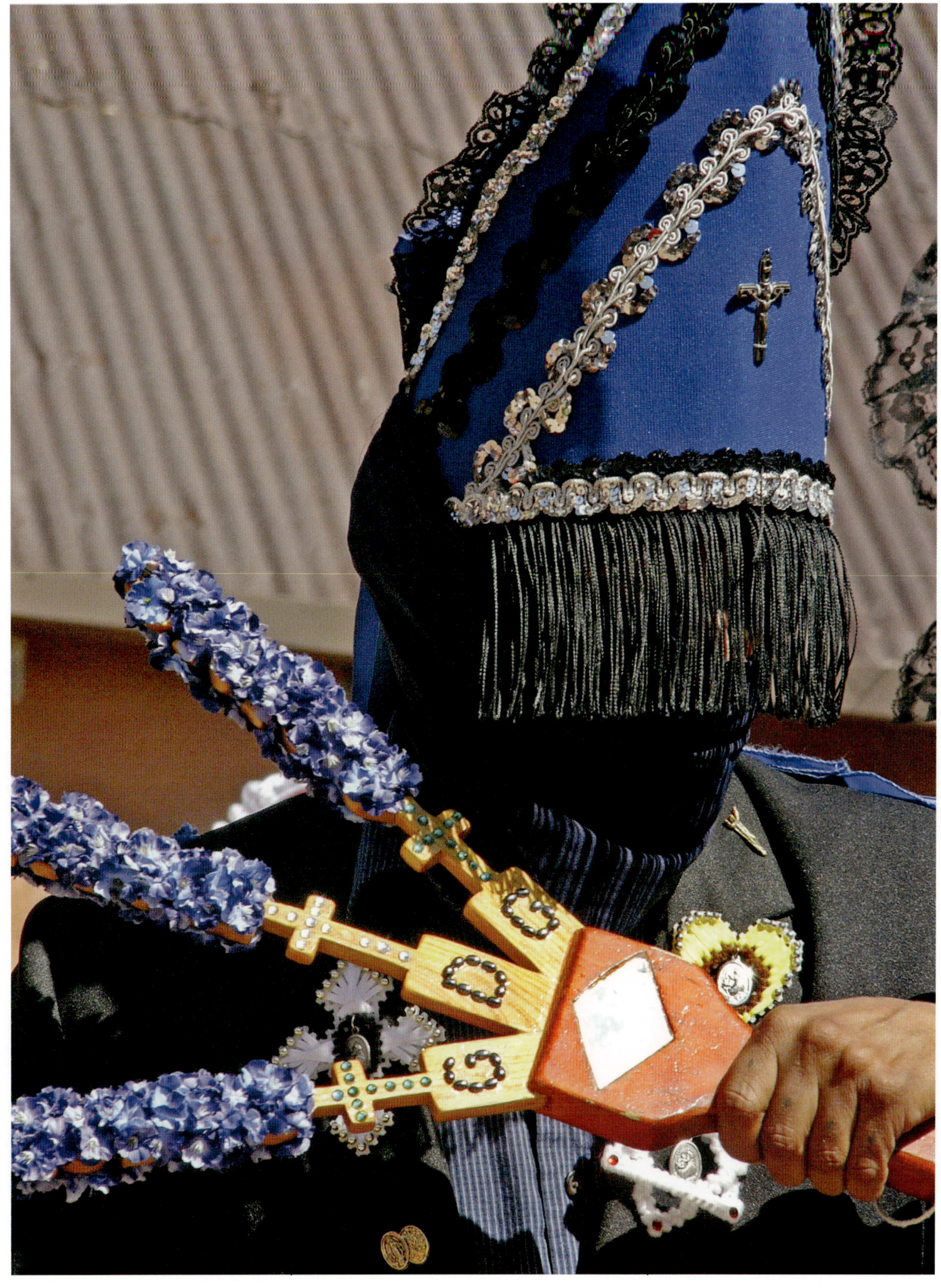

MATTE / in pottery, an unpolished clay **slip** or paint that fires to a dull, lusterless finish, to create a contrast with the stone-**polished** clay slip. A matte surface is also achieved by scratching (see **sgraffito**) or carving the polished surface of a vessel to reveal the matte surface below. The contrast between matte and polished surfaces is one of the distinguishing features of the **black-on-black** and **red-on-red** pottery techniques established in the early twentieth century. The New Mexico Pueblos of **Acoma**, **Santa Ana**, and **Zia** are well known today for pottery with matte finishes and matte-painted decoration.

Among the contemporary potters who have included matte surfaces as an integral part of their art are Nathan Youngblood (b. 1954) of Santa Clara Pueblo who uses matte areas to accentuate the polished surfaces of his intricate carvings; Tony Da (1940–2008) of San Ildefonso who created all-matte vessels and bears in the 1970s; and Jason Garcia (b. 1973) of Santa Clara who paints his **tiles** and vessels with all-natural, matte, clay paints. See also **glazeware** and **pigments—mineral**.

MEDICINE BUNDLE / Offering Bundle / objects tied onto the back of some Zuni **fetish** carvings that can consist of pieces of **turquoise**, **shell** and/or **coral** beads, **heishi**, **feathers**, a stone arrow, and other small items. These items may be used as an offering to the fetish, to evoke its spirit, or to increase the strength of the fetish. In some instances, the bundles or offerings include small hide containers in which a pinch of **cornmeal** (intended as a blessing), as well as other items of significance such as ground turquoise are placed. Traditionally, the bundles/offerings are tied to the fetish with strips of animal gut or **sinew**. It is important to note that

"true" medicine bundles are made and held by the priests, curers, *hatahlis*, and medicine men of Native peoples of the Southwest, and contain objects important to that particular culture, ritual, or religious practitioner.

MELON POTS (Turbinos) / a **clay** bowl, jar, or other form with distinctive ribs on the surface, created by Native potters of the region, by pushing the clay in and out by hand or with the use of a tool. Despite the name, these pots are more evocative of the various types of squash plants that Native peoples of the Southwest have traditionally grown. This style of pottery has been made by Pueblo potters in New Mexico, particularly at Santa Clara Pueblo, since at least 1910. Melon pots, typically red or black in color, continue to be popular with artisans and collectors today. Some contemporary potters have created variations on the style. For instance, Santa Clara Pueblo potter Nancy Youngblood (b. 1955), granddaughter of famed potter Margaret Tafoya (1904–2001), was inspired to create a dynamic style of deeply carved "S-swirl" melon-ribbed bowls, for which she has become well known. Contemporary potters in **Mata Ortiz**, in the state of Chihuahua, Mexico, create a similar type of design called *turbinos*—hand-formed ribs or ridges that swirl or spiral downward from the rim to the base of the clay pot.

MERINO WOOL / a type of wool that is short, greasy, crimped, and difficult to card and **dye**, historically used by weavers of the Southwest. Merino (or Rambouillet) is a European breed of sheep that was issued to the Navajos in the late 1860s during and after their internment at Bosque Redondo (Fort Sumner, New Mexico). At that time thousands of the Navajos' own churro

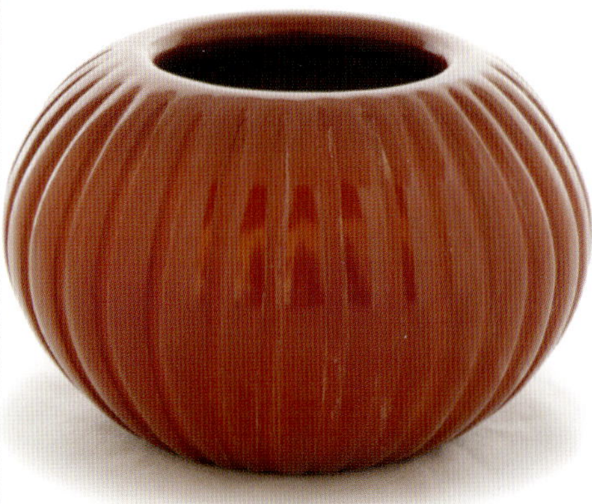

Angela Baca (Santa Clara), "melon" bowl, 2000, clay.

sheep were destroyed. These events led to the deterioration in the quality of wool available for hand spinning, and as a result Navajo weavers, who preferred **churro sheep wool**, became more dependent on commercially spun **yarn**, including three-ply Saxony yarn from Europe and three- and four-ply **Germantown yarn**. Hispano and Pueblo weavers of the region used merino wool as well, which also led to the decline in the quality of blankets they made from hand-spun wool yarns in the last quarter of the nineteenth century.

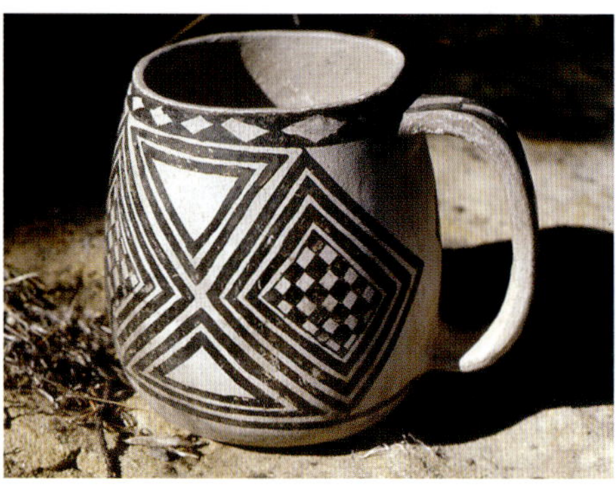

Mesa Verde black-on-white mug.

MESA VERDE POTTERY / a distinctive pottery type made by the prehistoric inhabitants of the Mesa Verde region in southwestern Colorado, consisting of white-**slip** clay with elaborate patterns executed in black carbon paint, or with mineral paints, or a combination of the two. Design motifs are primarily geometric, though zoomorphic and a few anthropomorphic figures occur. Among the common decorative motifs are opposed stepped triangles, interlocking scrolls, zigzag lines and frets, combinations of parallel lines, and a multitude of dots. One of the most common types of Mesa Verde **black-on-white** ware extant is the

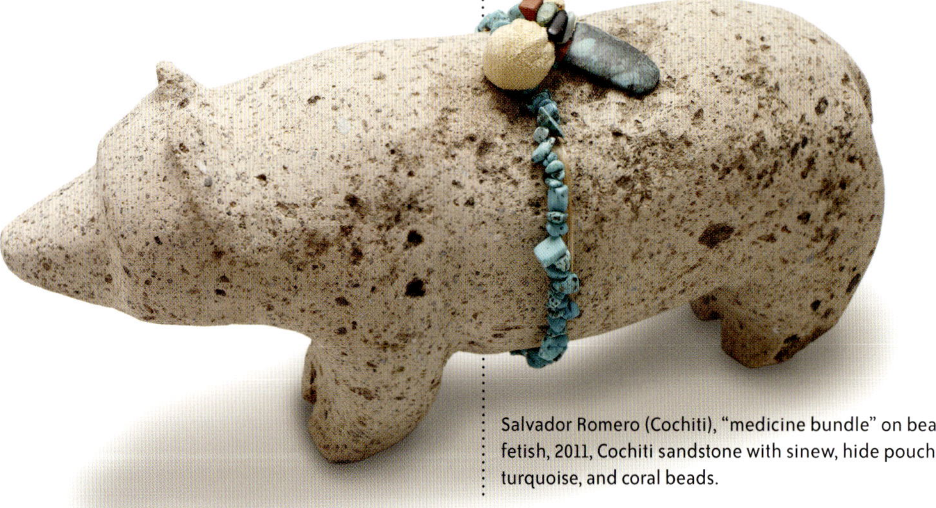

Salvador Romero (Cochiti), "medicine bundle" on bear fetish, 2011, Cochiti sandstone with sinew, hide pouch, turquoise, and coral beads.

drinking vessel resembling a mug. Other forms were bowls, jars, dippers, and pitchers. See also **black-on-white pottery**.

MESQUITE (Prosopis) / a large native desert plant that ranges from shrubs to large trees with long, compound leaves made up of tiny leaflets and long thorns on the branches, found below 5,000 feet around the springs, flood plains, rivers, washes, hillsides and in grasslands in the warm Sonoran, Mojave, and Chihuahuan deserts. There are several different species and hybrids of mesquite, which is a member of the legume family. Historically, in addition to being one of the most important food plants for Native Americans living in these regions, mesquite has been used by Native peoples in Arizona for a variety of uses from building material to firewood to making bows and arrows. The thorns were once used to make sharp, durable needles used for sewing; the inner bark, when stripped and dried, was woven into mats, baskets, and other utilitarian items. Early settlers in the Tucson, Arizona, area used mesquite wood to fashion fence posts, wagon wheels, furniture, and doors. Mesquite is still used by Native artisans in the area; for example, the wood is a favored fuel source for **firing** pottery and a black paint is made from the sap to paint designs on **clay** vessels. Due to the natural beauty of mesquite wood (with its dark coloring, semi-coarse grain, and deep golden swirls), currently there is a resurgence in the manufacture of mesquite furniture and flooring. See also **friendship bowls**.

METATE AND MANO / a metate is a concave slab, stone, or sometimes a piece of wood, utilized by Native Americans and early Hispano settlers for grinding **corn**, grains, seeds, and beans; a small hand-held stone called a mano was used to grind the food in the metate into a coarse meal or fine powder, usually mixed with water to create mush, to make flour for tortillas, or other dishes. Some Native peoples first ground seeds and pods in a small wooden mortar, using a stone pestle, and then ground the flour even finer in a larger metate. Pueblo potters of the region have also used metates and manos to grind their **temper** for making **clay** vessels. The type of stone used varied by the region, though it was usually basalt or another type of igneous or metamorphic rock. A prehistoric milling quarry was discovered near the Antelope Hill **petroglyph** site in southwest-

ern Arizona, where it is believed members of many Indian tribes came to obtain rock for their metates, manos, and pestles. Some cultures, such as the Western Apaches, also scavenged metates and manos off prehistoric sites for their own use. In the Hopi mesa villages of Arizona, women typically had two to four stone metates in varying degrees of coarseness for processing corn. The metates would be placed in a wooden frame and the Hopi women kneeled and ground the corn with the mano, moving the **cornmeal** from one metate to the next, until it was almost of powder-like consistency. Examples of prehistoric metates can often still be seen *in situ* at archaeological sites and national parks in the Southwest; manos and metates can also be seen in museum collections.

MICA / a group of silicate minerals that contain atoms of aluminum, oxygen, and silicon bonded into flat layers that can be split cleanly into thin, flexible sheets. Deposits of mica exist throughout the world, including in **clay** deposits found in the northern Rio Grande region of New Mexico. Historically, Hispano and Pueblo people of the area used mica for a variety of purposes: it was separated into thin transparent sheets to cover windows (even after glass was introduced to the region); it was added to **tierra amarilla** paint to decorate the interior walls of **adobe** homes; homemade mica-based paints were used with stencils to apply designs to adobe walls (using tufts of sheep's wool as a brush); and mica-rich clay was (and continues to be) used to create utilitarian pottery (see next entry).

MICACEOUS POTTERY / undecorated and unglazed earthenware made since prehistoric times by the Pueblo people, and since the eighteenth century by Hispano residents of the region, from **clay** containing bits of **mica** that produces tiny golden flecks upon the golden-colored or gray/black surface. The earliest types were often tempered with micaceous rock (potters added crushed rock to the clay) or covered with a wash of mica-rich clay to form a **slip**; eventually micaceous clay was used for the entire vessel. Early forms included ceremonial items as well as jars, bowls, cups, pitchers, water bottles, and cooking vessels.

Because micaceous ware is very strong and durable, it is superior ware for cooking. In contrast, the painted and polished non-micaceous wares made by Southwestern peoples were more suitable for storing and serving food. Because of

the grittiness of mica in the clay, no **tempering** agent needs to be added. Micaceous clay vessels and those slipped with micaceous clay can be fired to a sparkling black or golden color depending on the amount of oxygen present during **firing**. Often the beauty of micaceous pottery is enhanced by the natural **fire clouds**, or dark smudges, created during the firing process. To seal the porous clay, the inner surfaces of the cooking pots are often cured with animal fat before being used for the first time.

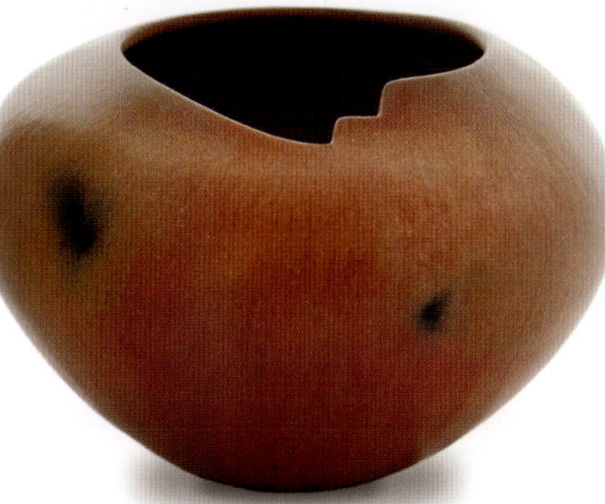

Rowena Gibson (Taos), micaceous pot (with stepped edge), 2010, micaceous clay with natural fire clouds.

The earliest examples of American Southwest micaceous pottery, found along the Gila River in southern Arizona, were made by the Hohokam culture (ca. AD 200).

Found throughout northern New Mexico, especially near Taos and Picuris pueblos, micaceous clay has been used to produce ceremonial and utilitarian vessels at **Picurís**, **Taos**, **Nambé**, **Tesuque**, **Santa Clara**, Pojoaque, and **Ohkay Owingeh**—all pueblos situated in the valleys and foothills of the Sangre de Cristo Mountains.

In the 1860s simple bowls and jars were the most common form, some of which were decorated with "piecrust" rims or "rope fillet" designs on the neck or shoulder. These early forms were shaped with corncob scrapers that left a brushed surface.

Micaceous pots were sold in curio shops as early as 1880, but were not regarded by collectors and traders with the same aesthetic value as the Pueblo painted wares. Novelty items made of micaceous clay for tourists over the decades include miniature figurines, **rain gods**, animal **effigies**, **horno** incense burners, ashtrays, candlesticks, pueblo models, and salt-and-pepper shakers. Some small items, such as little clay images of pueblo dwellings, were made by potters as gifts to friends and family.

Durable micaceous ware continued to be made

at these pueblos, and by Hispanos in the region, into the twentieth century and well after metal and enamel pots and pans arrived by way of the Santa Fe Trail (1820–80) and the railroad (beginning in 1879–1880). Some utilitarian micaceous wares were made by Pueblo potters for sale to tourists; these wares typically had impressed or incised designs.

Beginning in the 1970s, there was a resurgence in micaceous clay vessels made by Hispano artisans, some of whom elevated the craft of pottery to fine art. One example is Jacobo de la Serna (b. 1965) who used the traditional coil and scrape method and outdoor firing to create elegant, minimalist, and highly sculptural micaceous pottery. By the 1990s, Pueblo potters were also experimenting with turning micaceous pottery into purely an art form. It was the last Southwestern Pueblo ceramic tradition to make the transition from cooking wares and other utilitarian pots to different forms of art pottery and sculpture. A key figure in this transformation was Lonnie Vigil (b. 1949) of Nambé Pueblo.

In the twenty-first century, micaceous pottery with minimalist design has been experiencing a resurgence among Native American and Hispano potters of the Southwest. Some are using mica in innovative ways. For instance, potter Linda Tafoya-Sanchez of Santa Clara Pueblo uses micaceous slip to highlight designs and to complement the polished and **matte** surfaces of the pottery, and Hispano potter Annette Morfin of Youngsville, New Mexico, is using **horsehair** to create decorative flourishes on her micaceous vessels. Others are decorating their micaceous pots with relief carvings of stylized figures, animals, ears of **corn**, or other shapes that are cut out of clay slab and **appliquéd** on the surface. Some create **kiva**-style pots with cut-out steps on the rim. In addition to the micaceous "art pottery" sold at markets, galleries, and studios, an enormous amount of micaceous ware is still made by Native American and Hispano potters for domestic purposes (and also for ceremonial purposes by Native artists). See also **Jicarilla Apache pottery** and **pottery—Hispano**.

MILAGROS / the Spanish word for "miracles," miniature votive objects originally commissioned and handmade by silversmiths from the sixteenth to the early twentieth century. More recently, milagros are stamped or cast from a mold in a variety of materials—iron, tin, **copper**, brass, pewter, pot-metal, wood, or wax—with hand-

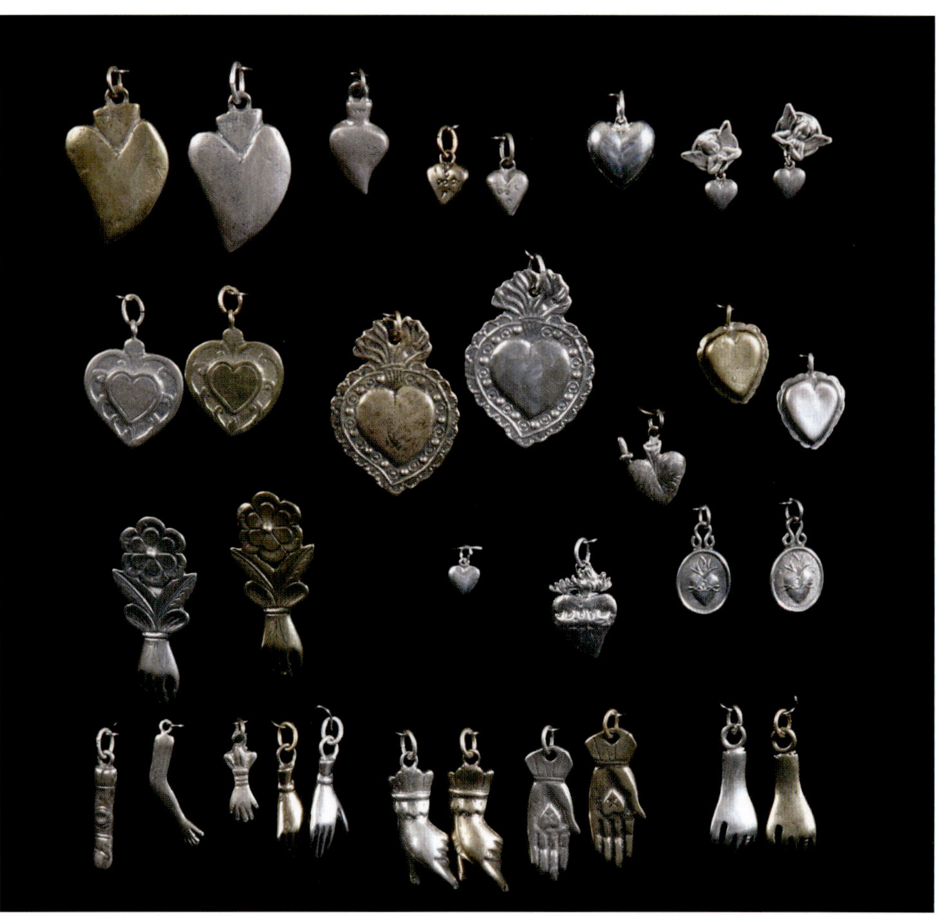

Silver, bronze, and tin milagros, votive offerings used to petition a saint for a miracle or to give thanks for an answered prayer.

finishes. Milagros are made in the form of figures, animals, plants, various body parts such as hearts, arms, legs, breasts, torsos, eyes, and inner organs, and other shapes portraying the needs/petitions of the faithful. A popular early subject was kneeling/praying figures, used by the devoted to indicate a prayer was successfully answered.

Whatever the form, milagros serve as offerings at churches, chapels, home shrines, and at pilgrimage sites to give thanks for an answered prayer or to petition a particular saint for a miracle. The tradition has long been popular in Mexico and other Latin American countries, where they can be found adorning vestments and altars of popular **santos**, and in more recent times in the American Southwest. Milagros should not be confused with three-dimensional cast-silver *dijes*, or charms, which are milagro-like miniatures that are used in Latin American countries and the American Southwest to adorn one's clothing, worn as jewelry, or attached to personal items.

Votive offerings have been made for deities since prehistoric times; after Christianity took root, the custom was re-appropriated for Christian use and milagros became offerings for saints. Milagro votive offerings are part of an ancient folk custom derived from Mediterranean Catholic traditions, specifically those of the Spanish and Portuguese—a custom brought to the New World by Cortés and other early Spanish conquerors and explorers.

By the colonial period, milagros, likely imported from Mexico, were part of Hispano folk beliefs in the American Southwest; today they play an important role in the region's devotional practices, as well as in craft production. Artisans encrust wooden crosses, hearts, and other forms with milagros, most often made from cast **silver** or silver-

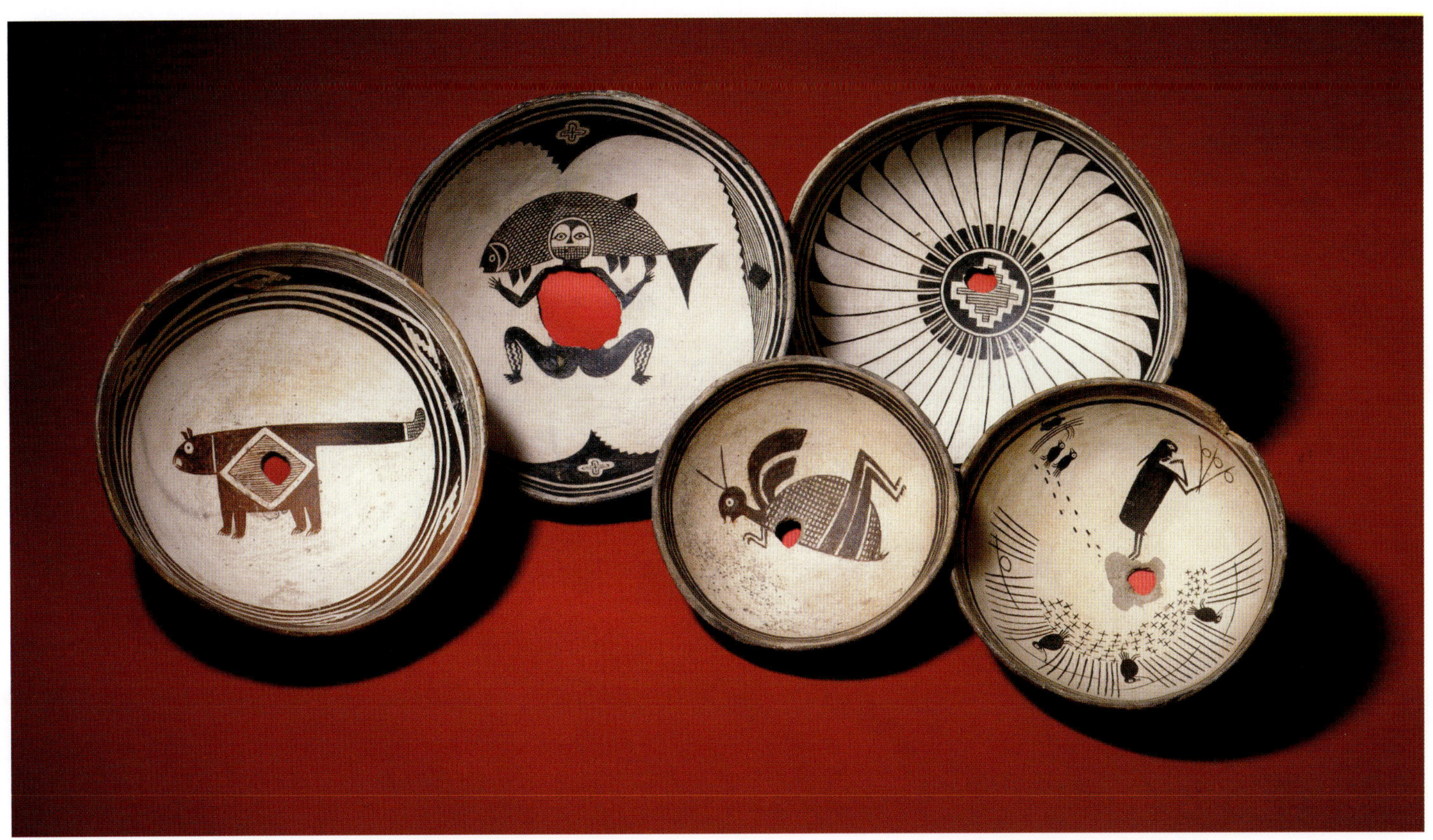

Mimbres black-on-white "story bowls," ca. 12th to 13th centuries.

coated metal (and occasionally gold), thus creating folk art that is both beautiful and spiritual.

The practice of offering milagros is still common today and many Hispano churches across the Southwest are filled with them. They can be found attached to walls, shrines, **crosses**, altars, and the clothing of saints. In San Miguel Chapel, Santa Fe, New Mexico, a large standing cross is almost completely encrusted with milagros that the faithful have left behind as petitions. At Santuario de Chimayó, Chimayó, New Mexico, milagros are hung in a side chapel along with crutches, braces, photographs, letters, and other **ex-voto** offerings and testimonials of cures and answered prayers. At the Mission of San Xavier del Bac, south of Tucson, Arizona, a reclining wood statue of San Xavier is the recipient of many offerings from the devoted, including numerous milagros. Cast, mass-produced milagros can be purchased today from a variety of sources including museum shops, gift stores, and religious-goods shops and vendors; often they are sold with brightly colored ribbons, ready for the faithful to pin or hang on the gown or altar of his or her favorite saint. Historical one-of-a-kind milagros by skilled **plateros** can sometimes still be found for sale in antique stores in Mexico and the Southwest.

MIMBRES POTTERY / a unique prehistoric utilitarian and ceremonial pottery characterized by its sophisticated and complex surface decoration of painted figural and animal forms and fine-line abstract and geometric designs on light-colored **clay**. It is also known as Mimbres **black-on-white** ware, a misleading term as the paint used was sometimes brown or red rather than black and the background color used was often gray, cream, or buff rather than white. The imagery on Mimbres pottery is important, for it tells us much about prehistoric life.

The Mimbres culture flourished between about AD 1000 and 1150 in small, isolated villages and farms in southwestern New Mexico, near the Mimbres River—named by early Spanish settlers for the abundance of mimbres or small willows found along its banks. The name Mimbres was adopted as the official name of the culture at the turn of the century. Their painted and fired pottery was likely made by women and usually took the form of relatively deep bowls—as well as globular jars, **ollas**, and **effigy** jars—with a central image and additional designs painted around the inner rim. The detailed imagery that appears on the bowls ranges from elaborate storytelling scenes of figures hunting, fishing, weaving, or engaged in ritual dances; to patterns of interlocking geometric shapes; to stylized portrayals of deer, lizards, rabbits, birds, fish, and other animals.

In Mimbres burial sites, the most frequently found offerings have been the black-on-white (or off-white) bowls, placed over the head of the deceased, and deliberately broken by having had a hole struck through the bottom with a pointed tool. Some Pueblos call them a "breath hole," which allowed the deceased's breath or spirit to escape through to the next world. The holes have also been called "kill holes" by scholars and archaeologists. In recent years, in compliance with the Native American Grave Protection and Repatriation Act (NAGPRA), funerary objects such as these bowls, formerly in public collections, have been returned to the appropriate pueblos for reburial.

Unearthed at ancient village sites in the Mimbres Valley beginning in the late-nineteenth century by military personnel, collectors, and amateur excavators and archaeologists, Mimbres pottery was not excavated by professional archaeologists until the 1920s. Since then, archaeologists have excavated thousands of Mimbres bowls along the Mimbres River in southwestern New Mexico. When the pottery became a highly valuable commodity beginning in the late 1960s, unscrupulous looters wreaked havoc on archaeology sites, a practice that continued into the 1990s.

Geometric Mimbres pottery designs were appropriated by Pueblo artisans of the Southwest beginning in the 1920s, when Julian Martinez of San Ildefonso Pueblo first adapted Mimbres motifs to his **black-on-black** pottery. Among the designs he revived was the radiating feather-fan pattern that has since become an extremely popular motif with Pueblo potters.

Much later, in the 1960s, San Ildefonso painter and potter Tony Da (grandson of Julian Martinez) reintroduced Mimbres animal imagery to Pueblo pottery. He incised (and later carved in low-relief) Mimbres-style antelope, deer, lizards, frogs, buffalo, and other animals on his red, black, black-and-sienna, and sienna plates, jars, and boxes. Native American artists continue to revive Mimbres patterns with integrity and respect in easel paintings and pottery—see for example the clay vessels of Diego Romero of Cochiti Pueblo. Additionally, many of the talented potters of **Mata Ortiz**, a village in the state of Chihuahua, Mexico, incorporate Mimbres animals in the highly intricate designs of their clay pots. In recent decades, Mimbres-style motifs have been (and continue to be) produced in many non-Indian contexts, ranging from inexpensive and mass-produced key rings to porcelain dinnerware.

MISSION / a religious complex built throughout the world by missionaries; in the Americas they were built by Spanish Catholics of the Franciscan Order, beginning in the seventeenth century (in New Mexico), for the purpose of educating, converting to Christianity, and "civilizing" the Native Americans of the region. The complex was usually comprised of a church with an attached *convento* consisting of the friar's quarters, kitchen, and multiple rooms including those for workshops, classrooms, dining, meeting area, etc., all of which faced an interior **courtyard**. A wall was typically placed around the courtyard in front of the church. With the use of local labor and materials, they were constructed in the Southwest by missionaries from Spain, Italy, Germany, and other countries, as part of Spain's colonizing efforts in the region.

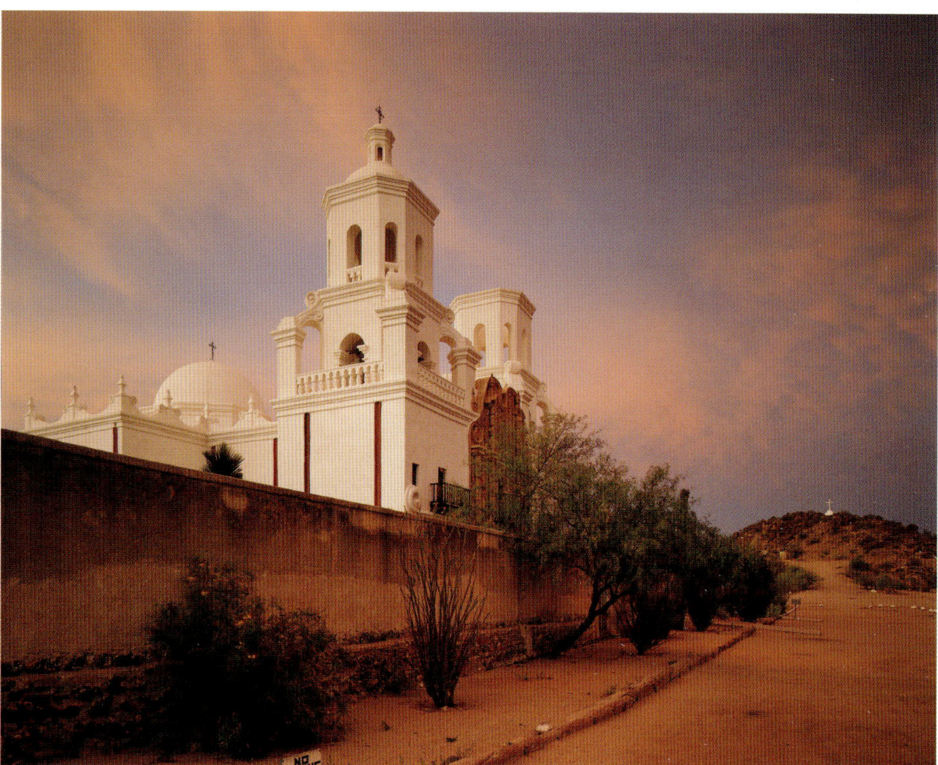

San Xavier del Bac Mission, Tucson, Arizona.

MISSION CHURCHES / Arizona / under Austro-Italian Jesuit missionary Eusebio Francisco Kino, the Jesuits established more than twenty-five missions in the northern Sonoran Desert of present-day Arizona and Sonora. Among them was San Xavier del Bac (first called the "White Dove of the Desert" around 1921), perhaps the finest mission of the Spanish Colonial era, and certainly the most elaborate, built beginning about 1783 and completed in 1797, on the site of a thriving Tohono O'odham farming community, nine miles south of Tucson, Arizona. Built of fired-**clay** brick, stone, and lime mortar and roofed with masonry vaults, the church's **Churrigueresque** central portal with **estípite columns**, and ornate **buttressed** towers, reflect Spanish Baroque design. Between 1992 and 1997 the interior was restored under the leadership of Paul Schwartzbaum, the head of conservation of the Guggenheim Museum and a member of the Vatican's technical commission that oversaw and evaluated the conservation of Michelangelo's Sistine Chapel. Schwartzbaum worked on San Xavier del Bac with a team of conservators from Italy, Turkey, England, and the U.S., including Tohono O'odham men who worked as apprentice conservators. The remains of another less elaborate mission church, San José de Tumacácori, dating to the late eighteenth/early nineteenth century with a single bell tower and walls of mud **adobe** and fired bricks, can be seen at Tumacácori National Historic Park, in southern Arizona.

MISSION CHURCHES / New Mexico / these churches were erected beginning in the seventeenth century by Franciscan friars, using Pueblo Indian labor, as part of the Spanish missionizing efforts in the Southwest. Mission churches were often constructed in the center of the **pueblo**, sometimes even within the most significant **plaza** area, in order to display the dominance of the church and Spanish control. Following their own building traditions, as well as those of the Pueblo people, the Franciscans built the churches with local materials—sand, **clay**, and water mixed and molded into sun-dried **adobe** brick, wooden beams, and stone.

Generally, Pueblo men made the adobe bricks and hauled them to the building site and Pueblo women constructed the walls and finished them with **mud plastering**. The finished churches typically featured a tall and elongated interior nave with a choir loft over the main entrance. Interior walls were usually plastered and painted

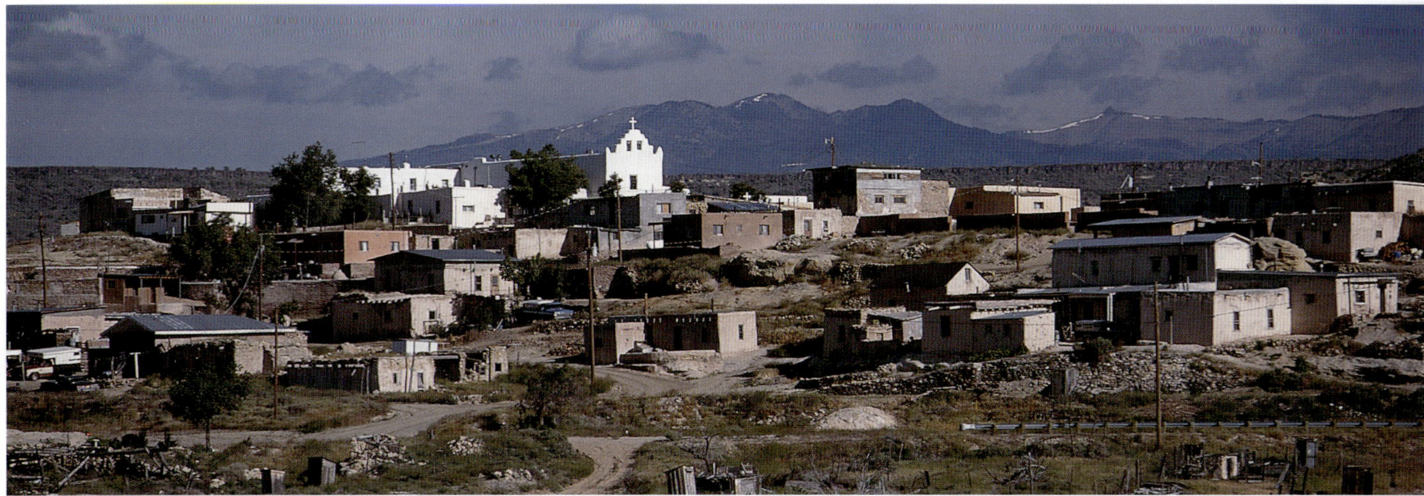

San Jose de Laguna Mission and Pueblo, Laguna, New Mexico.

in colorful designs. In addition, most had a line of small windows, or clerestory, between the roof of the nave and the roof of the transept in cruciform churches and between the nave and sanctuary roofs in single nave churches. Exterior facades were embellished with single or twin towers and capped walls and balconies. The flat roofs were constructed with **vigas** and **latillas** and carved **corbels**. (According to local tradition, in some instances vigas were chopped down and floated down the Rio Grande and then taken by horse and wagon to the church construction site.) By the late eighteenth century, modifications in the design appeared, such as the introduction of the cruciform plan. Surviving original examples can be seen at several pueblos including Zia, Isleta, Laguna, and Acoma.

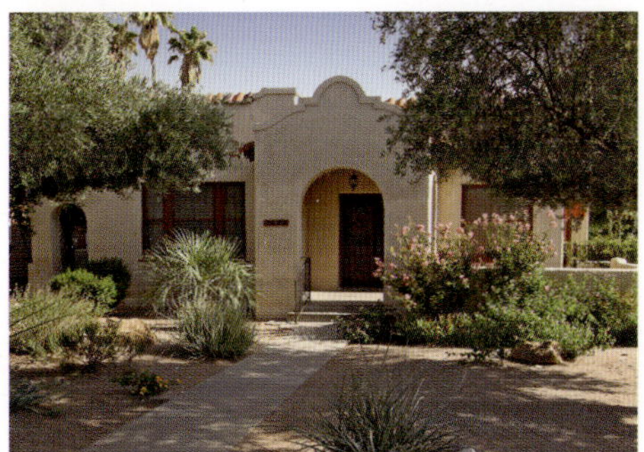

Mission Revival–style home, ca. 1928, Tucson, Arizona.

MISSION REVIVAL STYLE (California Mission Revival) /

loosely based on the architecture of eighteenth-century missions (of Roman and Moorish influence) in California, and built in the Southwest from about 1895 to 1930, this style typically features **stucco** walls usually painted white, extensive use of semi-circular arches, red clay **barrel-tile** roofs of low pitch, curved **parapet** gables, balconies, projecting eaves with exposed rafter ends, wrought-iron **grilles**, and sometimes towers or turrets capped with domes or pyramidal tiled roofs. Interiors are characterized by their wooden floors and trim, white walls, and built-in cabinets. **Courtyards**, **portals**, and/or gardens were also characteristic of the style, providing outdoor rooms within the walls of the building. An important source of inspiration for the style was A. Page Brown's California Building designed for the 1893 World's Columbian Exposition in Chicago.

MOKI STYLE (Moqui) /

a style of **sarape**, or shoulder-blanket pattern dating to at least 1750, originally consisting of simple arrangements of alternating narrow stripes of blue and white or blue and white with some brown, often used for trade among the Native peoples of the Southwest. The pattern was named Moki because of its strong association with Hopi-made wool blankets of this type—Moki, or Moqui, was a term the early Spanish used to identify the Hopi people of Arizona. Early dealers in Southwestern textiles assumed that the Hopis should be credited with originating the design and weaving most of these blankets. However, Moki-patterned blankets were also woven by the Navajos, the Zunis, and Spanish colonists throughout the early historic period. Later Moki-style textiles incorporated designs of stepped diamonds, crosses, and other geometric motifs interspersed on the stripped field.

MORADA /

a Spanish word for "dwelling," the term refers to the meeting place or chapter house where the Penitente Brotherhood prays and meditates. The penitente is a lay religious confraternity of Hispano men—also known as the Brotherhood of Our Father Jesus of Nazarene, or Los Hermanos Penitentes—who assisted area priests in colonial times and remain active in their faith today, primarily in northern New Mexico and southern Colorado. The term morada can also refer to the congregation as a whole.

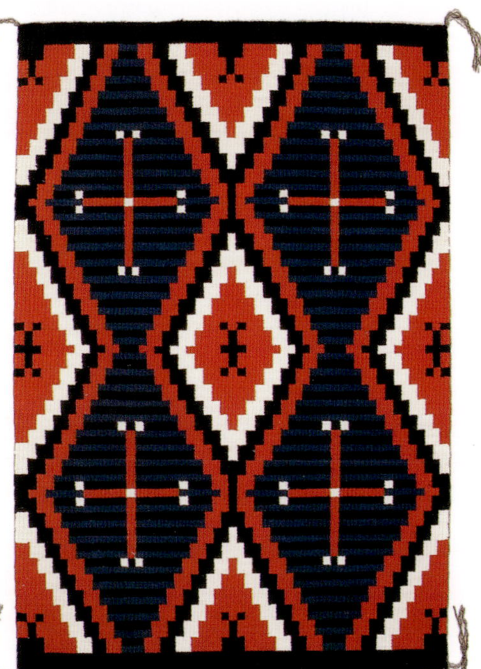

Barbara Teller Ornelas (Navajo), Moki blanket revival tapestry, ca. 1990, 26" x 18".

Moradas in the Southwest, largely built between about 1850 and 1930, are generally small structures featuring from one to several rooms, constructed of indigenous materials—**adobe**, **adzed** logs, and stone—in a wide range of simple architectural designs, usually topped with flat roofs. Moradas have very few windows, and those present are generally boarded up or shuttered closed. Heating was originally from a large **fogón** (fireplace). Later, pitched metal roofs, plaster interior walls, wooden floors, and wood stoves or other heating units were commonly added. Typically, there is a small inner wash area where penitente brothers cleanse after days of meditation and prayer. One or more large **crosses**—possibly up to six or eight feet tall, often painted white, and sometimes elaborated with subsidiary arms—stand in front of a morada, or lean against its walls.

Situated in remote areas to provide the secluded facilities members required, moradas have traditionally been open only to members. The Penitentes are associated with the Catholic Church: as early as 1856 the Bishop of Santa Fe (and later Archbishop) Jean Baptiste Lamy issued rules for the brotherhood; in 1947 the archbishop of Santa Fe recognized the Penitentes as an official society of the Catholic Church. The Penitentes' religious observances are focused on Lent and Holy Week, during which they engaged (and continue to engage) in secret practices.

In addition to meeting the spiritual needs of their communities, they have also traditionally undertaken charitable work. In recent years, membership in the brotherhood has increased.

Traditionally, the brotherhood has housed a large amount of religious art in the moradas, including hand-crafted **retablos**, **bultos**, and realistic life-size figures of Christ (some of which have movable limbs so the figure can be dressed and carried in processions). Also, the traditional penitente death figure, **Doña Sebastiana**, can often be found keeping watch in the morada, from her rickety wooden cart. These objects fill the central altar and other areas of the main room. Some of the historical morada pieces are now in museum collections, where they serve as inspiration for today's **santeros/santeras**. Some historians credit the moradas with helping to keep the **santo**-making tradition alive in the Southwest.

MORMON TEA (*Ephedra viridis*) / a densely branched shrub of the desert with yellow-green and blue-green stems depending on the species, that is boiled to make a red **dye** for coloring grasses and reeds used by Native Americans, particularly Hopis, to hand-weave baskets.

MORTISE-AND-TENON JOINT / a type of wood joint used in framing furniture and buildings, in which a projection formed on the end of a piece of wood (the tenon) fits into a rectangular hole or slot cut into another piece of wood (the mortise). Sometimes the joint is further secured by a peg through the tenon. Blacksmiths also used iron mortises to construct gates, **grilles**, and locks.

MOSAIC INLAY/OVERLAY / a jewelry technique dating to prehistoric times, and for many decades the trademark style of jewelers at Santo Domingo and Zuni pueblos in New Mexico, in which tiny pieces of **turquoise**, white abalone **shell**, red **spiny oyster**, black cannel coal or **jet,** and other stones are arranged and then adhered to shell bases (that are left in their natural form or carved into a shape) and then ground down until they are flush with each other. The Hohokam people were among the first to use a mosaic overlay technique—pendants were crafted by coating a shell (usually clam) with the natural adhesive **lac** and then overlaying turquoise and shell chips on top of the shell base. Common designs of Hohokam mosaic overlay were frogs and birds.

In the late nineteenth century, Hopi, Zuni, Santo Domingo and possibly other Native jewelers made mosaic tab earrings by hand grinding

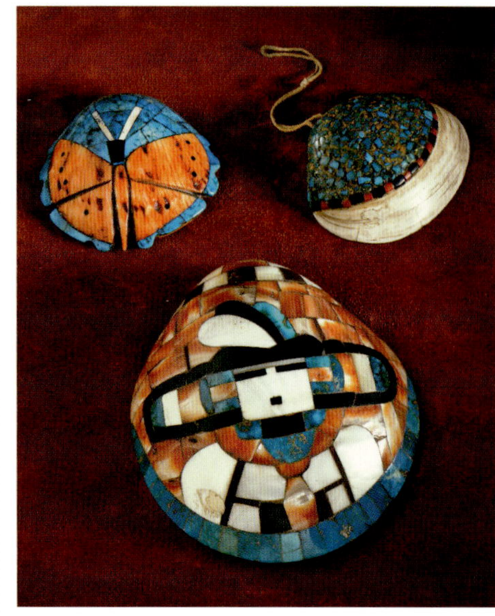

Zuni pendants: mosaic overlay on *Glycemeris* shell, early 1900s.

small pieces of turquoise and gluing them with piñon pitch to backings of tab-shaped **cottonwood** or shell. By the 1920s, lapadaries at Zuni were combining the mosaic method with silverwork: using **silver** backings, **bezels**, and sometimes a silver frame when making bracelets, buckles, pins, pendant earrings, etc.

Zuni and Santo Domingo jewelers during this period also excelled at mosaic "inlay," in which the tiny pieces of natural materials are set directly into the shell, stone, bone, or silver base. Jewelers

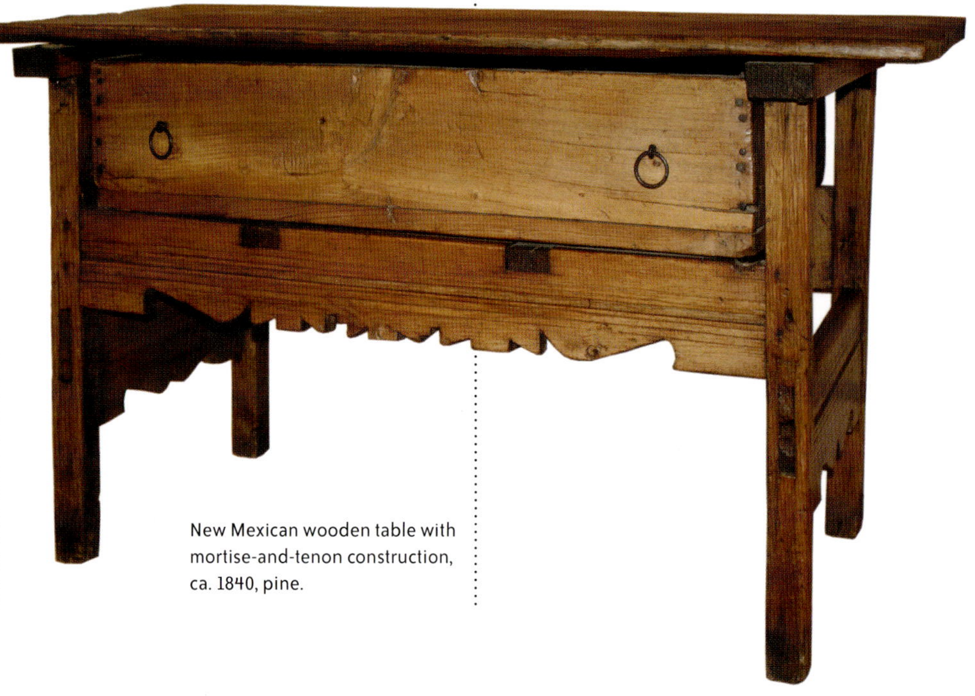

New Mexican wooden table with mortise-and-tenon construction, ca. 1840, pine.

at both pueblos made necklace pendants, **bolo tie** slides, bracelets, rings, and pins using the inlay and overlay method. In some instances, inlay was used to embellish mosaic overlay figures: such as spots on butterflies or dragonflies. Some of the favored designs of the 1930s to 1950s included geometric patterns (such as stepped triangles) and figures such as the **Rainbow Man** (which has become particularly popular), **Knifewing**, Rainbow Dancer, and the **thunderbird**.

During the 1930s and 1940s, Santo Domingo and Zuni artisans used pieces of old car batteries and Edison, and later vinyl records as a base for their mosaic jewelry and to simulate jet inlay. These items were cheaper than coral or spiny oyster shell, or in the case of battery casings, free.

In the early 1970s mosaic inlay was revived at Santo Domingo by Angie Reano Owen, who researched the Hohokam style of mosaic jewelry. Santo Domingo jewelers then adapted the mosaic style, sometimes combining it with silver, to a wide variety of jewelry items: pendants, bracelets, earrings, hair pieces, belt buckles, and **bolos.**

Today many Pueblo jewelers base their inlaid mosaic jewelry after styles and patterns of pieces unearthed at archaeological sites, which can now be seen in museum collections. Some, however, use nontraditional colors, modern materials, and contemporary imagery.

MOUNTAIN MAHOGANY (_Cercocarpus montanus_) / a shrub that grows in the canyons and on mesa tops throughout the Southwest uplands. Its stems and roots were used by the Navajos and some Pueblo people to make a reddish-brown **dye** for coloring wool and leather for mocassins, before the common use of aniline dye. In addition, some Jicarilla Apache, Navajo, San Juan Paiute, and other Native artisans have used the plant to make a dye for the sewing strands used to weave baskets. The Hopi people of northeastern Arizona have used the shrub's very hard wood for making their weaving battens and combs.

MUD PLASTERING (Enjarre) / the finish applied to the exterior and interior of **adobe** walls, as well as to adobe fireplaces, consisting of a mixture of mud or **clay** and straw with **caliche** or lime added to make the mud plaster water resistant while still allowing the organic materials to breathe. In some instances, **micaceous** soil was used for the plaster; when the mica flecks in these walls catches the light it creates a sparkling effect. Typically, a heavy coat of plaster is applied

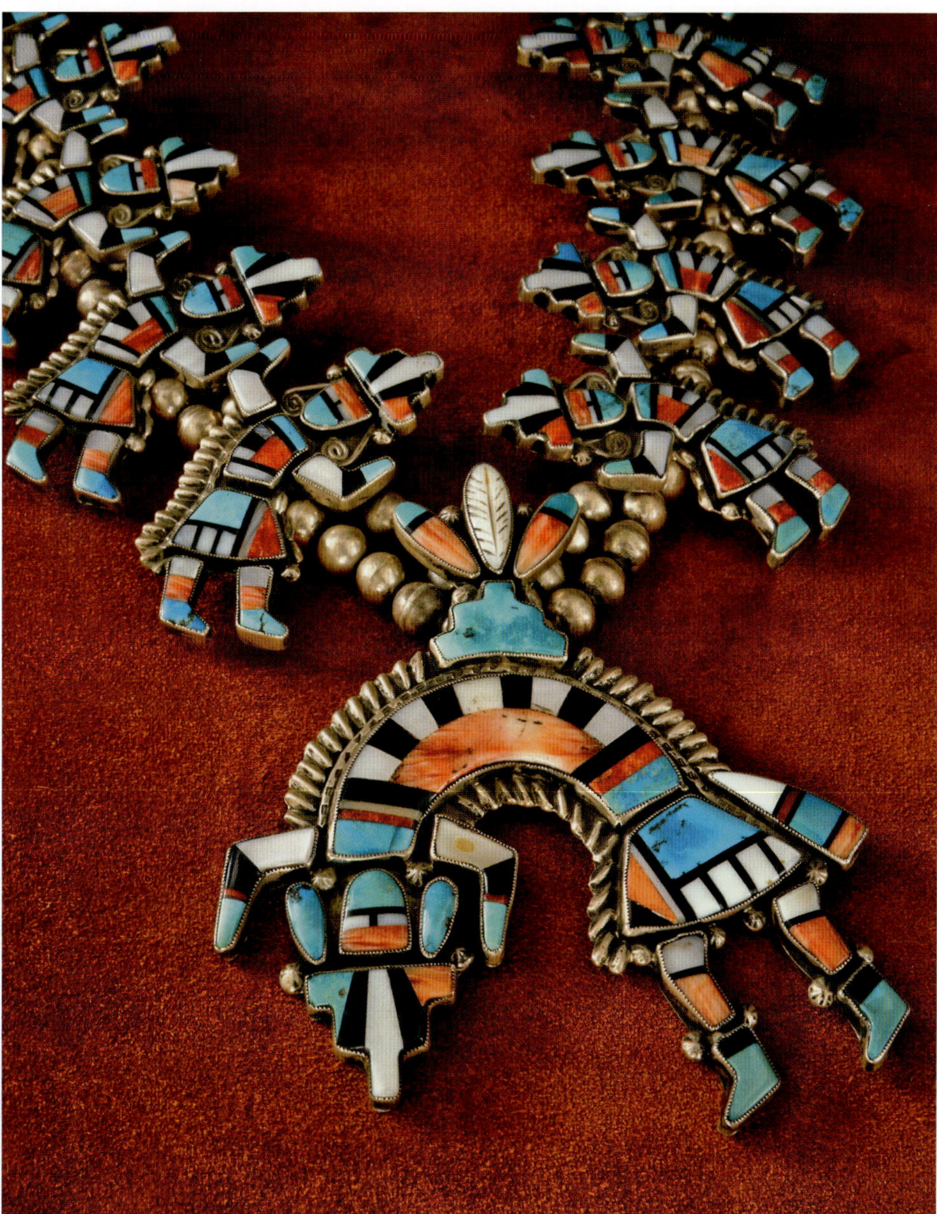

Zuni mosaic-inlay necklace with Rainbow Man design.

by hand, and after it dries another coat is applied by trowel, and when that dries completely the final alíze, or mud **slip**, is added to the surface with a sheepskin. The slip finish covers up any cracks in the mud plaster. On exterior walls, mud plastering was generally redone annually to repair weather-related damage. In both Hispano and Pueblo communities in the Southwest, this arduous task has been traditionally undertaken by women, who are called _enjarradoras_. However, men often participate in the mud plastering by setting the heavy scaffolding in place and mixing

the plaster with a shovel, trowel, or other tool. In the 1920s and '30s, when **Spanish Pueblo Revival–style** homes were all the rage in New Mexico, women from small villages in northern New Mexico were often hired by home builders and architects, such as John Gaw Meem, to execute traditional mud-plaster finishes on homes and fireplaces. During the twentieth century, older adobe homes were sometimes plastered with cement to reduce the high maintenance of the softer mud or lime plasters. This proved disastrous, as the hard cement plaster was not

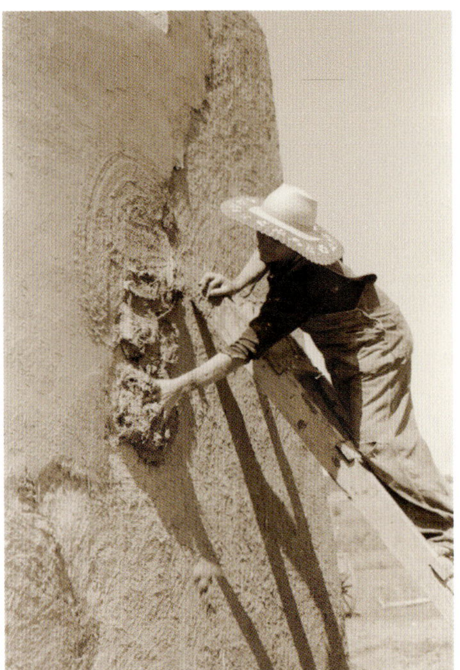

ABOVE: Mud plastering an adobe wall, Chamisal, New Mexico, 1940. **TOP RIGHT:** Rose Herbert, Woman with Cats, 2010, sun-dried mud and commercial paint.

compatible with adobe; it did not allow the adobe walls to breathe (or transpire moisture). The tradition of mud plastering adobe facades continues to this day; in some of the small Hispano villages of New Mexico (such as Ranchos de Taos and Corrales), the annual mud plastering of the church is an important community affair.

MUD TOYS / simple toys shaped like animal or human figures made by Navajos as early as the 1870s, from sifted dirt and water and dried in the hot Southwestern sun. Today mud toys are created from dirt dug from the landscape, baked in the sun, and painted with pigments made from natural materials or with commercial paints. Originally made by children as well as adults living in rural areas, before the days of store-bought toys, the earliest mud toys portrayed horses, cows, sheep, dogs, cats, cradleboards, and people. Some scholars have noted the resemblance between early mud toys and **fetishes** found at Southwestern archaeological sites. Antique and modern mud toys are sometimes decorated with animal hair and hide, a bit of stone or wood, cloth, **beads**, paper, **feathers**, sequins, or whatever else happened to be readily available. Mud toys were first sold commercially in 1983, when Jack Beasley of Farmington, New Mexico, discovered a market for mud toys made by

Elsie Benally, a Navajo from the remote Sweetwater region of Arizona. Beasley encouraged other Navajo women to fashion mud toys, including Mamie Deschillie (b. 1920) who decorated her toys in scraps of cloth and painted details. When the demand for this charming folk art increased, other Navajos began making mud toys. Like the earlier ones, the mud toys found for sale today are often whimsical and drawn from Navajo life, revealing the fertile imagination and versatility of Navajo artisans.

MUDHEAD (Koyemsi or Kooyemsi Katsina) / a nickname for the Hopi and Zuni dancers and carved dolls representing Koyemsi Katsina, distinguished by the ochre-colored mud covering their bodies, grotesque-looking masks on their faces, as well as their bulbous ears, topknots, kilts, and dance rattles. Mudheads, considered curers and messengers between humans and the supernaturals, serve many important functions in Hopi and Zuni ceremonies held in the **plazas** of their villages. They lead dances, drum, sing, play games with spectators, distribute seeds and gifts, battle clowns, carry prizes, and announce the beginning of **kiva** dances. Today they are popular figures reproduced in various Native American art forms, including pottery, carved figures, jewelry, and **quilts**. See also **katsina** and **katsina dolls**.

NACIMIENTO / the Spanish word for nativity scene or *crèche*, composed of figures around a crib in which baby Jesus sleeps, often accompanied by angels, shepherds, animals, and the Three Wise Men bearing gifts, made by Native American and Hispano artisans of the Southwest, in a variety of materials and designs, and intended for display in homes. Potter Manuel Vigil (1910–2003) of Tesuque Pueblo is credited with being the first Southwest Native American to have created a full ceramic nativity set in 1959, at the request of art patron Sallie R. Wagner (1913–2006) of Santa Fe. Shortly thereafter other potters, including Helen Cordero and Seferina Ortiz of Cochiti Pueblo and Alfred Aguilar of San Ildefonso began making small clay nativity figures primarily using traditional techniques from local, hand-coiled clay, left plain or painted with natural pigments, and fired outdoors. Once collectors discovered

these Native-made nacimientos, the demand for them rose and the art form quickly spread. Now clay nativity sets are made in various styles (redware, blackware, and polychrome) from miniature to seven inches in height, by potters at most New Mexico Pueblos, including Laguna, Jemez, Isleta, Taos, Ohkay Owingeh, Santa Clara, Zuni, and Cochiti. These sets of clay people and animals have deep roots in the figurative traditions of Pueblo pottery (see for example **storytellers**).

They also reflect the melding of Pueblo traditions with the rituals of the Catholic Church, and the custom practiced at all New Mexico Pueblos of celebrating Kings' Day, the January 6 feast day of the Three Wise Men. Still popular today, nacimientos are being made by some contemporary Pueblo

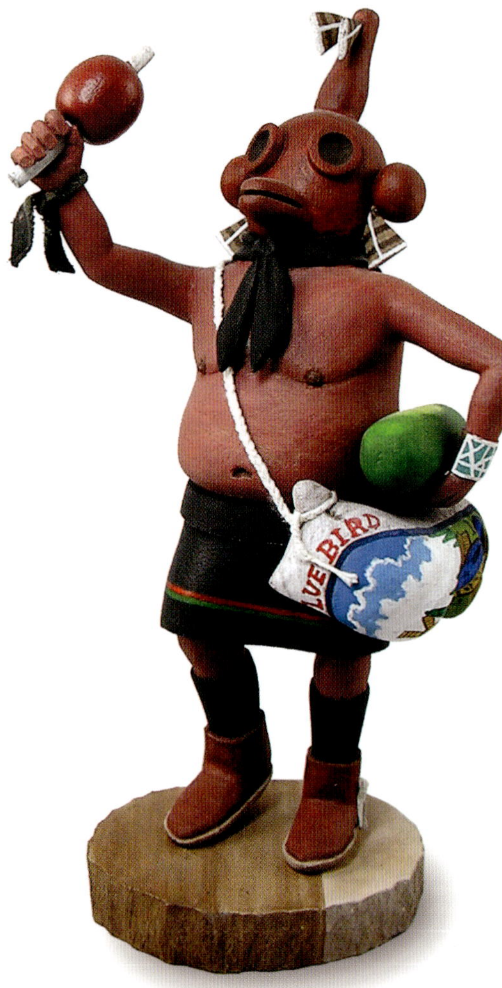

Andrew Grover (Hopi), Koyemsi katsina, 2010.

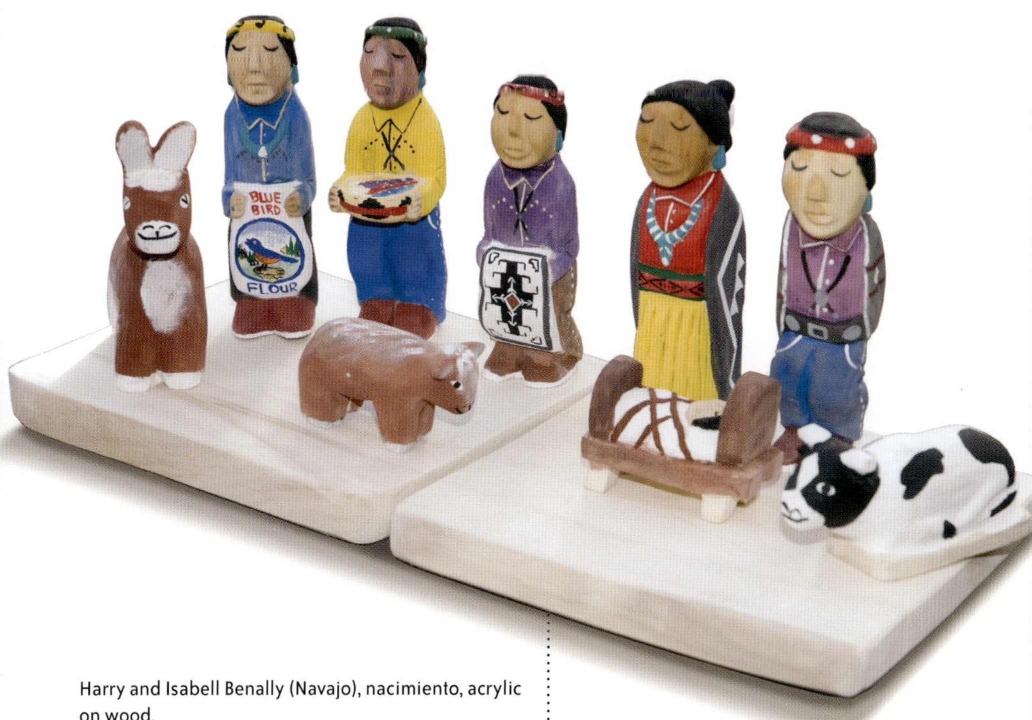

Harry and Isabell Benally (Navajo), nacimiento, acrylic on wood.

artisans with less traditional materials. Troy Slice of Zuni is carving them from antler and inlaying the figures with **turquoise**, **coral**, malachite, lapis lazuli, and other semi-precious stones, and Wilson Romero of Cochiti is carving them in a simple, stark manner from native stone found on Pueblo lands.

Although the birth of Jesus is not generally celebrated as part of the Navajo religion, since the 1960s some Navajo folk artists have carved nacimiento figures out of **cottonwood**, using hand-held tools, then sanded and painted them in bright acrylic paints with intricate details. They typically range in size from three inches to several feet in height. Among the first Navajo carvers to do so was Tom Yazzie (b. 1930), who is known for his nativity figures dressed in traditional Navajo attire—wrapped in **trade blankets** and adorned with silver and turquoise **squash blossom** necklaces and **concha** belts—and his baby Jesus is wrapped in a **cradleboard**.

Another prominent Navajo carver making nacimientos is Harry Benally (b. 1951), whose wife Isabell paints his figures. Together they create nativity figures with their eyes reverently closed, dressed in traditional Navajo attire, accompanied by the Three Wise Men bearing gifts of a sack of Blue Bird flour (to make frybread), and a Navajo-style basket and weaving.

Nativity scenes are also artistic expressions of indigenous people in Mexico, where the scenes originated in the early days of European contact.

Made of clay, wood, or tin, the Mexican nacimientos often include depictions of folklife alongside the scene of the birth of Christ. The tradition of the nativity or the crèche has long been deeply important to Hispano artisans in the Southwest, as well as in Spain and Mexico. An 800-piece nacimiento consisting mostly of miniature painted terra-cotta figurines collected throughout Mexico can be seen on permanent exhibit at the Tucson Museum of Art's historic La Casa Cordova. Begun in 1977 and completed in 2009, it was created by Maria Luisa Leon Tena in honor of her mother. Potters in **Mata Ortiz**, Chihuahua, Mexico, carry on the tradition today with their clay nacimientos.

Although a subject that has not been well studied, the nativity or crèche has long been deeply important to Hispano artisans of the Southwest, where they have been made through the centuries. Among those who have made them (and continue to do so) are **Córdova woodcarvers** in New Mexico.

Navajo naja, ca. 2012, sterling silver with coral.

NAJA (Nazha) / an anglicized form of the Navajo word *nazha* meaning "crescent," and a design motif dating to ancient times in several parts of the world (especially around the Mediterranean Sea) with a complex history and symbolism, it is a term used in the Southwest to refer to a crescent-shaped pendant of wrought or cast **silver** made by Navajo silversmiths to hang from the forehead plates of **horse bridles/headstalls** and later also from **squash-blossom** silver-bead necklaces. The crescent-shape design of the naja was adapted by the Navajos from bridle ornaments made by Mexican smiths, who in turn copied the motif from the Spaniards (who also used it on their horse gear). Najas were also popular among southern and central Plains Indians, who hung it on their mounts and used them as personal decoration. They were initially hammered from annealed silver coins or ingots; as early as 1870 some najas were cast; and by the turn of the twentieth century most were made by the **casting** technique. Early Navajo-made najas are single; as silverworking knowledge increased, elaboration of the motif followed, and najas were made with double "arms," one set within the other, and sometimes triple arms. Decoration on the arms varies from none to simple file markings and stamps to elaborate **stamp work** or rows of inlaid stones. Arm terminals are finished in a variety of ways: they may be tapered into one or more points, domed like a Navajo-made silver **button**, flattened into a round disk with or without stampwork, or shaped into tiny hands.

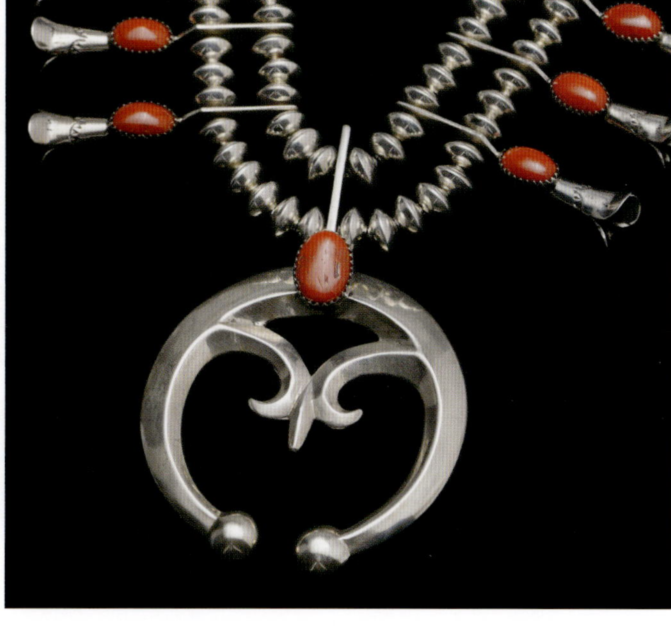

Originally, sandstone and later a lightweight volcanic stone called **tufa**, or tuff, was used to make the two-piece molds for casting. Once the naja is removed from the mold, files and other abrasives are used to smooth and finish the form. By the early 1880s Navajo smiths were ornamenting najas with **turquoise** stones set in **bezels**; the turquoise might dangle inside the curve or rise above the naja, hiding the loop used for attaching it to the necklace. There is essentially no stylistic difference between the najas intended for Navajo leather horse bridles and those intended for necklaces. However, najas for bridles have a more substantial loop for attaching them to the forehead plate, and these loops have a flat surface on the back so the naja will rest comfortably against the horse's forehead.

Contemporary Navajo jewelers continue to cast traditional najas and sell them individually or use them to adorn squash-blossom or simple-beaded necklaces. When making the traditional naja pendant, however, they add their own artistic touch and continually experiment with new techniques, different tools, innovative designs, and use of unusual stones. Najas as well as the squash-blossom necklaces have become quitessential, highly sought-after examples of the creativity and tradition of Southwestern Native American jewelry.

NAMBÉ PUEBLO POTTERY / primarily **micaceous** clay cooking pots, fired to a glittering black or golden color. After the arrival of the railroad in the region in 1880, Nambé potters began creating some pieces for the tourist market, including miniature pitchers and dog **effigies**. In the early 1990s, utilitarian micaceous ware was transformed into a form of art pottery. A key figure in this transformation was Nambé potter

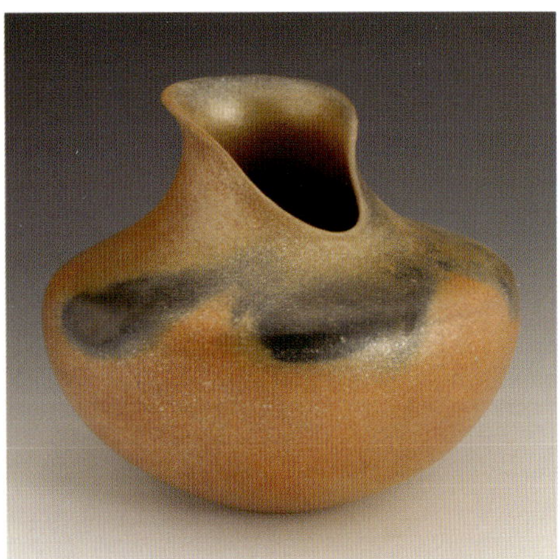

Lonnie Vigil (Nambé), micaceous jar.

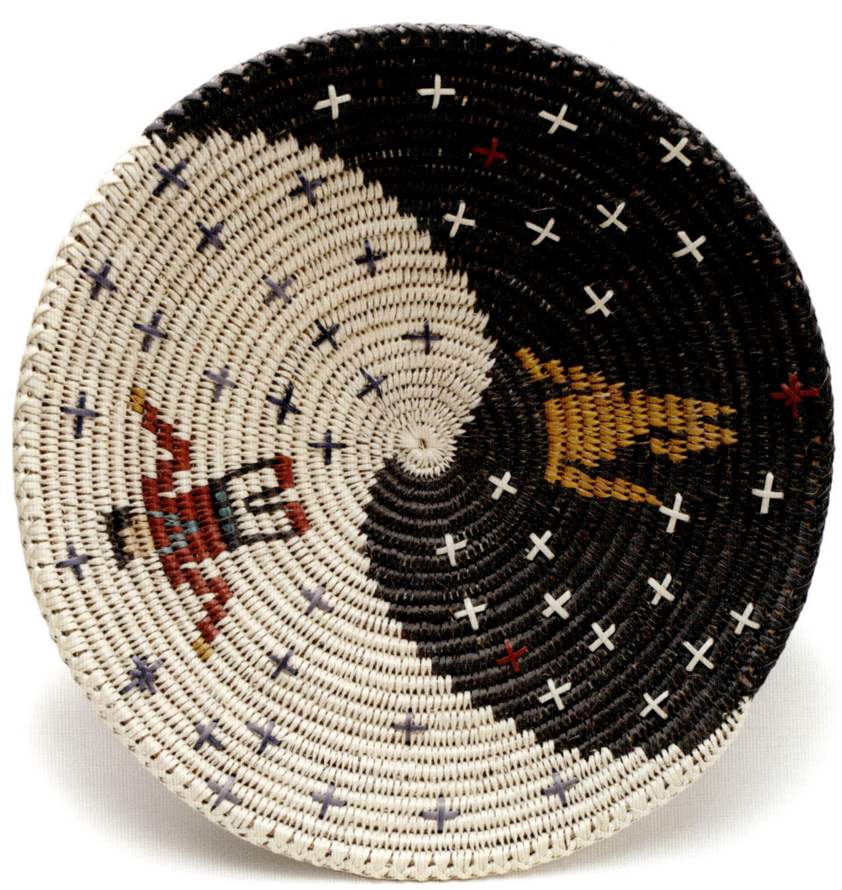

Sally Black (Navajo), pictorial coiled basket ("Story of Creation" or "Placing The Stars"), 2003, sumac, commercial and natural dyes.

Lonnie Vigil (b. 1949), who became known for the remarkable symmetry, large size, and simplicity of his stark, glittering, micaceous pots in black or bronze. Vigil, who credits Clay Mother for teaching him the art of pottery, uses clay from the Nambé hills to create the incredibly thin walls of his contemporary pieces. It is through Vigil's work that pottery making has been kept alive at Nambé.

NAVAJO BASKETS / after their arrival in the Southwest, sometime between AD 1200 and 1500, the Navajos learned basketry skills from Pueblo weavers. Spanish accounts dating to the seventeenth century mention the importance of Navajo baskets as items of trade with the Spanish and other Native Americans. The early Navajo baskets created for utilitarian purposes and for trade include: **twined** or **coiled** cone-shaped burden baskets for collecting wild and cultivated plant foods; **coiled** basketry **water jars** (coated inside and out with **piñon pitch**) called *tó'shjeeh*; and a coiled shallow bowl or tray (about 12 to 14 inches in diameter and several inches deep) called *ts'aa'*, used in the household for serving and pre-

paring foods and for various ceremonial rituals.

In the late 1800s, the Navajo basketmaking tradition began to decline—the utilitarian wares were largely replaced by factory-made metal buckets and pans, and basket production was replaced by rug weaving as the most profitable enterprise. The decline was also due in part to a set of strict taboos that came to be associated with the Navajo creation of ceremonial baskets. The Navajos acquired, for instance, the coiled trays or *ts'aa'*—more familiarly known as the **wedding basket**—used for ceremonial purposes (and still one of the most widely recognized basket styles of the Southwest today) from other Native peoples, especially the San Juan Paiutes and Utes.

Thanks to the establishment of basket-making classes, the support of Anglo post traders in the region, and the creativity of Navajo weaver Mary Holiday Black (b. 1935), coiled basket weaving experienced a dramatic revival and renaissance in the Navajo Nation beginning in the mid-1960s. Black was particularly inspirational and influential: she taught her family and extended family the art of basket weaving, and she experimented with dyes and new designs. In her imaginative pictorial trays, she portrayed designs based on traditional Navajo stories such as "Placing the Stars."

In recent decades, there has been an explosion of innovation among Navajo basket makers, especially by the Black family, who continually create coiled trays (with **sumac** sewing elements, sumac foundation rods, and aniline **dyes**) featuring new, colorful designs that reflect Navajo culture and history. These works of art are intended to be displayed prominently on a collector's wall. Some Navajo basket weavers, however, remain firmly entrenched in the past: these women have revived the old-style piñon-pitch basketry water jars. See also **basketry**, **basketry materials**, **close stitch**, **coiling—basketry**, **pictorial baskets**, **piñon pitch/sap**, **Spider-Woman Cross**, **water jars**, and **wedding baskets**.

NAVAJO FOLK ART / made on the Navajo reservation since at least the 1970s, folk art—ranging from polka-dotted wooden chickens to horses sculpted out of mud to pottery with tiny **appliquéd** figures and animals—is both a creative outlet and successful commercial venture for numerous Navajos. Traditionally, it was considered taboo for a Navajo to carve a human or religious figure: if the carving was inaccurate or destroyed or broken, it could bring bad luck to both the creator and the person or spirit it depicted. Even the decoration of pottery with appliquéd or painted figures was initially prohibited. Among the first to challenge the taboo was Navajo medicine man Charlie Willeto (1897–1964), who carved wood figurines beginning in 1961. Most of the work made by self-taught Navajo folk artists can be categorized—see for example: **beaded folk art**, **dolls**, **mud toys**, **Navajo pottery**, **nacimientos**, **Navajo woodcarvings**, and **pictorial rugs**—while other pieces are unique. One of the most widely acclaimed and important figures in Navajo folk art whose work defies categorization is Mamie Deschillie (b. 1920), who grew up in the small sheep-herding community of Burnham, New Mexico, and has created imaginative mud toys, cardboard collages, cardboard cut-out figures, and watercolor paintings on cardboard.

NAVAJO POTTERY / handcrafted pottery that has been made for personal and ceremonial use for at least three hundred years. Today Navajo potters are best known for pots created from coarse **micaceous** clays that turn a range of colors from golden brown to a rich dark brown when fired outdoors. Primarily made by women, Navajo pottery has traditionally been hand-**coiled** and thick walled, featuring relatively simple decoration. The forms have mainly been utilitarian cooking and storage vessels, as well as water **drums** and other ceremonial objects. The Navajos use similar techniques as Pueblo potters in forming and firing ceramics with some variations. For instance, Navajo potters sometimes use cedar wood for **firing** because it burns efficiently and at high temperatures. They also typically coat the interior and exterior of their pots with refined, melted **piñon**-tree sap (a golden brown color) to make them waterproof. (A wood stick wrapped in a rag is dipped into the pitch and then the pitch is brushed on the surface, and once it has hardened the pot is watertight. The sap is polished to a high sheen with a cloth after the pot has cooled.) Often the only decorative elements on a Navajo pot are the traditional **appliqué** "beaded necklace" just below the rim, known as a **biyo'**; the natural dark smudges known as "**fire clouds**" that occur on the surface during the firing process; and sometimes incised design elements.

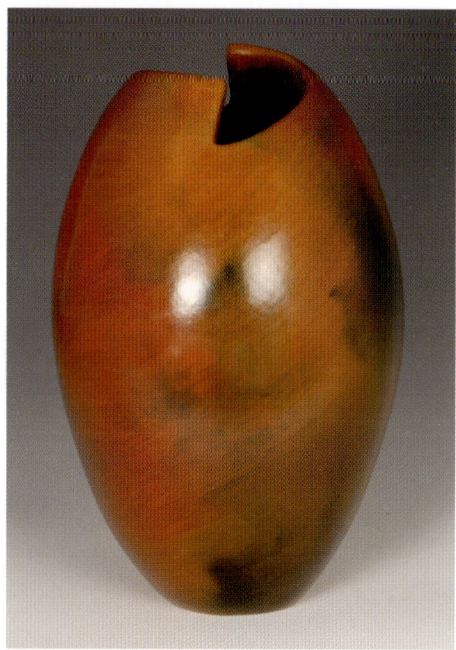

Alice Cling (Navajo), pot with fire clouds.

In the early twentieth century, commercially made wares largely replaced utilitarian pottery. Beginning in the mid-twentieth century, some potters began to produce works for the outside market. By the late 1960s Navajo pottery was experiencing somewhat of a revival. By the mid-1980s, urged on by Indian art trader William "Bill" Beaver at Sacred Mountain Trading Post near Flagstaff, Arizona, potter Alice Williams Cling (b. 1946), who learned pottery from her mother Rose Williams, was inspired to make innovative pots and to establish an important place for Navajo art pottery in the Southwestern ceramic market. Today her pots, with their elegeant forms, high luster from iron-rich piñon pitch, and distinctive fire clouds, are collected by pottery connoisseurs nationwide. The Williams/Cling family, led by Alice, paved the way for other Navajo potters to experiment with new shapes and designs, including the award winning potter Samuel Manymules (b. 1963).

Among the innovations is the appliqué of clay animals and figures to traditional forms of pottery—such as **wedding vases**, jars, bowls, and **tiles**—that has become the hallmark of the Manygoats family and other Navajo folk art potters in the Cow Springs-Shonto area. In addition, other potters have been incising their pots with traditional Navajo design motifs, such as stylized **Yé'ii** figures (Navajo deities).

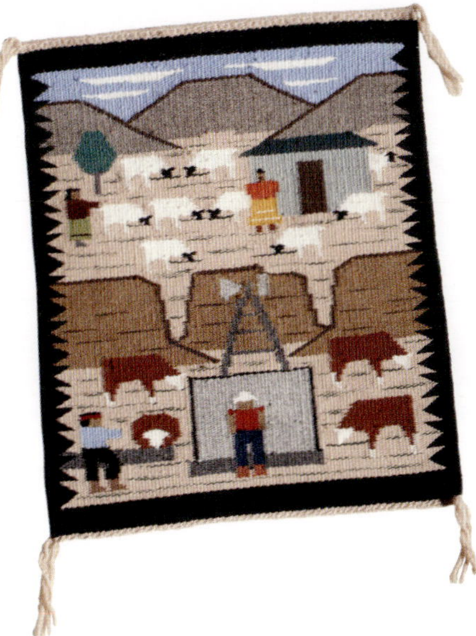

NAVAJO SILVERWORK / after learning the craft from Mexican and Spanish silversmiths around 1870, the Navajos were the first Native Americans in the Southwest to practice silverwork, fabricating **silver** ornaments for themselves and for their horses. Atsidi Sani is credited with being the first Navajo silversmith. Prior to this, the Navajos (as well as other Native peoples of the region) gained their metal jewelry (**copper**, brass, and **silver**) in trade from the Mexican silversmiths who plied their trade in the region. Silver bracelets, **tobacco canteens**, and **conchas**, all popular for trading, were among the earliest silver items the Navajo made.

Initially, the primary source of silver was Mexican pesos and later American coins from soldiers stationed at the posts near the Navajo Reservation. Coins were melted into a mold forming an ingot, which was then cooled and hammered into the desired shape. Once the separate shapes had been made, they were joined together by soldering and fashioned into various pieces of jewelry. The silver was decorated by using **cold chisels**, files, and stamps or **dies**.

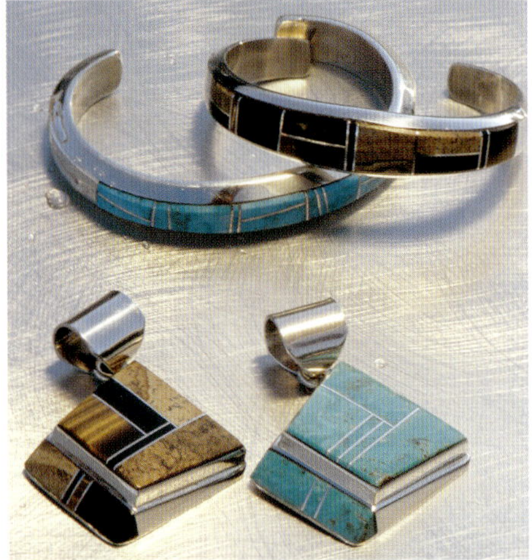

ABOVE: Bracelets and pendants by Wayne Muskett (Navajo). **TOP:** Navajo cuff bracelet, silver with overlay design and a turquoise stone.

By the early 1880s, the Navajo smiths had mastered soldering and were cutting and shaping **turquoise** stones and setting them in the silver. They made simple rings, bracelets, earrings (often just consisting of a loop of silver through a drilled turquoise bead or pendant), **buttons**, **ketohs**,

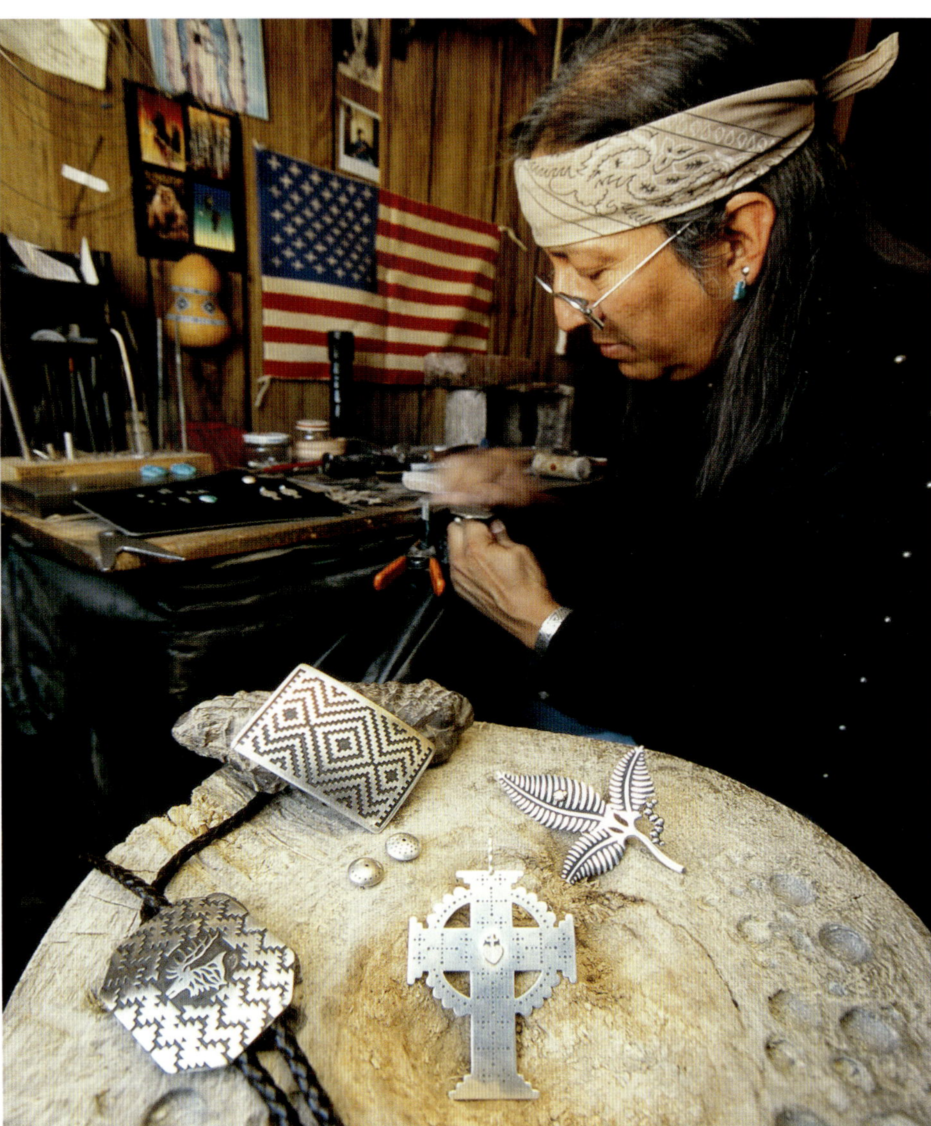

Roland Brady (Navajo) works on intricate silver jewelry.

squash blossom necklaces, **concha** belts, and decorations for **horse bridles.** By 1880 Navajo silversmiths living near military forts and railroad depots were making souvenir objects such as **spoons**, letter openers, and watch fobs. Historically, and continuing to the present, silver jewelry is considered an important sign of prestige and wealth among the Navajos (and other Native peoples of the region) and serves as items for barter with traders and others.

The availability of sheet silver and wire in the 1920s and 1930s saved silversmiths a lot of time and encouraged the increased production of simple items like bracelets and pins. Around this time, increased tourism to the region encouraged the sale of Native American jewelry, and factory-like curio shops cranked out cheap versions of

Navajo pieces. Navajo and Pueblo silversmiths demonstrated their art for the public in these stores. In the 1930s modern equipment and commercially cut stones brought more precision and ease to silversmithing. At the same time, various Indian and non-Indian organizations and agencies began encouraging a revival of traditional craftsmanship and styles, later leading to a flowering of silversmithing among the Navajos and other Native peoples of the Southwest. In the 1930s and '40s, jewelry made in **curio** shops and in artisans' homes became an important element of the Pueblo and Navajo economies. Presently, there is an abundance of Navajo jewelers working in the art; they are constantly expanding the range of materials and designs, and often setting various gems and semi-precious gems in their pieces.

NAVAJO TEXTILES / see **bayeta**, **blanket**, **Burntwater rugs**, **Chief's Blankets**, **Chinle style**, **cochineal**, **yarn—commercial**, **Crystal style rugs**, **dyes—aniline**, **dyes—vegetal**, **eyedazzler**, **Gallup Throw**, **Ganado style**, **Ganado Trading Post**, **Germantown yarns/rugs**, **yarn—handspun**, **Klagetoh Rug style**, **lac**, **loom—upright**, **manta**, **Merino wool**, **Moki style**, **pictorial rugs**, **pound blankets**, **raveled yarn**, **round-shaped Navajo rugs**, **saddle blankets**, **sampler rugs**, **sarape**, **sandpaintings—textiles**, **Slave Blankets**, **Spider Woman**, **Spider-Woman Cross**, **spindle**, **spirit line**, **storm pattern**, **tapestries**, **Teec Nos Pos**, **Tree of Life**, **twill weave**, **two-faced weave**, **Two Grey Hills**, and **Wide Ruins rug style**.

NAVAJO WOODCARVINGS / a folk art tradition established in the early 1960s by pioneering Navajo artist and healer Charlie Willeto (active ca. 1961–1964), who was encouraged and supported in his endeavor by Indian art traders in Arizona, and made hundreds of animal and human figures as artistic expressions intended for sale. Over time, other Navajos began carving and painting wooden figures as well. Ranging in size from five inches to five feet, these figures are simply carved out of wood, usually **cottonwood**, with basic tools—axe, hatchet, hammer, saw, or pocketknife—and painted with house paint, watercolors, or acrylic, and sometimes adorned with horsehair, sheep wool, bark, and other natural materials or found objects. These highly original forms derive from the personal influences and experiences of each woodcarver.

Some of the more elaborate examples are adapted from Navajo ceremonial narratives, depict everyday life on the reservation, or are likenesses of Navajos dressed in typical Navajo clothing—men in jeans, shirts, and **trade blankets** and adorned with **turquoise** necklaces and earrings; women in cotton skirts and crushed velvet blouses with **silver** buttons and wearing turquoise and silver jewelry. Among the more popular of the whimsical Navajo woodcarvings made today are the colorful chickens and ravens made by the Herbert family.

NEEDLEPOINT / a subcategory of **cluster work** jewelry, developed by jewelers at Zuni Pueblo, New Mexico, by the 1930s, in which small, narrow, elongated stones (usually **turquoise** or **coral**) are set in parallel or concentric rows to

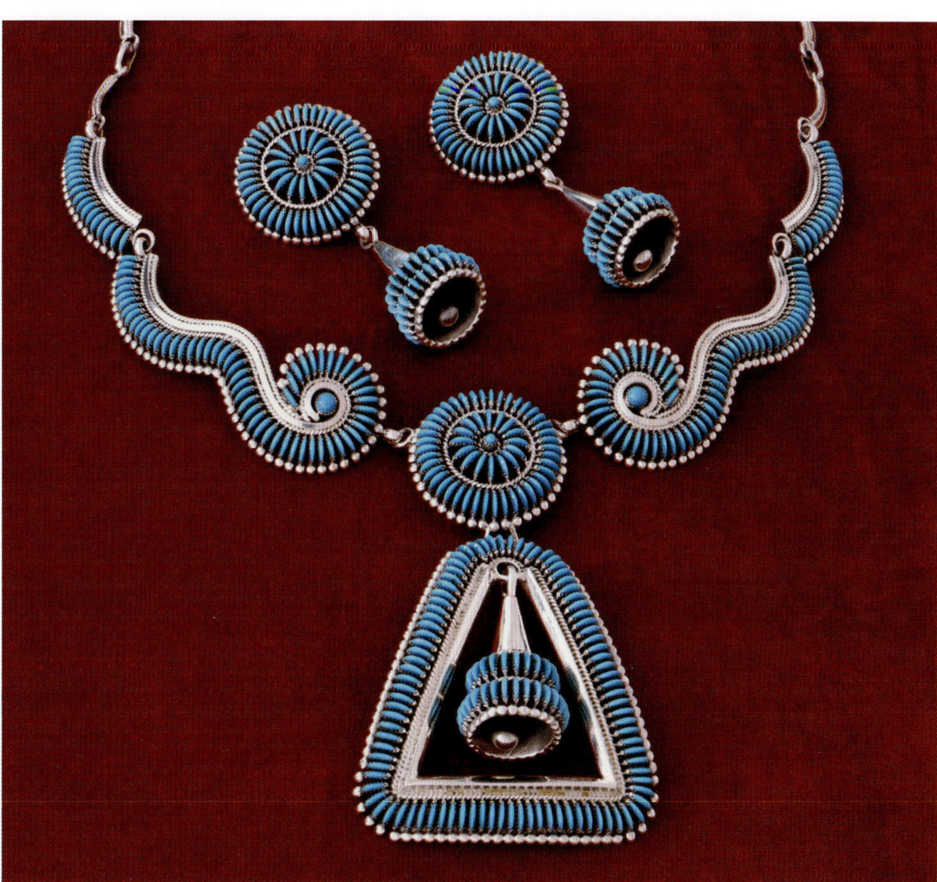

Edith Tsaybetsaye (Zuni), needlepoint-style necklace with turquoise set in silver.

form a cluster of various patterns in bracelets, pins/pendants, or earrings. In early examples, the materials were often separated by bands of twisted wire. Later on, **silver** panels were added between rows to create more complex designs. Post trader C. G. Wallace encouraged Zuni jewelers to use the intricate and difficult small-stone techniques of needlepoint and **petit point**, in the hope that these styles would prevent the mass-production of machine-made Native-style jewelry. In recent decades, Navajo jewelry artists have also adopted the needlepoint technique, generally using treated turquoise. See also **petit point** and **Zuni Pueblo jewelry**.

NICHO (niche) / an arched (or sometimes rectangular) recess or hollowed-out space in an interior (and sometimes exterior) **adobe** wall, used to display three-dimensional objects, in particular **bultos** or other religious objects. The term can also refer to freestanding wood or tin cabinets typically used to house **retablos**, bultos, or prints of saints. The early tin nichos, a popular New Mexican folk art since the mid-nineteenth century, are often made from tinplate recycled from tin containers that is punched or **embossed** (using punches or **dies**) with decorative patterns and then painted. Another form of decoration added to tin nichos is scraps of commercially made wallpaper or hand-painted paper.

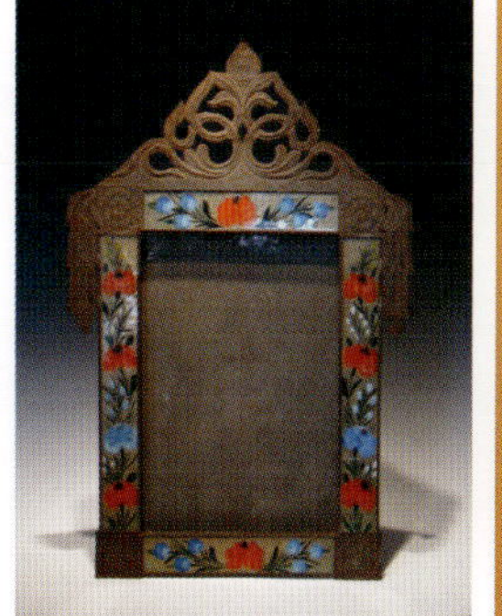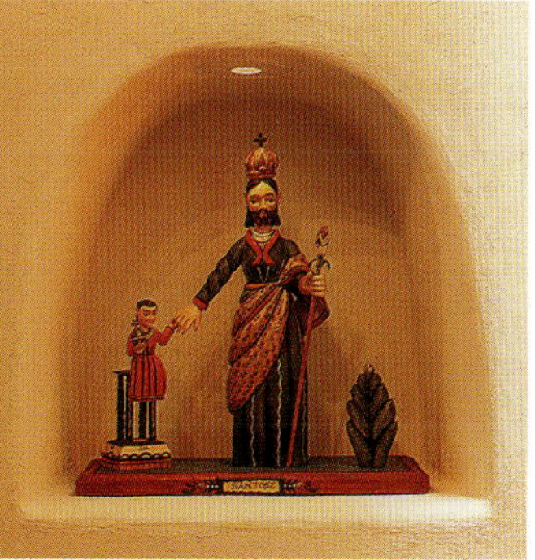

Tin nicho (left) and recessed adobe wall nicho (right).

NUESTRA SEÑORA DE GUADALUPE (Our Lady of Guadalupe, Earth Mother Tonantzin) / the patron saint of Mexico and the single most potent and popular religious and cultural image associated with the Southwest, especially for the region's **santeros** and **santeras**, who frequently portray the Virgin in their **retablos** and **bultos**. The miraculous apparition of Our Lady of Guadalupe occurred on December 9, 1531, when she appeared to an Aztec Indian convert named Juan Diego, while he was walking past Tepeyac Hill, outside Mexico City. She told him to instruct Bishop Zumárraga to build a church for her on the spot where she had appeared. The bishop denied Juan Diego's request, twice, insisting on seeing proof of the vision. During a third apparition, the Virgin instructed Juan Diego to gather roses he found growing on the hillside and take them to the bishop. When he placed the roses at the bishop's feet he discovered that the Virgin's image had miraculously imprinted itself on his cloak (or *tilma*), in which he had carried the roses.

The tilma, which still hangs above the main altar in the Basilica of Nuestra Señora de Guadalupe in Mexico City, bears the image of a young woman with dark hair, eyes downcast and hands folded, surrounded by rays of light, clad in a blue robe sprinkled with gold stars, and balancing on the crescent moon. The Basilica, with its miraculous tilma, is now the most visited pilgrimage site in the western hemisphere.

Today the Virgin of Guadalupe is celebrated on her feast day, December 12, in the southwestern U.S., Mexico, and elsewhere with special Masses, processions, and dramatic presentations. For the devotees of Guadalupe she serves as a model of the benevolent mother and Christian virtues including faith, hope, and charity; she also intercedes on the behalf of supplicants. Throughout the Southwest, there are many churches and chapels named in her honor.

Her now iconic image—ranging from detailed replications of her "portrait" on the tilma to creative interpretations that reflect an artist's individual expression—appears in home shrines and chapels *(capillas)*, in churches, on stone grave markers, on wall murals and low-rider cars, on glass candle holders, on ceramic tiles embedded in walls and niches in homes and on public edifices, on body tattoos and t-shirts, set in stained glass, in sacred folk art (retablos and bultos), in tin and wood and clay, in jewelry and cloth, in **colcha** embroidery, in **relicarios**, and on a wide variety of other devotional objects.

OBSIDIAN / a hard, dark, volcanic glass formed when rhyolitic lava cools rapidly, used by prehistoric peoples for chipped- and flaked-stone tools, such as knives and arrow points, because this raw material fractured in a predictable way resulting in razor-sharp edges. Typically, the sharpened obsidian was secured to the shaft of arrows or the wood handles of knives with deer **sinew**. Obsidian was a common early trade item among the Native peoples of the Southwest. Today some Zuni artisans carve small **fetishes** such as **bears** and other forms out of brown or snowflake obsidian and some Native American jewelers in the region set pieces of obsidian in **silver**.

OCOTILLO (*Fouquieria splendens*) / a native desert plant with leafy pole-like branches (or canes) topped with bright orange-red tubular flowers (especially after rainfall) in the spring, summer, and occasionally fall, found growing on the coarse-soiled alluvial plains and hillsides from the Sonoran desert in Arizona to the Chihuahuan desert of New Mexico and western Texas. Typically leafless most of the year and covered with woody spines, ocotillos produce many leaves after significant precipitation; they can grow up to fifteen feet tall. Native Americans in the Southwest have traditionally used every part of the ocotillo plant. For instance, the branches have been used to build fences to protect crops from rodents and burrowing animals; to construct ceilings; and to build **ramadas** or other structures. The Hualapai people in Arizona are known to have used ocotillo branches for building huts; the Tohono O'odham have used fibers from the plant for building huts and as ribs in dome-shaped homes; and the Pimas made dethorned branches into shelves by binding the branches with rawhide. Today, the branches are still utilized in Arizona to make various types of fences and sometimes ceilings in traditional-style homes. See also **latillas**, **living fences**, and **pit structures**.

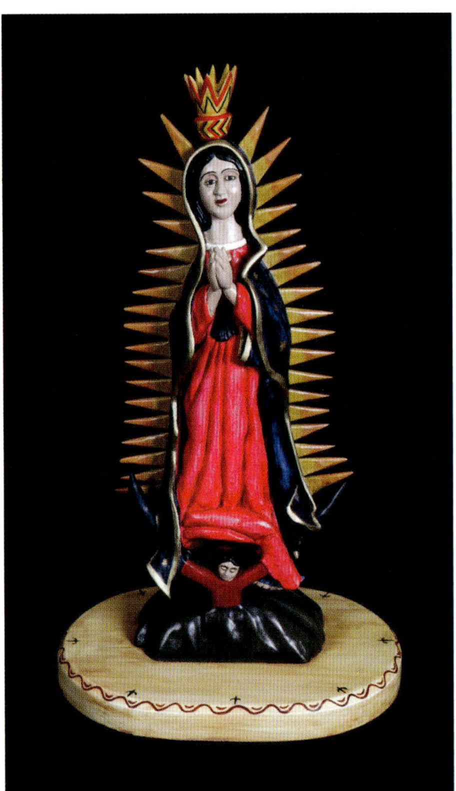

Rodolfo Parga (New Mexico), Nuestra Señora de Guadalupe bulto, natural pigments.

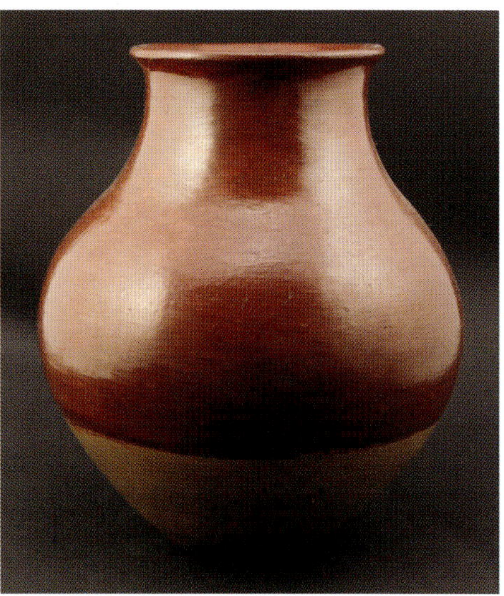

Tomasita Montoya (Ohkay Owingeh), redware pot, ca. 1955.

OHKAY OWINGEH (San Juan) PUEBLO POTTERY / pottery that historically consisted of cooking ware of **mica**-rich clay, as well as painted and **blackware** types of utilitarian pottery. Today the pueblo is recognized for its polished and highly decorated **redware**, distinguished by an unslipped and buff-colored band around the middle, lightly incised with designs—geometric shapes, floral patterns, cross-hatchings, and other forms—that are often highlighted with white, red, and **micaceous** clay paints. A handful of potters revived this style in 1930s, based upon **potsherds** discovered at a fifteenth-century ancestral pueblo located across the Rio Grande. The natural occurrence of **fire clouds** on the surface of pottery are highly prized at Ohkay Owingeh. At present potters work in a wide variety of styles, from **carved** wares to incised **polychrome**.

OLLA / a Spanish word for "jar," a term most often used to refer to pottery jars or baskets made to contain food or water, made by Pueblo, Maricopa, and other Southwest Native American tribes, as well as by Hispano artisans of the region. Generally smaller and lighter than storage jars, clay ollas were used to carry and store water and had concave bases that facilitated carrying them upon the head. They have also been used for cooking. Olla is also the inclusive term used for **Mata Ortiz** clay pots, made in the state of Chihuahua, Mexico.

OVERLAY / a jewelry construction technique developed in the late 1930s by the Hopis, in which a design is traced on a sheet of sterling **silver** (or sometimes gold) and then carefully cut out with a jeweler's saw by hand, creating a top design layer that is then soldered to another sheet of silver, called the bottom layer. Usually the overlay piece is slightly thicker than the bottom piece. The negative areas of the design are textured, using a hammer and a small punch, and then oxidized to blacken those areas for contrast; the positive areas are polished to either a shiny or matte finish. In addition to skillfully cutting out the design, this intricate technique involves filing, **appliqué**, and **stamping**.

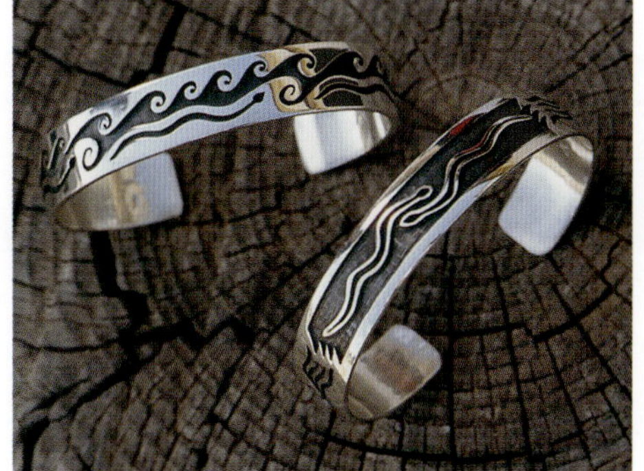

Hopi overlay bracelets by Dorothy Poleyma and Raymond Kyasyousie.

Now famous for this type of jewelry, the Hopis formerly made silver jewelry in the manner of Navajo silversmiths. The unique overlay style emerged in the late 1930s, during a research project sponsored by Dr. Harold and Mary-Russell Colton, co-founders of the Museum of Northern Arizona in Flagstaff, when old Hopi design elements, mainly from pottery, were rediscovered; at the same time the Coltons encouraged Hopi silversmiths to develop their own style of jewelry. Hopi artist Fred Kabotie was among the early smiths that used the overlay technique.

The new style of simple and bold jewelry—bracelets, **conchas**, pins, rings, earrings, belt buckles, pendants, and other forms—has flourished ever since. Most of the designs are drawn from, and symbolize, centuries-old Hopi cultural and ceremonial traditions: **bear-paw**, badger-paw, and parrot designs for Hopi clans; **kiva** steps and **katsina** figures relating to ceremonial life; and cornstalks and rain clouds as symbols of growth and fertility. Other images that frequently appear, especially on older pieces, are abstract renderings of lightning, **corn**, rain, the Hopi sun, and animals such as lizards and birds. In the 1970s Hopi jewelers began adding **turquoise** and other stones to the overlay. Today the silver overlay technique is being used by other Native peoples as well, including talented Tohono O'odham silversmiths.

OVERSTITCHING / a type of ornamentation sometimes applied to **coiled** baskets made by Hopi women, in which a decorative, light-colored stitch is placed over several darker-coiled stitches, in order to emphasize or to add features to the design.

PADDLE AND ANVIL METHOD / an ancient technique used by many cultures including the prehistoric Hohokam culture of south-central Arizona, and by some Tohono O'odham and Maricopa potters of the region today, to shape the walls of handmade pottery, by working the clay simultaneously from the outside with a wooden "paddle" and from the inside with a stone or wood piece that serves as an "anvil."

PAINTINGS ON HIDE / **Clothing** / **Objects** / an artistic tradition practiced by early Native Americans, using mineral and vegetal pigments to color and paint decorations on tanned-hide or rawhide (from buffalo, deer, or elk) clothing, shields, storage/carrying cases, and other items. Jicarilla Apaches, who arrived in the Southwest between AD 1300 and 1500, were known for this

Apache/Kiowa painted hide jacket.

work: Jicarilla women colored broad surfaces of clothing and equipment in brilliant gold, yellow, and green, and developed a distinctive geometric decoration on rawhide cases. Some early Jicarilla artisans painted realistic depictions on shields and on **parfleche**. Painting on hide largely died out in the late nineteenth century, when the Jicarillas and other Native people of the region settled on reservations and painted decoration on hide gave way to bold geometric embellishment with **beads** and other materials.

PAINTINGS ON HIDE / **Religious** / created with water-based paints on brain-tanned buffalo hides, and occasionally on elk and deer hides, portraying New Testament scenes, Catholic saints, and other holy personages, often surrounded with Baroque-style borders that imitated gilded wooden frames. They are the earliest surviving examples of Christian art in colonial New Mexico. The oldest extant examples date from the early seventeenth century. Church inventories indicate there were once hundreds of these paintings in eighteenth-century New Mexico; however, few have survived, as many clerics thought the hides unseemly and had the paintings destroyed.

Spanish **santeros** in the region had adopted this technique of using tanned leather in lieu of canvas and plants for vegetal dyes from Pueblo and Plains Indians. The surviving hide paintings suggest that these artists had knowledge of European techniques, including perspective, shading, and attention to architectural detail. Pueblo artists, probably under the direction of Franciscan friars, painted religious scenes on hide, some of which included Pueblo decorative motifs—pottery vessels, clouds, and rainbow motifs—designs still important in Pueblo culture today. Hide paintings were instrumental in helping the Franciscan friars spread the principles of Christianity throughout the Southwest.

In recent decades, there has been a revival of this painting technique; a small number of hide paintings are exhibited and sold at the Spanish Colonial Arts Society's annual Spanish Market, held in Santa Fe, New Mexico, in July and December. Among the contemporary artists recognized for their hide paintings are santeros Ramón José López and Joseph Manuel Chavez, both of whom have deep family roots in Santa Fe. Each of them uses natural pigments to paint traditional religious figures or historical scenes on brain-tanned hides of buffalo.

PAINTING ON POTTERY / before **firing**, designs are painted on the **clay** surface using colors made from organic or mineral-based materials. In some of the earliest pottery of the Southwest, glazes—mineral paints with fluxes, such as lead and **copper**, which become glassy when fired—were used for decoration. Traditionally, Pueblo and Hopi potters have used a fine brush made of narrow, flat **yucca** spears to apply the paint. Today both yucca and commercial brushes from art stores are used by Native potters. Among the many native pigments used in Pueblo pottery are: black paint, created from the brown juice made by boiling the leaves and stems of Rocky Mountain **Beeweed** (also called wild spinach), or made from tansy mustard mixed with **hematite** rock; and red paint, often made from ground stones of iron oxide or from clay.

PALMAS / See **Matachines dance wand**.

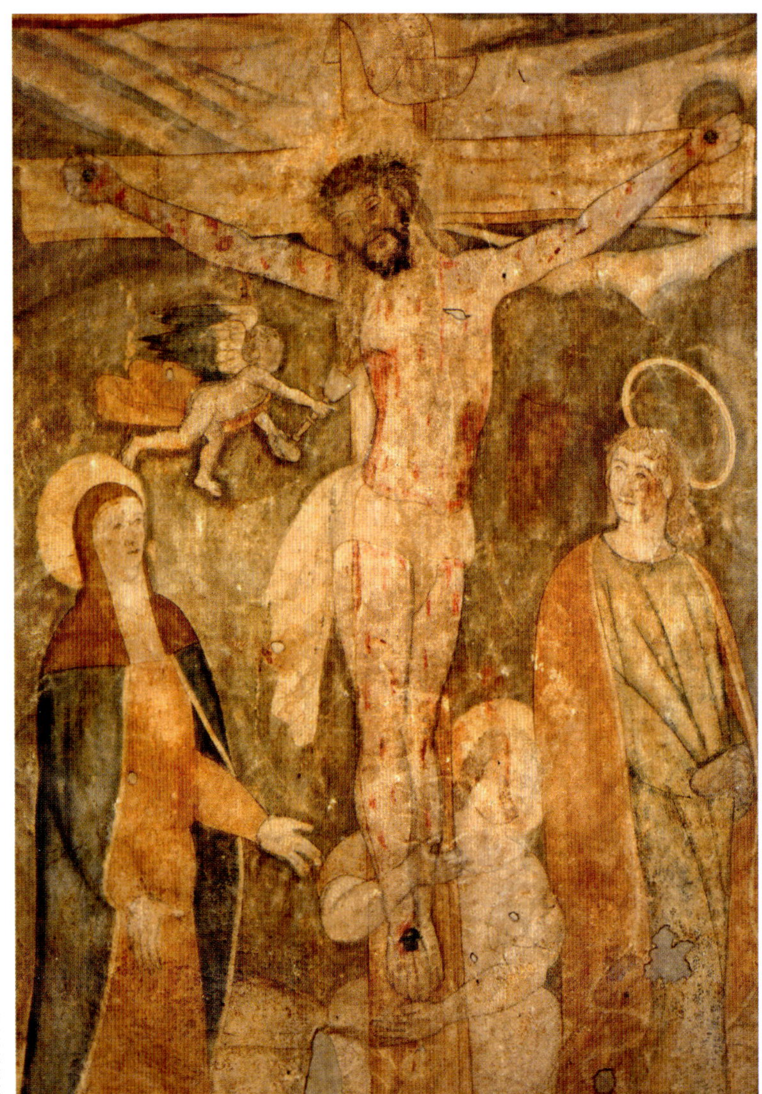

ABOVE: Franciscan F. (New Mexico), Crucifixion painting on hide, 18th century.
BELOW: Norma Ami (Hopi), paints a design on pottery.

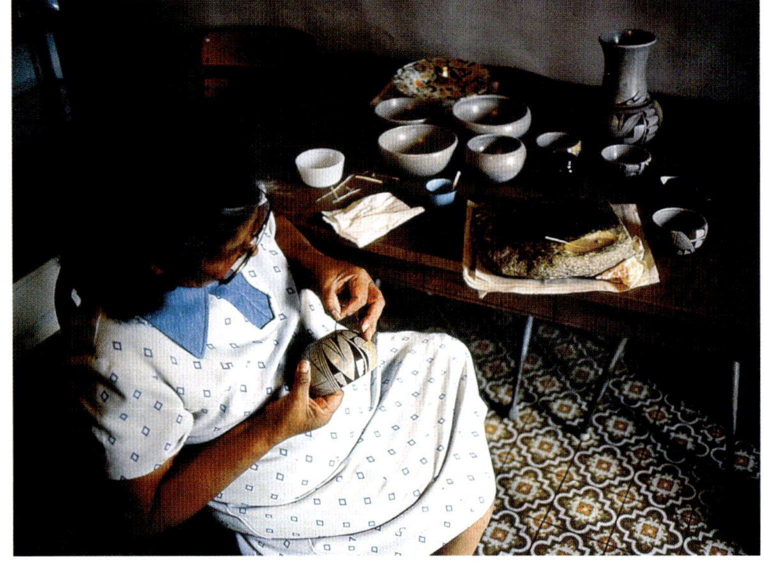

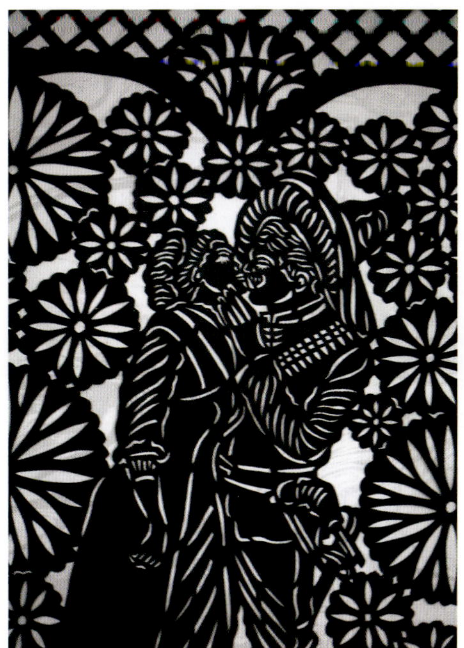

Catalina Delgado Trunk (New Mexico), papel picado.

PAPEL PICADO / meaning "perforated paper" in Spanish, a term used in the Southwest and Mexico to refer to a traditional Mexican folk art with its roots in ancient times, in which intricate patterns are cut out of brightly colored tissue paper using a pattern, a hammer, and sharp chisels (*fierritos*) of different sizes and/or scissors. A fusion of European, Asian, and Pre-Columbian artistic traditions, the fine art of making papel picado is a skill that continues to be passed down from generation to generation in Mexico. These cut tissue papers are strung together as a banner and used as a temporary decoration under the **portals** of homes and across the narrow streets of colonial Mexico villages, as well as throughout the American Southwest, for fiestas, christenings, and a variety of other celebrations, especially El Día de los Muertos (Day of the Dead).

For the latter, skeletal figures engaged in everyday activities of the living are portrayed. Among the other common images depicted are the Virgin of Guadalupe, nativity scenes, historic figures such as artist Frida Kahlo, floral and garden scenes, birds and animals, and hearts. When making papel picados for the banners, skilled craftsmen cut through as many as fifty sheets of tissue paper at a time. Borders of the cut-out sheets may be straight, scalloped, zig-zagged, or fringed.

For the individual artist, the methods and tools of papel picado have not changed much over time. Some have developed the craft into a fine art and create one of a kind works of papel picado, sold at various venues including folk art markets held throughout Mexico and the Southwest. In recent years, companies have begun to mass produce the banners using plastic or mylar instead of tissue paper, and special cutting blades instead of chisels. Although not as authentic as the tissue paper versions, the plastic banners are made in similar colors and with traditional images; they are also much sturdier and thus can be used over and over again.

PARAPET / an extension of the exterior wall that is flat, stepped, or curved, above the roof line; it conceals the roof and is often capped with brick or tile. Used in buildings of all different types of construction materials, parapets in the Southwest are typically seen in traditionally built **adobe** houses (or houses built of "adobe-like" materials). Today they are most often used to hide mechanical equipment situated on the roof.

PARFLECHE / a French Canadian word derived from the French term *parer* (to parry or turn aside) and *fleche* (arrow), referring to war shields of heavy buffalo rawhide that are tough enough to turn away an arrow, and in the Southwest referring to hand-painted folded Native American-made rawhide storage bags. These bags are usually shaped like an envelope, box, or in rare instances cylinders, and are decorated with boldly colored geometric designs of water-based paints and often tanned-hide fringe. The development and production of parfleches is most closely associated with nomadic tribes of the Great Plains. However, by the late 1860s, they were also an important part of the lifestyle of the Ute people of Colorado and Utah, who used the durable lightweight containers to carry a variety of possessions—clothing, utensils, food, and valuable medicinal or sacred objects. In addition, the Jicarilla and Mescalero Apaches made beautifully deco-

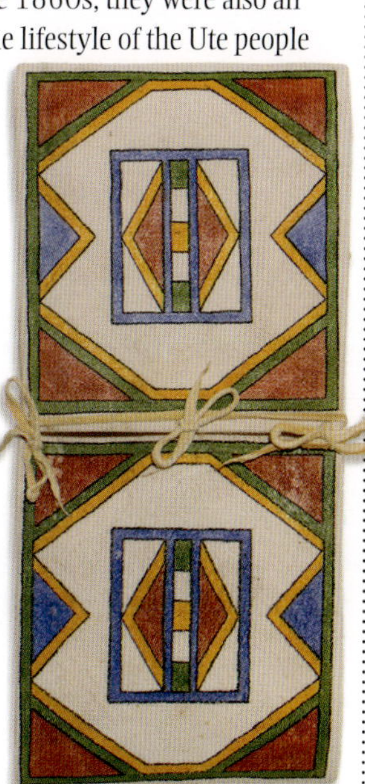

Debra K. Box (Southern Ute), parfleche, 2005.

rated parfleches in the form of large envelopes, smaller flat bags, and cylinders; they were traded to Pueblo people, some of whom incorporated parfleche designs in their pottery.

Primarily a woman's art, parfleches were made by taking rawhide—initially from elk and buffalo and later also from cow and horse—and soaking it and then stretching it over a wooden frame to dry in the sun. Then it is scraped to remove the hair and to make the hide somewhat flexible, and finally the hide is decorated with water-soluble paints of native or commercial pigments, mixed with glue, in patterns of red, yellow, green and/or blue, with the design units outlined in black. A varnish-like coating, traditionally made from prickly pear cactus juice, was applied to make the patterns water resistant. The parfleche was then cut from the dry hide and folded or assembled into the desired form.

Pueblo artisans made parfleches well into the twentieth century. The artform gradually declined among the Utes; by the 1930s they were producing fewer and fewer hide containers. They were rarely made from World War II until the late 1980s, when Ute artist Debra K. Box and her father, Austin Box, revived the art. The Boxes, who used traditional materials—cow rawhide and earth pigments—and techniques, ensured that the art of parfleche survived into the twenty-first century. Examples by the small number of Native artisans practicing the craft are displayed at Native American art fairs and at galleries in the Southwest.

PARROT / See **Acoma pottery**.

PASCOLA MASKS (Pahkola Masks) / small masks carved from soft wood such as **cottonwood**, traditionally painted black with red and white design elements—triangles, insects, animals, plants, and other symbols representing man's closeness to and respect for nature—with a cross (or sun symbol) at the forehead and sometimes on the chin, and tufts of tail hair from goats, horses, or cows placed above the eyes and under the mouth. The masks are made by Yaqui people living in Arizona.

An important part of Yaqui arts and tradition, the masks are worn by *pahkolam*—"old men of the fiesta" who serve as hosts of the tribe's rituals and celebrations during ceremonial dances, including the Lenten–Easter drama, the major ceremony of the Yaqui ritual year. Masks representing humans or goats are the most common,

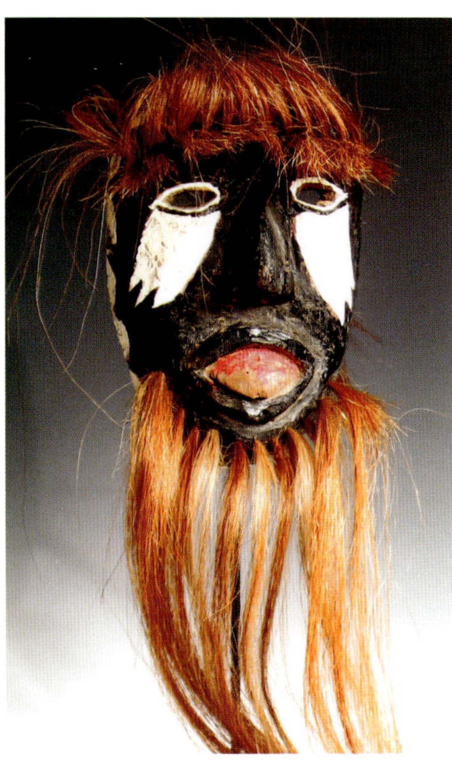

Pascola mask, Sonora/Arizona, ca. 1960, polychrome, wood with hair.

but coyotes, lions, and roosters have also been portrayed by *pahkola* carvers.

Pascola masks were a flourishing art form in the 1980s and into the 1990s; among the more prominent carvers of the era was Frank Martinez. In recent years the Yaqui mask-carving tradition was in danger of disappearing (it should be noted that traditionally the masks are burned at the end of the ceremony). However, at the time of writing this book, two artists who live in the tiny town of Guadalupe were carrying on this important tradition: Merced Maldonado, a Pascola dancer, storyteller, and artist, and Norberto Coronado, a painter and mask maker chosen as an Arizona Indian Living Treasure in 2002.

PAWN / Native American jewelry that is left as security with a post trader in exchange for goods, food, or money. For some, it was the only resource with which they could obtain food and other necessities. The original owner of the piece has a specified period to reclaim the jewelry before it becomes available for sale to the public. This system was customary on the Navajo Reservation until 1975; it was once part of an economic system that allowed the Navajos and traders on the reservation to do business in between the wool season and lambing seasons, when both were able to generate income.

Some dealers define "old pawn" as pawn jewelry dating from before 1900 and refer to pawned jewelry that was not retrieved by the agreed upon date as "dead pawn." Dead pawn was usually sold or entered into the private collection of the trader or dealer. Dead pawn jewelry—the personal property of a Native American, usually designed and executed for the wearer, not originally intended for sale—has become among the most coveted and sought after type of Native American jewelry in the Southwest, prized for its historical and cultural significance, as well as its artistry and beauty. Today the pawn system continues at select trading posts throughout the Southwest.

PETIT POINT / a subcategory of **cluster work** jewelry developed by jewelers at Zuni Pueblo, New Mexico, by the 1930s, in which exceptionally tiny round, oval, or teardrop-shape pieces of stone (usually **turquoise** or **coral**) are set in individual **silver** bezels in orderly rows, geometric patterns, or flowerlike clusters. In early examples, the materials were often separated by bands of twisted wire. Later on, silver panels were added between the rows to create more complex designs. Zuni jewelers have used petit point stone work to create exquisite rings, earrings, pins, **squash blossom** necklaces, and other forms.

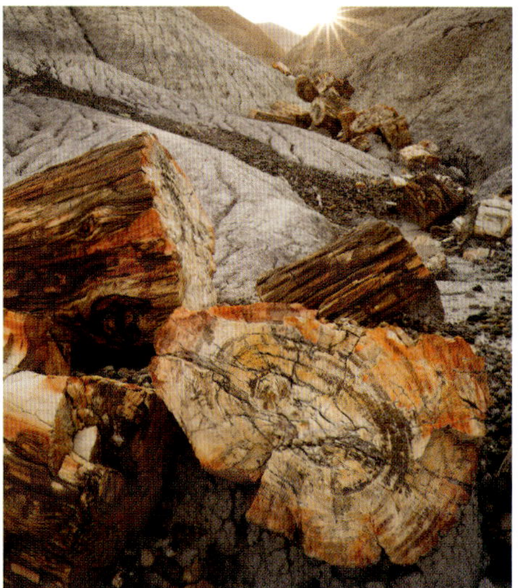

Petrified wood at Petrified National Forest, Arizona.

PETRIFIED WOOD (Fossilized Wood) / wood that has hardened over thousands or millions of years, as a mineral composition of quartz, jasper, chalcedony, or opal replaced the organic material. This type of wood has been used by Navajo jewelers as a semi-precious gemstone in their work. In the 1930s and '40s it was introduced to the Na-

vajos by Indian art traders who had the petrified wood cut and polished with lapidary equipment not available to most Native smiths. For instance, Julius Gans of Southwest Arts & Crafts in Santa Fe provided his Pueblo and Navajo smiths with cut and polished petrified wood from vendors in Tucson and Phoenix, Arizona. The colors of the hard yet brittle material become stronger after cutting and polishing. Today it is still used by Navajo artisans for fine jewelry and **inlay** work. The most significant occurrence of petrified wood is near Holbrook, Arizona, and the Petrified Forest National Park; the petrified wood used in jewelry is from private lands adjacent to the park.

Most of the petrified wood found in the region is almost solid quartz, created over 200 million years ago, when logs were washed into an ancient river system and buried by massive amounts of sediment and debris that cut off oxygen to the wood. Over thousands or millions of years the minerals absorbed into this porous wood, crystallized, and replaced the organic material.

PETROGLYPHS / a prehistoric and historic art form consisting of images pecked, ground, incised, abraded, or scratched into a rock surface, often portraying stylized human, zoomorphic, or other motifs drawn from nature, and found across the Southwest. Many were made by holding a pointed stone chisel against the drawing surface and hitting it with a hammer stone, thus carving away the dark layers of "desert varnish" on the surface, revealing the lighter-colored stone beneath. Desert varnish is the naturally occurring patination on the rock surface, resulting from airborne particles such as iron oxide and manganese oxide settling on the surface and eventually turning into a concrete-like substance; a process that can take thousands of years.

Ancestral Puebloan– and Hohokam-period petroglyph sites number in the thousands throughout Arizona, New Mexico, Utah, Colorado, Nevada, and California. Over time, historic travelers, livestock herders, and residents left their own inscriptions on rock surfaces too, often in the same vicinity as prehistoric and historic Native American petroglyphs and **pictographs**. The wide variety of images that have been depicted in petroglyphs over the centuries are too numerous to include here, however the following is an abbreviated list: mountain sheep, deer, **coyotes**, birds, lizards, rattlesnakes, **bear paws**, and insects; handprints; stylized human figures and narrative scenes such as people dancing, hunting, or riding

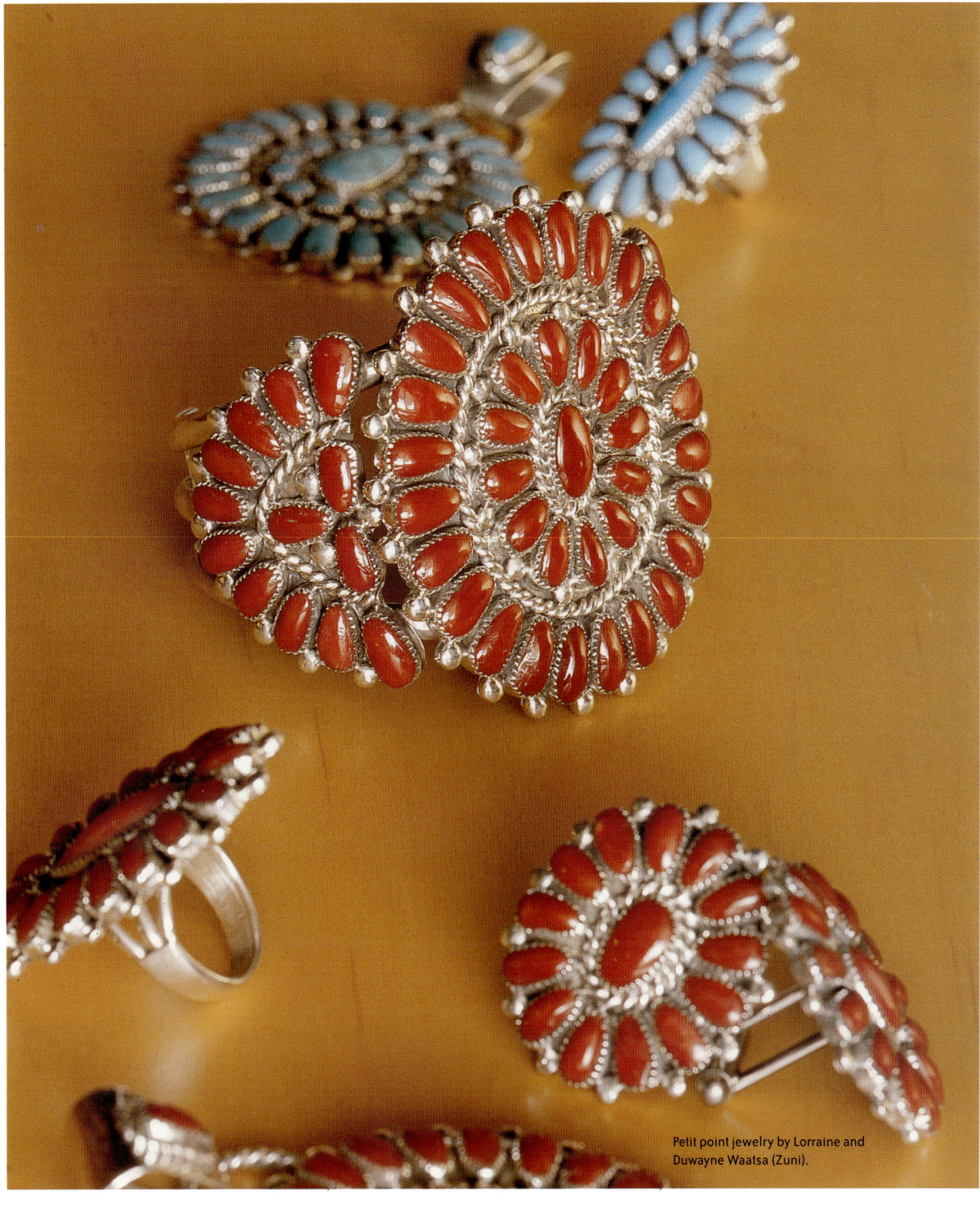

Petit point jewelry by Lorraine and
Duwayne Waatsa (Zuni).

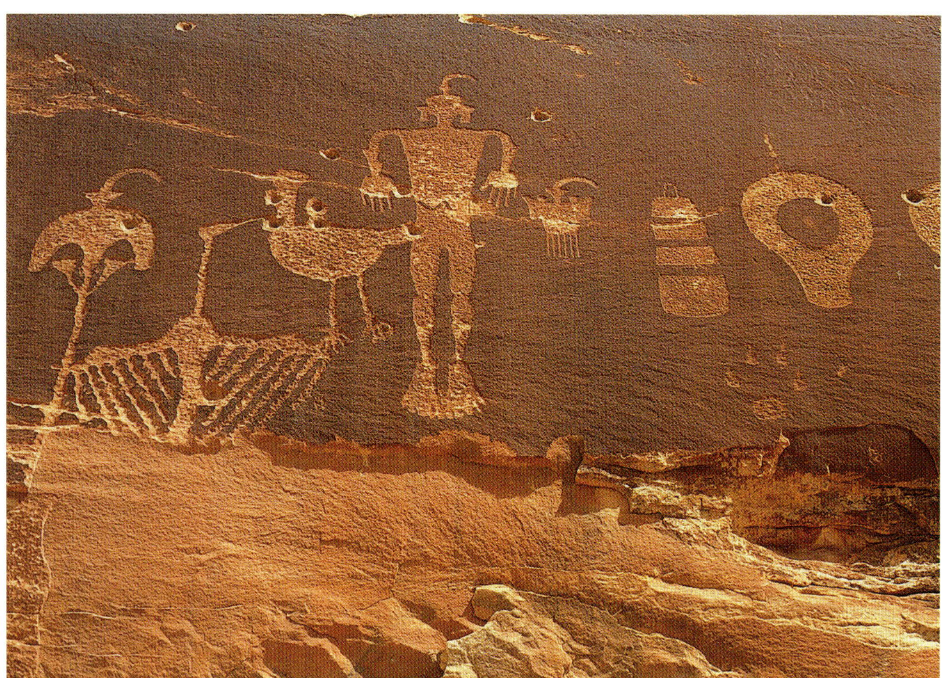

Petroglyphs at Wolfman Site, Utah.

horseback; abstract or geometric shapes like spirals, mazes, circles, and dots; textile or pottery designs; and **Yé'ii** figures. Petroglyphs on Hopi lands in Arizona sometimes include **katsina** figures and symbols for different clans. In fact, the Hopi word for petroglyph is *tutuveni* and means "clan marks of the Hopi people."

Petroglyphs have been extensively studied by archaeologists, who have distinguished several distinct styles that are characteristic of particular locations and time periods. The specific meaning of the prehistoric and historic symbols and forms depicted continue to remain a mystery. However, present-day tribal members and rock art specialists have been attempting to associate some glyphs with meanings. For example, tribal elders at Hopi and Zuni Pueblos have interpreted the many spiral and maze designs as symbols of the emergence portion of their creation story; the images, therefore, are migration markers left by the clans when traveling through the region. Some images have been determined to be ancient solar calendars used by Ancestral Puebloans to time their ceremonies; examples have been found at various sites in the Southwest, including at Puerco Pueblo in Arizona and in Chaco Canyon, New Mexico.

Whatever their meaning, petroglyphs were clearly important to their creators: etching or carving into rock is difficult and the images are permanent. To date petroglyphs and pictographs, scholars primarily rely upon: patination (fresher/brighter-looking images are generally younger, while darker ones are older—but this can be misleading, as some images may be better protected from weathering and appear brighter); association with nearby habitation sites that have been dated by archaeologists; images that appear similar to motifs on dated pottery or textiles; and known dates of the subject portrayed (such as the first use of bows and arrows).

Because of the cultural, spiritual, and archaeological importance of petroglyphs, many sites have been placed under the protection of the federal government, or are carefully managed by Native American communities. Contemporary Native American artists, weavers, and jewelers who grew up in areas abundant with petroglyphs have incorporated the motifs from the sacred rock art into their own work. See also **geoglyphs** and **pictographs**.

PICTOGRAPHS / a prehistoric and historic art form consisting of paintings or drawings in one or more colors, using mineral pigments and plant dyes, painted by splattering or with a finger or a brush (probably made from a spear of **yucca**), on a rock surface. Often pictographs were combined with the **petroglyph** technique of pecking images into the rock; some art rock specialists refer to these as pictoglyphs. The pigments in pictographs were made from a variety of natural sources—for example, red from iron oxides, white from **kaolin**, yellow from limonite, black and grays from charcoal, blue from ground azurite, and green from copper oxide or malachite. The pigments were then mixed with a binder such as saliva, urine, water, tallow, or blood to make a liquid paint. Sometimes, a small indentation in the rock floor where the pigments were ground into fine powder can be discovered near pictograph sites.

The earliest pictographs, such as those discovered at Chaco Canyon in northwestern New Mexico, are mostly human stick figures painted in dark-red ochre on the ceilings or back walls of rock shelters. The motifs and designs used in pictographs changed over time and varied by region. Among the images portrayed are abstract shapes—zigzags, parallel lines, dots, circles—and representational forms, such as human figures, animals, plant forms, handprints, paw prints, shield-like images, **Kokopellis**, and hunting and warfare scenes. Known to have spiritual, culturwal, and religious significance, these images have been extensively studied by archaeologists. However, the meaning behind most remains a mystery.

Pictographs are generally less common than petroglyphs, as in many instances the fragile paint materials used to make pictographs have faded or were washed away over the centuries. However, traces of fine examples can still be seen, especially in pictographs painted in protected locations such as in caves, under ledges, and in rock shelters. These culturally significant images, which record centuries of human presence in the region and catalog the passage of time, were made by the ancestors of the Native Americans who still inhabit the Southwest today. See also **geoglyphs** and **petroglyphs**.

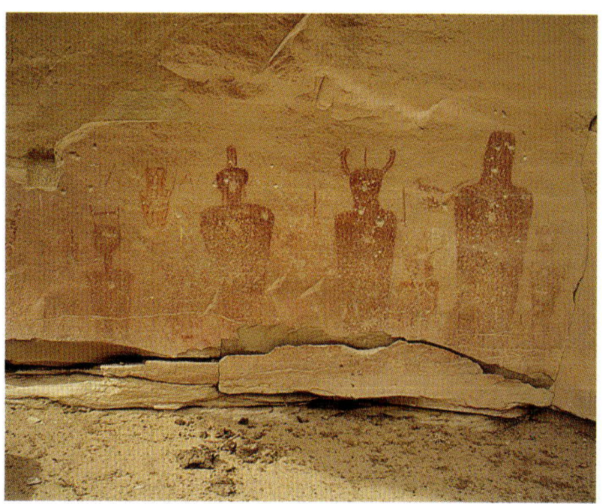

Pictographs at Sego Canyon, Utah.

PICTORIAL BASKETS / **Plaques** / handwoven baskets of natural and commercial materials made by the Native peoples of the Southwest, for utilitarian or ceremonial purposes, that incorporate recognizable images—including cultural activities, creation stories, legends, animals, native plants, and sacred symbols. Among the first to create them were the Pima, Tohono O'odham, Yavapai, and Apache peoples. Today they are woven as traditional **wicker plaques**, or as **coiled** baskets, either with all natural materials or combined with modern materials. Contemporary Navajo weavers, including Mary Black and her daughters Sally, Lorraine, and Agnes are renowned for their wide variety of imagery: people, dogs, horses, stars, blanket designs, insects, turtles, eagles, **coyotes**, and **squash blossoms**. Some contemporary Native pictorial basket weavers have chosen to specialize in one or two particular images for which they have become known. For example, San Juan Paiute weaver Rose Ann Whiskers is famous for her colorful **butterflies** added to the traditional Navajo **wedding basket** design; Hopi (Third Mesa) weaver Abigail Kaursgowva is known for her **katsina** imagery; and Hopi (Second Mesa) artisan Griselda Saufkie, chosen as an Arizona Indian Living Treasure in 1998, is renowned for her turtles and katsinas woven into her traditional coiled plaques.

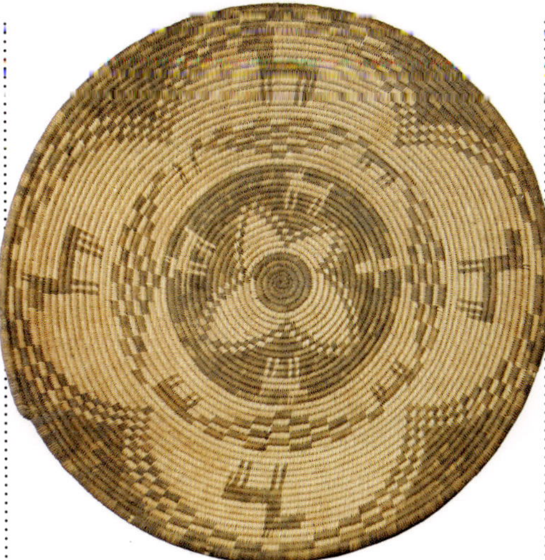
Apache pictorial tray, ca. 1900.

PICTORIAL RUGS / considered the earliest form of Navajo folk art, they are handwoven textiles that incorporate recognizable images, both realistic and highly stylized, such as scenes from daily life on the reservation, **Yé'ii** figures, **Trees of Life**, birds, trains, people, animals, and American flags. Typically, pictorial rugs are woven using wool **weft** and wool **warp**; in some instances a cotton warp may be used. The images implemented in these rugs are developed through experimentation and some, like the Yé'ii figures, are derived from Navajo religion. These pictorial blankets and **tapestries** were made as early as the 1840s, but became widespread by the 1880s, after the establishment of trading posts on the reservation and the advent of railroads in the Southwest. After World War II, they became yet more popular, due in large measure to the non-Indian demand for them. In the beginning the images consisted of "floating" design elements; by the 1930s the floating images became the main focus of the textiles. Today they are intended as wall hangings or tapestries, although some contemporary weavers, like Navajo Fanny Pete, create fuzzy, thick-woven pictorials with tassels at the corners that are intended as floor coverings. In earlier years, the subject matter of pictorials was dictated by the demands and orders of traders and tourists (including personal names, business names and logos, seasonal designs such as Christmas scenes, and landscapes). Today a variety of innovative imagery appears, including prehistoric dinosaurs, circus scenes, and Navajo legends of creation. Depictions of daily activities on the Navajo reservation remain among the most popular subjects. Contemporary weavers are creating pictorials in either the older, simpler style with figures portrayed in a naïve two-dimensional manner, or in a newer style that represents more realistic and defined figures with accurate three-dimensional perspective.

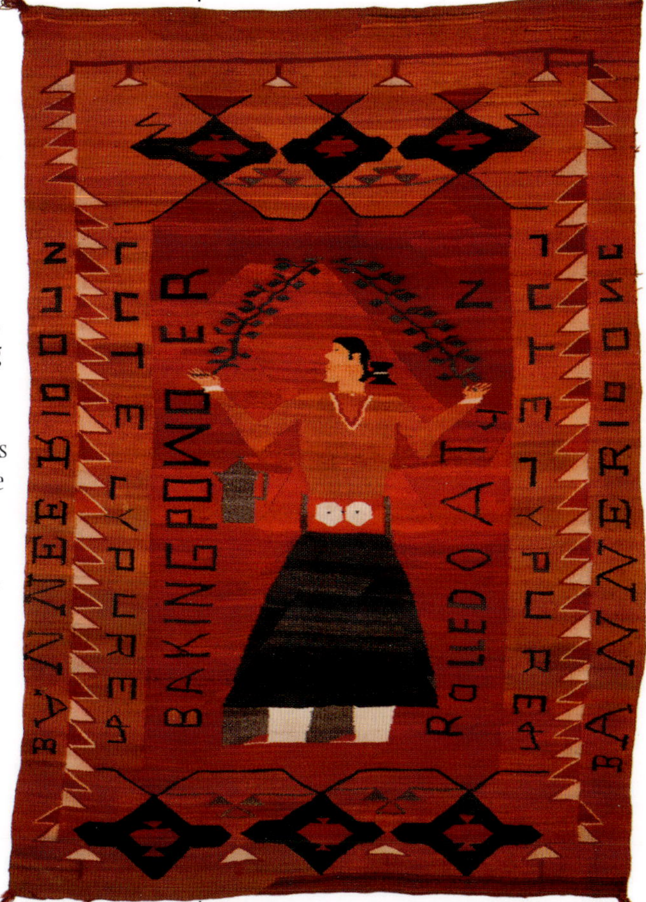

Navajo pictorial textile, ca. 1900, 78" x 54".

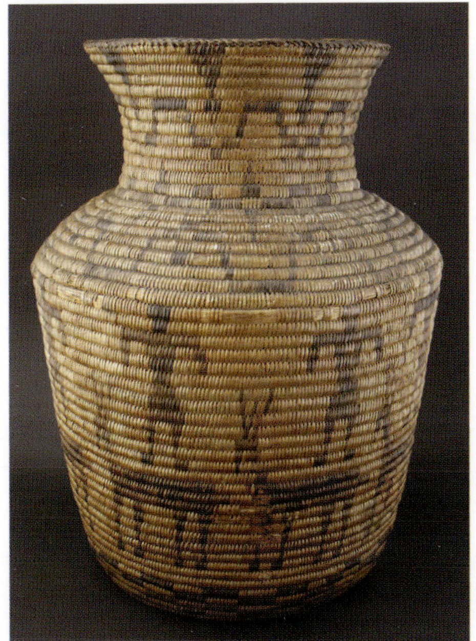
Pima pictorial olla, ca. 1900.

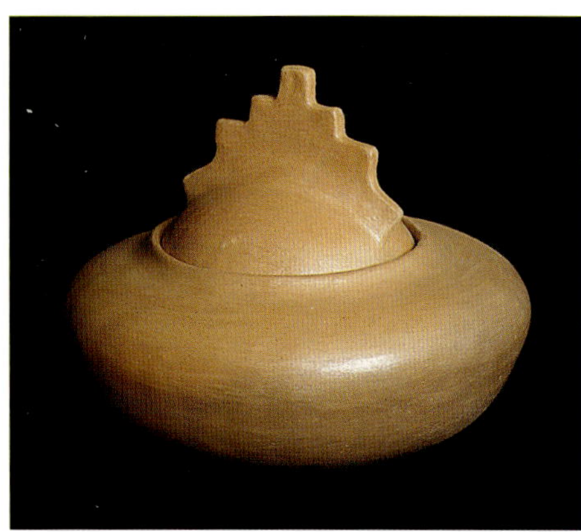

Ralph Sena (Picuris), pot with kiva-step design.

PICURIS PUEBLO POTTERY / known today for vessels of mica-rich clay distinguished by a luminous golden surface, Picuris Pueblo once made painted and blackware pottery. By the 1720s, however, thick-walled **micaceous** ware—unslipped, unpainted pottery made from **clay** with **mica** flakes that produce a glittery surface—**fired** a dark gray was the principal pottery made at Picuris.

Almost two hundred years later, when anthropologists and traders were encouraging the revival of Native American arts and crafts in the region, Picuris potters were only making the durable micaceous wares, likely because they are so superior for cooking and heating foods. After the arrival of the railroad to the region in 1880, some Picuris potters also made pottery for the tourist trade, including **rain gods**, miniature **adobe** houses, and bird, bison, and bear **effigies**. After 1930 Picuris potters began making thinner micaceous utilitarian wares that were fired in an oxygen-rich atmosphere that produces the luminous golden finish for which they have become known. No **temper** needs to be added to the coarse Picuris clay, as the mica serves as a natural tempering agent.

By the mid-twentieth century Picuris potters were experimenting with simple surface designs on their micaceous utilitarian wares; by the 1990s they had begun creating micaceous "art pottery" for sale, along with making more traditional wares. Some potters cover their pots with a **slip** consisting of high-luster micaceous material. Favored forms are distinctive tall, round-bottomed vases and bean pots with handles and lids that are bronze or reddish-orange in color.

Today potters are experimenting with different forms of minimalist designs, such as simple **appliquéd** coils, piecrust rims, or various patterns impressed in the moist clay with a variety of homemade tools. Potter Anthony Durand is known for the addition of nubs or "bosses" on the shoulders of his plain vessels, a design inspired by fragments found in the ruins of Old Picuris Pueblo. Many potters still use a corncob to shape the pot—the first step in thinning and smoothing the surface. Another decorative feature often seen is **fire clouds**—dark smudges on the surface resulting from the firing process—considered to be a prized effect at Picuris Pueblo.

PIGMENTS / Carbon (Vegetal) / a type of black pigment made from the residue of boiled stems and leaves of plants such as Rocky Mountain **beeweed** (to make a substance called guaco), tansy mustard, or other herbs, traditionally used by Native American potters to decorate clay vessels and by **santeros/santeras** to paint their **retablos** or **bultos**. In pottery, carbon paints have a watery brown appearance that turns black when the pot is **fired**. Many artisans of the Southwest continue to use these natural pigments, which are also now available commercially.

PIGMENTS / Mineral / matte pigments made from mineral substances, such as iron oxide for red or manganese oxide for black, mixed with water and sometimes with a vegetal base (such as **beeweed** juice or extract) that acts as a binder. Matte pigments are used by Native American potters for decorating clay vessels and by **santeros/santeras** for painting their **retablos** or **bultos**. The mixing of mineral paints is a fine art in itself; the potter must know the exact proportions of the ingredients. Many artisans of the Southwest, as well as the potters of **Mata Ortiz** in Mexico, continue to use the natural mineral pigments, which are also now available commercially.

PIKI TRAYS / a large, rectangular, and flat woven basket tray made by Hopi women and used for serving wafer-thin corn piki bread—one of the traditional foods made for special occasions and ceremonies at the Hopi mesa villages. The central part of the mat is **plaited**, traditionally using scrub **sumac** and more recently using narrow-leaf dune broom (*Parryella filifolia*, or *siwi* in the Hopi language). The border is wound in the wicker technique using sumac or a commercial reed material to make the form rigid; and the rim is finished with a wrap of **yucca** splints. Piki trays are made for use within the Hopi community and are rarely made for sale. They are an important part of the bride's gift to the groom's family; when given, the tray is stacked with piki bread. The making of piki bread continues to be an important skill for Hopi women to master, as it is both a staple and ceremonial food. A type of piki bread has also been traditionally made by some Pueblos; for instance, at Tesuque Pueblo this type of bread is known by the Tewa word *buwa yaweh* (or "peel off bread"). Though the subject has not been thoroughly researched, it is believed that a special basketry tray was once woven by Pueblo weavers to serve piki bread.

PIMA (Akimel O'odham) BASKETS / known for a centuries-long tradition of fine, **coiled** utilitarian baskets. By the early twentieth century, some weavers were also making coiled pieces for the tourist/collector market. Typically, Pima baskets are made using an **awl**, with cattail stems (gathered in June and July) for the bundle foundation; river **willows** (gathered from May through September) for sewing splints; **devil's claw** for the black center and rims and design accents; and a herringbone-stitched rim. Some Pima baskets incorporate red willow or red **yucca** design elements; the red **dye** is made from cooking the roots of the **mountain mahogany** bush.

Because the Pimas live on lands beside the Gila and Salt Rivers, water symbols often appear in their basket designs. Other classic Pima patterns are the whorl, fret (sometimes used to create the **squash blossom** design), and stepped zigzags. After the Roosevelt Dam was built on the Salt River, north of Phoenix, Arizona, in 1911, the Salt River dried up and many willow trees died, leading some Pima weavers to stop making baskets altogether and others to use the more commonly available yucca for the main sewing element.

Beginning in the 1920s, Pima artisans made items for the tourist trade, including miniatures (replicas of larger baskets and fanciful tea cups, saucers, pitchers, and sugar bowls) and full-sized baskets, some ornamented with glass trade **beads**. The tourist baskets were woven with willow, devil's claw, and **beargrass** and the beads were sewn around the rim. The miniatures, a favored basket type made today, are difficult to fashion, for the sewing materials must be split twice and then shaved to make them as thin as possible for weaving. At present yucca splints over a beargrass foundation have become the common Pima basket-weaving materials and the designs are either traditional in origin or highly innovative. See also **basketry materials**, **beaded baskets**, **gíhos**, and **horsehair baskets**.

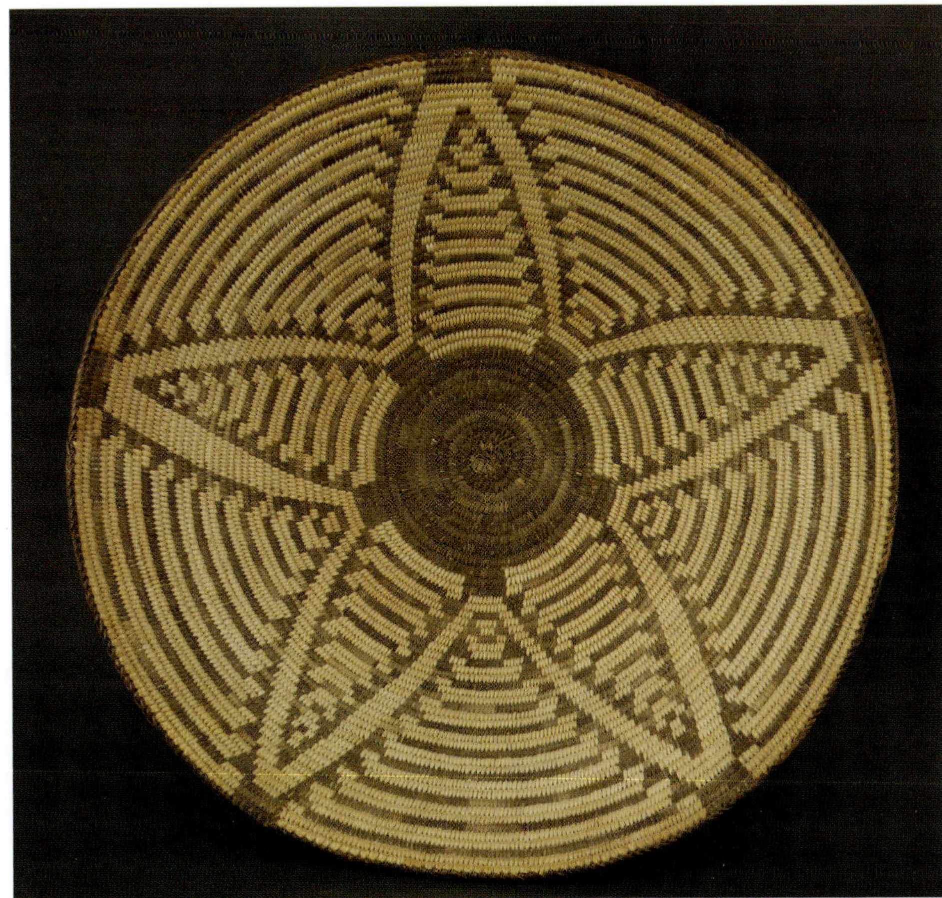

Pima star-design basket, ca. 1900.

PIÑON PITCH / Sap / pitch from piñon trees, which grow in abundance in the Southwest, has traditionally been used by Native and Hispano artisans for a variety of uses: basket makers coat handwoven **water jars/storage** baskets for waterproofing (see below); piñon sap mixed with grain alcohol was (and continues to be) used by **santeros/santeras** as a final protective varnish on their **bultos** and **retablos**; and some contemporary **Navajo pottery** is coated with melted piñon pitch for an attractive finish and for waterproofing. Some artisans add hematite to the pitch to give it a reddish hue.

PIÑON-PITCH BASKETS / pitch from piñon pine trees has traditionally been used by Native basket makers of the region to coat handwoven coiled **water jars** and **storage baskets** (rounded forms with either a straight or slightly out-flaring neck), both inside and out, for waterproofing. Baskets of this type are distinguished by their dark amber color, smooth glossy surface, and piñon scent. The Navajos call these baskets

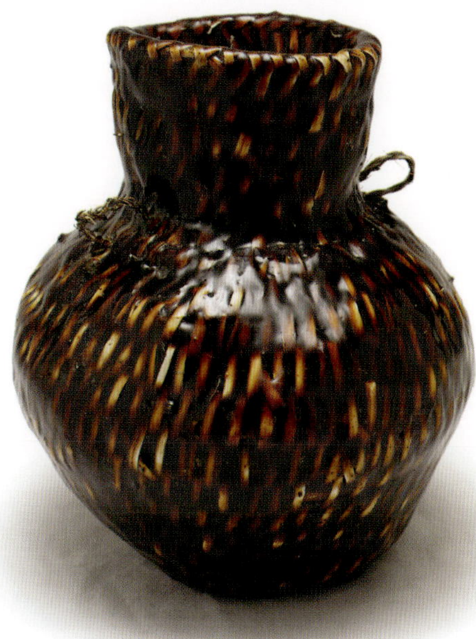

Etta Rock (Navajo), piñon-pitch basket, 2011, sumac, horse hair (handles), piñon pitch.

tó'shjeeh. First the basket is woven from split **sumac** and/or **willow**, usually with a herringbone rim and side handles of braided, looped horsehair; then the exterior (except for the handles) and interior surfaces are covered with the hot pitch; and the basket is allowed to cool. To fix any imperfections, such as air bubbles, the pot is warmed in the flames of an outdoor fire or cookstove and then the artisan uses his or her fingers to smooth out the surface.

Some tribes such as the Jicarilla Apaches and Utes also traditionally applied a thin layer of white **clay** to the outside to decorate and further waterproof the basket. Ute examples also had stoppers of juniper, bark, or clay. Western Apache piñon-sealed water jars called *tus'* were used for aging an alcoholic beverage called *tulapai*—a corn beer made from fermented ground corn and maguey.

Pitch baskets were made and used by Navajos, Utes, Jicarilla Apaches, San Juan Paiutes, and other Southwestern Native people until the early twentieth century, when these baskets were largely replaced by factory-made metal and ceramic items. However, the tradition of using piñon-pitch coating can still be seen today on replicas of old-style basket **jars**. Among the best contemporary piñon-pitch basket makers is Navajo Etta Rock, who weaves sumac baskets dipped in hot piñon pitch, with horsehair handles, at her home in Monument Valley. She has taught her grandson Lester to carry on this traditional and rarely seen art form.

PINTLE HINGE / a type of door hinge formed by two wooden dowels (pins that secure two pieces of wood together by fitting into holes on each piece) or pintles (pivot pins) mortised into the **lintel** and sill. This type of door hinge was used during the Spanish Colonial period, when iron was scarce. Pintle hinges can also be found on chest lids and **alacenas**.

PIT STRUCTURES / the earliest architectural form in the Southwest, consisting of a single-room dwelling partially excavated into the ground, built and used by a variety of prehistoric cultures. Early settlements (ca. AD 200 to 750) consisted of one or more pit structures, while later settlements (ca. AD 750 to 900) featured pit structures and associated surface rooms. The pit structures were multi-purpose; among the variety of activities that likely took place there were: preparing food, making tools, and sleeping.

In New Mexico, these houses typically consisted of a circular (and sometimes square or rectangular) room dug from the earth—about 14 to 22 feet in diameter and from a few inches to more than 3 feet in depth—with a superstructure above such as walls and a roof built of wood poles and brush chinked with mud that was then completely plastered over with mud. The "pit" area of the house allowed the house to stay cool in the summer and warm in the winter. In Arizona, the Pima and Tohono O'odham people built pit structures (called *ki*) consisting of domed shelters of brush and mud partially sunken into the ground; beside the pit house a **ramada** (or *wa:tho*) was typically erected, providing both shade and cross ventilation.

In New Mexico, pit structures were generally entered via a ladder through an opening in the roof or from a narrow entryway extending from one of the walls. Often a smooth layer of **mud plaster** was laid for the floor. A small, circular hearth or fire-pit, lined with clay or stone, was built into the floor near the entryway; the hearth provided heat and light (with a smoke hole in the roof for ventilation). Smaller rock-lined or mud plaster-lined pits were used for cooking and depressions in the floor held pots.

Pit structures were lived in throughout the prehistoric Southwest in the earlier phases of the Ancestral Puebloan, Mogollon, and Hohokam cultures, each of them having developed their own particular building technique. For example, the Hohokam typically dug a large pit (using digging sticks, **potsherd** scoops, or baskets); then dug postholes and erected heavy **mesquite** or pine posts to support the roof. They constructed a framework for the walls of **cottonwood** and **willow** posts that were covered with brush or bundles of reeds and then built the roof by placing beams across the major supports and placing a network of **saguaro** and **ocotillo** ribs across the beams, and finally a layer of brush. The last step was to cover the whole structure with mud plaster and dirt (a building method called **waddle-and-daub** or **jacál**).

Archaeologists believe that when the Pueblo people of New Mexico began to build aboveground living spaces with mud and **masonry** walls, the pit house was retained as a place for ritual activities and naturally evolved into what is known today as the **kiva**—a below-ground ceremonial chamber.

PLACITA (Patio, Courtyard) / a little **plaza** or inner **courtyard** surrounded in all or part by buildings or rooms. In New Mexico and Arizona

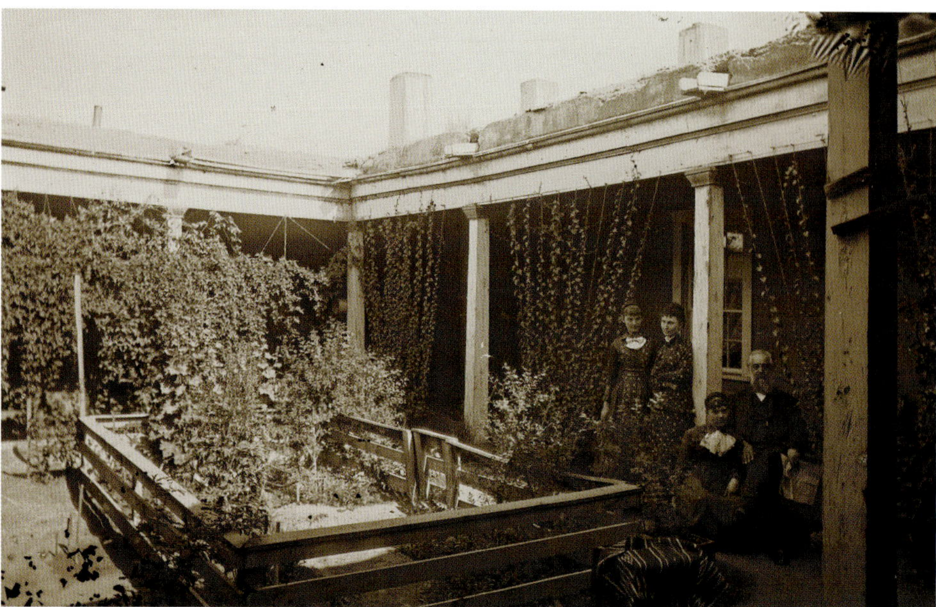

Placita in Santa Fe house, ca. 1882.

early houses of the Spanish settlers began as a simple one or two-room box. As families expanded and resources increased, additional rooms were added, often at right angles to the existing one, thus forming a partly or completely enclosed courtyard. In isolated places, these placitas served as spaces for small animals, laundry, and for defensive purposes. In towns and cities, where there was a communal defense against enemies, the courtyard was primarily an urban retreat filled with shade trees and flowering shrubs. The Hacienda de los Martinez built in 1804 in Taos, New Mexico, features an example of the fortress-type placita. See also **haciendas**.

PLAITING / an ancient and simple technique used to make baskets, in which single strands of material, flexible or rigid, are alternately passed over and under each other. When one strand passes over or under more than one strand at a time, it results in a decorative pattern known as **twilling**. The plaiting technique likely arrived in the Southwest from Mexico and was historically used by Native Americans to: create mats for sleeping, eating, and drying foods; head rings for carrying **ollas** and loaded baskets; to make the headband and back mat required for carrying collapsible **burden baskets**; and in the production of trinkets, clothing, and ritual items.

The most commonly used materials are **yucca**, which is flexible, and rigid materials such as **willow** branches, rabbitbrush, **sumac**, and dune broom. The weaver creates patterns by alternating

the sequence of the weave or by using different colored and/or textured materials. Basket makers at the Rio Grande Pueblos of New Mexico—Jemez, Ohkay Owingeh, Santa Clara, and Santo Domingo—and at Hopi villages in Arizona continue to use this ancient technique. See also **piki baskets**.

PLAQUES / See **Hopi plaques**.

PLATERO / the Spanish word for "silversmith."

PLAZA / a Spanish word for "square," a term used in the Southwest to describe an open area or central square in a town, city, pueblo, or Native village that serves as the hub of religious, political, cultural, and social activity. Popular to this day throughout Mexico and Latin America as well, the plaza was and still is an expression of civic pride. It is the physical as well as symbolic center of a town. In early times, plazas in the Southwest also served defensive purposes; in some New Mexico villages, they were fortified with protective walls, guarded gates, and a **presidio**.

According to the 1573 royal decrees of King Philip II (later incorporated into a larger body of legislation known as the Laws of the Indies, in 1681), which detailed the laying out of Spanish towns in the New World, *villas* were to be arranged around a central plaza. Public, commercial, religious, and institutional buildings, as well as merchant homes—all fronted by **portales**—were to face the plaza. These open spaces served as the military parade grounds *(plaza de armas)* for the Spanish garrisons, and it was where religious processions and markets took place. The townspeople were to build their homes on the streets surrounding the plaza. This plan produced a dense, compact arrangement.

Some original Spanish Colonial–era plazas still exist in the Southwest. One is the plaza of Santa Fe, New Mexico; planted with shade trees and graced by benches and a gazebo (or bandstand), it is still the commercial and social center of the city. Other examples exist at many New Mexico pueblos. Well before the Spanish arrived, Pueblo people of the area were building their terraced houses and **kivas** clustered around one or more plazas. Likewise, in Arizona the Hohokam, Pima, and Tohono O'odham people built their villages around a central plaza.

In contrast to the Spanish plazas, Pueblo plazas are less formally arranged and appear more like simple open communal spaces. In the plaza of San Ildefonso a giant, ancient **cottonwood** tree grows, while at Taos Pueblo a river runs diagonally through the middle. However, like the Spanish plazas, the Pueblo plazas had a defensive purpose, intended to protect the villages from raids by other Indians. More importantly, the Pueblo plaza was (and continues to be) the physical, spiritual, and symbolic center of the village. Constructed and arranged with an orientation based upon cosmological reference points, these spaces are where Pueblo people hold their most important social and religious activities and ceremonial dances.

POLISHING (Burnishing) / an important and traditional finishing technique in pottery making, in which a smooth stone (some potters may use other objects such as a wooden Popsicle stick) is used to burnish or smooth the surface of a **clay** piece to give the surface a lustrous, shiny appearance. The term also refers to the smoothing of wood surfaces in handcrafted furniture; like pottery, the traditional way to burnish wood is to use a polished stone to achieve a fine finish. In pottery, the process (done before the pot is **fired**) is arduous and painstaking and once started

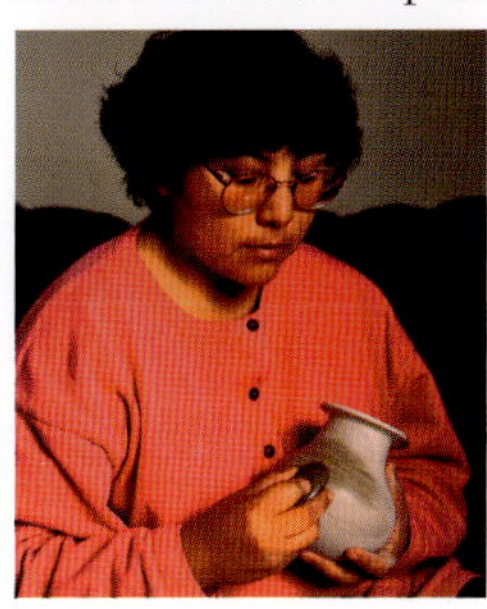

must be finished; if a potter stops partway through, streaky lines and/ or an uneven sheen will be the result. Some potters apply one or more coats of **slip** (watery clay)

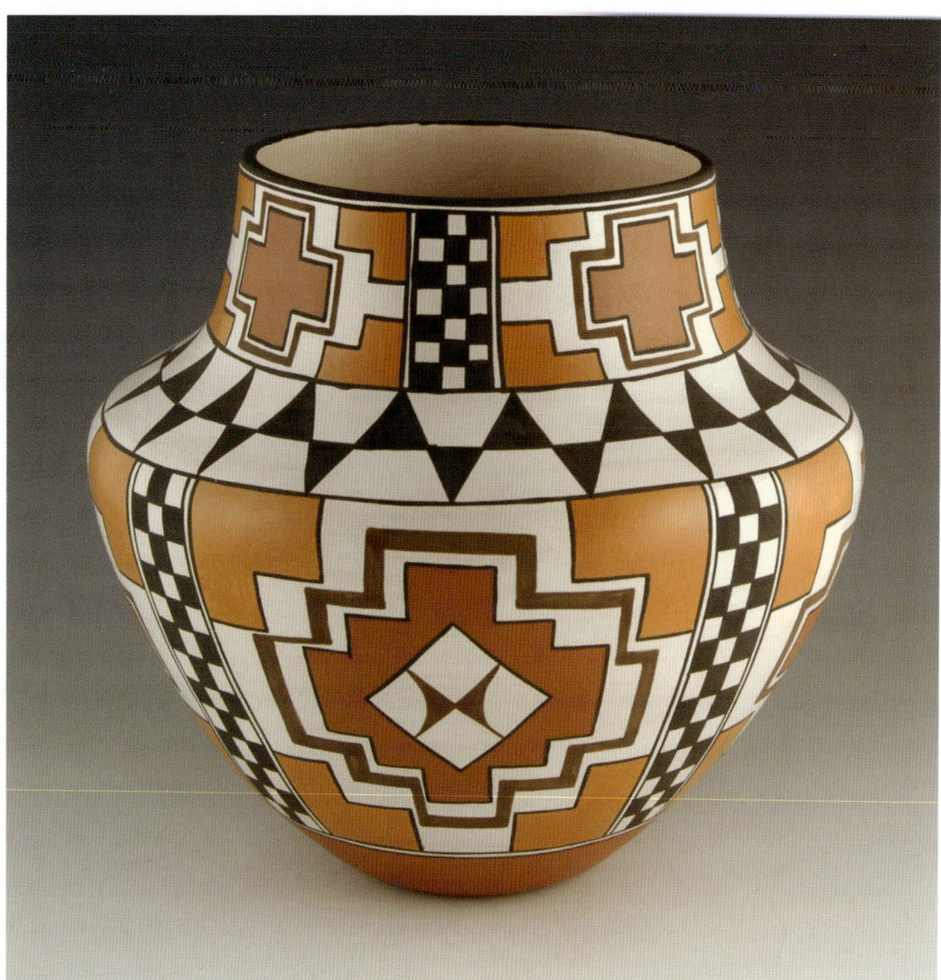

ABOVE: Marquis Lente (Laguna), polychrome jar. **BELOW:** Dawn Navasie (Hopi) polishes a jar prior to painting.

to the surface as they are polishing. The longer a piece is polished, the higher the shine. Polishing stones, the most favored "tool" used for polishing, have a very smooth surface (often they are river-washed) and come in a variety of shapes and sizes. Treasured heirlooms, the stones are handed down from generation to generation.

Originally, Native American pottery was polished to create a surface that would help keep moisture from entering or exiting the walls of a vessel; when pieces were no longer used for utilitarian purposes, polishing began to be done for aesthetic reasons, as it is today. Some contemporary Southwestern potters and woodworkers still use the traditional method of burnishing, while others use fine sandpaper to achieve a smooth surface.

The contemporary potters of **Mata Ortiz**, in Chihuahua, Mexico, polish their vessels by covering the surface with oil (vegetable, saddle, castor, or baby), then applying water conservatively to

the entire pot using a soft cloth, followed by the smoothing of the surface with a stone.

POLYCHROME / decoration consisting of multiple colors. In pottery, it refers to the use of two or more colors to decorate the pot surface. For **retablos**, it refers to the use of several colors of paint on the prepared wood surface. In **pictographs**, it refers to a style in which multiple colors are employed.

PONY BEADS / large glass beads (averaging 4 mm, or $^1/_8$ inch, in diameter) primarily produced on the island of Murano, Italy, used for decoration by Native Americans on hides or cloth, so named because they were brought to the American West as trade items by itinerant traders on pony pack teams. They were also called "pound" beads by traders—one pound of beads could typically be traded for one buffalo robe or one sturdy horse. Pony beads were likely the type of bead traded by the Spanish in the Southwest in the eighteenth century. These beads appeared in the Plains about 1800 and shortly thereafter were being used by the Utes of Colorado. Too large and expensive for intricate work, they were used sparingly to make bands of decoration for hide clothing, bags, cradles, and moccasins. Initially, the beads came in sky blue, white, dark blue, light red, dark red, and beige.

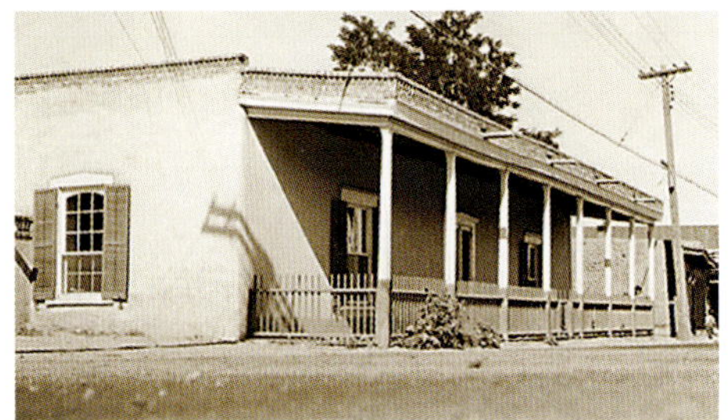

Portal, Borrego House, Santa Fe, New Mexico, 1936.

PORTAL (Portales/Portals) / a Spanish word referring in New Mexico to a covered porch-like structure, usually placed at the front of a building to provide protection from the elements. Portales (or portals in English) originally consisted of one or more hand-hewn log posts topped by a **zapata** or **corbel** supporting a long horizontal beam, typically roofed with packed earth, brush, and branches over **vigas** and **tablas** (split, hand-**adzed** boards) or **latillas**. Used on both residential and commercial buildings, portales were particularly prevalent in Santa Fe, New Mexico, where they can still be seen today, extending across the fronts of structures, providing protection from the blazing hot sun or monsoon rains.

POTSHERDS (Shards, Sherds) / fragments of broken pottery, usually prehistoric. The pottery sherds of the Hohokam, Ancestral Puebloans, and other ancient peoples of the Southwest are studied by archaeologists to learn more about the lifeways of the region's earliest inhabitants.

They examine scrape marks, chips, and residues to understand how they were used. For example, a sherd with soot deposits was likely from a pot used for cooking. They also study the form, decoration, materials, manufacturing method, and context of the sherds.

Native people of the Southwest today believe that their ancestors deliberately left sherds as evidence of their lives. The Hopis, for example, call these potsherds "the footprints of the ancestors." Over the centuries and up to the present day, sherds have been used for practical purposes by Native American potters. When **firing** clay vessels in outdoor kilns, some potters cover the pots with sherds to keep the pots from touching the fuel. These sherds tend to be large and are from the potter's own failed pots or are sometimes **clay** slabs made expressly for this purpose. When **coiling** a clay pot, potters may use a sherd as a tool to scrape and smooth out the surface, both the interior and exterior. Furthermore, the designs and symbols discovered on ancient potsherds have inspired many contemporary Native American and Mexican potters to replicate or rework in their own pots these important visual connections to their past. Another way some Native potters connect to their past is by grinding up old sherds and using them for **temper**. In this way their pots contain remnants of the clay creations of their ancestors.

Historic pottery sherds can be found scattered on the ground at many archaeological sites, **pueblos**, and national parks throughout the region. Native people ask that visitors do not remove these precious objects. In addition to damaging the cultural and spiritual nature of these ancient homelands, the removal of sherds has been illegal since the passing of the Archaeological Resources Protection Act of 1979.

POTTERY / Ceremonial / clay vessels made for ceremonial use. Native peoples of the Southwest have made ceremonial pottery for centuries, and continue to do so today. It is considered an honor for a potter's work to be used as a ceremonial bowl. The types of clay vessels made by Pueblo potters for **kiva** leaders include stew bowls to carry food to the gods, **canteens** for rain priests to carry water from the sacred springs, and two-spouted **wedding jars** for sacred medicines. Also, clay vessels may be made for certain ceremonial occasions, such as a birth or death. Perhaps the most classic ceremonial

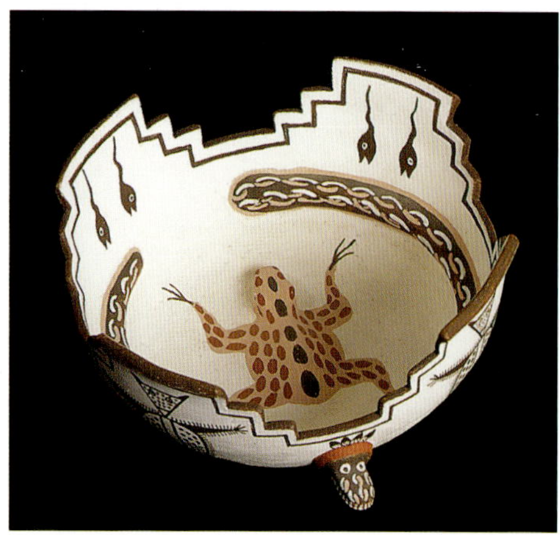

Jack Kalestewa (Zuni), kiva bowl.

ceramic shape is the prayer-**cornmeal** bowl—often called a "kiva" bowl—made at a number of pueblos in the region, which typically have edges cut with steps or terraces. They have been made of **micaceous** clay, in highly polished red or black ware, and **polychrome**.

During their rain ceremony, the Tohono O'odham drink **saguaro** fruit wine, which is prepared and stored in red-on-brown or plainware vessels. Rain songs are sung over the jars while the liquid ferments. At Zuni Pueblo, New Mexico, artisans have decorated ceramic ceremonial bowls with terraced edges that represent clouds, and sometimes with painted animals also associated with water. See also **effigy vessels**.

POTTERY / Hispano / beginning in the late eighteenth century, Hispano potters living in villages from the Mesilla Valley in southern New Mexico to the San Luis Valley of southern Colorado created utilitarian vessels such as jars, pitchers, bowls, cups, serving pots, bean pots, stew pots, *comales* (griddles), candle holders, chamber pots, and eventually even chimney flues. In rare instances, they utilized pots for ritual or devotional purposes. The Hispano potters used locally available **clays**, the traditional **coil** and scrape method, a **slip** finish that was **polished** smooth with a stone (except on **micaceous** wares), and **fired** their pots outdoors on a platform of stones in a shallow depression in the ground. Among the types of pottery they made were polished redware, blackware, and brownware. In addition, micaceous clay was often used by early Hispano potters; they left these wares unpolished, usually finishing them with a thin micaceous slip applied with a rag before firing. Hispanos made wares with little or no decoration, for their own use and for sale. They also obtained large amounts of

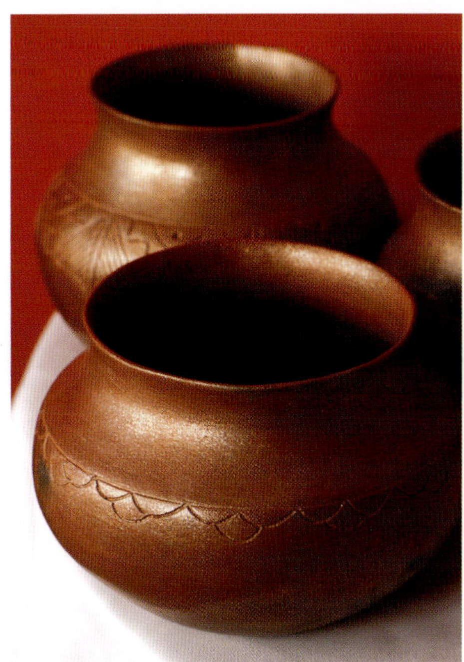

ABOVE AND RIGHT: Felipe Ortega (New Mexico), micaceous bean pots.

pottery through trade with nearby Puebloan and Apachean potters.

Although similar in style and technique to the pottery made at the New Mexico pueblos of Taos, Picuris, and Ohkay Owingeh, and by the Jicarilla Apaches, historic Hispano clay vessels have a few features that distinguish them from their Pueblo counterparts. For instance, Hispano potters primarily used a fine to medium sand **temper** (instead of tuff or **potsherds**); they fired vessels at higher temperatures using native woods (instead of animal dung); and they used certain surface decoration, such as that found on red-on-brown ware (known as Casitas), which has rag- or brush-applied red borders at the rim, red bull's-eye motifs or swirls, or simple splatters of red slip on the interior. Also, some Hispano potters formed smaller bowls by pressing a flattened disk of moist clay into a convex mold specifically made for that purpose, or over the inverted base of an existing larger bowl or pot (called "convex molding"); once the bowls were partially dried, the potters removed them from the mold or pot base and finished their work.

After the arrival of the railroad in New Mexico, in 1879–1880, Hispano-made pottery declined dramatically, gradually replaced in Hispano villages and settlements by metal wares and American-made crockery. Despite this trend, some

Hispano potters continued to make certain pots. For instance, because micaceous pottery was (and continues to be) so durable and superior for cooking and heating foods, Hispano potters continued to make micaceous bean pots or other cooking pots; they were especially popular for the Hispano villagers who preferred to eat food cooked in a traditional manner. Also, it has been (and continues to be) culturally and socially important for Hispano households to share with friends, family, and strangers food such as the stews, beans, and other recipes cooked in micaceous pots.

In the late 1970s micaceous pottery was revived by Felipe Ortega (b. 1951) (of Jicarilla Apache and Hispanic descent) of La Madera, New Mexico. And, in recent decades there has been a further resurgence of these wares, as is evident by the large amount of micaceous-clay pottery that is displayed and sold at the annual Spanish Market, held in Santa Fe, New Mexico, each July and December. In many instances, **fire clouds** and delicately inscribed designs play an important role in the surface decoration of these micaceous wares.

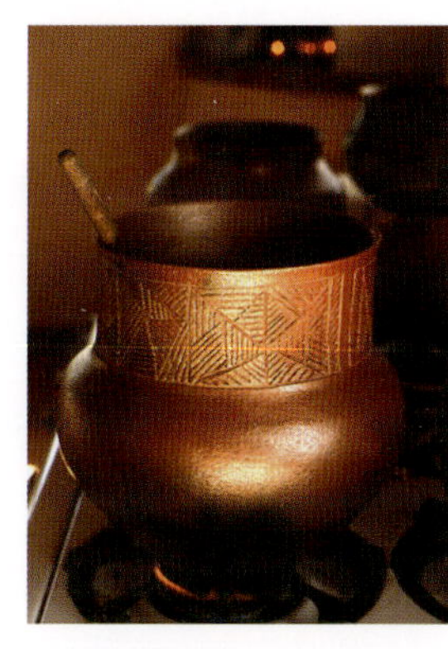

POTTERY / Prehistoric / utilitarian **clay** vessels that were made beginning about 300 BC by all the major prehistoric peoples who populated the Southwest, including the Ancestral Puebloan, Hohokam, Mogollon, Mimbres, Salado, and Sinagua peoples. Pottery is one of the first indicators of a sedentary lifestyle of these early peoples. See also **Hohokam pottery**, **Mesa Verde pottery**, and **Mimbres pottery**.

POTTERY / Pueblo / vessels made for centuries by Pueblo women in the Rio Grande villages of New Mexico, for use in their homes (for storing grains, carrying water, and serving meals), in ceremonies, and for trade among Pueblo and Hispano people. Since the late nineteenth century, they have made pottery for sale as **curios**, and more recently, as art objects.

With the advent of the railroad and the arrival of numerous collectors and tourists in the early 1880s, potters made smaller, decorative pieces (such as candlesticks, ashtrays, salt and pepper shakers, and miniature pots) to meet the new demand for souvenirs. At that time, there was a steady decline in handmade Pueblo utilitarian pottery, which was replaced by more durable cooking wares and bottles that were imported by train. Generally potters did not sign their works until the 1920s, when a few began signing at the request of pottery and curio dealers; it became more commonplace in the 1960s, and today virtually all potters sign their work. Typically, the woman who handcrafted the pot would sign her name on the bottom, even if several family members had worked on the piece.

The interest in Pueblo pottery ebbed and flowed over the decades until the 1970s, when there was a renewed enthusiasm for the pottery as part of a movement to preserve Native culture. Since then, Native-made pottery has evolved from a folk art to a fine art and the most refined and complex examples are in high demand among collectors.

Until recent decades, many Pueblos frowned upon men making pottery. Today the art form can be a family affair: with one person making the pots, another decorating and **polishing** them, and yet another **firing** them; or, more typically, one person will do everything. Most Pueblo potters strive to use the traditional method to create vessels—coil-built, stone-polished, and wood-fired or manure-fired outdoors—while others have modified the method somewhat with easier modern techniques, using one or more of the following: commercial **clay,** forming the vessel in a mold or making them on a potter's wheel, decorating with commercial pigments, and firing in an electric or gas kiln.

Hohokam Sacaton red-on-buff scoop from the Pueblo Grande site, ca. AD 900–1100.

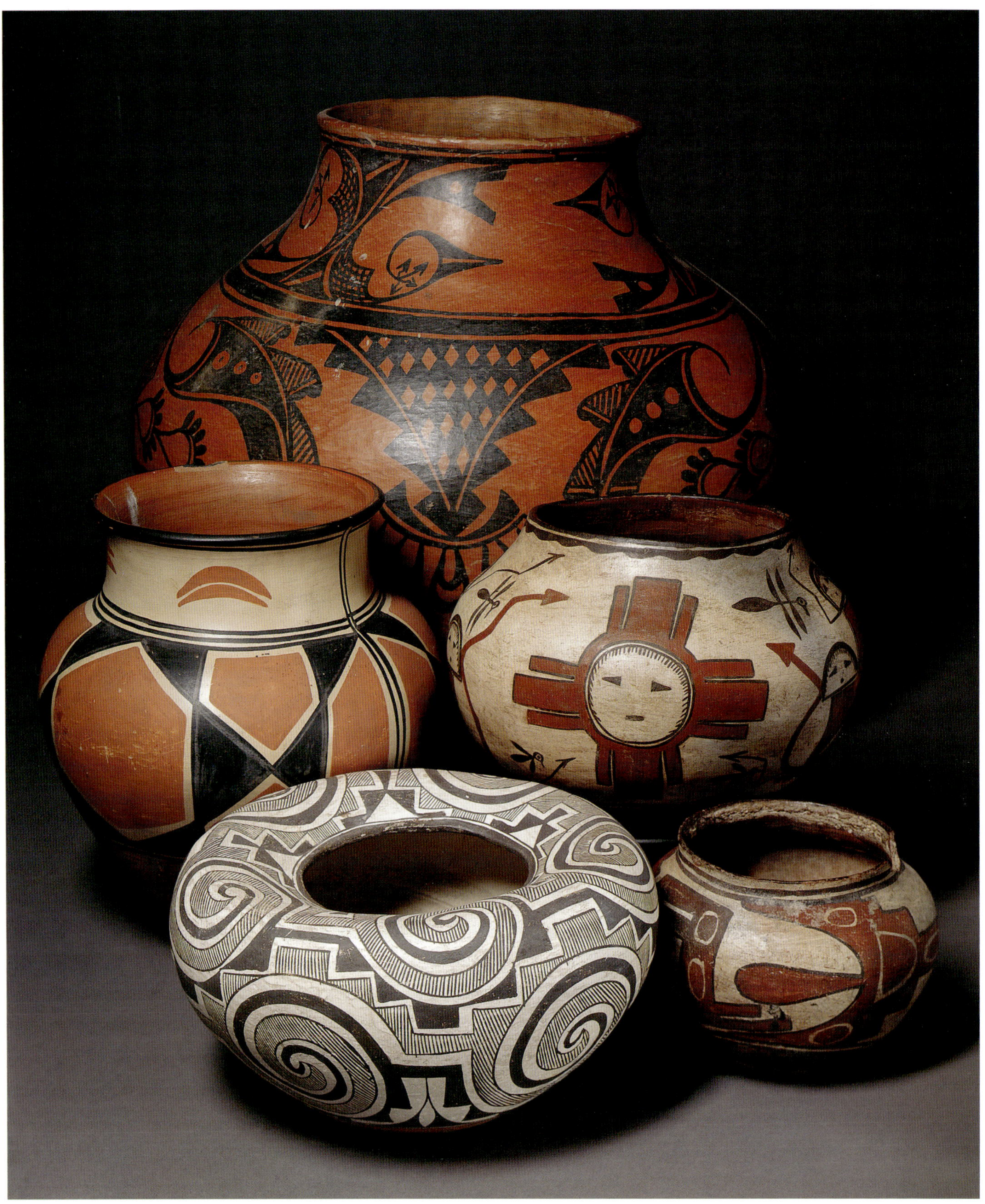

Pueblo pottery (clockwise from top): San Ildefonso storage jar, 1918; Zia pot, 1890; Santa Ana water jar, pre-1926; Acoma seed jar, pre-1925; Santo Domingo pot, 1915.

Each Pueblo is known for its distinctive style of pottery, and each potter decorates his or her work with designs that have special significance to their own culture or clan, including traditional symbols that have been passed down from generation to generation. Contemporary potters also draw upon their own experiences or imaginations and "push the envelope" by creating innovative designs on their pottery.

Since early times, Pueblo potters have had a profound spiritual connection to the earth and the clay. At each stage of the process, a traditional potter thanks the source of his or her materials and inspiration. "Mother Clay" guides these potters throughout the process of creating their vessels. Potters say prayers from the time of gathering the clay through the outdoor firing. By gathering clay, rocks, and plant material from their homelands, these potters connect to the natural world that embraces them.

POUND BLANKETS (Pound Rugs) / a term used to refer to the blankets or rugs handwoven with a few simple colors and designs by Navajo artisans from about 1890 to 1910, purchased and sold "by the pound" by post traders. A popular, though largely unsubstantiated story regarding these rugs suggests that in some instances weight was added by packing sand and/or dirt into the raw wool or finished rug/blanket, thus increasing the selling price. As many rugs were shipped via railroad by the bale, it is more likely they picked up lots of grit in railroad cars in the process.

PRIEST'S CHAIR / See **sillón frailero**.

PRESIDIO / a Spanish word referring to a walled garrison or fort, generally built from **adobe** bricks, arranged in a square with defendable entrances, and used to protect early Spanish settlers of the Southwest from raiding Native Americans and others. Presidios typically contained military quarters, supply stores, stables, living quarters, a chapel, and other buildings. In Arizona, two examples of presidios established by the Spanish in the eighteenth century can still be seen: San Agustín del Tucson and San Ignacio de Tubac.

PUDDLED ADOBE / a construction method in which **adobe**—earth (*tierra*) mixed with water— was "puddled" or molded in place by hand to form the walls of a structure. The damp earth was placed in layers, raising the walls gradually, layer upon layer, until the desired height was achieved.

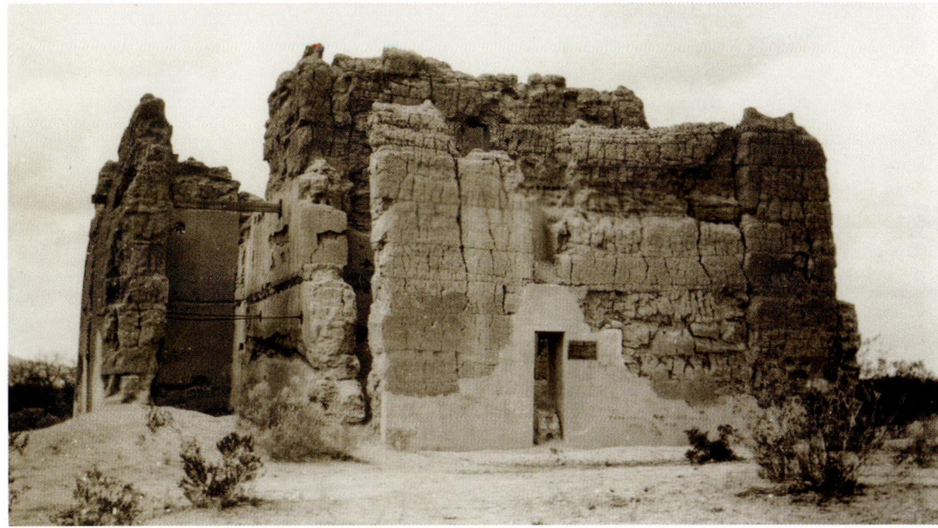

Puddled adobe ruins at Casa Grande Ruins National Monument, Arizona.

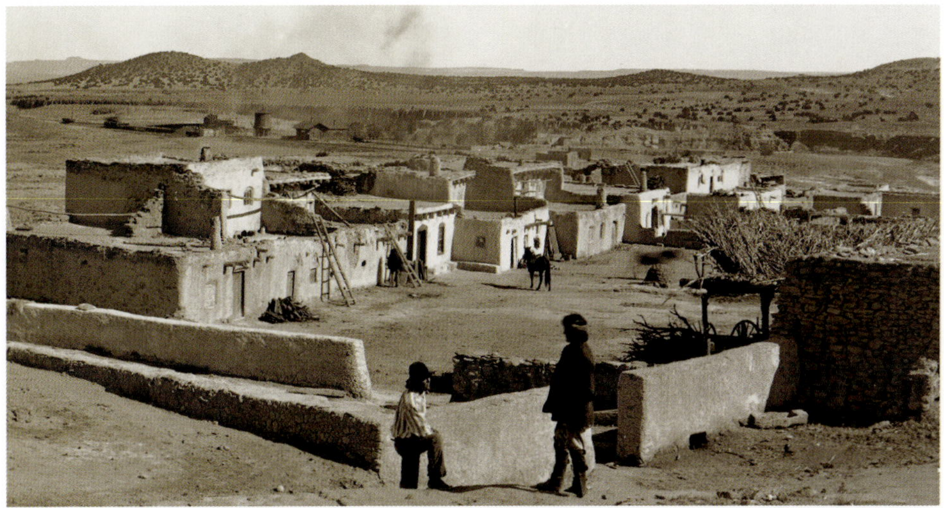

Laguna Pueblo, New Mexico, 1883.

The method was used by the Ancestral Puebloans and other early Native peoples of the Southwest before the arrival of Spanish explorers and settlers, who taught them how to form and sun-dry adobe bricks that could be laid in mortar and stacked in linear configurations for building.

The fourteenth-century Hohokam "Great House" at Casa Grande Ruins National Monument in southern Arizona is a rare surviving example of this ancient puddling technique. The local **caliche** soil used to build it is rich in calcium carbonate (or lime), a stabilizer that has helped preserve the puddled mud walls from deterioration, despite many centuries of exposure to rainfall. It has been estimated that the ancient Sonoran Desert people puddled together six million pounds of caliche-rich soil in building the multi-story "Great House." Another rare example of the puddling technique can be seen at the extensive ruins of Paquimé in Chihuahua, Mexico. See also **rammed earth**.

PUEBLO / a Spanish word meaning "village," this term is used today to refer to the communal Pueblo Indian villages of the Southwest, as well as the people who inhabit them and the buildings constructed in them. When Spanish explorers arrived in the Rio Grande region of New Mexico in the late sixteenth century, they found indigenous people living in large integrated villages, which they identified as "pueblos" because these earthen villages closely resembled the **adobe** architecture of their homeland. At first pueblos consisted of rectangular surface rooms constructed of stone, wood, and mud mortar with roofs of wood beams and brush, thatch, or mud, joined together to form a single unit. Over time pueblos grew in size and by the time the Spanish arrived, they were two to five-stories in height, and were built of coursed-adobe and stone, arranged in clusters or blocks of small, connected rooms (ranging in number from fifty to five hundred), with flat roofs comprised of poles, brush, and mud. Stepped **parapets** and exposed **vigas** are common features on the exterior. Most rooms were entered via roof hatches accessed by tapering pole ladders; however, some living quarters on the upper levels had doors opening onto the roof terraces of lower levels. Historically, the terraces served as workspaces where women might have made pottery, woven textiles, or prepared food. Interiors generally had a **fogón** (corner fireplace) and built-in **bancos**. Chimney tops were capped with ceramic pots to protect the adobe from erosion. The rooms and houses were arranged around a central community **plaza**—an open area where important social and ceremonial activities took place. The villages also featured ceremonial structures called **kivas**.

Currently inhabited by descendants of the original builders, New Mexico pueblos have greatly expanded in recent decades, with individual houses being built of modern materials in areas adjoining the main pueblo. The materials, forms, and details of the traditional structures heavily influenced the architects of the early twentieth-century in the Southwest; these buildings contributed to what became known as the **Spanish Pueblo Revival** style. For more than a century, the sculptural shapes of the pueblos have inspired artists and writers from around the world; in addition, the historic, well-built pueblo structures serve as inspiration for the organic architecture of today. See also **adobe** and **puddled adobe**.

PUEBLO DECO STYLE / a variant of the Art Deco style that developed in the Southwest during the first thirty years of the twentieth century, with imagery that blends the motifs of Native American and Hispano cultures and the aesthetics of Art Deco. Some Pueblo Deco buildings combine the irregular massing and wall color of Pueblo influence and the vertical and stepped decorative features typical of the Art Deco style. The angularity, repetitiveness, and abstraction of the Native American motifs that appear in some Pueblo Deco buildings share qualities with Art Deco ornaments such as chevrons and zigzags. Architects, interior designers, and craftspeople imaginatively applied

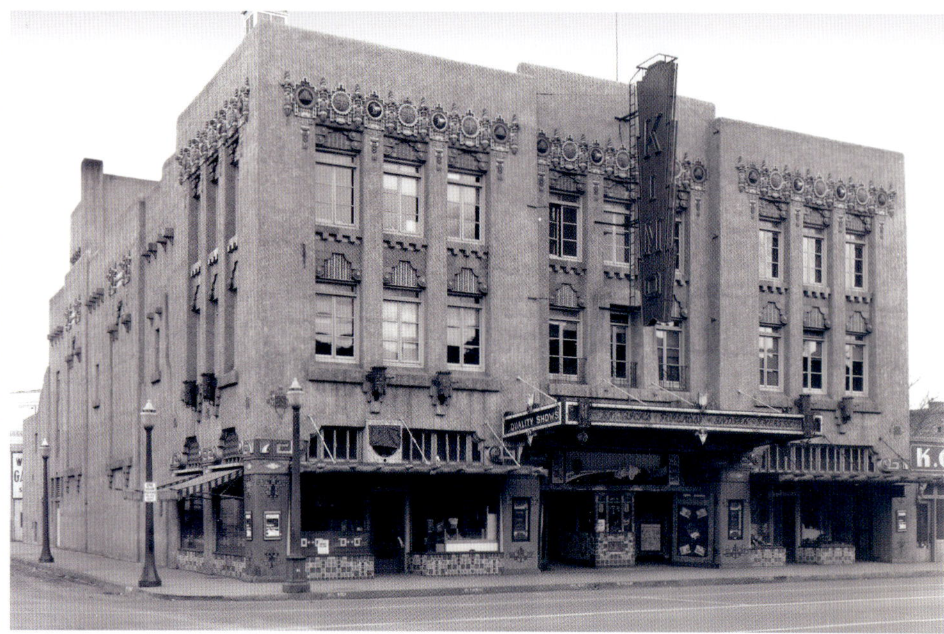

The Pueblo Deco–style KiMo Theatre, Albuquerque, New Mexico, 1940.

Deco details to a wide range of buildings in cities and towns throughout the Southwest. One of the finest examples to survive is the KiMo Theatre built in Albuquerque, New Mexico, in 1926–27, designed by Carl and Robert Boller, which has the massing of a Spanish mission and a multitude of Pueblo and Navajo motifs on the façade, including colorful **terra-cotta** ornamentation inspired by Pueblo pottery and textiles.

PUEBLO REVIVAL STYLE / See **Spanish Pueblo Revival style**.

PUEBLO TEXTILES / textiles made by Pueblo people of the Arizona–New Mexico region. They raised cotton in their fields, which, along with other vegetable fibers, they spun and wove on vertical **looms** into fine textiles, called *campeche* or **manta** cloth by sixteenth-century Spanish colonists. The Navajos adopted weaving techniques and tools from these Pueblo weavers in the seventeenth century. The primary weavers at the pueblos were men. Pueblo weavers sometimes sewed or twined on strips of fur (typically rabbit) into their textiles for decoration or warmth. Among the nineteenth-century Pueblo textiles were **saddle blankets**. See also **kilt** and **rain sash**.

PUKI / the Tewa word for a shallow, bowl-shaped support such as a basket or **clay** bowl used by Native American potters to support, shape, and turn the bottom of a clay pot while it is being initially formed with **coils** of clay. It may also be used to rotate the vessel while building up its walls to help ensure symmetry. The "puki ridge" is the indentation left by the puki on the pot. In the **pueblos** of New Mexico the puki was originally a curved indentation in the dirt floor of the home. The shape of the puki determines the angle or rise from the base to the shoulder of the clay vessel; thus, potters use pukis of varying sizes and shapes depending on the type of ceramic form desired. Highly valued by Pueblo families, pukis are often passed down from generation to generation.

QUILTS / **Quilt Making** / a craft in which scraps of cloth are pieced together in patterns, usually with **appliquéd**, **embroidered**, or quilted designs on each scrap, sewn to a backing material and filled with batting (cotton, wool, feathers, or down). Traditionally quilts were used to provide warmth—as bedcovers, bedrolls, shawls, swaddling for babies, and as coverings over doorways and windows of early Native-built shelters. Anglo schoolteachers and missionaries introduced quilt making to Native Americans of the Southwest in the late 1800s, as part of their effort to "civilize" Native peoples by teaching them Euro-American domestic arts.

By the early years of the twentieth century, quilting had become a common pastime of many Native peoples in the region, including the Hopis and San Carlos Apaches. Early Native quilters typically followed simple patterns, made use of scrap instead of purchased cloth, and gleaned batting from natural and cultivated sources. Because quilts were so heavily used, worn, and recycled, few of these early examples survived. In addition to making traditional patterns—pinwheel, log cabin, spools, and lone star—Native quilters incorporated their own cultural motifs into their quilts, including designs drawn from **sandpaintings**, **Navajo textiles**, **basketry**, religion (**katsinas**), and **beadwork**.

Since the late nineteenth century, Native quilters have shown their work in tribal exhibitions, fairs, and powwows. Among the native groups who make quilts today are the Tohono O'odham, Navajo, Southern Ute, Isleta Pueblo, and Hopi. Navajo artisans also create quilts that reflect traditional woven rug and **silver** jewelry designs.

Quilt cooperatives are a vital source of economic activity for some of these communities. Contemporary Native American quilters make quilts and wall hangings using both hand and machine quilting, and machine-pieced and appliquéd fabrics, and sometimes enhance the work with beadwork, **yarn**, and other items. They also regularly employ polyester batting and purchase new cloth.

For the quilting patterns used to stitch together the three layers of cloth (top, batting, and backing), many contemporary Native American textile artists prefer stars, tipis, **thunderbirds**, pipes, war bonnets, and arrowheads in addition to the clamshells, fans, or outline quilting used by non-Native quilters. The colors chosen by contemporary quilters often reflect the Native quilter's close spiritual ties to nature. Some present-day quilters use their quilts as a forum for expressing feelings about issues important to Native Americans. Beginning in the latter part of the twentieth century, there has been increased interest in historical and contemporary Native American quilts, making them highly collectible items. A gift of a quilt is literally a gift of warmth, as well as a symbolic blessing. See also **Hopi quilts**.

QUIVER / a case of tanned (or raw) hide (often from a deer or bobcat) stitched together with a rawhide thong or **sinew**, used in the nineteenth century to hold bows and arrows for hunting large game animals including pronghorns. Handcrafted by Ute, Apache, and other Native peoples of the region, quivers were left plain or adorned with fringe and/or painted geometric designs of red, green, and blue. If the animal skin used had a nice tail, it was left on for decoration. The cases usually had long leather loops for carrying them over the shoulder. Some quivers were also made from mountain lion; early twentieth-century curio dealers commissioned artisans at Tesuque Pueblo (and possibly at other Tewa pueblos) to make mountain lion quivers for sale.

RADIOCARBON DATING (Carbon-14 Dating) / a method of determining the age of historic objects ranging from pottery to baskets to textiles that are made from carbon-bearing organic material—such as **yucca** fibers, wood, cotton cloth, and bones—by measuring the radioactivity of their carbon content. Constantly produced in small amounts in the atmosphere, carbon-14 (or radiocarbon) is found in all living organisms. When the plant or animal dies, the absorption rate ceases and radiocarbon begins to decay. Archaeologists have developed a method to measure the minute amounts of carbon-14 left in samples, thus providing a date of the "death" of the animal or plant material, and thus an approximate date of the object being tested.

RAIN GODS / small, seated, clay figurines made for the tourist trade beginning in the 1880s by Tesuque Pueblo potters. These figures, which rarely exceed ten inches in height, were hand-molded, smoothed with a gourd fragment (or another type of tool, or the potter's fingers), and then covered with a **micaceous** or cream-colored **slip**. Often also decorated with water-based or poster paint after being fired, these figures are distinguished by their rounded head, slender arms, slit eyes, open mouth, "mitten" hands, and extended legs. In some instances, the figurines were made with genitals, or holding small children, animals, or objects. The ones holding pots on their laps became known as "gods of rain" or rain gods—one of several types of "idols" or "gods" made and aggressively marketed for tourists.

Although some early documents describe the rain gods as figures "chanting prayers for rain," they had nothing to do with Tesuque religion; they evolved from figurines made by the early 1870s and offered for sale in Santa Fe and the surrounding region. Rain-god figures became an important part of the economy at late-nineteenth and early-twentieth century Tesuque Pueblo, where they were made in the thousands. During this period, they were mass-marketed by Santa Fe **curio** dealers Aaron and Jake Gold and J. S. Candelario, who sold them to stores, dealers, and customers across the country. Potters at Tesuque had difficulty meeting the demand, leading some artisans to shape and fire them too quickly and improperly. Many writers at the time maligned the rain god as representative of the bad influences of non-Indians on Pueblo culture. Beginning in 1908, when a recession caused all curio sales to decline, the rain gods began to decline in popularity as well. In recent decades, however, the rain god has experienced a revival; they are still made in small quantities at Tesuque Pueblo today.

RAIN SASH / woven on a **back-strap loom**, of white cotton and wool thread/yarn, with long flowing fringe at both ends that moves like liquid and are said to represent rain falling, and with knotted tassels that represent clouds. The sash is worn at the waist over a Pueblo man's kilt. In the Hopi tradition, young Hopi men are given a sash of this type, as well as a handwoven belt and **kilt**, by their godfathers when they are initiated into manhood. Hopi women also wear white sashes of this type around their waist for weddings or ceremonial dances. Rain sashes may also be made using the sprang technique, an ancient method in which **warp** threads are set on a rectangular frame or between a pair of beams and the weaver uses her fingers to generate fabric (or a sash) by interlinking the warp threads. The Hopi term for belt or sash is *mötsapngön kwewa*.

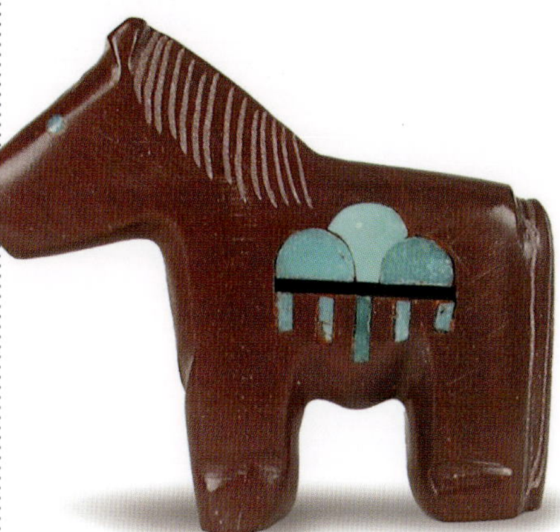

Emery Boone (Zuni), "Rain Maker" horse fetish with rain symbol, pipestone, turquoise, mother-of-pearl.

RAIN SYMBOLS / Native American artisans of the arid Southwestern U.S. (as well as in Mexico and South America) have long used designs that symbolize rain, lightning, clouds, thunder, rainbows, and water animals in their work to represent their sincere wishes and prayers for rain and the good life that comes with it. Historically, several Native cultures have associated snakes, tadpoles, and frogs with rain, including the Hopis, who believe snakes carry prayers for rain to spiritual deities. The Hopis also believe that birds are the messengers to cloud spirits. The Hohokam carved animals associated with rain (especially frogs) in shells and stone. Ancestral Puebloan people (ca. AD 950 to 1300) used stepped or terraced elements on pottery and in murals that resemble the cloud symbols of modern day Pueblo cultures. And beginning in the fourteenth century, Ancestral Puebloan people painted murals including **katsina** figures that were important cloud spirits and bringers of rain.

Today Pueblo artisans frequently depict designs that symbolize rain. For instance, at Zuni Pueblo, New Mexico, a **dragonfly** is an old and important water animal that appears on pottery and other art forms. At the Hopi villages, cloud (terraced designs) and rain symbols are embroidered on **kilts** and sashes that are worn by men throughout their annual cycle of ceremonies.

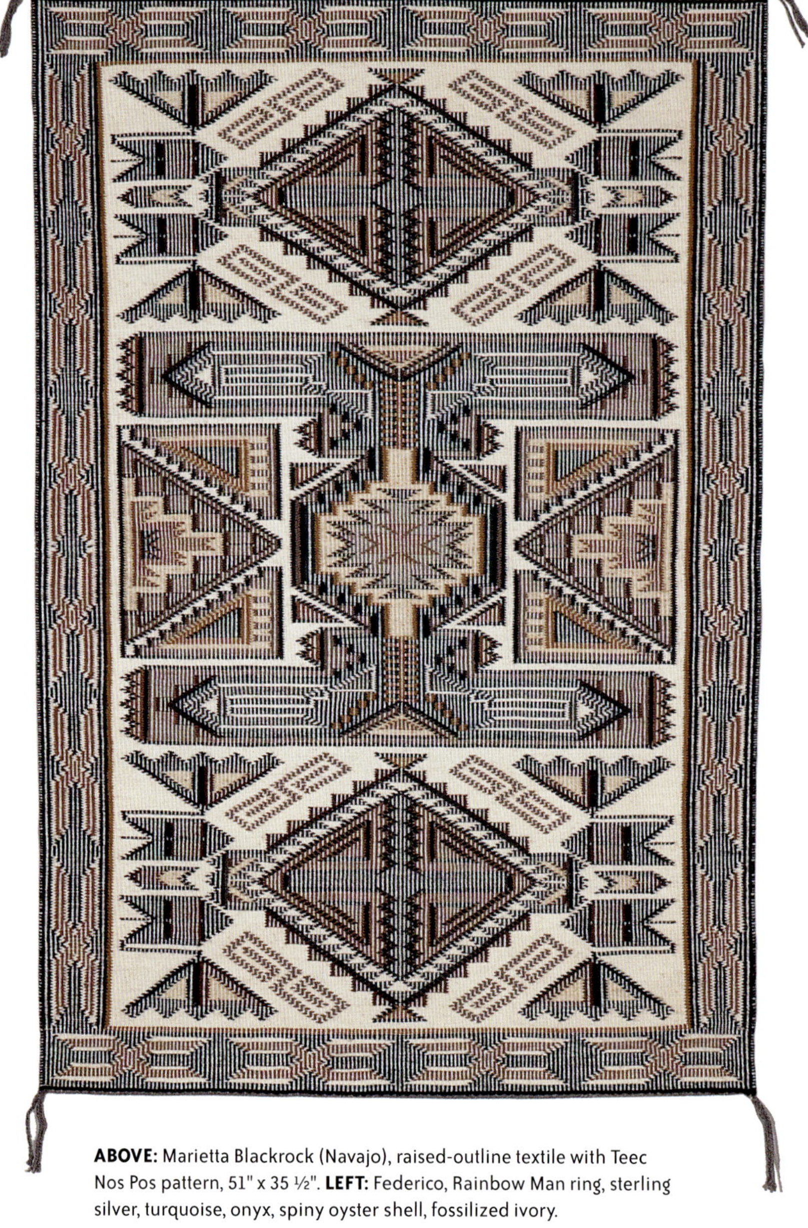

RAINBOW GOD (Rainbow Man) / Rainbow People / the rainbow, important to Pueblo, Navajo, and other Native peoples, has various meanings, but generally represents a link to rain and is a good omen. Rainbow God—usually depicted with an arched body forming a stylized rainbow, wearing a ceremonial **kilt**, moccasins, and cloud-shaped headdress with prayer **feathers**—appears today in various Native-made art forms. Rainbow People (Nááts'íílid Yé'ii in Navajo), depicted in a similar manner with arched bodies and feathered-headdresses, appear in Navajo **sandpaintings**, usually in pairs, much as rainbows do in nature.

A figure of some importance in the ceremonial life of Zuni Pueblo, New Mexico, the Rainbow God first appeared as a decorative feature in Zuni jewelry beginning in the late 1920s or early 1930s. Sold by post traders, it quickly became popular among tourists and other purchasers of Native jewelry. The figure has a long history in Zuni culture as well; anthropologist Frank Hamilton Cushing, who lived with the Zunis from 1879 to 1884, documented this form, as well as the **Knifewing** figure, as appearing on the shield of the Bow Priesthood (or Bow Priest Society). Featured in a wide range of jewelry, the Rainbow God shows

ABOVE: Marietta Blackrock (Navajo), raised-outline textile with Teec Nos Pos pattern, 51" x 35 ½". **LEFT:** Federico, Rainbow Man ring, sterling silver, turquoise, onyx, spiny oyster shell, fossilized ivory.

off the skills of Zuni lapidaries, who typically use **turquoise**, **jet**, white **shell**, mother-of-pearl, and clamshell set in sterling **silver** to create the figures. They are still made by Zuni jewelers today.

RAISED-OUTLINE TEXTILE / a Navajo weaving technique in which all or most of a rug is filled with fine vertical pinstripes of various colors and raised three-dimensional ridges outline the edges of the design elements. As the ridges appear only on one side of the textile, this type of weaving has a definite front and back. Among the more frequent designs used in raised-outline textiles is

the **storm pattern**. The earliest known example of a raised-outline rug was woven in the Ganado area of Arizona in 1934.

The region most associated with the technique is Coal Mine Mesa, Arizona, where Ned Hatathli, manager of the Navajo Arts and Crafts Guild, helped develop it in 1950. Another major supporter of raised-outline textiles was post trader Bruce Burnham of Sanders, Arizona, who encouraged weavers relocated from the Coal Mine Mesa area to use the **Teec Nos Pos** pattern with pastel colors, in the 1980s. Burnham renamed these rugs and patterns "New Lands."

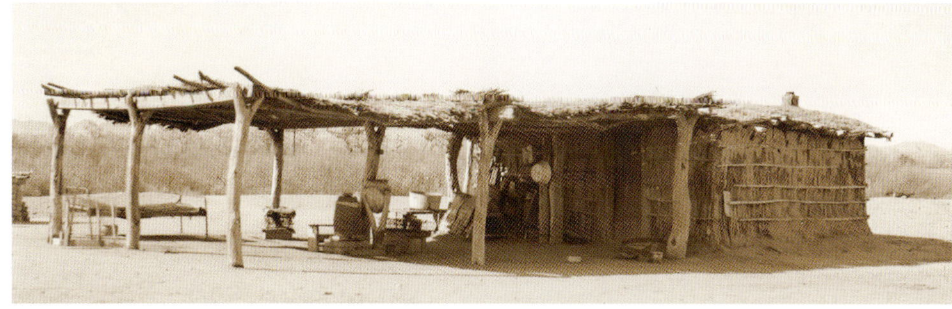

Wattle-and-daub farmhouse with ramada, Gila River, Arizona.

RAMADA / from the Spanish word *rama* (branch) and *ramaje* (arbor), the term refers to rustic, free-standing, wood post-and-beam shelters open on all four sides and covered with lightweight brush (and occasionally with **saguaro** ribs in Arizona) and sometimes a layer of mud. Their primary purpose is to provide shade from the hot desert sun. Occasionally, side panels of woven plant material were used for additional protection. The ramada dates back to about AD 450, when they were built by the Hohokam people in the Tucson Basin. Erected beside their **pit structures** from sturdy wood posts and a roof of saguaro ribs and brush, ramadas were the center of the Hohokam living area. The Tohono O'odham of Arizona have also traditionally constructed ramadas (which they call *wa:tho*) out of **mesquite** posts and **ocotillo** stalks.

Historically, in the pueblos of New Mexico, ramadas were placed in front of **adobe** and/or **masonry** buildings and used to protect work areas from the summer heat. They have also been an important architectural element of Navajo summer **hogans**, where they are used for a variety of purposes. Both the Navajo and Pueblo peoples have traditionally erected ramadas for use during plaza dances and other ceremonies.

Today ramadas are popular with homeowners across the Southwest; they are built in a variety of styles—from vine-covered rustic wood to solid masonry structures with steel roofs—and are often used by landscape architects as focal points in garden designs and by homeowners as a shady refuge. The Native peoples of the Southwest continue to build ramadas out of natural materials for ceremonial and daily use.

RAMMED EARTH (Pisé Construction, Tierra Apisonada) / among the oldest building techniques dating back at least six thousand years (in ancient Egypt), in which moistened earth is tamped between temporary movable forms of wood and/or steel, creating walls of high thermal mass that are ideal for hot, arid climates. This method was brought to the New World by European explorers and settlers. The technique is somewhat similar to the ancient method of **puddled adobe** except that the earth is tamped into a compact form. Beginning in the late 1970s, rammed earth construction was increasingly used by people living in the West and Southwest to construct homes ranging from simple, small owner-built structures to elaborate multi-million-dollar estates designed by architects. Although labor-intensive and expensive, rammed earth homes are admired for their aesthetic qualities and for being energy-efficient and environmentally friendly. They are ideal for passive solar strategies—the thick, dense walls absorb the warmth from the sun gradually throughout the day, and then this heat is slowly released into the interior at night. Among the important early proponents of the technique were Quentin Branch of Tucson, Arizona, and Paul McHenry Jr. in New Mexico.

To build rammed-earth walls, mineral-laden soil (a mixture of mostly sand with some clay) is mixed with a small amount of Portland cement for stabilization (making rammed-earth more durable than adobe), then moistened with water, and placed into boxlike forms—usually made of plywood and metal straps, about 18 to 36 inches in depth—that have been placed atop concrete stem walls and foundation. Each eight-inch layer of soil is rammed by hand or by mechanical or pneumatic tampers (called "jumping jacks") into the boxlike form, until it is about five inches high and of rock-hard density.

The final rammed earth wall, which has a slightly textured surface, adheres to the stem wall through gravity and pressure; a steel and concrete bond beam placed at the top of the wall reinforces its strength. Once the finished wall section has been rammed and the walls are stable, the forms are removed and reused to build other wall sections. The color of the wall depends on the color of the soil mixture. Interior walls are covered in a clear sealant or with plaster or **stucco**; exterior walls are sometimes finished with a layer of rigid foam insulation and then covered with stucco.

RATTLES / Gourd (Dance Rattles) / hollowed-out and cleaned gourds with painted decoration (and sometimes with feathers), filled with pebbles or another rattling material, and with a **cotton-wood** handle attached, were (and continue to be) used frequently by dancers in Native American ceremonies as a percussion musical instrument to mark the rhythm during a dance. The noise a shaking rattle makes is also associated with the sound of falling rain or driving hail. Gourd rattles, or *guajes*, are held in the left hand of dancers in los **Matachines**, a historic dance and music ritual still performed by both Hispano and Native American communities in the Southwest. In contrast, dancers in all other Native American ceremonies hold rattles in the right hand. During the Hopi Powamuya or Bean Dance, gourd rattles are among the special gifts given to boys by the **Katsinam**, to encourage them to practice the katsina songs they hear. Traditionally, the gourd rattles have been painted with colorful geometric designs and with black cross-stitched lines around the side (a design convention harkening back to the old-style **hide** rattles that were stitched

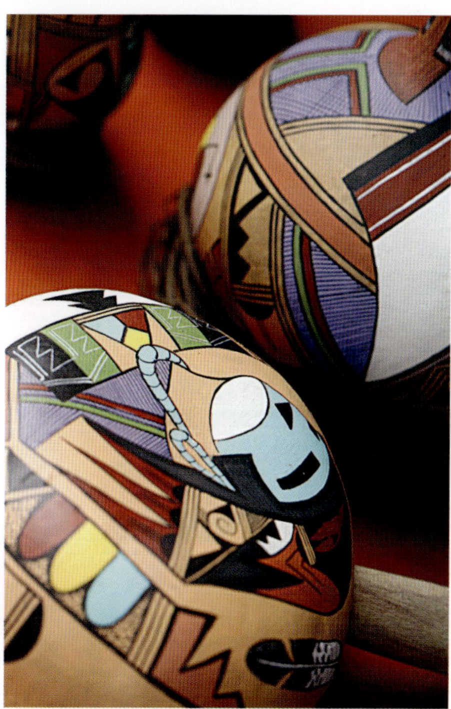

Frank Poolheco, painted-gourd rattles.

together). In recent years, Hopi artisans have been painting their gourds with a variety of motifs, including animals or the face of a **katsina** (a spirit being), and attaching cottonwood appendages—such as ears, nose, beak, eyes, and horns. These "new" style rattles are primarily made for the tourist market.

RATTLES / Hide / simple rattles made since ancient times, by stitching together two rawhide halves while the hide was still damp. Like the gourd rattle, they are used as dance rattles or to accompany the rhythm of the drum during Native American ceremonial dances. By about 1890, artisans at Tesuque Pueblo, outside Santa Fe, New Mexico, were making rattles from discarded cowtails and horsetails, shaped and sewn to form a hollow bulb and to cover a wooden handle. Rocks were inserted in the bulb and the tail was sewn into the small end of the handle. They were purely ornamental and intended for the tourist trade. Early **curio** dealers in Santa Fe such as Jake Gold and J. S. Candelario, as well as Española, New Mexico, dealer Thomas S. Dozier, are known to have commissioned and sold these Tesuque hide rattles.

RAVELED YARN / a type of yarn created by unraveling the yarn out of a piece of woolen commercially made trade cloth (such as **bayeta**). This type of yarn was used in the mid- to late nineteenth century by Navajos (and sparingly by Pueblo and Hispano artisans) to weave the figures and ground of shoulder blankets or dresses. Before aniline **dyes** became available, weavers used this method to obtain a deep-red colored yarn that could not be obtained with native dyes. The imported cloth used for raveling was dyed with **lac** and/or **cochineal** dyes. After about 1870, the Native weavers used orange-red aniline-dyed American flannel cloth as a source of raveled yarn for their textiles. The raveled yarn was soon after replaced with **Germantown yarns**.

RED / Red-on-red Pottery / a type of pottery made by artisans at New Mexico Pueblos, characterized by its rich red hue, created by using an iron-rich clay **slip** on the vessel that stays red during the **firing** process when oxygen is allowed to reach its surface. To create a glossy surface, the potter applies a **clay** slip and **burnishes**

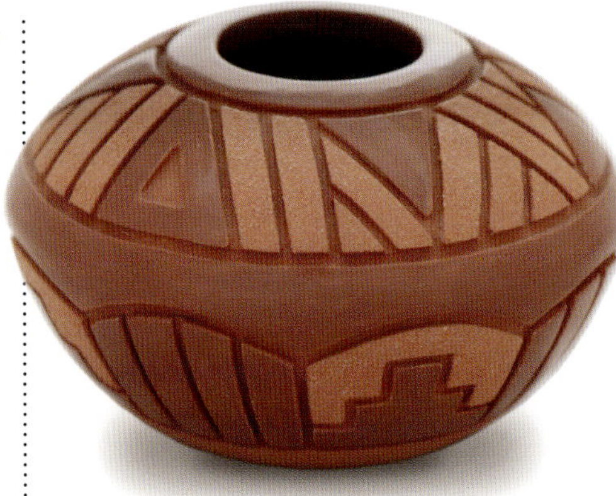

it with a stone before firing. For the designs, the potter applies the red slip and leaves it unpolished, to create a contrast between the polished surface and the unpolished or matte design motifs. The consistency and hue of red pottery has changed over the decades, as different sources of clay have been used, as some sources were lost when potters passed away or when supplies were depleted.

Potters at San Ildefonso Pueblo experimented with red-on-red pottery before 1920; some examples incorporated a matte slip that fired white, used for small accents. In the 1930s Tonita Roybal (1892–1945), along with her husband Juan Cruz Roybal (1896–1990), made superb examples of this style. At Santa Clara Pueblo, Lela Gutierrez (1895–1966) and Van Gutierrez (1870–1956) developed a type of red-on-red ware with several matte colors. Today potters

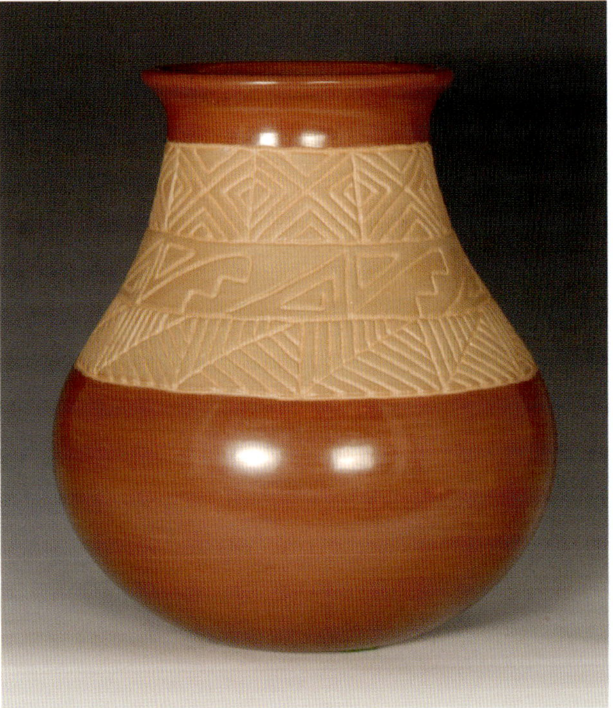

at Santa Clara use natural red-clay slips that are high in iron oxide that creates a deep, blood-red coloration. Other contemporary potters known for their red-on-red wares are from San Ildefonso and Ohkay Owingeh pueblos.

RED AND BUFF POTTERY / a type of pottery made by artisans at Ohkay Owingeh Pueblo, consisting of polished red-hued **clay** with a distinctive un-**slipped** and buff-colored band around the middle on which geometric and sometimes floral motifs are incised and/or painted in red, light brown, and other natural colors. Based on **potsherds** found in a fifteenth-century ancestral pueblo across the Rio Grande, this style was revived by a handful of Ohkay Owingeh potters in the 1930s. Prehistoric **Hohokam pottery** was also red on buff.

REJA / See **grille**.

RELICARIOS (Reliquarios) / a Spanish word for reliquaries and/or lockets, referring to images of saints, Christ, or the Virgin Mary placed in a metal frame (and sometimes in lockets) with a ring at the top so it may be worn on a necklace. In some instances, early relicarios were made of fabric and stitched with metal thread with a loop of metal thread for hanging. Relicarios are related to the reliquaries of the Middle Ages that contained a piece of a saint's bone or other relic. The image in a relicario may be a painting, print, or carved ivory, wood, or alabaster; the frame is usually metal (**silver,** silver gilt, brass, tin, or gold); and the necklace on which it hangs ranges from a simple metal chain to an elaborate string of gold-**filigree** beads, **coral**, jet, crystal, and/or other precious materials. Relicarios can vary in style from a simple mass-produced trinket of base metal or silver encasing a religious print to an exquisite pendant of chased gold set with jewels encasing a skillfully painted or sculpted image. They were worn throughout Latin America, especially during the colonial period. In the New World, Spanish and Portuguese colonists adorned themselves with relicarios to provide comfort and protection against the dangers of life on the frontier.

ABOVE: Sue Tapia (Laguna), red-on-red pot, ca. 2007, clay with natural slip.
LEFT: Mary Ester Archuleta (Ohkay Owingeh), red and buff clay jar.

Devout colonial women often gave a relicario as a votive offering to an image of the Virgin or saint in a church or chapel. Generally made by metalsmiths and treasured as heirlooms, these devotional items were imported into New Mexico beginning in the 1700s. In the mid-nineteenth century, some residents in the region's isolated mountain villages purchased relicarios from itinerant Arab peddlers. Eventually New Mexico artisans made relicarios for sale; an early popular form consisted of a small, rectangular, tin frame with a religious print encased behind a sheet of **mica** and a loop at the back for hanging. Today Hispano jewelers of the Southwest fashion elaborate relicarios out of gold or silver in which they set tiny original paintings or prints of saints, or depictions of the beloved **Nuestra Señora de Guadalupe**.

REPISA / a small single- or double-wooden shelf, usually handcrafted from pine, that hangs on a wall, typically found in Spanish Colonial (and later **Spanish Colonial Revival**) New Mexico homes, as well as in Arizona, in buildings such as the mission sites of Tubac and Tumacácori. These shelves, especially later examples, have been decorated with carved and/or painted (with water-based paints) patterns or motifs.

REPOUSSÉ (Repoussage, Embossing) / a decorative technique in which the surface of a piece of **silver** jewelry or other metalwork is hammered with variously shaped tools or **dies** from the reverse (or back) side to create an embossed or raised design on the front (or top) of the piece. The design on the front is often further refined and enhanced with chisel and/or **stamp work**.

Repoussé is commonly used by Native American silversmiths, especially the Navajos. Historically, the technique has been used to decorate the silver ornaments on **horse bridles**, **ketohs** (bow guards), buckles, **conchas**, bracelets, and other objects of adornment. Contemporary jewelers continue to use this technique, often in combination with other methods, to create new and modern forms. Repoussé can also be used with pottery, to push the **clay** out from the inside to create a design or stylized form such as the ribs in **melon pots**. For example, renowned Laguna Pueblo potter Andrew Padilla creates the ribs of his white-clay melon pots by pushing the clay from the inside; and Hopi artist Al Qoyawayma uses the method to create ears of **corn**, figures, and other shapes in relief on his clay vessels.

REREDO / a word of Anglo origin meaning "altar screen," this term has been used since the early twentieth century in the Southwest for a large decorative screen consisting of a hand-carved architectural framework inset with individual images of saints and other religious figures painted on wood panels, placed behind an altar in a church or chapel; the reredo may be free-standing or part of the altar structure. The term is also used for miniature hand-painted wood altar screens intended for display in the home, made by **santeros/santeras** in New Mexico. The term may have been first introduced to the region by Anglo American artists/collectors in the 1920s. Previous to that, altar screens were generally called retablos both in New Spain and in Spanish Colonial New Mexico. They continue to be called retablos in modern-day Mexico and Spain. See also **altar screens**.

RETABLO / derived from the Latin *retro tabula* (meaning behind the "altar" table), a term for paintings and large **altar screens** of devotional religious images on wood. Beginning about 1800, in New Mexico, the term became used only for small painted panels, while throughout New Spain it continued to be used for large altar screens.

Traditionally, in New Mexico, the wood panel for a retablo was shaped from ponderosa pine trees felled in a forest, smoothed with a hand **adze** or drawknife, and covered in layers of **gesso** (a white plaster-like substance made from gypsum). After the gesso dried, the **santero/santera**—using mineral and vegetal **pigments** that were gathered and ground into paints, and a brush made from **yucca** leaves, horse hair, or human hair—painted a saint and its attributes on the prepared panel. The retablo was then sealed

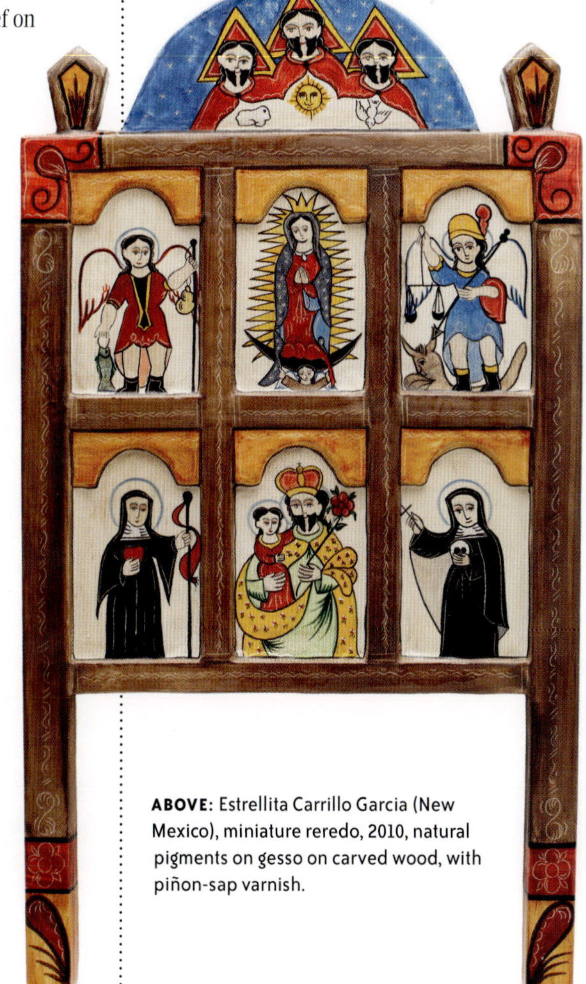

ABOVE LEFT: Holy Child of the Three Potencies relicario, 18th-century Mexico or Guatemala, silver and paint on metal.

ABOVE: Estrellita Carrillo Garcia (New Mexico), miniature reredo, 2010, natural pigments on gesso on carved wood, with piñon-sap varnish.

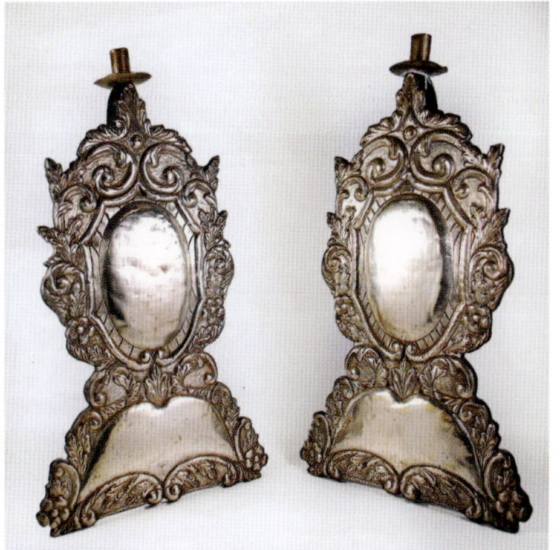

LEFT: Spanish Colonial silver repoussé candlesticks, 19th century.

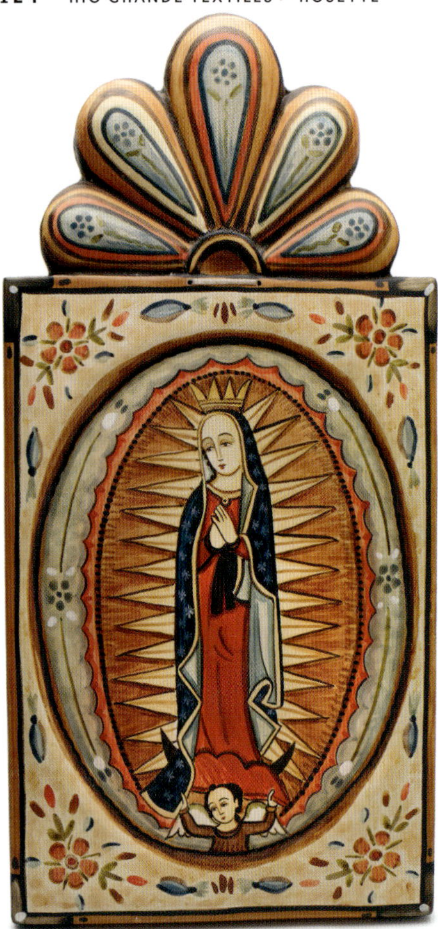

Nicolás R. Otero, Nuestra Señora de Guadalupe retablo, ca. 2010, natural pigments on gesso on chiseled wood.

with a native resin varnish, such as sap from a **piñon** tree. Beginning in the 1700s and through the mid-1800s, the source of imagery for New Mexico retablos was illustrated prayer cards, missals, bibles, oil paintings, and sculptures brought up from Mexico by the Spanish colonists on supply caravans. The early retablos based on these images consisted of rather flat and abstracted figures.

By the end of the nineteenth century the demand for retablos in the Southwest had declined because of the availability of mass-produced religious imagery. The art form experienced a resurgence, however, in the 1920s in New Mexico, when writer Mary Austin and artist Frank Applegate founded the Spanish Colonial Arts Society to preserve and perpetuate traditional Hispano arts.

Contemporary artisans carry on the art form today, some using traditional methods and materials—including adzed pine, natural pigments, and gold leaf—while others use modern materials such as milled lumber, commercial gesso, and commercial paints. In recent years, artisans have used piñon-sap varnish to protect

the surface, and some use **sgraffito** to add detailing. Artisans now sign their pieces, market them to collectors, and enjoy a vast following. See also **reredos**, **santos**, and **santeros/santeras**.

RIO GRANDE TEXTILES / a handwoven blanket created with handspun **churro wool** dyed with muted hues—first with vegetal **dyes** and from the nineteenth century onward with synthetic or aniline dyes as well as vegetal dyes—with visible **warp** fringe (hand-knotted) at both ends. Rio Grande blankets, also known as *frazadas* (or as *frezada* in northern New Mexico and southern Colorado) are longer than wide and woven on a treadle **loom**. They were developed by Hispano artisans living along the Rio Grande and its tributaries in New Mexico, in the seventeenth and eighteenth centuries.

This vibrant textile tradition—a melding of Spanish, Mexican, and Navajo weaving influences —was established after the Spanish introduced some 4,000 churro sheep to New Mexico, in 1598. The earliest surviving examples, which date to the nineteenth century, feature wide bands and zones of narrow stripes, in the natural colors of **churro wool**—white and brown—sometimes combined with natural-dyed **yarns**—especially **indigo**, yellow, pinks and reds (made from the madder root and the **cochineal** insect), and reddish to golden tan. Later Rio Grande–style blan-

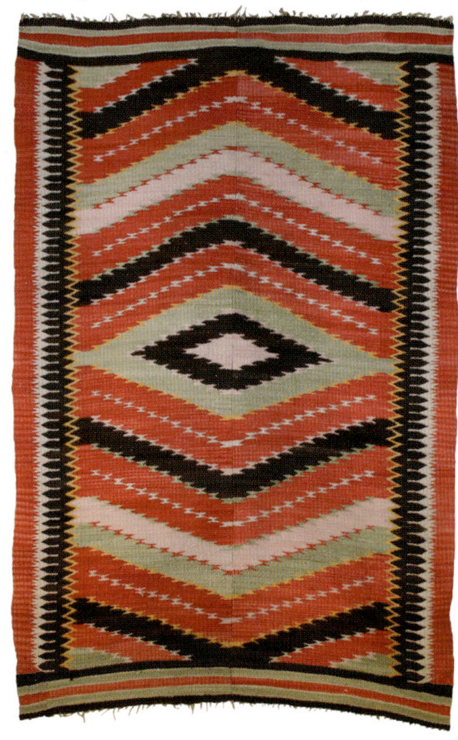

Rio Grande blanket, ca. 1890, 77" x 51".

kets are more complex, with intricate geometric patterns such as chevrons, leaf forms, and serrated diamonds, in imitation of traditional Mexican **Saltillo sarapes**, and were typically made with **Merino wool** yarns brilliantly colored with synthetic dyes. Beginning in the mid-1880s, strong and smooth commercial cotton "string" gradually replaced wool as the favored warp used by Hispano weavers.

The blankets were produced for domestic use— for wearing during the day and bedding at night— and for commercial export. In fact, they were the most widely distributed of nineteenth-century New Mexican Spanish goods: traded down south into Mexico, east into the United States, west to California, and to Native Americans at various locations. Hundreds of such blankets were distributed to Navajos during their forced exile at Bosque Redondo (Fort Sumner, New Mexico) from about 1864 to 1868, and influenced the designs of Navajo handwoven textiles of the period. For instance, the eight-pointed **Vallero star**, a motif commonly used in blankets woven in the Spanish villages, later appeared in Navajo textiles.

Striped Rio Grande-style blankets continue to be made today in New Mexico and in southern Colorado; the Hispano weavers producing them use either the traditional handspun and hand-dyed wool fibers or commercially manufactured yarns and cotton warp.

ROCK ART / See **geoglyphs**, **petroglyphs**, and **pictographs**.

ROCKER ENGRAVING / a decorative technique found on nineteenth-century **Navajo silverwork**, in which a design is impressed by "rocking" an **awl** or short-bladed chisel or the corner of a file back and forth on the surface. The finished effect is a line comprising lightly impressed, continuous zigzags. Likely learned from Mexican smiths, the method was common before the Navajos learned to use **stamp work** and other **silver** techniques in the late nineteenth century. See also **souvenir spoons**.

ROSETTE / a carved or painted circular or oval pattern that is a highly stylized (or abstract) representation of a flower, used extensively since antiquity as a decorative motif in architecture, furniture, and decorative arts; it appears frequently on **tinwork**, furniture (especially on chests), **corbels**, and other woodwork of the Spanish Colonial era in New Mexico. Some writ-

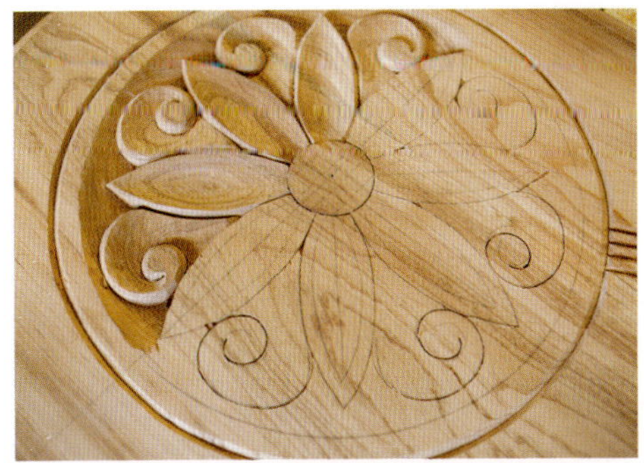

Hand-carved rosette.

ers have referred to the shape of **silver** Navajo **conchas** as "rosettes." Revived in the 1930s by **WPA furniture** makers and artisans in New Mexico, the design is a common motif used by contemporary artists and artisans throughout the Southwest. Many variations of the rosette exist; one of the more common usages is on the crest (or top) of **trasteros** and **retablos**, in which only half a rosette appears. The latter is also sometimes referred to as a **lunette**. The rosette has been variously interpreted by scholars; for instance, some suggest the rosette is not a floral element at all and actually represents a cockleshell and is a symbol of pilgrimage, while others have said the circular motif represents a Navajo **hogan**.

ROUND-SHAPED NAVAJO RUGS / an innovative style of rug first made by Navajo weaver Rose Owens in the late 1960s, after dreaming about **Spider Woman** weaving in a circle. Her husband helped with the first rug by bringing her the metal rim of a wagon wheel to help create the round shape. The style remains popular among Navajo weavers today.

ROUTE 66 / the legendary 2,448-mile-long highway extending from Chicago, Illinois, to Santa Monica, California, and crossing the heart of the Southwest. Formally established in 1926 and completed by 1938, Route 66 was an important outlet for the sale of Native American arts and crafts. Pottery, textiles, jewelry, **katsina dolls**, and a variety of novelty items were made for this tourist trade. **Thunderbird** folk art jewelry made by Santo Domingo Pueblo artisans out of repurposed and found materials and hand-carved/tempera-

Mary H. Yazzie (Navajo), round textile, 68" diameter.

painted wooden Hopi **katsina dolls** were favorite items for sale in Route 66 **trading posts**.

By the 1930s the majority of travel in the Southwest had shifted to automobiles, and Route 66 was a busy thoroughfare along which roadside stands and trading posts flourished. In fact, Route 66 traders became the intermediaries between Native American artists and buyers. By initiating designs and marketing specific types of wares they thought would sell, they directly influenced the designs and types of objects that Native people made.

One of the more famous trading posts of the era was Maurice Maisel's store on West Central Avenue (Route 66) in Albuquerque, New Mexico, where customers could watch Navajo silversmiths handcraft jewelry. Among the items made specifically for Route 66 retail businesses, which are highly collectible today, are small Hopi-style katsina dolls and **Navajo silverwork** including vintage lipstick holders, cosmetic compacts, card holders, belt buckles, hat bands, boxes, and so on.

By the 1950s many trading posts on the route no longer offered high quality Native-made goods; instead they sold cheap mass-produced items of inferior quality.

Arizona has the longest stretch of Route 66 still in use today, running from Seligman to Kingman. Portions of the highway—especially in places like Gallup, New Mexico, and near Holbrook, Arizona—are still enlivened with neon signs advertising galleries, **curio** stores, and trading posts that offer both fine Native American art, as well as kitschy items recalling an earlier time on the "Mother Road."

ROW WORK / a style of **silver** jewelry made by **Zuni Pueblo jewelers** since at least the 1930s, similar to **cluster work**, in which small stones, usually **turquoise** or **coral**, are set in individual silver **bezels** and arranged in one or more matching rows. The rows may be straight, as in bracelets and rings, or may frame the sides of **cluster work** pieces such as bracelets and pins. The stones used in this technique may be large in size composed in a single row, or small in size with numerous rows. Sometimes the stones are set with tiny silver drops.

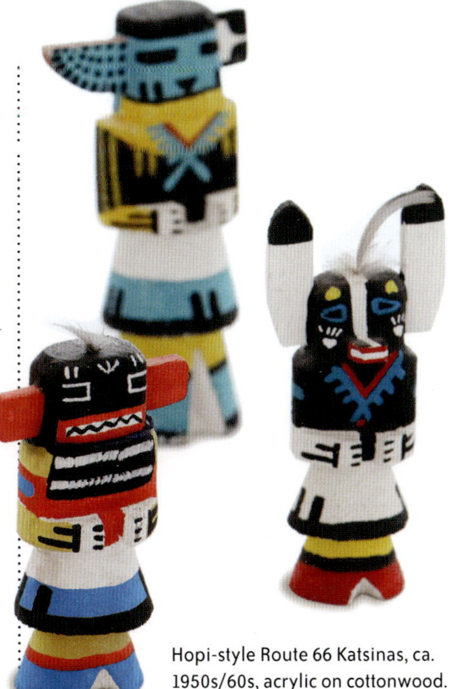

Hopi-style Route 66 Katsinas, ca. 1950s/60s, acrylic on cottonwood.

RUG STYLES / the naming of regionalized Navajo rug patterns—such as **Crystal**, **Two Grey Hills**, **Ganado**, etc.—were started by post traders in the 1920s, to help distinguish the weaving style that one post represented from that of others, as part of a marketing plan. By the 1950s, when Navajo weavers began moving around the region more, these regional patterns did not have the same validity. They are still used today, however, to distinguish certain patterns.

SABANILLA / the diminutive of the Spanish word *sábana* (sheet), a type of plain- or **twill**-weave cloth of fine-to-medium weight, made with handspun natural-white **churro-wool** yarn, made in Spanish Colonial New Mexico and used for a variety of purposes including clothing, sheeting, mattress sacks, and bedcovers, as well as the foundation cloth for wool-on-wool **colcha** embroidery. Produced on a horizontal treadle **loom**, the fabric has the same number of **warp**

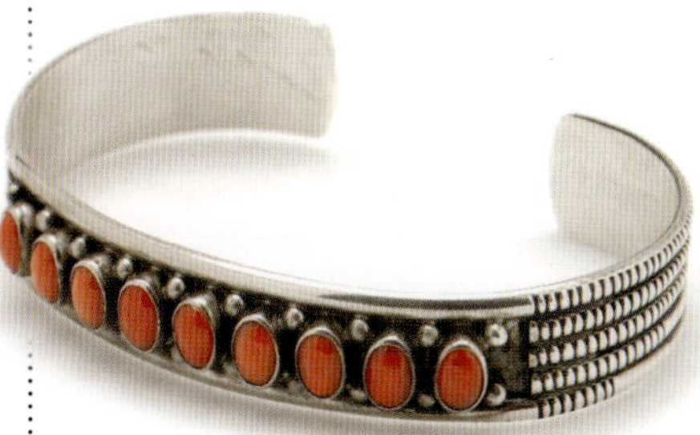

Zuni row-work bracelet, ca. 1970s, sterling silver and coral.

(lengthwise) threads as **weft** (horizontal) threads and ranges from 22 to 28 inches in width. To make a bedcover or altar cloth, three widths of sabanilla were typically sewn together. Sabanilla was considerably finer than other yardage produced on New Mexico looms.

SADDLE BAGS / tanned-hide bags sewn together with **sinew**, usually with tanned-hide fringe at either end, with a slit in the center fold through which the bag is opened and through which items were placed. They were attached to a saddle or packed on the back of a horse and used to carry supplies and equipment. Among the typical items placed in a saddle bag were foods such as bread or dry meat and clothing and blankets. They were made by Native Americans of the Southwest beginning shortly after horses were introduced to the region by the Spanish in the seventeenth century. By the nineteenth century, the Colorado Utes embellished their saddle bags with intricate **beadwork** designs and tanned-hide fringe, while the Western Apaches decorated theirs with designs cut out of the rawhide, revealing red and/or black cloth below. See also **saddle blankets—Ute**.

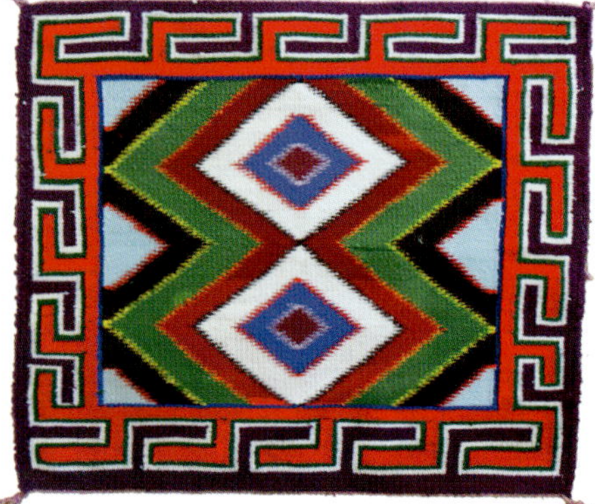

Navajo "fancy" single saddle blanket, ca. 1970s.

SADDLE BLANKETS / Saddle Covers / Navajo / originally functional pads made from thick animal pelts and hides, saddle blankets became a necessity for Native Americans after the Spanish introduced horses to the Southwest in the 1600s. As new materials became available and weaving skills developed among tribes, the blankets became highly decorated woven textiles. Since at least 1860 they were produced by Navajo weavers for use and for trade (called *'ak'idahi'níli* in Navajo).

These blankets were intended for placement beneath a leather-covered saddle on the back of a horse, as a pad to keep the horses from getting saddlesore on long rides. They were woven in a

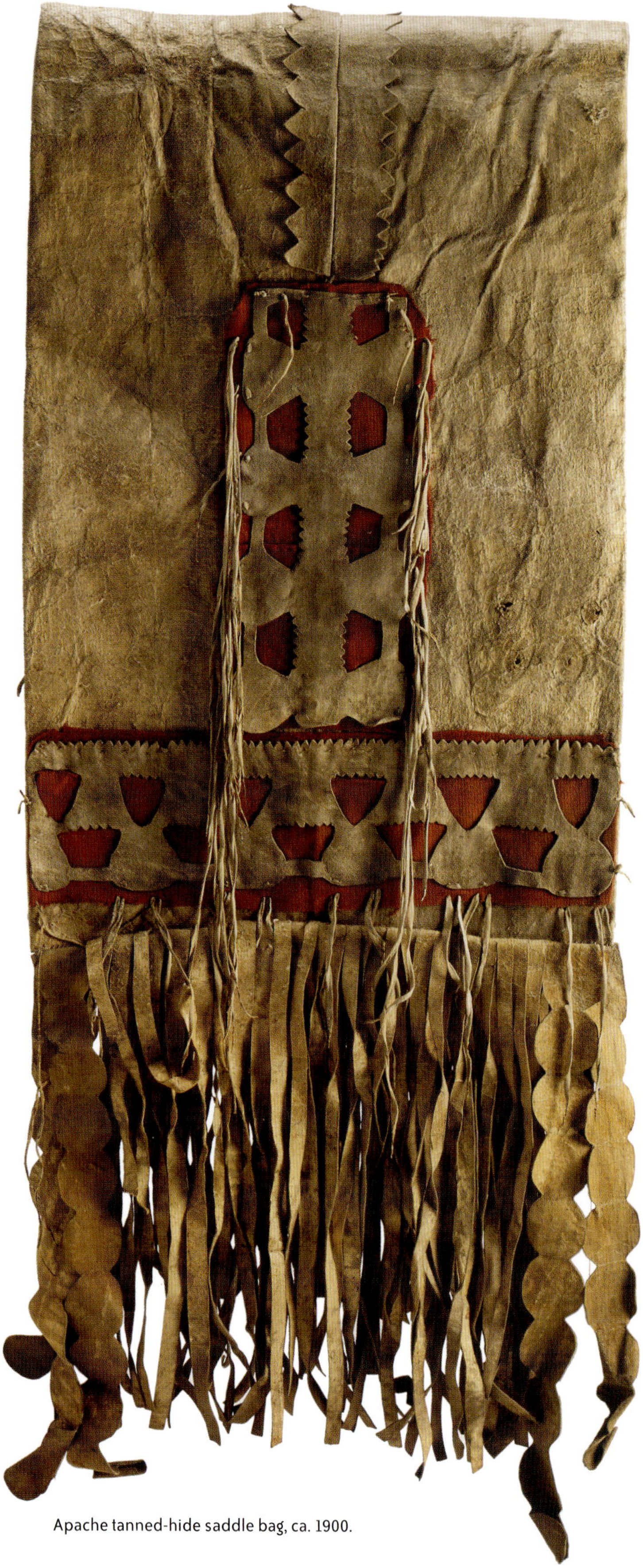

Apache tanned-hide saddle bag, ca. 1900.

single and double style; the singles were about 30 inches square and the doubles were of similar width but about twice as long and were doubled over when in use to provide extra padding. Saddle blankets were also placed over the saddle for the rider's comfort or to provide a fancy saddle decoration. The single-style blankets were occasionally decorated with fringe or pom-pom tassels in the corners.

By the late nineteenth century the thinner, finer blankets were being replaced by thicker saddle blankets woven by Navajos using the **twill** technique. They learned this method from Pueblo weavers. Because it created a much thicker, sturdier textile than the plain weave, twill was an excellent method for weaving saddle blankets that received so much wear and tear on the back of a horse. By 1900 the saddle-style textiles had become popular with tourists and were sold at **trading posts** as **curios.** Around that same time, some Navajo saddle blankets were woven with colorful four-ply commercial **yarns**, with added fringe and tassels, and became known as "Sunday saddle blankets." These "fancy" saddle blankets were for special occasions. Navajos still make twilled saddle blankets for their own use today.

SADDLE BLANKETS / Ute / blankets made by the Southern Utes of Colorado in the mid- to late-nineteenth century from tanned hide were embellished with colorful glass beads and hide fringe. The Utes were among the first Native Americans in the Southwest to have horses, which they stole or bartered from Hispano settlers, beginning in the mid-1600s. Horses were introduced to America by the Spanish, who first settled in New Mexico in the late sixteenth century.

SAGRADA CORAZÓN / a simple but powerful design consisting of a heart with flames emitting from the top (suggesting a halo, divine light, or the transformative power of love) and encircled by the crown of thorns (alluding to the manner of Jesus's death) and sometimes surmounted by a **cross**, together representing the Sacred Heart and the passion, love, and suffering of Jesus Christ. The Sagrada Corazón is often depicted by Hispano artists in **tinwork**, **retablos**, **bultos**, paintings, carvings, and **straw appliqué**. Sometimes, the heart is shown pierced by the lance wound or with a spear and nails to symbolize the crucifixion. For some, it is purely an artistic design, while for others, it is an intensely spiritual element and important symbol of Catholic religious tradition. See also **crosses.**

SAGUARO (_Carnegiea gigantea_) / a native cactus of the Sonoran Desert that can reach fifty feet in height, distinguished by its spiny green trunk and branches and its plum-sized fruit, used for a variety of purposes including as a building material in the early architecture of the region. The strong, woody ribs of dried saguaro cactus were traditionally implemented in the ceiling construction of the prehistoric homes of Arizona's Sonoran Desert. Because timber was scarce, the Salado people (farmers in the Salt River Valley) used saguaro ribs for the ceilings of their **cliff dwellings** in the thirteenth and fourteenth centuries. Dried saguaro ribs (or _savinas_) were sometimes used in traditionally built homes of the pre-railroad period, and later in the **Spanish Colonial Revival-style** houses of the 1910s through the 1930s in Arizona.

For centuries, the Tohono O'odham and Pima peoples have harvested the fruits of the saguaro that grow at the top of the spiny branches and trunk, which must be dislodged with a tool,

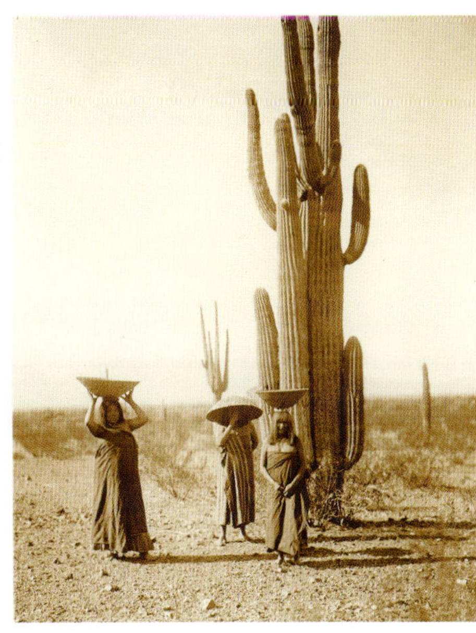
Maricopa women among saguaros, 1907.

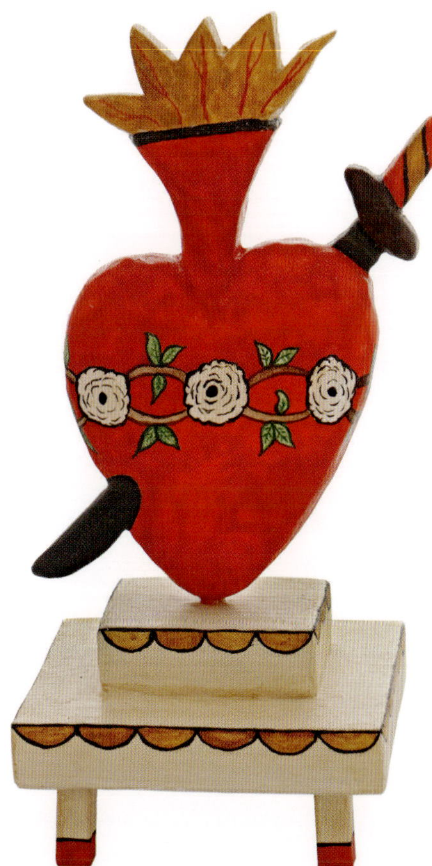
Margarito R. Mondragón (New Mexico), El Sagrado Corazón de María bulto, 2011, natural pigments on gesso on carved pine, with piñon-sap varnish and beeswax.

usually consisting of a long wood pole (often two saguaro ribs attached together) with a small stick at the tip to function as a hook. The fruit's pulp (eaten fresh, boiled into a sweetener, or boiled and fermented into wine) and the seeds (ground with water into a gruel to make bread) were an important food source; the wine was used for rain-bringing ceremonies. Saguaros, as well as scenes portraying saguaro fruit-picking, a culturally important activity, have appeared as decoration on various art forms made by the Native peoples of Arizona. For example, since at least the late nineteenth century, the spiny cacti and fruit-picking images are popular decorative patterns used in the handwoven baskets of Tohono O'odham and Pima artisans. The saguaro is an iconic motif of the Southwest and today appears on everything from magnets to dish towels to ceramics. See also **ramada** and **Sonoran row house**.

SALA (Living Room, Parlor) / a relatively large multipurpose room of Spanish Colonial–era and territorial-era homes in the Southwest, where guests were entertained, food was cooked and served, and the residents sometimes slept. Because it was the most formal room in a dwelling, it often contained more elaborate woodwork and a finished ceiling.

SALTILLO BLANKETS / Sarapes / a term used by the early nineteenth century for handwoven Mexican sarapes/blankets featuring intricate patterns: usually a central serrated or diamond figure, borders, vertical zigzag striping of the background, and small "floating" elements such as hourglass shapes and serrated diamonds. When woven with a slit in the center, it could be slipped over the head and worn like a poncho; ones woven without a slit could be folded over the shoulder or wrapped around the body. These sarapes/blankets, which are labor-intensive to make, are named after Saltillo, a city and major marketing center in the state of Coahuila, Mexico, where this style of textile was developed and produced; it was, however, also produced in a number of other towns in northern and central Mexico. In Mexico, the Saltillo sarape was typically an exceedingly fine, intricately detailed, **weft**-faced **tapestry**; in addition to its functionality, the sarape had high value in Mexican society and indicated the prestige and wealth of its wearer.

These widely traded blankets were introduced into the Rio Grande Valley of New Mexico in the early 1800s; the distinctive designs strongly influenced local Spanish weavers, who imitated Saltillo patterns in their own textiles. These sarapes/blankets ranged in decoration from simple bands of striping to more elaborate Saltillo-derived design elements. By the 1860s, some Navajo and Pueblo weavers were also imitating the style. Saltillo sarapes worn as an outer garment became extremely popular among men living throughout Mexico and the Southwest. It became the custom of rich Spanish *vaqueros* (cowboys) to tie their colorful Saltillo sarapes and ponchos to the backs of their saddles, as a sign of wealth and pride. See also **eyedazzlers** and **Rio Grande textiles**.

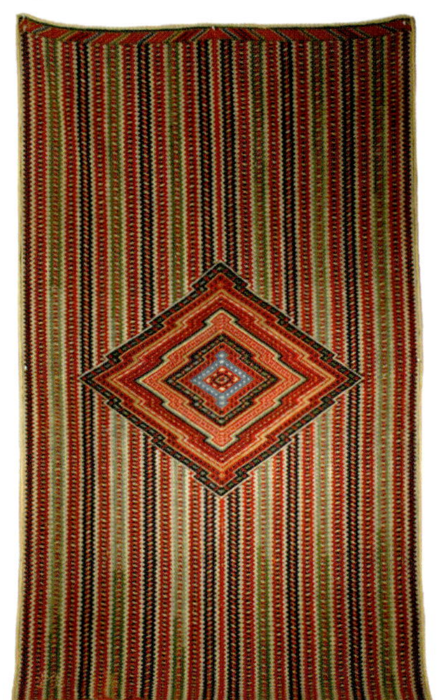

Classic Saltillo sarape, ca. 1840, natural wool with natural dyes, 89" x 52".

SALTILLO TILE / an unglazed, handcrafted floor tile made in Saltillo, in the state of Coahuila, Mexico, varying in color from a yellowish ochre to a reddish brick (depending on where the tiles were stacked in the kiln), with an overall earthy and rustic look much admired by homeowners in the southwestern United States.

To make Saltillo tiles, **clay**—excavated from natural deposits in Mexico—is mixed with water and then hand-packed into wood frames to form the tile shapes, and dried outdoors in the sun for several days. After drying in the sun, the tiles are fired in a wood- and fuel-fired kiln. In addition to their unique aesthetic qualities, Saltillo tiles are practical flooring material for they are extremely sturdy and easy to clean. Similar tiles made elsewhere in Mexico are generally referred to as "pavers," or terra-cotta floor tiles. See also **tiles—Mexican/Spanish**.

SAMPLER RUGS / multiple Navajo rug designs of different styles woven into one single rug, first appearing in the late nineteenth century. The term also may refer to small, almost miniature textiles woven for sale or trade to tourists (see also **loom samplers**). The sampler rugs typically range from four-in-one (the most common) to nine-in-one to fifteen-in-one. Additionally, some Navajo weavers have made "a rug within a rug" in which one pattern is symmetrically centered over what appears to be another rug beneath it. In some examples, the inner rug pattern may have tassels projecting from each corner, thus further heightening the illusion of a rug in a rug.

SAN FRANCISCO DE ASÍS (St. Francis of Assisi) / the patron saint of small animals, a popular figure with New Mexican **santeros/santeras**, traditionally portrayed wearing a friar's habit, cowl, and knotted-cord belt, bearded and tonsured, and often marked with the stigmata on his hands (the wounds identical to those received by Christ when crucified on the cross). He also typically holds a cross in one hand and a skull (or book) in the other, and is standing or kneeling. St. Francis was born in 1181 to a wealthy merchant of Assisi, and after a vision of Christ, he devoted

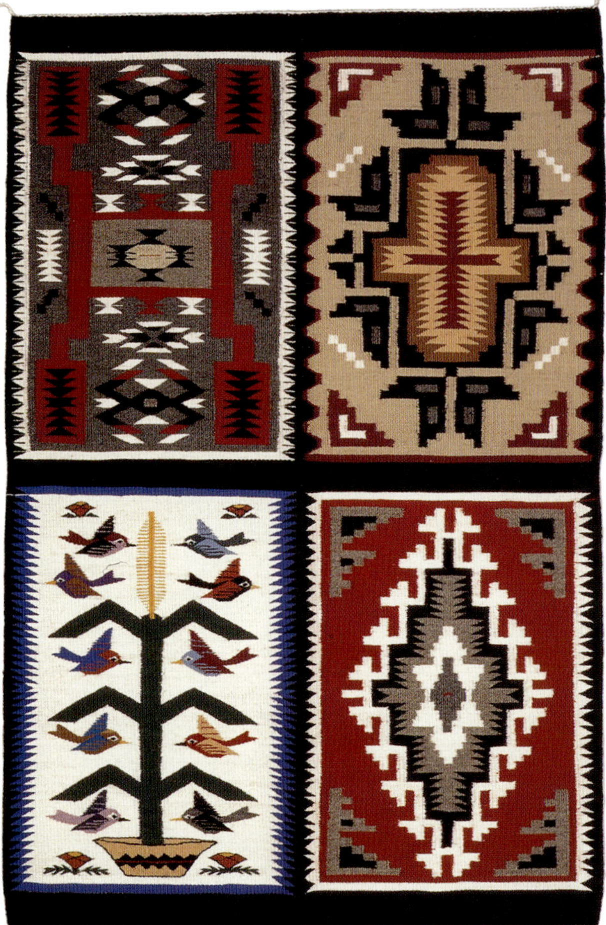

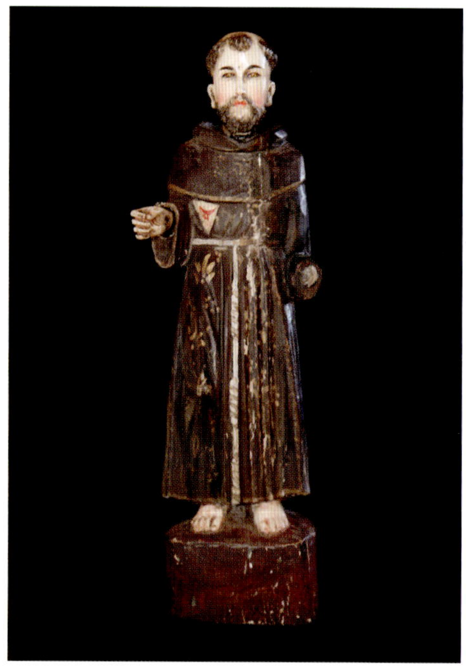

ABOVE: Priscilla Endischee (Navajo), sampler textile, includes (clockwise from upper left): storm pattern, Teec Nos Pos variant, Ganado, and bird pictorial styles.
BELOW: Painted-wood bulto of St. Francis, ca. 1890.

himself to a life of poverty and the care of the sick and the poor. He attracted followers and began the order of Friars Minor, popularly known as the Franciscans; until the end of the eighteenth century, this order had sole responsibility for New Mexico. St. Francis was devoted to the Christ Child and according to legend he preached to the birds; he also experienced an ecstatic vision during which he received the stigmata. This influential saint died in 1226 and his feast day is celebrated on October 4. In recent times, St. Francis has been portrayed by santeros in a brown habit (the dress of modern Franciscians), with small birds and animals perched on his shoulders or in his hands. He is the patron saint of New Mexico's capital city of Santa Fe (traditionally known as La Ciudad Real de la Santa Fe de San Francisco de Asís).

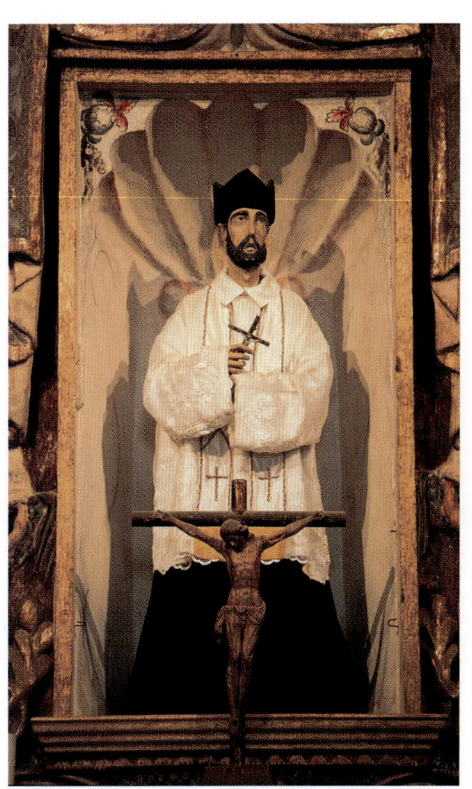

San Francisco Xavier figure at Mission San Xavier del Bac.

SAN FRANCISCO XAVIER / the personal patron of Father Eusebio Francisco Kino, the Jesuit explorer-missionary who brought Christianity and European culture to present day Arizona and Sonora. Born in Spain in 1506, San Francisco studied in Paris, became a Jesuit, and was sent as a missionary to the East Indies. After his death in 1552 off the coast of China, his body was packed in lime and returned by sea to Goa, India, where

it is said to have arrived in a perfect state of preservation—many believed this was a sign of Xavier's strong spiritual qualities. Thousands of pilgrims each year celebrate his feast day on December 3, and travel to the church of Bom Jesus in Goa, where his body lies in state. The Mission San Xavier del Bac near Tucson, Arizona, was named for him; within this mission church are carved wooden sculptures depicting San Francisco Xavier.

SAN ILDEFONSO PUEBLO POTTERY / potters at this pueblo were making black-on-cream or **polychrome** water jars and other utilitarian wares from the time the pueblo was established at its present location in the fourteenth century. Over the centuries there were many innovative potters at San Ildefonso, especially between 1880 and the 1920s. Among them were the renowned potters Maria Martinez and her husband Julian, who together helped create the now famous style of pottery with matte-black designs on polished black vessels, known as **black-on-black** ware. First created around 1919–20, the black-on-black pots were made by painting a **clay** design on a burnished red pot, and at the end of the **firing** process, oxygen is removed by smothering the fire with manure and ashes.

Other influential San Ildefonso potters of this period were Martina Vigil (1856–1916) and her husband Florentino Montoya (1858–1918), who began making polychrome pots around 1875, and whose shapes and painted designs (in red and black on cream-colored **slip**) were copied by many other potters, including Maria and Julian.

Among the favored images of San Ildefonso potters is **avanyu** (the water serpent), which Julian Martinez began painting on the **black-on-black** jars made by his wife beginning in 1919. Another common design, dating to prehistoric times, is the stylized repetition of **feathers** encircling a pot, plate, or other form. Maria's son, Popovi Da (1923–1971), experimented with several new techniques including black-and-sienna ware and pots with inlaid turquoise. These techniques, along with the introduction of **sgraffito** or scratched designs, became more refined by his son, Tony Da (1940–2008).

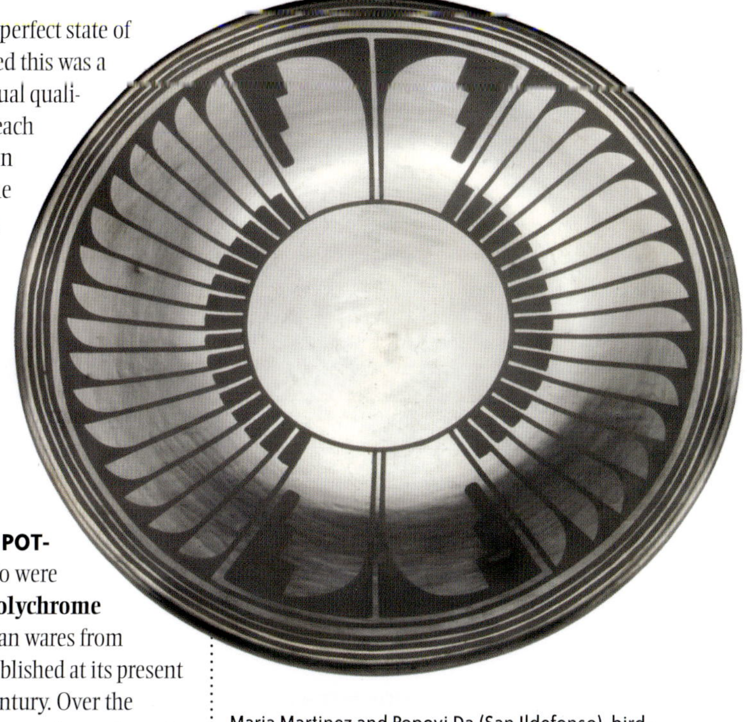

Maria Martinez and Popovi Da (San Ildefonso), bird-wing plate.

In the 1930s San Ildefonso artisan Rose Gonzales (1900–1989), and some potters at Santa Clara Pueblo, began making the innovative **carved** blackware, by deeply carving pots and figurines with various designs. Among the innovative potters working at San Ildefonso today are the award-winning Russell Sanchez (b. 1963) and Dora Tse-Pé (b. 1939, Zia Pueblo). Both are known for their highly polished forms and intricate inlay work.

SAN ISIDRO LABRADOR (San Ysidro, St. Isidore the Farmer) / patron saint of farmers and the city of Madrid, Spain, an important figure in Spanish Colonial New Mexico, and frequently portrayed in the religious art of New Mexican **santeros** today. Generally, he is shown as a humble peasant dressed in everyday colonial garb (the red-and-blue **bayeta** wool uniform of the frontier settler), with a broad-brimmed hat, and holding a staff or ox goad in one hand, accompanied by an angel guiding a plow pulled by two oxen. In **retablos** he is often shown in a field amid a recognizable New Mexican landscape or inside a church.

The legend of this saint is deeply rooted in the traditions of Spain. Born in the eleventh century outside Madrid, Isidro was a poor farmer who became renowned for his legendary powers of

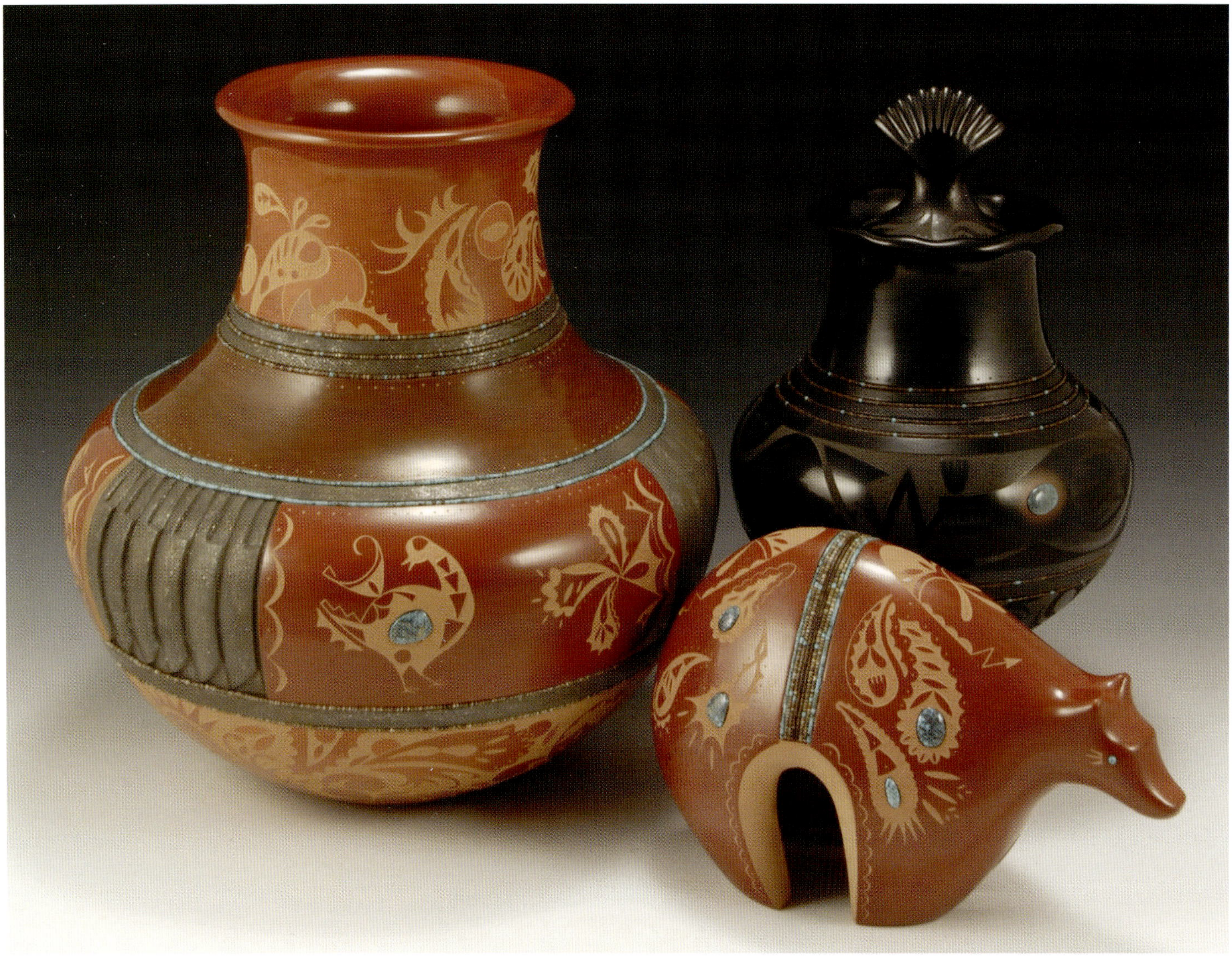

ABOVE: Russell Sanchez (San Ildefonso), group of pottery with inlay and sgraffito details.

prayer that led to bountiful harvests and tales of miracles on the farm. For instance, according to legend while Isidro prayed angels miraculously took his place behind the plow. Many other miracles were attributed to him. After his canonization in 1622, San Isidro Labrador's reputation spread throughout the New World, as far as seventeenth-century rural New Mexico, where Spanish colonists had transplanted their agrarian lifestyle and where the saint became an important part of local lore and life. Traditionally, when his feast day is celebrated on May 15 (as it still is today), Hispanos pray to the saint for abundant rainfall and bountiful crops.

RIGHT: José Mondragon (New Mexico), San Isidro bulto, ca. 1959–1990.

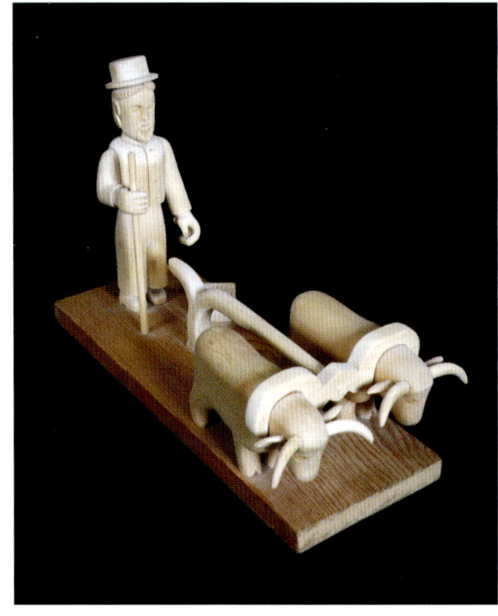

SAN JUAN PAIUTE BASKETS / historically, the San Juan Paiutes made both **twined** and **coiled sumac** (and sometimes **willow**) baskets used for ceremonies and essential for the gathering and preparation and storing of food, such as **piñon-pitch**-covered **water jars**, small vase-shaped **ollas**, bowl-trays, "boiling bowls," conical **burden baskets**, winnowing trays, and seed beaters (or "harvesting fans"). They also made basket cradles, and twined-basketry hats for women (to protect their foreheads from the weight of the carrying straps used to transport burden baskets). In the 1870s, after the San Juan Paiutes developed a trading relationship with their Navajo neighbors, they provided the Navajos with basketry water jugs sealed with pinon-pitch. By about the 1930s they also made for trade with the Navajo the so-called "**wedding basket**"—a ceremonial form of coiled basket with a predominantly red, black, and white (or natural) design, which the San Juan Paiute weavers learned from Navajo women.

Wedding baskets became a reliable and important source of income for the Paiutes; it remains the type most often made by Paiute weavers today. One reason the Navajos purchase these baskets from the Paiutes (and also from the Utes) is that the Navajo creation of ceremonial baskets was (and still is) governed by a set of taboos (such as when a woman can and cannot weave). San Juan Paiute women are not restricted by these taboos. Eventually, San Juan Paiute women added their own artistic touch to the classic wedding design, including bright colors, geometric shapes, and pictorial elements. By the early twentieth century manufactured containers purchased at trading posts gradually began to replace basketry vessels; however, the San Juan Paiute never completely abandoned the tradition of weaving utilitarian basket forms.

San Juan Paiute basketry experienced a resurgence beginning in the 1960s, due in part to trader William Beaver, who purchased the Sacred Mountain Trading Post in Arizona (located between Cameron and Flagstaff) in 1960. He devoted his time to supporting and promoting Paiute baskets (as well as **Navajo pottery**); for instance, in the 1970s, he provided weavers with photographs from the Fred Harvey basket collection at the Heard Museum and various books and pictures to encourage them to weave "old-timer" baskets. In 1985–86 the Wheelwright Museum of the American Indian in Santa Fe, New Mexico, held an influential exhibition of Beaver's collection of San Juan Paiute baskets, resulting in greater interest in their work.

Today basketry is still a vital economic and ceremonial aspect of San Juan Paiute culture. Weavers continue to make utilitarian old-timer baskets, as well as wedding baskets to trade with the Navajos and to sell in the marketplace, and baskets with interpretations of traditional designs from other tribes. They also weave innovative "design baskets" that exhibit much creativity in their bold, new patterns and colors. In addition to the traditional sumac and willow, some now use **yucca** splints to weave coiled tray shapes and other forms; colors are made by using natural and/or commercial **dyes** and black splints used for decoration are sometimes **devil's claw**. One of the more popular patterns features one or more rows of **butterflies** encircling the basketry form.

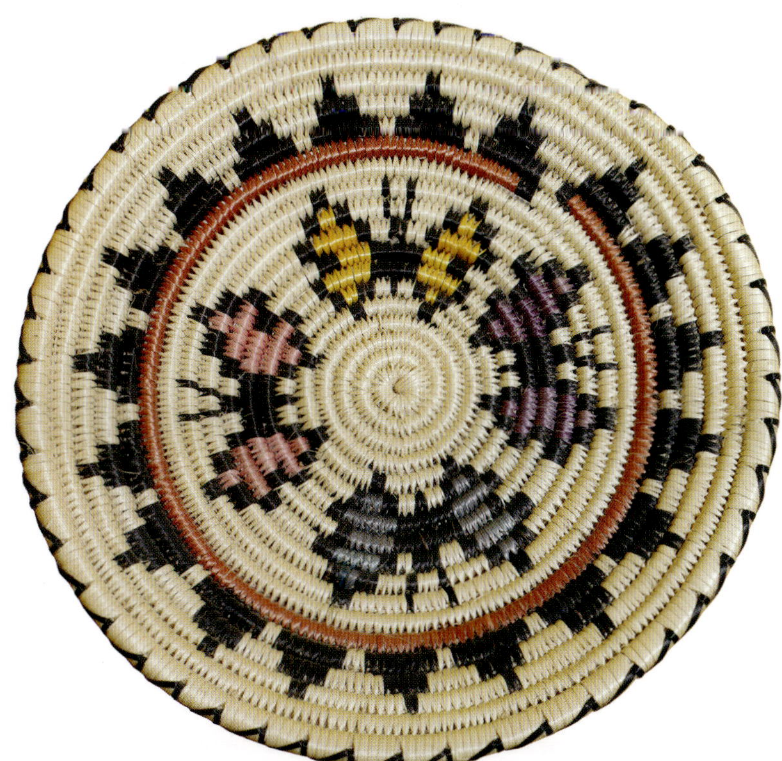

ABOVE: Rose Ann Whiskers (San Juan Paiute), "Butterfly" coiled plaque, 2003, natural and commercially dyed yucca.
BELOW: Navajo sand-cast brooch, sterling silver.

SAND CASTING / a long-practiced European technique of creating jewelry or metalwork (often confused with **tufa casting**), used by Navajo and Pueblo silversmiths beginning sometime in the twentieth century, involving the pouring of molten **silver** or gold into a mold carved into sand (sometimes mixed with a fixative and packed into a wood or iron frame), in which the artisan has hand carved with a knife or file the exact shape and design of the desired object. After the material has cooled and hardened, the artisan removes the piece from the mold, the extraneous bits are cut off, the edges are filed smooth, and surfaces are ground and polished. Some Navajo and Pueblo silversmiths continue to use this method of forming silver or gold today. Some refer to the method as "cement and oil" and use cement mixed with oil instead of sand, a slightly different process that allows the jeweler to make a duplicate quite easily and quickly. Others use a commercial product called French sand, which according to some scholars, was used as early as the 1930s by some Native jewelers.

SANDPAINTINGS (Dry Paintings) / Ceremonial / ephemeral religious works of art created on the ground out of natural materials including sand, earth, and ground chalk, charcoal, leaves, and pigments by the Pueblo, Hopi, Tohono O'odham, and Navajo peoples. Sand or "dry" paintings play a particularly important role in Navajo ceremonies and curing rituals—including treating of illnesses, offering of blessings, expelling of evil, or restoration of the world to balance.

These highly stylized and abstract designs (as befitting the depiction of a sacred personage) are drawn on the floor of a **hogan** by a Navajo *hataalii* (a Navajo expression that translates as "singer" and a term used for a medicine man) and one or several apprentices. First, natural-colored sand is placed on the floor as the base. Second, the designs and imagery are added with natural pigments—including sandstones, mudstones, crushed **turquoise**, charcoal from oak, **cornmeal**, powdered flower petals, and plant pollens. The design elements used are strictly prescribed; in healing ceremonies, the sandpaintings depict the supernatural being or beings most capable of curing the particular illness of the patient.

A sandpainting is usually completed in one day, used in a ceremony at night, and destroyed before sunrise the following day. In multi-day/night ceremonies, a different painting is created each day. A wooden stick, with prayer feathers attached to it, is used to destroy the painting, and then the sand is ceremonially disposed of. Because of the supernatural power and sacred nature of the sandpaintings, it was considered taboo for anyone other than the medicine man to recreate them and they were rarely reproduced outside of ceremonial settings. The designs were (and continue to be) committed to memory by medicine men and passed down from one generation to another.

The earliest reproductions of sandpaintings are the watercolors and colored-pencil drawings made in the late nineteenth century by Anglo ethnologists and traders, who sought to record Navajo ceremonial knowledge. One of the first times sandpainting motifs were used as decorative art was in 1923, at the Hotel Navajo in Gallup, New Mexico, where architect/designer Mary Elizabeth Jane Colter (1869–1958) used twelve large "sandpaintings" on interior walls.

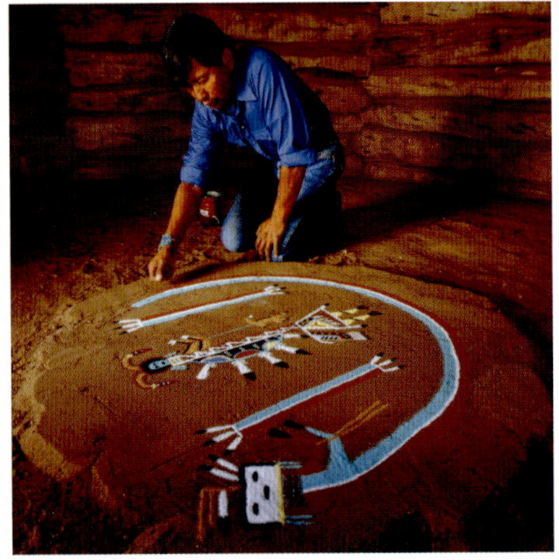

Since the mid-twentieth century, sandpainting imagery has been replicated in handwoven textiles, pottery, "permanent" sandpaintings, and in other art forms. To avoid summoning the gods and to protect them from harm, Navajo artisans who portray sandpaintings may undergo the Blessingway ceremony before creating a work, and they avoid exact copies of the sacred sandpaintings. By changing slightly the imagery, colors, symbolism, or composition, they believe the paintings are secular objects. See also **sandpaintings—permanent** and **sandpaintings—textiles**.

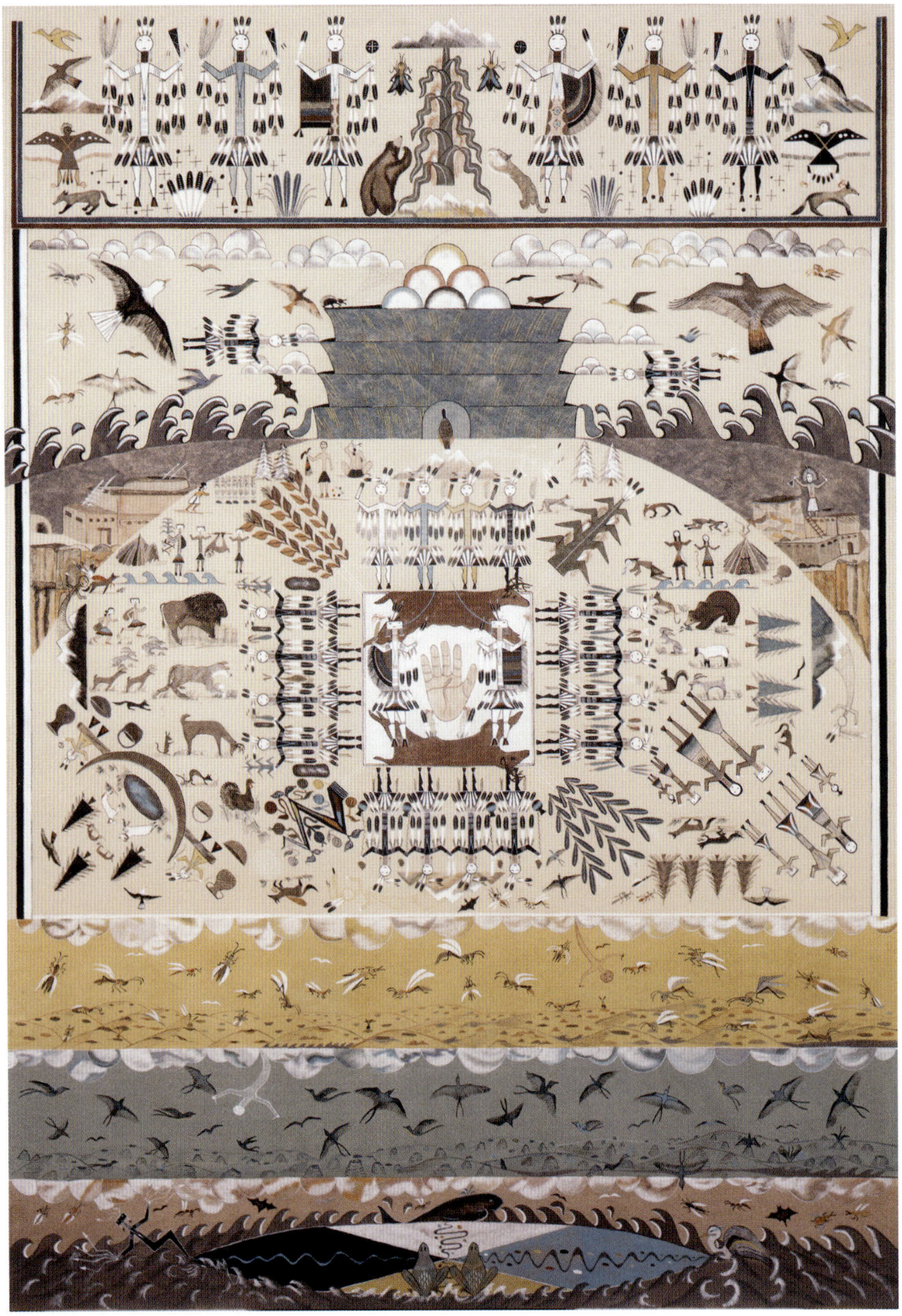

ABOVE: Rosie Yellowhair (Navajo), "Emergence Story" permanent sandpainting, 2004, 60 ½" x 42 ¼".
LEFT: Art Etcitty (Navajo) creates a dry sandpainting at Hubbell Trading Post.

SANDPAINTINGS / Permanent / the exacting art form of replicating traditional ceremonial Native American sandpainting motifs using naturally colored sand glued onto pressed wood (or Masonite) boards. Among the earliest to practice the art was Navajo artist Fred Stevens (or Grey Squirrel) of Sheep Springs, New Mexico; he began making permanent sandpaintings in the 1950s. Traditionally, the first step is to gather different rocks—such as limestone, **turquoise**, vanadium, gypsum, azurite, chrysocolla, and sandstone—from within Navajoland (Dinétah), often keeping the exact locations a secret. After the rock is broken into small pieces, it is left to dry and then ground using a mano and **metate** (mortar and pestle), or sometimes a hand-operated coffee grinder. After grinding, the sand is sifted. (Today many artists skip this process and purchase ready-made colored sands from stores and trading posts, primarily in northwestern New Mexico). Then, a sheet of particle board (from 3/8 inch to 1/2 inch in thickness) is covered evenly in white glue or another adhesive. The background sand is carefully applied and the board left to dry in the sun, after which it is lightly sanded. The design is drawn in glue using fine brushes, applying only one section at a time, and then the sand is applied by hand—trickled onto the surface with the artist's fingers. Once this process is complete, the work is left to dry for a day or two and then the entire surface is sprayed with a matte fixative or shellac to secure the sand permanently to the board. The colors and design elements used are highly symbolic: images range from figures to animals to plants to geometric motifs.

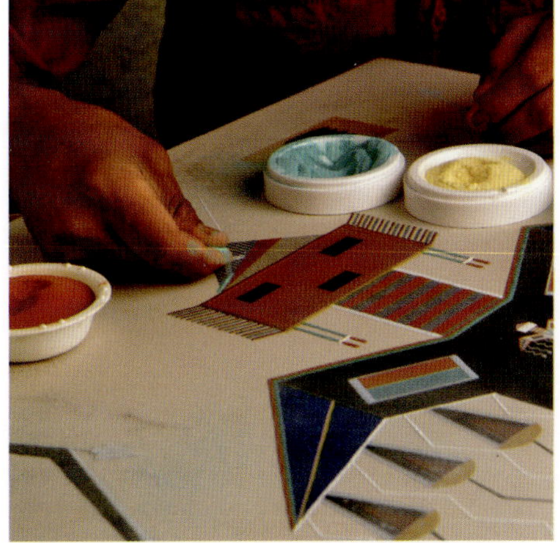

Joe Ben, Jr. (Navajo) adds ground sandstone to his permanent sandpainting.

To avoid an exact copy of a religious sandpainting, when Navajo artists make sand-on-board paintings for sale they always deliberately include "errors," or variations of the religious imagery. Some contemporary artists use non-traditional materials in their paintings, such as lapis lazuli, and have developed their own unique styles and techniques. The healing designs of sandpaintings have also been painted on muslin cloth and paper, and have been carefully woven into Navajo rugs, **tapestries**, and baskets. See also **sandpaintings—ceremonial** and **sandpaintings—textiles**.

SANDPAINTINGS / **Textiles** / a highly detailed, **pictorial** Navajo rug/tapestry style representing sacred sandpaintings that are traditionally created by a Navajo *hataalii*, or medicine man, as an essential part of Navajo ceremonies and curing

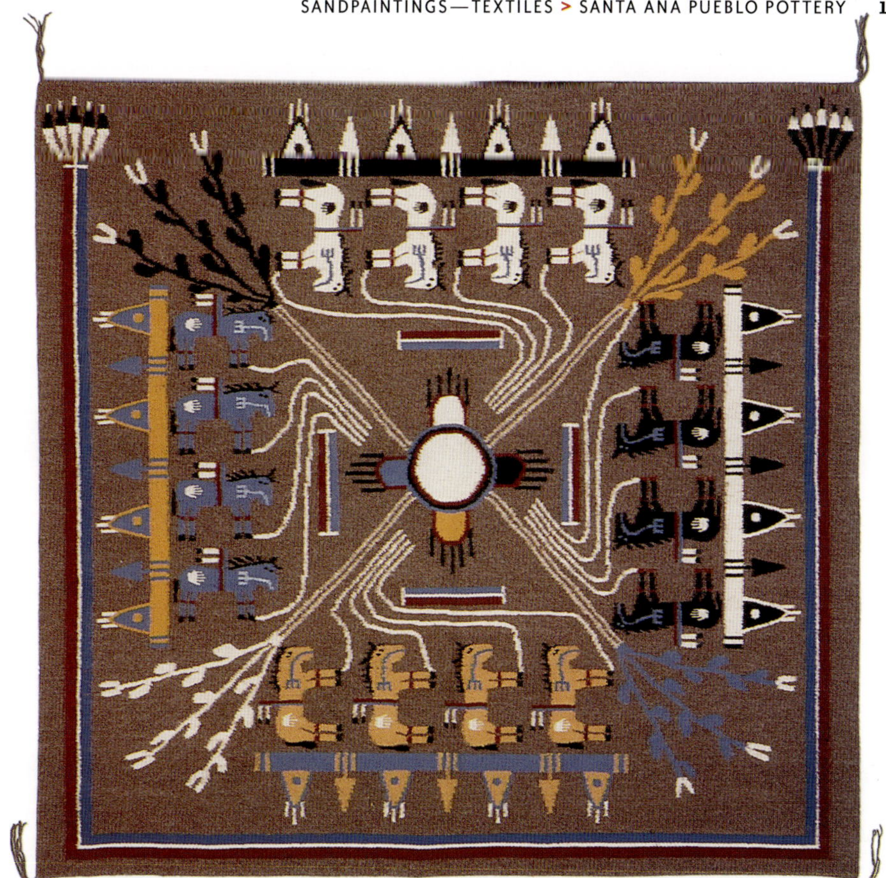

Mary Rose Tyler (Navajo), "Home of the Buffalo" sandpainting textile, 52 ½" x 49".

rituals. Because of the sacred nature of sandpaintings, it was long considered taboo among the Navajos to reproduce them—anyone who did so risked blindness or severe illness.

The first recorded sandpainting rug was created in 1896, for a member of the Hyde Exploring Expedition to the Chaco Canyon region of New Mexico. In the early 1900s Navajo weaver Yanabah created vertical textiles of figures from sandpaintings, a style unique from textiles depicting full sandpainting designs. About 1919, Franc Newcomb, wife of trader Arthur Newcomb of Newcomb, New Mexico, convinced a hataalii named Hastiin Klah (ca. 1867–1937) to weave a sandpainting rug for her. Klah, who was concerned with the preservation and recording of Navajo ceremonies, encouraged his niece, Gladys Manuelito, to weave sandpainting rugs as well. These highly intricate, time-consuming, and costly rugs are still woven today. The weaver may hire a medicine man to perform a ceremony before or after the rug is woven to ensure protection for the weaver. Also, when Navajos weave figures taken from sandpaintings they do so with modifications, to preserve the sanctity of the curing ceremonies the figures are used in. More

importantly, because sandpaintings are essentially an invitation to the depicted Holy People to make themselves present and effect a cure, in permanent textiles of sandpaintings the artisan must avoid creating images that invite their presence. See also **sandpaintings—permanent** and **sandpaintings—ceremonial**.

SANTA ANA PUEBLO POTTERY / known for vessels featuring matte-mineral grayish white or buff **slip** over brick-red **clay**, with simple and bold designs—such as clouds, lightning, scallops, and triangles—executed in red and usually outlined in black. Evidence suggests they have been making this style of pottery since at least the mid- to late eighteenth century. Historic Santa Ana pottery resembles the ceramics made at Zia Pueblo, where the Keres language is also spoken.

Since the eighteenth century, Santa Ana potters have collected their clay adjacent to the old pueblo on the Jemez River, and have used fine, water-worn sand for the **temper**. One of the important early utilitarian forms made at Santa Ana (as well as at other Pueblos in the region) is the large bowl used for mixing bread dough; it is believed that these dough bowls should never be

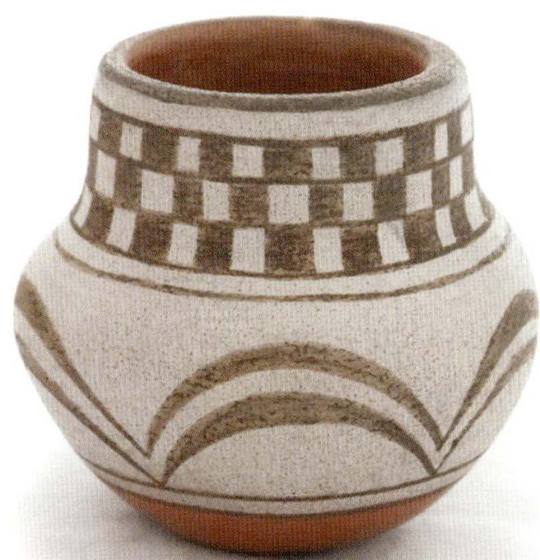

Stirapama Tamara (Santa Ana), polychrome small vase, 2004, clay with natural slips.

cleaned, so that the spirits of the previous batch of dough can be incorporated into the substance of each following one.

In the early 1900s, Santa Ana ceramics declined in quality and quantity. Some utilitarian and decorated wares were made into the 1930s. The tradition almost disappeared completely, but was kept alive in the twentieth century by a handful of potters: Eudora Montoya (the only potter at Santa Ana in the 1960s, who began teaching other women there in the 1970s), Elveria Montoya, Lucille Montoya, and others. In the 1970s the expansion of awareness for Native Americans and their art forms, the enlargement of Indian fairs and markets, and other factors encouraged the making and collecting of Pueblo pottery, even at Santa Ana.

Today a small number of potters are active; among them are Jean Robbins, Laura Peña, Donna Pino, and Diane Menchego. They create small to medium-size **polychrome** bowls and jars of white-clay slip, polished interiors, and orange-red and black designs adapted and revived from early 1900-era Santa Ana styles. Fine examples of Santa Ana pottery, of both the past and present, remain rare.

SANTA CLARA PUEBLO POTTERY / plain, polished **black-on-black** and **red pottery** are perhaps the two most noteworthy types of pottery made at Santa Clara, and among the most prevalent images portrayed on their vessels are the **bear paw** (impressed in the wet clay before **firing**), a motif revived in the early twentieth century, and **avanyu**, the water serpent who according to Santa Clara legend once saved the village from a flood. Potters have painted, **carved**, or etched avanyu encircling vessels and plates, with its tongue and tail intersecting.

Another Santa Clara innovation is highly pol-

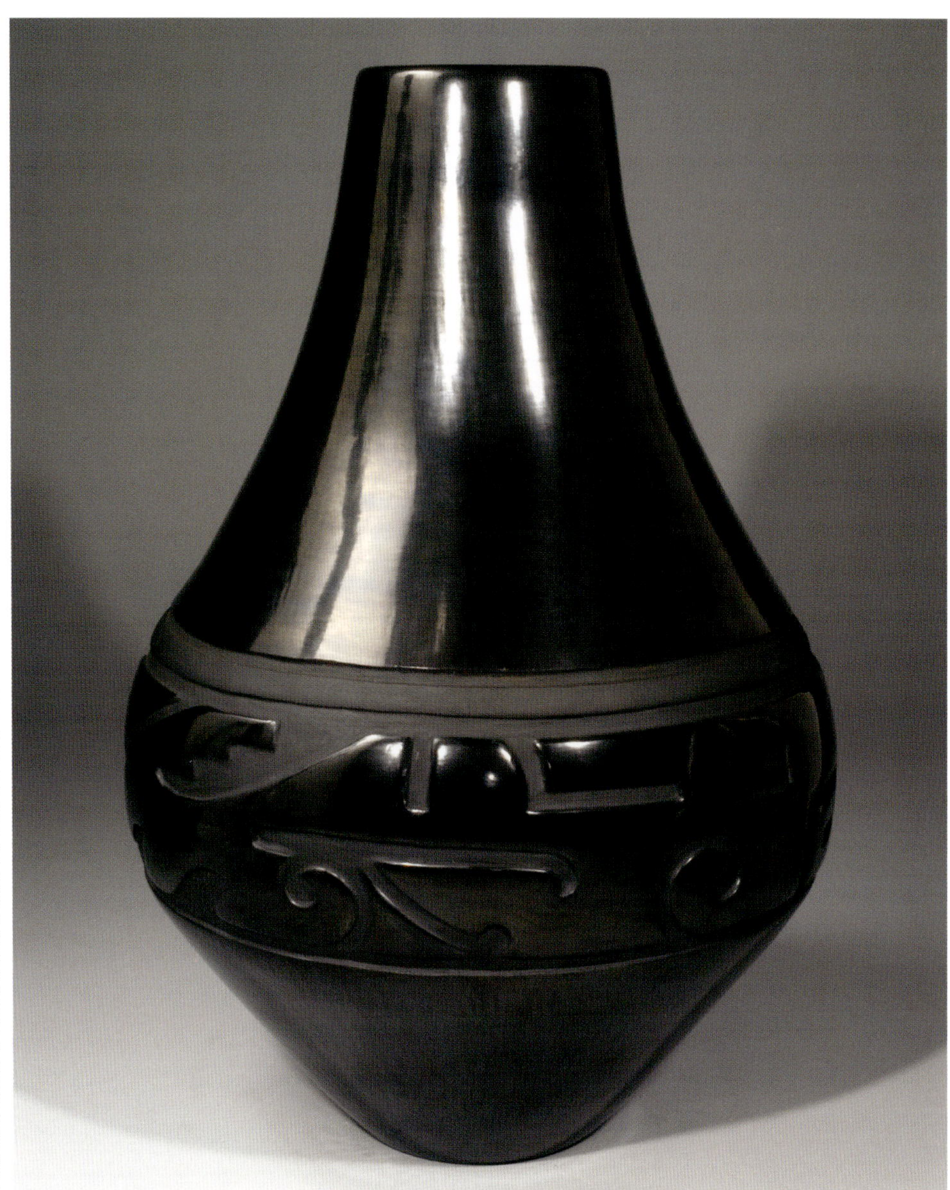

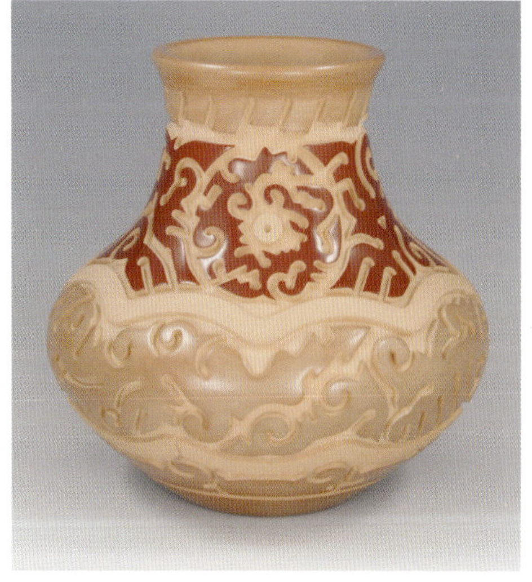

ABOVE: LuAnn Tafoya (Santa Clara), black jar. **RIGHT:** Nathan Youngblood (Santa Clara), large tricolor water jar.

ished pottery with deeply carved designs; Sara Fina Tafoya (ca. 1863–1949) is credited with establishing this method. Also, for at least one hundred years, potters at this pueblo have been creating small, polished redware and blackware clay animals (or *animalitos*), some with **matte** designs etched or impressed in the clay. During the Great Depression, a large number of these figures were made, for it was easier to sell the smaller, less expensive figures than larger, pricey bowls or jars. Also, during the 1930s, Lela and Van Gutierrez were among the potters who revived the tradition of **polychrome** wares at Santa Clara. Originally inspired by kiva murals and Pueblo paintings, they went on to create many of their own designs and developed an intricate and complicated painting style on their pottery.

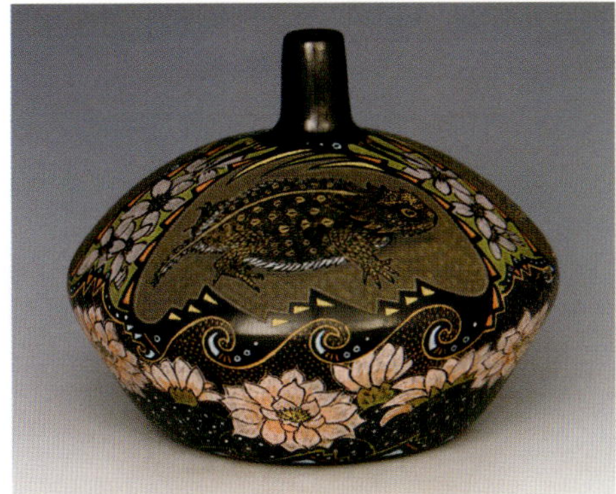

Jennifer Moquino (Santa Clara), jar with horned lizards.

Today polished redware and blackware with carved motifs or **sgraffito** designs are widely created by Santa Clara potters. In recent decades, they have added **storyteller** figures to their repertoire. And, like so many other Pueblo potters, artisans at Santa Clara are constantly seeking to explore new avenues in ceramics. Many now combine traditional materials, forms, and designs with contemporary, non-traditional features, including inlaid **turquoise**, **coral**, **heishi**, **silver**, and other materials.

SANTERO/SANTERA / a Spanish word meaning a "maker of religious images" (such as **santos**, **bultos**, and **retablos**); santero refers to a male "saint maker" and santera refers to a female "saint maker." Traditionally, santeros were holy men, often sacristans of a church, involved with the care and sometimes repair of holy images. It was long believed that the more religious the santero, the more powerful the image created by him. By the mid-eighteenth century there were Hispano santeros creating devotional art in the Southwest; since at least the early twentieth century, Hispano women have also created religious art in the region.

The earliest santeros working in northern New Mexico and the San Luis Valley of Colorado were largely self-taught, though some learned their skills as apprentices to masters. They used native pine, aspen, **cottonwood**, and oil paints to create religious art based on Spanish and Mexican examples that were imported to the region from Mexico in the colonial period. These early works reflected the same subjects, iconography, and baroque style of their colonial counterparts, but with a distinct local character and style. Among the innovations established by the New Mexican santeros was the practice of combining oil paints and gold leaf with the natural mineral and vegtal paints that the region's Pueblo people had taught them to use.

By the late eighteenth century the work of New Mexican santeros was highly valued and placed alongside the imported religious objects in churches, chapels, and homes. And by the early nineteenth century there were at least a dozen santeros active in the area.

Today there are a large number of santeros/santeras working in the Southwest, especially in New Mexico and southern Colorado. Many continue to make and use the traditional materials (natural or mineral pigments, gesso, and **piñon-pitch** varnish) for their santos, while others, for aesthetic reasons, use acrylics or oil paints and manufactured varnishes. Many present-day santeros/santeras sell their bultos and retablos in the commercial marketplace, however, for most of them the craft is primarily an act of devotion.

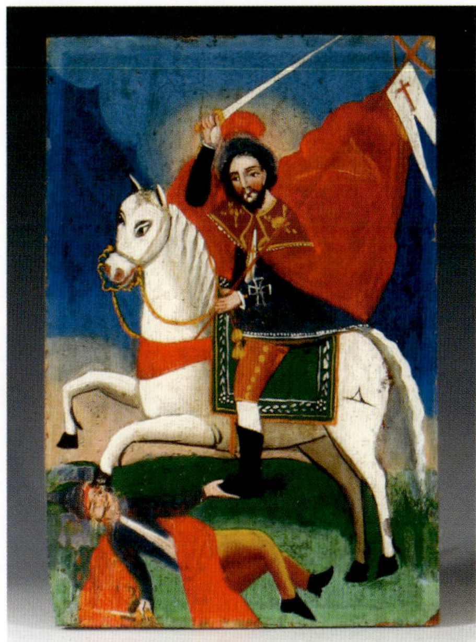

Santiago de Compostela, Mexican retablo, 19th century, oil on wood.

SANTIAGO DE COMPOSTELA (Saint James, Santiago Matamoros) / the patron saint of Spain, horsemen, horses, and the military, and a popular figure with New Mexican **santeros/santeras**. He is generally portrayed bearded, riding a white horse, armed with a spear or sword, and riding over a field covered with the bodies of slain Moors. According to legend, Apostle James, a Galilean fisherman, traveled to Spain to convert the pagan peoples, and after his martyrdom in Jerusalem, his body was transported miraculously back to Spain, where it was discovered eight hundred years later at Compostela.

Saint James was seen as a valiant warrior who helped the Christian Spaniards with their long battle against the Moors, and he was also associated with the militant expansion of Spanish Christianity throughout the Americas. Thousands of visitors annually make the pilgrimage to Compostela to celebrate Saint James's feast day on July 25. A famous statue of Santiago, made by an unknown santero (circa 1810–1820), can be seen enclosed in a glass case near the altar in the Santuario de Chimayó, in Chimayó, New Mexico. It was once customary for supplicants to place miniature boots, bridles, quirts, and sombreros near the statue as offerings to Saint James, the militant defender of Christians.

SANTO / a Spanish word meaning saint or holy, as well as "image of saint," which in the Southwest refers to a carved (**bulto**) or painted (**retablo**) image of a Catholic saint, the Virgin Mary, an angel, or Jesus Christ. Santos, serving as a bridge or intercessor between the human and the divine, are intended to be displayed in churches and **moradas** and in private homes.

Sacred images were first brought to the Americas around four hundred years ago by explorers from Spain, Portugal, and elsewhere in Europe. By the late eighteenth century in New Mexico the tradition of making santos had been established, and the development of distinctive regional styles and subjects quickly followed. A small number of historic santos of northern New Mexico, in private and public collections, have been identified by scholars as being created by Hispano **santeros/santeras** as early as the 1760s. Most, however, date from between the end of the colonial period (the 1820s) and the arrival of the railroad in 1880.

Today the primary centers of santo production in the Southwest are the villages and cities of central and northern New Mexico and southern Colorado. Scholars have identified a "Colorado Style" among modern santeros/santeras that is distinguished by deep carving and imagery combining unpainted and painted areas. The most commonly portrayed and most popular santos of the Southwest are: San Miguel Arcángel, San Raphael Arcángel, Ángel de la Guardia, La Purísma Concepción, Nuestra Señora del Carmen, La Conquistadora, Nuestra Señora del Rosario, Nuestra Señora de Dolores, **Nuestra Señora de Guadalupe**, **El Santo Niño de Atocha**, San

Antonio de Padua, San Agustín, Santa Bárbara, San Cayetano, Santa Clara, **San Francisco de Asís**, **San Francisco Xavier**, **San Isidro Labrador**, **Santiago de Compostela**, San Juan Bautista, San José, San Judas Taddeo, Saint **Kateri Tekakwitha**, San Pascual Bailón, San Pedro, San Ramón Nonato, Santa Rita, and Santa Teresa de Ávila.

While many contemporary santeros/santeras continue to make traditional devotional santos, others continue to experiment by producing less-well-known saints and by portraying politically and/or socially charged images that "push the envelope" and express modern messages. In recent years, some, including the organizers of the Spanish Colonial Arts Society's Spanish Market in Santa Fe, have encouraged this experimentation.

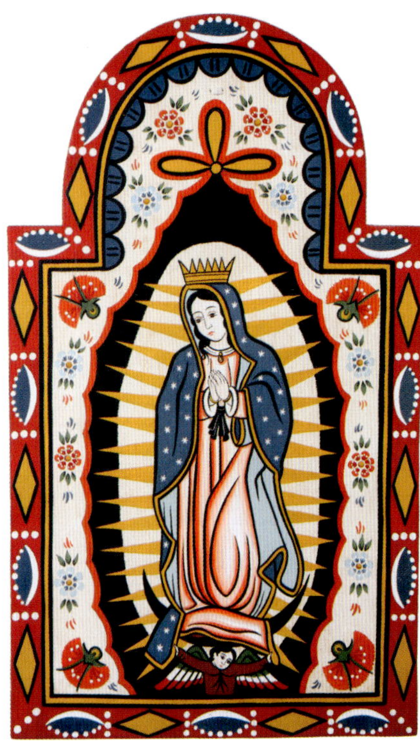

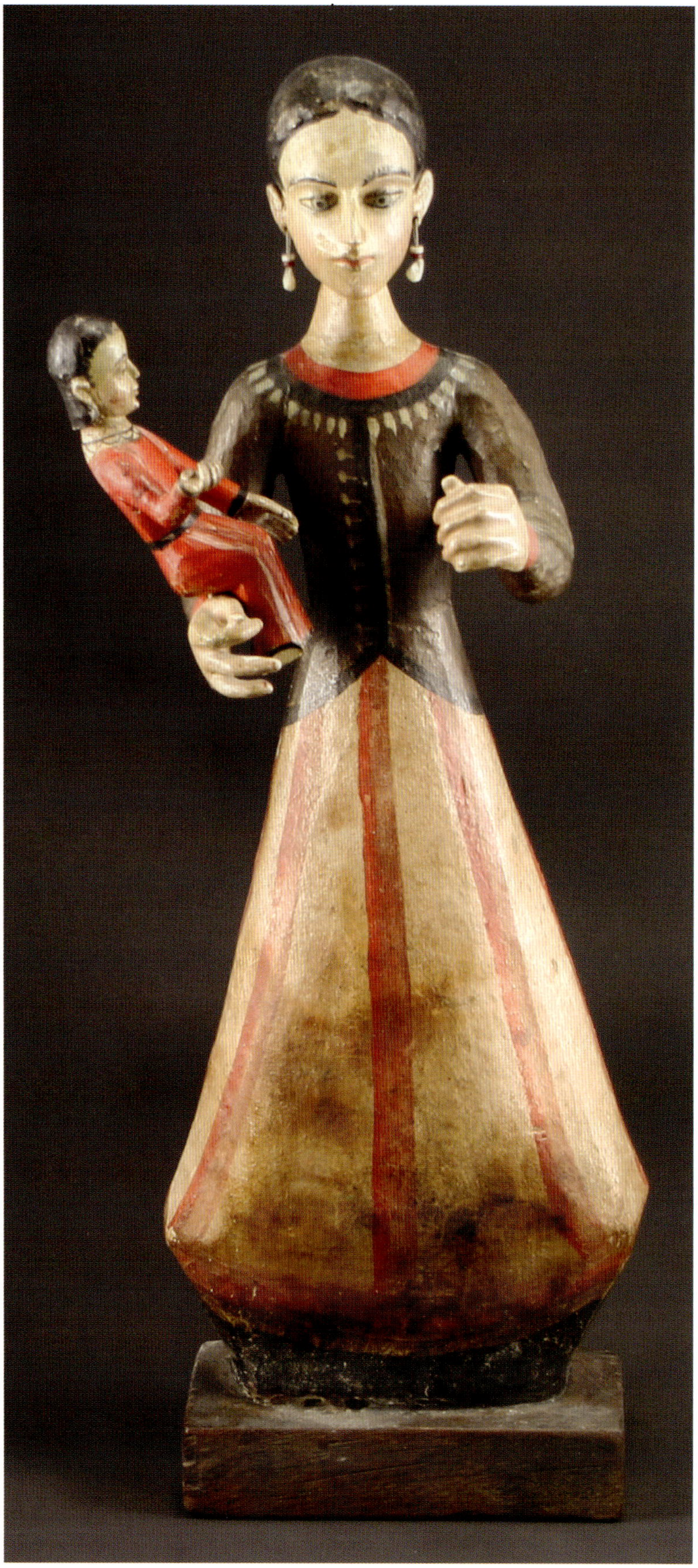

ABOVE: Gabriel Vigil (New Mexico), Nuestra Señora de Guadalupe retablo. **RIGHT:** José Aragón (New Mexico), bulto, ca. 1840.

SANTO DOMINGO (Kewa) PUEBLO JEWELRY /
made for centuries by the Santo Domingo people, who have been known for their masterful use of **turquoise** (which they mined in the nearby Cerrillos Hills), **shells** from the Gulf of California and the Pacific (obtained through extensive trade routes), and other natural materials in **beads** and **mosaic** jewelry. The Santo Domingo people, whose **pueblo** was founded in north-central New Mexico about 1700, traveled throughout the Southwest to trade their jewelry for Navajo

textiles, buffalo hides, food, and other items.

By the mid-1920s jewelers at Santo Domingo were producing necklaces with bone or shell tabs (pendant-like beads) covered with turquoise mosaic, set off by contrasting pieces of **jet** and strung with bone or shells. They were popular with Native American and Anglo women. During this time, the Santo Domingo villages, located on the banks of the Rio Grande, had direct access to **Route 66** and the Santa Fe Railway, where they sold their wares.

A short while later, when the region's turquoise mines were controlled by American companies and other materials used for traditional jewelry and trade were difficult to find, Santo Domingo jewelers learned to adopt other, more plentiful resources for their jewelry. For instance, in the 1930s they developed a unique type of folk art jewelry made entirely from repurposed and found materials: local gypsum (fashioned into beads), tiny chips of turquoise (for mosaic inlay), sun-bleached animal bone, and modern plastics (including photograph records, celluloid combs, and battery-case rubber). The signature motif of this jewelry (necklaces with matching earrings) was the **thunderbird**.

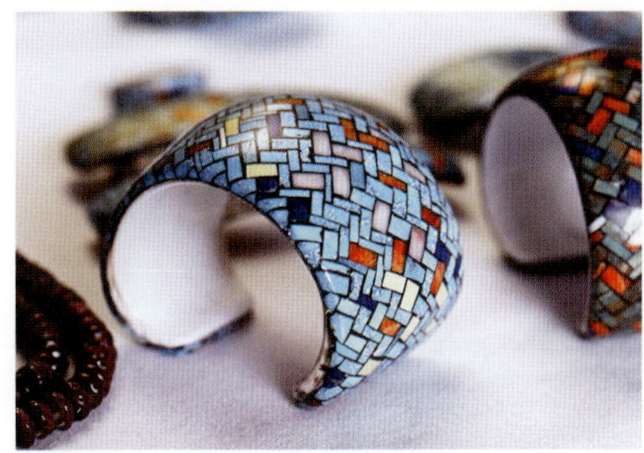

Angie Reano Owen (Santo Domingo), mosaic-overlay herringbone-style cuff bracelets.

By the 1950s the manufacture of thunderbird jewelry was dying out, as other forms of jewelry traditionally made at Santo Domingo began to thrive—including "mosaic-on-shell" work. Santo Domingo artisan Angie Reano Owen (b. 1946) is credited with reviving the tradition of **mosaic inlay** jewelry—a technique that involves adhering tiny bits of turquoise, coral, jet, and other stones to a shell base in intricate patterns. After studying Ancestral Pueblo jewelry in museums and private collections, she fashioned cuff bracelets, earrings, pendants, and other forms after ancient styles but with her own artistic touch. She eventually started inlaying in a herringbone style that has since become her signature; lapis lazuli is one of the non-traditional stones she uses.

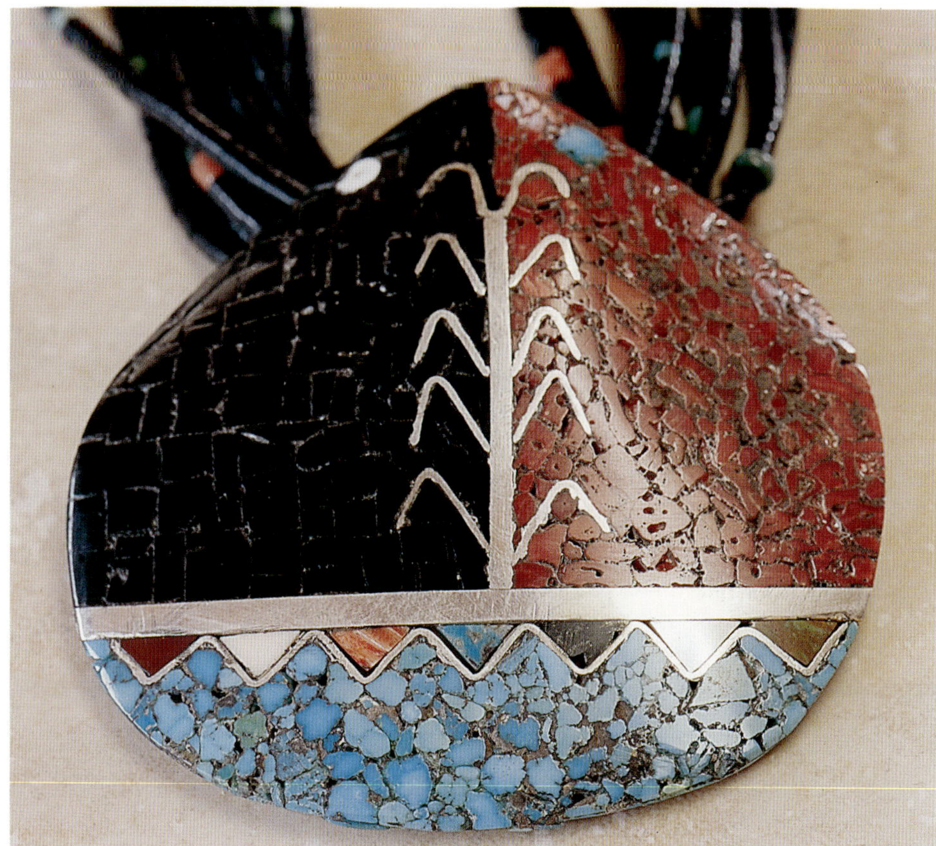

Mary Coriz Lovato (Santo Domingo), mosaic-overlay pendant with corn motif.

Some Santo Domingo jewelers have incorporated **silver** into their mosaics. In fact, Santo Domingo Pueblo also has a history of fine silversmithing. Beginning in the late 1930s, Santo Domingo jewelers made silver pins with **stamp work** designs based on the patterns and imagery found on historic Santo Domingo pottery. Some of the skilled silversmiths working at the prominent **trading posts** in Albuquerque, New Mexico, from the 1920s to the 1940s, were from Santo Domingo, including Leo Coriz (1913–1997), who became widely respected for his **tufa-cast** jewelry and is credited with preserving the silversmithing tradition at Santo Domingo. Coriz's tufa-cast work is being carried on by his descendants—including his daughter Mary Coriz Lovato, grandson Anthony Lovato (b. 1958), and great-grandson Joel Pajarito (b. 1984)—all of whom create jewelry that blends traditional and contemporary motifs and techniques.

Today Santo Domingo artisans are renowned for their high-quality shell, coral, jet, and turquoise single- and multi-strand necklaces, intricate **heishi** (shell) beadwork, and **shell pendants** with mosaic overlay/inlay work. The latter is strikingly similar to the thousand-year-old pieces of Ancestral Pueblo jewelry unearthed at Chaco Canyon (New Mexico) and Mesa Verde (Colorado). See also **liquid silver**.

SANTO DOMINGO (Kewa) PUEBLO POTTERY /

Santo Domingo Pueblo has a long tradition of making **polychrome** pottery with large and bold geometric designs of ancient origin. Until 1700, Santo Domingo potters created design motifs using a pigment containing a lead-oxide that melted during the **firing** and became glossy. After 1700 (and to the present), they have used vegetal-black and mineral-red paints on ceramic wares, with cream **slip** on the body and red slip used sparingly on the base (and sometimes on the interior rim of a jar). One style of Santo Domingo pottery originated in the late eighteenth century and featured black geometric decoration on cream slip; a similar style of pottery was made at Cochiti Pueblo.

Besides geometric motifs, Santo Domingo potters have long favored large floral patterns, stylized birds, and other animals, usually enclosed within circular bands. Depictions of the human form traditionally have never occurred in the arts of this Pueblo, including on pottery.

Today stew bowls, dough bowls, and full-size **water jars** are common forms made at the pueblo. They are made to serve food on feast days and other utilitarian purposes, as well as for sale. Some artisans are expanding the subject matter portrayed on **clay** vessels; William Andrew Pacheco, for instance, is known for his whimsical dinosaur figures. Most use the traditional methods of natural paints and outdoor firing to make their wares.

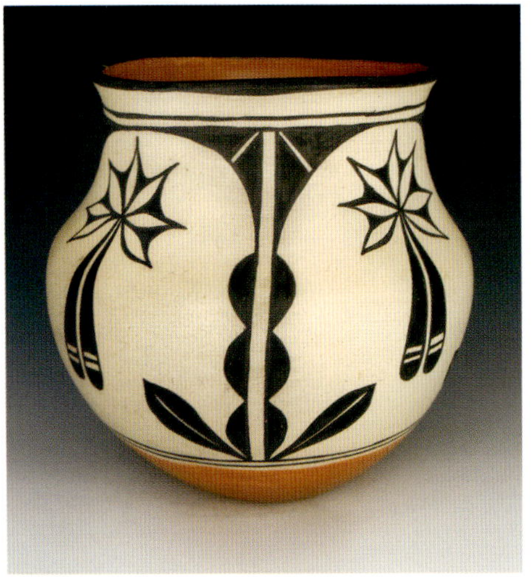

Santana Melchor (Santo Domingo), jar.

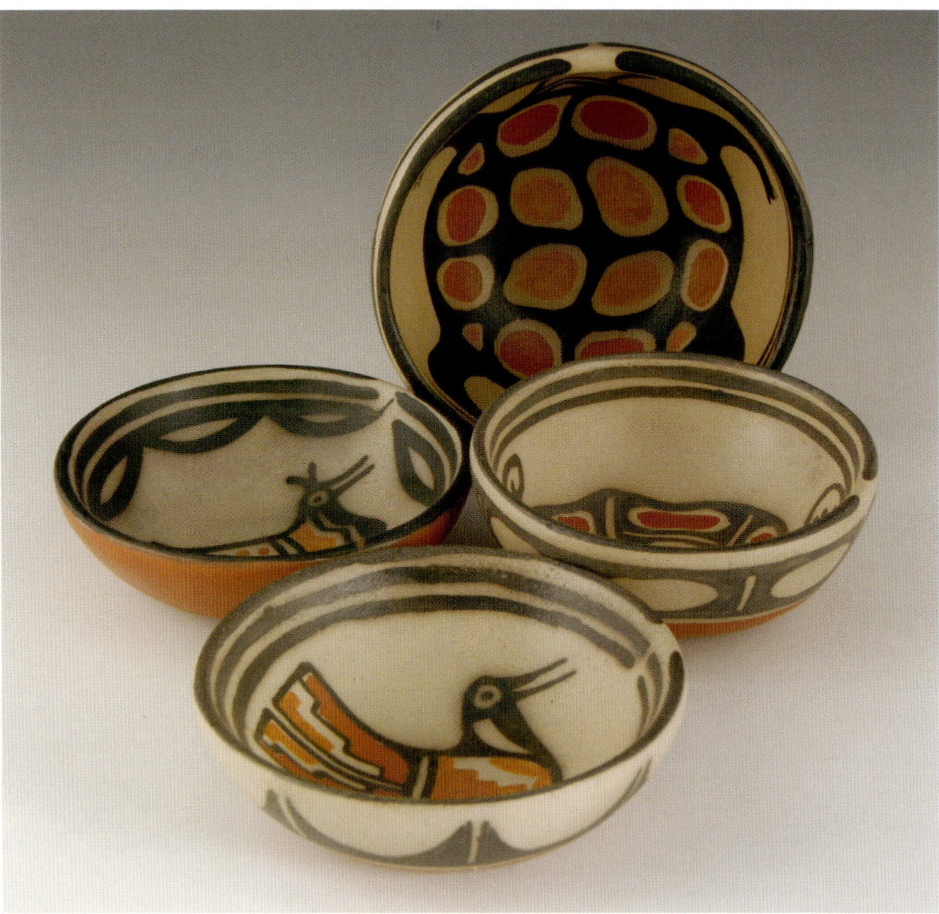

Warren Coriz (Santo Domingo), group of polychrome, animal-themed bowls.

SANTO NIÑO DE ATOCHA, EL (The Holy Child of Atocha) / the patron saint of pilgrims, a special manifestation of the young Christ, and one of the most popular folk themes for **retablos** and **bultos** in New Mexico and southern Arizona, typically depicted as a seated boy in pilgrim's dress—a wide-brimmed hat with feather, a cape, a staff, and buckled sandals or shoes. In addition, the figure is often shown with a water gourd, shafts of wheat, or a basket containing flowers or bread, and sometimes a cockleshell—the traditional symbol of a pilgrim. Throughout the Southwest, he is associated with healing powers and his feast day is Christmas.

According to popular legend, the origins of this image can be traced to Atocha, Spain, where during the Moorish invasion the Moors forbade anyone except for young children to visit incarcerated Christians. The starving prisoners prayed for deliverance and their prayers were answered when a young child dressed as a pilgrim with a staff, a water gourd, and a basket of food arrived. Miraculously, after all the prisoners were fed there

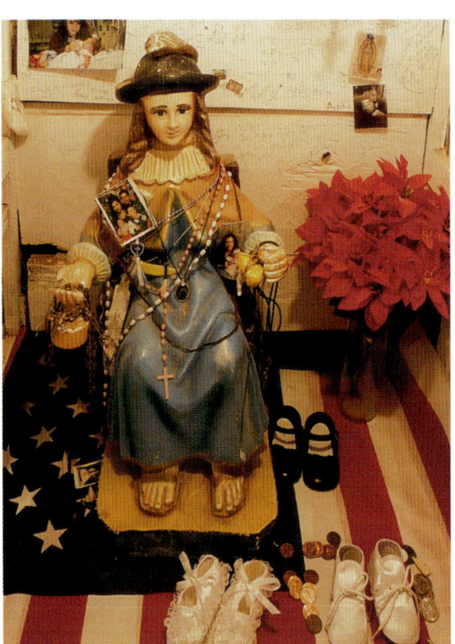

El Santo Niño de Atocha in his shrine in the Santuario de Chimayó, in Chimayó, New Mexico.

was still food in his basket and water in his gourd.

Another story suggests the devotion for this figure originated in Plateros, Zacatecas, Mexico, where a statue of the Christ Child, once attached to the image of Our Lady of Atocha, was somehow separated from his mother and took on a life of his own. Today El Santo Niño de Atocha is the patron saint of protection from violence, safety during travel, and the freeing of prisoners. In fact, during World War II he was the patron of the New Mexico National Guard when imprisoned at Bataan in the Philippines. A shrine devoted to Niño de Atocha can be seen in the Santuario de Chimayó, in Chimayó, New Mexico, where supplicants often leave photographs of babies and pairs of baby shoes.

SARAPE (Serape, Zarape) / a Spanish word used to describe a woolen blanket or shawl, woven longer-than-wide of plain weave, worn in the Southwest as an outer garment; they had an important role in the trade and economy of the region. Adopted in colonial New Mexico, it was

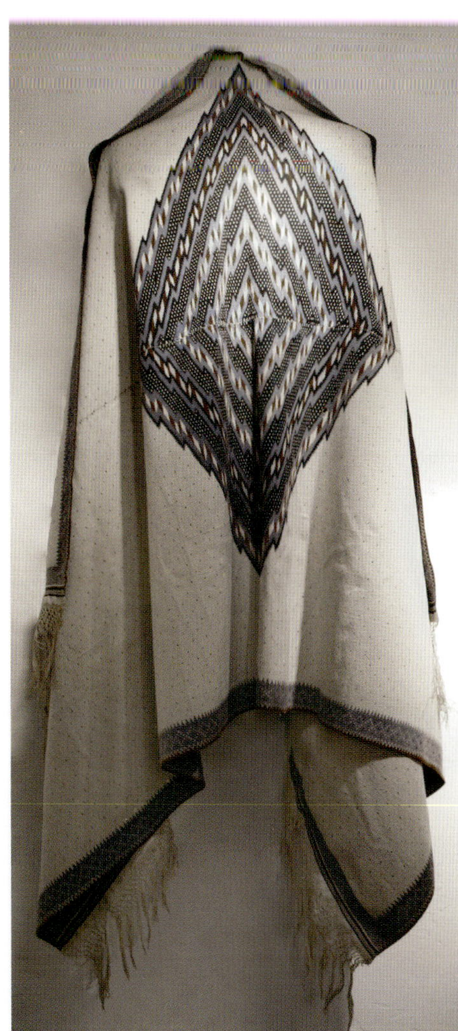

Classic Saltillo sarape, ca. 1850, 77" x 45".

worn by Hispano, Navajo, and Pueblo people as shoulder blankets and as Mexican-style **ponchos** (with a tapestry slit in the center allowing the blanket to fit over the head). Also, sarapes were used as sleeping blankets. The earliest sarapes are patterned with narrow brown or black, **indigo** blue, and white stripes. Striped blankets of this kind are often referred to as "**Moki**-patterned." Navajo-made sarapes are woven of fine-threaded, handspun, **cochineal**- or **lac-dyed** yarns from **raveled cloth**. They feature diamond patterns, along with X shapes or grouped zigzag lines and terraced triangles. The latter also usually have predominantly red backgrounds contrasting the native handspun indigo blue and white **churro-wool** designs. See also **bayeta**.

SCRAPER / a stiff tool used to smooth and connect the **coils** of a piece of pottery as it is being made. Traditionally, Native American potters made the scraper from natural material, such as a small, shaped piece of gourd. Today any object that is readily available and does the job might be used, including a credit card or Popsicle stick.

SEED JARS / **Pots** / a spherical, utilitarian ceramic vessel of relatively small size with an opening in the center through which seeds are dropped, made by Native potters since prehistoric times. It was designed to store and protect precious seeds during the winter months. After the jar was filled, the opening was usually covered with a small dish and then sealed with mud, making the jar impenetrable to rodents.

Today contemporary Pueblo potters make the classic shape for purely aesthetic purposes and embellish the surface with a wide variety of designs. Many also reduce the size of the center hole to demonstrate the potter's technical proficiency.

Since about 1975, silversmiths have made miniature seed pots in **silver** (generally no bigger than 3 inches in diameter), drawing upon the classic forms and designs of ceramic seed pots.

Navajos Norbert Peshlakai and White Buffalo (a.k.a. Mike Perez) are credited with making the first examples. Using **stamp work**, **appliqué**, **overlay**, **embossing**, **tufa casting**, cutouts, hand-hammering, texture made by a crosscut-tip or punch-tip hammer, and other techniques, Navajo artisans have created a variety of designs on the silver seed pots. Among them are: life-sustaining **corn**, animals, insects (especially butterflies), mesas, **feathers**, flowers, rug patterns, **pueblos**, the sun, the stars, **Yé'ii** figures, narrative scenes, abstract or geometric shapes, and other motifs that are ancient, traditional, or contemporary that tell a story and reflect Native American art and culture. In some instances, Navajo smiths have **inlaid** small pieces of **coral**, **shell**, or **turquoise** on the surface; used gold to fashion the seed pot; or made animal-shaped stoppers.

SGRAFFITO / an Italian term, used for the technique of shallow etching or scratching of the surface of pottery, stone, and other materials, using a tool with a sharp tiny point, to create unique designs. Pueblo potters of New Mexico, who call

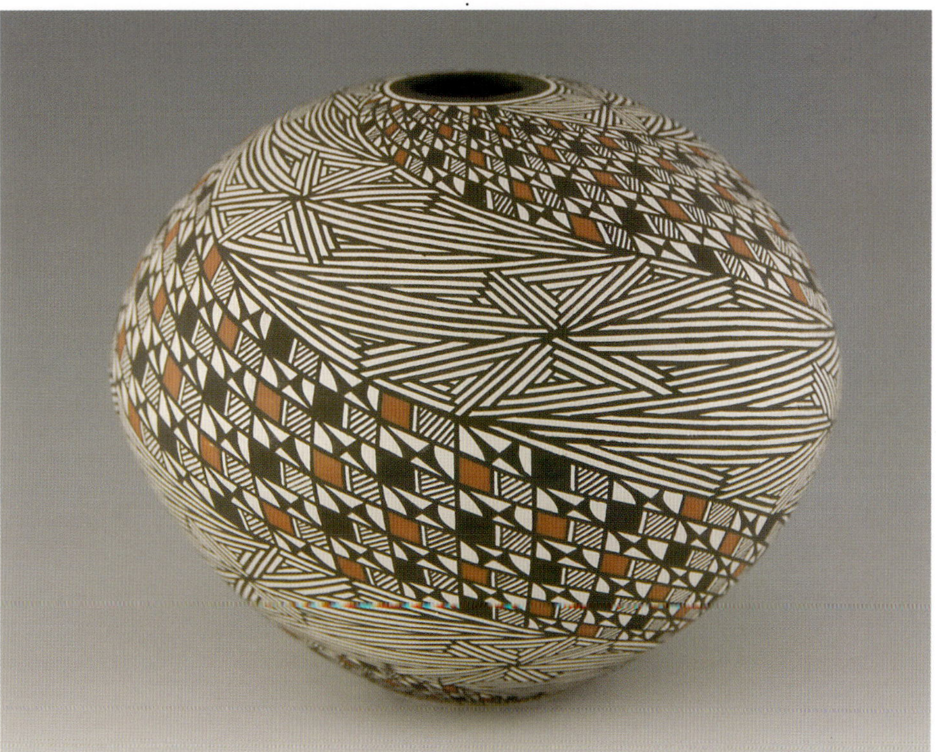

ABOVE: Roger Kasero (Laguna), seed pot with swirl design. **TOP:** Daniel Sunshine Reeves, miniature seed pot, 2011, sterling silver with stamp work.

this method "etching," create sgraffito patterns by "scratching" the polished slip surface of **clay** vessels either before or after firing to expose the color of the clay beneath. San Ildefonso potter Tony Da (1940–2008) was among the first Pueblo potters to master and refine this technique in the late 1960s. Da used an X-ACTO® knife to lightly incise **Mimbres**-style animals in the polished surfaces of his plates, boxes, and jars. Santa Clara Pueblo potters Joseph Lonewolf (b. 1932), his father, Camilio Sunflower Tafoya (1902–1995), and his sister, Grace Medicine Flower (b. 1938), also introduced this technique in the late 1960s, by lightly etching intricate designs onto the stone-**polished** surfaces of their miniature and larger-sized pots.

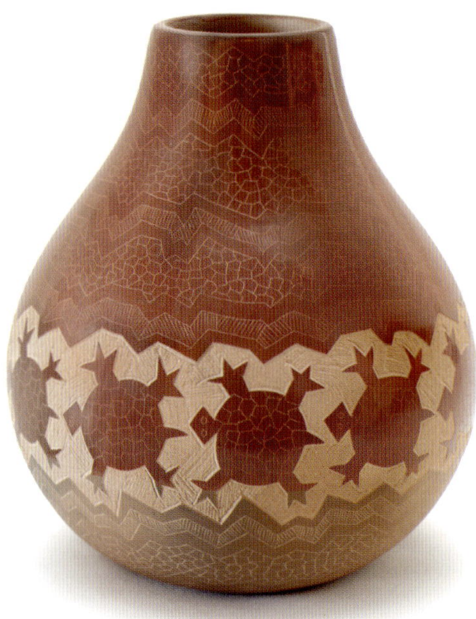

Jody Naranjo (Santa Clara), sgraffito on clay vessel, 2005, clay with natural slips.

Contemporary artisans such as Jody Naranjo of Santa Clara Pueblo have brought this technique to new heights with elaborate sgraffito ranging from highly intricate geometric shapes to figural images to illustrations of churches and pueblo buildings. Since the 1980s, Zuni Pueblo artisans have used this method to create designs on their intricately carved **fetishes**: they lightly cut lines in the surface of animals carved in black marble, red pipestone, and other stones, typically using an X-ACTO® knife or dental tool. Contemporary Hispano artisans in New Mexico also use this technique for carving lines in the **gesso** surface of wooden **retablos**, to provide detailed design elements.

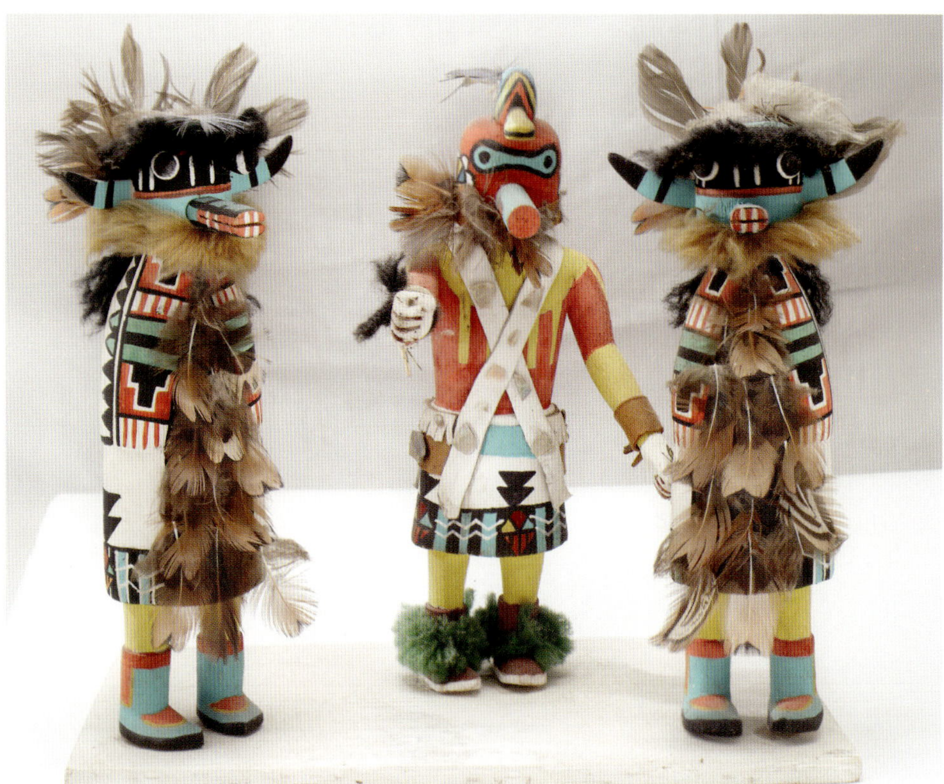

Zuni Shalakos (left: Zuni Warrior; center: "Salimopaiyakya" or Duck Shalako; right: Zuni Warrior), ca. 1940s/'50s, painted cottonwood with feathers and wool yarn decoration, attached to wood base.

SHALAKOS (Salako) / ten-foot-tall katsinam who are the principal gods represented at the winter house-blessing ceremony, a six-week reenactment of Zuni emergence and migration beliefs that begins the first week in December. A communal prayer for rain, the health of the Zuni people, and the propagation of plants and animals culminates in the arrival of the Shalakos in the village. Today the Shalako figure is portrayed in jewelry, carved dolls, and in other Zuni art forms.

SHELLS / imported from the Pacific Coast and Gulf of Mexico (also known as the Sea of Cortez) to the Southwest by way of overland trade routes during prehistoric times, shells such as abalone, **spiny oyster** (*Spondylus*), olive (*Olivella dama*), and clam (*Glycymeris gigantea*) were turned into **beads**, pendants, bracelets, earrings, and other decorative ornaments by Native peoples and used for personal adornment and ceremonies. The Hohokam of Arizona is believed to be the first of the ancient Native cultures to develop shell jewelry (and shell **fetishes**). Shells were a highly important trade commodity; the Hohokam traded their surplus to the Mogollon people, who in turn supplied the Ancestral Puebloans of the Four Corners region.

The most common ornaments made by the Hohokam were bracelets, manufactured by grinding down a clam shell with a stone tool, leaving only a ring of shell big enough to fit over a wrist. Some were carved with geometric designs or animal shapes. Shell necklaces were made by stringing whole shells or flat disc beads; the ends of shells were ground away to make an opening so they could be strung, or a hole was drilled.

Today Pueblo and other Native jewelers use shells such as olivellas and abalones in creating **heishi** and other pieces; and Zuni Pueblo artisans use a wide variety of shells to carve fetishes, including mother-of-pearl, olivellas, conch, clam, and spiny oyster. See also **beads**, **fetishes**, **heishi**, **shell etching**, **shell pendants**, and **spiny oyster**.

SHELL ETCHING / a creative technique native to the American Southwest and dating to prehistoric times, in which seashells were etched with a design using an acid produced from the fermented fruit of the **saguaro** cactus. The **shell** was coated with a resistant substance—usually pitch from the **mesquite** or **lac** from the creosote bush—on or around the design, then the shell was placed

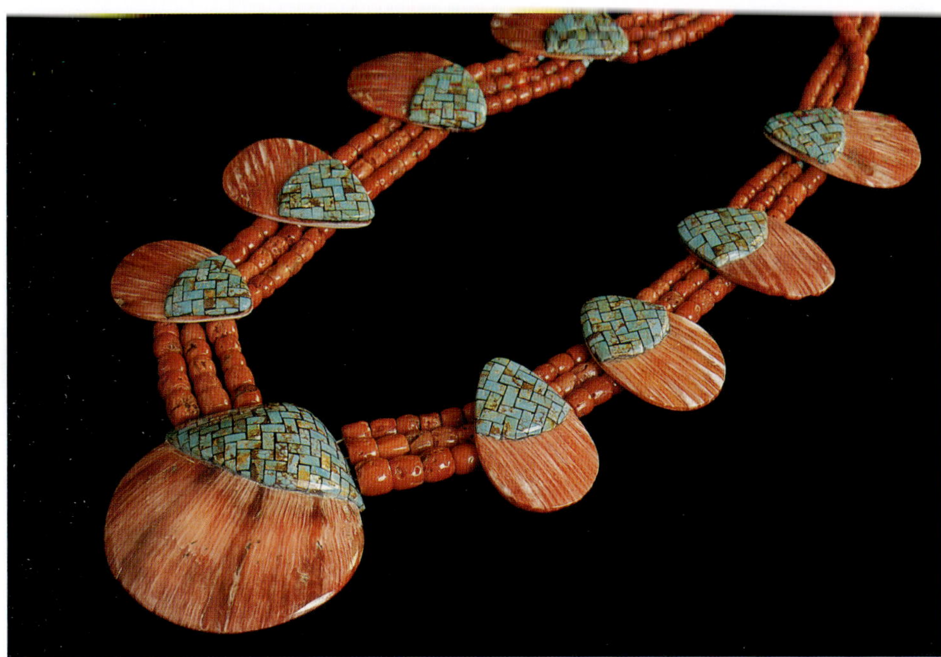

Angie Reano Owen (Santo Domingo), necklace of spiny oyster shell, turquoise, and machined coral beads.

in the saguaro acid (for up to several days), and any unprotected areas on the surface were eaten away. Once the desired depth of the etching was reached, the shell was taken out of the acid and the pitch was then scraped away, revealing a raised design. The etching was done on the interior and/or exterior of the shell. In rare instances, the raised design was painted with mineral pigments.

Etched shells were used as ornaments or turned into jewelry forms including pendants and earrings. The Hohokam people, who inhabited parts of present-day Arizona from circa AD 300 to 1300, are credited with being the first in the world to develop and master the art of etching with acid. They obtained shells through trade with west coast tribes or by making trips on foot to the Gulf of California. The preferred shell for etching was the *Laevicardium elatum*, commonly called the giant egg cockle. Some of the geometric designs that appear on Hohokam etched shells are similar to those designs that appeared on **Hohokam pottery**.

Today only a handful of Native artisans etch shells in the traditional way. Among them is Timothy Terry, of the Pima tribe in Arizona, who gathers his own fruit from the saguaro cactus to make the acid for decorating his shell necklaces, bracelets, and earrings. Terry also cuts and carves his shells, and uses designs and symbols drawn from the ancient Hohokam etched shells that were unearthed at archaeological sites and are now in museum collections.

SHELL PENDANTS / among the earliest jewelry found at archaeological sites in the Southwest are pendants comprised of a seashell base (left natural or carved into a shape) and inlaid (or overlaid) with tiny pieces of blue or green **turquoise** from the Southwest, as well as chips of orange-red **spiny oyster** shells *(spondylus)*. Such pendants were made by the prehistoric Hohokam, Salado, and Sinagua peoples of Arizona, who obtained the **shells** from the Pacific Coast or Gulf of Mexico through trade or by traveling to the region on foot. Archaeological evidence suggests that the Hohokam used **lac** to adhere stones and shells chips to the shell base. Some Hohokam marine-shell pendants were left unadorned and consisted of carved shapes such as frogs and animals associated with water. The use of oceanic shells so far inland illustrates the existence of extensive ancient trade routes among America's earliest inhabitants, and the symbolic importance of seashells over the more readily obtainable freshwater shell. The tradition of making shell pendants is carried on today by jewelers at Santo Domingo (Kewa) Pueblo. See also **mosaic inlay/overlay**

SHIELD / a disk of heavy rawhide about two feet in diameter, with wood and/or leather handgrips attached to the back and typically decorated on the front with paints and feathers and later glass **beads** and **tinklers**, made by Native Americans. They were used by warriors on foot or on horseback in combat, to shield themselves and to disorient the enemy by holding them at arm's length and twirling them rapidly. Most have designs of cultural and religious significance painted on the front. Such shields have a long history in the Southwest, as suggested by the many images of them in regional rock art. By the early twentieth century, shields were being made for the **curio** trade. Among the traders who sold them was Thomas S. Dozier of Española, New Mexico, who commissioned shields made from bull hides for his clients, beginning in 1902. Some Native artisans continue to make shields; for instance, the Southern Utes of Colorado make them using rawhide, commercial paints, cloth, and **yarn**, as well as other decorations including **feathers**, human hair, and **sinew**.

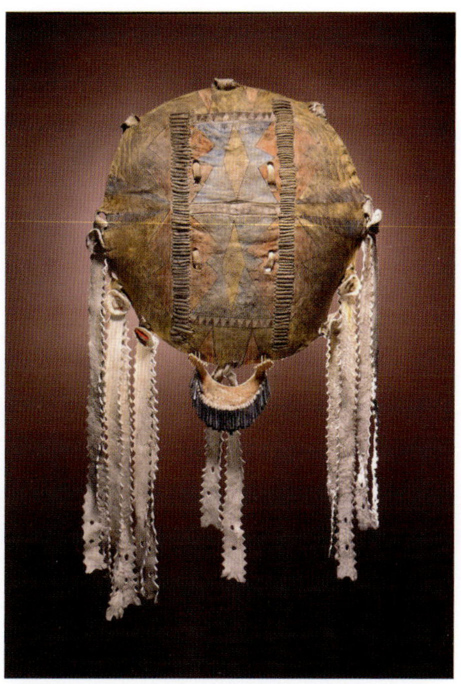

Mescalero Apache leather shield, 19th century.

SIFTER BASKETS (Ring Baskets, Tutsaya) / consisting of loosely **plaited** natural materials—typically narrow-leaf **yucca** or **beargrass**—attached to a wood ring that serves as the circular rim, with a fringed self-selvedge rim finish. Sifter baskets were originally used for washing grains with all the impurities being sifted out through the open-weave design. They were also used for winnowing grains and sometimes the storing and serving of food. Yucca sifter baskets date to about 2000 BC and continue to be woven the same way today by artisans at Jemez Pueblo and at all three

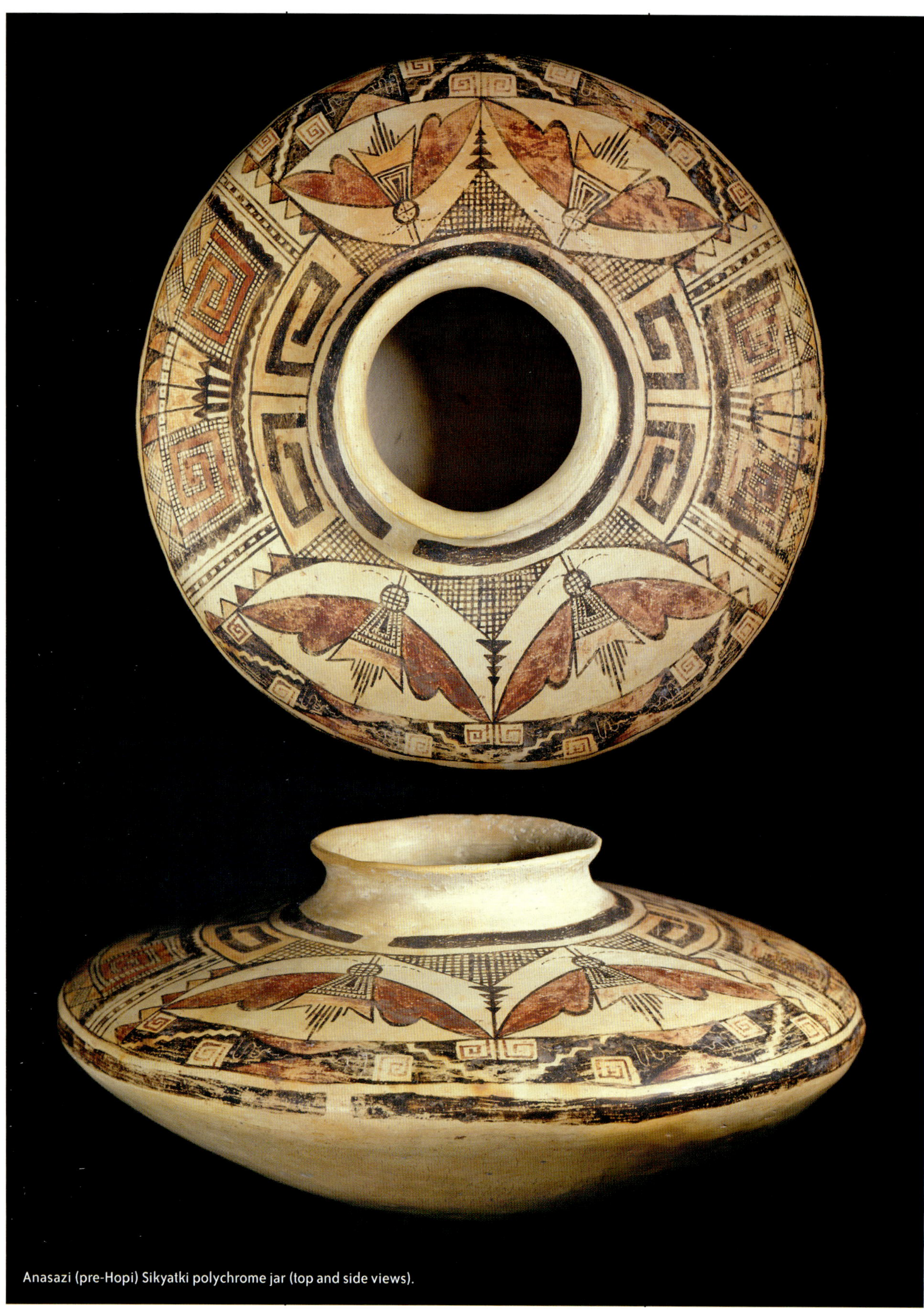

Anasazi (pre-Hopi) Sikyatki polychrome jar (top and side views).

Hopi mesa villages. The Hopi name for these baskets is *tutsaya*.

Traditionally made by women, sifter baskets have been made by a few Hopi men in recent years. In making these baskets, the color of the yucca depends upon what time of year the plant was collected, which part of the leaf was used, and how long the yucca leaves were bleached in the sun. **Awls** of different sizes are used to split the yucca leaves for weaving. Originally, the ring or rim of Hopi sifter baskets was made from **sumac** or **willow** branches; today Hopi weavers use a variety of different materials, from tamarisk-bush branches to willow or sumac branches, and sometimes commercially made metal rings. (If the basket is made using a steel ring, it cannot be used for ceremonies.)

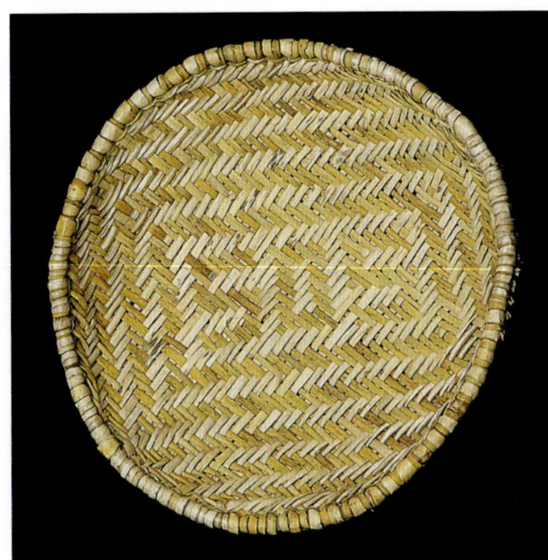

Hopi sifter basket, yucca on a willow ring.

In recent decades Hopi weavers have been using green yucca blades and white yucca blades (natural, sun bleached, or dyed with commercial dyes) to create diamond and other geometric patterns, as well as more complex pictorial designs. For example, Kevin Navasie of First Mesa (Hopi-Tewa) is known for using letters and pictorial images such as **katsina** faces in his sifter baskets. At present, the baskets of Navasie and other Hopi weavers are used for holding and storing food, as colanders for washing **corn** and beans, for sale to the tourist market, and for ceremonial purposes —as part of the Basket Dance (when they are held by young girls) and for wedding paybacks.

SIKYATKI POTTERY / highly developed ceramics made by Hopi descendants of the Ancestral Puebloans, in which they combined complex **polychrome** designs with abstracted symbols and animal imagery, a style that is closely related to contemporaneous types from the Hopi village of Awatovi. The village of Sikyatki flourished in the fifteenth and sixteenth centuries on First Mesa. Sikyatki potters used several painting methods, including spattering and stippling, with black paints mixed from vegetal and mineral **pigments** and red-clay paints. After archaeologists excavated Sikyatki pottery during the late 1800s at ruins near First Mesa, Hopi, images of the pots were published and appeared on everything from **Fred Harvey Company** postcards to books. The Sikyatki pottery designs—stylized birds and insects along with scrolls of fine-line decoration—and shapes including wide-shouldered flattened jars, low bowls, and **seed jars** have inspired the Hopi women potters of First Mesa villages ever since.

Among them was a Hopi-Tewa woman from Hano named Nampeyo (ca. 1860–1942). She studied Sikyatki vessels and **potsherds** she found exposed after storms in the soil of Sikyatki's ruins, located the old sources of clay, and created vessels with imaginative designs based on the prehistoric pottery. At first creating white-slipped vessels, she eventually abandoned these and polished the yellow clay body itself. Some scholars consider Nampeyo the first "celebrity" potter. Encouraged by anthropologists collecting their work and the growing tourist market, she and other potters of First Mesa brought about a renaissance in Hopi pottery. Nampeyo's descendants, including famed potter Dextra Quotskuyva (b. 1928), have carried on her tradition, becoming internationally known for their work. The new versions of the old Sikyatki designs also include **butterflies**, **katsina** faces, and a variety of stylized animals.

SILLA / a Spanish word for "seat," a term used in Spanish Colonial New Mexico for chair, which appears frequently on estate inventories of the period. The word *silleta* (little chair) probably referred to a chair without arms. The different components of a chair are called: crest (the decoration on the top rail); rails (horizontal wood members above the stretchers); stretcher (a horizontal rail, sometimes a spindle, connecting the lower portions of the legs); and splat (a flat, upright wood shape used to join the seat and front stretcher, or join the seat and top rail). Spanish Colonial and Spanish Colonial Revival-style chairs had carved wood or leather seats. The use of leather seating can be traced back to Spanish fifteenth-century

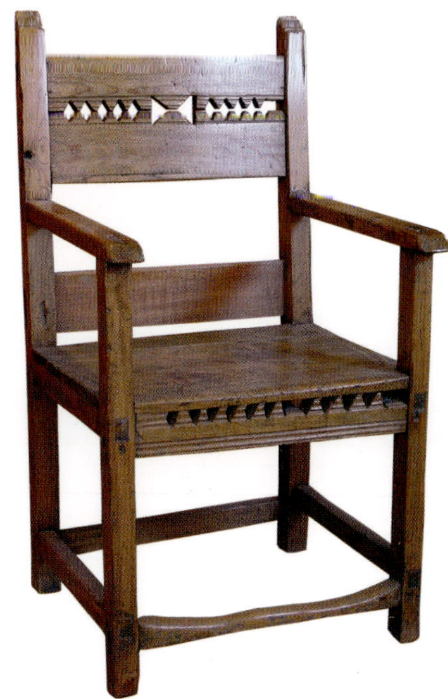

New Mexican sillón frailero, 19th century, pine.

side-saddle chairs that had draped leather seats used for carrying people on the back of animals. During the Spanish Colonial period, leather was widely used as an alternative to textiles; both pigskin and cowhide were used as upholstery. See also **sillón frailero**.

SILLÓN FRAILERO (Priest's/Friar's Chair) / a carved wooden armchair, believed to have been originally used in churches and reserved for the use of priests or friars in the Spanish colonies. They were of **mortise-and-tenon** construction with simple lines influenced by the style of early Spanish armchairs, usually consisting of slightly inclined back posts, narrow arms resting on extended front legs, low side stretchers, and a distinctive decorative front stretcher known as a *chambrana* that was usually carved or fretted. Some fraileros were covered with tooled leather or embroidered fabric. Also used in domestic settings in Spanish Colonial New Mexico, this type of chair was identified as the "master's chair" and used by the head of the household; it was considered a highly valued possession. Some scholars suggest the term sillón frailero was developed in the twentieth century by Anglo Americans, who assumed that all such chairs were only reserved for and used by priests.

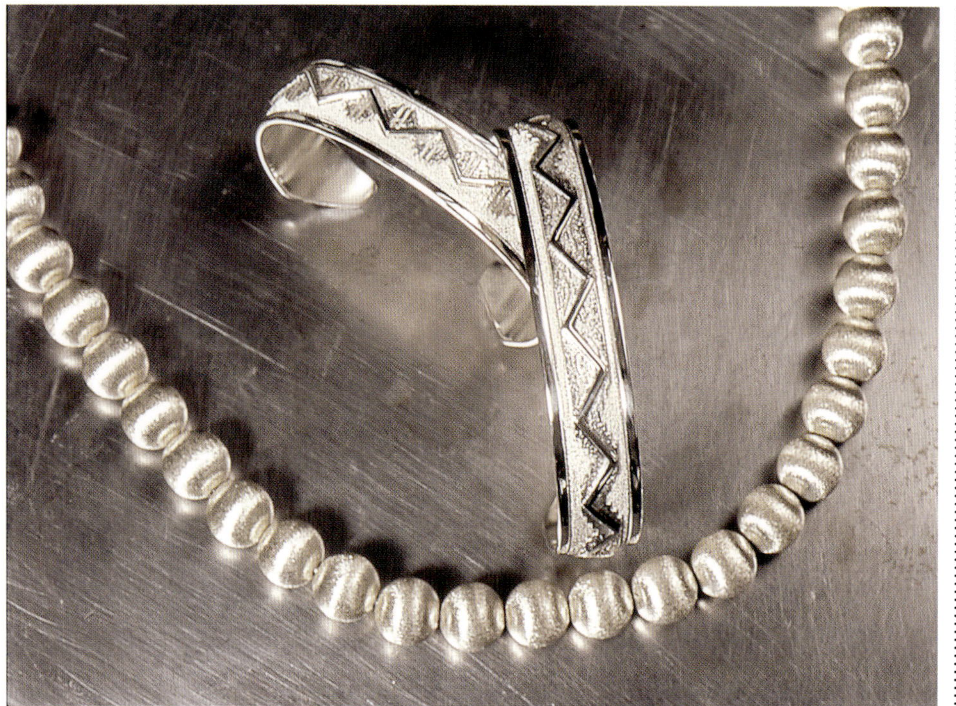

TOP AND LOWER RIGHT: Silverwork by Raynard Scott (Navajo).

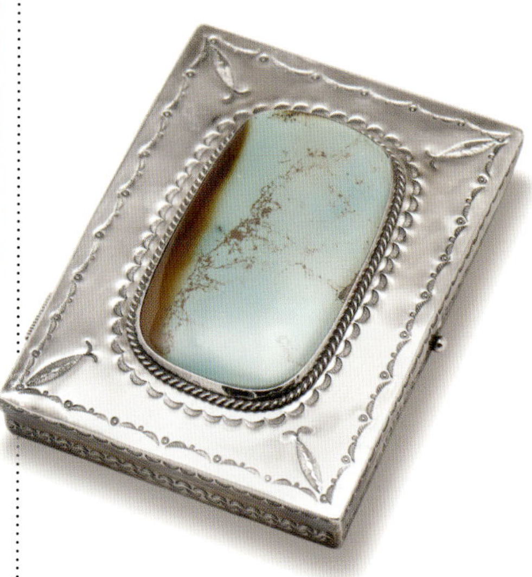

BELOW AND OPPOSITE: Navajo silver boxes, early 20th century, sterling silver with stamp work, hand tooling, and/or repoussé work, and some are inlaid with turquoise.

SILVER / the most common metal used in Native American jewelry. Today silver is available in three different types: sterling, 92.5 parts silver and 7.5 parts other metal; coin silver, 90 parts silver and 10 parts other metal, so-named because the 90/10 formula had become the standard for coinage; and "drawn" silver, silver wire drawn through progressively smaller holes in a draw-plate to the desired diameter and shape (round, triangular, or square). So-called **German silver**, sometimes referred to as nickel silver, is really an alloy of 60 parts **copper**, 20 parts zinc, and 20 parts nickel, and is very similar to brass.

SILVER BOXES / decorative boxes made by Navajo silversmiths at the encouragement of post traders, for the tourist trade, beginning about 1900. The boxes were initially small, but larger ones were produced later with the availability of sheet silver and improved methods of rolling out ingot silver. The decoration of the boxes, especially the lid, became the focus and provided opportunities for elaborate **stamp work** patterns, stone settings, and **mosaic** or **channel work**. Hinges for the lids were handmade of silver wire, pins, and sheet silver; or soldered and commercially made. Front closures ranged from simple buttons to hinged flaps. In some mid-twentieth century boxes, feet made of **silver beads** or but-

tons were soldered to the bottom of the boxes. Some Native American silversmiths still make boxes; among them is the award-winning Navajo silversmith Edison Cummings (b. 1962) who combines **repoussé** with fine stamp work.

SILVER OVERLAY / See **overlay**.

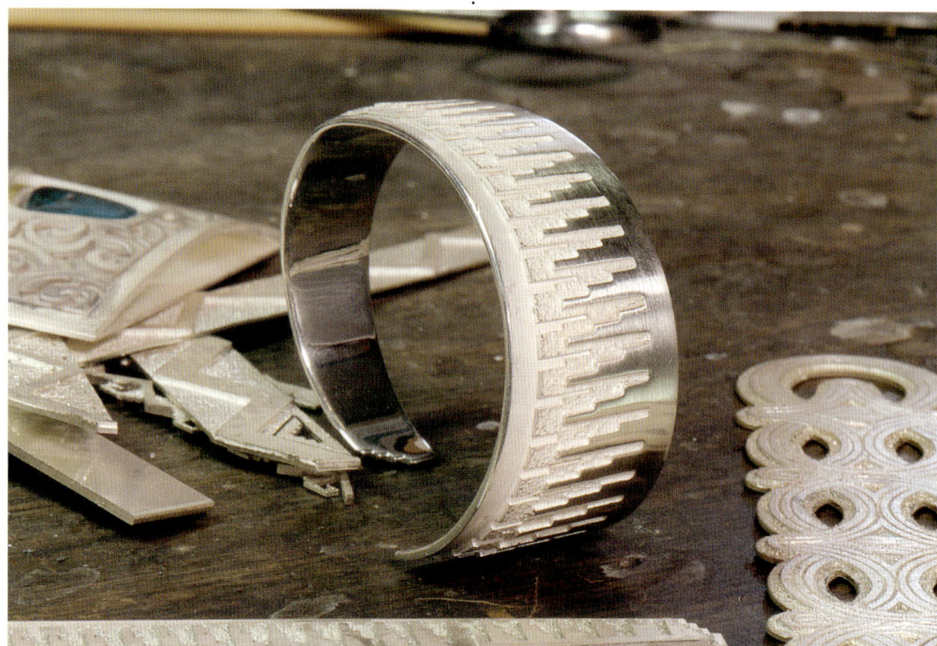

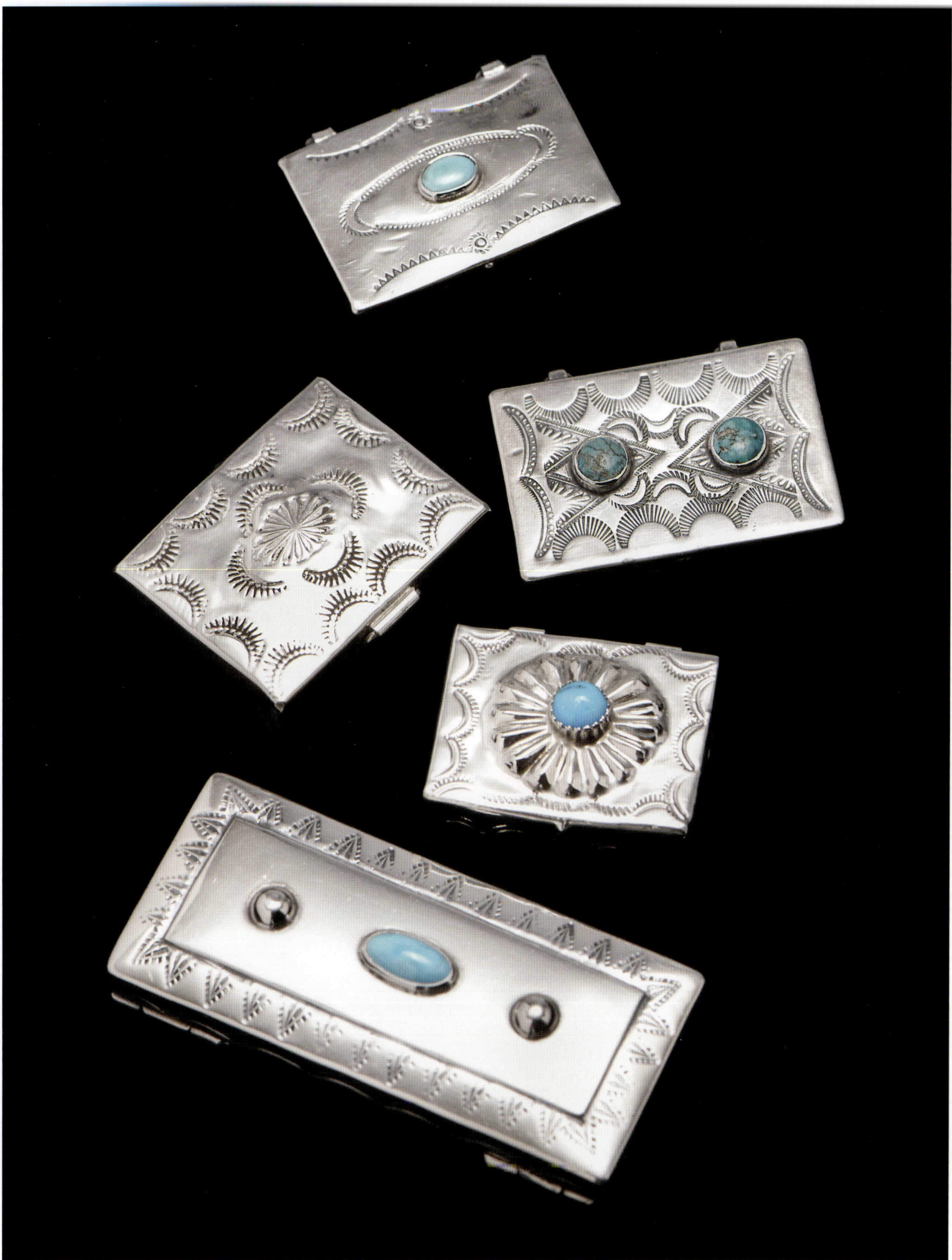

SINEW / a tough band of fibrous connective tissue, also known as a tendon—stripped from the sides of the spinal column or from the leg bones of animals hunted for food such as deer, caribou, buffalo, or moose—converted into separate, thin, durable fibers (or threads) through a process of cleaning, drying, and moistening (to make the stiff strands pliable), and used historically by Native Americans in the Southwest for sewing hide clothing, attaching **beadwork** to hide or feathers to arrows, the wrapping of **fetishes**, and for a variety of other purposes such as lashing tool blades to shafts. For instance, early indigenous people of the region used sinew to secure sharpened **obsidian** points to the shafts of arrows or the handles of knives. Traditionally, in the sewing of clothing, an **awl** of sharp bone was used to punch a series of holes in the hide pieces to be sewn, and then the sinew was threaded through these holes. After the arrival of Europeans in the region, in the late sixteenth century, sinew was gradually replaced with imported cotton thread. Some artisans continue to use sinew today to sew traditional hide clothing or for other purposes (considered a mark of fine craftsmanship), while others have replaced it with commercially made materials (such as waxed polyester threads) that replicate the look and feel of sinew.

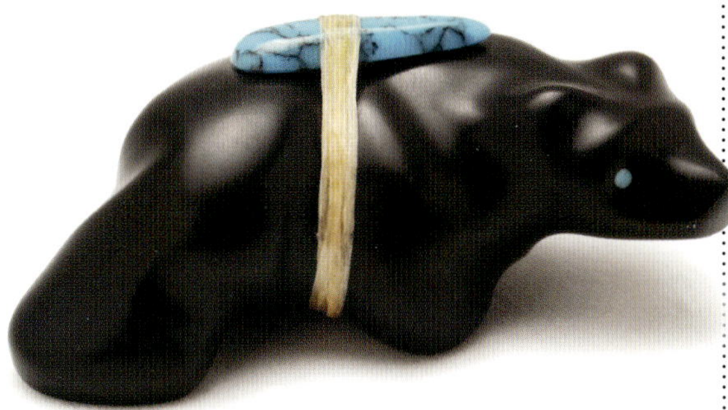

Herbert Halate (Zuni), bear fetish, ca. 2006, jet with turquoise and sinew.

SLAVE BLANKETS (Servant Blankets) / nineteenth-century blankets believed to have been woven by Navajo, Pueblo, or other Native Americans who were captured and indentured as slaves/servants by the Spanish. These blankets combine the features distinctive to Navajo upright **loom** weaving (such as twined selvages and **lazy lines**) and Hispano **Rio Grande blankets** (with two-ply **warps**, soft colors, and banded designs). Some slave blankets have the characteristics of textiles produced on Hispano treadle looms (horizontal looms with a flying treadle and two-ply warps) and Navajo stepped motifs.

SLIP / a very fine, liquid mixture of **clay** and water applied with a rag or brush to all or part of the surface of a clay vessel prior to **firing**, used to create areas of color or to make a uniform surface onto which pigments adhere or soak into. It is most often from a different type of clay than that used in the body of a pot. After being wiped or brushed onto the pot, the slip is usually **polished** with a smooth stone. If left unpolished, the slip will fire to a dull or **matte** finish. Some slips were (and continue to be) highly treasured and traded between pueblos. For example, the old stone-polished red used in Tewa-Pueblo pottery was acquired in trade from Cochiti or Santo Domingo and the beautiful stone-polished white used in the Tewa pueblos, especially San Ildefonso and Tesuque, was obtained in trade from Spanish New Mexicans near Chimayó.

In some instances, traditional sources for slips have been destroyed or used up. For example, a type of clay once used for white slip by Cochiti Pueblo potters is no longer available; the Cochiti Dam, completed in 1975, was built over the place where the slip was acquired. This scarcity of traditional slip has forced some Pueblo potters to use commercial slips in their work.

SOLOMONIC COLUMN (Salomónica, Spiral-Rope Carving) / a spiral or twisting column used extensively in the architecture of Europe and Mexico during the Baroque period, as well as in Spanish Colonial New Mexico beginning in the seventeenth century, as a decorative element on **altar screens**, **retablos**, **furniture**, and **tinwork** (especially frames and **nichos**). Later, they were incorporated into the design of buildings in Arizona; for example, architect Josias Joesler used them throughout St. Philips In The Hills Church, which he designed and built in Tucson in 1936, in the **Spanish Colonial Mission Revival** style. According to legend, these columns are derived from the biblical descriptions of the two columns that flanked the entrance to King Solomon's Temple in Jerusalem. Also known as spiral-rope carving, this design element may also represent the Franciscan order of monks, in reference to the rope belts they use to tie their robes. In furniture, the "Solomonic" column, or rope design, may be freestanding, but is usually carved along the edge of a surface.

SONORAN ROW HOUSE / a popular building style among Hispano (and other) settlers of northwest New Spain (present-day Arizona) from about 1850 to 1890, influenced by the architecture of northern Mexico. Its roots can be traced

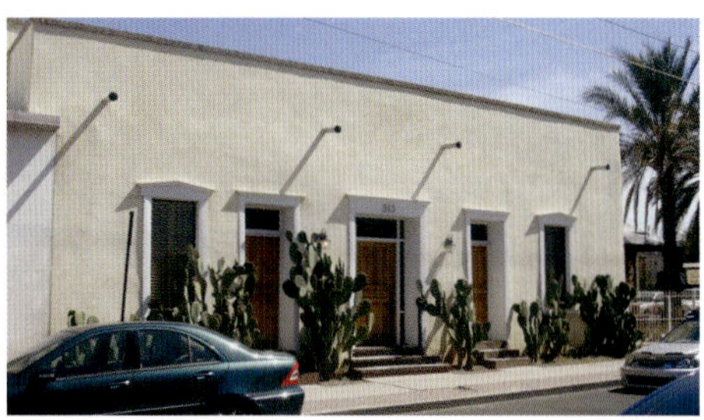

Sonoran row house, Tucson, Arizona.

to southern Spain and northern Africa. Sonoran row houses were constructed in a simple square or rectangular plan, with thick **adobe**-brick walls (from 18 to 24 inches in depth) finished with lime or **mud plaster** (to prevent erosion), ceilings of exposed **saguaro** ribs (or *savinas*) and **vigas** (beams), with pounded dirt floors, flat earthen roofs (drained by **canales**), hand-hewn timber **lintels** (over door and window openings) usually of **mesquite**, no foundation (or possibly one made of stone), few and small openings, little or no trim, and initially no glass. Doors were typically brush or saguaro cactus ribs tied together with twigs or rawhide strips. Windows were small and set even with the outside of the wall, thus forming deep interior windowsills. These single-story homes were typically built close to the front property line with shared walls (saving time, materials, and space). Corner adobe fireplaces (**fogones**) were generally built in every room. The basic row house had a central hallway (or **zaguán**) leading from the street façade directly to the **courtyard**, off of which are the rooms (one or two deep). This ensemble was repeated in a sequence that filled out a city block, gradually growing over time from a linear form to an "L" shape to a "U" shape, ultimately becoming a square around a fully defined courtyard. Fine examples of the Sonoran row house have been preserved in the Barrio Viejo in Tucson, Arizona. See also **Sonoran Transformed** and **Sonoran Transitional**.

SONORAN TRANSFORMED (Transformed Sonoran) / Sonoran row houses built between 1863 and 1912 in Arizona, modified with the addition of a waterproof pitched roof, as well as materials brought to the region via wagon (or via the railroad after 1880), such as bricks for **coping**, milled lumber for roofs or window and door trim/casings, and sheet metal or tin for pitched roofing. Floors, originally of compacted earth, were covered with wood planks. See also **Sonoran row house** and **Sonoran Transitional**.

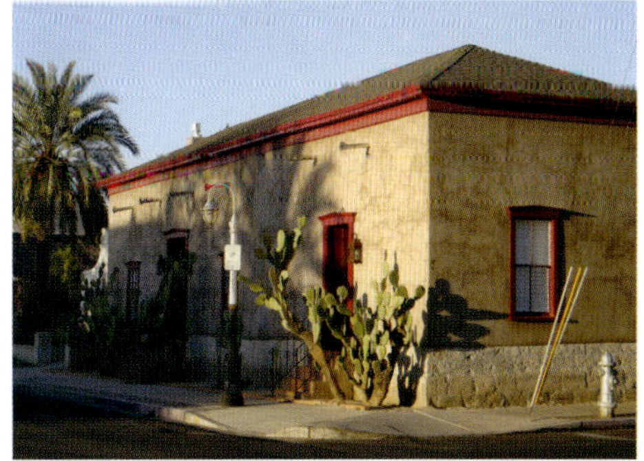

Sonoran Transformed house, Tucson, Arizona.

SONORAN TRANSITIONAL / houses built from around 1880 to 1900 in Arizona, in a style drawn from the architectural traditions of the East and Midwest—including Greek Revival–style wood pediments over windows and doors and brick **dentils** as **coping**, and Victorian-style wood trim on the exterior and interior including beadboard wainscoting, lathe-turned balusters, milled-wood brackets, and rows of turned **spindles**. Other features introduced were wood-framed porches with decorative columns, bay windows, and French doors. These design concepts were brought to the area by Anglo-American immigrants, who wished to have familiar architectural features from their homes back East (or elsewhere in the U.S.) in their new Southwestern dwellings. Some architectural historians refer to these Sonoran houses as "hybrids," because they combine the building traditions of Hispanic vernacular homes with designs brought to the region by the Anglos. See also **Sonoran row house** and **Sonoran Transformed**.

SOUVENIR SPOONS / spoons (along with other small **silver** or metal items such as letter openers and shoe horns) were fashioned for the **curio** trade beginning in the 1880s when the railroad reached the Southwest. They were originally made by melting down Mexican *pesos* or American coins into a mold forming an ingot, and then hand-hammered into shape, by Navajo and some Pueblo smiths. The earliest examples were decorated with **rocker engraving**, and later involved more elaborate **die** or **stamp work**. Eventually these souvenir spoons featured a wide variety of motifs atop the handle and/or in the bowl—including human profiles, **swastikas**, arrows, cats, birds, lizards, deer, and **feathers**.

Some Native-made spoons were later engraved by Anglo jewelers with dates, initials, or names, to

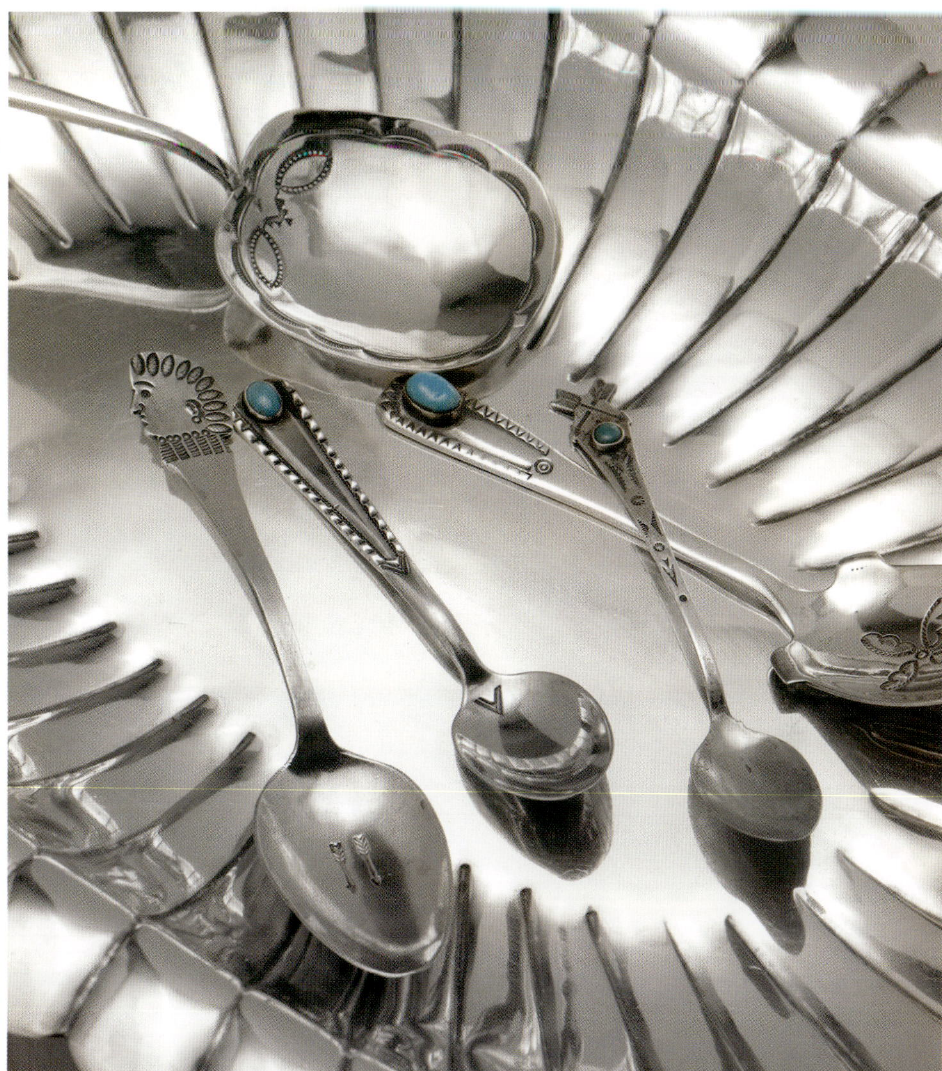

Navajo souvenir spoons, ranging in date from ca. 1910s to early 21st century, sterling silver, some with turquoise, and various designs (mostly stamp work).

identity the person to whom it was presented as a gift, or locations to commemorate the location where the spoon was purchased. Initially, Navajo and Pueblo souvenir spoons were priced by their weight in silver. They were sold at **Fred Harvey Company** hotels along the train routes, and by 1902 by traders such as Juan Lorenzo **Hubbell** in Ganado, Arizona, and John B. Moore in **Crystal**, New Mexico.

Other important outlets for Native-made souvenir spoons were the world fairs and expos—such as the 1904 St. Louis World's Fair and the 1915–16 Panama-California Exposition in San Diego. During the same time, collecting souvenir spoons of specific sights and cities had become a national pastime in the U.S. By 1904 manufacturers began to copy Indian-designed/themed spoons

(as well as other silver items) and cranked them out in silver or cheaper metals by the hundreds. In the 1920s souvenir spoons declined in popularity, and Navajo silversmiths increasingly crafted spoons for utilitarian purposes, such as salad sets, iced tea sets, and butter knives. After **turquoise** became widely available in the early 1900s, Navajo smiths sometimes used this gemstone to decorate utilitarian spoons. In the 1920s and '30s sheet silver became available, saving the silversmiths a great deal of time in crafting spoons and other items. Silver spoons are still made today by Native artist-jewelers who sign their pieces and receive wide recognition for their work. These spoons have become a way for artists to showcase their talents and creativity.

SPANISH COLONIAL ART / artwork from the Spanish empire was introduced to Spanish colonies in the New World by the late sixteenth century, and reflected the artistic traditions then taking place in Spain (which also reflected the artistic trends of greater Europe). The imported devotional images were used to decorate churches and private chapels, and were used in religious ceremonies. By the mid-eighteenth century an abundance of local resources inspired a group of area artisans (in what is now Santa Fe and its outlying villages, and later Rio Abajo) to create artwork and other objects of their own, including **santos**, **bultos**, textiles, furniture, jewelry, and other devotional, decorative, and utilitarian objects. Made with local materials and a local aesthetic, these objects were primarily based on traditional Spanish and Mexican colonial designs (which again also reflected European design trends).

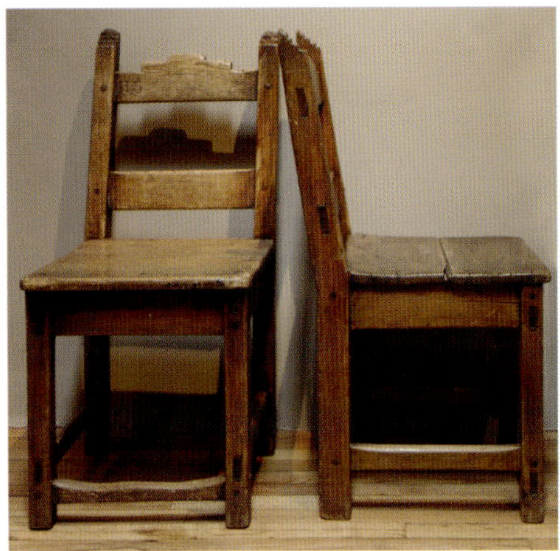

Spanish Colonial–style New Mexican chairs, ca. 1930s, ponderosa pine with terraced finials and back rests.

SPANISH COLONIAL FURNITURE / a type of furniture handcrafted in colonial New Mexico characterized by simple, sturdy, and elegant designs based on sixteenth-century Spanish prototypes that were constructed using **mortise-and-tenon** or dovetail **joinery**, and sometimes iron hardware. However, unlike the ornately carved motifs on Spanish furniture, New Mexican furniture had simple **chip-carved**, incised, or relief-carved details. This difference was primarily due to the soft nature of the local pine wood and the limited availability of tools.

These early New Mexican **carpinteros** hand-planed or hand-**adzed** the surfaces of their furniture and to burnish the surface they used the traditional method of using a polished stone to achieve a smooth, shiny finish. Hand-rubbed

finishes of natural stains and/or wax were also used. Designs were typically drawn directly on the surface or transferred using a template or pattern. The early carpenters (who first arrived in the region in 1598 with the Oñate expedition) produced beds, stools, chairs, tables, benches, **repisas**, storage boxes and **chests**, and **trasteros**. In addition to carved motifs, some furniture pieces were painted with water-based paints. By the early seventeenth century, Pueblo Indians in the region were being trained as carpenters and making furniture, doors, and window frames at mission workshops. The Pueblos of Cochiti and Pecos became well known for their fine furniture throughout the colonial period.

After Mexico won its independence from Spain in 1821 and the Santa Fe Trail opened in 1822, more tools, materials, and furniture styles influenced the woodwork of Hispano and Pueblo carpenters. Motifs on the pieces reflected the popular and prevalent European styles, including Gothic, Renaissance, Baroque, Rococo, and later Neo-classical.

Spanish Colonial–style furniture experienced a revival in New Mexico in the 1930s, through the beginning of World War II, when the government-sponsored Works Progress Administration (WPA) supported the making of this style of furniture in a number of schools and public buildings throughout the state.

Today the style flourishes once again, as evidenced by the number of beautiful handcrafted examples exhibited and sold at the annual Spanish Market in Santa Fe, New Mexico (held in July and December). As with the earlier pieces, the contemporary furniture is distinguished by its carved surfaces, variety of stains, and designs rooted in the Spanish Colonial and Mexican traditions. See also **WPA furniture**.

SPANISH COLONIAL-STYLE DOMESTIC ARCHITECTURE / built during Spanish occupation and colonization of the region (1598–1821 in New Mexico; 1740–1821 in Arizona), this style is typified by **adobe**-brick walls, a one-story house around a **courtyard** (or **placita**), ceilings constructed of **vigas**, a flat roof with **canales** extruding from a paparet, a long narrow **portal** facing the street or courtyard, and small windows (facing the street) often covered with protective wood or iron **grilles.** Rooms were initially built in a single file, and typically grew into L-shaped, then U-shaped, and sometimes square-shaped plans that surrounded central courtyards. All the interior doors opened onto the covered portal or

courtyard. Few examples remain from this era: portions of the Palace of the Governors in Santa Fe, New Mexico; a section of the Otero family **hacienda** in Tubac, Arizona, now a part of the Tubac Country Club; and the Plaza del Cerro in Chimayó, New Mexico.

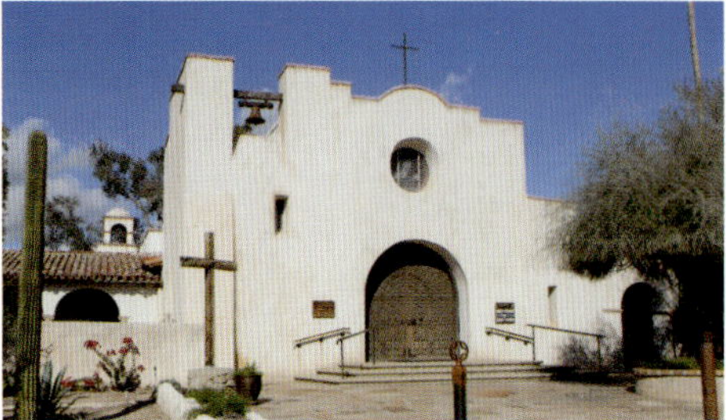

Josias Joesler (architect), St. Philip's in the Hills Church, Spanish Colonial Revival style, 1936, Tucson, Arizona.

SPANISH COLONIAL REVIVAL STYLE (Spanish Revival) / an eclectic architectural style popular in the Southwest from about 1915 through the 1930s, for structures ranging from cottages to mansions to movie cinemas to churches, inspired in part by eighteenth-century Spanish missions of California. The characteristics of the style include the following: red **barrel-tiled** roofs; white, rough-textured **stucco** exterior walls (and rough, white-plastered interior walls); elaborate entryways with carved or cast ornaments and columns; decorative **tiles**, arches, and tile-capped **parapets**; wrought-iron or wood **grilles** in the windows, and round-arched and quatrefoil-shaped windows; and staircases with iron spiral balusters and scroll elements.

Like the similar but less elaborate **Mission Revival** style, Spanish Colonial Revivals usually featured **courtyards**, **portals**, and gardens that offered outdoor rooms within the walls of the building. The style was publicized and widely spread as a result of the romantic fair buildings designed by East Coast architect Bertram Grosvenor Goodhue (1869–1924) for the 1915–16 Panama-Pacific Exposition in San Diego, California. Among the finest architects working in the Spanish Colonial Revival style were Josias Joesler (1895–1956) in Tucson, Arizona, as well as George Washington Smith and Richard Requa in southern California.

SPANISH PUEBLO REVIVAL STYLE (Pueblo Revival, "Santa Fe Style") / an architectural style popular in the region from about 1905 to 1940 (and revived in recent decades), consisting of earth-colored walls (of **stucco**, **adobe**, brick, or wood-frame), flat roofs with rounded and

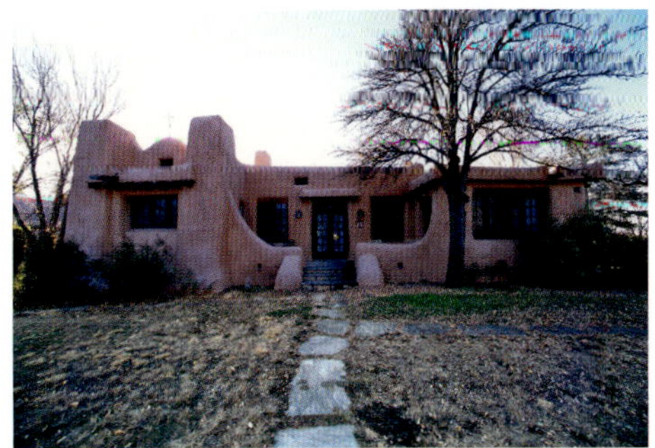

Frank and Rosina Smith House, Spanish Pueblo Revival style, ca. 1920, Santa Fe, New Mexico.

stepped parapets, **canales** (drain spouts), **vigas** projecting from the exterior walls (more often decorative than structural), rough-hewn wooden **lintels** spanning window and door openings, and **portals** with carved wooden **corbels**. On the interior, ceilings typically feature hand-hewn vigas separated by **latillas** (in the case of Arizona by **saguaro** ribs), and carved wood corbels. Traditionally built versions have two- to three-foot-thick adobe walls finished in **mud plaster**. Some have terraces and sculptural buttresses that imitate pueblo architecture.

The revival appeared as early as 1905, when architect Mary Elizabeth Jane Colter (1869–1958) built Hopi House for the **Fred Harvey Company** at the Grand Canyon—a building that evoked the historic dwellings she had seen in Oraibi, an ancient Hopi village in northeastern Arizona. The New Mexico Building, erected at the 1915–16 Panama–Pacific Exposition in San Diego, California, designed by the firm of Rapp and Rapp and based on the mission church at Acoma Pueblo, helped spread the popularity of the Spanish Pueblo Revival manner.

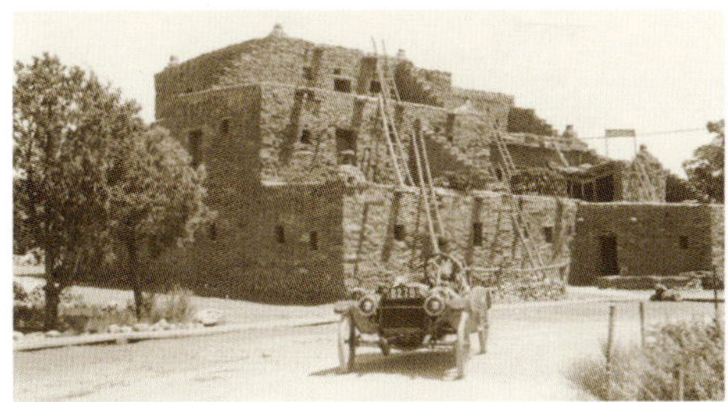

Hopi House, built in 1905, Grand Canyon, Arizona.

It is also referred to as "Santa Fe Style," because it was particularly popular in Santa Fe, New Mexico. In the 1910s business leaders sought to revive the city's declining economy through the development of tourism. They adopted this style—based on the city's remaining Spanish- and Mexican-era buildings and nearby Pueblo villages—for public and residential buildings, believing this would help attract tourists. Owners of Santa Fe–style homes throughout the Southwest often integrated traditional regional work, including **retablos**, **bultos**, **tinwork**, **colcha**, **Pueblo pottery**, Navajo rugs, and Native American basketry into their interiors.

The Spanish Pueblo Revival style remains a popular residential manner today in New Mexico and Arizona, where it is valued for its picturesque and romantic qualities, as well as its appropriateness for the Southwestern desert climate and landscape. See diagram on page 186.

SPIDER WOMAN / one of the Navajo Holy People who, according to the stories of many Navajo clans, originally taught **Changing Woman** (another Holy Person) the art of weaving, with the stipulation that she would in turn teach the Navajos how to weave. She was assisted by Spider Man, who taught the Navajos how to make the loom and tools out of sacred natural materials. According to Navajo legend, Spider Woman lived atop Spider Rock, a majestic red stone pillar in the depths of Canyon de Chelly, Arizona, a sacred place to the Navajos who made this their homeland beginning in the seventeenth century. Many Navajos believe that before weaving a textile, a Blessingway ceremony must be performed by a medicine man and prayers offered to grant the weaver permission. The sacred origin of weaving demonstrates the significance of this art form within the Navajo religion. Spider Woman was a powerful deity for the Hopis as well. According to Hopi belief, she led the Hopis to this world and, among other things, taught the people language.

SPIDER-WOMAN CROSS (Hubbell's Cross, Rain Cross) / a term likely introduced by post traders that describes a **cross** with four equal arms and two small squares at the end of each of the four arms. This motif was often used in Navajo

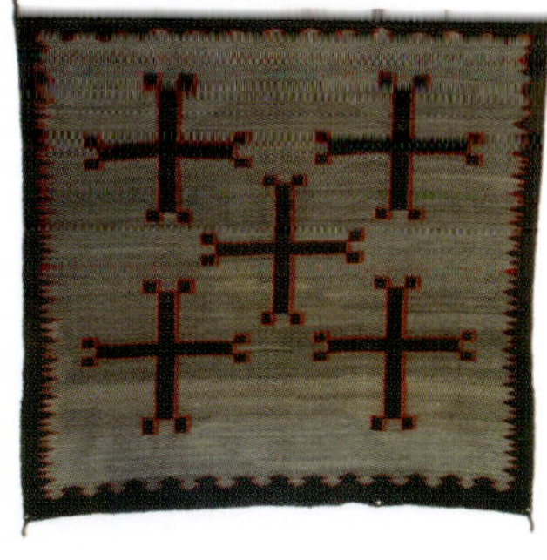

textiles, especially rugs made in the **Ganado** region of Arizona, as well as in Navajo baskets. The coiled **sumac** basketry **trays** (or shallow bowls), in which four **Spider Woman** (or "rain")- crosses appear, were used in certain Navajo ceremonies to hold sacred **cornmeal**. Many older baskets with this design have a cloth plug in the bottom so the cornmeal or other contents will not spill out. A similar design has been used in the basketry of San Juan Paiutes of northern Arizona, who refer to the shape as the rain cross. The traditional Spider-Woman cross is utilized by Native artisans today in basketry, textiles, and jewelry. See also **Ganado Style** and **Hubbell Trading Post**.

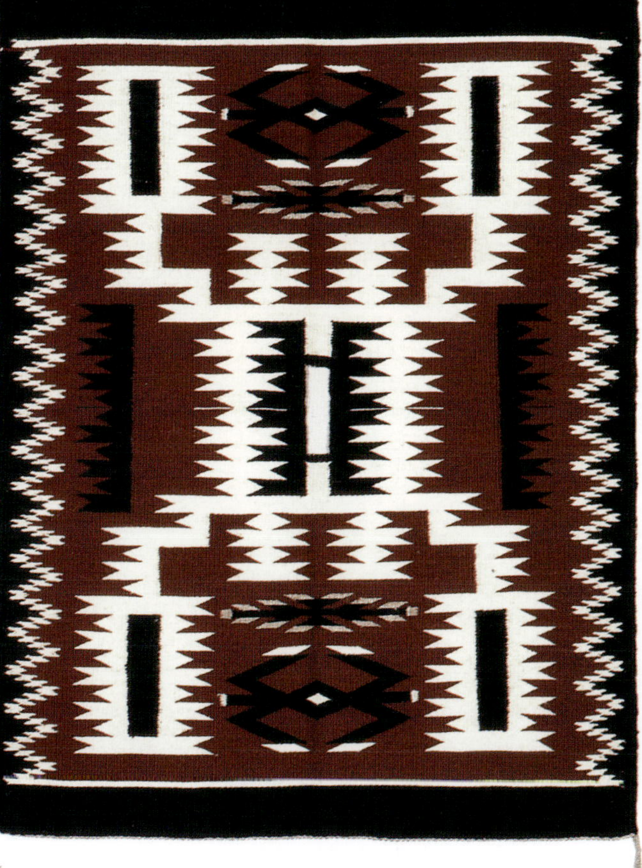

ABOVE: Navajo Ganado-style textile, ca. 1900, with five Spider-Woman crosses. **BELOW:** Tomacita Sloan (Navajo), Spider Woman rug, 36" x 28".

SPINDLE (Malacate) / a tool that dates back to ancient Puebloan times, comprising a wooden stick or rod with a wooden disk at the bottom end for weight, still used by some Navajo and Hispano weavers today, for hand-spinning wool, cotton, and other fibers into **yarn** or thread of different shapes and thickness. As fibers are drawn onto the spindle from a mass (or mat) of carded fibers, the spindle is rotated and a twist is transferred to the fibers, forming the thread/yarn. When weavers need thin yarn for **tapestries**, they will spin the fibers over and over again to achieve the desired tightness and thinness. The spindle ranges from a wooden shaft with a fairly large, flat wooden disk for spinning a large amount of heavy wool yarn to ones with a small fired-clay weight for spinning thread. In addition to the Navajo and Pueblo people, the spindle has been used by Hispano weavers of the Southwest, who call it a *malacate*. (Hispano weavers also spin wool on a spinning wheel.) In furniture and architecture, a spindle refers to a thin turned rod or baluster, sometimes tapering at each end and sometimes ornamented. See also **yarn—handspun**.

SPINY OYSTER (*Spondylus*) / a reddish-orange or red oyster shell from the Pacific coast of Baja California, highly prized by Native American jewelry makers for over a thousand years. Among the earliest to use these shells were the Hohokam (300 BC–AD 1450) and the Salado (circa AD 1100) people of Arizona, who acquired the shells through trade. They combined spiny oyster with **turquoise** from the Southwest in **shell pendants**. The use of oceanic shells so far inland illustrates the existence of extensive ancient trade routes among America's earliest inhabitants, as well as the symbolic importance of seashells. Spiny oyster was the only source for a red-orange material for Native-made jewelry until **coral** was introduced.

SPIRAL-ROPE CARVING / see **Solomonic column**.

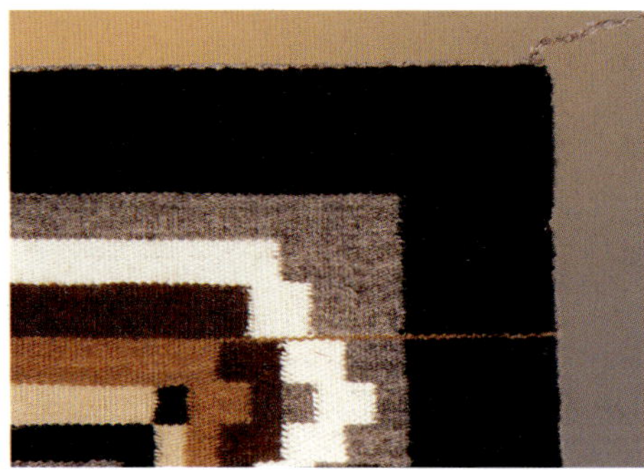

Close-up of spirit line in a Two Grey Hills textile by Dorothy Lowe (Navajo).

SPIRIT LINE (Line Break, Spirit Trail, Ceremonial Break, Weaver's Pathway) / an intentional break (or line) in the design of a wool rug, ceramic pot, woven basket, and other Native American art forms, with various meanings generally associated with healing rituals, emergence, and origin narratives. Some Native American artisans say that it provides an exit or a "way out" for their creative energies, so their spirit will not be trapped inside the work and they can remain "free" to make additional rugs, baskets, or pottery. For the Navajos, this break in the design is called *'atiin* (pathway) and is related to the Emergence story, which describes the Navajos' emergence from previous worlds into the present one. It is a mandatory design element in ceremonial baskets (such as the **wedding basket**) and enables medicine men to orient the baskets to the east, providing a pathway for healing. In Navajo rugs, the spirit line consists of a small, thin line that extends from the design field across the border to the outside edge of the rug, often near a corner. In Jicarilla Apache baskets, the ceremonial break symbolizes the "sun ladders" that played a major role in the Jicarilla creation story.

SPLIT STITCH (Spaced Stitch) / a technique used in coiled baskets made by Native basket makers in the Southwest. In split-stitch work, the stitches are more widely spaced, exposing the foundation coil for contrast. It is a faster weaving technique and was generally used for utilitarian baskets, notably the large storage baskets among the Pimas. This method, along with the **close-stitch** technique (in which stitches buttress each other and totally cover the foundation) are used today by the Tohono O'odham of Arizona to create mesmerizing designs such as rattlesnakes, "**man-in-the-maze**," fret, and other patterns. See diagram on page 186.

SQUASH BLOSSOM / a term used in the Southwest to refer to a **silver** pendant in the shape of the trumpet-like squash blossom, as well as for a necklace style comprising of silver **beads** interspersed with silver squash-blossom pendants (and usually a **naja**), made by Navajo silversmiths beginning in the 1870s/1880s. They were one of the earliest necklace styles made by Navajo craftsmen and widely traded. Although the form does resemble the flower of the squash plant (an important part of the Southwest diet since ancient times), some scholars believe its use in jewelry was possibly inspired by the fruit of the pomegranate—a design motif of early Christian, Islamic, and Jewish origins that was also a favorite Spanish decoration for centuries. In particular, silver-ball buttons/beads fashioned to resemble the pomegranate were used to decorate Spanish and Mexican trousers and jackets. Another possible influence on the Navajo "squash blossom" form are the early-nineteenth-century Mexican Indian necklaces comprised of **coral** and glass trade beads with silver pomegranate beads interspersed.

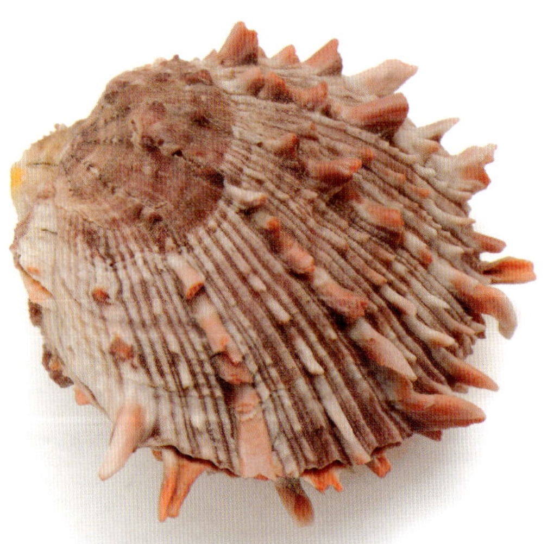

ABOVE LEFT: Shell pendant by Tonita Coriz and Abenicio Crespin (Santo Domingo), 2011, spiny oyster shell overlaid with turquoise, jet, and shell, with sterling silver stamp-work loop.
FAR LEFT: Natural spiny oyster shell.
LEFT: Polished spiny oyster shell.

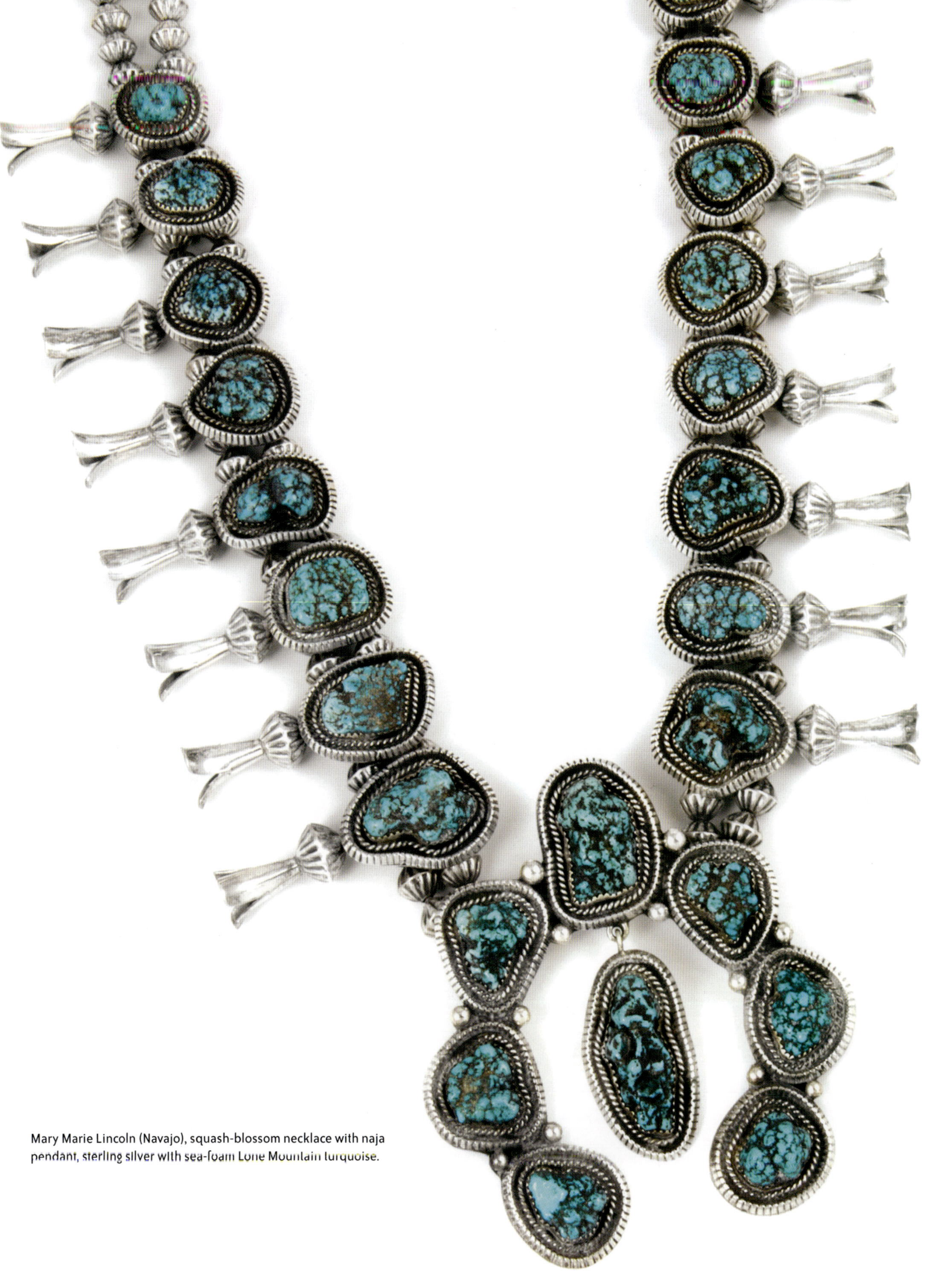

Mary Marie Lincoln (Navajo), squash-blossom necklace with naja pendant, sterling silver with sea-foam Lone Mountain turquoise.

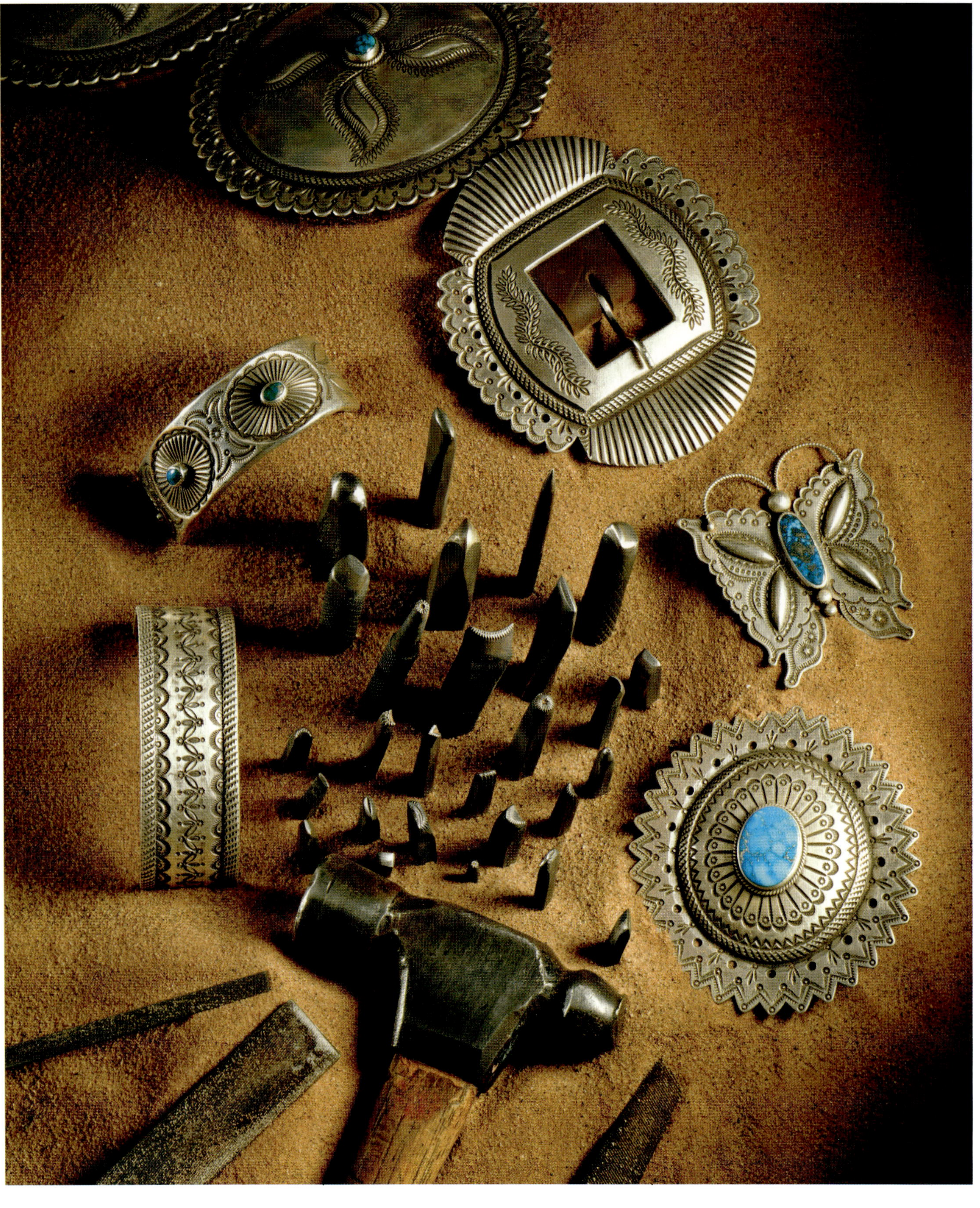

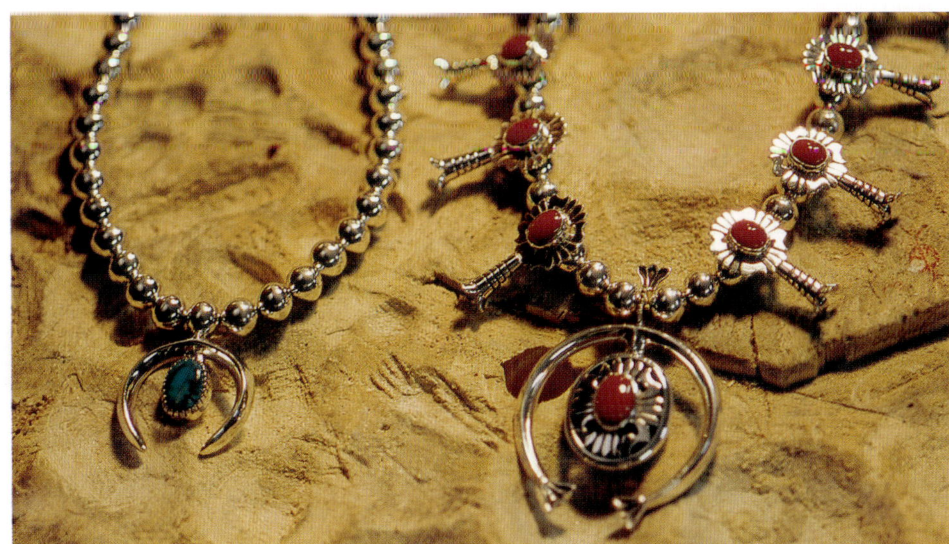

ABOVE: Allison Lee (Navajo), naja (left) and squash-blossom (right) necklaces. **OPPOSITE:** Silverwork with stamped designs by Perry Shorty (Navajo). Perry makes his own stamps, many from concrete nails.

Typically, squash blossom pendants were (and continue to be) formed by **doming** two halves to create a bead, then cutting sheet silver to form the oblong shank/petal shape, which is then soldered to the bead. A small tab of silver drilled with a hole or a silver ring is soldered to the top of the bead, through which the necklace string is passed. The squash blossom pendants may be plain or decorated with notched edges, knobs, or simple incised or stamped designs. Sometimes matching silver earrings, formed by doming or fashioned from short hollow tubes of silver attached to a solid silver ball, have been made to accompany necklaces. In addition, squash-blossom necklaces usually feature a large single or double crescent-shaped center pendant called a naja (or nazha), and sometimes is decorated with inlaid pieces of **turquoise**, **coral**, or other stones. In some early versions of the necklace, likely made by Pueblo smiths, small silver **crosses** were substituted for or added to the pendants and beads. The squash blossom necklace style has sustained its popularity to the present day; contemporary Navajo smiths and other Native jewelers continue to experiment with materials, forms, techniques, and designs when creating the traditional squash-blossom pendants and necklaces.

STAMP WORK (Stamping, Stampwork) / a

technique of impressing designs on the surface of leather, **silver**, or other metals with a **die** or stamp. The die, typically made of iron, is placed on the surface and the other end is struck with a hammer. The source of the iron ranges from railroad spikes to chisels to files to nail sets. The stamping of silver items is usually done on a flat surface, before the shaping of the silver into final form. It is painstaking and risky work: if a stamp is misplaced, the only way of correcting it is to melt down the silver and start over. Individual stamps with simple designs can be used to create a repeating design, or can be combined with other stamps to create more elaborate patterns.

Beginning in the 1880s, Navajo silversmiths, influenced by the stamped designs on early-nineteenth-century Mexican leather saddles, have used this technique to decorate silver jewelry. In the 1880s and 1890s, traders in Arizona and New Mexico imported tools for Navajo smiths that included fine files that were used to shape dies and also could be turned into dies themselves. By the late 1880s they were making their own stamps from a variety of metal forms, even railroad spikes. Some dies with arrowheads, **swastikas**, and other motifs were added to the Navajo silversmith's toolkit once the railroad entered the Southwest and **curio**-store owners and traders introduced new design ideas for the tourist market. Navajo smiths became widely regarded for their intricate stamp-work silver made from dies with designs ranging from simple shapes such as crescents, circles, **rosettes**, and wavy and zigzag lines to more complex animal or human forms, impressed on jewelry, boxes, spoons, **conchas**, and other items.

Contemporary Native smiths are carrying on the stamp work tradition, to which they bring their own individual design skills and aesthetics. One Navajo artisan known for his complex stamp work is Norbert Peshlakai (b. 1953). A fourth generation silversmith, he is especially well known for his miniature **seed pots** with his characteristic stamped designs including a rabbit, horse, butterfly, and a cowboy figure.

Some silversmiths use a figurative individual stamp, such as a bird or a goat, as an identifying mark, or **hallmark**, on their work. However, Navajo smiths share stamps and purchase stamps from each other, so it is not a definitive method of identification.

STORAGE BASKET (Granary Basket) / a very

large, traditional, utilitarian basketry form of the Pimas that was used to store grain. It was handwoven using the **coil** and **split stitch** techniques, from fibers of plants that grow in the region. Originally wheat straw was sewn together with split stitches of **mesquite** bark, and later split **willow** was used for the light-colored areas of the basket design and **devil's claw** for the dark areas. This tall, round basket, often up to four feet high and three feet in diameter, was so large that the woman who was coiling it had to sit or stand inside.

STORAGE JAR / a classic utilitarian Pueblo

pottery shape that dates back to prehistoric times, commonly tall (not less than 20 inches in height, and in some cases more than three feet high) and round or elongated in shape with the widest part at mid-body, strong thick walls, a proportionally small opening at the top with an upright or slightly flared rim, intended for storing grain or

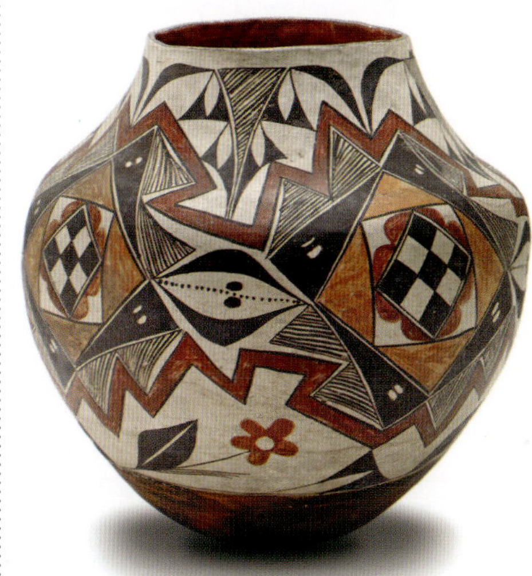

Laguna Pueblo polychrome storage jar, ca. 1880s, clay with natural clay slips.

corn. The small opening could be readily sealed to protect the contents from animals and insects. In some of the earliest surviving examples there are indentations placed in the base on either side to make it easier to handle the pot when full. In general, these pots were a necessary part of household equipment for every Ancestral Puebloan family.

In the nineteenth century, storage jars—too big and bulky for tourists to easily transport as souvenirs—were made for home use and as shipping containers. Technically more difficult to make because of their large size, these vessels were hand-**coiled** and wood-**fired**, and **pukis** were usually utilized to help create the round, globular shapes.

Many fine examples of the form exist dating from the 1880s to early 1900s. Among the renowned potters to make storage jars was Santa Clara Pueblo potter Sara Fina Tafoya (1863–1949). She used a stylized **bear paw** design as a hallmark on the surface of her jars and made them for sale as well as for home use. The form was continued and refined by her daughter Margaret Tafoya (1904–2001). Today a mere handful of Pueblo potters (such as Nambé potter Lonnie Vigil) are actively making large storage jars using the traditional coil and outdoor wood firing process.

STORM PATTERN / a Navajo rug style woven primarily in the western part of the Navajo Reservation in Arizona, featuring zigzag connecting lines (symbolizing lightning bolts), a center box or space (according to some it represents a Navajo **hogan**), and squares at each of the four corners (indicating the Four Sacred Mountains of the Navajo homelands). Traditionally, the colors were red, black, and white on a gray background. Scholars have long debated the origin of the pattern. However, it is known that when **Crystal Trading Post** proprietor John B. Moore issued a mail-order catalog in 1911 he included an example of a storm pattern rug and claimed it was connected to Navajo mythology. Made in a region of the Southwest known for its violent storms and lightning, storm pattern textiles are still woven today.

STORYTELLER BOWLS / small ceramic bowls made by Pueblo artisans, generally hand-**coiled**, **fired**, and painted with natural or commercial paints, usually with children (and occasionally

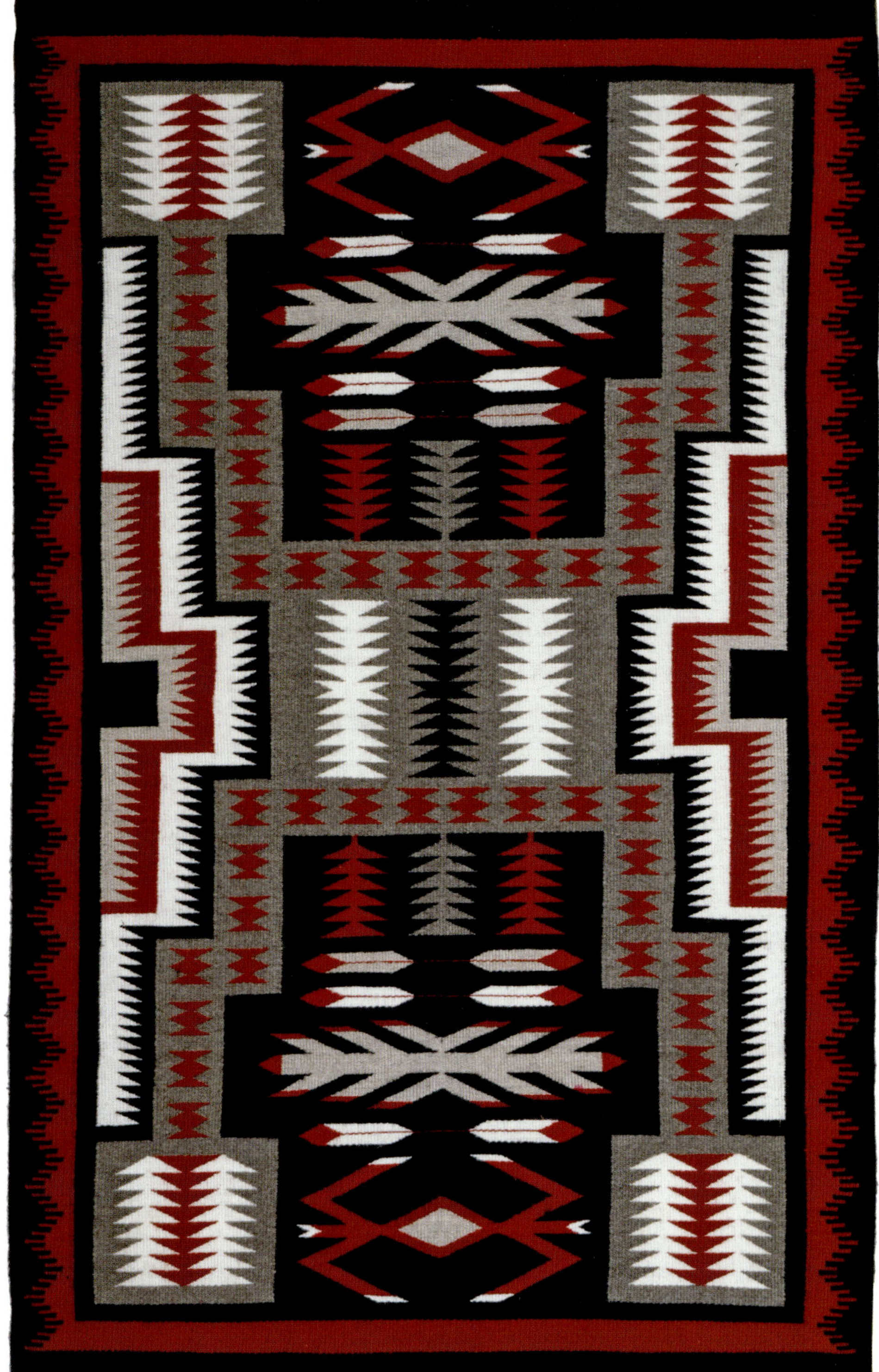

Rose Dan Begay (Navajo), storm-pattern textile.

with animals) gathered around the rim, sometimes looking at figures (usually animals) inside on the bottom of the bowl. The design was originally inspired by the natural rock cisterns atop Acoma mesa where children play and animals come to drink the rainwater. Among the Acoma potters who make storyteller bowls are Marilyn Ray and Corrine Garcia. Garcia uses the ancient **corrugated** technique to make her **clay** bowls and then adds the figures.

STORYTELLER FIGURES / a hollow **clay** figurative piece composed of a seated adult with small clay figures of children perched on his or her legs, arms, or shoulders. The main figure is usually depicted with his or her mouth open as if in the middle of telling a story, representing the Pueblo custom of passing on historical and cultural traditions and beliefs through stories and songs. They have traditionally been made using the color scheme of orange-red, off-white (or cream), and black (or dark gray).

Although a figurine known as the "Singing Mother"—a woman holding one or more children—dates back to the turn of the twentieth century, the first true storyteller was made in 1964 by Helen Cordero (1914–1994) of Cochiti Pueblo. Cordero's first storyteller, consisting of a Pueblo man with five children on his lap and shoulders, was inspired by and made in memory of her grandfather, Santiago Quintana, a famous and gifted Cochiti storyteller. Also influenced by the earlier tradition of clay figures made at Cochiti, and encouraged by the well-known folk art collector Alexander Girard, Cordero's storyteller figures immediately became popular collector's items. In 1986 Cordero was selected as a National Heritage Fellow by the National Endowment for the Arts.

Storytellers were eventually made by potters at other pueblos—Jemez, Taos, Isleta, Tesuque, Santa Clara, Acoma, Santo Domingo, and Zuni—as well as by Navajo and Hopi potters. Made in distinct styles sometimes specific to a particular pueblo's traditions, storyteller figures portray not only humans but sometimes animals (such as **bears**, turtles, **coyotes**, and owls), and whimsical figures such as mermaids, **koshares**, and **mudheads**. Cordero and other storyteller makers often painted the surface of their figures with images relating to Christian and/or Pueblo iconography.

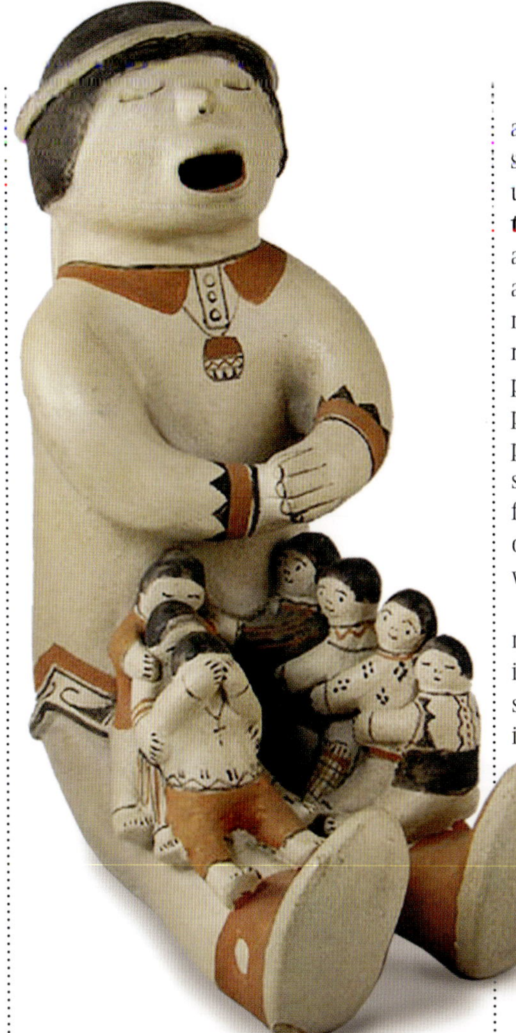

Today storytellers are made by hand building and pinching the clay into the desired form, then scraping and sanding the surface until smooth using a piece of **gourd** or small wedge of **cottonwood**. Once the form has dried a clay **slip** is applied (which some potters **polish** with a stone), and then the potter paints the figure. Traditionally mineral and vegetal paints were used, though in recent years some artists have used commercial paints, such as acrylic, which is applied after the piece is fired. Some potters at Taos and other pueblos are making bronze-hued **micaceous**-clay storytellers with no added surface decoration. The figurines are usually **fired** in a gas or electric kiln, or by using the traditional outdoor method with wood, coal, or animal dung as fuel.

Over time, storyteller figures have become more and more elaborate. They sometimes include a plethora of tiny clay **appliquéd** details, such as replicas of baskets, pottery, or drums, insects such as ladybugs or **butterflies**, and domesticated cats or dogs. This style is evident, for instance, in the storytellers of award-winning Acoma pottery Marilyn Ray and Cochiti potter Martha Arquero. In addition to being made in the traditional seated pose, storyteller figures are also being formed in reclining positions. Pueblo people continue to keep their native storytelling alive as a significant part of village life. As a result, storyteller figures remain popular as commemorations and celebrations of this tradition. See also **storyteller bowls** and **storyteller jewelry**.

ABOVE: Helen Cordero (Cochiti, 1915–1994), storyteller. **BELOW:** Storytellers, clay with natural pigments/clay slip, from left to right: Judy Lewis (Acoma), ca. 2009; Christian Fragua (Jemez), ca. 2006; Phyllis Nez (Navajo [in the style of Cochiti]), ca. 2007; Dorothy Herrera (Cochiti), ca. 2008; Joanna Herrera (Cochiti), ca. 2005; and Felerta Eustace (Cochiti), ca. 2004.

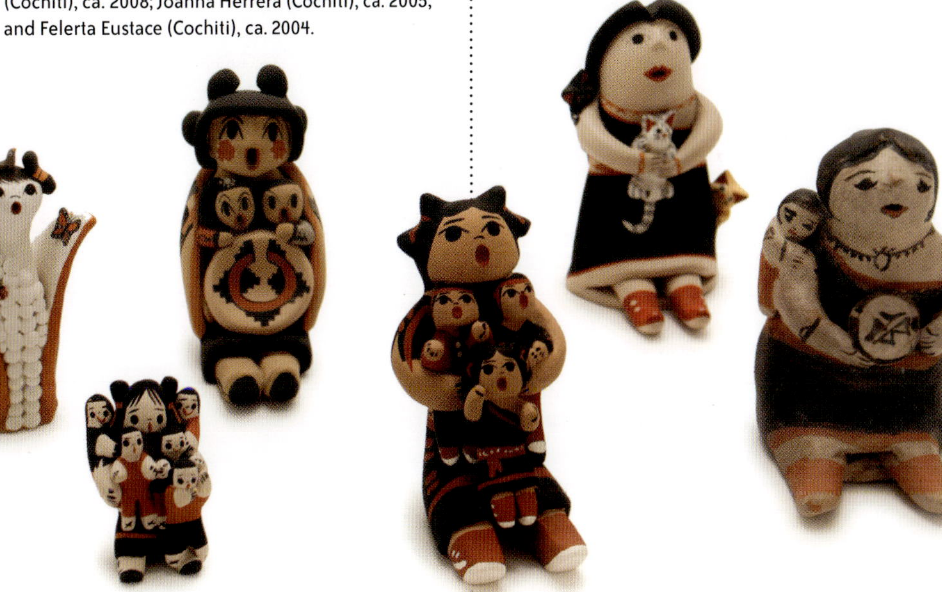

STORYTELLER JEWELRY / made using the silver **overlay** technique, most commonly by Navajo silversmiths, featuring scenes of daily life on the reservation such as a Navajo **hogan**, a woman weaving a rug, a figure making frybread, and sheep tended by a Navajo man. The most common form used is a cuff bracelet. In some instances, the designs are in gold overlaid onto **silver** and/or the piece may be further embellished with **stamp work.** See also **storyteller figures**.

STRAW APPLIQUÉ / a technique that may have developed in Europe, in which flattened pieces of straw, cornhusks, or other plant material are torn or cut into shapes, laid out in a design, and then adhered to wood (usually pine or fir) that has been smoothed and painted a dark color. The entire surface is then protected with a pine-resin based varnish. The straw's natural, golden sparkle provides a striking contrast to the dark painted background. Inspired by the elaborate and popular **marquetry** of Mexico, Spain, and elsewhere in Europe—which was created from expensive woods, ivory, and shell—straw appliqué may have been used as early as the seventeenth century by Spanish Colonial artisans in New Mexico.

Primarily used to adorn devotional items such as **crosses** or **nichos** in **mission** and village churches, as well as in private chapels in homes along the Rio Grande, the technique flourished in late-eighteenth and nineteenth-century New Mexico. The imagery featured in the early straw appliqué was geometric and floral, in imitation of designs found on Hispano-Moresque chests and other decorative objects from Spain and its colonies. Later, additional items were embellished with straw, including furniture, candlesticks, chests, mirror frames, and boxes.

The technique began to decline in the late-nineteenth century; however, in the 1930s, Eliseo Rodríguez of Santa Fe, New Mexico, under the auspices of the Federal Art Project (FAP), revived the art of decorating with straw. Also an accomplished painter, Eliseo, along with his wife Paula, introduced narrative imagery into the craft, a direct result of his training as a painter.

In recent decades straw appliqué has flourished once again, becoming one of the most popular traditional Spanish Colonial art forms in New Mexico, with more and more artisans selling their wares at the annual Spanish Market (in July and December) in Santa Fe. Among them is Vicki Rodríguez,

daughter of Eliseo and Paula, who has received much praise for her work, worldwide. Contemporary artisans, using traditional and in some cases modern materials (such as commercial **gesso** to smooth the wood surface, glue to adhere the straw, polyurethane for the protective finish, and straw dyed different colors), decorate a vast array of objects—**retablos**, **bultos**, dance wands, cradles, **crosses**, frames, and much more.

In addition to Spanish marquetry, straw appliqué is said to have emulated the more expensive gold-leaf decoration of Spanish art. Sometimes referred to as "poor man's gold," the bits of straw in these appliqué pieces do indeed glitter like gold when lit by candlelight. See also **encrusted straw**.

STRAW BALE / an environmentally friendly construction technique in which stacked, machine-formed blocks of straw (commonly wheat, rice, barley, hops, or oats) bound with baling wire or polypropylene twine are used to build the walls of structures. In the United States, it was first used to build homes in the 1880s by pioneer farmers in Nebraska and elsewhere on the Great Plains—places where trees and lumber were scarce and baled straw was plentiful. Settlers realized that straw bales retained warmth and provided protection from the elements. Over time, two types of straw bale construction

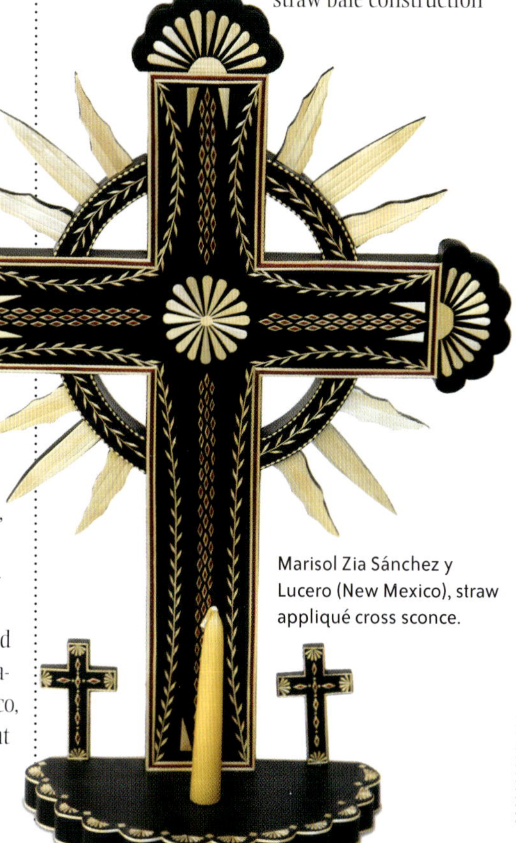

Marisol Zia Sánchez y Lucero (New Mexico), straw appliqué cross sconce.

developed: straw bales were stacked with staggered joints like brick construction, called "Nebraska style" after its place of origin; or bales were fitted into a wood or steel framework in a "post and beam" system. Straw bale waned after World War II, when modern frame-construction subdivisions sprang up across the country. However, in the 1970s, when a "back-to-the-land" movement emerged, straw bale construction experienced a renaissance in the Southwest. By the early 1990s it had become increasingly popular; the first legally permitted, insured, and bank-financed "post and beam" straw bale house was built in Tesuque, New Mexico, in 1991, and two years later the first permitted load-bearing Nebraska-style straw bale house was completed in Tucson, Arizona.

When building two-foot-thick straw-bale walls of high insulation, suited to a wide range of climates including the hot and arid Southwest, the bales are stacked in the desired configuration and then finished with plaster (such as **stucco** or **clay**). The plastering of interior and exterior surfaces is important to protect the straw from moisture, insects, and fire. In some instances, the walls are further clad with some type of ventilated siding. And straw bales may be combined with other wall materials. The size of the bales used varies depending on the type of baler used and local practice.

Straw bale is preferred by some builders and homeowners today because the material is eco-friendly, relatively easy to work with, and inexpensive. At first used to build simple, one-story square or rectangular homes with pitched roofs, straw bale has in recent decades been used for a wide variety of styles and forms—including contemporary, organic forms designed to fit into historical contexts and multi-story structures. Intensely proud of their homes, owners of straw-bale homes have established a tradition of including a "truth window"—a small area of the interior wall left uncovered (but protected with glass or sometimes a little door) that reveals the straw bale construction.

STUCCO (Plaster) / a paste-like material that is applied to a wall or ceiling and allowed to dry into a hard surface, used as a weatherproofing coat on exterior walls and for decorating/sealing interior walls and ceilings. Some of the earliest "stucco" used in the Southwest consisted of almost pure lime with some sand mixed in. In the desert regions of Arizona, stucco was mixed with nopal cactus juice to add "stickiness," as well as to provide the right chemical additive that allows the finished product to be both waterproof and "breath-able" (so the stucco would expand/contract at the same rate as the **adobe** walls). By the early 1900s various binders were used in stucco/plaster, such as lime, gypsum, sand, or Portland cement. Beginning about 1915, earth-colored plaster or stucco was used over wood frame or brick to imitate adobe—a construction technique that gained popularity in the Southwest when the cost effectiveness of adobe construction receded. By the late 1920s the Portland Cement Association and other companies were making cement stuccos in a variety of textures and colors that Southwestern architects used to create the softly curving faux-adobe walls of **Spanish Pueblo Revival**–style buildings. In some instances cement stucco has been used to sheath adobe walls, causing the adobe wall to destabilize and crumble due to the incongruous nature of the two materials.

SUMAC (*Rhus anacardiaceae, Rhus trilobata*) / one of the plants most frequently used by Native American basket makers in the Southwest for the foundations and sewing splints in **coiled** or **twined** baskets, as well as for a **dye**. Sumac is harvested in the late fall after the first frost, or in the early spring. To prepare it for use as sewing strands, the sumac is split into three parts by utilizing the teeth and both hands. Then it is peeled, pithed, and smoothed with a piece of leather before being colored with synthetic aniline dye or vegetal dye. Sumac is used for basket weaving by the Hualapai, Havasupai, Western and Jicarilla Apache, Ute, San Juan Paiute, Hopi, and Navajo peoples. See also **dyes—vegetal**.

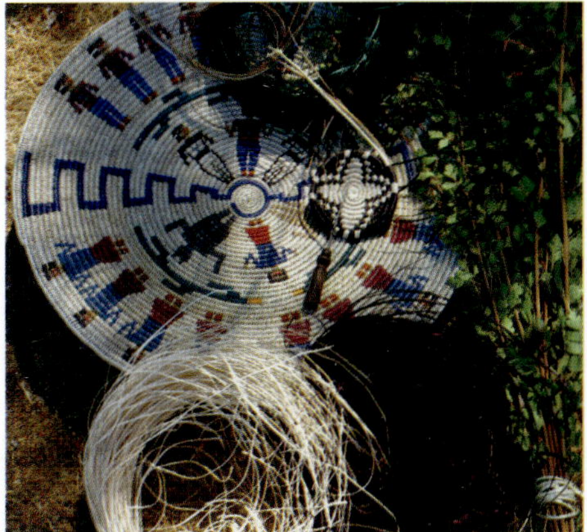

Large basket by Agnes Gray (Navajo), small basket by Sally Black (Navajo) with fresh sumac and natural and dyed sumac strips.

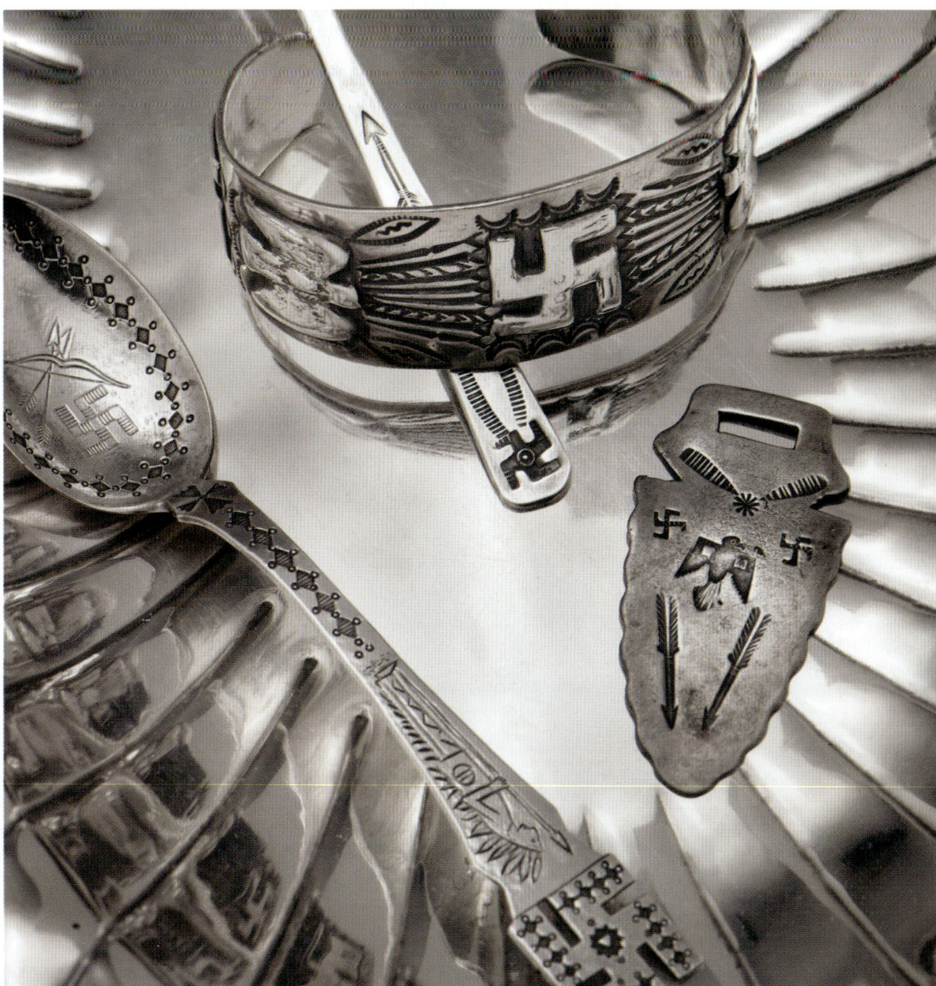

Swastika motif on sterling silver (most with stamp work, some with hand tooling): Navajo teaspoon, ca. 1920s; Hopi cuff bracelet, ca. 1920s; souvenir spoon (Mansfield Co.), ca. 1907 (trading post); watch fob (trading post), ca. 1920s.

SWASTIKA / Whirling Logs (Fylfot, Crooked Cross) / from the Sanskrit words *su* and *vasti*, meaning "well-being," the swastika—a symbol and design motif consisting of four intersecting arms—flourished in textiles, **curio** jewelry, stamped silverwork, pottery, and basketry made for the tourist trade by the Tohono O'odham, Hopi, Navajo, Pueblo, and Apache peoples, from about 1890 to 1940. The symbol became popular following the publication of Thomas Wilson's 1894 report entitled "The Swastika, The Earliest Known Symbol and its Migration." By 1900 reservation post traders and curio dealers were encouraging the use of the swastika for use in Native American art, especially Navajo textiles, and inventing lore about its importance in Navajo and Pueblo culture.

An ancient design used by many cultures around the world and associated with various meanings—perfection, happiness, pleasure—the swastika was popular in twentieth-century North America as a symbol of good luck. Among the popular items on which it appeared as a "good luck" symbol was **Navajo silverwork**, especially **souvenir spoons**.

The Navajos call the four-armed motif "whirling log" after a story that occurs in the Nightway and Featherway ceremonies. It also generally represents the four directions and the sacred number four: representing the four seasons, the four sacred mountains in Navajo country, or the four corners of the earth. The whirling log appeared in early Navajo **sandpaintings** and mythology; in the Navajo language it is called *tsil'ol-ni*, or "that which revolves," and is the basis on which the Nightway and Featherway sandpaintings are laid out.

Due to the negative connotations of the swastika owing to its adoption by Adolf Hitler's Nazi Party in Germany, around 1938 traders asked artisans to stop using it on their pieces. On

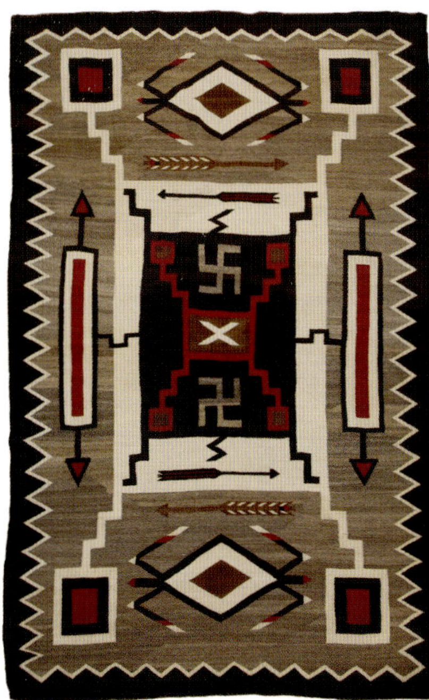

Navajo Crystal storm-pattern rug with whirling log (swastika) symbols, ca. 1920, 86" x 56".

February 28, 1940, in Tucson, Arizona, representatives from the Hopi, Navajo, Apache, and Tohono O'odham tribes signed a proclamation banning the use of the symbol in their artwork. In the document, the tribal leaders described the ornament as "a symbol of friendship among our forefathers for many centuries [that] has been desecrated by another nation of peoples." In recent years, the whirling-log motif has begun to reappear in some Native American work.

TABLAS / short, split, hand-**adzed** wood boards used in the ceilings of rooms, and sometimes as part of the roofing material in **portals**, beginning as early as the sixteenth century in Spanish settlements of the New World.

TABLITAS (Tabletas, Headpieces) / deriving from the Spanish word meaning "little board," these flat headdresses are constructed from wooden boards that are brightly painted with designs—often plants, fertility, and **rain symbols**—and frequently decorated with feathers. Leather and string are used to hold the boards together and to tie the tablita to the dancer's head. They are worn by Pueblo women in religious dances in the Rio Grande pueblos and in the Hopi Butterfly Dance. They are also part of the masks of certain Hopi **katsinas**, most famously the Hemis katsinas that appear in the Niman or Home

Dance held in the summer. Tablitas usually have a terraced or stepped design carved out along the top representing clouds. Yarn and cornhusks may also embellish the design. In the Hopi language, they are called *kopatsoki*.

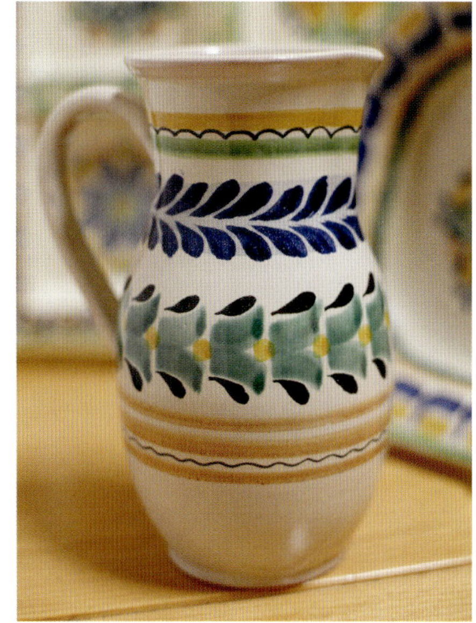

Gorky González (Mexico), talavera pitcher, 2011, glazed earthenware.

TALAVERA (Mexican majolica) / a type of tin- and lead-glazed earthenware decorated with hand-painted designs based on ceramics made in Talavera de la Reina and other Spanish cities. Talavera pottery has been made in the workshops of Puebla, Mexico, since the second half of the sixteenth century, in the form of tableware, architectural tiles, and utilitarian ware that has long been imported to the United States, especially to the Southwest.

Pottery found during excavation of historic sites in New Mexico indicates that during the eighteenth and nineteenth centuries Mexican *majolica* was used by the Hispano colonists and settlers there. Originally, talavera was made from one or more types of **clay** sifted for impurities, mixed together to get the right consistency, and then soaked in water tanks. It was then shaped on a potter's wheel to the desired form; given a soft firing and covered with an opaque, white glaze made from tin and lead; then decorated with mineral pigments and fired a second time. The hand-painted designs reflect a combination of influences, including Islamic, Moorish, Spanish, Italian, Chinese, and Mexican.

Talavera tiles *(azulejos)* have been particularly popular in the Southwest, where they are used to

create an "exotic" effect on the interior and exterior of homes and public buildings.

Despite a decline in production during the early nineteenth century, the art of talavera is still practiced in Puebla, as well as in Dolores Hidalgo and other cities in the state of Guanajuato, and is strictly regulated. Among those responsible for the revival of the art is Gorky González (b. 1939), who expanded his pottery skills by studying Oriental techniques in Japan.

Today a broad selection of handmade, labor-intensive, once-fired and twice-fired tableware and tiles, embellished with designs using non-lead glazes, are produced. In particular, tiles are still popular as decoration in buildings, furniture, and other items. Still made entirely by hand, authentic Talavera tiles and tableware are renowned for their bright mineral pigments, slightly raised designs, and high gloss. The tiles are also noteworthy for their concave and convex surfaces giving them a "pillowed" look when installed and for the "crazed" or **crackled** finish that becomes more pronounced with age.

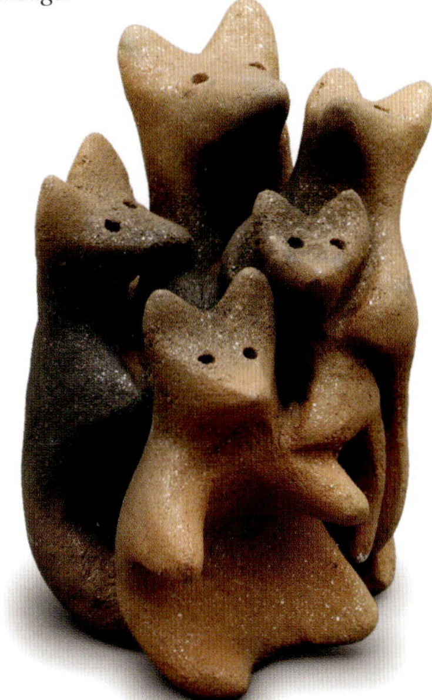

Jason Mondragon (Taos), micaceous storyteller pottery with fire clouds.

TAOS PUEBLO POTTERY / historically, Taos potters made traditional blackware pottery, as well as vessels of **mica**-rich clay. At the beginning of the twentieth century, when anthropologists and traders encouraged the revival of Native American arts and crafts, potters at this Pueblo were only making the durable **micaceous** wares that were superior for cooking and heating foods. Today Taos potters are primarily known for micaceous pottery—unslipped, unpainted, utilitarian golden-color wares of **clay** with mica flakes that produce a glittery surface on the pottery when fired. Taos micaceous clay pots, for which no **temper** is needed, have been handmade the same way for centuries: the walls of the vessel are built up by **coiling** the clay; the coils are smoothed and scraped with a file or other tool and sometimes minimal incised or **appliquéd** decoration is added; and finally the piece is **fired** outdoors. Most Taos pieces have **fire clouds**, the natural dark smudges that result during the firing process. High-fired micaceous clay vitrifies and becomes waterproof; however, some Taos potters use oil to further seal the inside of their bean pots and other cookware. Bean pots, one of the more traditional forms made at Taos, often have twisted-clay handles on the sides and on the lid. Among the other micaceous clay forms made at Taos today are bowls, vases, jars, and **storytellers**.

TAPESTRY / an extremely fine and technically difficult technique of weaving that dates back hundreds of years in Europe, used by both Native American and Hispano weavers of the Southwest, consisting of at least 80 **wefts** per linear inch (the average Navajo or Hispano textile is 30 wefts per inch) of extremely finely-spun yarn. The finer weave allows for designs of intricate geometric forms. The term tapestry is also generally used today for finely woven Native American textiles that are used as wall hangings or decorative fabrics (as opposed to wearing blankets or rugs), as well as for Hispano **Saltillo** sarapes. Among the first and most famous of the Navajo weavers to use the technique, in the 1940s, was Daisy Taugelchee (1909–1990) of the **Two Grey Hills/Toadlena** region in New Mexico. Encouraged by Charles Herring of the Toadlena Trading Post, Daisy, by the time she was thirty-five, had won numerous prestigious awards for her four-by-six-foot tapestries, woven in upwards of 115 wefts per inch in the colors of natural wool (tans, grays, browns, and golds). The tapestry technique continues to be carried on by weavers today, especially Navajos living in the Two Grey Hills/Toadlena area; their dazzling designs featuring muted natural hues and intense blacks continue to draw high praise, high prices, and win textile competitions.

TEEC NOS POS / meaning "trees in a circle," this term refers to a unique style of Navajo weaving distinguished by its elaborate and bold patterns and handspun yarn in a wide range of colors. The style developed about 1900 in the region around

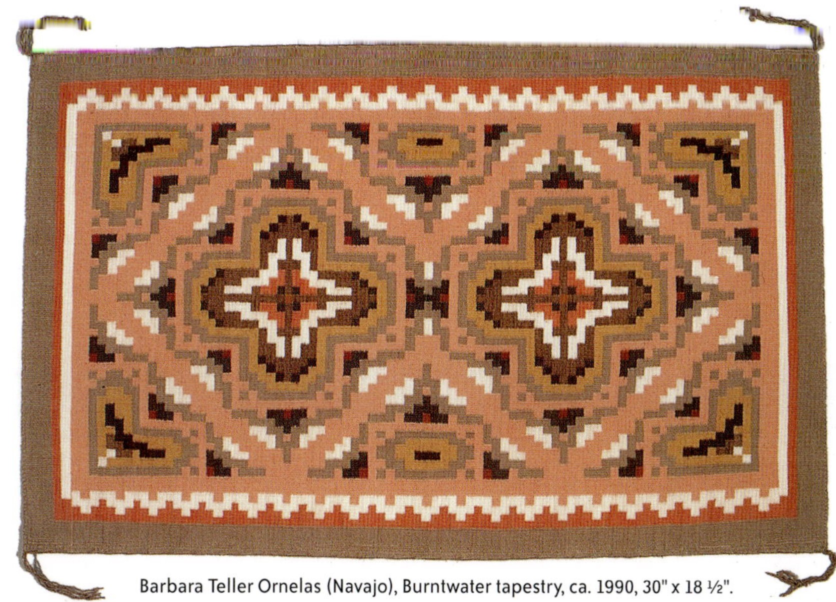

Barbara Teller Ornelas (Navajo), Burntwater tapestry, ca. 1990, 30" x 18 ½".

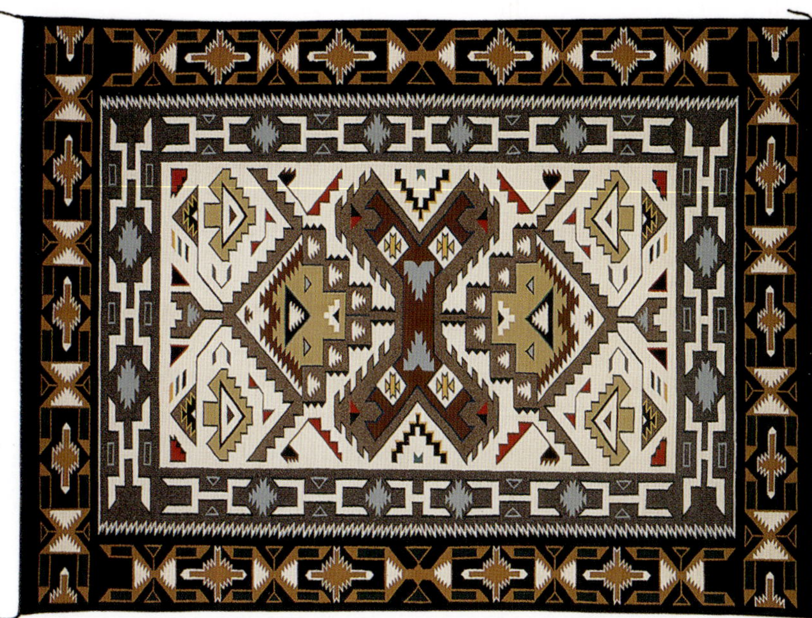

Pearl Ben (Navajo), Teec Nos Pos textile, 81 ½" x 59".

Teec Nos Pos—a **trading post** in the Four Corners region, where Arizona, Utah, Colorado, and New Mexico meet. Inspired by the Oriental rug patterns introduced to Navajo weavers by traders on the reservation, Teec Nos Pos rugs have figured borders, double-cross patterns, Xs, and hooked figures. Contemporary weavers working in this style primarily use commercial **yarns** of bright colors.

TEMPER / a coarse, stable material—such as sand, **shell**, tuff (or tufa), sandstone, or **potsherds**—crushed to a powder and added to raw **clay** to facilitate workability, promote even drying, and to prevent the risks of shrinkage and cracking during the drying and **firing** stages of pottery making. The clay and temper—a mixture sometimes referred to as "paste"—are blended together using hands (or feet) to get the right consistency. Some Pueblo potters use **metates** and manos to grind their temper. Because potters tended to use locally available materials as temper, archaeologists can identify the area in which historic pots were produced by examining the temper. A petrographic microscope is used to examine thin slices of pottery and determine the temper used. The rock or mineral fragments can then be matched to samples from specific areas of the Southwest.

TERNEPLATE (Terne) / a lead-tin alloy over iron or steel, darker in color and duller in finish (*terne* means "dull" in French) than tinplate, available in flat small sheets and used beginning in the mid-nineteenth century for pitched roofs, and from the beginning of the early twentieth century for **tinwork** by Hispano artisans of New Mexico. Tinworkers like the lovely, dark patina that develops on terneplate over time. Sheets of terneplate for roofing, which afforded longevity and reliable protection from the elements and fire, were small enough to be carried on wagon trains over the Santa Fe Trail. Terne was cheaper than steel coated with pure tin, a roofing material used elsewhere in the country as early as 1800.

Pitched and seamed metal roofs in the Southwest were a welcome change from the traditional flat earthen roofs that leaked water and dirt. However, in places like Santa Fe, New Mexico, in the early twentieth century they were banished as being ugly and not in keeping with the **Spanish Pueblo Revival style** of architecture then in vogue.

As a roofing material, terneplate was eventually replaced by corrugated metal. After the railroad reached New Mexico in 1880, corrugated iron was brought to the region in railway cars, making the price of pitched roofs even more affordable. A few historic houses in Santa Fe still have terneplate roofing, including the Felipe B. Delgado House, built circa 1890–91 on Palace Avenue. See also **tin sconces**.

TERRA-COTTA CONSTRUCTION / hollow terra-cotta blocks often laid in a manner evoking the irregularity of **adobe** walls and finished with coats of adobe-colored **stucco.** This building method was favored, beginning in the early 1920s, by such renowned Southwest architects as John Gaw Meem (1894–1983), who believed this material was much easier to maintain than authentic adobe (and therefore ultimately less expensive). In Santa Fe, New Mexico, the terra-cotta blocks were called "pentile" because most of them were made at the state penitentiary. The blocks were typically striated, so the mortar would adhere more readily to the surface.

TERRITORIAL REVIVAL STYLE / an architectural revival style established in the early twentieth century and still popular today, that draws upon elements from the provincial Greek Revival-style buildings of the American territorial period (especially those erected between the United States occupation of the Southwest in 1846 and the advent of the railroad in 1880). Typically constructed of **adobe**, these buildings are more angular versions of the **Pueblo Revival** and **Spanish Pueblo Revival** styles, featuring squared corners (instead of round), brick **dentils** or **coping** around the roofline, milled woodwork details such as pedimented **lintels** on window frames, and square **portal** posts. This popular revival style is still built in New Mexico today (generally with wall materials replicating the look of true adobe), as well as in Arizona (with gabled tin and shingled roofs). See also **Territorial Style—Arizona** and **Territorial Style—New Mexico**.

TERRITORIAL STYLE / Arizona / a freestanding, pitched-roof house centered on a lot, often constructed on a stone foundation with walls of fired brick and a gabled, pyramidal, or hipped roof often sheathed in tin tiles, built from about 1880 to 1910, and named after the period in which Arizona was a territory of the United States (1863–1912). Other characteristics include windows and doors topped with a flat **lintel** or a segmental arch; broad front porches with wood floors, rafters, and slender lathe-turned columns and trim; and floor plans that range from square (with one corner devoted to the exterior porch) to irregular (with bay-window projections). An architectural manner heavily influenced by the Anglos who migrated to the Southwest from the East or Midwest, the Territorial-style home features a number of prefabricated materials brought to the region via the railroad, including bricks, milled lumber, tin shingles, and cast iron. These homes were not well insulated and thus offered poor protection from extreme heat, unlike its predecessor—the **adobe**-constructed home (see **Sonoran row house**, **Sonoran Transformed**, and **Sonoran Transitional**).

TERRITORIAL STYLE / New Mexico / a mid-nineteenth-century architectural style unique to New Mexico, made possible by the introduction of whitewashed milled lumber, window glass, and kiln-fired brick brought to the region by Anglos who sought to "civilize" and improve the territory's rustic **adobe** buildings. The notable features of the style included a flat earthen-packed roof, adobe walls with sharp-edged corners, Greek Revival–style trim over windows and doors (including triangular **lintels** that recall temple pediments), white posts with molding capitals supporting porches, and fired-brick **coping** placed along the roofline in a pattern resembling classical Greek **dentils**. Typically, these one-story (and occasionally two-story) Territorial-style homes had milled posts and beams instead of the rough-hewn logs used as **vigas** and columns in **Spanish Colonial–style** homes. Named for the time period when New Mexico became a territory of the United States, beginning in 1848, the style flourished until about 1900.

TERRONES / from the Spanish name for a sod brick *(terrón)*, a form of earthen construction used along the Rio Grande River and more rarely in other areas of the Southwest, in which mud and sod bricks are cut from grassy river bottoms, stacked to dry thoroughly in the sun, and then laid in courses to build the walls of homes and other structures. This technique was mainly used in eighteenth- and nineteenth-century New Mexico, especially at Isleta Pueblo (south of Albuquerque) and in Rio Abajo—the lower Rio Grande Valley around Albuquerque, where marshland and sod was plentiful.

Typically, the bricks were cut from sod that had fairly deep roots (with the roots acting as a binder), using a shovel or flat spade, into long, rectangular

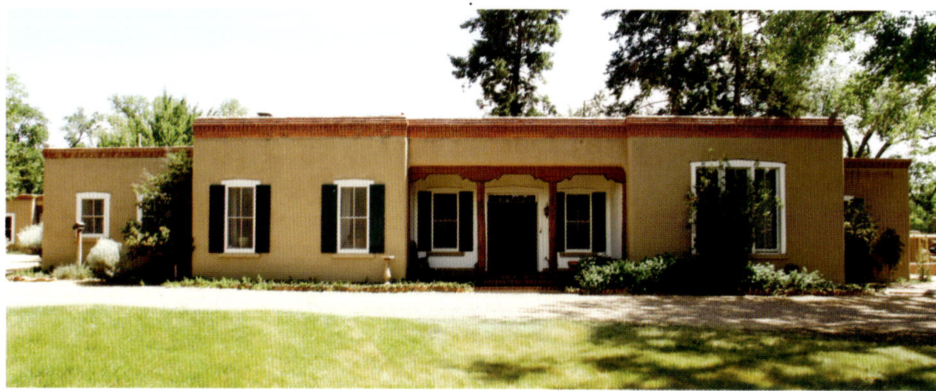

New Mexican Territorial Revival–style home, Acequia Madre House, 1925–26, Santa Fe.

bricks of about 7 x 7 x 14 inches. Terrones, sometimes used in combination with **adobe** bricks, provided tough, durable walls. However, surviving early examples of the technique are rare; among them are a few houses in Old Town Albuquerque and at Isleta Pueblo, where terrones were used for construction as late as the 1980s. Additionally, San Agustin Mission Church at Isleta, originally built in 1612 and one of the oldest extant Spanish Mission complexes in New Mexico, was built with a combination of terróne and adobe bricks.

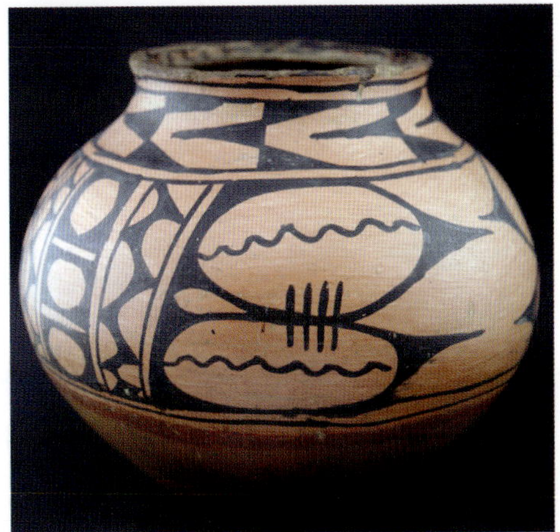

Tesuque Pueblo black-on-red pot, ca. 1890.

TESUQUE PUEBLO POTTERY / this Tewa-speaking pueblo, situated just outside Santa Fe, New Mexico, is known today for its **rain gods**, **micaceous** ware, burnished **black pottery,** and pieces brightly decorated with poster paints after **firing**. In its early history, beginning about 1600, Tesuque potters made polychrome vessels in styles that were very similar to other Tewa-speaking pueblos in the region.

By the early nineteenth century, they had developed their own distinctive motifs, including little hooks around diamond shapes, six-pointed flower motifs, prominent crosshatched key-shaped figures, and horizontal stems with paired leaves. Later in the century, they were still making micaceous ware in such forms as large jars and double-bellied water bottles. Beginning about 1880, when the railroad first reached the region, Tesuque potters began the tradition of making small micaceous novelty items for the tourist trade. Among the items they made over the following decades were rain gods; deer, frog, and bird **effigies**; and salt-and-pepper shakers.

Of all the northern Rio Grande pueblos, Tesuque made the largest number of **curio** items

(especially rain gods), probably because of its proximity to Santa Fe. The pottery making tradition seriously declined at Tesuque at the turn of the twentieth century, when work was limited to pieces that were sun-dried rather than fired and decorated with poster paints. The latter are known as "poster paint pots" and were made in many miniature forms such as a teacup and saucer. At present, Tesuque potters create micaceous wares, rain gods, **polychrome** vessels, and other forms.

THUNDERBIRD / a design featuring a bird with outstretched wings often stepped to symbolize clouds (sometimes confused with the **Knifewing** Dancer), possibly derived from the nighthawk. The thunderbird first appeared in ancient Native American art such as rock art, and rarely on **Mimbres** and **Sikyatki** bowls. Although the thunderbird has no known significance in Native American cultures of the Southwest, it became one of the most popular images ever to appear on **curio** and souvenir items made by Native Americans beginning in the early twentieth century. It was also a favored design motif in the early twentieth-century Hispano handwoven textiles made in Chimayó, New Mexico.

The word "thunderbird"—meaning a mythical, giant bird that represented thunder, lightning, and rain—appeared mainly in scholarly literature about the cultures of the Eastern Woodlands and Northwest Coast. It appeared in the Southwest in 1895 when archaeologist Jesse Walter Fewkes used it to describe imagery he observed on an ancient Sikyatki bowl fragment. Beginning in 1908, the thunderbird was used extensively by the **Fred Harvey Company** in their advertisements, publications, and **silver** jewelry (some of which was made by Native American silversmiths). According to some scholars, the design was inspired by a **pictograph** of a "thunderbird" seen by Fred Harvey Company employee Herman Schweizer near the ruins at Abó, near Mountainair, New Mexico.

Quickly embraced by tourists as an authentic Southwest "Indian symbol," the thunderbird appeared on spoons, brooches, watch fobs, and other

Santo Domingo Pueblo thunderbird mosaic pendant and necklace with tab beads, ca. 1930s/'40s, turquoise, plastic, vinyl record (or battery casing), shell, bone, and heavy string.

items. The stylized thunderbird with its broad chest, squared-off shoulders, stepped wings, and head facing to one side has an Art Deco appearance. Postcards and curio catalogues of the early twentieth century assigned the motif symbolism, such as the "sacred bearer of happiness," but these are of unknown origin. The motif continued to be used for many decades for silver jewelry by the Harvey Company and others, but with less precision and often mass-produced in "factories" where Native employees worked at benches stamping out imitation Native-themed designs.

Beginning in the Depression era and up until the 1960s, jewelers at Santo Domingo Pueblo made thunderbird mosaic pendant necklaces and matching earrings out of repurposed and found materials: hard rubber battery casings (for backings of the thunderbird mosaics); celluloid (to substitute for ivory and tortoise shell); tiny chips of **turquoise**; bakelite (for the bright reds, yellows, and other colors); and vinyl phonograph records (to replicate jet). This folk art jewelry was sold to tourists at roadside stands, on railroad platforms, and in curio shops by the thousands. Among the Santo Domingo jewelers to make them was Mary C. Lovato, who made her necklaces from pieces of plastic dishware, records, and even combs, mixed with turquoise and **beads** made from gypsum from a mine in the nearby Sandia Mountains. Today the thunderbird remains in use by Native artists as a "retro" motif and appears in various art forms from jewelry to bronze sculpture.

TIERRA AMARILLA / meaning "yellow earth" in Spanish, a type of **clay** deposit found in the Chama River Valley of New Mexico and elsewhere, used for the **mud plastering** of **adobe** walls and fireplaces in Spanish Colonial–era homes of the Southwest. It is also the name of a small community in northern New Mexico.

TIERRA BLANCA / meaning "white earth" in Spanish, a type of bright white **clay** found in New Mexico, used for the **mud plastering** and white-washing of **adobe** walls and fireplaces in Spanish Colonial–era homes of the Southwest. It was applied by hand, typically with a piece of sheepskin, and was intended to give an attractive finish to the mud walls.

TILES / Mexican / Spanish / handmade glazed-ceramic tiles used as a decorative feature in homes built in Spanish Revival styles, particularly during the 1910s through the 1930s. The tiles were imported from Spain and Mexico and eventually replicated by American manufacturers. Often hand painted or sometimes incised with relief designs, and generally featuring a rustic and uneven look, they were used to outline windows and door openings, to decorate stair

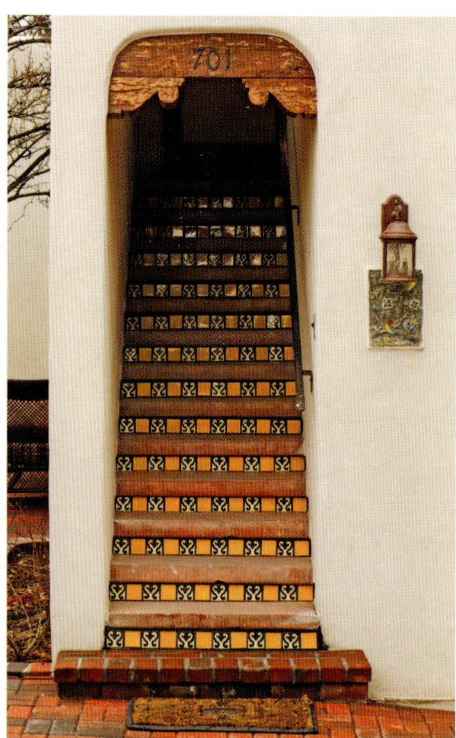

Mexican-tiled staircase, ca. 1930s, Santa Fe, New Mexico.

risers, as floor paving inside and out, for kitchen counters and back splashes, and for a variety of other ornamental uses. The subtle "crazed" or **crackled** and uneven surfaces, the imaginative and colorful painted designs, and the water resistance and sturdiness of Mexican tiles continue to make them popular decorative folk-art features of many houses throughout the Southwest today. They perfectly complement the earthen-colored **adobe** or whitewashed plaster walls typical of the region's homes. See also **Saltillo tiles** and **Talavera**.

TILES (Ceramic Plaques) / Native American / small slabs of **clay** of varying shapes that have been painted and fired, featuring decorative patterns or figures, made for the commercial market by Pueblo Indian potters of the Rio Grande valley, New Mexico, and of the Hopi villages in northern Arizona. Ceramic tiles have been made for utilitarian, decorative, and ceremonial purposes. Concerning the latter, ethnologist Alexander M. Stephen observed that in the early 1890s flat slabs of clay were being used at Hopi for various religious ceremonies.

Tiles and plaques became a popular tourist item in the mid-1890s due in part to the influence of Englishman Thomas V. Keam, who owned

a **trading post** near the Hopi villages. Tiles were made at New Mexico pueblos by the 1890s. When the **Fred Harvey Company** opened its Indian Department in 1902, tiles were a featured item. Often pierced by tiny holes to be used for hanging, tiles created for the curio trade are decorated with a vast array of images—Hopi **katsina** faces or figures, birds, flowers, and geometric designs. One of the more difficult pottery forms to make (they often curl or crack during the drying process, or explode during **firing**), tiles have become increasingly popular in recent years as an artistic outlet for Native Americans across the Southwest. Some, like Santa Clara Pueblo potter Jason Garcia, use the traditional tile form as a two-dimensional canvas for depicting various aspects of Pueblo life.

TINKLERS (Bells, Tin Cones, "Jingles") / small cone-shaped ornaments about one inch long, made from bone, stone, or **copper** and later primarily in tin (often cut from the lids of cans) and sewn onto Native American clothing, bags, pouches, baskets, and other items. The cones hanging from ceremonial dresses, shirts, or other ceremonial attire make a jingling or "tinkle" sound when struck together as the wearer walks or dances. For some Pueblo cultures, the tinklers are used on ceremonial garb because the sound they make resembles the sound of rain.

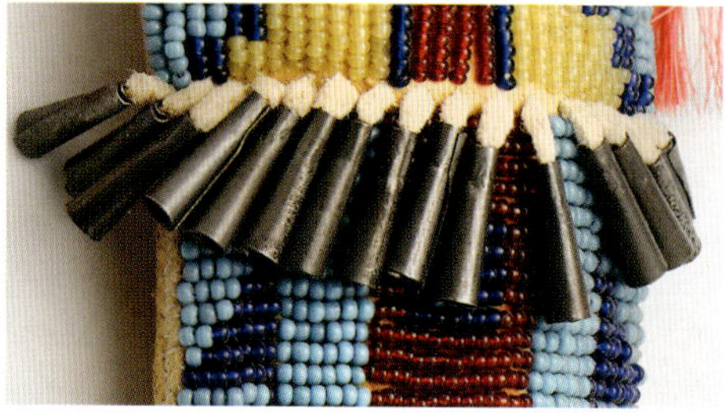

Dave Chavarria, tin tinklers on knife sheath, 2005.

Beginning in the late nineteenth century, Mescalero and Western Apache basket makers attached these small tin cones on the end of buckskin strips hanging from the rim, bottom, or sides of **burden baskets**. Western Apache basket maker Cecilia Nelson Henry (1902–1996) reintroduced and popularized this decorative technique on her burden baskets in the 1950s and 1960s. Henry cut the cones—called bells by Apache weavers—from Clabber Girl Baking Powder cans. Tinklers have been a hallmark on Western Apache baskets ever since. At the annual

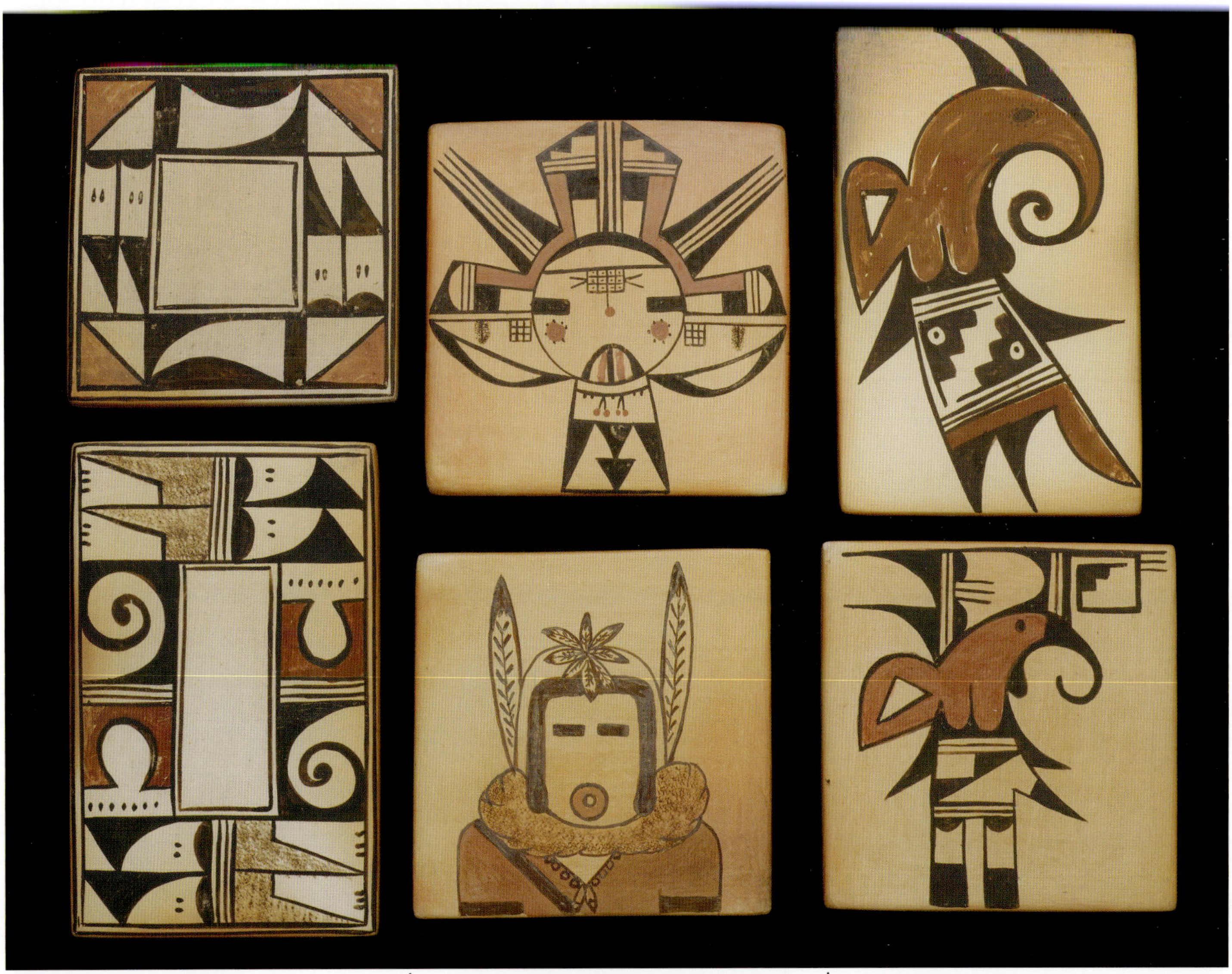

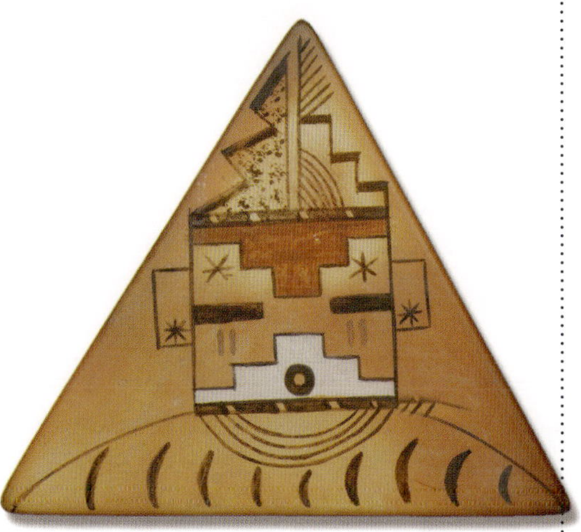

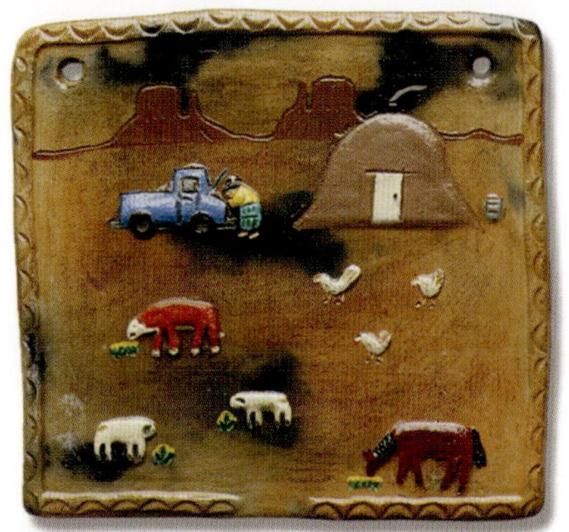

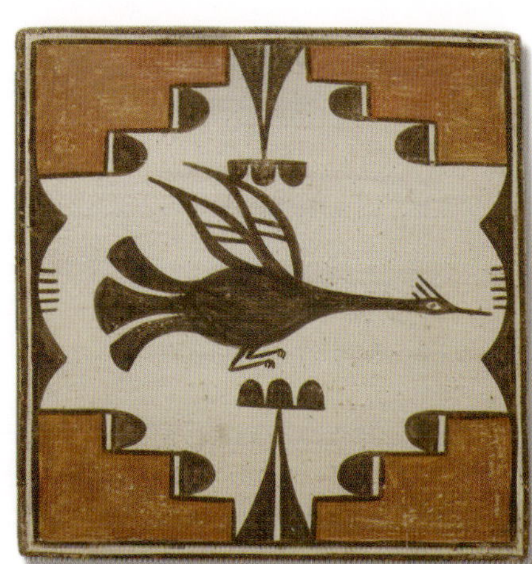

Clay tiles. Top row: Sadie Adams (Hopi–Tewa), ca. 1940s–'70s. Middle row: Sadie Adams, ca. 1940s–'70s; Lorna Lomakema (Hopi), ca. 1970s, Sadie Adams, ca. 1940s–'70s. Bottom row: Darlene James (Hopi), Elizabeth Manygoats (Navajo); Harviana Toribio (Zia), ca. 1940.

Gathering of Nations Powwow in Albuquerque, New Mexico, there is a special competition category called Women's Jingle Dress, for which Native women wear dresses adorned with an abundance of conical-shaped jingles, or tinklers. Today tinklers are commercially made in tin, aluminum, brass, and copper; but some Native artisans still fashion the cone shapes by cutting tin cans.

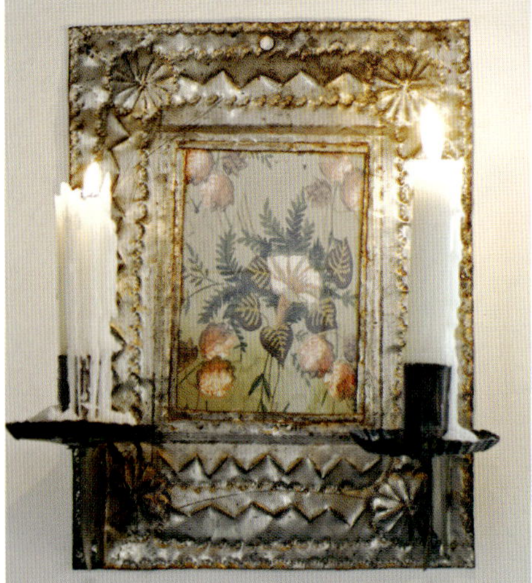

Wall sconce, early 20ᵗʰ century, tin and wallpaper.

TIN SCONCES / handcrafted from American tin containers—such as those used for lard and kerosene—using hammers, small punches, shears, and a soldering iron, and designed to be hung on the wall in homes, churches, and **moradas**. Some early tinsmiths also decorated the finished sconces with paint. In New Mexico, they are also called *candelabro de pared*. They were made by the mid-nineteenth century, after the opening of the Santa Fe Trail and arrival of U.S. troops in New Mexico. By the end of the nineteenth century, when lamp oil began replacing candles as the primary source of light, the demand for tin sconces declined dramatically. Many antique tin sconces were later electrified.

As with other **tinwork** forms, the tin sconce was revived in the 1920s and 1930s, when Spanish Colonial–style decorative arts and architecture gained renewed popularity in New Mexico, in part due to the founding of the Spanish Colonial Arts Society, establishment of the annual Spanish Market, and the opening of stores devoted to such work. At that time, tinsmiths had begun pur-

Nicolas Madrid (New Mexico), tinwork mirror with Mesilla combed glass and Apdodaca-inspired rosettes, 2011.

chasing sheets or rolls of tin, called **terneplate** (thicker and darker in color than the tin used in cans), to create sconces and other tin forms. Many descendants of the artisans who participated in the revival of tinwork in New Mexico, including Bonifacio Sandoval (now deceased), Angelina Delgado Martínez, and the Romero family of Santa Fe, are continuing the art form in the state today and passing the tradition down to yet another generation.

TINPLATE / sheet-iron coated with a thick layer of pure tin used from the mid-nineteenth century as a roofing material in the Southwest. Tinplate was a low-cost, lightweight, and low-maintenance roofing material. Tin shingles with embossed designs were popular for Victorian-style homes in the late nineteenth century in the Southwest and elsewhere in the country.

TINWORK / decorative and utilitarian items made of tin (also known as "poor man's silver"), typically hand-shaped with cutting shears, and decorated with designs made using **stamps**, punches, and a hammer, and a soldering iron to join separate parts. Tinwork is an art form that flourished in New Mexico after 1846, when the region became a territory of the United States and tin became readily available. Previous to that period, tinwork was imported to the region from Mexico. When large tin containers of food supplies were brought over the Santa Fe Trail to U.S. troops, tin cans became the favored source of material for New Mexican *hojalateros* (tinsmiths).

Throughout the latter half of the nineteenth century, Hispano artisans in New Mexico produced a variety of wares in tin, such as frames for European religious prints, **nichos** for **bultos**, *candelabros de pared* (**sconces**), *arañas* (chandeliers), *candeleros* (candlesticks), *faroles* (lanterns), and even the cone **tinklers** or "jingles" used on Spanish horsegear and popular among Native Americans for decorating their leather bags and ceremonial clothing. Early tinworkers were influenced by international styles, such as rococo and neoclassical, but many New Mexican artisans also developed their own motifs. Sometimes glass, strips of wallpaper (manufactured in Europe and eastern United States), or painted floral designs were incorporated into the tin objects.

By the end of the nineteenth century the Industrial Revolution, along with modern improvements such as gas and coal lighting, lessened the need for handmade tin such as wall sconces

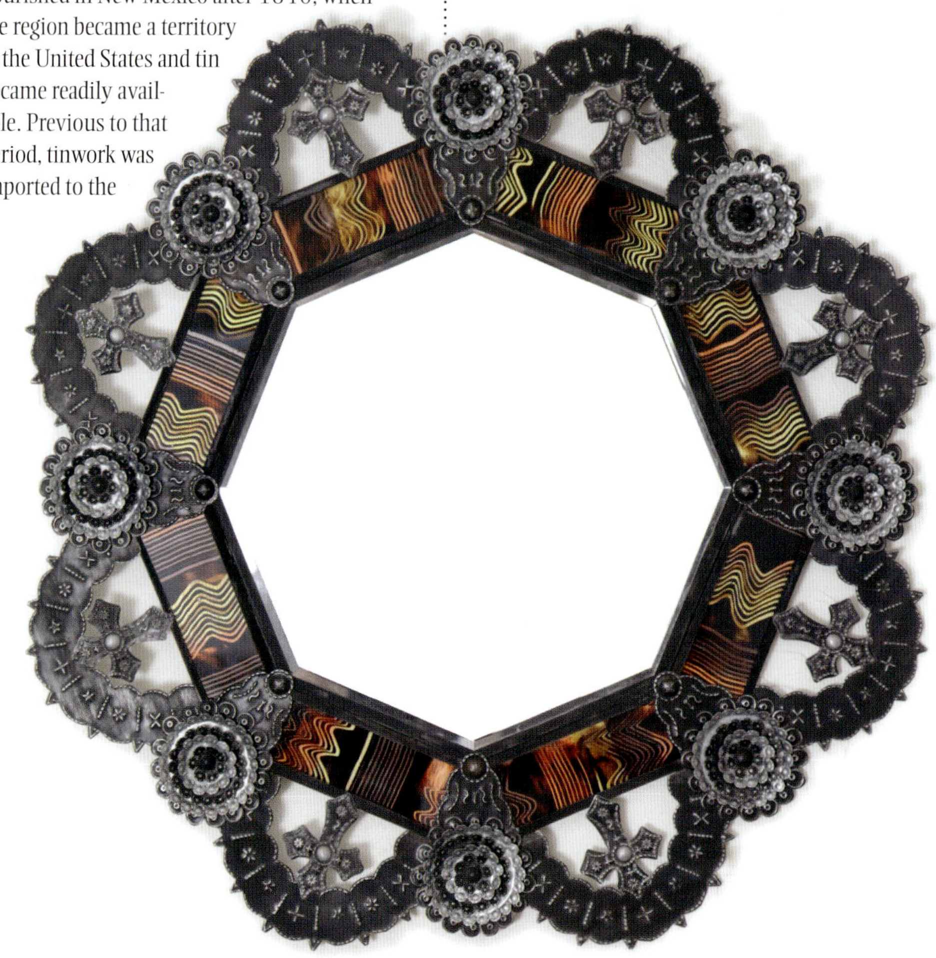

and other items. It was not until the 1920s and
'30s that the craft experienced a resurgence, due
in part to renewed public interest in traditional
Spanish Colonial crafts and a surge in popularity
of **Spanish Pueblo Revival–style** architecture that required regional decorative arts. The
revival was also due to the Spanish Colonial Arts
Society, which established the Spanish Market in
1926 (now an annual event held in Santa Fe in
July and December) and the opening of the Native
Market shop in Santa Fe in 1933. To meet the new
demand, artisans replaced cast-off tin cans with
terneplate—iron or steel sheets coated with an
alloy of lead and tin—a relatively rust-proof and
easy-to-shape metal. Terneplate also takes on an
appealing, darker patina over time. Important
figures in the revival were: Francisco Sandoval,
Francisco Delgado and Ildeberto Delgado, and
Emilio and Senaida Romero. In the mid-twentieth
century, Senaida Romero established the tradition
of putting **colcha** embroidery behind glass in tinwork crosses, boxes, frames, and other tin objects;
this innovation is still popular today.

Tinwork flourishes in twenty-first-century New
Mexico, where contemporary artisans experiment
with innovative uses of tin and add their own
artistic flourishes to this historic tradition. Many
continue to hand-shape and hand-punch tin with
ornate designs. Some **santeros/santeras** use
tin as frames for their **retablos** or for decorative
elements in their bultos. The favored material is
sheets of galvanized-steel, which does not take on
the same aged appearance as the old terneplate.

TOBACCO CANTEENS / Flasks (tabaqueras)

small containers made of **silver**, **copper**, or
leather, miniaturized versions of army canteens,
made in the nineteenth century by Native
American and Hispano artisans. They were common forms, particularly in New Mexico because
smoking was a popular pastime among men and
women of all classes during this period. Initially
made of plain buckskin, tobacco flasks were
hand wrought in silver by Navajo smiths by the
late 1800s; they were popular souvenirs among
the U.S. soldiers stationed at the nearby forts of
Wingate and Defiance. Difficult to make, silver
flasks were created by soldering together two
dome-shaped silver discs and attaching a silver
neck with a lid. Often Navajo smiths hid the seam
running around the edge with a strand of twisted
wire. First decorated with simple rocker-engraving,
silver canteens were later decorated with elaborate
stampwork designs and sometimes set with a

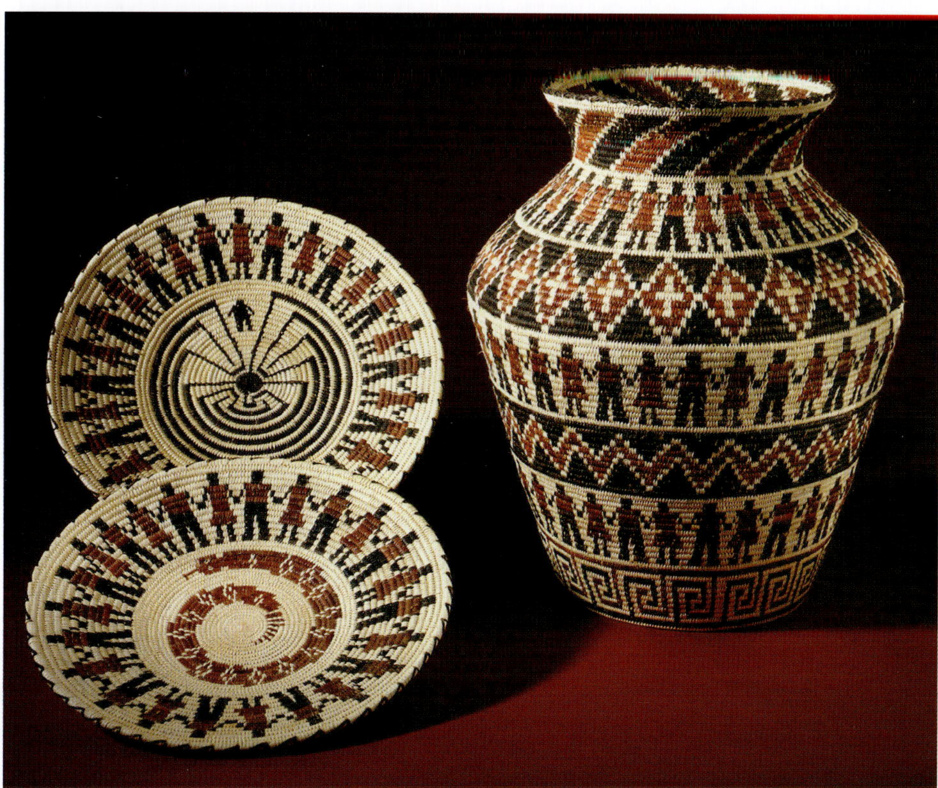

Mary Thomas (Tohono O'odham) baskets.

few small pieces of **turquoise**. Usually a leather
cord or chain was attached to one or two silver
rings soldered to the canteen seam and attached
to a ring in the top of the stopper, to keep the
stopper from being mislaid. A handful of skilled,
contemporary Native silversmiths still fashion
silver canteens for sale today.

Beginning in the nineteenth century, New
Mexican *plateros* (silversmiths) produced containers for locally grown tobacco (known as *punche*),
called *tabaqueras*, which were fashioned from
copper or silver and featured stamped decoration
or rocker-engraved dates or the names or initials
of the flask's owner. In addition, some Hispano
artisans made small, flat tabaqueras out of hardened buckskin or rawhide, molded into circular or
oval shapes with a round opening at the top, and a
wooden stopper.

TOHONO O'ODHAM BASKETS (Hoh) /

handwoven **coiled** baskets, **close-stitched** or
split-stitched, using the native plants of the
Sonoran Desert in southern Arizona, typically
beargrass (*Nolina microcarpa*, called *moho* by the
Tohono O'odham) for the foundation (or **warp**),
and sewn with bleached white **yucca** (*Yucca elata*,

or *tokway*) and black from the seed pod of the
devil's claw plant (*Proboscidea parviflora*, or
eehuk). Occasionally, a basket weaver may use red
from the root of the Spanish dagger or Shin Dagger plant (*Yucca arizonica*, or *oo'ee-dok*).

Traditionally, the Tohono O'odham used baskets
to carry water and firewood, prepare food, store
household items, in trade with other Native and
non-Native peoples, and for ceremonies. For
example, tightly woven bowl-shaped baskets were
made to hold the **saguaro** wine during the rain
ceremony; Tohono O'odham men sat in a circle
and took turns drinking from the baskets until
they were empty. By the twentieth century some
weavers were making finely coiled jars and trays (or
shallow bowls) for the tourist market. They were
distinguished by black-and-white geometric and
occasionally figurative designs. During the 1920s
coiled miniature baskets of **willow** and devil's
claw became popular. Tohono O'odham weavers
have traditionally relied on natural colors of the
plants to create patterns rather than utilizing dyes.

Before beginning, they spend countless hours harvesting and preparing their materials. The growing,
collecting, and preparing of the natural fibers requires
respect for and great knowledge of the natural world.

In the early 1900s most Tohono O'odham women were coiling baskets with willow stitching in a loose fashion. Well after World War II, coiled baskets with split stitches of willow or yucca spaced to create a variety of decorative patterns became common. Yucca became the favored sewing element, due in part to a drought on the reservation that caused willow trees to die off, and because yucca is much easier to harvest and work with. Therefore, willow baskets have become increasingly rare. Native devil's claw (*Martynia annua*) is still used extensively for the black decoration. In recent decades, some women have planted small gardens of devil's claw to use in their own baskets and to trade and sell to other basket makers.

Among the favored Tohono O'odham designs used today are: traditional geometric patterns, the **man-in-the-maze**, and pictorial imagery such as dancers, birds, cacti, desert animals (Gila mon-

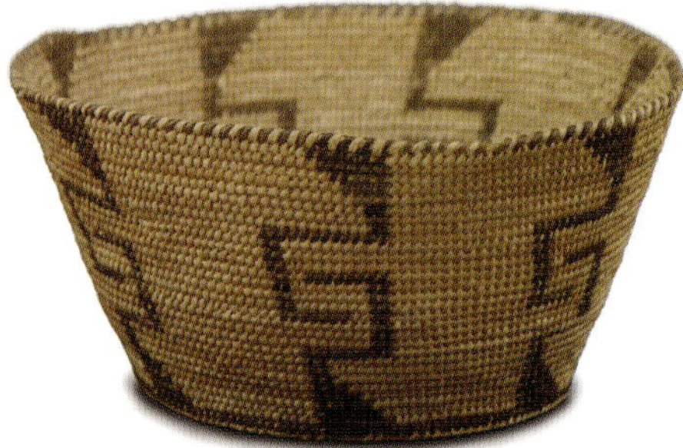

Tohono O'odham pictorial basket, ca. 1950.

sters, scorpions, etc.), and **crosses**. Also, some contemporary basket weavers (such as Annie Antone) have been inspired to replicate prehistoric **Hohokam** pottery motifs. The so-called "**friendship**" pattern has become increasingly popular on Tohono O'odham (as well as Pima) baskets, in which a group of men and/or women (usually shown from the back), holding hands, encircle the perimeter of the basket. The friendship pattern was influenced by an indigenous California (Yokuts) design. See also **basketry materials**, **basketry—ceremonial**, **horsehair baskets**, and **wire baskets**.

TONGUE-AND-GROOVE / a type of wood joint in which a raised area on the edge of one board fits into a corresponding groove in the edge of the other board, to produce a flush surface.

TORREÓN / a Spanish word for "defensive tower" (or "watchtower"), referring to typically round, two-story buildings with two- to three-foot thick **adobe**-brick or stone walls enclosing a space

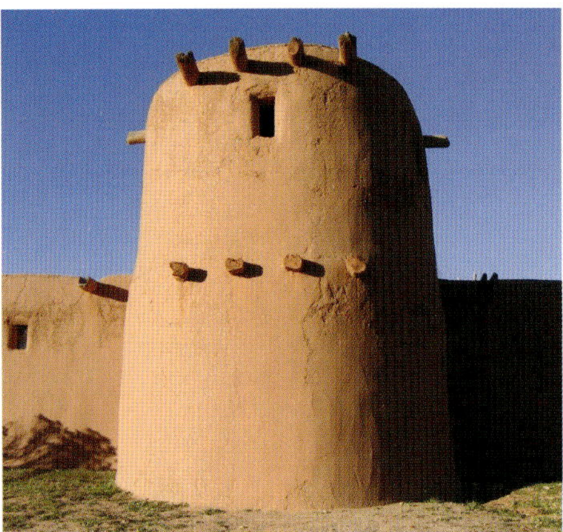

Torreón at El Rancho de las Golandrinas, Santa Fe, New Mexico.

up to 15 feet in diameter, with a flat **parapeted** roof reached through a trapdoor. They usually had one strong door and peepholes, or a few small barred windows, placed high in the walls. Constructed primarily for military purposes, torreones were built in Spanish Colonial New Mexico and Arizona at the corners of plazas to provide a rooftop vantage point for soldiers to ward off attackers, and refuge for women and children (in the upper room) and animals (in the lower room). They were also built to defend isolated farmsteads. Only the ruins of several torreones exist at several locations in the region. Re-creations may be seen at Arizona's Presidio San Agustín del Tucson and at the open-air museum El Rancho de las Golondrinas in La Ciénega, New Mexico. In the 1920s, when the **Spanish Pueblo Revival style** was popular in New Mexico, several Santa Feans built picturesque, round adobe houses that resemble Spanish torreones; among them was artist Frank Applegate and historian Ralph Emerson Twitchell.

TRADE BLANKET (Pendleton Blanket, Indian Pattern Blanket) / a high quality, machine-woven, commercially produced, woolen reversible blanket—made in a variety of colors and featuring bold geometric and/or **pictorial** designs, some of which have their roots in Navajo and other Native textiles (motifs such as crosses/stars, arrows, stepped-patterns, **swastikas/whirling logs**, and zigzags)—originally intended for the Native American market and sold at **trading posts** (and later through mail-order catalogs) in the Southwest (as well as on reservations elsewhere in the United States) beginning about 1892. It was

around this same time that post traders were encouraging Navajo weavers to concentrate on making rugs for the tourist trade, instead of weaving wearing robes for personal use and trade. Fringed blankets were manufactured for women and advertised as "shawls;" unfringed blankets were made for men and advertised as "robes." The earliest trade blankets were made entirely of wool and later on they were made of wool and a cotton **warp**.

These relatively inexpensive, commercially made trade blankets were embraced by the Navajo, Pueblo, and other Native peoples in the early twentieth century in the Southwest, and their appeal has never waned completely. They were originally worn as everyday attire, as well as used for bedding and as ceremonial dance shawls (as they are today) by Native American women. Some tribes (such as Zuni Pueblo) have buried their dead in trade blankets. Among the prominent early manufacturers of trade blankets were the Pendleton Woolen Mills of Oregon (established in 1896); Oregon City Woolen Mills; J. Capps and Sons, Jacksonville, Illinois; and Buell Manufacturing Company, St. Joseph, Missouri. Production of manufactured Indian trade blankets came to a halt in 1942, with the onset of World War II; however, Pendleton resumed making them in 1947, offering a much-reduced number of patterns. Pendleton, as well as Canada's Hudson's Bay Company (which has been marketing its "point" trade blankets in North America since

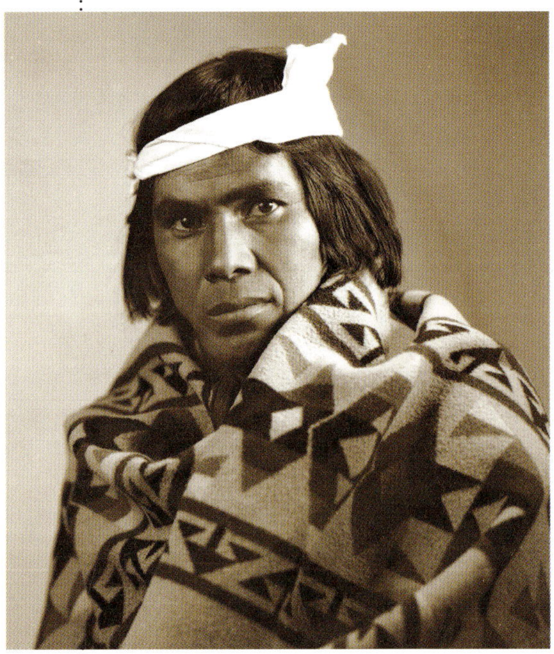

Bennie Garcia wearing a trade blanket, Santo Domingo Pueblo, ca. 1925–1945.

1780), are the only surviving major manufacturers of traditional "trade blankets" today. A large portion of Pendleton's blankets are still purchased by Native Americans. From the beginning, manufactured trade blankets were also marketed to the non-Indian trade, which also embraced (and continue to do so) these finely woven, colorfast, beautifully designed wool blankets. They have become a serious collector's item for individuals and museums.

TRADING POSTS / in 1796 Congress, under President George Washington, passed a bill intended "for the protection of Indians" that authorized the establishment of "trading houses" or posts among the Native Americans. The earliest traders were licensed by the government and were allowed to use Indian land without paying rent. The first trader to be licensed on the newly created Navajo Reservation was Lehman Spiegelberg of Santa Fe, New Mexico, on August 28, 1868.

By the late nineteenth century at various locations on Indian reservations throughout the Southwest, trading posts operated by non-Indian business men and women, often aided by Navajos hired as managers, offered an important link between the reservation and the rest of the world. They heavily influenced the production and sale of Native arts and crafts. In exchange for dry goods and groceries they purchased sheep, wool, rugs, **silver** jewelry, and baskets from the Native peoples. Trading-post owners also provided Native Americans with materials, designs, and a steady and secure market for their handmade wares.

By encouraging the production of crafts for the increasing number of tourists arriving by train, new shapes, sizes, and colors of baskets, textiles, pottery, and jewelry were produced for the **curio** trade. In seeking a competitive edge over one another, post owners developed regional styles— as seen in the **Two Grey Hills**, **Ganado** Red, and other rug weaving patterns that are associated with specific trading posts.

In some instances, trading post owners introduced or encouraged the manufacture of certain crafts. For example, C. G. Wallace helped create a market for Zuni jewelry and encouraged the styles of silver and **turquoise** jewelry that are now closely identified with Zuni Pueblo, enabling many Zunis to earn a living or supplement their income by making jewelry.

Today, controlled through a series of regulations and by the terms of leases, traders on Indian lands continue to play an important role in

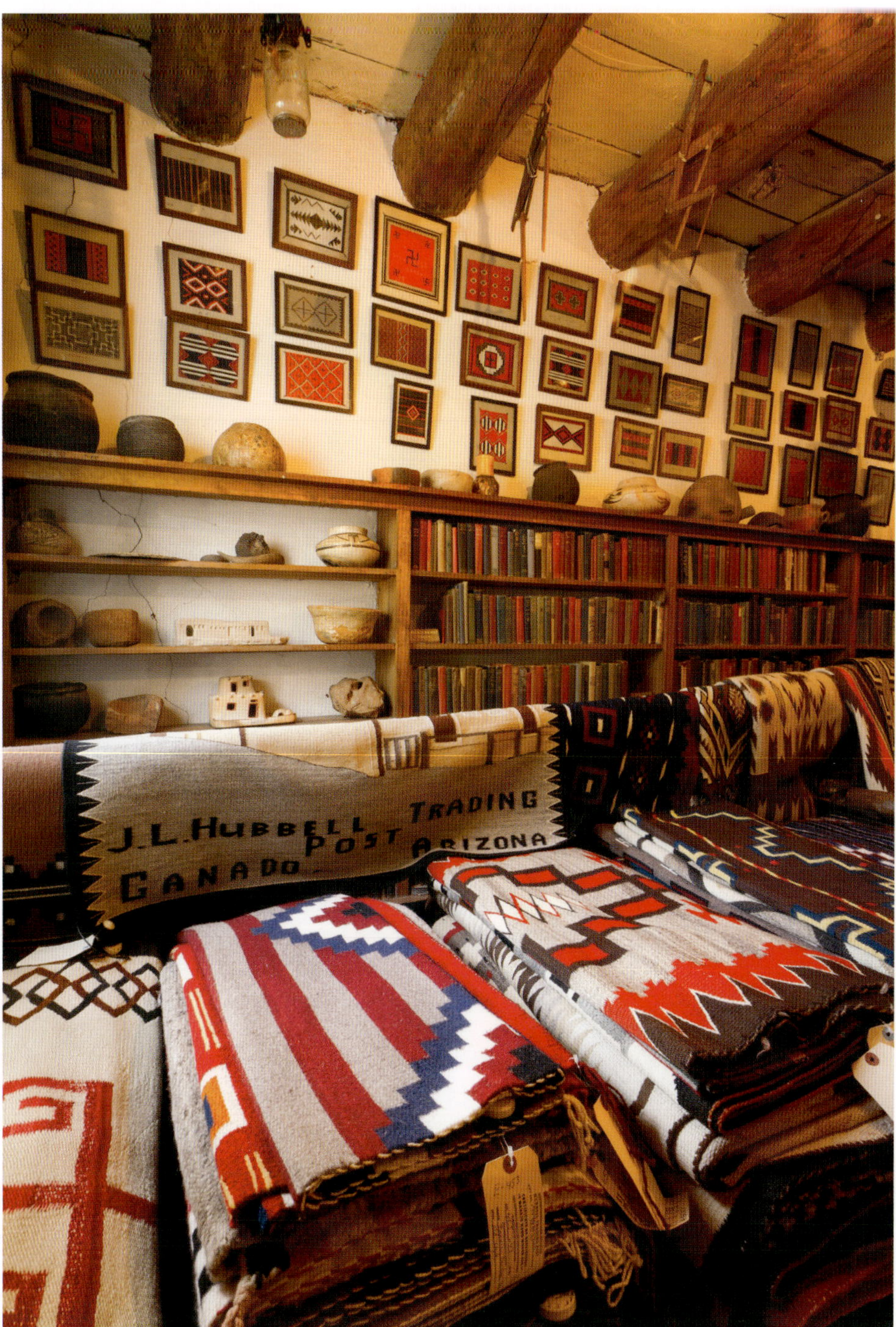

Handwoven rugs stacked in piles at Hubbell Trading Post, Ganado, Arizona.

encouraging and supporting new ideas in Native American decorative arts. They also help Native weavers, silversmiths, and other artisans get fair prices for their work and offer them opportunities to demonstrate their crafts for visitors. See also **Burnt-water rugs**, **Crystal Trading Post**, **Ganado Trading Post**, **Hubbell Trading Post**, **Keams Canyon Trading Post**, **Klagetoh Rug style**, **Route 66**, **Teec Nos Pos**, **Two Grey Hills textiles and Trading Post**, and **Wide Ruins Rug style and Trading Post**.

TRASTERO (Cupboard) / a tall freestanding cabinet of framed construction, often divided into upper and lower sections, made in Spanish Colonial New Mexico and used for storage. The double doors are either solid or embellished with spindles, cutouts, or other decorative patterns. Spindles, a traditional element on Spanish cupboards used to store food, allowed ventilation for the food storage areas in trasteros. In the eighteenth century, cresting (a grooved, decorated top section) began appearing in trasteros both in Spain and in the New World. The most popular crest designs were (and continue to be) **rosettes** and scalloping. Contemporary furniture makers frequently create trasteros, often adding their own innovative flair to this historical cabinet form. See also **armarios**.

TRAYS / a term used in the literature on Native American basketry to describe **coiled** handwoven trays, which are a shallow, round basket shape that have been made for centuries by a number of different Southwestern Native basket-weaving traditions. They have a variety of uses, both ceremonial and utilitarian—such as winnowing wheat, collecting grains, seeds, and fruits, and for dispensing food and other items. Among the tribes to make them are the O'odham, Apache, and Paiute tribes. **Coiled** trays remain a popular basket form today; they lend themselves well to **pictorial** designs.

TREE OF LIFE / an ancient motif usually consisting of a tree, and sometimes biblical figures, birds, and other animals. The Tree of Life is a traditional and popular subject of artists throughout the ages, including those of the Southwest and Mexico, where the design appears in a variety of forms and mediums including **clay**, wood, and wool. The Tree of Life is drawn from the Book of Genesis and traditionally has symbolized fertility, the life cycle, and rebirth. However, the specific meaning and purpose can vary depending on the region in which it is made, as well as the artists' culture and preferences.

Clay candelabra-style Trees of Life created in central Mexico were originally intended to teach the Biblical story of creation to native peoples during the early colonial period. Today Trees of Life are still made in Mexico for religious and decorative purposes. The Mexican Trees of Life are adorned with flowers, birds, animals, and leaves and feature a base figure that can vary from Madonnas and saints to Adam and Eve or skeletons, depending on the purpose of the piece. Varying in size from miniatures to large-scale sculptures, Mexican Trees of Life are typically made from mold-made and hand-formed pieces of clay joined together, sometimes

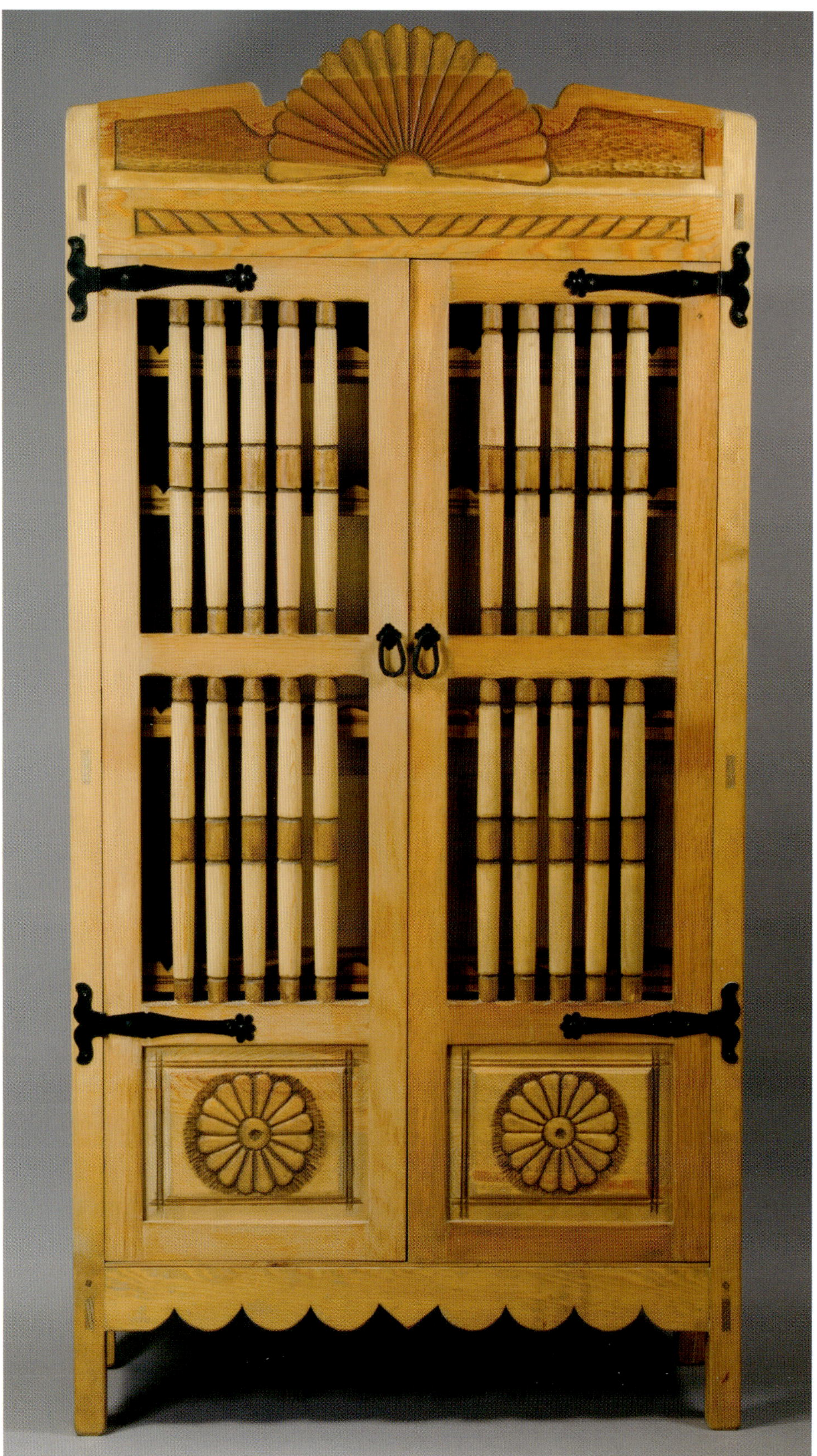

Abad Eloy Lucero (New Mexico), trastero, 1999, hand-carved pine and ironwork.

with galvanized wire to hold together large tree sections. They are then single-fired in a kiln. The trees are either left plain, **slip** decorated, or elaborately painted. To achieve the latter, after firing the piece is whitewashed with a mixture of zinc oxide and calcium carbonate, painted with a mixture of aniline **dyes** and tempera, and then coated with a homemade varnish of tree resin mixed with prickly pear cactus juice.

The term Tree of Life is also used in the Southwest to describe a Navajo **pictorial** rug design in which a tree is depicted in the form of a sacred corn stalk, usually growing out of a **wedding**

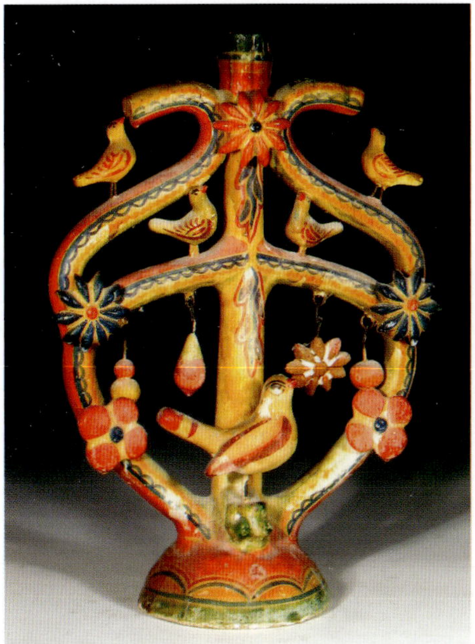

Heriberto Castillo (Mexico), Tree of Life, ca. 1960, cold-painted ceramic.

basket, and accompanied by paired birds or other animals such as butterflies or cows. Based upon a **sandpainting** motif from the Blessingway Ceremony, the Tree of Life motif first appeared in Navajo textiles around 1900. **Corn** is considered a life-giving force to the Navajo; the "Tree of Life" pattern is an example of how the Navajos transformed an ancient motif into a meaningful symbol relating to their own religion.

In New Mexico, Trees of Life have also been made by various artisans including the López family, woodworkers known throughout the Southwest for their **chip-carved**, unpainted religious figures. From the small village of Córdova, these artisans carve the trees (usually with branches and small birds or other animals attached) out of aspen and cedar, and they use pegs and/or glue to join the separate pieces. See also **Córdova woodcarving**.

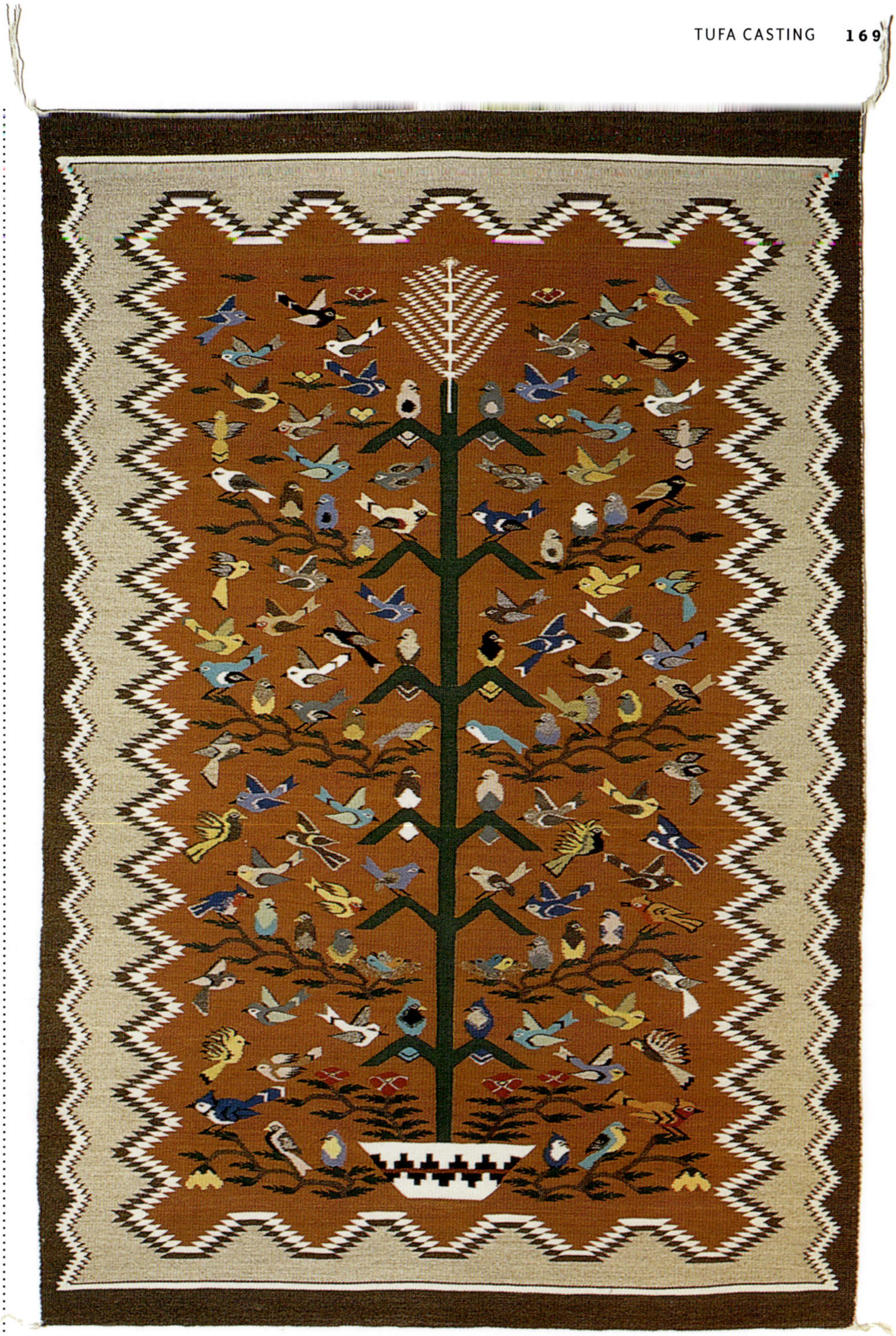

Evelyn Tsosie (Navajo), Tree of Life textile.

TREE-RING DATING / See **dendrochronology**.

TUFA CASTING / a technique in which lightweight, porous, compressed volcanic ash, which occurs in several areas of the Southwest, especially on and near the Pajarito Plateau, and is called tufa or tuff, is used to make a mold for casting **silver** or gold jewelry pieces. The shape and design is carved into the stone (the mirror image

of what the artist wants the finished piece to look like). Then, a funnel is carved to allow the molten silver to flow and small air channels are added, leading from the extremity of the design, to allow air to escape and the silver to flow more smoothly. The stone is blackened with smoke (to prevent the molten metal from sticking to the mold), and finally hot liquid silver or gold is poured into the design. When the silver or gold has cooled, the hardened piece is pulled from the cast. Tufa is easy

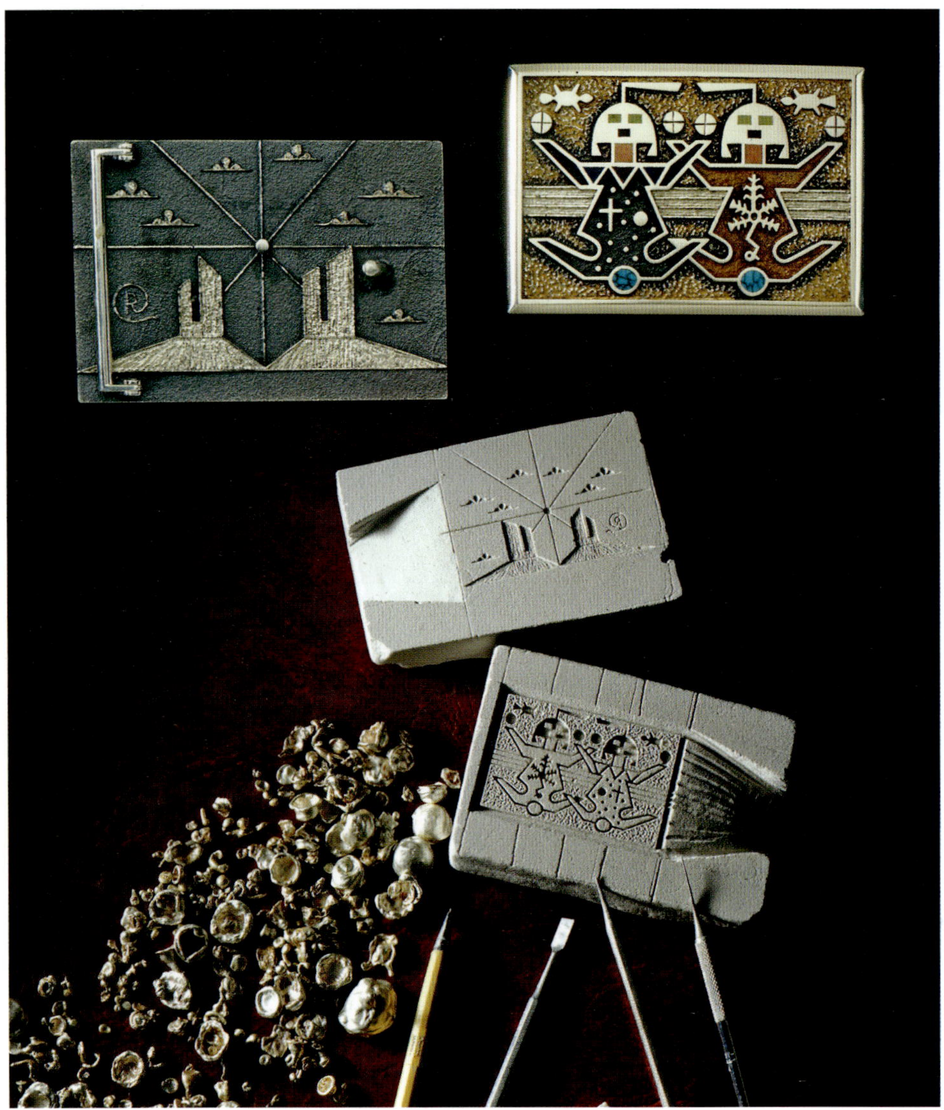

Tufa-cast jewelry by Ric Charlie (Navajo), showing the double tufa mold used for this two-sided belt buckle.

green), and often all three may appear together in the same rock.

Historically, turquoise was **inlaid** on a variety of objects from **shell pendants** to ceremonial masks to combs; was used to create **beads** for necklaces; and **fetishes** used for religious purposes were carved out of it. Turquoise was also an early and important commodity for exchange. The stone received its name from Turkish traders who called it *turceis*. English speakers adopted the French word for the stone—*turquois*—and added the letter "e." The Navajo and other peoples of the American Southwest referred to the stone by its Nahuatl name, *chalchihuitl*, a term they used until the late 1800s.

Artifacts adorned with turquoise, raw turquoise stones, and turquoise beads have been discovered in over two hundred Ancestral Puebloan mining sites of the Southwest, indicating that Native Americans have mined turquoise for almost two thousand years. One ancient mine is located in the Cerrillos Hills, about twenty miles southwest of Santa Fe, New Mexico. The stone's sacredness is evidenced by the numerous turquoise offerings recovered in ancient burial rooms and at **kiva** sites throughout the Southwest, including at Chaco Canyon, New Mexico.

Turquoise has a variety of meanings and uses for the Native cultures of the Southwest. For the Navajos, turquoise symbolizes cosmic harmony and beauty—a concept called *hozho*. Traditionally, Navajos have carried a piece of turquoise in a medicine pouch for its healing and protective powers. Because the Navajos also considered turquoise a token of well being, the stone has long been a favored gift for family and friends. Turquoise represents the color of water and is therefore an important stone in Navajo prayer offerings for rain. Apache warriors and hunters once attached tiny bits of turquoise to their bows

to carve and is resistant to high temperatures, but the molds break easily and do not hold up well to repeated use.

The method was first used by Navajo silversmiths in the mid-1870s for creating bracelets, **ketohs**, and other items. Today it is used by Navajo and Pueblo smiths—including the famed Coriz family jewelers at Santo Domingo Pueblo and the highly accomplished Navajo jewelers Darryl and Rebecca Begay—for a variety of items from jewelry to buckles to **canteens** to **seed pots**.

TURQUOISE / a semi-precious stone—hydrous aluminum phosphate colored by **copper** salts—ranging in hue from very pale green to deep sky blue (those with more copper content appear bluer). Turquoise varies in strength from soft and somewhat porous to very hard and of gemstone grade, and is found in the arid and semi-arid mountainous regions of the American Southwest including Arizona, Colorado, Nevada, New Mexico, and Utah. The stone has been of spiritual, economic, and decorative significance to native peoples since at least AD 300. Turquoise, uniform in color or containing matrix—distinct patterns of lighter or darker lines of other natural elements—was typically found with its mineralogical cousins: azurite (a deep blue), malachite (a deep green), and chrysocolla (blue or

Kirk Smith (Navajo), Kingman turquoise bracelet, sterling silver.

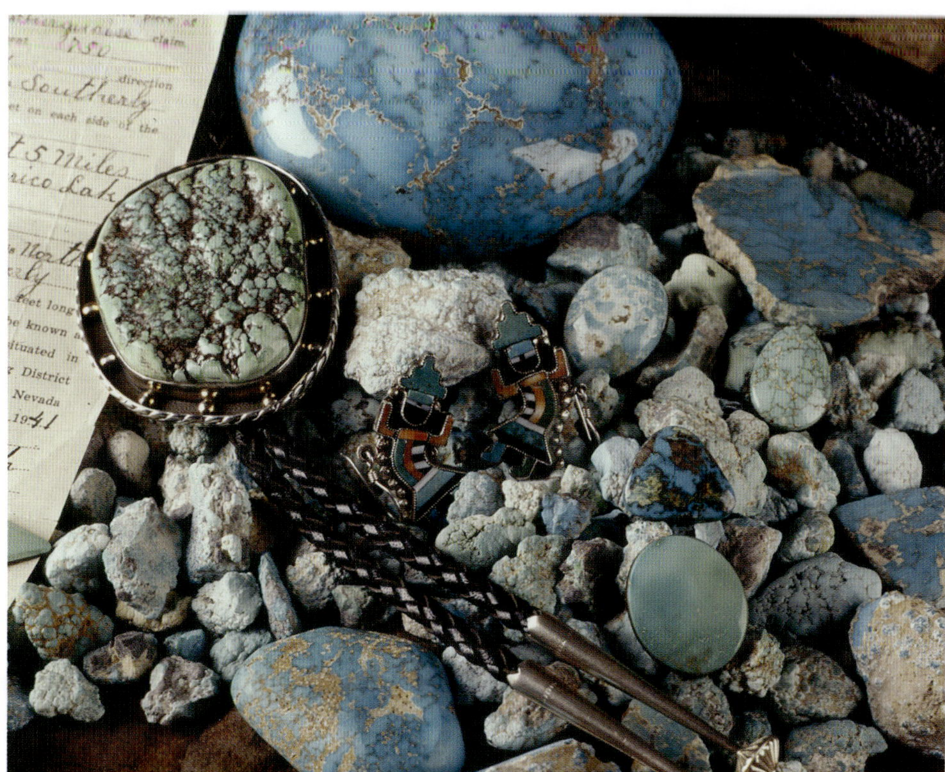

ABOVE: Turquoise from the Carico Lake district in Nevada, with a Navajo bolo tie and Zuni inlay earrings.
RIGHT: Arland Ben (Navajo), Candelaria turquoise ring, sterling silver with gold petroglyph overlay.

Many Southwestern mines are no longer active; much of the turquoise used in jewelry and silverwork today is imported from China with some also coming from turquoise mines in Iran, Chile, and Mexico. In recent years, some grades of turquoise have gone up so much in value that they are worth more per ounce than gold or platinum. Only ten percent of the turquoise mined is of gem quality; most turquoise seen on the market today has been stabilized—meaning it has been injected with clear, colorless acrylics to toughen and harden the stone and enhance its color. The Indian Arts and Crafts Association (IACA) does allow stabilized turquoise to be used; however, they do not allow low-grade turquoise that has been treated with a blue dye to enhance its color, or turquoise that has been reconstituted—turquoise pulverized into tiny chips mixed with epoxy and worked into cakes or stones used just like natural stones. Under Federal Trade Commission guidelines, consumers must be told if a stone has been treated and how. Most of the finest Native American jewelers use stabilized turquoise; natural gem-quality turquoise is used primarily by top jewelers and commands much higher prices.

TWILL WEAVE / a textile structure in which the **weft** passes over and under two or more **warps** and the floats are aligned to form diagonal lines, zigzags, or diamond shapes. The technique typically creates a fabric that is a durable textile and one with geometric patterning. Historically, Pueblo weavers employed twill in a balanced format (equal amounts of warp and weft showing) to make solid-colored **mantas** and other garments. Navajo weavers formerly used a complex twill tapestry weave to create weft-faced mantas and saddle cinches. Since the late nineteenth century, they have used this method for multi-colored weft-faced rugs that work well as **saddle blankets**. After about 1900, Anglo-Americans and other visitors to the region purchased these thick twill-weave blankets to take back as souvenirs. Initially made using handspun natural-color wool (grays, black, tans, off-white), later vegetal- or synthetic-dyed **yarns** of various colors were incorporated. Navajos still make twilled saddle blankets for their own use, and some contemporary weavers incorporate twills innovatively in their rugs.

to make their arrows fly straight, and wore turquoise as protection against enemies. The Pimas of Arizona carried turquoise to ward off illness. The Zunis of New Mexico, who associate blue turquoise with Father Sky and green turquoise with Mother Earth, carve fetishes from turquoise or use inlaid turquoise for eyes, mouths, or attachments to enhance their power. **Katsina** dancers at both Zuni Pueblo and the Hopi villages wear turquoise necklaces, and powdered turquoise is a common offering to accompany a prayer.

TURQUOISE SILVER JEWELRY / considered by many in the Southwest to be more precious than gold, **turquoise** has been used in **silver** jewelry, as an enduring expression of Navajo and Pueblo aesthetics and culture, since at least 1880. Among the first Native American silversmiths to set turquoise in silver and other metal objects was Atsidi Sani and his brother Slender-Maker-of-Silver, and a Zuni craftsman named Kineshde. With the arrival of the Atchison, Topeka and Santa Fe Railway in northern New Mexico and Arizona in the early 1880s, the enthusiasm for authentic, handcrafted silver and turquoise jewelry among settlers and tourists from the East increased. The

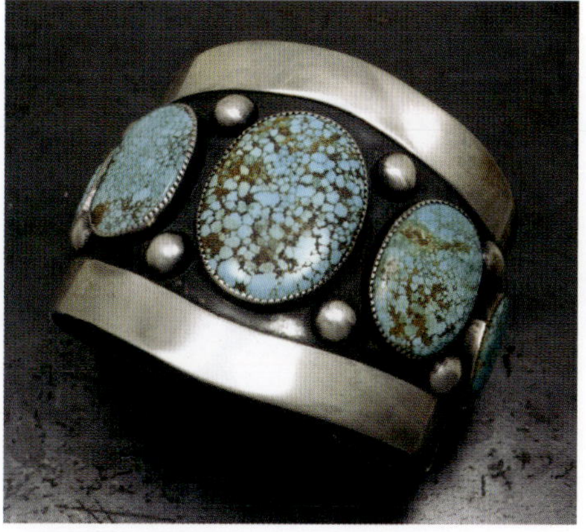

Number 8 turquoise and silver cuff bracelet.

trade provided Native artisans of the American Southwest with much-needed income.

By the first decade of the twentieth century, precut turquoise became available; after 1940, machine-cut turquoise stones, cut in uniform and standardized shapes and sizes, were widely available for purchase. Individual jewelers, however, also continued to cut their own stones, with the aid of machinery, from the end of World War II to the present, many of them excelling at the skill of matching and cutting of stones.

TWINING / an ancient technique used for making the earliest baskets in the Southwest and in other regions, in which two or three slender and flexible splints (the **weft**) are twisted around rigid foundation elements (the **warp**). The different types of twining are called twisted, plain, and diagonal. When open areas exist between warp and weft elements in twined pieces, it is called "open-work." The method produces a lightweight but sturdy container, and thus was used for **burden baskets**, jar forms, and bowls. Peoples of the Desert Archaic era (beginning in 6000 BC) are the earliest known artisans to use twining. The materials they used were **willow**, **sumac**, mulberry, and **yucca** leaves. Today twining is still used by the Havasupai, Haualapai, San Juan Paiute, and Western Apache peoples. See diagram on page 186.

TWO GREY HILLS/TOADLENA / Textiles and Trading Posts / a Navajo rug and **tapestry** style known for its technical virtuosity and distinguished by its exclusive use of fine handspun wool (from locally raised sheep) in natural colors—browns, greys, tans, golds, and whites—and its sophisticated harmonious designs that incorporate one or more borders and complicated highly detailed motifs (such as terraced diamonds and triangles). The rug style developed in the mid-1920s, and the tapestry style in the 1940s, and is named after the Two Grey Hills and Toadlena trading posts, situated nearby one another in northwestern New Mexico. Weavers in the area have taken work to both posts for generations.

In developing this distinctive style Navajo weavers collaborated with two traders: Ed Davies, who bought the Two Grey Hills Trading Post in 1909, and George Bloomfield, the resident trader at Toadlena. Together they encouraged Navajo women in their communities to improve the quality of their textiles by cleaning the wool more thoroughly, spinning the wool finer, and by creating new designs. By the 1960s the popularity of the Two Grey Hills/Toadlena textiles and the prices they achieved had soared and smaller textiles became more common. Weavers expanded the traditional palette, creating works that contained as many as ten different shades of natural wool.

In the 1970s and '80s weavers began focusing on fine tapestries and conducted business through shops and galleries off the reservation. By the late 1990s many master weavers had passed away and tourism to the region declined, resulting in

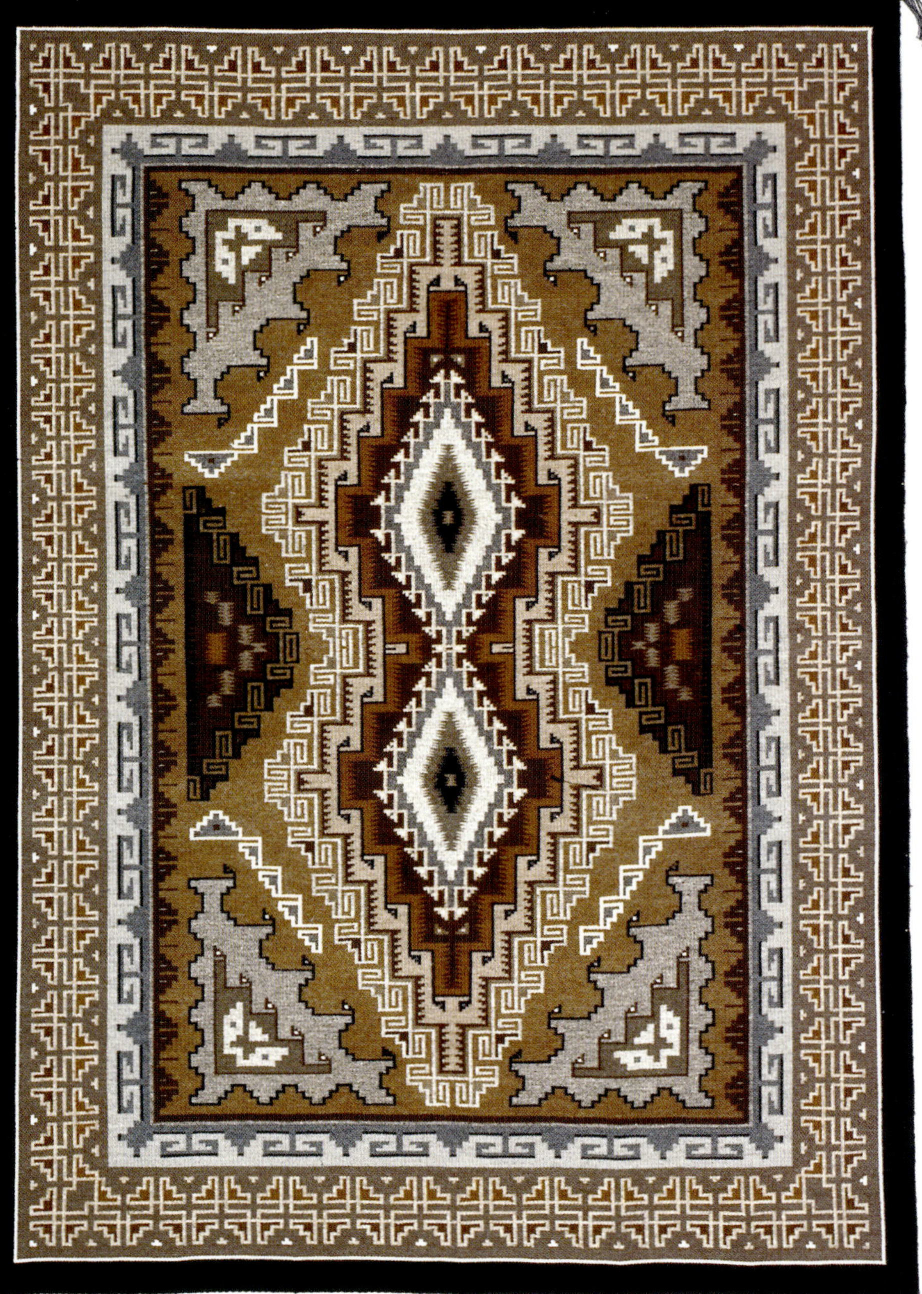

Rita Bedah (Navajo), Two Grey Hills textile, 72 ½" x 53".

diminishing sales of these textiles. Currently, however, the Two Grey Hills/Toadlena style is flourishing once again, made by a new generation of weavers. This revival is due to the dedication to the weaving tradition of Navajo families, especially the Teller-Ornelas family, and is due in part to the encouragement of post traders like Mark Winter, who purchased the Toadlena Trading Post in 1997 and provided a ready market for Two Grey Hills/Toadlena–area weavers. Characterized by its fineness of weave (from 80 to 120 wefts per inch) and high quality wool, and intricately executed highly detailed designs, Two Grey Hills/Toadlena has proven to be one of the most popular and enduring of the Navajo textile styles.

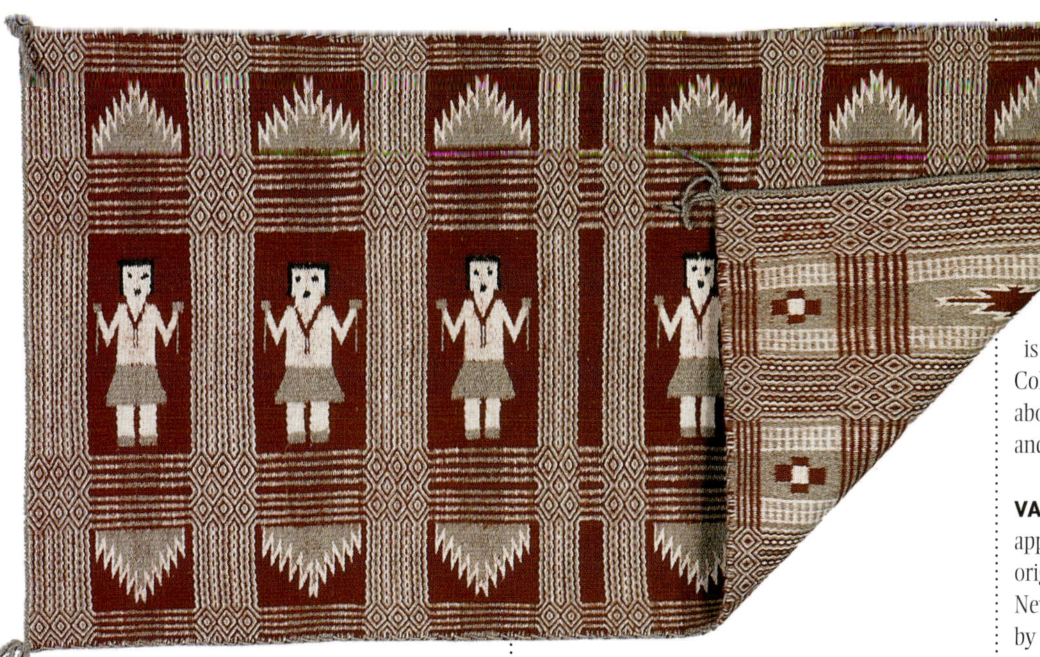

yarns colored with synthetic dyes (both available to weavers in the region by 1860). Named after the small village of El Valle, the Vallero star pattern was borrowed by some Navajo weavers and incorporated into their own blanket styles. Textiles with this pattern were also made in the village of Trampas, New Mexico; thus, the pattern is sometimes referred to as "Trampas Valleros." Colorful blankets of this type almost died out about 1900; however, they are still being woven and are much admired today.

VARA / a standard unit of measurement equal to approximately 33.6 inches (or 84 centimeters), originating in Medieval Spain and used in colonial New Mexico by carpenters to make furniture and by builders in constructing homes.

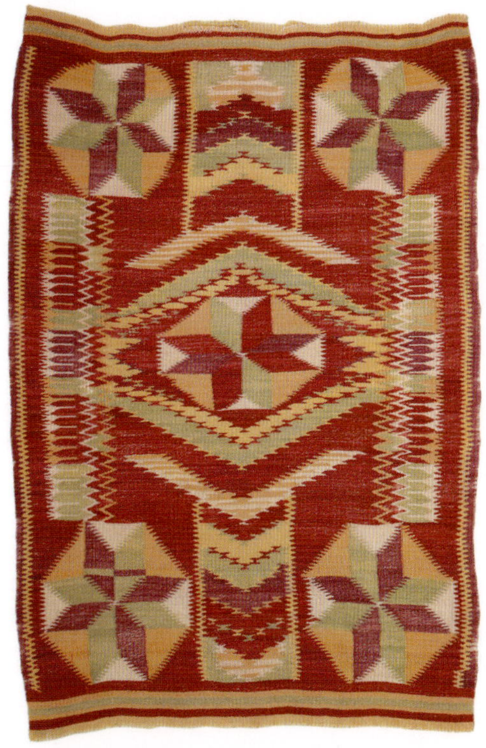

ABOVE LEFT: Harriet Snyder (Navajo), two-faced textile, 44 ½" x 23 ½". **BELOW:** Spanish Colonial blanket with Vallero star pattern, ca. 1880.

TWO-FACED WEAVE / a technically difficult Navajo weaving technique dating back to the nineteenth century, involving four **heddles**— two throwing long **weft** floats to the foreground of the textile and two throwing long weft floats to the back, allowing one pattern to be built up on the front and an entirely different, usually simple, pattern on the reverse. Today two-faced rugs are generally a diamond-**twill weave** surrounding panels of plain weave or bead stitch; sometimes they incorporate geometric designs and/or **Yé'ii** figures.

UMBILICAL CORD FETISHES AND BAGS / made by members of the Plains nations, particularly the Sioux, they were traditionally made by placing a baby's umbilical cord in the center of a turtle form, stuffing it with down, and sewing up the sides. Originally umbilical fetishes were hung on the baby's **cradleboard** or from the mother's belt. The Ute tribe of Colorado made tanned-hide and elaborately beaded umbilical-cord holders or bags; they were worn as necklaces and also were attached to cradleboards. At the turn of the twentieth century, these fetishes became popular with collectors who perceived them as exotic curiosities. As a result, traders began having Native bead and quill workers produce imitations for the tourist market.

UNITED INDIAN TRADER'S ASSOCIATION (UITA) / founded in 1931 to encourage and perpetuate authentic Native American arts and crafts, and to discourage "machine production." The association implemented a stamping system in 1946 for jewelry and spoons comprising the initials UITA and a number indicating the place where it was made. The UITA established stringent standards: the stamp could only be used on silverwork entirely handmade with hand-powered tools by Navajo or Pueblo craftsmen; prefabricated ring shanks and bezels, power dies and power punches, and other mechanical tools were prohibited. In 1977 the UITA was renamed the Indian Country Business Association and was essentially dissolved in 1997, when it donated its remaining funds to the Cline Library at Northern Arizona University, to help fund interviews with old-time **trading post** owners and managers. **Silver** jewelry and spoons with the UITA stamp are highly sought after today, for it indicates the work is handcrafted using traditional methods. See also **Indian Arts and Crafts Board**.

VALLERO STAR PATTERN / a symmetrical eight-pointed star motif of contrasting colors, used by Hispano weavers of northern New Mexico in blankets made from handspun or commercially processed **yarn**, since the mid-nineteenth century. The pattern was possibly influenced by American patchwork **quilt** patterns, although the use of this motif can be found on Mexican textiles as well as many other textiles worldwide. When making Vallero star-pattern textiles, Hispano weavers often took advantage of the new palette of colors afforded by commercial **dyes** and/or commercial

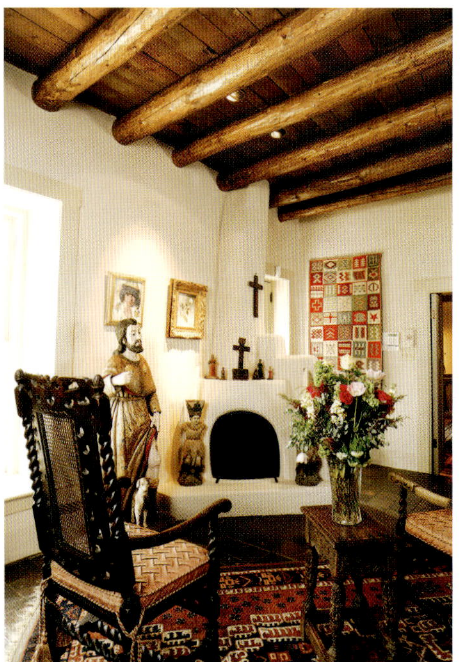

Vigas in ceiling of sitting room, Prada–Dietrich House, ca. 1820/renovations 1920s, Santa Fe, New Mexico.

VIGA / a large, peeled, round log or beam (usually 6 to 12 or more inches in diameter) used in ceiling construction and generally left exposed. Vigas are laid out horizontally at uniform intervals across the top of **adobe** walls, with **latillas** or wood planks (and sometimes plaster) laid between them. Often the vigas project beyond the exterior wall surface making them visible on the facade; the original purpose for this was to extend the spanning capacity of the viga. Generally hand-**adzed**, vigas are most often found in adobe **pueblos**, **Sonoran row houses**, and in **Spanish Colonial** and **Spanish Pueblo Revival–style** homes. Today they are a classic feature of the "Santa Fe Style." In some instances, faux viga ends made of wood, plastic, or metal are placed on the exterior of buildings purely for aesthetic reasons, to suggest or imitate traditional building methods.

WARP / in weaving, the warp is the yarn strung in vertical lines on a loom and which forms the foundation or "bones" of the rug, while the **weft** yarns, woven over and under the warp, form the pattern or design and make the warp invisible. In basketry, it refers to the

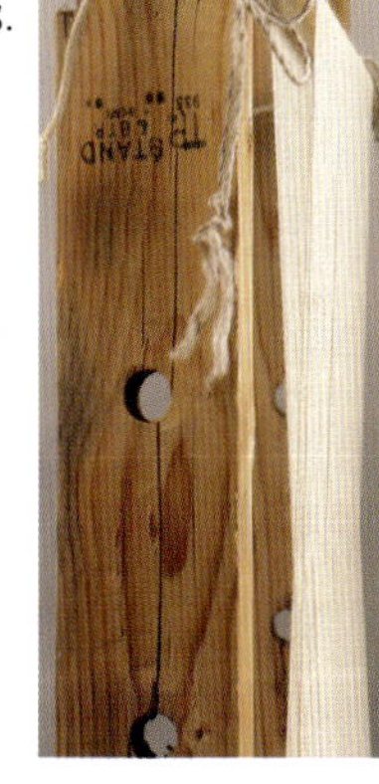

foundation: in the **coiling** method the warp consists of a bundle, one or more branches, or a combination of both; in **twining** the warp is the rigid sticks around which the pliable splints (weft) are woven. See diagram on page 187.

WATER JARS (Water Jugs, Tus') / woven **coiled** baskets of rounded form with either a straight or slightly out-flaring neck, typically made of **sumac** and/or **willow**, usually coated inside (and often outside) with hot **piñon pitch** to make them watertight. Hematite is sometimes added to the pitch to give it a warm reddish hue. The Apache word for pitched water jars is *tus'*. See also **piñon-pitch baskets** and **Western Apache Basketry**.

WEAVING / Hispano / since their arrival in the region in the late sixteenth century, Hispano residents of the Southwest have enjoyed a rich tradition of weaving textiles. Spanish Colonial women wove rugs, bedding, clothing, blankets, church decorations such as altar cloths, and other utilitarian fabrics. Some of their textiles were exported south to Mexico. Using traditional four-harness, counterbalanced, horizontal floor **looms**—initially constructed out of rough-hewn logs and later milled lumber with metal fittings —they created distinct types of fabric. To create the yarn for weaving, Hispano artisans cleaned, **carded**, spun, washed, and **dyed** sheep's wool. In the early twentieth century one of the largest weaving centers was in the northern New Mexico town of Chimayó. The term "Chimayó" became used in the **curio trade** during that time to describe all Spanish New Mexican textiles. See also **Chimayó textiles** and **Rio Grande textiles**.

WEAVING / Native American / long before the Spanish conquest in the late sixteenth century, Native peoples of the Southwest were proficient in weaving with cotton, plant fibers, turkey feathers, rabbit fur, and human hair. Remnants of prehistoric woven garments, blankets, sandals, belts, bags, and other artifacts, as well as tools for weaving textiles, have been recovered from archaeological sites in the Southwest that clearly indicate that skilled weavers lived in what are now present-day New Mexico, Arizona, Colorado, and Utah as early as AD 200.

After the Spanish introduced domesticated sheep and European weaving methods, the Native American textile industry flourished, with large workshops for the weaving of commercial textiles in Santa Fe and other locations in New Mexico established by the 1630s. These Native American weavers used an upright **loom** and made their own yarn by cleaning, carding, spinning, washing, and dyeing sheep wool.

An art form that flourishes to this day, especially among the Navajos (whose term for blanket or rug is *beeldléí*), handwoven rugs are being made by Native American artisans in about sixteen different regional styles in New Mexico and Arizona.

WEDDING BASKET (Ceremonial Basket, Medicine Basket) / called *ts'aa'* in Navajo, it is the most familiar and one of the oldest Navajo **coiled**-basket designs, and one of the few with known symbolic significance, typically woven with three-lobed **sumac** splints sewn around a

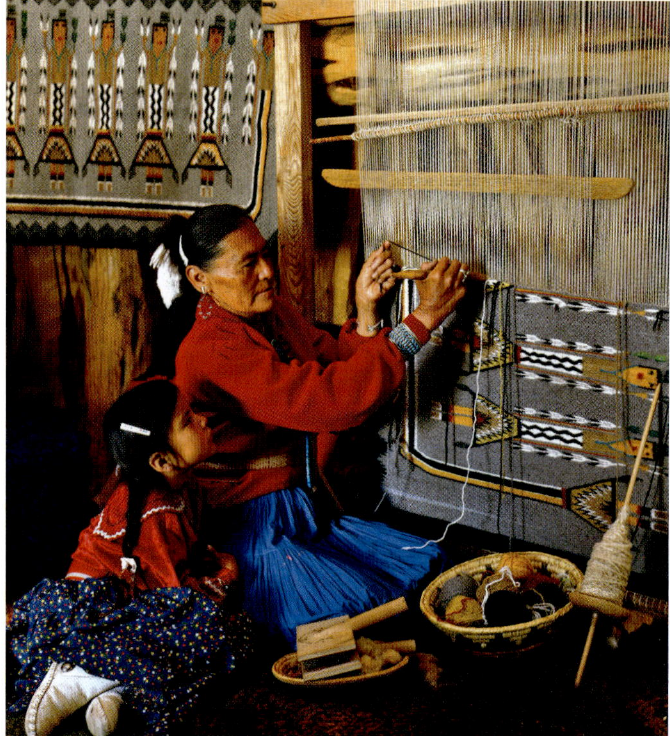

ABOVE: Susie Yazzie (Navajo) shows her daughter the art of weaving.
LEFT: Unique figure-eight structure of the warp of a Navajo textile stretched on temporary beams.

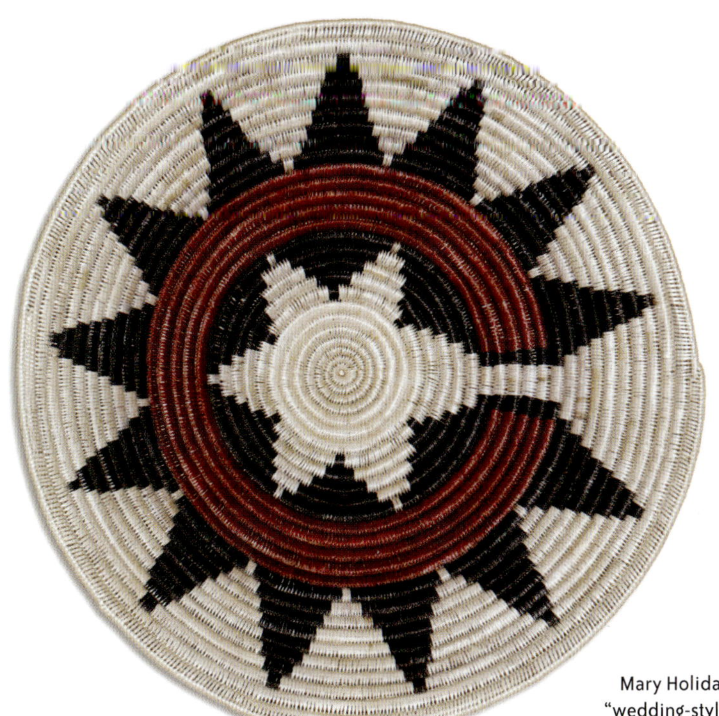

Mary Holiday Black (Navajo),
"wedding-style" plaque, 2009,
sumac, natural and synthetic dyes.

sumac rod foundation, with decoration of natural vegetal **dyes** (and more recently commercial dyes), in a shallow bowl or **tray** form. There are different interpretations of the wedding design, but it is generally agreed that the white center represents the earth or beginning of life, the black stepped terraces denote clouds or mountains, and the encircling bands of red symbolize the sun's rays or a rainbow.

These baskets also have the ceremonial break or pathway (*'atiin* in Navajo) aligned with the small ridge of the last coil—a mandatory design element that helps the medicine man orient the basket to the east and provides a pathway for healing—and a **herringbone** rim finish.

These coiled trays play an important role in various Navajo ceremonies: they are used to serve the special cornmeal mixture during marriage nuptials, to hold ritual paraphernalia, and are given as payment for the medicine man. Historically, wedding baskets have also been inverted and used as a drum. After a wedding basket was used in a ceremony, the medicine man generally traded it for goods or cash, a custom that resulted in the distribution of these baskets around the Navajo reservation, with the traders buying and selling them repeatedly.

Since the late nineteenth century, Colorado Ute and San Juan Paiute and Jicarilla Apache weavers have made wedding baskets and trays for intertribal trade with the Navajos, supplying them to traders as well as directly to Navajo buyers. For Navajos, the weaving of these baskets involves dealing with many taboos, thus it is easier for them to purchase wedding baskets from Native weavers who are not affected by these taboos. The colors and design motifs of the traditional wedding basket appear in some early Navajo textiles; contemporary Navajo weavers often include it in "**Tree of Life**" tapestries.

In recent decades creative basket weavers have invented variations of the traditional wedding design. For example, Mary Holiday Black (b. 1935), who was instrumental in reviving the art of Navajo basketry in the 1960s and '70s, has designed a basket in which **Yé'ii Bichaii** figures emerge from the traditional wedding pattern, and San Juan Paiute basket maker Rose Ann Whiskers has incorporated colorful **butterfly** images into her traditional wedding-basket design. Some Native American jewelers replicate the popular wedding basket design in pins, earrings, and pendants.

WEDDING JAR / Vase (Double-necked Jars) / a double-spouted **clay** vessel connected by a graceful arched handle in the middle, dating back to prehistoric times, and made today by Pueblo and Navajo potters. Beginning in the early 1900s, when the form was dubbed "wedding vase," it became a fashionable item sold by **curio** dealers and collected by tourists. Wedding vases have been made by Native potters with various decorative features, including incised patterns,

appliquéd figures, animals, and **corn**, and traditional and contemporary designs painted with clay **slip**. They have also been made of bronze-hued **micaceous** clay and left unadorned. In some pots the handle consists of a rope like coil. The building and **firing** of wedding vessels is tricky, as the spouts tend to separate and crack, particularly during the drying stage (before being sanded, slipped, and fired).

The origin of the name "wedding jars" is unknown and there are many different stories relating to the form's meaning. Some have described the pot as having one spout representing man and the other representing woman, united or bound together as one by the handle. Early curio dealers referred to these clay pots as "double bottle necks" or "Love Cups." Contemporary Hopi-Tewa potter Rainy Naha refers to wedding vases as "medicinal jars"—in which medicine goes in one side and pours out the other—and are kept safe in **kivas**. Books on pottery, some Native

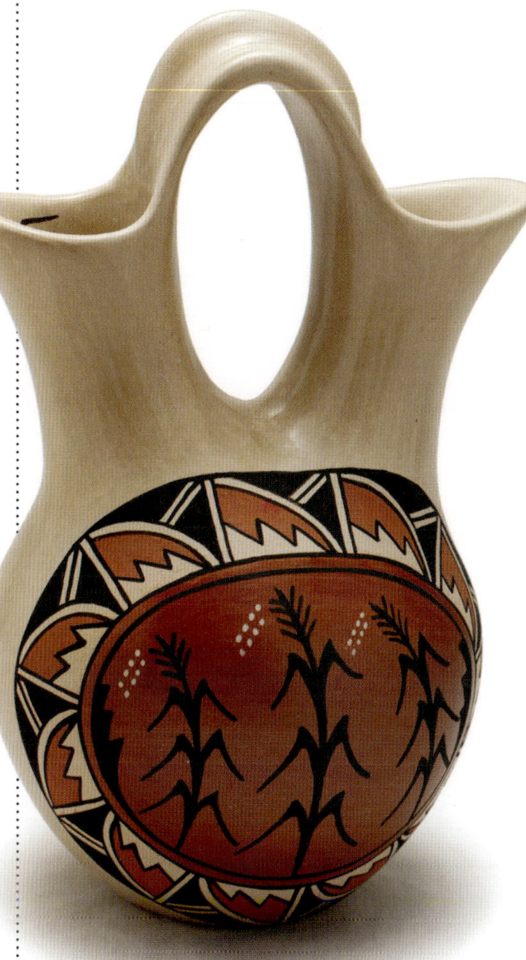

Juanita C. Fragua (Jemez), wedding vase, 1998, clay with natural slips.

potters, as well as some dealers continue to refer to these pots as "wedding" vases or jars. As in the early twentieth century, the form is largely made today for the tourist market. Called *matrimonios* in Mexico, these double-spouted and handled jars are also made by potters of **Mata Ortiz**, a village in the state of Chihuahua, Mexico.

WEFT / in weaving, the yarns woven over and under the vertical **warp** yarns, which are attached to a **loom**. Essentially, they are the "visible" threads going across the face of the textile. In basketry, it refers to the pliable sewing strands also called "sewing element" that are wrapped around the foundation (warp) in a **coiled** basket. In **twined** baskets, it is the two or three strands that pass over and under the rigid foundation (warp). See diagram on page 187.

WESTERN APACHE (Indé) BASKETRY / baskets were a practical necessity for the early semi-nomadic Western Apaches in facilitating the transportation of possessions. Beginning in the 1870s, when the Western Apaches—including the White Mountain, San Carlos, Cibecue, Northern Tonto, and Southern Tonto bands—were placed at the San Carlos Reservation, they made finely **twined** and **coiled** baskets primarily from **sumac**, **willow**, mulberry, **cottonwood**, and **devil's claw**. The main forms woven were coiled plates and shallow bowls for preparing and serving foods; **twined burden baskets** with rounded bottoms decorated with buckskin fringe used for gathering and transporting goods; and twined jars and bottles covered with **piñon pitch** used for carrying and storing water. Specific types of baskets were used in the Sunrise Ceremony: burden baskets were used to hold foods and gifts for those in attendance, and coiled **trays** (or round baskets) were employed to carry the sacred pollen.

In the late nineteenth and early twentieth century, Western Apaches made vase-shaped **ollas**, frequently several feet high and taking up to a year or longer to complete; they were popular among collectors and tourists. Other baskets from this period include coiled plates and shallow bowls with designs featuring human and animal figures executed in devil's claw (first appearing about 1900, they were likely in response to the tourist market); **polychrome** baskets with reddish patterns made from **mountain mahogany** or **yucca** roots; and twined burden baskets with commercial dyes (especially red and green) and buckskin fringes tipped with **tinklers**.

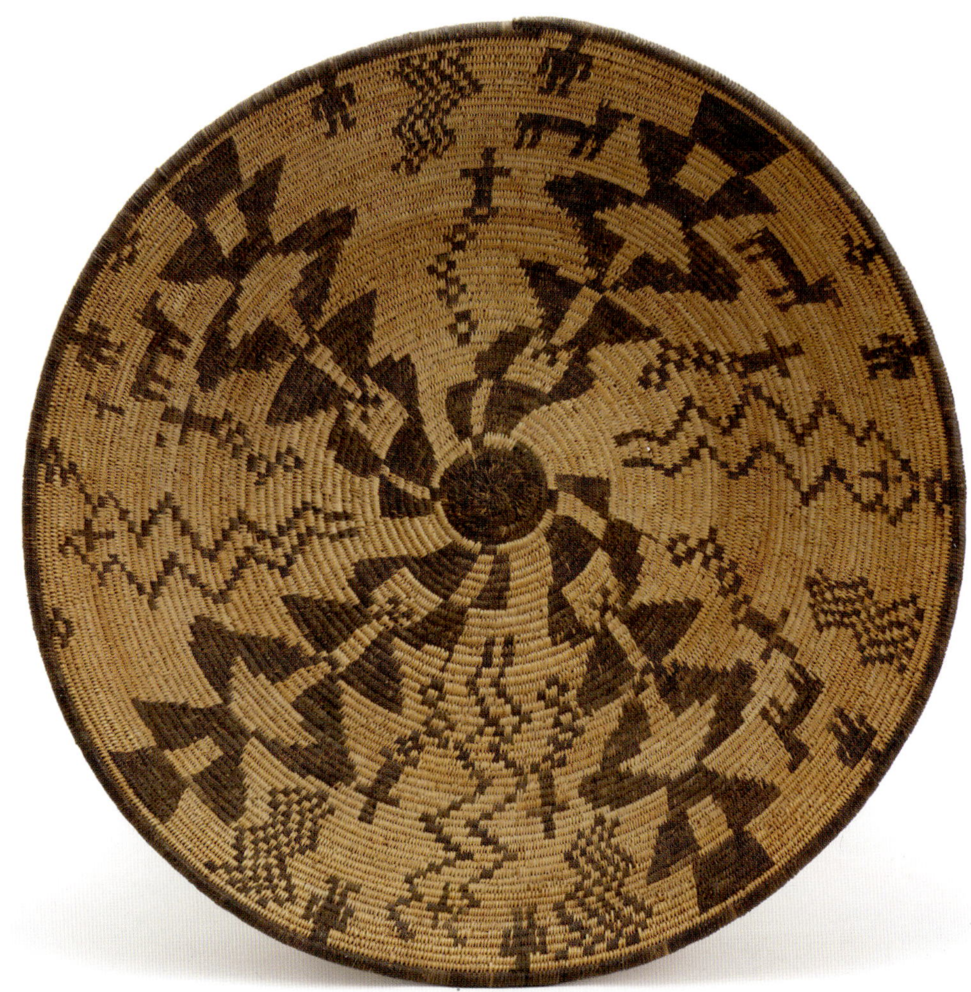

Western Apache basket, early 1900s, willow and devil's claw.

From the 1930s to 1960s Western Apache basketry severely declined. However, in the late 1960s the craft experienced a revival because of the establishment of basket-making classes on the reservation and the encouragement of Melvin and Joyce Montgomery, who purchased the Peridot Trading Post on the San Carlos Indian Reservation in 1968 and provided a consistent outlet for baskets. Among the forms made during this period were *tus'* (**water jars**) that were sealed with piñon pitch and used for aging an alcoholic beverage called *tulapai*.

The difficult and time-consuming coiled basket-making method is near extinction among the Western Apaches today. At the date of publication, there was only one remaining weaver of traditional Western Apache coiled baskets: Teri Goode of the San Carlos Apache Reservation. She learned the craft from her mother and her grandmother. She weaves her coiled baskets using sumac, devil's claw, wild mulberry, and redbud, materials that she harvests during the fall months.

WHEAT STITCH / a two-stitch technique used in the **coiled** baskets of the Tohono O'odham in Arizona. The first stitch is used in a **split stitch** method that splits the lower coil stitch, and a second stitch is then added to the right of it.

WHIRLING LOGS (Tsil'ol-ni) / See **swastika/ whirling log**.

WICKER PLAQUES / See **Hopi plaques**, **wicker**.

WICKERWORK BASKETS / a type of handwoven basket created from rigid sewing elements of **willow** branches, dune broom (*Parryella filifolia*, called *siwi* by the Hopi), or rabbit brush by Pueblo and Hispano artisans since the early twentieth century. Variations in color may be made by juxtaposing peeled and unpeeled branches. Originally made primarily by men, wickerwork baskets are traditionally used for everyday household tasks—carrying, storing, and serving foods such as **corn**, beans, breads, and fruits—and to bring food to the **kiva** on Pueblo feast days. They are particularly valued for the ceremonial Pueblo Basket Dances because the plants used to weave them come from along the Rio Grande. Many Pueblo, as well as Hispano, people like to hang wickerwork baskets on the wall for decoration. Among the few skilled weavers still carrying on the wickerwork or willow basket tradition is Joseph Gutierrez of Santa Clara Pueblo; his sturdy red-willow bowls are in high demand at his village. He gathers his willow as he needs it, spends a day processing his materials, and then four to five hours weaving each basket using the **plaiting** method. His baskets are distinguished by a decorative rim, created by bringing the bunched **warps** to the outside of the basket and working them into a braid.

Functional willow wickerwork baskets have also traditionally been made by Hispano residents of New Mexico, who harvested twigs of river willow from along the riverbeds in the northern part of the state. According to contemporary Hispano basket makers, weaving willow baskets is a laborious process that can only be done during certain times of the year (the red willow shoots can only be collected in winter months when the plant is dormant and then the shoots must be cured, or dried, for a year, and then soaked to make them pliable) and is a craft being handed down from generation to generation. Among the few Hispano artisans making them currently is Jenny Valencia Baeza, a third generation basket weaver.

Apache wickiup, 1903.

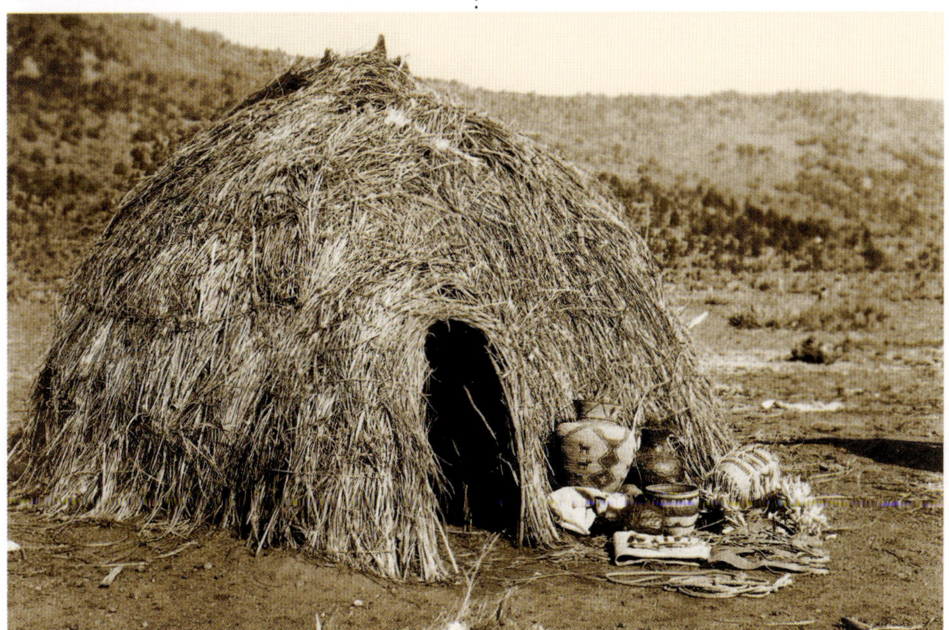

WICKIUP (Brush Lodge) / from the Mesquakie or Fox word *wiikiyaapi* meaning "lodge" or "house," an ancient Native American house type consisting of a circular, domed, brush shelter, in which the Utes, Apaches, and other tribes of the Southwest resided, especially in the summer months. The construction varied depending on the availability of materials, but typically they were built over a framework of three or four wood poles joined in the center, covered with an outer surface of bark and/or brush or grass and an encircling band of **willow** to hold the outer covering in place. It usually contained a central fire-pit (and a smoke hole above), and when sleeping, the inhabitants oriented themselves with feet towards the fire. A hide usually covered the entranceway. By the early 1700s the Utes had also adopted the use of the conical tipi covered with buffalo and other animal hides (and later with canvas), which afforded more protection from the elements in the winter and was easily transported by horse when the Utes changed location.

WIDE RUINS RUG STYLE AND TRADING POST / established in the early 1900s as the Kinteel Trading Post in the southeast corner of the Navajo Reservation in Arizona, the post was purchased in 1938 and renamed Wide Ruins by William and Sallie Lippincott. The Lippincotts,

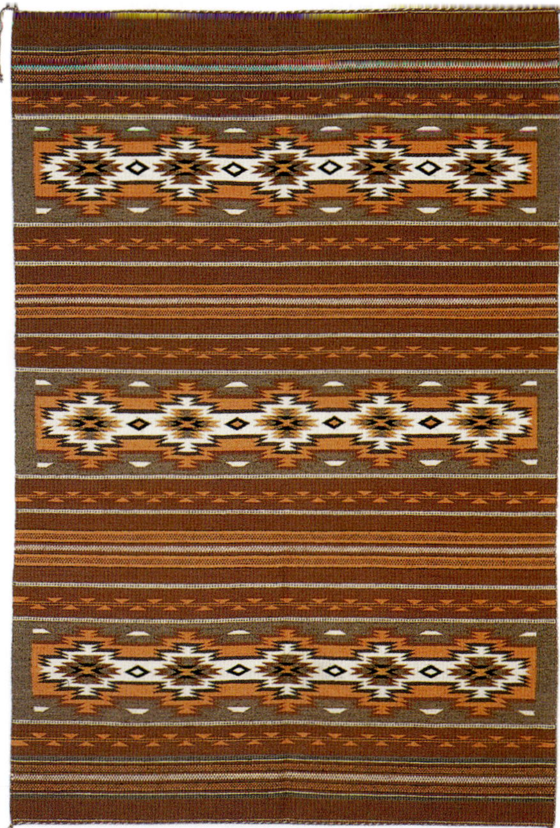

Peggy Lynch (Navajo), Wide Ruins textile, 52 ½" x 36 ½".

who traded at the post until 1950, encouraged area weavers to create high-quality rugs with simple horizontal stripes and bands (with no borders) using vegetal-**dyed**, handspun-wool **yarn**. Sallie kept a plant recipe book that weavers could consult; her husband Bill promoted the building of an addition to the schoolhouse so that weaving classes could be offered to the younger Navajo women; and together they initiated craft festivals that featured awards for weaving and silversmithing.

Later operated by the Navajos, the historic Wide Ruins Trading Post burned in a fire in 1986. The Lippincott's rug style, however, is still made today by Navajo weavers. These Wide Ruins rugs are characterized by their fine workmanship and handspun wool of earth and sunset pastels—pinks, yellow, beige, deep corals, grays, olive greens, tans, browns, and lilacs. The rug style that bears the post name also features some design motifs within the stripes and bands: a bead stitch of alternating **weft** colors (sometimes referred to as "railroad tracks"), hatch work, wavy lines, arrows, chevrons, and **squash blossoms**. See also **Chinle Rug Style**.

WILLOW (Salix nigra) / Desert Willow (Chilopsis linearis) / several varieties of willow are utilized by Southwestern basket makers in one capacity or another for **coiling** or **twining** baskets. The willow shoots are gathered and peeled for foundation rods; they are also utilized for the sewing strands in baskets, but because they do not hold the **dye** well willow is usually used for white backgrounds or tan elements.

The desert willow—a large shrub that can reach 20 feet high, with long, slender leaves and pink to purple flowers in July, usually found growing in dry desert water courses—was important to Native Americans in the Sonoran Desert, especially prior to contact with Europeans in the seventeenth century. They used the strong but flexible branches for framing rectangular or domed houses and for weaving enormous basket-like structures called granaries that were used to hold mesquite pods or other large quantities of food.

Also, some Native cultures such as the O'odham and Maricopa of Arizona used the branches to make bows (with fibers of the **agave** plant for string), and to hold round-bottomed ceramic jars and pots. Today willow is most often found in the coiled baskets of Pima, Tohono O'odham, and Jicarilla Apaches, and in the **burden baskets** of Western Apaches. Some Tohono O'odham weavers combine the willow sewing strands (or splints) with cattail foundations.

WIRE BASKETS (Wainom Hua) / a distinctive, sturdy type of basket traditionally made from heavy-gauge baling wire (used in ranching), by male Tohono O'odhams in southern Arizona, since at least the mid-twentieth century. Originally wire baskets held food and were lowered into wells to keep the food cool and fresh. A small number of men continue to make these baskets, from **copper** and other types of wire, for household use and for sale. Tohono O'odham artisan Eugene Lopez is credited with bringing the art of wire basket making to the public. Using only a few tools such as pliers and a hammer, they are handcrafted by a looping technique that is related to the "lace coiling" method used in making **burden baskets**. Among the forms made are baskets with handles, shallow bowls, lidded baskets, vase shapes and, rarely, serving utensils. Also, miniature wire-basket forms have been made, including some that have been transformed into earrings.

WIRE JEWELRY / some of the earliest Southwestern bracelets were made from commercially

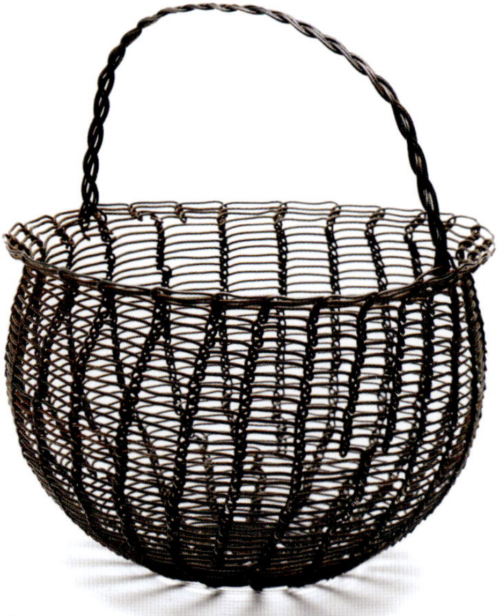

Eugene Lopez (Tohono O'odham), wire basket, ca. 1970.

produced brass and **copper** wire obtained through trade. Later, Navajo silversmiths produced their own **silver** wire by using a drawplate. By the early 1900s, round, square, and carinated (or triangular) fabricated silver wire was commercially available, though many smiths continued to draw their own wire into the 1940s and some still use drawplates today. A popular bracelet style originating in the 1920s consisted of one or more of these wires twisted together. This style is still made today.

WPA FURNITURE / distinguished by its carved surfaces, dark stains, and designs rooted in the Spanish Colonial and Mexican traditions, this type of furniture was made for the Works Progress Administration (WPA)—and the Federal Art Project (FAP), the WPA division devoted to the arts—in New Mexico, from the 1930s to the beginning of World War II. The WPA/FAP and local sponsors supported the making of **Spanish Colonial Revival–style** furniture (and fabric arts and religious art) in a number of vocational schools throughout the state. Native Americans were trained along with other furniture makers; one school near Cochiti Pueblo is credited with originating a "bead-and-groove" carved design in the early 1940s.

WPA-style utilitarian items—chairs, desks, dining tables, dressers, blanket boxes, storage chests, small boxes, lamps, picture frames, *roperos* (wardrobes), and **trasteros**—were commonly made for public buildings, private individuals, or an artisan's own home. **Chip-carved** motifs—especially **rosettes**—frequently adorn the furniture. Some WPA-trained craftsmen

produced pieces with more modern elements such as geometric Art Deco patterns, inlays, and painted imagery.

WROUGHT IRON / See **ironwork**.

YARN / Commercial / machine-spun wool yarn, manufactured in textile mills by industrial processes, first available in limited quantities to Navajo and Hispano weavers in the Southwest as early as the 1820s/30s, as a result of trade over the Santa Fe Trail. At first these yarns were used in small amounts in textiles, as accents to design motifs. These three-ply, naturally dyed, Saxony yarns were imported from Europe. Identifiable by their regularly ridged texture and solid coloring, commercial yarns (sometimes respun by weavers) introduced a new range of vibrant colors, such as red, orange, yellow, purple, blue, and green.

Throughout much of the nineteenth century, commercial yarns were acquired in trade with other cultures, the United States military, **trading posts**, and other outlets. After 1875, when commercial wool yarns became available to pueblos in New Mexico, Pueblo weavers used them with increasing frequency to weave traditional items such as **mantas**. By the 1880s these yarns were

WPA chair, northern New Mexico, ca. 1935, Ponderosa pine with red cedar.

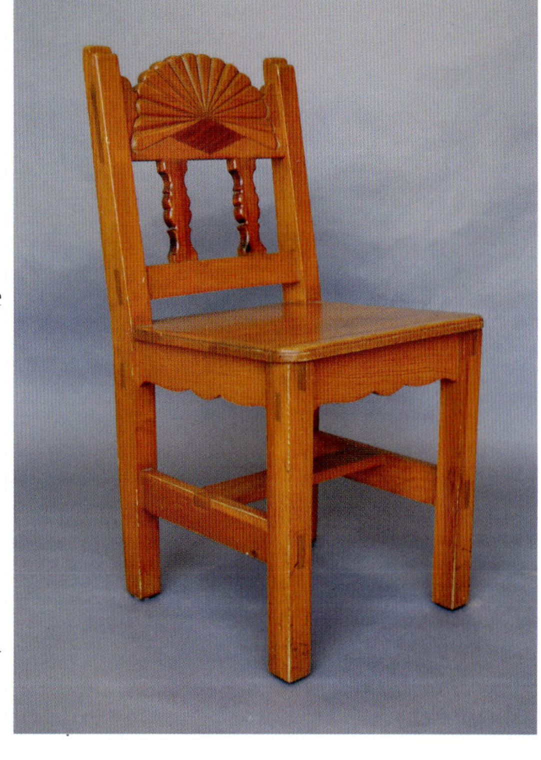

highly sought after by most Native weavers of the Southwest, from the Navajo to the Pueblo to the Hispano. Commercial yarns not only provided an array of bright colors but also saved countless hours otherwise spent **carding**, cleaning, spinning, and **dyeing** natural wool. See also **Chimayó textiles** and **Germantown yarns**.

YARN / Handspun / also called homespun, it is yarn produced from raw wool fibers, twisted to form a continuous thread (or yarn) by hand or with the aid of a **spindle** or spinning wheel. Navajo, Hispano, and Pueblo peoples of the Southwest have used handspun yarn for their handwoven textiles for centuries. For Hispano weavers, the spinning process is called *hilar*, the spindle is *malacate*, and the spinning wheel is *torno de hilar*. In New Mexico, spinning was typically done with a hand spindle rather than a spinning wheel. As early as the 1820s/30s, limited quantities of commercially made (and machine-spun) yarns became available to Spanish and Navajo weavers as a result of trade over the Santa Fe Trail. However, the art of handspinning yarn has never died out; to this day, many weavers in the Southwest prefer to handspin their own yarns from natural-dyed or undyed fibers.

YÉ'II (Yei) / supernatural beings, or Holy People, from the Navajo religion, often depicted in a stylized form in Navajo **pictorial rugs**, **tapestries**, basket **trays**, and other art forms, intended for sale and not for ceremonial use. Depictions of Yé'ii figures first appeared on Navajo textiles in the late nineteenth century. Made with brightly colored **yarns** (with a wool **warp** and sometimes cotton), they were a stylistic departure from the geometric non-representational textiles for which the Navajo weavers were known.

Yé'ii rugs became widely woven in the early twentieth century, at the urging of post traders. Among the earliest to make them was Yanabah Simpson, a weaver married to Richard Simpson, who lived near Farmington, New Mexico; she made large single- or double-figure vertical Yé'ii rugs in the early 1900s. Yé'ii rugs were also woven in Shiprock, New Mexico, where trader Will Evans helped develop multiple-figure Yé'ii textiles in the 1920s. In the Lukachukai area, a similar horizontal

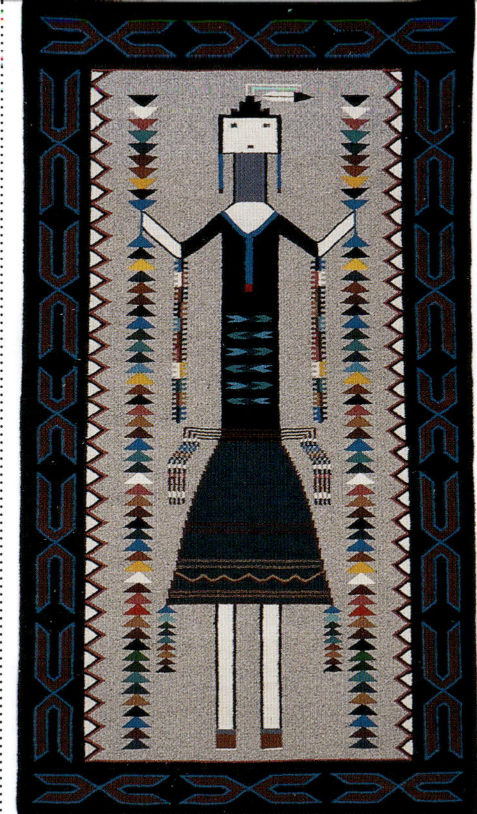

Marjorie Dee (Navajo), Simpson Yé'ii revival textile, 60" x 34".

Yé'ii rug was developed that was larger in size and coarser from the use of handspun yarns. Many traditional Navajo people and medicine men raised objections when these sacred figures were first woven into rugs (and appeared in other art forms) outside of a ceremonial context.

By the 1960s the market appeal of Yé'ii imagery, as well as increased secularization among Native peoples, led to the acceptance of the Yé'ii and the **Yé'ii bichaii** (a Navajo dancer who portrays the Yé'ii) as a well-established and popular category of Navajo arts and crafts. Yé'ii and Yé'ii bichaii appear on pottery, baskets, tapestries, rugs, and in a variety of other art forms. However, to this day, many Navajo women will consult with a *hataalii*—which translates as "singer" in Navajo and is a term used for a healer or medicine man—for permission or advice on using such imagery, even when stylized, so as not to represent a specific figure.

YÉ'II BICHAII (Ye'ii bicheii, Yeibichai) / the Navajo name for "Grandfather of the Gods," or "Talking God of the Holy People," commonly used in reference to the dancers who portray Yé'ii divinities and are often represented in Navajo rugs, **tapestries**, baskets, and other art forms. The sacred Yé'ii Bichaii dance occurs at the conclusion of the nine-day Nightway (or winter Night Chant) ceremony. Talking God is traditionally shown with a white face and facing forward, while the other masked dancers are shown in profile to highlight their distinction from the divine beings.

YESO / See **gesso**.

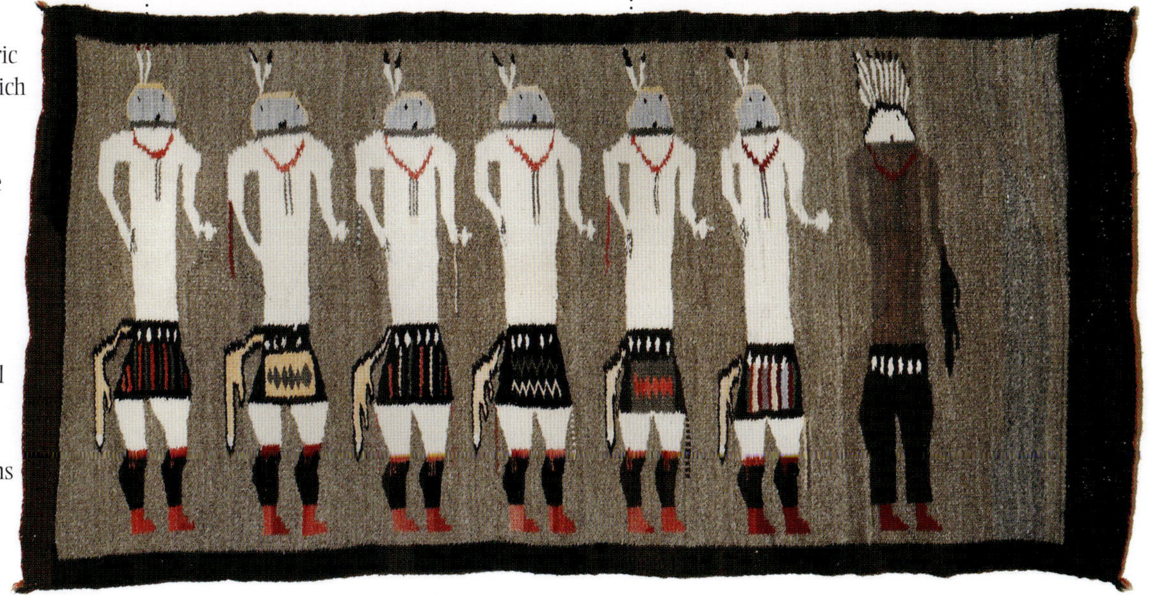

Navajo Yé'ii Bichaii pictorial textile, ca. 1920s, natural and commercially dyed homespun yarns.

YUCCA (*Yucca Elata, Yucca Baccata*) / a spike-leafed desert plant with white to pale yellow blossoms and one of the most useful resources in the prehistoric and historic Southwest. Highly revered by Native Americans in the region, the yucca provided a source of food (in its fruit), soap, and pliable but strong fibers (obtained by shredding the plant leaf) that were woven into baskets, sandals, ropes, mats, clothing, nets, and mattresses. Fragile prehistoric yucca textiles have been discovered preserved at various Ancestral Puebloan sites in the Southwest; for instance, sandals made of **twined** and **dyed** yucca-fiber were found in the shallow, dry caves of Grand Gulch, in southeastern Utah.

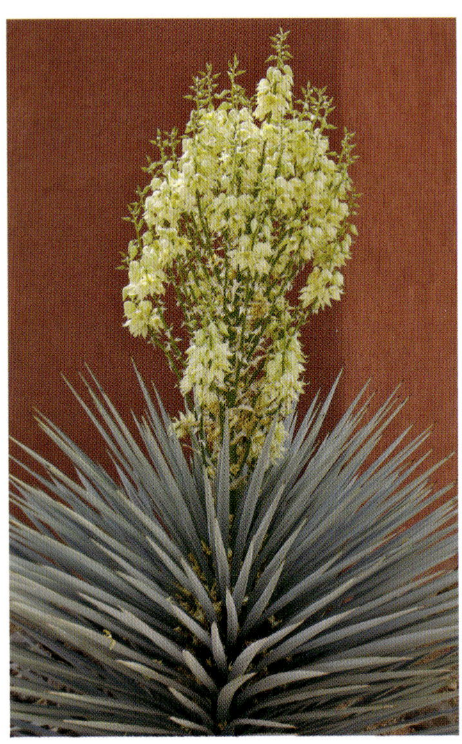

Yucca leaves have traditionally been used as paintbrushes by the Pueblo potters of New Mexico. Narrow brushes for fine line work are trimmed from a yucca spear and left narrow and flat; wider brushes, sometimes used for painting larger solid areas, are trimmed from the spear and the soft tissue between the fibers at one end are chewed and pulled out with the artisan's teeth.

The yucca root was (and continues to be) used to make a reddish-brown dye on sewing strands employed for designs in the **coiled** baskets of the Tohono O'odham in Arizona. In addition, the white and green yucca leaf is used for sewing splints on coiled baskets by the Hopis of Second Mesa and the Tohono O'odham; for splints on **plaited** yucca-ring **sifter baskets** of the Hopis and of Pueblo people; and to bind the rims of Hopi **wicker plaques**. For white yucca sewing splints, the center leaves of the plant are gathered in late summer and allowed to bleach in the sun; for yellow splints, leaves are placed in the sun and rain and allowed to turn yellow; and for the green yucca splints, the outside leaves of the plant are used and can be gathered during any time of the year. To prepare the leaves for weaving, they are dampened with water and kept damp (usually rolled up in a towel). Only the amount needed for that day is dampened, otherwise mildew or mold will grow on the yucca.

YUCCA-RING BASKETS / See **sifter baskets**.

ZAGUÁN / a Spanish word for entrance, hall, or vestibule; a term used in the Southwest for a covered, central entryway (or hallway) that leads from the street to the **courtyard** of a traditionally built **adobe** home. Of Arabic origin, the zaguán served as the transition from public space to private, and provided additional ventilation for the house. Originally, these entranceways were wide enough for the passage of a carriage or wagon. In the American Southwest, the zaguán was intended to protect all who entered (on horseback, in carriages or wagons, or on foot) from possible attacks by raiding Native Americans. The term also once referred to a large double-door entrance to a fortified **plaza** or village compound (in which all the windows and doors of the buildings opened onto the plaza). Later in the nineteenth century, a zaguán typically consisted of a wide covered corridor, or entrance hallway, which was quite high, and with or without doors that joined two separate buildings or a string of rooms. Another term used for this feature is "breezeway."

ZAPATA / Zapato / a Spanish word for "shoe," used in the Southwest to refer to the double-ended, carved-wood structural and ornamental element placed at the top of a post and used to support a wood beam joint, often used in **portals** on the exterior of buildings in the region. See also **corbel**.

ZAPOTEC TEXTILES / a type of textile of extraordinary diversity, beauty, and craftsmanship handwoven by Zapotec Indians of Teotitlán del Valle, a small village in the State of Oaxaca, Mex-

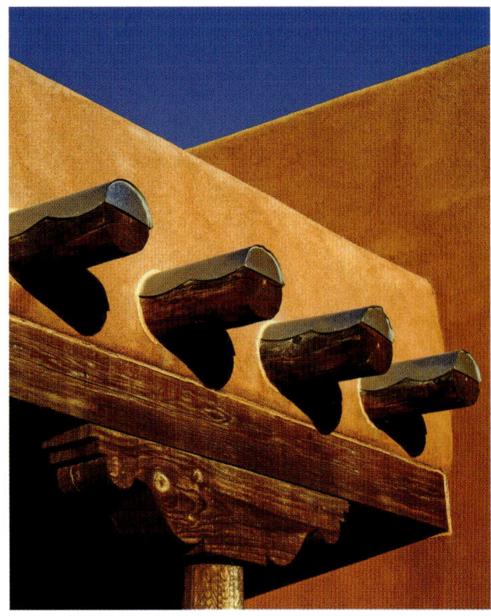

Zapata, the wood element shown at the top of the post.

ico. The Zapotecs, an ancient people and one of the first groups to settle in Central America, have woven textiles since pre-Columbian times. Originally, they used yarn derived from native plants such as cotton and **agave** and the backstrap **loom** to weave cloth for the immediate needs of their families. In the early sixteenth century, the Spanish introduced to the Zapotecs **churro** sheep (which yielded thick wool yarns for weaving), the spinning wheel, carding paddles, scissors, steel needles, and the fixed-frame pedal or treadle loom (a type of loom still in use by Zapotec weavers today). Following these innovations, Zapotec weavers produced clothing such as wearing blankets, **sarapes**, and ponchos for their own use and for trade with other Indians and the Spanish. Over the following centuries, the Zapotec weaving industry continued to thrive and produce tightly woven, highly sought-after textiles. When the textile market shifted from Native people to tourists, especially after 1948 with the opening of the Pan-American Highway (which provided easier access to Oaxaca's craft markets), the Zapotecs wove **tapestries** for display in the home as well as blankets for sale. In the 1960s, they began producing rugs for the tourist trade, with larger looms built to accommodate the new larger-size textiles. A decade later, American importers further energized Zapotec textile production by inspiring the use of new designs—from modernist motifs to Navajo geometric patterns—as well as new color schemes.

As in the past, weaving among the Zapotec today is a family affair. Some use factory made wool for their rugs, while most still hand card, hand spin, and hand **dye** (using natural vegetal and/or aniline dyes) wool from churro sheep to produce yarn. Rugs and tapestries are woven on the treadle loom; once completed the **warp** threads are tied together, usually to form braided or twisted fringe, or the weaver may further refine the ends by weaving the warp threads back into the piece or sewing a braid over its edges.

Zapotec textiles are distinguished by a vast array of colors, from subdued palettes to bright vivid hues, and an equally large array of intricate designs: including motifs from ancient patterns—such as the stone carvings on Pre-columbian temples and traditional **Saltillo sarapes**; motifs drawn from classic Navajo textiles; modernist paintings—by Paul Klee, Pablo Picasso, and others; and "**Tree of Life**" designs with birds, animals, and flowers. Some weavers are producing completely original compositions as well.

ZIA PUEBLO POTTERY / fine pottery has been produced at Zia Pueblo for nearly 700 years, mostly from the same brick-red **clay** and finely ground black basalt (hard volcanic rock) **temper**. Originally, Zia's clay vessels—especially serving bowls and large **storage jars** to hold water, grain, or other foodstuffs—were traded or sold to the nearby pueblos of Jemez, Santa Ana, San Felipe, and Santo Domingo (Kewa) for food and other essentials.

Water jars were an important form to the Zias. Until 1928, when a water hydrant was installed in the village, women gathered water every day from the Jemez River, transporting full water jars up the mesa on their heads until they reached home and emptied them into a larger storage jar. In 1939, when a bridge finally reached the formerly remote village, Zia potters began making small, non-utilitarian pots strictly for sale to tourists and collectors.

Today Zia produces pottery distinguished by thick walls and matte painted decoration of orange-red and black on white-, buff-, or tan-**slipped** pots that have been partially stone-**polished**; usually the base of the pot is left unslipped to reveal the red clay. Among the prominent design features used on Zia pots are curved arches, wide undulating bands, and rainbow-like bands that enclose the hallmark "Zia bird"—suggested by some to represent a roadrunner, usually depicted with fanned, two- or three-part tail

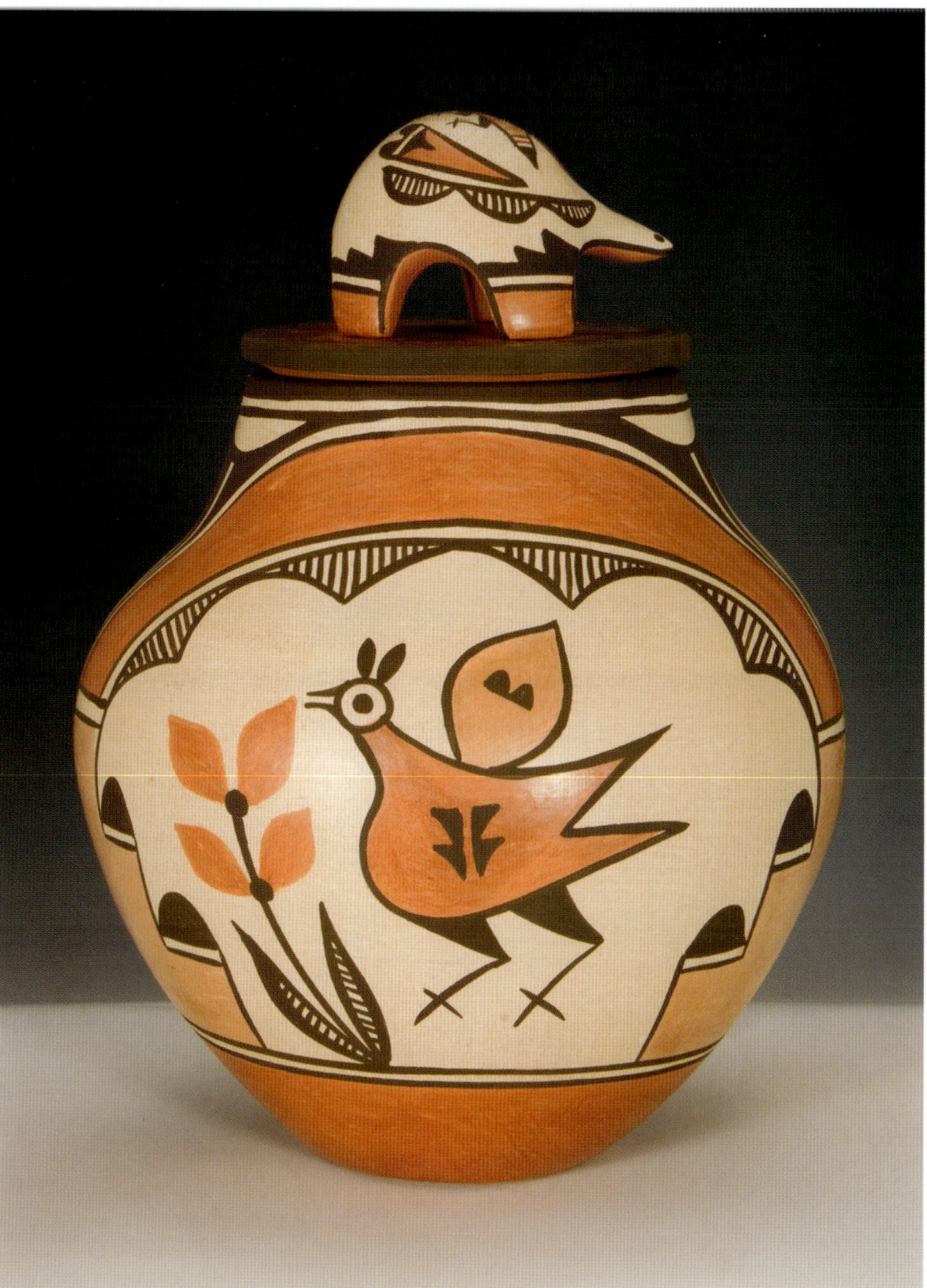

Elizabeth Medina (Zia), traditional "Zia bird" water jar with turtle lid.

feathers, tear-drop shaped wings, wide eyes, and open claws. According to local legend, this bird is believed to have led the people to water during a drought long ago. In addition, the bird is a sacred emblem of speed and the bearer of prayers; on pottery it is typically shown in flight, swiftly carrying the people's prayer for rain up to the skies.

Other favored designs on Zia pots include parrots, deer, flowering plants with large petals, abstract feathers, clouds, lighting, and geometric motifs. Contemporary potters use the same red clay and basalt temper, as well as the same red, white, and black pigments used at the pueblo for at least five centuries. The black pigment is made from manganese-rich iron concretions found on sandstone cliffs near Zia. Potters at the pueblo today use both kiln and traditional sheep-manure **firings**.

ZUNI CARVINGS / See **fetishes**.

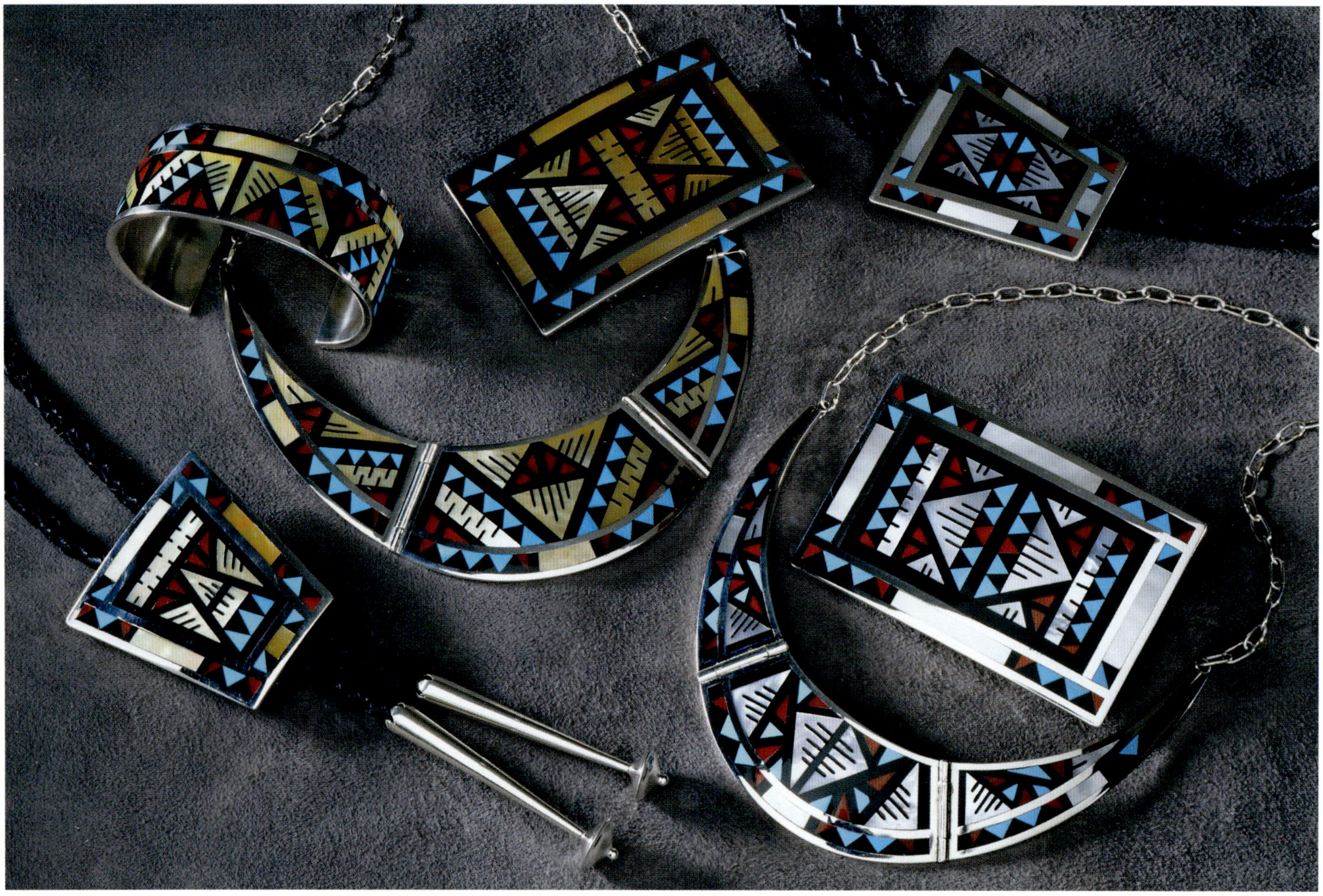

Alex and Marylita Boone (Zuni), silver inlaid with turquoise, coral, jet, gold, and mother-of-pearl.

ZUNI PUEBLO JEWELRY / with its origins traced to prehistoric times, early Zuni Pueblo jewelry consisted of strands of beads made from **shell**, seed, bone, or stone, worn around the neck or wrist, and pendants of carved stone or shell were made as ear ornaments (**jaclas**) or spacers on necklaces. Metalwork at the pueblo consisted of brass and **copper** items such as twisted wire bracelets and rings. In the early 1870s Zuni artisans learned the art of silversmithing from the Navajos and began making simple **silver** wire hoop earrings, **beads**, and buttons.

Eventually, sophisticated tools such as chisels, files, **stamps**, and **dies**, and the first use of **turquoise** on silver in the 1890s, encouraged Zuni smiths to create more elaborate jewelry. One of the finest early Zuni jewelers was Leekya Deyuse (1889–1966), who was initially known for his large tab, nugget, and disc-bead necklaces. He later became famous for his **fetish necklaces** and other fetish jewelry featuring carved animals in

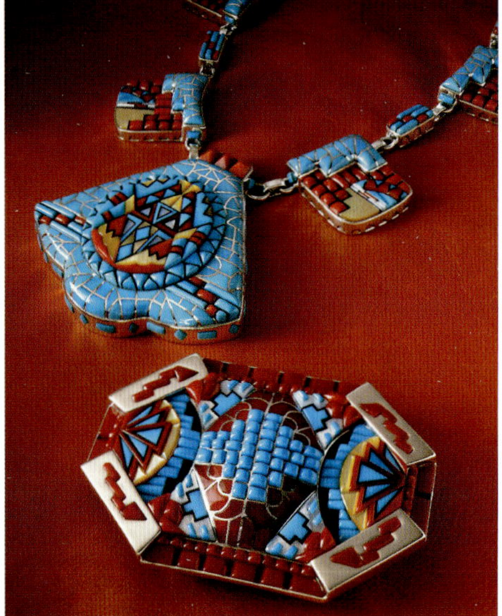

Carolyn Bobelu (Zuni), turquoise, coral, jet, and shell set in multiple levels.

coral, turquoise, shell, and **jet**.

By 1910 Zuni smiths were developing a unique style of jewelry called **cluster work**, in which a number of tiny cut turquoise stones are set in silver around a large central turquoise. As more turquoise became available, Zuni smiths increasingly made these clusters and used them to decorate bracelets, **ketohs**, **conchas**, rings, buckles, **squash-blossom** necklaces, and other jewelry forms.

For the Zunis, the silver was of secondary importance, only used as a means to hold turquoise stones in place. From cluster work they developed two more elaborate and intricate styles that were used in pins, bracelets, earrings, pendants, and other items: **petit-point**, in which a large number of tiny teardrop or oval shaped turquoise is set in silver, and **needlepoint**, in which the turquoise stones are pointed at both ends.

C. G. Wallace (1898–1993), a post trader active at Zuni Pueblo beginning in 1920, had a

profound effect on the development of silver and
lapidary arts at the pueblo in the early twentieth
century. He hired Zuni and Navajo smiths to
make jewelry in his post workshop. His **trading
post** sold silverworking tools and equipment,
and a wide variety of materials such as silver
and copper, turquoise and other semi-precious
stones, shell and coral, and other exotic materials
(tortoise shell, ivory, and **petrified wood**).

In the 1940s Zuni lapidarists revived several
ancient jewelry techniques, including **mosaic
inlay** and **mosaic overlay**, methods found
on shell and wood ornaments at prehistoric and
historic sites in the region. Zuni carver Teddy
Weahkee (ca. 1890–1965) was among the first
artists to create mosaic overly and inlaid pieces for
commercial sale. Also around this time, the Zunis
originated **channel inlay**, a technique in which
the silver dividers remain visible and part of the
decorative pattern. Traditional designs of Zuni
inlay artists include birds, butterflies, **Rainbow Man**, **Knifewing**, flowers, figures, and
geometric designs; and the items covered with the
inlay range from pins to conchas. Zuni jewelers
also cast pieces such as **crosses**, Knifewings, belt
buckles, and other pieces using **tufa**, hard stone,
or **sand** mold methods.

Zuni carver Leekya Deyuse (1889–1966) is
credited with originating fetish necklaces: in the
1940s he began making small fetish-type animals
and strung them on **heishi** necklaces that were
purchased from Santo Domingo jewelers. These
necklaces, made with a variety of animals and
semi-precious gemstones, are now handcrafted
by Zuni and other Native artists and are among
the most popular Southwestern jewelry forms
today. Traditionally, silverwork was a family affair
at Zuni, where many family members helped and
some specialized in certain tasks. Today the Zunis
continue to be known for their fetish necklaces
and superb lapidary skills in setting multiple
stones in silver.

ZUNI PUEBLO POTTERY / polychrome pottery has been created at Zuni Pueblo for centuries.
The early historic period pots are known as
Ashiwi Polychrome (ca. 1680–1750) and are
characterized by white kaolinite background **slip**
and designs—geometric elements such as stepped
areas and triangles, and abstract feathers and
birds—painted with deep red and black pigments.

The early forms included water jars with concave bases to facilitate being carried on the head;
Zuni women used them to carry water from the

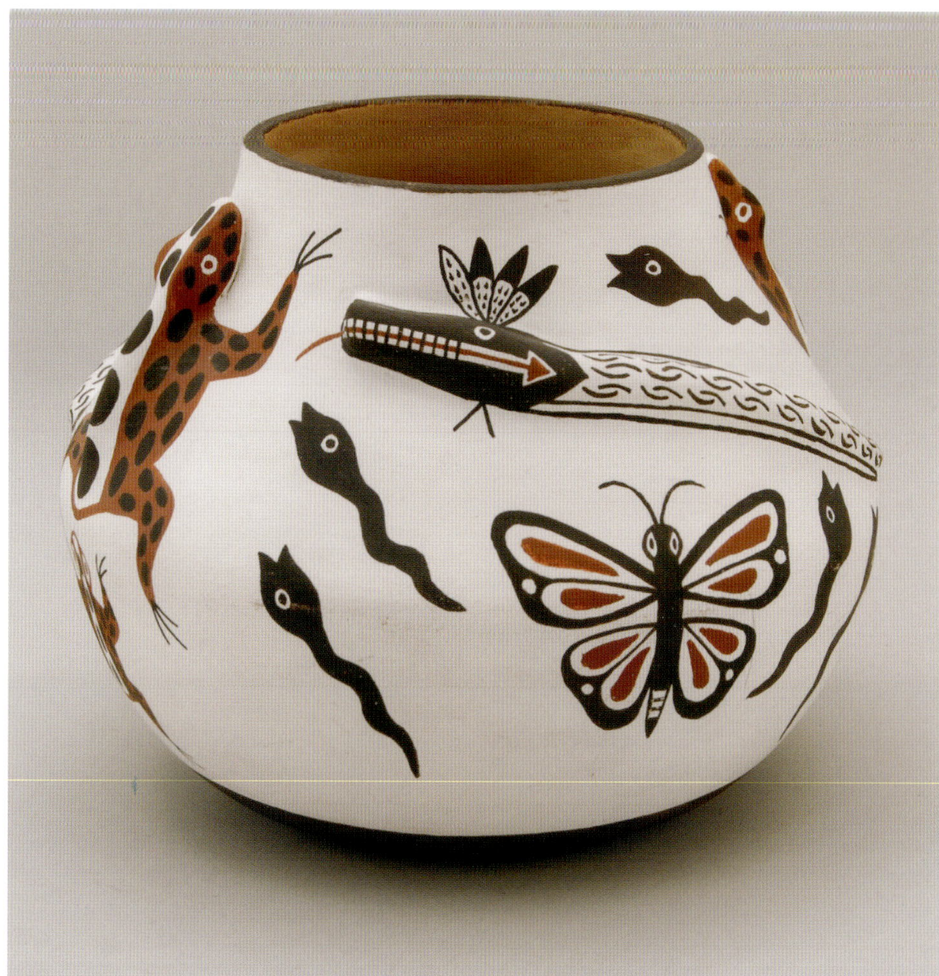

Jack Kalestewa (Zuni), jar with frogs.

pueblo's central well back to their household. Because they would have been highly visible in the
home, potters lavished more attention on decorating water jars than other vessel forms. Beginning
in the twentieth century, Zuni "olla maidens"
have celebrated traditional water-carrying skills
at public and private ceremonies by marching,
singing, and dancing while balancing water jars on
their heads.

In the second half of the nineteenth century
Zuni ceramics experienced a flowering; among the
finest potters to work in the Zuni tradition during
this period, and into the early twentieth century,
is a woman named Tsayutitsa.

In the very early 1900s Zuni potters developed
a form that remains popular today: chubby owl
figures, with stubby wings and ears, and sometimes
with little owls on their backs. Except for pots made
for religious ceremonies, the craft nearly disappeared later in the twentieth century when jewelry
making became the pueblo's dominant craft form.

Today Zuni is primarily known for its
white-slipped wares with red base and overall
elaborate designs in red and black. Among the
popular designs are the deer with a **heart line**,
large medallions or sunflower motifs said to be
emblematic of the six directions, various creatures
associated with water such as **dragonflies** and
frogs, and various simple design elements such
as spirals and stylized feathers and hatching (to
symbolize rain). The recent revival of the craft is
based on studies of nineteenth-century pottery in
museum collections. Zuni potters continue to use
potsherds as the **temper** in their **clay**, and most
use gas or electric kilns to **fire** their work.

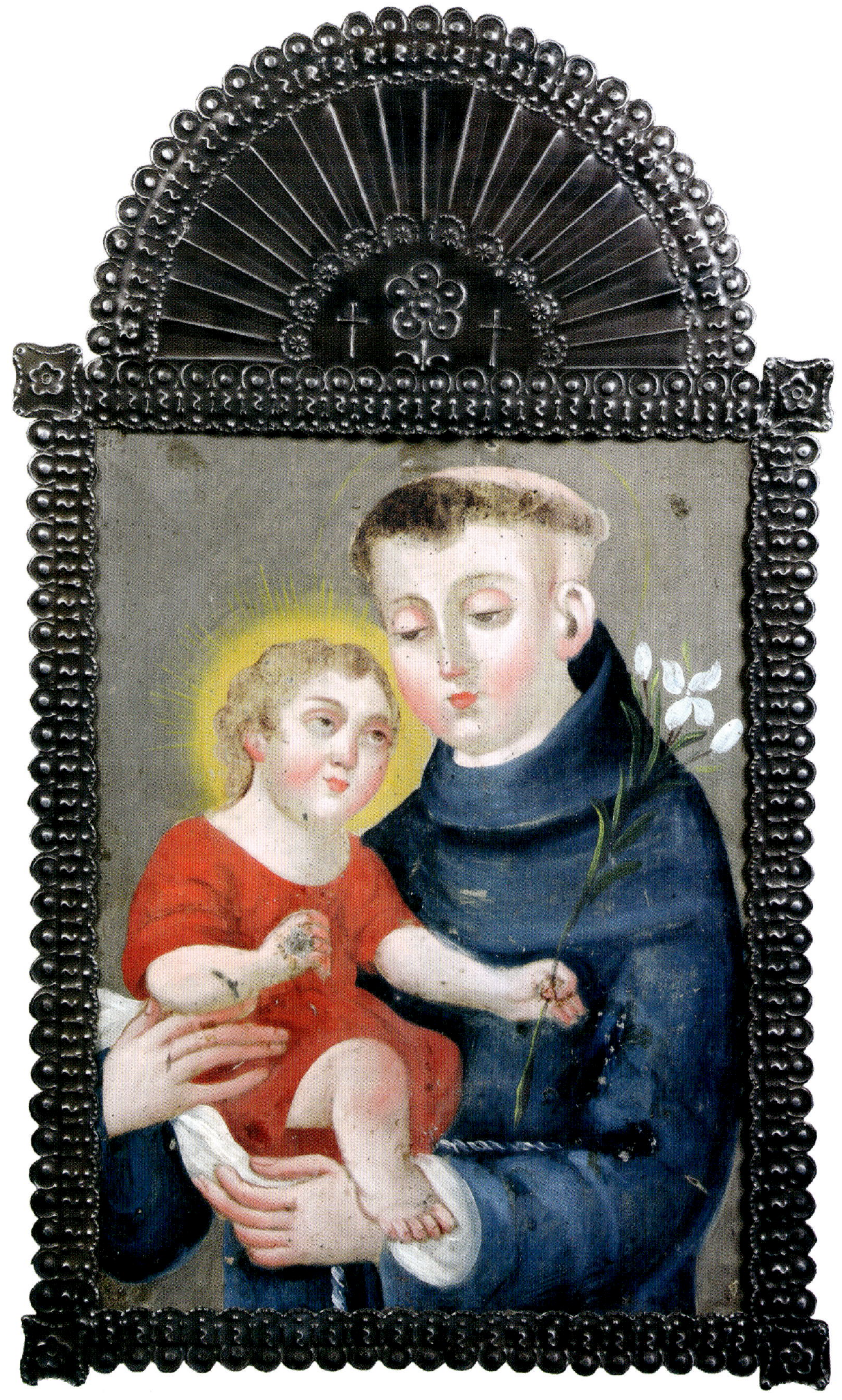

ACKNOWLEDGMENTS

A book of this magnitude could not have been completed without the aid of important scholars, who out of the kindness of their hearts took the time to carefully review terms relating to their areas of specialization. The project also could not have been done without the many artists and artisans who shared their techniques, materials, and philosophies with me—over the years and in recent months specifically for this book.

My heartfelt gratitude to the following three scholars/historians, who joined the "reviewing team" at the end of the project and provided us with crucial input concerning terms in their areas of specialization: Carmella Padilla, award-winning author, editor, and native Santa Fean; Jonathan Batkin, Director, Wheelwright Museum of the American Indian, Santa Fe, New Mexico; and R. Brooks Jeffrey, Director, Drachman Institute, College of Architecture and Landscape Architecture, University of Arizona.

I am also extremely grateful to the following scholars who generously devoted a great deal of time in assisting me with my research and reviewing the manuscript: Ann E. Marshall, author and Vice President, Curation and Education, Heard Museum, Phoenix, Arizona; Robin Farwell Gavin, author and Curator, Museum of Spanish Colonial Art, Santa Fe, New Mexico; and Charles King, author and owner of King Galleries, Scottsdale, Arizona. In particular, I wish to thank Mark Bahti, author and proprietor of Bahti Indian Arts in Tucson, Arizona, and Santa Fe, New Mexico, who went above and beyond the call of duty in reviewing term definitions and offering advice on a myriad of subjects.

Additionally, a very big thank you to the following reviewers/research consultants, who helped "polish up" certain terms: Walter Parks, author of *The Miracle of Mata Ortiz*; Diana Purdue, Curator of Collections, Heard Museum; Wendy Weston, Director of Special Projects, Heard Museum; Terry DeWald, owner, Terry DeWald American Indian Art, Tucson, Arizona; Jake and Susanne Page, authors of several books on Southwestern art; Kent McManis, owner, Grey Dog Trading Company, Tucson; Carleen C. Lazzell, editor, *La Cronica de Nuevo Mexico*; Jim Turner, historian and author of *Arizona: A Celebration of the Grand Canyon State*; Nora Trulsson, editor at *Sources + Design* magazine and co-author of *Living Homes: Sustainable Architecture and Design*; Bernard Fontana, author of several books including *A Gift of Angels: The Art of Mission San Xavier del Bac*; Mark Sublette, author and proprietor of Medicine Man Gallery (Santa Fe and Tucson); and Linda Cordell, Senior Scholar, School of Advanced Research, Santa Fe, New Mexico.

Most importantly, my sincere thanks to the team at Rio Nuevo Publishers for taking on this massive, complicated, and yet highly worthwhile project: W. Ross Humphreys, Publisher; David Jenney, Co-Publisher; Robin Stancliff, freelance photographer; and most especially Caroline Cook, Editor, whose patience, knowledge of the Southwest, and superb editing skills guided me through every step of this publication.

Lastly, I am deeply appreciative of my husband, Martin, whose enduring patience and love, as well as his extensive knowledge of southwestern art, guided me during the long journey of researching, writing, and reviewing this book. Together we share a never-ending passion for collecting objects that tell the unique story of the Southwest. And many thanks to my dog, Lily, who kept my feet warm, got me outside for breaks from long hours at the computer, and generally provided much joy and comfort.

OPPOSITE: Nicolas Madrid (Mexico), Saint Anthony retablo in tin frame.

APPENDIX—*technical diagrams*

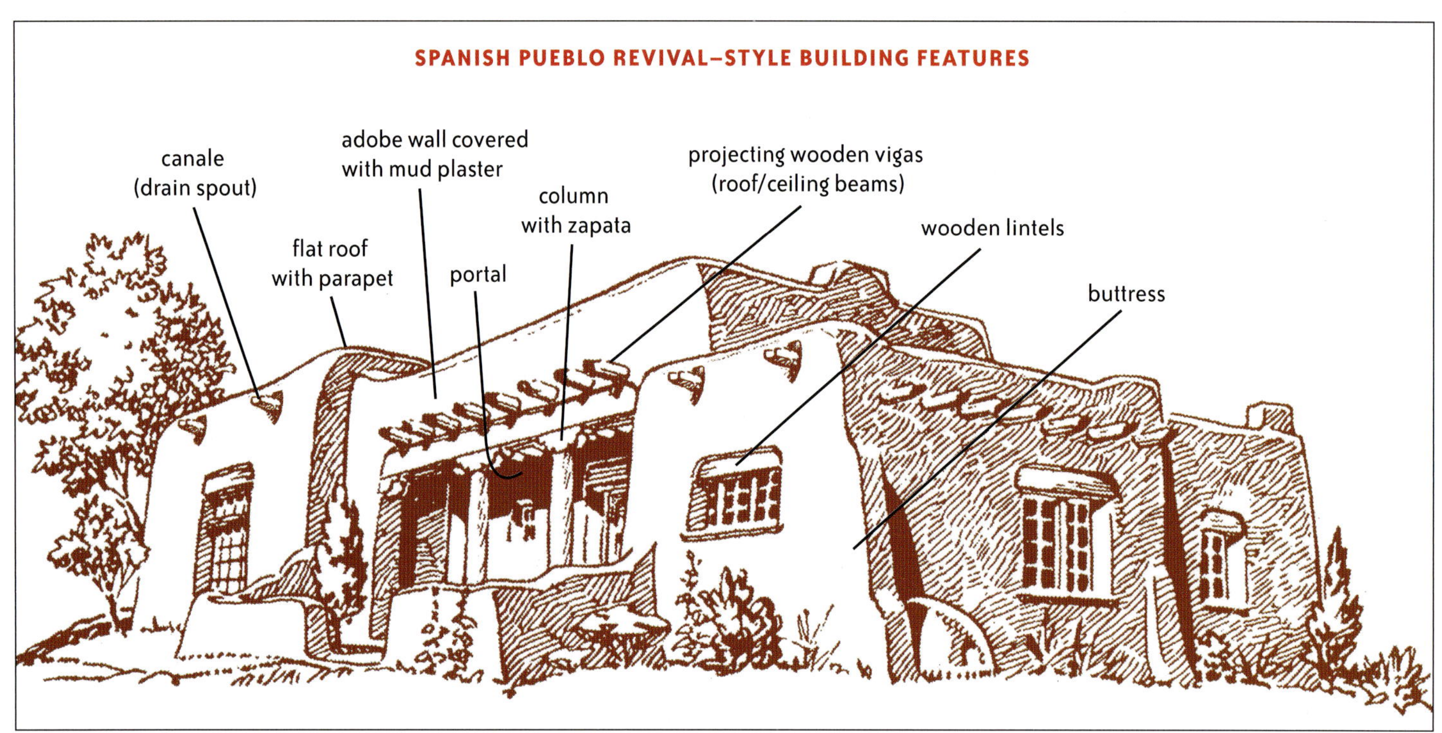

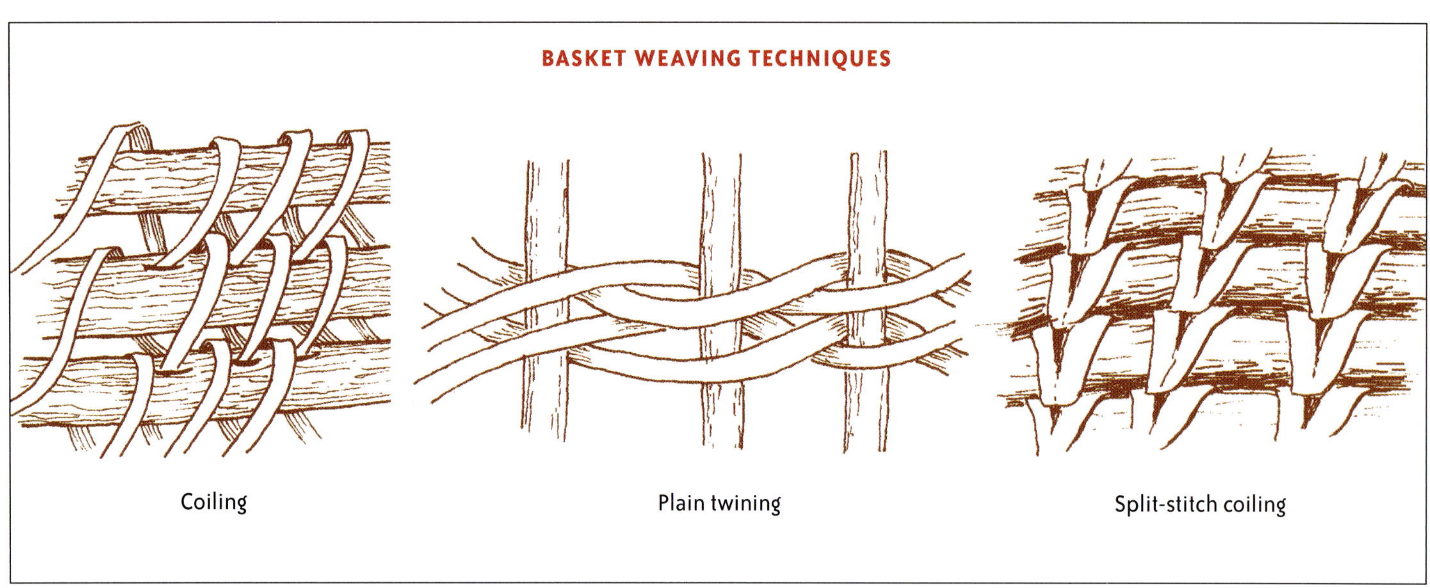

NAVAJO LOOM

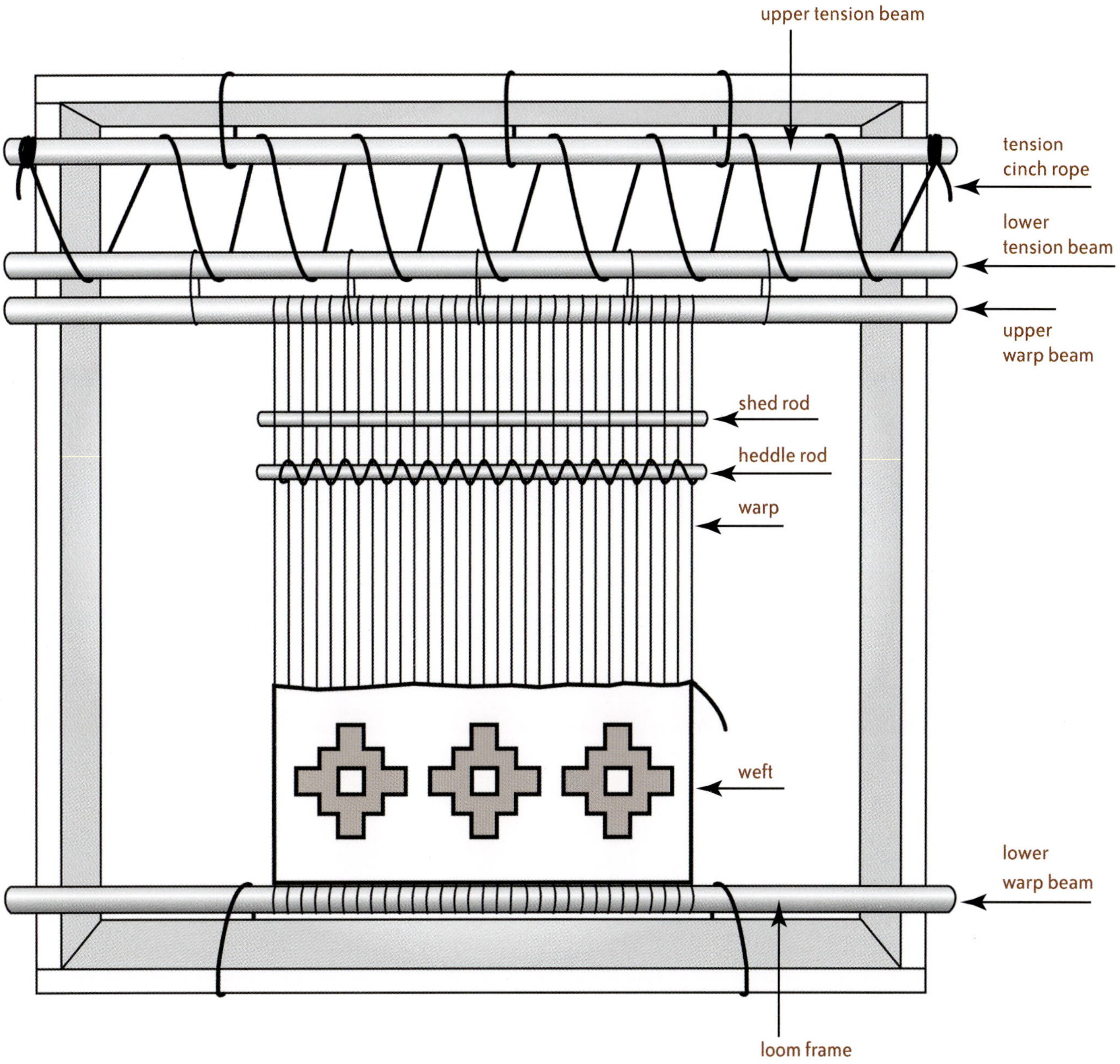

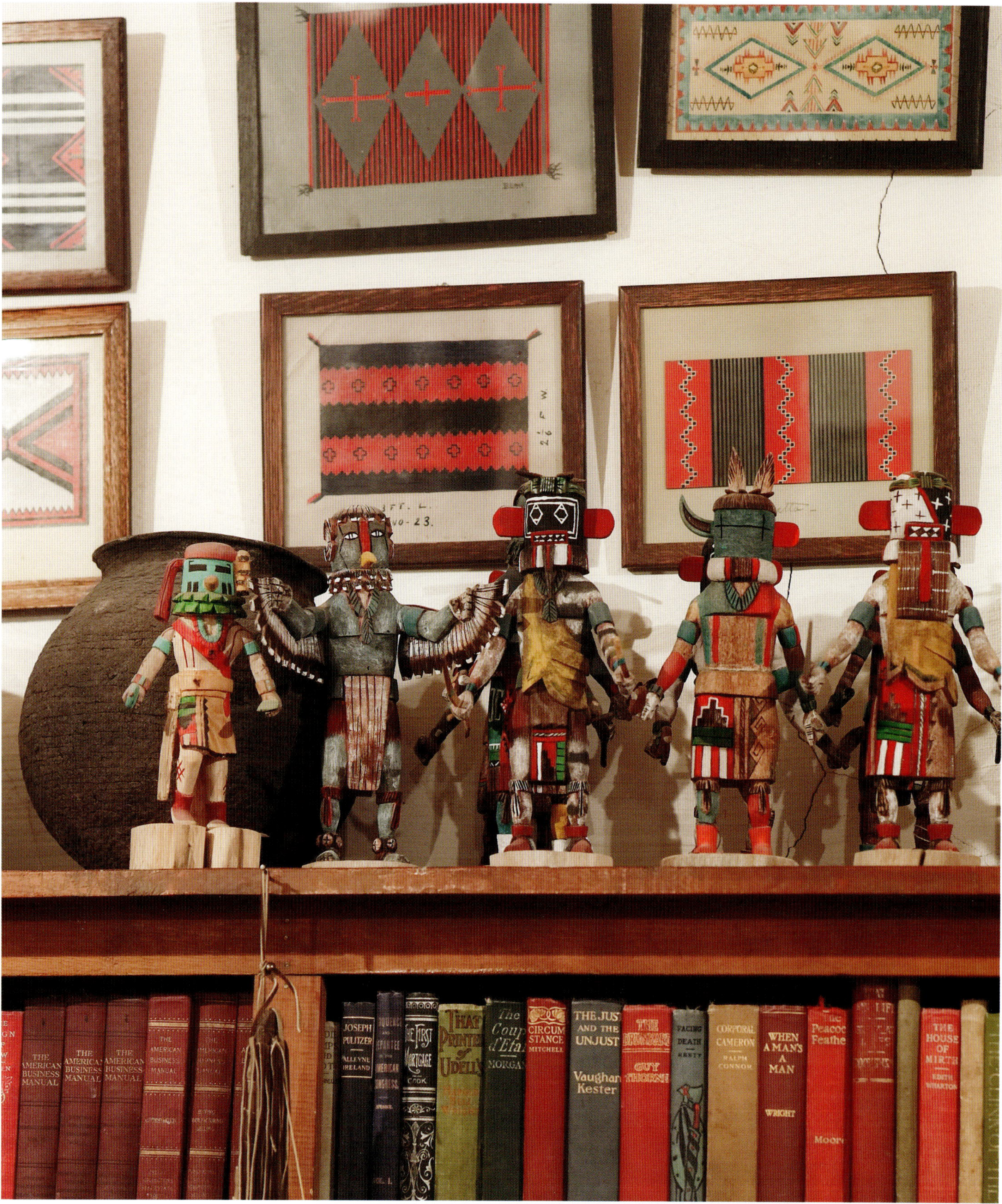

upper tension beam
tension cinch rope
lower tension beam
upper warp beam
shed rod
heddle rod
warp
weft
lower warp beam
loom frame

Rug room at Hubbell Trading Post, decorated with framed rug designs, corrugated pot, and katsinam.

Places to See ART IN THE SOUTHWEST

ARIZONA

AMERIND FOUNDATION
2100 North Amerind Road, Dragoon, AZ 85609
(520) 586-3666, www.amerind.org

ARIZONA STATE MUSEUM
1013 East University Boulevard, Tucson, AZ
85721, (520) 621-6302,
www.statemuseum.arizona.edu

BAHTI INDIAN ARTS
4330 North Campbell #73, Tucson, AZ 85718
(520) 577-02990, www.bahti.com

BLUE RAIN GALLERY
4164 North Marshall Way, Scottsdale, AZ 85251
(480) 874-8110, www.blueraingallery.com

CAMERON TRADING POST
466 Highway 89, Cameron, AZ 86020
(877) 608-3491, www.camerontradingpost.com

**CASA GRANDE RUINS
NATIONAL MONUMENT**
1100 West Ruins Drive, Coolidge, AZ 85128
(520) 723-3172, www.nps.gov/cagr

GARLAND'S INDIAN JEWELRY
3953 North State Route 89A, Sedona, AZ 86336
(928) 282-6632, www.garlandsjewelry.com

GARLAND'S NAVAJO RUGS
411 State Route 179, Sedona, AZ 86336
(928) 282-4070, www.garlandsrugs.com

GRAND CANYON NATIONAL PARK
PO Box 129, Grand Canyon, AZ 86023
(928) 638-7888, www.nps.gov/grca

GREY DOG TRADING COMPANY
4320 North Campbell Avenue, Tucson, AZ 85718
(520) 881-6888, www.greydogtrading.com

HEARD MUSEUM
2301 North Central Avenue, Phoenix, AZ 85004
(602) 252-8840, www.heard.org

HEARD MUSEUM NORTH
32633 North Scottsdale Road, Scottsdale, AZ
85266, (480) 488-9817, www.heard.org

HOPI CULTURAL CENTER
Route 264, Kykotsmovi Village, AZ 86043
(928) 734-2401, www.hopiculturalcenter.com

**HUBBELL TRADING POST
NATIONAL HISTORIC SITE**
PO Box 150, Ganado, AZ 86505
(928) 755-3476, www.nps.gov/hutr

KING GALLERIES
Ste A, 7100 East Main Street, Scottsdale, AZ
85251, (480) 481-0187, www.kinggalleries.com

MEDICINE MAN GALLERY
7000 E. Tanque Verde Road, Suite 16, Tucson, AZ
85715, (800) 422-9382 or (520) 722-7798,
www.medicinemangallery.com

**MONTEZUMA CASTLE
NATIONAL MONUMENT**
PO Box 219, Camp Verde, AZ 89005
(928) 567-3322, www.nps.gov/moca

MUSEUM OF NORTHERN ARIZONA
3101 North Fort Valley Road, Flagstaff, AZ
86001, (928) 774-5213, www.musnaz.org

NAVAJO NATION MUSEUM
Hwy 264 and Post Office Loop Road, Window
Rock, AZ 86515, (928) 871-7941,
ggsc.wnmu.edu/mcf/museums/nnm.html

NIZHONI RANCH GALLERY
P.O. Box 815, Sonoita, AZ 85637
(520) 455-5020, www.navajorug.com

OLD TERRITORIAL SHOP
7077 E Main Street # 7, Scottsdale, AZ 85251
(480) 945-5432, www.oldterritorialshop.com

PATANIA'S STERLING SILVER ORIGINALS
174 East Toole Avenue, Tucson, AZ 85701
(520) 795-0086

PETRIFIED FOREST NATIONAL PARK
PO Box 2217, Petrified Forest, AZ 86028
(928) 524-6228, www.nps.gov/pefo

PUEBLO GRANDE MUSEUM
4619 E. Washington Street, Phoenix, AZ 85034
(602) 495-0900, www.pueblogrande.org

SAN XAVIER DEL BAC MISSION
1950 West San Xavier Road, Tucson, AZ 85746
(520) 294-2624, www.sanxaviermission.org

TEEC NOS POS TRADING POST
Highways 160 & 64, Teec Nos Pos, AZ 86514
(928) 656-3224, tnptradingpost.com

TLAQUEPAQUE ARTS & CRAFTS VILLAGE
336 State Route 179, Sedona, AZ 86324
(928) 282-4838, www.tlaq.com

TUMACÁCORI NATIONAL HISTORICAL PARK
PO Box 8067, Tumacácori, AZ 85640
(520) 398-2341, www.nps.gov/tuma

TWO DOGS SOUTHWEST GALLERY
PO Box 6204, Chandler, AZ 85246
(602) 739-2821,
www.twodogssouthwestgallery.com

WADDELL TRADING COMPANY
7144 Main Street, Scottsdale, AZ 85251
(480) 755-8080, waddelltradingco.com

CALIFORNIA

AGUA CALIENTE CULTURAL MUSEUM
219 South Palm Canyon Drive, Palm Springs, CA 92262, 760-323-0151, www.accmuseum.org

ANTELOPE VALLEY INDIAN MUSEUM
15701 East Avenue M, Lake Los Angeles, CA 93535, www.avim.parks.ca.gov

THE BOWERS MUSEUM
2002 North Main Street, Santa Ana, CA 92706 (714) 567-3600, www.bowers.org

CALIFORNIA HERITAGE MUSEUM
2612 Main Street Santa Monica, CA 90405 (310) 392-8537, www.californiaheritagemuseum.org

COLONIAL ARTS
151 Vermont Street, Suite 6, San Francisco, CA 94103, (415)-505-0680, www.colonialarts.com

HACIENDA ANTIQUES & ART OF OLD CALIFORNIA
8559 North Ventura Avenue, Ventura, CA 93001 (805) 613-8003, www.trocadero.com/Hacienda

HISTORIA – JAMES CASWELL
1322 Second Street, Suite 2, Santa Monica, CA 90401, (310) 394-3384, historia-antiques.com

MISSION INN MUSEUM
3696 Main Street, Riverside, CA 92501 (951) 788-9556, www.missioninnmuseum.com

MISSION SAN JUAN CAPISTRANO
26801 Ortega Highway, San Juan Capistrano, CA 92675 , (949) 234-1300, missionsjc.com

OLD TOWN SAN DIEGO STATE HISTORIC PARK
4002 Wallace Street, San Diego, CA, 92110 www.parks.ca.gov

COLORADO

CENTER OF SOUTHWEST STUDIES
1000 Rim Drive, Durango, CO 81301 (970) 247-7456, swcenter.fortlewis.edu

DENVER ART MUSEUM
100 W. 14th Ave. Parkway, Denver, CO 80204 (720) 865-5000, www.denverartmuseum.org

DURANGO SILVER COMPANY
17897 Highway 160, Durango, CO 81301 (970) 375-2401, www.durangosilver.com

KOSHARE INDIAN MUSEUM
115 West 18th Street, La Junta, CO 81050 (719) 384-4411, www.kosharehistory.org

MESA VERDE NATIONAL PARK
PO Box 8, Mesa Verde, CO 81330 (970) 529-4465, www.nps.gov/meve

NATIVE AMERICAN TRADING COMPANY
213 West 13th Avenue, Denver, CO 80204 (303) 534-0771, www.nativeamericantradingco.com

SANGRE DE CRISTO ARTS CENTER
210 N Santa Fe Avenue, Pueblo, CO 81003 719-295-7200, www.sdc-arts.org

TOH-ATIN GALLERY
145 West 9th Street, Durango, CO 81301 (970) 247-8277, toh-atin.com

NEW MEXICO

ADOBE GALLERY
221 Canyon Road Santa Fe, New Mexico 87501 (505) 955-0550, www.adobegallery.com

ALAN KESSLER GALLERY
836 Canyon Road, Santa Fe, NM 87501 (505) 986-0123, www.trocadero.com/ack45/

ALBUQUERQUE MUSEUM OF ART AND HISTORY
2000 Mountain Road Northwest, Albuquerque, NM 87104, (505) 242-4600, www.cabq.gov

ANDREA FISHER FINE POTTERY
100 West San Francisco Street, Santa Fe, NM 87501, (505) 986-1234, www.andreafisherpottery.com

ANDREWS PUEBLO POTTERY
303 Romero NW (Old Town) Albuquerque, NM 87104, www.andrewspueblopottery.com

A:SHIWI A:WAN MUSEUM AND HERITAGE CENTER
02 East Ojo Caliente Road, Zuni, NM 87327 (505) 782-4403, www.ashiwi-museum.org

BAHTI INDIAN ARTS
119 East Palace Avenue, Santa Fe, NM 87501 (505) 983-4542, www.bahti.com

BANDELIER NATIONAL MONUMENT
15 Entrance Road, Los Alamos, NM 87544 (505) 672-3861, www.nps.gov/band

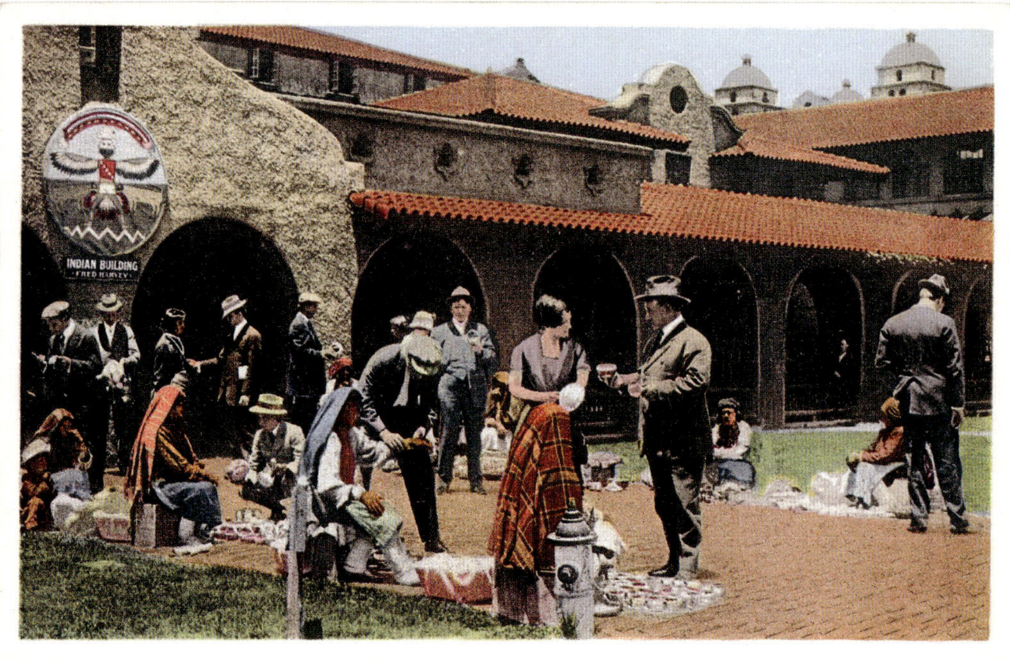

Antique postcard portraying entrance to Alvarado Hotel "Indian Building," Albuquerque, New Mexico.

BLUE RAIN GALLERY
130 Lincoln Avenue, Suite C, Santa Fe, New
Mexico 87501, (505) 954-9902,
www.blueraingallery.com

CHIMAYÓ MUSEUM
13 Plaza De Cerro, Chimayó, NM 87522
(505) 351-0945, www.chimayomuseum.org

CHIIMAYÓ TRADING & MERCANTILE
Highway 76, Chimayó, NM 87522
(800) 248-7859, www.chimayoarts.com

COULTER BROOKS ART AND ANTIQUES
924 Paseo de Peralta #4, Santa Fe, NM 87501
(505) 577-7051, www.coulterbrooks.com

INDIAN PUEBLO CULTURAL CENTER
2401 12th Street N.W., Albuquerque, NM
87104, (505) 843-7270, www.indianpueblo.org

JEMEZ STATE MONUMENT HERITAGE AREA
Sandoval County, NM, (505) 867-5351,
www.nmmonuments.org/jemez

MAXWELL MUSEUM OF ANTHROPOLOGY
MSC01 1050, 1 University of New Mexico,
Albuquerque, NM 87131
(505) 277-4405, www.unm.edu/~maxwell

EL MUSEO CULTURAL
555 Camino De La Familia, Santa Fe, NM 87501
(505) 992-0591, www.elmuseocultural.org

MILLICENT ROGERS MUSEUM
1504 Millicent Rogers Road, Taos, NM 87571
(505) 758-2462, www.millicentrogers.org

MORNING STAR GALLERY
513 Canyon Road, Santa Fe, NM 87501
(505) 982-8187, www.morningstargallery.com

MUSEUM OF CONTEMPORARY NATIVE ARTS
108 Cathedral Place, Santa Fe, NM 87501
(505) 983-8900, www.iaia.edu/museum

MUSEUM OF INDIAN ARTS AND CULTURE
710 Camino Lejo, Santa Fe, NM 87505
(505) 476-1250, www.indianartsandculture.org

MUSEUM OF INTERNATIONAL FOLK ART
706 Camino Lejo, Santa Fe, NM 87505
(505) 476-1200, www.internationalfolkart.org

MUSEUM OF SPANISH COLONIAL ART
750 Camino Lejo, Santa Fe, NM 87501
(505) 982-2226, www.spanishcolonial.org

NATIONAL HISPANIC CULTURAL CENTER
1701 4th Street Southwest, Albuquerque, NM
87102, (505) 246-2261, www.nhccnm.org

THE OWINGS GALLERY
120 East Marcy Avenue, Santa Fe, NM 87501
(505) 982-6244, www.owingsgallery.com

NEDRA MATTEUCCI GALLERIES
1075 Paseo de Peralta, Santa Fe, NM 87501
(505) 982-4631, www.matteucci.com

PACHAMAMA GALLERY
223 Canyon Road, Santa Fe, NM 87501
(505) 983-4020, www.pachamamasantafe.com

PALACE OF THE GOVERNORS
105 West Palace Avenue, Santa Fe, NM 87501
(505) 476-5100, www.palaceofthegovernors.org

PEYTON WRIGHT GALLERY
237 East Palace Avenue, Santa Fe, NM 87501
(505) 989-9888, www.peytonwright.com

POEH MUSEUM
78 Cities of Gold Road, Santa Fe, NM 87501
(505) 455-5041, www.poehmuseum.com

EL POTRERO TRADING POST
17 Santuario Dr # A, Chimayó, NM 87522
(505) 351-4112, www.potrerotradingpost.com

THE RAINBOW MAN
107 East Palace Road, Santa Fe, NM 87501
(505) 982-8706, www.therainbowman.com

EL RANCHO DE LAS GOLONDRINAS
334 Los Pinos Rd, Santa Fe, NM 87507
505) 471-2261, www.golondrinas.org

EL RINCON TRADING POST AND MUSEUM
114 Kit Carson Road, Taos, NM 87571
(575) 758-9188

SANTA FE GALLERY AT CAFÉ PASQUAL'S
121 Don Gaspar, Santa Fe, NM 87501
(505) 983-9340, www.pasquals.com

SHIPROCK TRADING POST
301 West Main Street, Farmington, NM 87401
(505) 324-0881, www.shiprocktradingpost.com

TAOS HISTORIC MUSEUMS
222 Ledoux Street, Taos, NM 87571
(575) 758-0505, www.taoshistoricmuseums.com

TWO GRACES TAOS
68 St. Francis Church Plaza, Ranchos de Taos,
NM 87557, (575) 758-4101,
www.twograces.blogspot.com

TWO GREY HILLS TRADING POST
HCR 330, Tohatchi, NM 87325
(505) 789-3270, www.twogreyhills.com

**WESTERN NEW MEXICO UNIVERSITY
MUSEUM**
1000 West College Avenue, Silver City, NM
88061, (575) 538-6386,
www.wnmumuseum.org

**WHEELWRIGHT MUSEUM OF THE
AMERICAN INDIAN**
704 Camino Lejo, Santa Fe, NM 87505
(505) 982-4636, www.wheelwright.org

WRIGHT'S INDIAN ART
1100 San Mateo Boulevard, NE, Suite 21, Albuquerque, NM 87110
(505) 266-0120, www.wrightsgallery.com

UTAH

CHASE HOME MUSEUM OF UTAH FOLK ART
900 S 700 E, Salt Lake City, UT 84105
(801) 236-7555

EDGE OF THE CEDARS STATE PARK MUSEUM
660 West 400 North, Blanding, UT 84511
(435) 678-2238, www.utah.com/stateparks/
edge_of_cedars.htm

GOULDING'S TRADING POST
Goulding's Lodge, Monument Valley, UT 84536
(435) 727-3231, www.gouldings.com

TWIN ROCKS TRADING POST
913 East Navajo Twins Drive, Bluff, UT 84512
(435) 672-2341, www.twinrocks.com

UTAH MUSEUM OF FINE ARTS
410 Campus Center Drive, Salt Lake City, UT
84112, (801) 581-7332, umfa.utah.edu

BIBLIOGRAPHY *and Suggestions for Further Reading*

NOTE: In addition to the sources listed in the bibiography, information in this book was drawn from the wall text of museum exhibitions (permanent and temporary) in the Southwest—including those at the Heard Museum, Phoenix, Arizona; Maxwell Museum of Anthropology, University of New Mexico, Albuquerque; Museum of Spanish Colonial Art, Santa Fe, New Mexico; National Hispanic Cultural Center, Albuquerque, New Mexico; Museum of Indian Arts and Culture, Santa Fe. Also, in addition to the specific articles listed here, other articles in issues of the *American Indian Art Magazine*, a scholarly journal published quarterly, were used as a resource. The websites of Native peoples living throughout the region and websites of organizations such as the Spanish Colonial Arts Society, Santa Fe, were consulted as well. The books are separated loosely into categories; many of the books contain information on subjects other than just the category heading it is listed under.

ANCESTRAL PUEBLOAN PERIOD

Vivian, R. Gwinn and Bruce Hilpert. *The Chaco Handbook: An Encyclopedic Guide.* Salt Lake City: The University of Utah Press, 2002.

"What's in a Name?" *Archaeology* 59, no. 4 (July/August 2006).

ARCHITECTURE

Bunting, Bainbridge. *Early Architecture In New Mexico.* Albuquerque: University of New Mexico Press, 1976.

Clark, Victoria. *How Arizona Sold Its Sunshine: Historical Hotels of Arizona.* Sedona, AZ: Blue Gourd Publishing Inc., 2004.

Fontana, Bernard L. *A Gift of Angels: The Art of Mission San Xavier del Bac.* Tucson: University of Arizona Press, 2010.

Gidwitz, Tom. *Counting Rings: Tree-Ring Dating.* Western National Parks Association, 2008.

Gellner, Arrol. *Red Tile Style: America's Spanish Revival Architecture.* New York: Viking Studio, 2002.

Iowa, Jerome. *Ageless Adobe: History and Preservation in Southwestern Architecture.* Santa Fe: Sunstone Press, 1985.

McGregor, Suzi Moore and Nora Burba Trullson. *Living Homes: Sustainable Architecture and Design.* San Francisco: Chronicle Books, 2001.

Moore Booker, Margaret. *The Santa Fe House: Historic Residences, Enchanting Adobes, and Romantic Revivals.* New York: Rizzoli, 2009.

Nequette, Anne M. and R. Brooks Jeffery. *A Guide to Tucson Architecture.* Tucson: The University of Arizona Press, 2002.

Patterson, Ann and Mark Vinson. *Landmark Buildings: Arizona's Architectural Heritage.* Phoenix: Arizona Highways Books and Arizona Department of Transportation, 2004.

Vint, Bob and Christina Neumann. *Southwest Housing Traditions: Design, Materials, Performance.* Washington, D.C.: U.S. Department of Housing and Urban Development, 2005.

Weigle, Marta ed. *Hispanic Arts and Ethnohistory In the Southwest.* Santa Fe: Ancient City Press, 1983.

Whiffen, Marcus and Carla Breeze. *Pueblo Deco: The Art Deco Architecture of the Southwest.* Albuquerque: University of New Mexico Press, 1984.

Wilson, Chris. *The Myth of Santa Fe: Creating A Modern Regional Tradition.* Albuquerque: University of New Mexico Press, 1997.

BASKETRY

Dalrymple, Larry. *Indian Basketmakers of the Southwest: The Living Art and Fine Tradition.* Santa Fe: Museum of New Mexico Press, 2000.

Finger, Judith W. and Andrew D. Finger. *Circles of Life: Katsina Imagery On Hopi Wicker Basketry.* Ukiah, CA: Grace Hudson Museum and Sun House, 2006.

McGreevy, Susan Brown. *Indian Basketry Artists of the Southwest: Deep Roots, New Growth.* Santa Fe: School of American Research Press, 2001.

McGreevy, Susan Brown and Andrew Hunter Whiteford. *Translating Tradition: Basketry Arts of the San Juan Paiutes.* Santa Fe: Wheelwright Museum of the American Indian, 1985.

Simpson, Georgiana Kennedy. *Navajo Ceremonial Baskets: Sacred Symbols, Sacred Space.* Summertown, Tennessee: Native Voices, 2003.

Teiwes, Helga. *Hopi Basket Weaving: Artistry in Natural Fibers.* Tucson: The University of Arizona Press, 1996.

BEADWORK

Houk, Rose. *A Guide to American Indian Beadwork of the Southwest.* Tucson: Western National Parks Association, 2008.

CLOTHING AND ACCESSORIES

Brasser, Theodore. *Native American Clothing: An Illustrated History.* Ontario, Canada: Firefly Books, 2009.

Paterek, Josephine. *Encyclopedia of American Indian Costume.* New York and London: W. W. Norton & Company, 1994.

COLCHA

Benson, Nancy C. *New Mexico Colcha Club: Spanish Colonial Embroidery & The Women Who Saved It.* Santa Fe: Museum of New Mexico Press, 2008.

DECORATIVE ARTS / HISPANO ARTS

Cirillo, Dexter. *Across Frontiers: Hispanic Crafts of New Mexico.* San Francisco: Chronicle Books, 1998.

Egan, Martha J. *Relicarios: Devotional Miniatures from the Americas.* Santa Fe: Museum of New Mexico Press, 1993.

Montaño, Mary. *Tradiciones Nuevomexicanas: Hispano Arts and Culture of New Mexico.* Albuquerque: The University of New Mexico Press, 2001.

Morelli, Laura. *Made In The Southwest.* New York: Universe, 2005.

Padilla, Carmella, ed. *Conexiones: Connections in Spanish Colonial Art.* Santa Fe: Museum of Spanish Colonial Art, 2002.

Pierce, Donna and Marta Weigle, eds. *Spanish New Mexico, Volume One: The Arts of Spanish New Mexico.* Santa Fe: Museum of New Mexico Press, 1996.

Rosenak, Chuck and Jan. *The Saint Makers: Contemporary Santeras Y Santeros.* Flagstaff, AZ: Northland Publishing, 1998.

Weigle, Marta ed. *Hispanic Arts and Ethnohistory In the Southwest.* Santa Fe: Ancient City Press, 1983.

Wroth, William and Robin Farwell Gavin, eds. *Converging Streams: Art of the Hispanic and Native American Southwest.* Santa Fe: Museum of Spanish Colonial Art, 2010.

FETISHES

Bahti, Mark. *Spirit in the Stone: A Handbook of Southwest Indian Animal Carvings and Beliefs.* Tucson: Rio Nuevo Publishers, 1999.

McManis, Kent. *Zuni Fetishes & Carvings.* Tucson: Rio Nuevo Publishers, 2010.

Rodee, Marian and James Ostler. *The Fetish Carvers of Zuni.* Albuquerque: The Maxwell Museum of Anthropology, The University of New Mexico; Zuni, New Mexico: The Pueblo of Zuni Arts and Crafts, 1990.

Slaney, Deborah C. *Blue Gem, White Metal: Carvings and Jewelry from the C. G. Wallace Collection.* Phoenix: Heard Museum, 1998.

FURNITURE

Taylor, Lonn and Dessa Bokides. *New Mexican Furniture, 1600–1940.* Santa Fe: Museum of New Mexico Press, 1989.

Williams, A. D. *Spanish Colonial Furniture.* Salt Lake City: Gibbs M Smith, Inc., 1982.

Wroth, William, ed. *Furniture From The Hispanic Southwest.* Santa Fe: Ancient City Press, 1984.

JEWELRY

Bahti, Mark. *Silver and Stone: Profiles of American Indian Jewelers.* Tucson: Rio Nuevo Publishers, 2007.

Batkin, Jonathan. *The Native American Curio Trade in New Mexico.* Santa Fe: Wheelright Museum of the American Indian, 2008.

Bauver, Robert. *Navajo and Pueblo Earrings, 1850–1945: Collected by Robert V. Gallegos.* Albuquerque: Rio Grande Books, 2007.

Micaceous pottery at Spanish Market, Santa Fe, New Mexico.

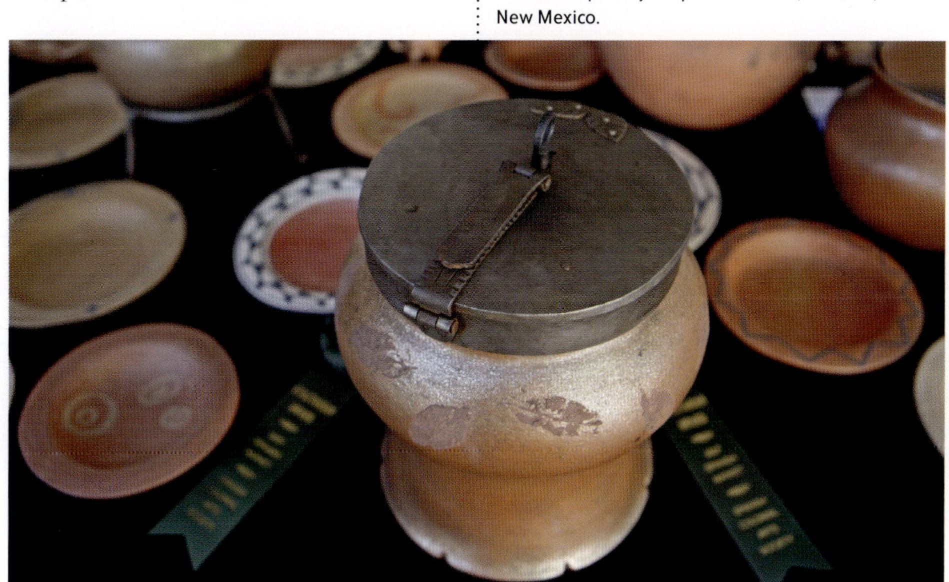

Bedinger, Margery. *Indian Silver: Navajo and Pueblo Jewelers.* Albuquerque: University of New Mexico Press, 1973.

Marchaza, Lauren M. "Selling Authenticity: The Role of Zuni Knifewings and Rainbow Gods in Tourism of the American Southwest." Master of Arts Thesis, College of Fine Arts of Ohio University, June 2007.

Pardue, Diana F. *Contemporary Southwestern Jewelry.* Santa Fe: Gibbs Smith, Publisher, 2007.

Pardue, Diana F. *Native American Bolo Ties: Vintage and Contemporary Artistry.* Santa Fe: Museum of New Mexico Press in association with the Heard Museum, 2011.

Simpson, Georgiana Kennedy. *A Guide to Indian Jewelry of the Southwest.* Tucson: Southwest Parks and Monuments Association, 1999.

Slaney, Deborah C. *Blue Gem, White Metal: Carvings and Jewelry from the C. G. Wallace Collection.* Phoenix: Heard Museum, 1998.

Tisdale, Shelby J. *Fine Indian Jewelry of the Southwest: The Millicent Rogers Museum Collection.* Santa Fe: Museum of New Mexico Press, 2006.

KATSINAM

Finger, Judith W. and Andrew D. Finger. *Circles of Life: Katsina Imagery On Hopi Wicker Basketry.* Ukiah, CA: Grace Hudson Museum and Sun House, 2006.

Houk, Rose. *A Guide to Hopi Katsina Carvings.* Tucson: Western National Parks Association, 2003.

McManis, Kent. *A Guide to Hopi Katsina Dolls.* Tucson: Rio Nuevo Publishers, 2000.

Pearlstone, Zena. *Katsina: Commodified and Appropriated Images of Hopi Supernaturals.* Los Angeles: UCLA Fowler Museum of Cultural History, 2001.

LANDSCAPE ARCHITECTURE AND DESIGN

Calhoun, Scott. *The Hot Garden: Landscape Design for the Desert Southwest.* Tucson: Rio Nuevo Publishers, 2009.

LeBlanc, Sydney. *Secret Gardens of Santa Fe.* New York: Rizzoli, 1997.

MISCELLANEOUS

Berke, Arnold. *Mary Colter: Architect of the Southwest.* New York: Princeton Architectural Press, 2002.

Cornett, James W. *Indian Uses of Desert Plants.* Palm Springs, CA: Nature Trails Press, 2011.

Hand/Eye Magazine: Global Art, Craft & Design (Spring 2012, New Mexico Issue): 5–45.

Martin, Ned and Jody and Robert Bauver. *Bridles of the Americas, Vol. I: Indian Silver.* Nicasio, CA: Hawk Hill Press, 2010.

Marshall, Ann, ed. *Home: Native People In The Southwest.* Phoenix: Heard Museum, 2005.

Marshall, Ann. *Rain: Native Impressions from the American Southwest.* Phoenix: Heard Museum; Santa Fe: Museum of New Mexico Press, 2000.

Pettit, Michael. *Artists of New Mexico Traditions: The National Heritage Fellows.* Santa Fe: Museum of New Mexico Press, 2012.

Stephenson, Claude, ed. *Matachines!* Santa Fe: New Mexico Arts, 2008.

Trimble, Stephen. *The People: Indians of the American Southwest.* Santa Fe: School of American Research Press, 1993.

MEXICAN ARTS

Egan, Martha. *Milagros: Votive Offerings from the Americas.* Santa Fe: Museum of New Mexico Press, 1991.

Lowell, Susan and Jim Hills, Jorge Quintana Rodríguez, Walter Parks, and Michael Wisner. *The Many Faces of Mata Ortiz.* Tucson: Rio Nuevo Publishers, 1999.

Oettinger, Marion Jr. *Folk Treasures of Mexico: The Nelson A. Rockefeller Collection.* New York: Harry N. Abrams, Inc., Publishers, 1990.

Powell, Melissa, ed. *Secrets of Casas Grandes: Precolumbian Art and Archaeology of Northern New Mexico.* Santa Fe: Museum of New Mexico Press, 2006.

Sayer, Chloë. *Arts and Crafts of Mexico.* London: Thames & Hudson Ltd., 1990; reprint 2000.

Stanton, Andra Fischgrund. *Zapotec Weavers of Teotilan.* Santa Fe: Museum of New Mexico Press, 1999.

Takahashi, Masako. *Mexican Tiles.* San Francisco: Chronicle Books, 2000.

NATIVE AMERICAN ART (GENERAL) / FOLK ART

Anderson, Duane, ed. *Legacy: Southwest Indian Art at the School of American Research.* Santa Fe: School of American Research Press, 1999.

Ferg, Alan, ed. *Western Apache Material Culture: The Goodwin and Guenther Collections.* Tucson: The University of Arizona Press, for The Arizona State Museum, 1987.

Lamb, Susan. *A Guide to American Indian Folk Art of the Southwest.* Tucson: Western National Parks Association, 2006.

Marshall, Ann. *Rain: Native Expressions From The American Southwest.* Phoenix: Heard Museum; Santa Fe: Museum of New Mexico Press, 2000.

McGreevy, Susan Brown. "I Never Saw A Purple Cow: Navajo Contemporary Animal Art," *American Indian Art Magazine* 22, no. 4 (Autumn 1997): 48–57.

Ortiz, Alfonso, ed. *Handbook of North American Indians, Vol. 10: Southwest.* Washington, DC: Smithsonian Institution, 1983.

Page, Susanne and Jake. *Indian Arts of the Southwest.* Tucson: Rio Nuevo Publishers, 2008.

Rosenak, Chuck and Jan. *Navajo Folk Art.* Tucson: Rio Nuevo Publishers, 2008.

Wroth, William, ed. *Ute Indian Arts & Culture: From Prehistory to the New Millennium.* Colorado Springs, Colorado: Taylor Museum of the Colorado Springs Fine Arts Center, 2000.

POTTERY / CERAMICS

Anderson, Duane. *All That Glitters: The Emergence of American Micaceous Art Pottery in Northern New Mexico.* Santa Fe: School for Advanced Research Press, 1999.

Anderson, Duane. *When Rain Gods Reigned: From Curios to Art at Tesuque Pueblo.* Santa Fe: Museum of New Mexico Press, 2002.

Bahti, Mark. *Pueblo Stories & Storytellers.* Tucson: Rio Nuebo Publishers, 2010.

Barstad, Jan. *Hohokam Pottery.* Tucson: Western National Parks Association, 1999.

Batkin, Jonathan, ed. *Clay People: Indian Figurative Traditions.* Santa Fe: Wheelwright Museum of the American Indian, 1999.

Batkin, Jonathan. *The Native American Curio Trade in New Mexico.* Santa Fe: Wheelright Museum of the American Indian, 2008.

Brody, J. J. *Mimbres Painted Pottery.* Santa Fe: School of American Research Press, 2004.

Carrillo, Charles M. *Hispanic New Mexican Pottery: Evidence of Craft Specialization, 1790–1890.* Albuquerque: LPD Press, 1997.

Dillingham, Rick. *Acoma and Laguna Pottery.* Santa Fe: School of American Research Press, 1992.

Harlow, Francis H., Duane Anderson, and Dwight P. Lanmon. *The Pottery of Santa Ana Pueblo.* Santa Fe: Museum of New Mexico Press, 2005.

King, Charles S. and Richard L. Spivey. *The Life and Art of Tony Da.* Tucson: Rio Nuevo Publishers, 2011.

Hays-Gilpin, Kelley. *A Quick Field Guide to Pottery Sherds in the Southwest.* Western National Parks Association, 2006.

King, Charles S. *Born of Fire: The Life and Pottery of Margaret Tafoya.* Santa Fe: Museum of New Mexico Press, 2008.

Lanmon, Dwight P. and Francis H. Harlow. *The Pottery of Zuni Pueblo.* Santa Fe: Museum of New Mexico Press, 2008.

Messier, Kim and Pat Messier. *Hopi & Pueblo Tiles: An Illustrated History.* Tucson: Rio Nuevo Publishers, 2007.

Peterson, Susan. *Pottery by American Indian Women: The Legacy of Generations.* Washington, D.C.: The National Museum of Women in the Arts, 1997.

Powell, Melissa S., ed. *Secrets of Casas Grandes: Precolumbian Art & Archaeology of Northern New Mexico.* Santa Fe: Museum of New Mexico Press, 2006.

Takahashi, Masako. *Mexican Tiles.* San Francisco: Chronicle Books, 2000.

Trimble, Stephen. *Talking with the Clay: The Art of Pueblo Pottery in the 21st Century.* Santa Fe: School for Advanced Research Press, 2007.

Verzuh, Valerie K., ed. *A River Apart: The Pottery of Cochiti and Santo Domingo Pueblos.* Santa Fe: Museum of New Mexico Press, 2008.

RELIGIOUS ART

Awalt, Barbe and Paul Rhetts. *Charlie Carrillo: Tradition & Soul/Tradición y Alma.* Albuquerque: LPD Press, 1995.

Dunnington, Jacqueline Orsini. *Guadalupe: Our Lady of New Mexico.* Santa Fe: Museum of New Mexico Press, 1999.

Griffith, Jim. *Saints of the Southwest.* Tucson: Rio Nuevo Publishers, 2000.

Rosenak, Chuck and Jan. *The Saint Makers: Contemporary Santeras Y Santeros.* Flagstaff: Northland Publishing, 1998.

ROCK ART

Cheek, Lawrence W. *Kokopelli.* Tucson: Rio Nuevo Publishers, 2004.

Farnsworth, Janet Webb. *Rock Art Along the Way.* Tucson: Rio Nuevo Publishers, 2006.

Slifer, Dennis and James Duffield. *Kokopelli: Fluteplayer Images in Rock Art.* Santa Fe: Ancient City Press, 1994.

Sullivan, Gordon and Cathie. *Roadside Guide to Indian Ruins & Rock Art of the Southwest.* Englewood, CO: Westcliffe Publishers, Inc., 2005.

SANDPAINTINGS

Bahti, Mark and Eugene Baatsoslanii Joe. *Navajo Sandpaintings.* Tucson: Rio Nuevo Publishers, 2009.

SILVERWORK

Batkin, Jonathan. *The Native American Curio Trade in New Mexico.* Santa Fe: Wheelright Museum of the American Indian, 2008.

Kline, Cindra. *Navajo Spoons: Indian Artistry and the Souvenir Trade, 1880s–1940s.* Santa Fe: Museum of New Mexico Press, 2001.

Kline, Cindra. "A Stirring Story: Navajo and Pueblo Spoons," *American Indian Art* 28, no. 4 (Autumn 2003): 60–69.

Loscher, Tricia. *Old Traditions in New Pots: Silver Seed Pots From The Norman L. Sandfield Collection.* Phoenix: Heard Museum, 2007.

Torres-Nez, John. *Beesh Ligaii in Balance: The Besser Collection of Navajo and Pueblo Silverwork.* Santa Fe: Museum of Indian Arts and Culture, 2004.

SPANISH COLONIAL PERIOD

Montaño, Mary. *Tradiciones Nuevomexicanas.* Albuquerque: The University of New Mexico Press, 2001.

Padilla, Carmella, ed. *Conexiones: Connections in Spanish Colonial Art.* Santa Fe: Museum of Spanish Colonial Art, 2002.

Padilla, Carmella. *El Rancho de las Golondrinas: Living History in New Mexico's La Ciénega Valley.* Santa Fe: Museum of New Mexico Press, 2009.

Wroth, William and Robin Farwell Gavin, eds. *Converging Streams: Art of the Hispanic and Native American Southwest.* Santa Fe: Museum of Spanish Colonial Art, 2010.

TEXTILES

Allen, Dodi and Carter Allen. *The Weavers Way: Navajo Profiles.* Tucson: Carter Allen, 2003.

Coulter, Lane, ed. *Navajo Saddle Blankets: Textiles to Ride in the American West.* Santa Fe: Museum of New Mexico Press, 2002.

Dedera, Don. *Navajo Rugs: The Essential Guide.* Flagstaff: Northland Publishing, 1996.

Fisher, Nora. *Rio Grande Textiles.* Santa Fe: Museum of New Mexico Press, 1994.

Friedman, Barry. *Chasing Rainbows: Collecting American Indian Trade & Camp Blankets.* Boston: Bulfinch Press, AOL Time Warner Book Group, 2002.

Kent, Kate Peck. *Navajo Weaving: Three Centuries of Change.* Santa Fe: School of American Research Press, 1985.

Kent, Kate Peck. *Pueblo Indian Textiles: A Living Tradition.* Santa Fe: School of American Research Press, 1983.

Lucero, Helen and Suzanne Baizerman. *Chimayó Weaving: The Transformation of a Tradition.* Albuquerque: University of New Mexico Press, 1999.

MacDowell, Marsha L. and C. Kurt Dewhurst, eds. *To Honor and Comfort: Native Quilting Traditions.* Santa Fe: Museum of New Mexico Press in association with Michigan State University, 1997.

McManis, Kent and Robert Jeffries. *Navajo Weavings.* Tucson: Rio Nuevo Publishers, 2009.

O'Bagy Davis, Carolyn. *Hopi Quilting: Stitched Traditions from an Ancient Community.* Tucson: Sanpete Publications, 1997.

Valette, Rebecca M. and Jean-Paul Valette. *Weaving The Dance: Navajo Yeibichai Textiles (1910–1950).* Albuquerque: Adobe Gallery, in association with University of Washington Press, Seattle and London, 2000.

Weigle, Marta ed. *Hispanic Arts and Ethnohistory In the Southwest.* Santa Fe: Ancient City Press, 1983.

Wheat, Joe Ben. *Blanket Weaving in the Southwest.* Tucson: University of Arizona Press, 2003.

Whitaker, Kathleen. *Southwest Textiles: Weavings of the Navajo and Pueblo.* Seattle and London: University of Washington Press, in association with Southwest Museum, Los Angeles, 2002.

TURQUOISE

Lowry, Joe Dan and Joe P. Lowry. *Turquoise Unearthed: An Illustrated Guide.* Tucson: Rio Nuevo Publishers, 2002.

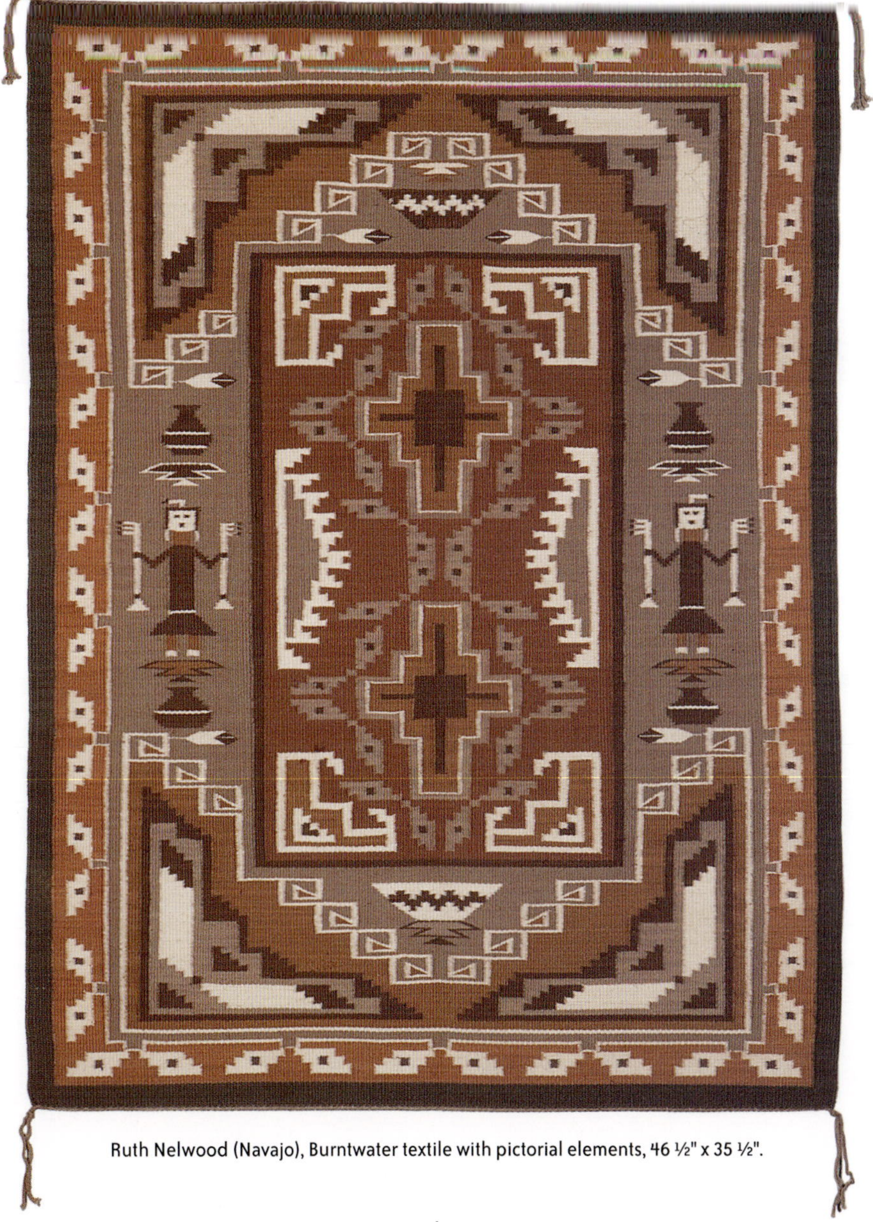

Ruth Nelwood (Navajo), Burntwater textile with pictorial elements, 46 ½" x 35 ½".

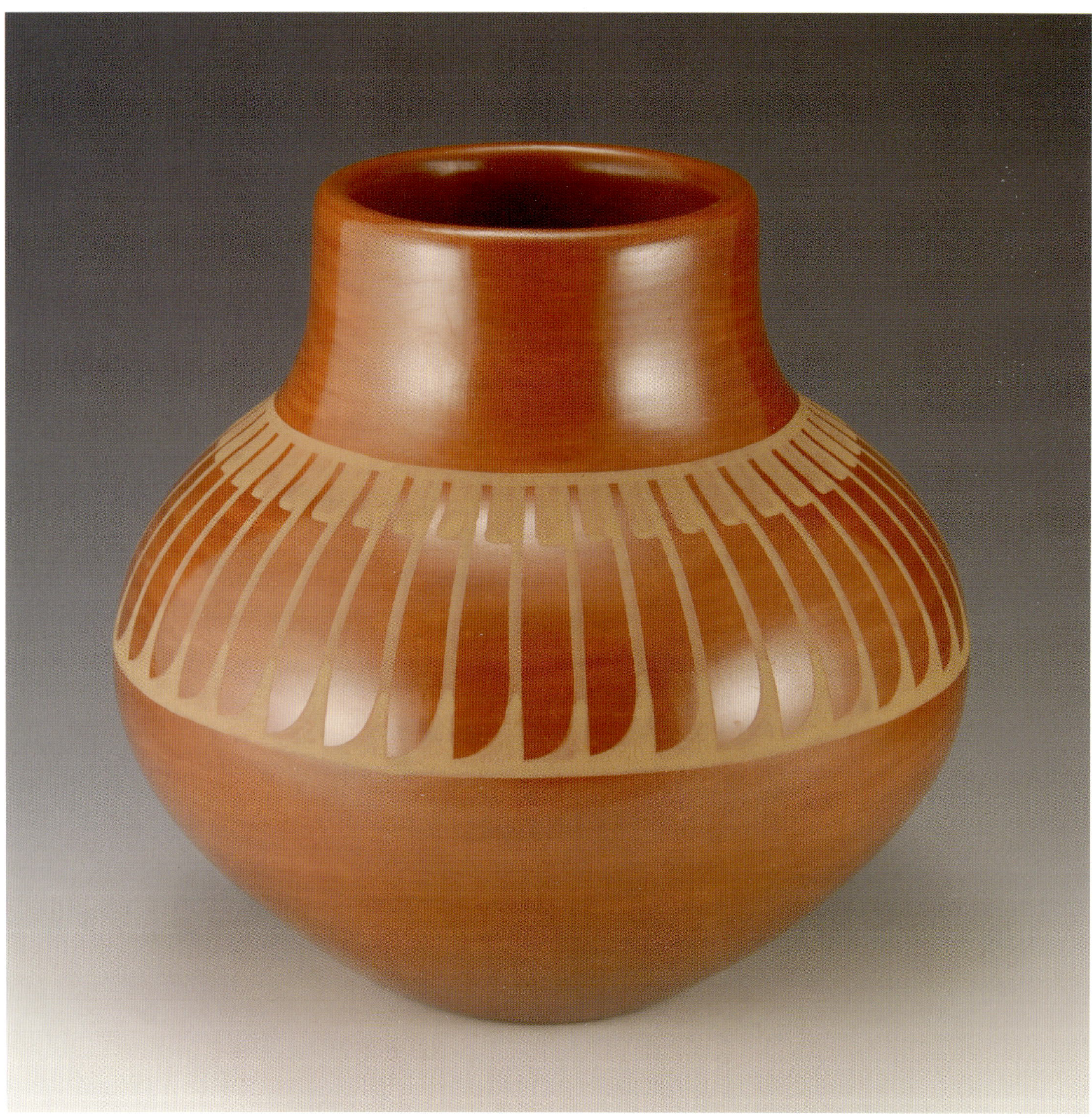

Maria Martinez and Popovi Da (San Ildefonso), redware jar with Mimbres-style feather design.

PHOTOGRAPHY & COLLECTIONS CREDITS

Adobe Gallery: p. 28 bottom left

Albuquerque Museum: p. 118

Arizona State Museum, University of Arizona (catalog #GP43855): p. 75 right

Bahti Indian Arts (photos by Robin Stancliff): p. 26 (antique buttons), 34 bottom, 39, 75 left, 97 bottom, 158 right

Blair's Dinnebito Trading Post (photos by Robin Stancliff): 128 top, 149 bottom right

Blue Rain Gallery: p. 28 bottom right (photo by Dorie Hagler), 29 (photo by Pat Pollard)

Booker Collection (photos on p. ix and 47 top left by Margaret Moore Booker, all others by Robin Stancliff): p. ix, p. 21 bottom left, 23 left, 25 bottom, 26 (contemporary buttons), 32 top, 38 right, 39, 40 bottom, 43 bottom, 44 bottom left, 45, 47 top left, 50 bottom, 52 bottom, 53 right, 54 top left, 55 middle, 62 right, 68 top, 71 left, 74 bottom, 78 top, 88 top and bottom, 89, 96 top right, 98 top, 99 middle and bottom, 111 bottom, 114 bottom, 122 top, 123 bottom right, 124 top, 125 top right and bottom right, 127 bottom, 131, 134 top left, 139 top right, 140, 144 middle, 145, 146 left, 147 right, 150 bottom, 153 bottom, 157 right, 158 middle, 161 right, 162 bottom, 175, 179 bottom, 198, 202

Café Pasqual's Gallery (photos by Kitty Leaken): p. 115 top and middle

Scott Calhoun: p. 14 top, 46 bottom left, 80 left, 180 left

Edgar Callaert: p. 30 middle

Carolyn O'Bagy Davis: 64 top

Centennial Museum, University of Texas, El Paso: p. 70 right

Colonial Arts: p. 128 bottom left

Colorado Historical Society: p. 112 (photo by William Henry Jackson, CHS.J1351)

Coulter Brooks Art & Antiques: p. 178 bottom

Cowan's Auctions: p. 103 right

Dreamstime.com: p. 61 right

Durango Silver Company: p. 19 left

Edward S. Curtis: p. 177 bottom

Garland's Indian Jewelry: p. 16 middle, 100 top left, 120 left, 170 bottom, 171 top right

Steve Getzwiller, www.navajorug.com, Sonoita, AZ: p. 31 top right

Rose Gonnella: p. 155 bottom

Grey Dog Trading Company (photos by Robin Stancliff): 56, 59 bottom right, 70 left, 74 top, 120 right, 125 bottom left, 159 bottom, 174 bottom left, 195

Jim Griffith: p. 15 left, 101 bottom right, 129 left, 138 bottom

Hacienda: p. 123 bottom left

Heard Museum, Phoenix, Arizona: plaque on front cover, p. 16 top, 20 top, 31 middle and bottom right, 43 top, 47 bottom left, 51, 57 bottom, 59 top right, 61 left, 72 bottom left, 82 bottom, 109 bottom right, 126 right, 132 right, 141 right, 176, 178 top

Bernadette Heath: p. 11, 108

Historia: p. 50 top right, 84 left, 101 bottom left, 106 top, 135 right, 169 left

Horsekeeping.com: p. 119

Hubbell Trading Post: p. 66 bottom, p. 67 (photo by Robin Stancliff)

W. Ross Humphreys: p. 16 bottom, 18 bottom, 19 top right, 21 top right, 24 middle, 49, 54 top right and bottom, 59 top left, 59 bottom left, 60, 73 top, 84 top and bottom, 85, 100 top right and bottom, 103 left, 107, 126 left, 137, 144 top and bottom, 149 top right, 153 top, 188

Jerry Jacka: p. 15 right, 17 top, 25 top (courtesy Garland's Navajo Rugs), 36 middle and bottom, 44 bottom right (courtesy Garland's Navajo Rugs), 46 bottom right, 52 top, 65, 72 top, 77 right, 81 top, 91 top, 94 top, 95, 101 top, 113 bottom, 132 left, 133 left, 142, 152, 154, 157 left, 165 (courtesy Terry DeWild), 170 top, 174 bottom right, 182

Pat Jessup: p. 93 bottom left

King Galleries: p. 9, 12, 20 bottom, 21 top left, 21 bottom right, 22, 36 top, 42, 63 bottom, 69 bottom left, 76 top, 98 bottom, 99 top, 113 top, 122 bottom, 129 right, 130 top, 134 top right and bottom, 135 left, 138 top left and right, 139 bottom, 181, 183, 196

Hermann Knechtle: p. 30 top

Steve Larese: p. 14 bottom, 27 middle and bottom right, 40 top, 46 top, 50 top left, 55 left, 77 left, 79 bottom, 149 top left, 160, 162 top, 164 left, 174 top, 180 right

Larry Lindahl: p. 4, 106 bottom, 167

Library of Congress
xii: Edward S. Curtis, 3c20925
p. 13: Russell Lee, 8a29082
p. 96 top left, Russell Lee, 8a29105
p. 114 top left, Frederick D. Nichols, HABS NM, 25-SANFE, 4
p. 121 top, Frederick A. Eastman, HABS ARIZ,11-POST.V,5--1
p. 127 top, Edward S. Curtis, 3c01181

Chris Marchetti, courtesy John Sharpe, The Turquoise Room, La Posada Hotel: p. 58 top, 68 bottom right

Nedra Matteucci: p. 174 top left

Medicine Man Gallery: p. i, plaque on p. vii, p. 48 left, 78 bottom, 102 right, 109 top and bottom left, 111 top, 124 bottom, 139 top left, 158 left, 161 left, 166 middle

Menaul Historical Library of the Southwest, Albuquerque, New Mexico: p. 4

Kim and Pat Messier: p. 163

Morning Star Gallery: p. 19 bottom right, 27 top, 79 top, 94 bottom, 148 left

Ann Murdy: p. 7, 81 bottom right, 82 top, 86, 87, 105 top, 121 bottom, 193

Museum of International Folk Art, IFAF Collection, in Memory of Oliver Seth. FA.1999.23.1: p. 168

Museum of Spanish Colonial Art, Collections of the Spanish Colonial Arts Society (photos by Jack Parsons): p. 31 left, 37, 41 top, 57 top, 69 bottom right, 104 top, 123 top, 143 right, 184

National Park Service: p. 88 middle, 117 top (photo by Dr. Albert P. Duryee), 149 bottom left

Native American Trading Company: p. 105 bottom

Mark Nohl: p. 35, 93 top, 116, 171 top left

Old Territorial Shop: p. 72 bottom right, 76 bottom, 96 bottom, 155 top

Owings Gallery: p. 24 left

Susanne Page: p. 17 bottom, 18 top, 24 right, 28 top, 30 bottom, 33, 41 bottom, 48 right, 53 left, 55 right, 63 top, 68 bottom left, 71 right, 74 middle, 80 right, 104 bottom, 110, 114 top right, 141 left, 143 left, 169 right

Courtesy Palace of the Governors Photo Archives (NMHM/DCA)
p. viii: T. Harmon Parkhurst, 043608
p. 3: T. Harmon Parkhurst, 003773
p. 5: William H. Jackson, 041729
p. 6: Ben Wittick, 016051
p. 8: Photographer unknown, 004487
p. 73 bottom: Ferenz Fedor, 100483
p. 117 bottom: Ben Wittick, 016051
p. 166 bottom: T. Harmon Parkhurst, 004307

Sam Patania, Patania's Sterling Silver Originals: p. 171 middle

Peabody Museum, Harvard University Photo T906: p. iii

El Potrero Trading Post: p. ii, 23 right, 38 left, 44 top, 90, 91 bottom, 102 left, 128 bottom right, 130 bottom, 136, 156, 164 right

Private collections (photos by Robin Stancliff): 93 bottom right, 159 top

Randy Prentice: p. 92

Pueblo Grande Museum: p. 10, 62 left, 83, 115 bottom

El Rancho de las Golondrinas: p. 64 bottom, 166 top

© Genevieve Russell, 2011: p. 32 bottom, 125 top left

Catherine Robles Shaw: p. 47 bottom right

Chuck Rosenak: p. 97 top

Shiprock Trading Post (photos by Robin Stancliff): p. 81 bottom left, 172, 177 top, 133 right, 173 top

Courtesy Taos Historic Museums (photo by Don Laine): p. 58 bottom

Tom Till: p. 34 top

Jim Turner: p. 146 right, 147 left

Twin Rocks Trading Post: p. 66 top, 150 top, (photo by Robin Stancliff), 179 top (photo by Robin Stancliff)

Two Dogs Southwest Gallery: p. 41 middle

University of Colorado Museum of Natural History, UCM # 1997.12.324. © 2004: p. 173 bottom

Waddell Trading Company: p. 151

Wright's Indian Art: p. 69 top

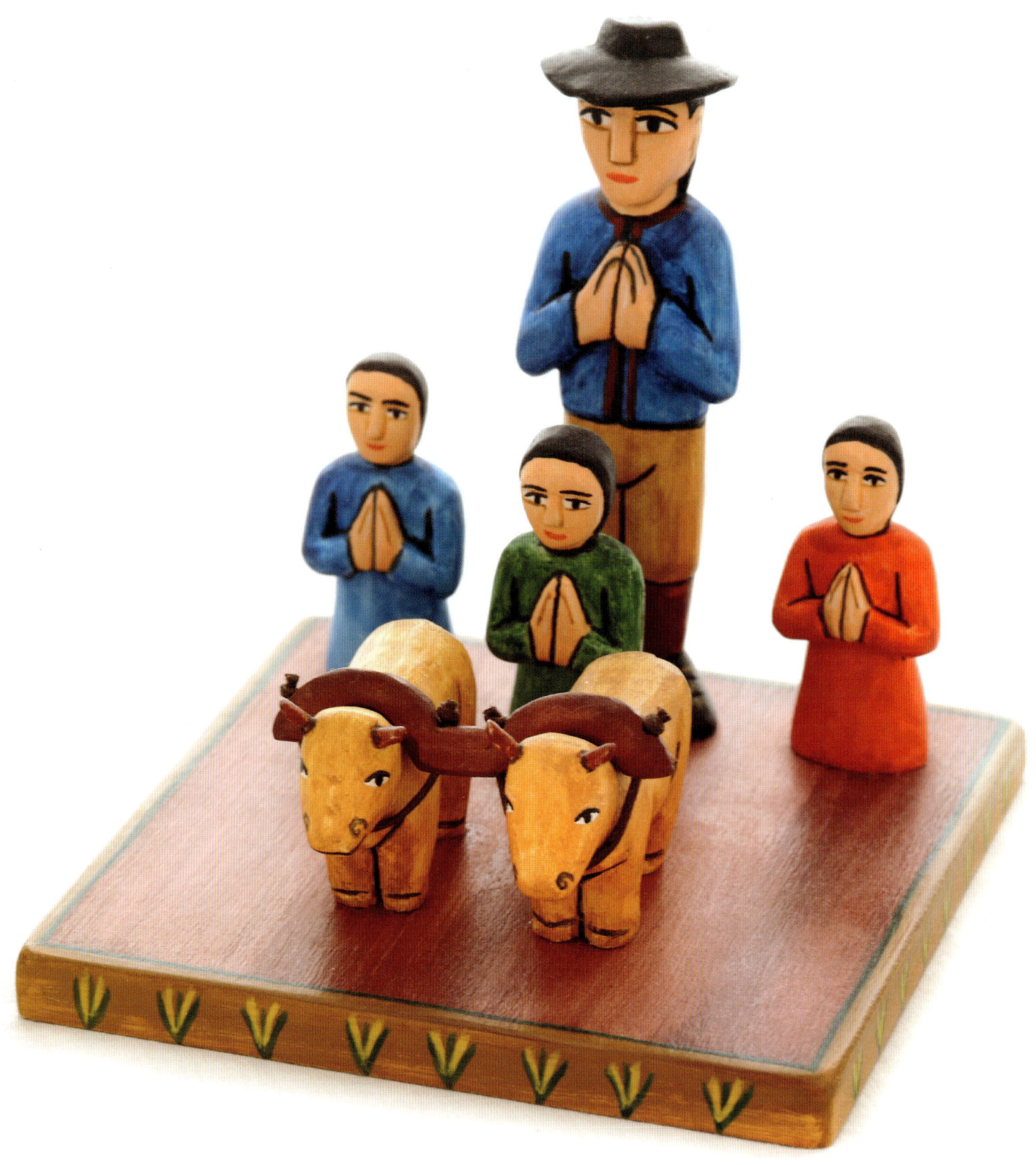

Ronald Samuel Garcia (New Mexico), San Isidro Labrador with three praying figures
and oxen (bulto), 2011, wood, natural pigments, piñon varnish, beeswax, leather.

INDEX

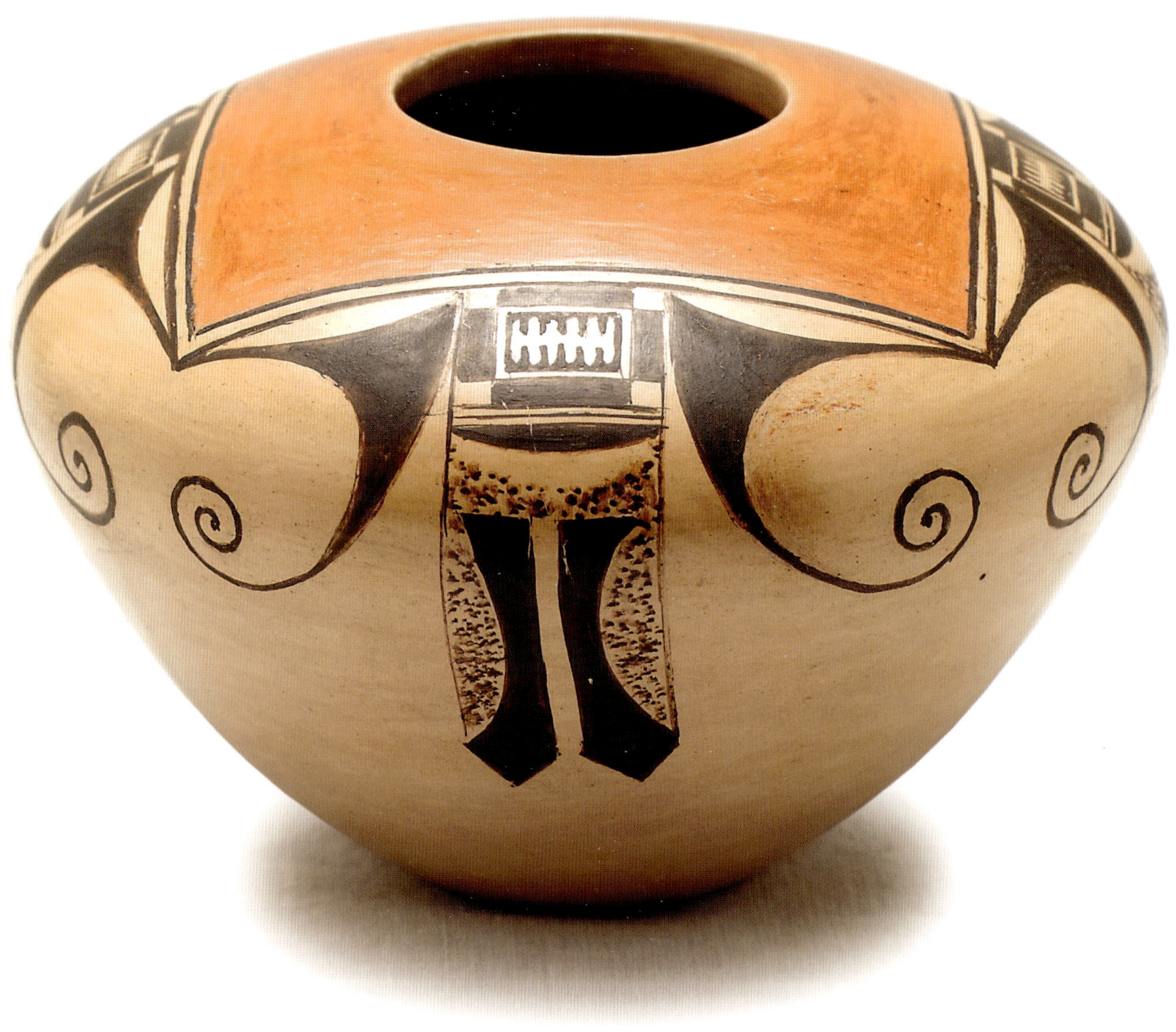

Dextra Quotskuyva Nampeyo (Hopi), small polychrome jar,
ca. mid-1980s, clay with clay slip design.

ABOUT THE AUTHOR

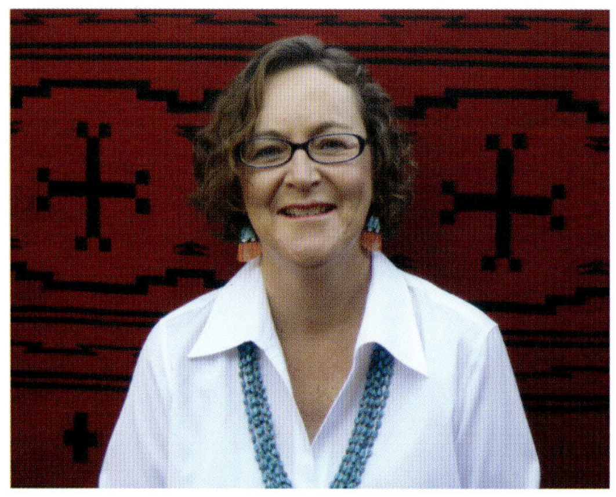

MARGARET MOORE BOOKER is the award-winning author of several books and numerous articles on art, decorative arts, architecture, and history, and biographies on prominent Americans. She wrote *The Santa Fe House: Historic Residences, Enchanting Adobes, and Romantic Revivals* (NY: Rizzoli, 2009), chosen "best art book" of 2010 by the New Mexico Book Co-op and winner of the Historical Society of New Mexico's 2010 Twitchell Award for "significant contribution to history." And she co-authored *Sea Captains' Houses and Rose-Covered Cottages: The Architectural Heritage of Nantucket Island* (NY: Universe, 2003), chosen by the *New York Times Book Review* as a "Notable Book of 2003." A resident of Santa Fe since 2004, she divides her time between writing projects and freelance work, with a focus on the art, architecture, decorative arts, and history of the Southwest.